QUALITIES OF
Effective Teachers

JAMES H. STRONGE

Association for Supervision and Curriculum Development
Alexandria, Virginia USA

Association for Supervision and Curriculum Development
1703 N. Beauregard St. • Alexandria, VA 22311-1714 USA
Telephone: 800-933-2723 or 703-578-9600 • Fax: 703-575-5400
Web site: http://www.ascd.org • E-mail: member@ascd.org

All Web links in this book are correct as of the publication date below but may have become inactive or otherwise modified since that time. If you notice a deactivated or changed link, please e-mail books@ascd.org with the words "Link Update" in the subject line. In your message, please specify the Web link, the book title, and the page number on which the link appears.

Printed in the United States of America.

July 2002 member book (pc). ASCD Premium, Comprehensive, and Regular members periodically receive ASCD books as part of their membership benefits. No. FY02-08.

ASCD Product No. 102007

ASCD member price: $18.95   nonmember price: $22.95

Library of Congress Cataloging-in-Publication Data
Stronge, James H.
  Qualities of effective teachers / James H. Stronge.
      p. cm.
Includes bibliographical references and index.
  ISBN 0-87120-663-3 (alk. paper)
  1. Effective teaching. 2. Teacher effectiveness. I. Title.
  LB1025.3 .S789 2002
  371.102—dc21
                              2002004844

08 07 06 05 04 03 02   10 9 8 7 6 5 4 3 2 1

To my wife, Terri, a gifted teacher of young children,

and

to devoted teachers everywhere

Qualities of Effective Teachers

Acknowledgments

The creation of a project is never an isolated endeavor. This was certainly true in the development of this book. To move from imagination to culmination required the encouragement, support, and assistance of many individuals. I take this opportunity to acknowledge the contributions of many friends, generous colleagues, and capable students.

I appreciate the support from colleagues in the Virginia Department of Education—George Irby, Dianne Pollard, Lillian Shearin, and Cheryl Strobel. Their faith in this project was expressed in initial funding for a field-based project related to effective teaching and student achievement.

Colleagues from the College of William and Mary offered invaluable support as the book and related projects unfolded. In particular, Patricia Popp, Thomas Ward, and Virginia McLaughlin offered technical support and encouragement for this research.

Many of my graduate students contributed significantly as the project developed. Christine Hill, Jeanne Struck, and Kimberly Chandler assisted with a review and synthesis of extant research related to effective teaching. Catherine Little helped refine the conceptual framework and develop an early draft for the manuscript. William Brown, Jennifer Hindman, and Linda Hutchinson worked extensively on the annotated bibliography included in the book. And Lisa Vernon and Jennifer Hindman, again, provided invaluable assistance in refining and editing a final version of the manuscript. I am, indeed, privileged to work with such outstanding doctoral students.

Several other friends and colleagues contributed significantly to the book's development. Among them, Pamela Tucker, a faculty member with the University of Virginia, provided suggestions for making the book more practical and insightful. John O'Neil, ASCD book acquisitions editor, saw value in this project for teachers and administrators. And, finally, Anne Meek helped significantly to shape the book through her early reviews, ongoing encouragement, and edit of the manuscript.

To everyone who contributed, I wish to express my admiration for your dedicated work as educators and my appreciation for helping to make this project a reality.

Introduction

The focus for this book is the teacher. The content is presented within the context of a person—the teacher—as opposed to viewing teaching skills as isolated processes. The book is research-based, and the style and format are designed to be user-friendly providing easy-to-use summaries and tools for teacher effectiveness.

If finding or becoming an effective teacher were simple, this book would not be needed. If a single method for developing an effective teacher existed, such a teacher would be in every classroom. Nonetheless, there are common attributes that characterize effective teachers.

Teachers have a powerful, long-lasting influence on their students. They directly affect how students learn, what they learn, how much they learn, and the ways they interact with one another and the world around them. Considering the degree of the teacher's influence, it is important to understand what teachers should do to promote positive results in the lives of students—with regard to school achievement, positive attitudes toward school, interest in learning, and other desirable outcomes. This understanding should be based both on what experts and stakeholders think teachers should do and on what educational research has shown to be significant in the preparation and practice of effective teachers.

Qualities of Effective Teachers chronicles the common background and identifies the common behaviors that characterize effectiveness in the classroom. Based on a comprehensive review and synthesis of research related to effective teaching, the book serves as a resource for teachers, administrators, and others interested in improving the quality of teaching and learning in our schools.

Defining an Effective Teacher

Effectiveness is an elusive concept when we consider the complex task of teaching. Some researchers define teacher effectiveness in terms of student achievement. Others focus on high performance ratings from supervisors. Still others rely on comments from students, administrators, and other interested stakeholders. In fact, in addition to *effective*, we vacillate on just how to refer to successful teachers. Cruickshank and Haefele (2001) noted that good teachers, at various times, have been called *ideal, analytical, dutiful, competent, expert, reflective, satisfying, diversity-responsive,* and *respected*.

A teacher's influence is far reaching, so it is challenging to define what outcomes might show effectiveness and how those outcomes should be measured. In addition, many variables outside the teacher's control also affect each of the potential measures of effectiveness.

Despite the various complexities and regardless of what we call them, we can agree that effective teachers do make an extraordinary and lasting impact on the lives of students. In recent years, as the field of education has moved toward a stronger focus on accountability and on careful analysis of variables affecting educational outcomes, the teacher has proven time and again to be the most influential school-related force in student achievement. Consequently, in an attempt to develop an understanding of what teachers do to cause significant student learning, researchers have begun to focus on the specific characteristics and teaching processes employed by the most effective teachers.

The growing body of research concerned with teacher effectiveness has reinforced the notion that specific characteristics and behaviors matter in teaching, in terms of student achievement as well as other desirable outcomes. Although looking across studies yields some inconsistencies in defining elements of effectiveness, careful exploration of the research, nevertheless, helps confirm which practices are most important and which require further investigation. Commonalities highlighted in *Qualities of Effective Teachers* include characteristics of the teacher as an individual, teacher preparation, classroom management, and the way a teacher plans, teaches, and monitors student progress. Put these jigsaw pieces together and a portrait of an effective teacher takes shape.

Overview

Qualities of Effective Teachers sheds light on the elusive concept of teacher effectiveness by summarizing research results accumulated across several decades to define specific teacher behaviors that contribute to student achievement and other measures of effectiveness. The book was developed by focusing specifically on the *teacher* and her or his preparation, personality, and practice, rather than on other influences such as student demographics, school and district administration, or organizational decision-making outside the teacher's control. The sources considered in creating this synthesis of teacher background and behaviors include broad-based studies of teacher practice as linked to student achievement, case studies of teachers identified as effective within specific contexts, surveys and interviews among stakeholders, meta-analyses of teacher effectiveness studies, and other reviews of research.

The research findings and recommended practices identified in this book should seem like old friends to many teachers. For these effective teachers, the book should serve as a review and reminder for continued improvement. For others, the same findings serve to build awareness as they take steps to enhance their effectiveness. By focusing on teacher effectiveness, our ultimate goal is to improve the educational experiences and achievement of the students we serve in our schools.

Organization of the Book

Qualities of Effective Teachers is designed to serve as a resource and reference tool for educators. It identifies elements of effective teaching within broad categories and points readers interested in further exploration to the research studies and reviews used in the preparation of the text. The book is divided into two parts. Part 1 focuses on the research useful in developing a profile of what an effective teacher is, and Part 2 contains myriad resources.

The first six chapters address major categories of teacher effectiveness. The first two chapters explore the teacher as an individual and as a professional.

• Chapter 1 investigates prerequisites of effective teaching, focusing on the influence of a teacher's background and professional preparation. The implications of verbal ability, content knowledge, educational coursework, and teacher certification are explored.

• Chapter 2 examines what the effective teacher is like as a person, focusing on a teacher's nonacademic interactions with students and on the aspects of a teacher's behavior that make her loved, respected, and remembered by students as personally effective. This chapter also explores the significance of the teacher's professional attitude. This discussion emphasizes dedicated and reflective practice among effective teachers.

Chapters 3 through 6 focus more specifically on aspects of a teacher's job responsibilities and practices.

• Chapter 3 considers the management and organizational skills an effective teacher displays, with emphasis on the establishment of an effective learning environment in which routines and discipline are established and maintained to serve as a backdrop for instruction and student engagement.

    • Chapter 4 investigates organization for instruction with a focus on maximizing the amount of time allocated for instruction, communicating expectations for student achievement, and planning for instructional purposes.

    • Chapter 5 focuses on implementation of instruction with an emphasis on communication and complexity of instructional content by using appropriate questioning techniques and supporting active learning.

    • Chapter 6 examines monitoring student progress and potential through discussing the importance of homework and applying findings of student learning outcomes, as well as responding to and meeting the individual needs of special populations within the classroom.

    Within each chapter, information is organized into categories of characteristics or behaviors that are supported by the existing research as important aspects of teacher effectiveness. Summaries of research are provided in a straightforward manner in each chapter, with a list of key references to guide the interested reader to further information on the topics. Chapter 7 contains a brief conclusion on what an effective teacher is and how teacher effectiveness can be improved.

    Part 2, the final section of the text, includes teacher skills assessment checklists, behaviors to look for in effective teacher performance, an annotated bibliography of selected sources, and a complete reference list. This portion of the book focuses on helping teachers improve—whether the improvement is self-diagnosed or the result of supervisor assistance. In particular, the checklists and qualities should be helpful in converting research findings into improved practice.

Uses for the Book

By closely aligning the attributes of high-quality teaching with curricula and assessments, we can be better equipped to identify links between classroom processes and desirable student outcomes. Thus, *Qualities of Effective Teachers* is aimed at improving the quality of teacher performance and learning opportunities for students. In this effort, the book can be a valuable resource for the following audiences:

    • Teachers who desire to improve their own performance through analysis and reflective practice.

• Teacher leaders who are engaged in mentoring, peer coaching, and collaborative school-wide improvement.

• School administrators and department heads who supervise and evaluate teachers.

• Staff development specialists who plan and deliver training focused on improving instruction.

• Human resource specialists who are responsible for recruiting and selecting high-quality teacher applicants.

• Teacher and administrator educators who can employ the book's research synthesis in their teacher training and instructional leadership programs.

• Policy makers and their staffs who are responsible for developing tools and strategies for state or district teacher development and evaluation processes.

Each group contributes to the education of students and has a vested interest in their success.

Key references: Archer, 1998; Cawelti, 1999a; Cotton, 1999, 2000; Cruickshank & Haefele, 2001; Darling-Hammond, 2000; National Board for Professional Teaching Standards (NBPTS), no date; Olson, 1997; Stronge & Tucker, 2000; Wright, Horn, & Sanders, 1997

1

What It Means To Be an Effective Teacher

Part 1 of *Qualities of Effective Teachers* focuses on the research useful in developing a profile of an effective teacher. Following the Introduction, the first six chapters of the book address major categories of teacher effectiveness. The first two chapters explore the teacher as an individual and as a professional; chapters 3 through 6 focus more specifically on aspects of a teacher's job responsibilities and practices. Chapter 7 contains a brief conclusion on what an effective teacher is and how teacher effectiveness can be improved.

1

Prerequisites of Effective Teaching

During the time observed, the students moved from desks to group to sustained silent reading on the carpet. The teacher gave all students work to do at their desks focusing on English skills that related to the social studies theme of the Wild West. During the small group instruction on dictionary skills, the students used their guide words to look up unfamiliar Wild West terms, with the students having a choice as to which words they would look up. Depending on the skill level of the group, the complexity of the words differed. Then, the teacher coached the students in a soft and nurturing tone. During a post-observation meeting, the teacher shared that she had been a classroom teacher for three years and worked as a teaching assistant for two years while earning a master's degree in Early Childhood Education with elementary teaching certification.

NOTES FROM CLASSROOM OBSERVATION
OF 3RD GRADE TEACHER

A major educational debate today concerns how to recruit and prepare teachers. Many educators, policymakers, and taxpayers question whether traditional preservice programs prepare teachers who can maintain excellent instructional programs that increase student achievement. Alternative programs for recruiting and preparing teachers have been devised, giving rise to research comparing the effectiveness of teachers from different types of preparation backgrounds. Beyond the issue of pedagogical preparation, the question of content knowledge and its relevance to effective teaching remains a legitimate concern.

This chapter explores the research on teacher preparation and reviews what has been learned through extensive studies and research regarding the background of effective teachers. Each section of the chapter summarizes research findings related to a specific aspect of a teacher's background, with a list of key references related to that topic. Figure 1.1, located at the end of the chapter, summarizes the relationships among each of the background aspects described in the chapter and provides the related references.

Verbal Ability and Effective Teaching

Does the teacher's intellectual ability or aptitude translate into improved effectiveness in the classroom? Over several decades researchers have investigated relationships between teacher ability, as demonstrated through teacher's scores on aptitude tests such as the SAT (Scholastic Assessment Tests) or GRE (Graduate Record Exam), and the achievement of students. The results of such studies have been mixed. Some show no relationship beyond the level of basic skills knowledge. However, other studies have shown connections, particularly linking teachers' verbal ability with their students' performance.

While research generally has not supported a link between the teacher's intellectual aptitude and student success, one key finding has emerged: students taught by teachers with greater verbal ability learn more than those taught by teachers with lower verbal ability. Thus, a discernable link exists between the effective teacher's vocabulary and verbal skills and student academic success. Since communication skills are a part of verbal ability, effective teachers with higher verbal abilities can better convey ideas to students and communicate with them in a clear and compelling manner.

The following conclusions can be drawn from the research:

• Teachers' scores on verbal ability tests were the only input found to have a direct positive relationship with student achievement.

• Students taught by teachers with high verbal skills perform better on standardized tests than those students taught by teachers with lower verbal ability.

• A positive relationship exists between teachers with high verbal ability and student achievement.

• General intellectual aptitude has not typically been linked to higher student achievement; however, when teachers perform well on basic skills tests, their students also tend to do better on academic measures.

Key references: Darling-Hammond, 2000; Darling-Hammond, 2001; Hanushek, 1971; Haycock, 2000; Murnane, 1985; National Center for Educational Statistics, 1992; Rowan, Chiang, & Miller, 1997; Summers & Wolfe, 1975; Thomas B. Fordham Foundation, 1999; Wenglinsky, 2000

Educational Coursework and Effective Teaching

Teacher preparation traditionally has included a series of courses focusing on child development, instructional and assessment techniques, and methods and materials related to specific content areas. However, in recent years, teacher preparation programs and their usefulness to the teaching field have been the source of considerable scrutiny. Some recommendations and programs for teacher certification have curbed traditional teacher training in favor of brief, more practical and focused preparation of individuals with subject area degrees and varying backgrounds, including those with military and business training.

Partly in response to these programs, several studies have focused on teacher effectiveness related to the amount and type of educational coursework in a teacher's preparation program. In addition to understanding how students learn and what and how they need to be taught, studies support the finding that fully prepared teachers with background knowledge of pedagogy are better able to recognize individual student needs and customize instruction to increase overall student achievement. Additionally, teachers with better professional preparation are able to provide students with more diverse opportunities to learn.

There is little research and evaluation on the long-term effects of alternatively prepared teachers, but studies indicate that they may have more difficulty in the classroom than traditionally prepared teachers. Teachers who are not formally prepared to teach know little about how children grow, learn, and develop, or about how to support learning differences. Teachers with little or no coursework in education consistently have difficulties in the areas of classroom management, curriculum development, student motivation, and specific teaching strategies. They are less able to anticipate student knowledge and potential difficulties or to plan and redirect the lesson to meet the individual needs of the students.

On the other hand, one strong predictor of teaching performance is the amount of coursework in education. Studies have consistently found positive effects of teachers' formal education training on supervisory ratings and student learning. In addition to educational coursework, content knowledge is important. For example, one study indicated that students' science achievement positively related to teachers' course-taking background in both education and science. Thus, we can have confidence that both content knowledge and pedagogical skills are vital aspects of teacher effectiveness.

The following points summarize important outcomes related to educational coursework in teacher preparation:

• A teacher's formal pedagogical preparation has been shown to have a positive effect on student achievement, especially in the areas of mathematics, science, and reading.

• The teachers who completed programs of study in education consistently perform better on state licensing exams than those teachers who did not attend a program of study in education.

• The more methods courses in a teacher's preparation program, the more likely the teacher is to emphasize conceptual understanding and hands-on learning techniques in the classroom.

• A teacher's subject matter expertise supports student learning up to a point, but educational coursework appears to have a substantive value-added influence on student achievement.

• A positive relationship exists between student achievement and how recently an experienced teacher took part in a professional development opportunity such as a conference, workshop, or graduate class.

• The teachers prepared in schools of education demonstrate stronger classroom management skills and can better relate content to the needs and interests of students.

• The ability to apply and integrate knowledge or skills to a particular population in a specific setting is the key characteristic of an effective teacher.

Key references: Ashton & Crocker, 1987; Blair, 2000; Darling-Hammond, 2000; Darling-Hammond, 2001; Druva & Anderson, 1983; Evertson, Hawley, & Zlotnik, 1985; Ferguson & Womack, 1993; Fetler, 1999; Hansen & Feldhusen, 1994; Hanushek, 1971; Holt-Reynolds, 1999; Mason, Schroeter, Combs, & Washington, 1992; Mathews, 1999; Miller, McKenna, & McKenna, 1998; Monk & King, 1994; Schalock, Schalock, & Myton, 1998; Scherer, 2001; Shellard & Protheroe, 2000; Southern Regional Education Board, 1999; Thomas B. Fordham Foundation, 1999; Wenglinsky, 2000; Wise, 2000

Teacher Certification and Effective Teaching

Another important and controversial issue related to educational preparation of teachers is licensure and certification. In most states, teacher certification status is related to educational background and to scores on some test of pedagogical or content knowledge, or both. However, alternative certification routes are becoming more common along with alternative recruitment and preparation programs. As with other elements of teacher background, the research findings on licensure and certification related to student achievement are mixed.

The research indicates that the number of well-qualified, certified teachers within the state is a consistent and significant predictor of student achievement in math and reading on standardized tests. Furthermore, one of the best predictors of low student performance in individual schools is the number of uncertified teachers in the building. However, anywhere from 10 to 30 percent of new public school teachers each year begin teaching without full certification. In addition, more than half of the schools in the United States have certified teachers who are teaching in content areas in which they are not certified.

One study indicated that this practice of out-of-field teaching actually harms the teacher, as well as the students. In fact, teaching a grade level or subject for which a teacher is not certified or has little training may convert a highly qualified and capable teacher into an ineffective one. Some studies concluded that uncertified teachers and out-of-field teachers achieve far less with students than teachers with proper, in-field certification.

Some important findings from research related to certification standards are

• Fully prepared and certified teachers have a greater impact on gains in student learning than do uncertified or provisionally certified teachers, especially with minority populations and in urban and rural settings.

• Teacher certification status and teaching within one's field are positively related to student outcomes.

• Teachers with certification of some kind (standard, alternative, or provisional) tend to have higher achieving students than teachers working without certification.

• Teachers certified within their field have significantly higher achievement rates among their students than teachers working out-of-field, especially in mathematics.

• Students of teachers who hold standard certification in their subjects score from 7 to 10 points higher on 12th grade math tests than students of teachers with probationary, emergency, or no certification.

• Some studies have demonstrated relationships between standard certification and teacher practices (e.g., hands-on learning, connections to student experiences). These teacher practices have themselves been found to be effective in supporting student achievement, thus illustrating a possible indirect relationship between traditional certification and student achievement.

Key references: Darling-Hammond, 1996; Darling-Hammond, 2000; Darling-Hammond, 2001; Darling-Hammond, Berry, & Thoreson, 2001; Dozier & Bertotti, 2000; Evertson, Hawley, & Zlotnik, 1985; Ferguson & Womack, 1993; Fetler, 1999; Goldhaber & Brewer, 2000; Hawk, Coble, & Swanson, 1985; Ingersoll, 2001; Lilly, 1992; Mathews, 1999; Miller, McKenna, & McKenna, 1998; Scherer, 2001; Strauss & Sawyer, 1986; Wise, 2000

Content Knowledge and Effective Teaching

A teacher's knowledge of the content that is taught is another important issue that has been extensively investigated in the research on teacher effectiveness. Strong content knowledge consistently has been identified as an essential element among those who study effective teaching. Clearly, subject matter knowledge positively affects teaching performance, however, it is not sufficient in and of itself. Teacher training programs that emphasize content knowledge acquisition and neglect pedagogical coursework are less effective in preparing prospective teachers to teach today's students than programs that offer both content and pedagogical knowledge.

Studies surveying educational stakeholders about teacher effectiveness place high priority on competence in content knowledge. Teachers with subject matter knowledge are better able to go beyond the basic textbook content and involve students in meaningful discussions and student-directed activities. Some researchers argue that the definition of subject matter expertise must include the ability to convey and teach the content to others, as well as having an acute awareness of the concepts and ideas being taught. Additionally, a strong background in content and subject matter assists teachers in planning and organizing lessons that are sequential and interactive.

Investigations of the importance of teacher content knowledge have yielded the following results:

• Students perform better when their teachers have majored or minored in the subject area that they are teaching.

• Teachers with a major or minor in content area are associated with higher student achievement, especially in the areas of secondary science and mathematics.

• Students, teachers, principals, and school board members have all emphasized the importance of subject matter knowledge in describing effective teaching.

• The ability to convey the content to students in a way that they can grasp, use, and remember is important, but it is not necessarily related to additional knowledge or coursework in the content area.

• Content area preparation is positively related to student achievement within specific subjects, especially in mathematics and science.

• Several studies have illustrated that teachers with greater subject matter knowledge tend to ask higher-level questions, involve students in the lessons, and allow more student-directed activities.

• Inconsistent results have been reported relating teacher scores on subject matter tests to student achievement, raising questions as to how well such tests measure aspects of content knowledge that are important for effective teaching of that content.

• Unfortunately, approximately 23 percent of all secondary teachers (30 percent of math teachers) do not have even a minor in the field they teach.

Key references: Berliner, 1986; Blair, 2000; Brookhart & Loadman, 1992; Carlsen, 1987; Carlsen & Wilson, 1988; Covino & Iwanicki, 1996; Darling-Hammond, 1996; Darling-Hammond, 2000; Darling-Hammond, Berry, & Thoreson, 2001; Druva & Anderson, 1983; Ferguson & Womack, 1993; Fetler, 1999; Goldhaber & Brewer, 2000; Holt-Reynolds, 1999; Johnson, 1997; Mitchell, 1998; Monk & King, 1994; National Association of Secondary School Principals (NASSP), 1997; NBPTS, no date; Peart & Campbell, 1999; Rowan, Chiang, & Miller, 1997; Shellard & Protheroe, 2000; Shulman, 1987; Traina, 1999; Wenglinsky, 2000

Teaching Experience and Teacher Effectiveness

Teaching experience matters in teacher effectiveness and student achievement, at least to a certain point. Experienced teachers differ from rookie teachers in that they have attained expertise through real-life experiences, classroom practice, and time. These teachers typically have a greater repertoire from which to incorporate and organize routines for monitoring students and creating flowing, meaningful lessons. Teachers who are both experienced and effective are experts who know the content and students they teach, use efficient planning strategies, practice interactive decision-making, and embody effective classroom management skills. These experienced and effective teachers are efficient—they can do more in less time than novice educators.

Researchers indicate that teachers develop from novices to masters at different intervals over time, taking from five to eight years to master the art, science, and craft of teaching. Therefore, the number of years in front of a classroom of students may not necessarily indicate that a teacher is expert. One study suggests that in order for a teacher to be considered experienced, the ability to apply the "book knowledge" from preservice training to both common and exceptional classroom situations should be observable. Through experience and awareness, teachers are able to improvise. Flexibility and adaptability are sometimes better than a well-written lesson plan because classrooms are dynamic. Novice teachers often hesitate to deviate from a plan, but the effective teacher can do it with ease and therefore capitalize on a teachable moment and accommodate a schedule change. The ability to improvise is a characteristic more common to experienced educators than to beginners.

Research supports the following findings related to teacher experience:

• Teachers with more experience tend to show better planning skills, including a more hierarchical and organized structure in the presentation of their material.

• Effective experienced teachers are better able to apply a range of teaching strategies, and they demonstrate more depth and differentiation in learning activities.

• Experienced teachers tend to know and understand their students' learning needs, learning styles, prerequisite skills, and interests better than beginners.

• The classrooms of more experienced teachers are better organized around routines and plans for handling problems than those of novices.

• Teaching experience has up to a 30 percent beneficial effect on student academic performance.

• Teachers with more than three years of experience are more effective than those with three years or fewer, but these differences seem to level off after five to eight years. Teacher expertise as defined by experience (as well as education and scores on licensing exams) accounts for as much as 40 percent of the variation in students' achievement.

Key references: Covino & Iwanicki, 1996; Cruickshank & Haefele, 2001; Darling-Hammond, 2000; Education Review Office, 1998; Fetler, 1999; Haycock, 2000; Kerrins & Cushing, 1998; Neilsen, 1999; Scherer, 2001; Tell, 2001; Virshup, 1997

Figure 1.1
Key References: Prerequisites of Effective Teaching

Reference	Verbal Ability	Knowledge of Teaching & Learning	Certification Status	Content Knowledge	Teaching Experience
Ashton & Crocker, 1987		●			
Berliner, 1986				●	
Blair, 2000		●			
Brookhart & Loadman, 1992				●	
Carlsen, 1987				●	
Carlsen & Wilson, 1988				●	
Covino & Iwanicki, 1996				●	●
Cruickshank & Haefele, 2001					●
Darling-Hammond, 1996			●	●	
Darling-Hammond, 2000			●	●	
Darling-Hammond, 2001	●	●	●	●	●
Darling-Hammond, Berry, & Thoreson, 2001			●	●	
Dozier & Bertotti, 2000			●		
Druva & Anderson, 1983		●		●	
Educational Review Office, 1998					●
Evertson, Hawley, & Zlotnik, 1985		●	●		
Ferguson & Womack, 1993		●	●	●	
Fetler, 1999		●	●	●	●
Goldhaber & Brewer, 2000			●	●	
Hansen & Feldhusen, 1994		●			
Hanushek, 1971	●	●			
Hawk, Coble, & Swanson, 1985			●		
Haycock, 2000	●				●
Holt-Reynolds, 1999		●		●	
Ingersoll, 2001			●		
Johnson, 1997				●	

Figure 1.1 *continued*
Key References: Prerequisites of Effective Teaching

Reference	Verbal Ability	Knowledge of Teaching & Learning	Certification Status	Content Knowledge	Teaching Experience
Kerrins & Cushing, 1998					●
Lilly, 1992			●		
Mason, Schroeter, Combs, & Washington, 1992		●			
Mathews, 1999		●	●		
Miller, McKenna, & McKenna, 1998		●	●		
Mitchell, 1998				●	
Monk & King, 1994		●		●	
Murnane, 1985	●				
National Association of Secondary School Principals, 1997				●	
National Board for Professional Teaching Standards, no date				●	
National Center for Educational Statistics, 1992	●				
Neilsen, 1999					●
Peart & Campbell, 1999				●	
Rowan, Chiang, & Miller, 1997	●			●	
Schalock, Schalock, & Myton, 1998		●			
Scherer, 2001		●	●		●
Shellard & Protheroe, 2000		●		●	
Shulman, 1987				●	
Southern Regional Education Board, 1999		●			
Strauss & Sawyer, 1986			●		
Summers & Wolfe, 1975	●				
Tell, 2001		●			
Thomas B. Fordham Foundation, 1999	●	●			
Traina, 1999				●	
Virshup, 1997					●
Wenglinsky, 2000	●	●		●	
Wise, 2000		●	●		

2

The Teacher as a Person

I just wanted to write you a little thank you note for everything that you have done for me over the past two years. I have learned a lot and had a whole lotta fun doing it. I loved the labs, and basically everything we did in your class because you made it fun. You made it so we learned without even realizing we were learning anything, but when it came time to show that we knew it, we were like, "Whoa! I guess I really did learn something!" Not only did you teach us about science, you put us in real case scenarios and helped prepare us for high school and even college. But even further than that, you were like a friend to me. That might scare you a little, but you really remind me of myself, and I hope I grow up to be at least a little like you. I feel like you genuinely care about your students and sincerely enjoy your job . . . Thank you for being such a great teacher and friend. You have sincerely contributed to the "awesomeness" of these years. Thanks 1,000 times!

STUDENT LETTER TO A MIDDLE SCHOOL SCIENCE TEACHER WITH FOUR YEARS OF TEACHING EXPERIENCE

Much of the recent research on teacher effectiveness focuses on relating teacher behaviors to student achievement. Quite a bit of the research, however, has delved into stakeholders' perceptions of good teaching—what students, administrators, and teachers themselves think makes an effective teacher. Studies suggest that instructional and management processes are key to effectiveness, but many interview and survey responses about effective teaching emphasize the teacher's affective characteristics, or social and emotional behaviors, more than pedagogical practice.

13

Moreover, the teacher's psychological influence on students has been linked to student achievement in various effectiveness studies. This chapter explores what we know about teachers' affective characteristics as they relate to effectiveness and to perceptions of effectiveness. Figure 2.1, at the end of the chapter, lists the major characteristics with key references for additional reading.

Role of Caring

Effective teachers care about their students and demonstrate that they care in such a way that their students are aware of it, as we see in the classroom example at the beginning of this chapter. Several studies exploring what makes a good teacher show the importance of caring in the eyes of teachers and students. Also, supervisors who rate teachers place priority on how teachers show students that they are caring and supportive.

Caring is a broad term, maybe as broad as effectiveness itself. One study defines caring as an act of bringing out the best in students through affirmation and encouragement. Obviously, the characteristics of caring go well beyond knowing the students to include qualities such as patience, trust, honesty, and courage. Specific teacher attributes that show caring include listening, gentleness, understanding, knowledge of students as individuals, warmth and encouragement, and an overall love for children.

Listening

Effective teachers practice focused and sympathetic listening to show students they care not only about what happens in the classroom, but about students' lives in general. These teachers initiate two-way communication that exudes trust, tact, honesty, humility, and care. In the act of listening, these teachers actually pay attention to and understand what the students say. They are dedicated to bettering student lives and demonstrate their understanding through tenderness, patience, and gentleness. Moreover, research indicates that children want to be nurtured, and they value teachers who are kind, gentle, and encouraging. Particularly for elementary students, gentleness in a teacher is a sign of caring and an important element in perceived effectiveness.

Understanding

Students highly value teachers' understanding of their concerns and questions. Interviews with students consistently reveal that students want teachers who listen to their arguments and assist them in working out their problems. They want teachers who hold them in mutual respect and who are willing to talk about their own personal lives and experiences. Through appropriate self-disclosure, teachers become human in the eyes of students. Being available to students, and the depth of the teacher's understanding of students, legitimizes the teacher as a person when demonstrating genuine concern and empathy toward students.

Knowing Students

Effective, caring teachers know students both formally and informally. They use every opportunity at school and in the community to keep the lines of communication open. Many educational stakeholders emphasize that effective teachers know their students individually, not only understanding each student's learning style and needs, but also understanding the student's personality, likes and dislikes, and personal situations that may affect behavior and performance in school. Effective teachers care for the student first as a person, and second as a student. They respect each student as an individual.

Research on caring teachers yields the following important points:

• Caring teachers who know their students create relationships that enhance the learning process.

• Effective teachers consistently emphasize their love for children as one key element of their success.

• Teachers who create a supportive and warm classroom climate tend to be more effective with all students.

• Caring teachers are intentionally aware of student cultures outside the school.

• Caring teachers truly believe that each student has a right to a caring and competent teacher.

• Caring teachers appropriately respect confidentiality issues when dealing with students.

• Caring teachers regard the ethic of care and learning as important in educating students to their full potential.

Key references: Bain & Jacobs, 1990; Brophy & Good, 1986; Collinson, Killeavy, & Stephenson, 1999; Cotton, 1999; Cotton, 2000; Cruickshank & Haefele, 2001; Emmer, Evertson, & Anderson, 1980; Good & Brophy, 1997; Johnson, 1997; National Association of Secondary School Principals, 1997; Peart & Campbell, 1999; Thomas & Montomery, 1998; Wang, Haertel, & Walberg, 1993a; Wang, Haertel, & Walberg, 1993b; Yamaguchi, Strawser, & Higgins, 1997

Role of Fairness and Respect

Beyond a demonstration of caring, an effective teacher establishes rapport and credibility with students by emphasizing, modeling, and practicing fairness and respect. Respect and equity are identified as the prerequisites of effective teaching in the eyes of students. In fact, students interviewed for their views on effective teachers consistently note the importance of fairness and respect at all levels of schooling—from elementary through high school.

The elements of fairness and respect are highlighted in many studies. Students stated that effective teachers respond to misbehavior at an individual level rather than holding a whole class responsible for the actions of one student or a small group of students. They know and understand the facts before responding to any disciplinary situation, and then tell students specifically what they did wrong. Moreover, they tell students what they need to do right. Furthermore, students expect teachers to treat them equitably—when they behave as well as misbehave—and to avoid demonstrations of favoritism.

Effective teachers continually demonstrate respect and understanding, along with fairness regarding race, cultural background, and gender. Students' perceptions of teacher effectiveness emphasize racial impartiality with equitable treatment of all students. The students expect teachers not to allow ethnicity to affect their treatment or expectations of students.

Interviews and surveys of perceptions of fairness in the classroom indicate the following key points:

• Students associate respect with fairness and expect teachers to treat them as people.

• Students perceive effective teachers as those who avoid using ridicule and who prevent situations in which students lose respect in front of their peers.

• Effective teachers practice gender, racial, and ethnic fairness.

• Students associate fairness and respect with a teacher being consistent and providing opportunities for students to have input into the classroom.

• Effective teachers offer all students opportunities to participate and to succeed.

Key references: Collinson, Killeavy, & Stephenson, 1999; Cotton, 1999; Cotton, 2000; Emmer, Evertson, & Anderson, 1980; Good & Brophy, 1997; McBer, 2000; National Association of Secondary School Principals, 1997; Peart & Campbell, 1999; Thomas & Montomery, 1998; Yamaguchi, Strawser, & Higgins, 1997

Social Interactions with Students

Teachers and students spend much of their day interacting academically. However, social interactions and those that give the teacher opportunities to demonstrate caring, fairness, and respect have been shown to be an important element of teacher effectiveness. A teacher's ability to relate to students and to make positive, caring connections with them plays a significant role in cultivating a positive learning environment and promoting student achievement.

Effective teachers use a wide variety of strategies to interact with students. However, the basis for these interactions goes beyond the four walls of the classroom. In fact, students revealed that effective teachers demonstrate interest in students' lives beyond the classroom. Teachers who attend sporting events, concerts, and other special programs in which their students participate are valued by their students. Additionally, researchers contend that constructive social interactions between teachers and students not only contribute to student learning and achievement, but also increase student self-esteem by fostering feelings of belonging to the classroom and the school.

Teachers who are aware of their own style of interacting with their students are able to provide a more favorable learning environment for all students. Through social interactions with students, effective teachers are able to individually, realistically, and successfully challenge each and every student to succeed.

Aspects of effective teaching related to social interaction involve the following:

• Effective teachers consistently behave in a friendly and personal manner while maintaining appropriate teacher-student role structure.

• Effective teachers work *with* students as opposed to doing things *to* or *for* them.

• Productive interactions involve giving students responsibility and respect; also treating secondary students as adults when appropriate.

• Teachers who are considered effective allow students to participate in decision making.

• Effective teachers pay attention to what students have to say.

• Students indicate that effective teachers spend more time interacting and working directly with them than ineffective teachers.

• When interacting with students, effective teachers demonstrate a sense of fun and a willingness to play or participate.

• Effective teachers have a good sense of humor and are willing to share jokes.

Key references: Bain & Jacobs, 1990; Bloom, 1984; Brookhart & Loadman, 1992; Collinson, Killeavy, & Stephenson, 1999; Cotton, 1999; Cotton, 2000; Cruickshank & Haefele, 2001; Darling-Hammond, 2001; Education USA Special Report, no date; Good & Brophy, 1997; Johnson, 1997; Kohn, 1996; National Association of Secondary School Principals, 1997; Peart & Campbell, 1999; Porter & Brophy, 1988; Thomas & Montomery, 1998; Wang, Haertel, & Walberg, 1993a; Wang, Haertel, & Walberg, 1993b; Yamaguchi, Strawser, & Higgins, 1997

Promotion of Enthusiasm and Motivation for Learning

The teacher's enthusiasm for teaching, learning, and for the subject matter has been shown to be an important part of effective teaching, both in supporting positive relationships with students and in encouraging student achievement. Based on student interviews, teachers can effectively motivate most students by encouraging them to be responsible for their own learning, maintaining an organized classroom environment, setting high standards, assigning appropriate challenges, and providing reinforcement and encouragement during tasks. These students see effective teachers as motivational leaders.

Research indicates that effective teachers have residual positive effects on their students' willingness to work to their potential and beyond. Consequently, less effective teachers may actually extinguish students' interest in the subject. Good teachers realize and deal with the fact that some students prefer to sit quietly on the sideline; however, they do not stop involving them.

By finding a way to motivate a student to learn, a teacher contributes to a student's evolving attitude toward a particular subject or activity. In other words, the teacher can bring out the best in that student. An effective teacher recognizes that students vary in their motivation levels. An effective teacher knows how to support intrinsically motivated students and seeks ways to provide extrinsic motivation to students who need it. Motivating students consists of making students receptive to and excited about learning, as well as making them aware of the importance and value of learning itself. By establishing positive attitudes and perceptions about learning, the effective teacher makes the learner feel comfortable in the classroom. As a particular example of establishing positive attitudes, teachers who provide mastery learning techniques for their students improve the attitudes of their students. They also increase academic self-concept, interest in the subject area, and the desire to learn more about the subject. Emphasizing higher mental processes along with mastery learning strategies tends to create a learning environment that is exciting and constantly new and playful.

Researchers have investigated the influence of teacher enthusiasm on student motivation and learning, with the following results and conclusions:

• High levels of motivation in teachers relate to high levels of achievement in students.

• Teachers' enthusiasm for learning and for the subject matter under study has been shown to be an important factor in student motivation, which is closely linked to student achievement.

• A teacher's involvement in graduate studies, which indicates enthusiasm for learning, may be a source of motivation and may translate into higher achievement among students.

• Some studies indicate that the enthusiasm factor is more significant with older students than younger ones, but effective primary teachers also have demonstrated enthusiasm for their work as part of their overall effectiveness.

Key references: Bain & Jacobs, 1990; Bloom, 1984; Brophy & Good, 1986; Collinson, Killeavy, & Stephenson, 1999; Covino & Iwanicki, 1996; Darling-Hammond, 2000; Johnson, 1997; Marzano, Pickering, & McTighe, 1993; Monk & King, 1994; Palmer, 1990; Peart & Campbell, 1999; Rowan, Chiang, & Miller, 1997; Wang, Haertel, & Walberg, 1993a; Wang, Haertel, & Walberg, 1993b

Attitude Toward the Teaching Profession

An important facet of professionalism and of effectiveness in the classroom is a teacher's dedication to students and to the job of teaching. Through examination of several sources of evidence, a dual commitment to student learning and to personal learning has been found repeatedly in effective teachers. A common belief among effective teachers, which reveals their dual commitment, is that it is up to them to provide a multitude of tactics to reach students. In essence, effective teachers view themselves as responsible for the success of their students.

The effective teacher truly believes that all students can learn—it is not just a slogan. These teachers also believe that they must know their students, their subject, and themselves, while continuing to account for the fact that students learn differently. Through differentiation of instruction, effective teachers reach their students and together they enjoy their successes.

Effective teachers also work collaboratively with other staff members. They are willing to share their ideas and assist other teachers with difficulties. Collaborative environments create positive working relationships and help retain teachers. Additionally, effective teachers volunteer to lead work teams and to be mentors to new teachers. Effective teachers are informal leaders on the cutting edge of reform and are not afraid to take risks to improve education for all students. These informal leaders are the ones administrators typically call on for opinions and help in effecting change.

Effective teachers invest in their own education. They model to their students that education and learning are valuable by taking classes and participating in professional development, conferences, and inservice training. Additionally, they discuss their participation in these activities with students in a positive manner. Effective teachers learn and grow as they expect their students to learn and grow. They serve as powerful examples of lifelong learners as they find ways to develop professionally.

The relationship between teachers' attitudes and effectiveness can be summarized:

• Effective teachers exude positive attitudes about life and teaching.

• Extra hours spent preparing and reflecting upon instruction are well worth the student outcomes—specifically achievement.

• Promoting and participating in a collegial, collaborative work environment results in more positive attitudes in teachers.

• Effective teachers do not make excuses for student outcomes; they hold their students responsible while also accepting responsibility themselves.

Key references: Bain & Jacobs, 1990; Blair, 2000; Brookhart & Loadman, 1992; Cawelti, 1999b; Covino & Iwanicki, 1996; McBer, 2000; Mitchell, 1998; National Board for Professional Teaching Standards, no date; Porter & Brophy, 1988; Rowan, Chiang, & Miller, 1997; Thomas & Montomery, 1998; Virshup, 1997; Wong & Wong, 1998

Role of Reflective Practice

Another element of professionalism often cited as part of effective teaching is a teacher's reflective practice, or careful review of and thoughtfulness about one's own teaching process. The role of reflection has been described repeatedly in studies of teacher effectiveness. Those studies include interviews and surveys of teachers judged effective according to their students' achievement rates, studies of teachers certified under the National Board of Professional Teaching Standards, and case studies of effective schools. Effective teachers continuously practice self-evaluation and self-critique as learning tools. Reflective teachers portray themselves as students of learning. They are curious about the art and science of teaching and about themselves as effective teachers. They constantly improve lessons, think about how to reach particular children, and seek and try out new approaches in the classroom to better meet the needs of their learners.

Some researchers define reflective teachers as introspective. They seek a greater understanding of teaching through scholarly study and professional reading. Through reflective practice, effective teachers monitor their teaching because they want to be better teachers and to make a difference in the lives of students.

Effective teachers are not afraid of feedback; in fact, they elicit information and criticism from others. Additionally, in the interest of improving their ability to have a positive impact on student learning, these teachers readily accept constructive criticism and reflect upon it. Reflective practice can initially result in confusion for the teacher; the process requires open-mindedness, honesty, and sufficient time to change teaching behaviors.

Thoughtful questions generated by research can guide teachers in reflecting on practice. Effective teachers realize that reflective practices are more than simply preservice or inservice exercises. Indeed, reflective practices are crucial to lifelong learning and a professional necessity.

Thoughtful reflection translates into enhanced teacher efficacy. And a teacher's sense of efficacy has an impact on how she approaches instructional content and students. While efficacy does change for teachers as they encounter new experiences, such as materials and grade levels, they are more likely to have additional positive experiences as they reflect on these new experiences. Educators' confidence in their ability to facilitate the learning and understanding of material by students is observable by others. In particular, when teachers are confident, they communicate the belief of their own efficacy to students.

Additional findings on the value of reflective practices include the following:

• Effective teachers may reflect on their work formally or informally; for example, they may review a day's work mentally, keep a journal or portfolio, meet regularly with a mentor or with colleagues, or assess a videotaped recording of their teaching. Regardless of the mode, the key is reflection.

• Teachers whose students have high achievement rates continually mention reflection on their work as an important part of improving their teaching.

• Belief in one's efficacy and maintaining high expectations for students are common among teachers who reflect.

Key references: Collinson, Killeavy, & Stephenson, 1999; Covino & Iwanicki, 1996; Cruickshank & Haefele, 2001; Demmon-Berger, 1986; Good & Brophy, 1997; Mitchell, 1998; National Board for Professional Teaching Standards, no date; Thomas & Montomery, 1998

Figure 2.1
Key References: The Teacher as a Person

Reference	Caring	Fairness & Respect	Interactions with Students	Enthusiasm & Motivation	Attitude Toward Teaching	Reflective Practice
Bain & Jacobs, 1990	●		●	●	●	
Blair, 2000					●	
Bloom, 1984			●	●		
Brookhart & Loadman, 1992			●		●	
Brophy & Good, 1986	●			●		
Cawelti, 1999b					●	
Collinson, Killeavy, & Stephenson, 1999	●	●	●	●		●
Cotton, 1999	●	●	●			
Cotton, 2000	●	●	●			
Covino & Iwanicki, 1996				●	●	●
Cruickshank & Haefele, 2001	●		●			●
Darling-Hammond, 2000				●		
Darling-Hammond, 2001			●			
Demmon-Berger, 1986						●
Education USA Special Report, no date			●			
Emmer, Evertson, & Anderson, 1980	●	●				
Good & Brophy, 1997	●	●	●			●
Johnson, 1997	●		●	●		
Kohn, 1996				●		
Marzano, Pickering, & McTighe, 1993				●		
McBer, 2000		●			●	
Mitchell, 1998					●	●
Monk & King, 1994				●		
National Association of Secondary School Principals, 1997	●	●	●			

Figure 2.1 *continued*
Key References: The Teacher as a Person

Reference	Caring	Fairness & Respect	Interactions with Students	Enthusiasm & Motivation	Attitude Toward Teaching	Reflective Practice
National Board for Professional Teaching Standards, no date					●	●
Palmer, 1990				●		
Peart & Campbell, 1999	●	●	●	●		
Porter & Brophy, 1988			●		●	
Rowan, Chiang, & Miller, 1997				●	●	
Thomas & Montomery, 1998	●	●	●		●	●
Virshup, 1997					●	
Wang, Haertel, & Walberg, 1993a, 1993b	●		●	●		
Wong & Wong, 1998					●	
Yamaguchi, Strawser, & Higgins, 1997	●	●	●			

3

Classroom Management and Organization

Before class began, the teacher walked around the room, laying the graded work from a previous class session face down on the students' desks. When the students walked into the room, they looked at the assignment that had been returned, and immediately copied down the daily objective and home-work assignment before beginning the math starter, a problem on the board. If a student needed a calculator, ruler, or other materials, the student simply went to where the materials were stored and got what was needed. The teacher circulated around the room and within a few minutes began class by asking students to explain their approach and solution to a partner or triad. They moved into this formation, conferred, and then volunteered to share with the class. Then the teacher moved on to addressing questions about the graded assignment before introducing a new mathematical concept. The whole process of getting the students into the room, settled, and focused on the starter and going over the graded work lasted about fifteen minutes and the teacher used additional routines to maximize the remaining forty minutes of the class period.

ALGEBRA AND GEOMETRY TEACHER WITH 27 YEARS OF EXPERIENCE

An effective teacher plans and prepares for the organization of the classroom with the same care and precision used to design a high-quality lesson. In a symphony, the conductor manages the various sections to produce a harmonious sound, much like the teacher conducts the components of a classroom to create the buzz of students engaged in learning. Components of the organizational plan of a classroom include room arrangement, discipline, the creation of routines, and a plan to teach the students how their learning environment is organized. To the extent possible, effective teachers envision what is needed to make the classroom run smoothly. A key difference between beginning and experienced educators is that the novice tends to leap into the content the first week of school, while the senior teacher works on creating a positive classroom climate and then works academics into that objective.

The effective teacher is not just someone who knows how to support student learning through instructional techniques, strong curricular materials, and rapport with the class. The effective teacher must create an overall environment conducive to learning. Orchestrating this supportive learning environment requires that a teacher practice skills in classroom organization and management. It also requires consistency in behavioral expectations and responses. The effective educator attends to these elements in a proactive way to establish a positive classroom climate oriented toward learning, much as a symphony conductor attends to many elements in performing a musical masterpiece. Figure 3.1 at the end of this chapter summarizes specific elements of the effective learning environment and links these elements to key references.

Using Classroom Management Skills

Successful classroom management involves much more than rules and discipline. Indeed, research into classroom management demonstrates that effective teachers are those who are proactive about student behavior, involving students in the process of establishing and maintaining rules and routines. Doyle (1986) defined management as "the actions and strategies teachers use to solve the problem of order in classrooms" (p. 397), rather than responses to disciplinary situations. Effective teachers establish responses to common classroom issues of order that allow them to focus maximum time and energy on the instructional process. When teachers make the classroom experience engaging, there is little time or inclination for students to misbehave.

Effective classroom managers are thoroughly prepared and keep their students actively involved in the teaching and learning process. The primary ingredient here for teacher effectiveness is readiness. Effective teachers are prepared for students on a daily basis, from the very first day of school to the very last. Creating a productive classroom environment includes practical planning, such as developing functional floor plans with teacher and student work areas, wall spaces, and furniture placed within the classroom for optimal benefit. Some studies also include self-preparation, both physical and attitudinal, as a key contributor to the organizational process. Classroom managers who are prepared for the ups and downs of the instructional day work to create a setting that responds to the ebb and flow of the students. A positive attitude conveys this preparedness to students.

In addition to arranging the physical setting, effective teachers establish and actively teach rules and procedures at the beginning of the school year and rehearse them in the context in which they will be applied. They consistently and fairly enforce the rules for all students. Good classroom managers are effective monitors of students, as well. These teachers are keen observers of student behaviors and adept at discerning and addressing potential disruptions. Over and over again, the term "with-it-ness," meaning awareness of surroundings, is used to describe teachers who are effective classroom managers. Moreover, effective teachers who are aware of student behaviors have a tendency to be near problems when they erupt, and so can quell them quickly.

Many studies show that classroom management is an influential variable in teacher effectiveness. Explorations of student achievement, surveys of perceptions, and meta-analyses on a range of studies have all supported the notion that effective management is a key component of effective teaching. Elements of effective classroom management include establishing routines and procedures to limit disruption and time taken away from teaching and learning, maintaining momentum and variety in instructional practices, and monitoring and responding to student activity.

Research findings on the classroom management skills of effective teachers consistently outline the following elements:

- Consistent, proactive discipline is the crux of effective classroom management.
- Effective teachers establish routines for all daily tasks and needs.
- Effective classroom managers orchestrate smooth transitions and continuity of momentum throughout the day.
- Effective teachers and classroom managers strike a balance between variety and challenge in student activities.
- Effective classroom managers can multitask.
- Effective educators have a heightened awareness of all actions and activities in the classroom.
- Classroom management skills include the use of space and proximity or movement around the classroom for nearness to trouble spots and to encourage attention.
- Anticipation of potential problems by effective teachers is a means to limit disruption.

• Effective classroom teachers resolve minor inattention and disruption before they become major disruptions.

• Effective classroom managers are able to increase student engagement in learning and make good use of every instructional moment.

• Effective teachers seem to have eyes in the backs of their heads.

Key references: Bain & Jacobs, 1990; Berliner, 1986; Brophy & Good, 1986; Cotton, 1999; Cotton, 2000; Covino & Iwanicki, 1996; Demmon-Berger, 1986; Doyle, 1986; Education USA Special Report, no date; Emmer, Evertson, & Anderson, 1980; Good & Brophy, 1997; Good & McCaslin, 1992; Johnson, 1997; Kounin, 1970; Peart & Campbell, 1999; Shellard & Protheroe, 2000; Teddlie & Stringfield, 1993; Wang, Haertel, & Walberg, 1993a; Wang, Haertel, & Walberg, 1993b; Wong & Wong, 1998; Yamaguchi, Strawser, & Higgins, 1997

Applying Elements of Organization

Organizational skills deserve special attention in our discussion of effective classroom management and its role in effective teaching. The teacher who is organized in terms of routines, behaviors, and materials typically is better prepared for class and sets an example of organization for students that supports their organization for learning. Emphasis on organization has been shown to contribute to effective teaching by freeing up as much as an extra hour per week from administrative or lost time that can be used as instructional time.

Most effective teachers admit that rules, procedures, and routines take precedence over academic lessons during the first week of school, noting that organization takes a considerable investment of time at first; however, it has tremendous payback benefits. When materials are organized, it allows for smooth transitions between activities and increases the amount of time on academic tasks. Consequently, as students focus on academic engagement, the potential for behavior problems to occur is greatly reduced.

Organized classrooms are easy to recognize. Instructors in well-organized classrooms prepare effective working environments by optimizing proximity to materials and students. Routines and procedures are established so that the classrooms seem to run automatically. Students know exactly what to do and when to do it. This orchestrated level of organization allows effective teachers to provide differentiated instruction when it is needed.

Good classroom organization is achieved in a variety of ways. One elementary school example is the use of color-coding to assist a teacher or student in quickly locating materials. If multiple preparations are required of a teacher, color-coding bins or folders (one color per subject) can optimize organization. Placing commonly used materials such as scissors, staplers, tape, hole punches, and crayons in easily accessible places for students saves the teacher from being the sole distributor of the resources. Dish tubs may be used to organize the materials needed for a hands-on activity and should be prepared in advance to save class time. A secondary school example is when science educators designate students to serve as laboratory assistants who help prepare for lab work. In elementary school, the assignment of classroom jobs encourages responsibility as students serve as line leaders and paper collectors on a rotating basis. Using a combination of strategies to organize the classroom can allow more class time to be allocated for instruction.

Taking the time to set up procedures for routine tasks in a classroom enables the teacher to cue students to perform them with a minimal amount of explanation. Training, feedback, and praise, however, are needed to establish the routine. Just as kindergartners must be taught what to do when the fire drill sounds, procedures must be taught so that they become automatic responses. Once taught, the routines can be adapted if the situation arises, but the groundwork is laid for a well-orchestrated classroom.

Many studies summarize these key elements of organization:

• Teaching is best described as a juggling act in which the teacher is able to multitask (e.g., activities and classroom experiences).

• Handling of routine tasks is prompt and efficient by effective teachers.

• Having materials prepared and ready for use in advance of the lesson, including extra materials in case of unexpected problems or sudden arrival of new students, is a mark of an organized instructor.

• Creating and maintaining practical procedures allows teachers to support students in knowing what they are to do, when, with minimum repetition of directions.

• Communicating to students the organization of space and where necessary materials are to be stored is common among effective teachers.

Key references: Bain & Jacobs, 1990; Berendt & Koski, 1999; Brophy & Good, 1986; Cotton, 1999; Cotton, 2000; Covino & Iwanicki, 1996; Emmer, Evertson, & Anderson, 1980; Shellard & Protheroe, 2000; Wang, Haertel, & Walberg, 1993a; Wang, Haertel, & Walberg, 1993b; Wong & Wong, 1998

Managing and Responding to Student Behavior

One of the most important organizational skills an effective teacher possesses is the ability to prevent negative behavior. Studies indicate that the majority of behavior problems occur because students do not know or do not follow routines and procedures. This supports the notion that proactive classroom management is the most effective deterrent to discipline problems. Praising students, reinforcing positive behaviors, and establishing trust within the classroom builds respectful relationships between teachers and students. Disciplinary actions are rare in environments where teachers and students respect and trust each other.

The key to minimizing discipline problems is good classroom management skills. Effective teachers manage and attend to the needs of all students within the class. Unfortunately, classroom observation reports reveal that most teachers direct their attention and instruction more frequently to some students and ignore others. In the same sense, they provide more positive feedback to some while ignoring others. This type of teacher behavior increases the likelihood of student misbehavior. On the other hand, effective classroom managers are able to recognize cues from students and decide if a predetermined procedure or routine should be able to handle the behaviors. If no routine was established in advance, the teacher quickly adapts to handle the situation with little or no disruption to the other students.

Teachers who set and reinforce clear expectations for student behavior have more success in classroom control and fewer discipline problems than those who fail to do so. Establishing rules and procedures at the beginning of the school year and involving students in the process is one approach effective teachers use to ensure students recognize the importance of the students' role in the classroom. Effective teachers clearly communicate and reinforce behavioral expectations. When an expectation is not met, the educator addresses the concern, gives the student an opportunity to identify the issue, and provides ample examples of other choices that the student could have made. Additionally, the teacher assists students in understanding the logic behind the rules and the reasonableness of the consequences for breaking the rules, as well as the rewards for following them. These teachers link consequences to the behavior displayed by the student. They handle discipline issues on an individual basis as opposed to having class consequences for the actions of a few. For situations that are unfamiliar to students, the teacher provides instructions on how to behave. Parents and administrators are involved in supporting and enforcing effective teachers' well-prepared discipline plans. Finally, effective teachers truly believe that students have the capacity to learn self-discipline.

For students in early grades, the explicitness of rules and routines is most important; for students in later grades, clarity of expectations is a more important factor. Equally important as establishing behavioral expectations is the consistency teachers show in carrying out responses to the breaking of rules. Such consistent response and appropriate management helps effective teachers achieve lower levels of off-task student behaviors in their classrooms. Effective teachers also use discipline carefully to support management of the learning environment. Of the disciplinary situations that do arise, effective teachers are able to handle the majority of them within the classroom, without involving administrators. They realize that by reducing disciplinary problems within the classroom, they may be able to significantly increase overall student achievement. Essentially, the less disciplining that takes place, the more time there is for instruction; the more time there is for instruction, the more students learn.

Research on effective teachers' ability to efficiently manage student discipline consistently indicates the following:

• The effective teacher minimizes discipline time and accentuates instructional time.

• The time a teacher spends on disciplining students inversely affects student achievement outcomes.

• The effective teacher interprets and responds to inappropriate behaviors promptly.

• The effective teacher maintains clear rules and procedures, and establishes credibility with students through fair and consistent implementation of discipline.

• The effective teacher reinforces and reiterates the expectations for positive behavior.

Key references: Bain & Jacobs, 1990; Bloom, 1984; Brophy & Good, 1986; Cotton, 1999; Cotton, 2000; Covino & Iwanicki, 1996; Doyle, 1986; Education USA Special Report, no date; Emmer, Evertson, & Anderson, 1980; Good & Brophy, 1997; Hanushek, 1971; Shellard & Protheroe, 2000; Wang, Haertel, & Walberg, 1993a; Wang, Haertel, & Walberg, 1993b; Wong & Wong, 1998; Yamaguchi, Strawser, & Higgins, 1997

Figure 3.1
Key References: Classroom Management and Organization

Reference	Classroom Management	Key Elements of Organization	Disciplining Students
Bain & Jacobs, 1990	●	●	●
Berendt & Koski, 1999		●	
Berliner, 1986	●		
Bloom, 1984			●
Brophy & Good, 1986	●	●	●
Cotton, 1999	●	●	●
Cotton, 2000	●	●	●
Covino & Iwanicki, 1996	●	●	●
Demmon-Berger, 1986	●		
Doyle, 1986	●		●
Education USA Special Report, no date	●		●
Emmer, Evertson, & Anderson, 1980	●	●	●
Good & Brophy, 1997	●		●
Good & McCaslin, 1992	●		
Hanushek, 1971			●
Johnson, 1997	●		
Kounin, 1970	●		
Peart & Campbell, 1999	●		
Shellard & Protheroe, 2000	●	●	●
Teddlie & Stringfield, 1993	●		
Wang, Haertel, & Walberg, 1993a	●	●	●
Wang, Haertel, & Walberg, 1993b	●	●	●
Wong & Wong, 1998	●	●	●
Yamaguchi, Strawser, & Higgins, 1997	●		●

4

Organizing for Instruction

An electrical engineer turned middle school teacher believed that her students could learn advanced math concepts. She channeled her students' energy through expecting excellence, affirming that they could do it, and supporting them. She moved a below-grade-level mathematics group to on-grade level by teaching them pre-algebra concepts. She made it a class goal to go on to pre-algebra or algebra the following school year. This high-energy educator planned lessons that filled the gaps in the students' knowledge base while teaching them complex skills. She applied pre-algebra to the students' lives to make it accessible. She organized her instruction around the students' academic needs—meeting them where they were and taking them where she knew they could go.

MIDDLE SCHOOL TEACHER WITH 8 YEARS OF EXPERIENCE

Teaching is a complex activity that involves careful preparation and the planning of objectives and activities on an hourly, daily, and weekly basis. In addition, long-term planning ensures coverage of curriculum across a marking period, semester, and year. Further, effective educators demonstrate high expectations for students and select strategies to propel the students' learning. Beyond planning and preparation of materials, effective organizing for instruction also involves the development of a conscious orientation toward teaching and learning as the central focus of classroom activity. Teaching and learning as a focus must be consistently communicated to students in the classroom and to observers. This chapter explores elements of organizing and orienting for instruction that have been identified as part of effective teaching practice. Figure 4.1 at the end of this chapter outlines key references relating to these elements.

Focusing on Instruction

The effective teacher recognizes academic instruction as central to his role. This focus on instruction guides not only the teacher's own planning and classroom behavior, but also comes across clearly to students and represents *the* major element in a robust learning environment. A teacher may say to students, "It is my job to see that you succeed," or, "I want you to be prepared for life beyond the schoolhouse door." Although effective teachers believe that students must be challenged, they also realize the need for them to experience success. Several studies have emphasized the importance of a focus on high-quality instruction in supporting student achievement, including the following findings and conclusions:

• Effective teachers see consistency and organization in their classrooms as important because they allow the central focus of classroom time to be on teaching and learning.

• Effective teachers who consistently prioritize instruction and student learning as the central purposes of schooling communicate an enthusiasm and dedication to learning that students reflect in their own behavior and practice.

• Effective teachers reinforce their focus on instruction through their allocation of time to the teaching and learning process, and through their expectations for student learning.

Key references: Bain & Jacobs, 1990; Berendt & Koski, 1999; Berliner & Rosenshine, 1977; Brophy & Good, 1986; Cawelti, 1999b; Cotton, 1999; Cotton, 2000; Covino & Iwanicki, 1996; Holt-Reynolds, 1999; Molnar et al., 1999; Wang, Haertel, & Walberg, 1993a; Wang, Haertel, & Walberg, 1993b

Maximizing Instructional Time

Time is one of the most challenging constraints a teacher faces in trying to achieve curricular goals and meet the needs of all students, while managing the administrative tasks that are a necessary responsibility of the job. Nonetheless, effective teachers do manage to maximize instruction by their thoughtful and careful use of time.

Research has demonstrated that student achievement is higher in classes where instructional time is maximized. The effective teacher prioritizes instruction—a process that is accomplished partially through allocation of time. One illustration of how effective teachers best use the scarce commodity of time is orchestrating smooth classroom transitions. They remain involved with the students during the entire class period, from start to finish, allowing for no idle or down time.

Use of time can be optimized in the classroom by using planning or pacing materials. Students often want to know what is next during class, coming up next week, or next month. So having a scope and sequence not only helps the teacher to plan, but addresses student needs for information. For example, the use of calendars for long-term, weekly, and daily planning, besides providing a visual reminder to the teacher, can help students plan for work. Effective teachers are not only organized, they also convey this vital skill to their students. Sharing with students how the teacher organizes time can serve as a model for students to assist in their own planning, thus equipping them with the tools of success in the larger world and instilling in them habits of efficiency.

Another way that the teacher can set up the classroom to maximize time allocation for instruction is by using staging areas. For example, a list on the back of the door of what the teacher needs to do if a new student arrives fulfills a dual purpose: the new student feels that the teacher is organized; and the teacher feels prepared for the student. Another time-saving device is to use a common place to keep materials such as attendance cards, hall passes, and extra paper—this saves time because the teacher does not have to search for the items. In essence, in the effective classroom there is a place for everything and everything is in its place.

Establishing a pattern so that students can anticipate academic transitions reduces the loss of instructional time. Students observe the routine and know what will occur. For example, a teacher who uses a class warm-up activity that is displayed on the board or at work stations when students enter the room accomplishes the following multiple purposes:

• Giving students a way to constructively use their time during a class change or morning arrival.

• Preparing the students for the day's activities.

• Offering the teacher an opportunity to take roll or respond to a note from a parent at the start of class while the students are engaged.

• Making use of time that otherwise would have been lost.

• Providing a focus for the first few minutes of class as the teacher addresses the warm-up that can be extended into an introduction for the lesson.

Some teachers follow the same routine virtually every class period, as they review homework, introduce a new concept, use the new skill in an activity, and, if there is time, have independent practice. Other teachers use visual cues to signal a transition as opposed to a routine set of activities. For example, playing music, ringing a bell, or flickering the lights may signal to students that they need to complete a task before the class can move to the next activity. Techniques and routines such as these can capture minutes a day that add up to instructional hours over the course of the school year.

Studies reveal that effective teachers exercise varying techniques and strategies to ensure maximum learning time. The practices suggested above and those that follow support the effective teacher's overall emphasis on instruction. Additionally, they provide the framework for maximizing not only instructional time, but also students' time on task. Effective teachers

• Follow a consistent schedule and maintain the procedures and routines established at the beginning of the year.
• Handle administrative tasks quickly and efficiently.
• Prepare materials in advance.
• Make clear and smooth transitions.
• Maintain momentum within and across lessons.
• Limit disruptions and interruptions through appropriate behavioral management techniques.

Key references: Bain & Jacobs, 1990; Berendt & Koski, 1999; Borich, 2000; Brophy & Good, 1986; Cawelti, 1999b; Cotton, 1999; Cotton, 2000; Covino & Iwanicki, 1996; Education USA Special Report, no date; Good & Brophy, 1997; Walker, 1998; Wang, Haertel, & Walberg, 1993a; Wang, Haertel, & Walberg, 1993b

Expecting Students to Achieve

The previous chapter discussed the importance, in the effective teacher's practice, of clear, specific expectations for student behavior. However, clarifying behavioral expectations isn't enough; an accompanying clear and consistent focus on achievement expectations is also essential to academic success. Effective teachers believe in their students and expect all of them to learn, regardless of their skill levels and starting points.

Moreover, effective teachers believe that students can learn; therefore, the students do learn. Unfortunately, this self-fulfilling prophecy works both ways. For example, if a teacher believes that students are low performing, unreachable, and unable to learn, the students perform poorly, seem unreachable, and do not learn.

The expectations a teacher holds for students, whether consciously or subconsciously, are demonstrated through her interactions with the students during instruction. Research on teacher expectations has demonstrated that the students in the bottom third of the class receive significantly lower expectations to achieve, and much less encouragement, from many teachers. Conversely, students in the top third of the class get the most teacher attention and encouragement. This pattern of teacher behavior can be eliminated through self-observation (videotaped or audiotaped lessons) and self-awareness, so teachers can then bestow the benefits of attention and encouragement on all students.

In several studies, teacher expectations have been shown to relate to student achievement, including the following findings and conclusions:

• High expectations are identified as a key component of student success.

• High expectations represent an overall orientation toward improvement and growth in the classroom, which has been demonstrated to be a defining characteristic of benchmark schools.

• Some studies have suggested that subtle communication of lower expectations for certain students from teachers can limit achievement, while clearly articulated high expectations can become a self-fulfilling prophecy.

• Effective teachers not only express and clarify expectations for student achievement, but also stress student responsibility and accountability for striving to meet those expectations.

Key references: Bloom, 1984; Cawelti, 1999a; Cawelti, 1999b; Cotton, 1999; Cotton, 2000; Covino & Iwanicki, 1996; Education USA Special Report, no date; Good & Brophy, 1997; Good & McCaslin, 1992; Johnson, 1997; Mason, Schroeter, Combs, & Washington, 1992; Peart & Campbell, 1999; Porter & Brophy, 1988; Price, 2000; Tschannen-Moran, Hoy, & Hoy, 1998; Wang, Haertel, & Walberg, 1993a; Wang, Haertel, & Walberg, 1993b; Wong & Wong, 1998

Planning and Preparing for Instruction

Organizing time and preparing materials in advance of instruction have been noted as important aspects of effective teaching. Both the organization of time and the preparation of materials are components of the broader practice of planning carefully for instruction. Once the plans are developed, evidence suggests that effective teachers follow the instructional or lesson plan while continuously adjusting it to fit the needs of different students.

During their instructional planning time, effective teachers assess or recall students' preconceptions and misconceptions about the subject matter. Pre-assessments can help gauge students' prior knowledge of the material. The point is that effective teachers take into account the abilities of their students and the students' strengths and weaknesses as well as their interest levels. To further assist with meeting individual needs, effective teachers typically plan a blend of whole-group, small-group, and individualized instruction. Planning for instruction involves careful preparation for specific lessons, as well as long-term planning to ensure coverage of curriculum. Some studies have demonstrated that student achievement is related to the amount of content coverage a teacher accomplishes. Consequently, careful, deliberate planning maximizes the amount of content a teacher is able to cover.

Since students learn at different rates, effective teachers plan academic enrichment and remediation opportunities for students. Through the teacher's knowledge of the students, it is possible to offer alternatives to a student or a small group of students who have mastered the material faster than the rest of the class. These students can study the concept on a deeper level or apply the concept in a different way. For students who may lack the prerequisite knowledge or skills, the teacher needs to provide time for them to learn the foundational material on which to build the new piece. Providing meaningful experiences for all students to learn is a goal of planning.

By planning a unit that takes into account the students' prior knowledge as well as their learning styles, a teacher can provide effective vehicles for instruction. Teachers tend to teach in the manner that they themselves learn best; however, effective teachers stretch beyond that comfort zone to incorporate different learning styles. For example, during a lesson on the water cycle, the teacher may solicit ideas of what the students already know, run an action simulation in which students roll dice to determine where in the water cycle the students will go next, incorporate a writing experience where the students personify the water droplet to tell about their journey, graph where the droplets went, and then discuss what they observed and compare it to what they had previously thought. Whatever the unit, students benefit if the material can be connected to something they are already familiar with from prior school experiences or real-life situations. In the water cycle activity, the teacher took what the students already knew, built upon it, and addressed some of their misconceptions. Conscientious planning for student instruction and engagement is a key to connecting the classroom to future success for students.

Research indicates that instructional planning for effective teaching includes the following elements:

• Identifying clear lesson and learning objectives while carefully linking activities to them is essential for effectiveness.

• Planning the instructional strategies to be deployed in the classroom and the timing of these strategies.

• Recognizing the importance of linking instruction to real life.

• Using advance organizers, graphic organizers, and outlines to plan for effective instructional delivery.

• Considering student attention spans and learning styles when designing lessons.

• Systematically developing objectives, questions, and activities that reflect higher-level and lower-level cognitive skills as appropriate for the content and the students.

Key references: Bain & Jacobs, 1990; Berliner & Rosenshine, 1977; Brookhart & Loadman, 1992; Brophy & Good, 1986; Cotton, 1999; Cotton, 2000; Covino & Iwanicki, 1996; Darling-Hammond, 2000; Darling-Hammond, 2001; Education USA Special Report, no date; Emmer, Evertson, & Anderson, 1980; Good & McCaslin, 1992; Johnson, 1997; Marzano, Pickering, & McTighe, 1993; Porter & Brophy, 1988; Rosenshine & Stevens, 1986

Figure 4.1
Key References: Organizing for Instruction

Reference	Importance of Instruction	Time Allocation	Teacher Expectation	Planning for Instruction
Bain & Jacobs, 1990	●	●		●
Berendt & Koski, 1999	●	●		
Berliner & Rosenshine, 1977	●			●
Bloom, 1984			●	
Borich, 2000		●		
Brookhart & Loadman, 1992				●
Brophy & Good, 1986	●	●		
Cawelti, 1999a	●	●	●	
Cawelti, 1999b	●	●	●	
Cotton, 1999	●	●	●	
Cotton, 2000	●	●	●	
Covino & Iwanicki, 1996	●	●	●	
Darling-Hammond, 2000				●
Darling-Hammond, 2001				●
Education USA Special Report, no date		●	●	●
Emmer, Evertson, & Anderson, 1980				●
Good & Brophy, 1997		●	●	
Good & McCaslin, 1992			●	●
Holt-Reynolds, 1999	●			
Johnson, 1997			●	●
Marzano, Pickering, & McTighe, 1993				●
Mason, Schroeter, Combs, & Washington, 1992			●	
Molnar et al., 1999	●			
Peart & Campbell, 1999			●	
Porter & Brophy, 1988			●	●

Figure 4.1 *continued*
Key References: Organizing for Instruction

Reference	Importance of Instruction	Time Allocation	Teacher Expectation	Planning for Instruction
Price, 2000			●	
Rosenshine & Stevens, 1986				●
Tschannen-Moran, Hoy, & Hoy, 1998			●	
Walker, 1998		●		
Wang, Haertel, & Walberg, 1993a	●	●	●	
Wang, Haertel, & Walberg, 1993b	●	●	●	
Wong & Wong, 1998			●	

5

Implementing Instruction

A 28-year veteran of the elementary school classroom uses a variety of instructional strategies in the morning. Her students appear engaged and eager to participate in the instruction that today is focusing on reviewing skills for the state's standardized test. She alternates activities that require movement with quiet work. The morning work started with editing sentences on paper. Then students were called to the chalkboard to share their edits with the class. Next, the students worked at their seats on a spelling activity, followed by an action activity in which every student was given a vocabulary word on a piece of paper. The students defined the word and then one by one left their seats to find their positions in the alphabetizing line. The students helped each other to find the proper place. The teacher channels the students' energy into the instruction and capitalizes on their desire to socialize and move. The final activity of the morning was quiet—buddy reading during which the teacher circulated around the room. Every instructional minute was used, and the students responded well to the pacing.

VETERAN TEACHER, 3RD GRADE

Beyond teacher training, beyond rapport with students, and beyond skills in classroom management and organization, what do effective teachers actually do in the classroom? All the previous chapters focus on the important personal qualities and social and organizational behaviors that surround the teaching process. Undoubtedly, a teacher's preparation, relationships with students, and classroom management techniques are inextricably linked with classroom success. When it comes to assessing a teacher's effectiveness, however, there is nothing more important to consider than the actual act of teaching.

While this chapter is intended to highlight an effective teacher's need to possess and use a repertoire of effective instructional strategies, to communicate effectively, and to support student engagement in the teaching-and-learning process, it is not an encyclopedia of what works and what doesn't in the classroom. Indeed, the contextual issues related to the art of teaching defy the creation of a single list of effective instructional behaviors. Rather, what is intended here is to provide a fundamental underpinning for academic success. In relation to this purpose, the chapter provides an overview of the effective teacher's instructional practice, focusing on research-based elements of teaching. Figure 5.1, at the end of the chapter, outlines key references relating to these elements.

Use of Instructional Strategies

After instruction has been planned and the classroom prepared, teachers must begin to actually interact academically with students and with the curriculum—they must teach. Many elements of the teaching process have been linked to effectiveness in teaching, including the strategies teachers use, the clarity of their explanation of material, and the types of questions they ask. In addition, the methods teachers use to keep students focused and engaged clearly are important in implementing instruction effectively.

A teacher's repertoire of teaching strategies is an important element of overall effectiveness. Studies emphasize not only a teacher's efforts at planning instruction and selecting appropriate activities prior to instruction, but also successfully implementing strategies appropriate to the content and instructional goals. The literature on instruction suggests that students whose teachers develop and regularly integrate inquiry-based, hands-on learning activities, critical thinking skills, and assessments into daily lessons consistently out-perform their peers.

Flexibility and adeptness with a variety of teaching strategies contribute to teacher effectiveness. Effective teachers are constantly searching for group instructional strategies that are as effective as one-on-one tutoring. Direct teaching is one example of an effective instructional technique; studies illustrate the effectiveness of other teaching strategies as well.

Teachers who successfully employ a range of strategies reach more students because they tap into more learning styles and student interests. They also can use different strategies to ensure that concepts are well understood. Effective teachers routinely combine instructional techniques that involve individual, small-group, and whole-class instruction. This allows them to monitor and pace instruction based on the individual needs of students.

Some of the strategies and activities deemed effective in terms of promoting student achievement include direct teaching as well as guided and independent practice. Studies indicate that using manipulatives along with an integrative approach to problem solving in mathematics improves student performance on standardized assessments. The use of concept mapping and graphic organizers to promote students' understanding and retention of content are also factors related to effective teaching. Furthermore, effective teachers consistently note problem solving across the curriculum as an important aspect of their success.

In addition to applying basic principles in their lessons, effective teachers stress the importance of higher mental processes, such as problem-solving techniques, analytical thinking skills, and creativity. These skills enable students to relate their learning to real-life situations and incorporate concepts into their long-term memory. Other important instructional variables found to affect student achievement include using student ideas and eliciting student comments.

The following findings related to instructional strategies are supported by the existing research:

• Techniques and instructional strategies have nearly as much influence on student learning as student aptitude.

• Lecturing, a common teaching strategy, is an effort to quickly cover the material; however, it often overloads and overwhelms students with data, making it likely that they will confuse the facts presented.

• Hands-on learning, especially in science, has a positive effect on student achievement.

• Teachers who use hands-on learning strategies have students who out-perform their peers on the National Assessment of Educational Progress (NAEP) in the areas of science and mathematics.

• Despite the research supporting hands-on activity, it is a fairly uncommon instructional approach.

• Students have higher achievement rates when the focus of instruction is on meaningful conceptualization, especially when it emphasizes their own knowledge of the world.

• Effective teachers recognize that no single instructional strategy can be used in all situations. Rather, they develop and call on a broad repertoire of approaches that have proven successful for them with students of varying abilities, backgrounds, and interests.

Key references: Bain & Jacobs, 1990; Blair, 2000; Bloom, 1984; Brookhart & Loadman, 1992; Brophy & Good, 1986; Cawelti, 1999a; Cotton, 1999; Cotton, 2000; Covino & Iwanicki, 1996; Darling-Hammond, 2000; Darling-Hammond, 2001; Education USA Special Report, no date; Good & McCaslin, 1992; Johnson, 1997; •Marzano, Pickering, & McTighe, 1993; Mason, Schroeter, Combs, & Washington, 1992; Molnar et al., 1999; NASSP, 1997; Palmer, 1990; Peart & Campbell, 1999; Rosenshine & Stevens, 1986; Shellard & Protheroe, 2000; Shulman, 1987; Wang, Haertel, & Walberg, 1993b; Wenglinsky, 2000

Communicating High Expectations to Students

A teacher's ability to give clear and focused explanations to students and to clarify expectations for achievement are important aspects of effective instructional delivery. Effective teachers expect students to learn—they take the responsibility, themselves, to make sure students do learn. They set high standards and ensure a challenging curriculum for all students. Although achievement is related to the range of teaching strategies a teacher employs, clarity of explanation and expectation is a separate skill that is also vital in teacher effectiveness.

Communication is fundamental to any profession that requires interaction among people and within an organization. Teaching is no exception. Clarity in explanation, an important communication skill, is manifested in two primary ways in the teaching process. The first relates to the teacher's ability to explain content clearly and in a focused manner, pointing out concepts and relationships. The second concerns the teacher's clarity in terms of explaining directions for how students are to complete an activity. Further, the teacher's job requires clear communication of expectations, encouragement, and caring. Moreover, the communication of content in teaching is far more than relating information. Effective communication in teaching requires teachers to clearly understand subject matter and how to share that subject matter with students in a way that they come to own it and understand it deeply.

Because, in the eyes of students, the teacher's affective characteristics are often of primary concern, teachers must constantly communicate a climate of support and encouragement to ensure that students participate actively in the two-way teaching and learning process. Furthermore, effective management and student learning are clearly related to communication of expectations.

In several studies, teacher expectations and the ability to effectively communicate those expectations have been shown to relate to student achievement:

• Students and teachers who are asked about teaching effectiveness consistently note the importance of clarity in explanation of content.

• Examples and guided practice (as appropriate to the lesson) are important parts of getting the point of the lesson across; additionally, these examples may represent clarity both in content and in directions and procedures.

• Teachers can improve the performance of students who normally exhibit average achievement by setting and communicating high expectations.

• Successful teachers cite high expectations for themselves and their students as a key part of their success.

• Expectations that are set high represent an overall orientation toward improvement and growth in the classroom. High expectations have been demonstrated to be a defining characteristic of benchmark schools.

• Teachers stress students' personal responsibility and accountability for striving to meet high expectations. Linked to this emphasis is the importance of teaching students metacognitive strategies to support reflection on learning progress.

Key references: Bain & Jacobs, 1990; Berliner & Rosenshine, 1977; Blair, 2000; Brophy & Good, 1986; Cawelti, 1999a; Cawelti, 1999b; Cotton, 1999; Cotton, 2000; Covino & Iwanicki, 1996; Demmon-Berger, 1986; Emmer, Evertson, & Anderson, 1980; Good & Brophy, 1997; Good & McCaslin, 1992; Johnson, 1997; Marzano, Pickering, & McTighe, 1993; Mason, Schroeter, Combs, & Washington, 1992; NASSP, 1997; Peart & Campbell, 1999; Porter & Brophy, 1988; Price, 2000; Rosenshine & Stevens, 1986; Wang, Haertel, & Walberg, 1993a; Wang, Haertel, & Walberg, 1993b

Understanding the Complexities of Teaching

Teaching occurs at the crossroads of complex disciplines interacting with diverse and complex student learners. The effective teacher must have sufficient knowledge of subject matter and of teaching and learning to appreciate these complexities. An understanding and appreciation of these complexities can help prevent the teacher from trivializing content and from underestimating the work it will take to prepare lessons and to implement them with students. The effective teacher also recognizes each student as a multifaceted person, understanding that each student brings a lifetime of ideas and experiences in and out of school to the classroom. Moreover, the effective teacher recognizes that a class is, itself, a dynamic and complex entity, made of many personalities, evolving into a corporate personality of its own. All these understandings contribute to a teacher's interactions with students, plans and practices for managing the environment, and preparation and differentiation for student learning needs. In a word, teaching is complex.

Effective teachers emphasize meaning. They encourage students to respond to questions and activities that require them to discover and assimilate their own understanding, rather than to simply memorize material. These teachers also present and engage students in content at various levels of complexity, using a broad range of objectives and activities and employing activities and questions that address higher and lower levels of cognitive complexity.

Research on effective teaching has yielded the following results with regard to cognitive complexity of classroom tasks:

• Effective teachers are concerned with having students learn and demonstrate understanding of meanings rather than merely memorizing facts or events.

• Effective schools and effective teachers place priority on reading because it affects success in other content areas and overall achievement gains.

• Students have higher achievement rates when the focus of instruction is on meaningful conceptualization, especially when it builds on and emphasizes their own knowledge of the world.

Key references: Berliner & Rosenshine, 1977; Blair, 2000; Brophy & Good, 1986; Cawelti, 1999a; Cotton, 2000; Demmon-Berger, 1986; Good & Brophy, 1997; Marzano, Pickering, & McTighe, 1993; Porter & Brophy, 1988; Shellard & Protheroe, 2000; Taylor, Pearson, Clark, & Walpole, 1999; Wenglinsky, 2000

Using Questioning Techniques

Questions and answers, from teachers to students and back again, represent much of the academic interaction that takes place in schools. This process supports student engagement in learning and a teacher's ability to monitor the learning process. Although effectiveness research supports the importance of questioning, the definitions of the kinds of questions that are most beneficial vary. What is clear, however, is that good questioning is definitely an important aspect of effective teaching.

Several studies have shown greater levels of student achievement relating to the teacher's use of lower-level, concrete questions, but other studies have supported the benefits of higher-level questions in encouraging student achievement. This variance in results suggests the importance of a variety of question types to meet student needs and support student learning. Several key points outlined by these studies about questioning are as follows:

• Questions are most valuable when they receive responses—correct or incorrect—because responses encourage student engagement, demonstrate understanding or misconception, and further the discussion.

• The level of difficulty and cognitive level of questions should reflect the context for an optimal match; the level of the question should reflect the type of content, the goals of the lesson, and the students involved, with sufficient variance of question type within and across lessons to maintain interest and momentum.

• Questions should be considered carefully and prepared in advance of a lesson to ensure that they support the goals and emphasize the key points, along with maintaining appropriate levels of difficulty and complexity.

• Questions within a lesson should be considered as a sequence, not as isolated units, in planning, implementing, and assessing.

• Studies indicate that questioning techniques are imperative for teachers who desire to increase their ability in assessing student learning.

• Wait time is an important aspect of questioning; longer wait times have related to higher student achievement in several studies. However, amount of wait time should also be considered in terms of maintaining student engagement and lesson momentum.

Key references: Berliner & Rosenshine, 1977; Brophy & Good, 1986; Cawelti, 1999a; Cotton, 1999; Cotton, 2000; Covino & Iwanicki, 1996; Darling-Hammond, 2000; Rosenshine & Stevens, 1986; Tobin, 1980; Tobin & Capie, 1982; Wang, Haertel, & Walberg, 1993a; Wang, Haertel, & Walberg, 1993b

Supporting Student Engagement in Learning

Along with the importance of time allocated to instruction by the teacher, the time the students spend "on task," or engaged in the teaching and learning activity, is an important contributor to classroom success. To encourage student involvement in activities and lessons, effective teachers use varying strategies including calling on students in random order, providing any necessary additional clarification and illustration, and finding something positive to say when students do respond or interact. Teachers who use positive reinforcement, praise students, and employ meaningful activities are more likely to actively engage students in learning.

Here are research results related to student engagement in learning:

• Student engagement with learning activities is supported by the teacher's attention to the momentum of the daily lesson, to appropriate questioning, and to clarity of explanation in terms of both content and directions.

• Effective teachers are accepting, supportive, and persistent in challenging and engaging students in all aspects of instruction.

• Effective teachers vary not only their own instructional strategies, but also the types of assignments and activities given to students to support increased student engagement.

• Student engagement tends to be higher when activities are led and paced by the teacher, and student engagement is lowest during presentations by other students.

• Step-by-step directions around procedures to be followed in a given activity have been shown to be an important part of student success in activities, and they also encourage high levels of student engagement.

• Student engagement is maximized when students engage in authentic activities related to the content under study; for example, in primary classrooms effective teachers engage all students in a variety of reading and writing tasks throughout the day.

• Successful student engagement has important affective benefits for students, as it encourages a more positive attitude toward school.

Key references: Bloom, 1984; Borich, 2000; Brophy & Good, 1986; Cawelti, 1999a; Cotton, 1999; Cotton, 2000; Covino & Iwanicki, 1996; Cruickshank & Haefele, 2001; Cunningham & Allington, 1999; Demmon-Berger, 1986; Doyle, 1986; Emmer, Evertson, & Anderson, 1980; Good & Brophy, 1997; Johnson, 1997; Wang, Haertel, & Walberg, 1993a; Wang, Haertel, & Walberg, 1993b

Figure 5.1
Key References: Implementing Instruction

Reference	Instructional Strategies	Content & Expectations	Complexity	Questioning	Student
Bain & Jacobs, 1990	•	•			
Berliner & Rosenshine, 1977		•	•	•	
Blair, 2000	•	•	•		
Bloom, 1984	•				•
Borich, 2000					•
Brookhart & Loadman, 1992	•				
Brophy & Good, 1986	•	•	•	•	•
Cawelti, 1999a	•	•	•	•	•
Cawelti, 1999b		•			
Cotton, 1999	•	•		•	
Cotton, 2000	•	•	•	•	•
Covino & Iwanicki, 1996	•	•		•	•
Cruickshank & Haefele, 2001					•
Cunningham & Allington, 1999					•
Darling-Hammond, 2000				•	
Darling-Hammond, 2001	•				
Demmon-Berger, 1986		•	•		•
Doyle, 1986					•
Education USA Special Report, no date	•				
Emmer, Evertson, & Anderson, 1980		•			•
Good & Brophy, 1997		•			•
Good & McCaslin, 1992	•	•			
Johnson, 1997	•	•			•
Marzano, Pickering, & McTighe, 1993	•	•	•		
Mason, Schroeter, Combs, & Washington, 1992	•	•			

Figure 5.1 *continued*
Key References: Implementing Instruction

Reference	Instructional Strategies	Content & Expectations	Complexity	Questioning	Student
Molnar et al., 1999	●				
National Association of Secondary School Principals, 1997		●			
Palmer, 1990	●				
Peart & Campbell, 1999	●	●			
Porter & Brophy, 1988		●	●		
Price, 2000		●			
Rosenshine & Stevens, 1986	●	●		●	
Shellard & Protheroe, 2000	●		●		
Shulman, 1987	●				
Taylor, Pearson, Clark, & Walpole, 1999			●		
Tobin, 1980				●	
Tobin & Capie, 1982				●	
Wang, Haertel, & Walberg, 1993a		●		●	●
Wang, Haertel, & Walberg, 1993b	●	●		●	●
Wenglinsky, 2000	●		●		

6

Monitoring Student Progress and Potential

A teacher was asked how he would assess student learning and he responded with "end-of-the-week tests, state standardized tests, skill sheets, homework, verbalizations, and applying the lesson skill to another lesson." He used testing to track student progress and target areas that needed to be revisited. During a lesson, he moved students from questions that required simple recall to those that required students to apply and synthesize material. He wanted students to share what they thought and why they thought it. Furthermore, he used the input from the students to provide feedback to them in terms of acknowledging a good question or responding by pushing the students to delve deeper. The teacher used written, verbal, and nonverbal cues from his students to monitor and assess their academic success.

POST-OBSERVATION INTERVIEW

WITH A 29-YEAR TEACHING VETERAN

Monitoring and assessing student development and work is a complex task. With an increasing number of states having high-stakes testing linked to graduation requirements as well as statewide testing programs in the lower grades, teachers feel pressure to prepare students to be successful on the tests by aligning their instruction with the state's standards. As teachers provide experiences for students to learn material, they still must check for individual student learning. There are a variety of means to teach content and just as many ways to monitor and assess understanding. Effective teachers employ all the tools at their disposal to make a positive impact on students, including the use of homework and feedback. Figure 6.1 provides a list of key references to the elements that effective teachers use to monitor student progress and potential.

Importance of Homework

The value of homework is often questioned today, especially when students participate in so many other activities outside school and when teachers become frustrated with the number of students who do not complete homework assignments. However, homework remains an important part of effective teaching when used as an extension of the classroom.

Studies have been conducted to assess the value of homework in terms of student achievement, yielding the finding that one of the most influential school-based factors contributing to student learning is the amount of time spent on homework. One study stated the basic purposes of homework: practice, preparation, elaboration. Practice homework is the reinforcement of familiar concepts that need to be refined. Preparation focused homework exposes a student to a concept that the class will study in-depth on the next school day. Elaboration facilitates the exploration of related concepts. Before assigning any type of homework, effective teachers establish guidelines that include the following information:

- Purpose for the assignment.
- Amount of homework that will be assigned.
- Expectations for completion of the homework as well as consequences for not completing it.
- Types and amount of assistance from parents considered appropriate.

In addition to setting these guidelines, effective teachers also clearly communicate them to their students and parents.

A partnership among school support programs, teacher, and parents forms a triangle with the student in the center. In the triad, the teacher and the parents have the greatest contact with the child. Still, effective teachers do not naively assume that parents will support their child doing homework; they equip parents with the tools to make homework time successful. Teachers share tips like these:

- Designate a well-lit space for homework.
- Establish a time to do the work or use the calendar to plan when the work can be done if schedules vary.
- Ask students specifics about the school day and what needs to be done each night.

• Explain the benefits of homework and provide statements that parents can use with their child.

• Assure parents that the teacher wants to hear if the student needs lots of coaching from parents.

When teachers give parents concrete ideas of how to support their children, the home-and-school connection is strengthened and the homework experience is more productive.

Effective teachers not only assign homework, but also check and review it regularly. Students of teachers who spend more time dispensing homework as well as providing considerable supportive feedback make higher gains than students whose teachers fail to spend this time on homework. Feedback on completed homework is particularly important. A teacher may choose to grade the homework assignment by simply indicating correct and incorrect answers or by providing written comments related to the content. By using these types of feedback on a regular basis, teachers can help increase students' learning gains by as much as 30 percentile points on a standardized test in one year, as indicated by one study. A teacher who does not provide regular feedback on homework only realizes a third of the gain made by the educator who gives feedback.

The quality of the homework assignments is the important issue, not the quantity. Effective teachers assign homework that does not necessarily involve a finished paper to be submitted by the student. Rather, they assign homework that provokes thought for subsequent use in class discussions or writing activities. In fact, some researchers suggest that homework assignments should empower students to learn. This empowerment takes place only if students actually complete the homework.

Effective teachers provide specific goals and guidelines for homework and allow students to meet those requirements in various creative ways, such as performances, creative literature, videotapes, or posters. They use homework as a tool to assess the learning needs of the broad range of students within their classroom.

Additional research-supported findings include the following keys to effective homework:

• Homework has positive effects on student achievement when it is clearly explained and related to the content under study in the classroom and to student capacity.

• Homework is more effective in influencing student achievement when it is graded, commented on, and discussed in class.

• Effective teachers list homework as an important element in students' success.

• Only 14 percent of teachers reported assigning homework for at least one half-hour per night.

• For every additional 30 minutes spent on homework a night, high school students may increase their grade point averages by half a point.

Key references: Cawelti, 1999a; Cawelti, 1999b; Covino & Iwanicki, 1996; Education USA Special Report, no date; Marzano, Pickering, & Pollock, 2001; Senge et al., 2000; Walberg, 1984; Walberg, 1994; Wenglinsky, 2000

Monitoring Student Learning and Providing Feedback

Assessment is a central element of the teaching process. Assessment is used to determine the effectiveness of a lesson in terms of student learning and student engagement, to evaluate student progress, and as a basis for continuing instruction. The effective teacher uses assessment efficiently to monitor student progress and to plan further instruction. Assessments of various formats provide feedback to the teacher about what strategies are working, which students need more targeted assistance, and what content needs to be revisited. The students of these teachers score higher on standardized tests than students of teachers who primarily use portfolio and project assessments as the culminating event in a unit and do not reflect upon the results and address areas of weakness.

Effective teachers use a variety of assessment practices to monitor student learning, including formal and informal assessments, and formative and summative assessments. They monitor student progress informally through such techniques as scanning and circulating around the room, or simply talking to individuals or small groups of students about specific tasks or activities. These teachers make notes about difficulties they observe and spend time thinking about how they can better reach students. More formal monitoring of student progress includes teacher-made or standardized tests, projects, or writing assignments. Assessment of student learning is not limited to just the individual; these approaches can be applied to a group of students as well.

Effective teachers frequently use in-class tests. They understand how to interpret and use the information discerned from standardized and teacher-made achievement tests. A common practice is to count how many students incorrectly answer a question and then to analyze that question to determine if it was misleading or if the students did not learn the material. They also look at the type of questions a student incorrectly answers and consider whether teaching test-taking skills can assist the student. Finally, teachers can group questions by the concept they are assessing to determine if the entire concept needs to be retaught with a different instructional approach. Effective teachers follow-up their assessments with re-teaching and enrichment as needed. In addition, effective teachers ensure that assessments are not only aligned with the curriculum, but with the actual instruction that takes place.

Educators recognize the importance of feedback to students on their work. Feedback is one of the most powerful modification techniques for increasing learning outcomes in students. Effective teachers provide feedback in a timely manner and ensure that it relates specifically to the criteria of the task. Studies found that the amount of time between the activity and the feedback has a critical effect on student achievement. In fact, the longer the delay in giving feedback, the less likely students will respond to the feedback and the less likely learning will be enhanced.

Effective teachers provide feedback that is primarily corrective. They avoid simply indicating right or wrong answers because this practice can actually have a negative impact on student learning. Effective teachers provide specific explanations of what students are doing correctly, what they are not doing correctly, and how to fix it.

Students need to learn how to critically examine their own work and to provide constructive criticism to others. Effective educators take the time to instruct students on how to perform constructive criticism. A useful tool for many teachers is a rubric in which students are provided the parameters of success before working on the assignment; students can then assess their own work prior to submitting it to the teacher. Then, the teacher can use the same rubric for feedback. Depending on the assignment, offering students an opportunity to incorporate the feedback and resubmit work for additional credit is a worthwhile venture that reinforces the value of revisions.

Without doubt, feedback gained from oneself, one's peers, and the teacher enhances the learning process. Effective teachers use a variety of inputs to monitor student progress, and they constantly probe and collect information from the learners with whom they work in class. A variety of techniques, including mental notes, work samples, and feedback can assist the teacher in creating improved, more meaningful instruction for the students.

Here are additional findings related to the ongoing assessment process and teacher feedback:

• Teachers in schools with high achievement rates use pre-assessments to support targeted teaching of skills important to learn for standardized tests, as well as to group students for reteaching.

- Effective teachers plan and implement good monitoring strategies by targeting questions to the lesson objectives.
- Effective teachers carefully choose the information sources they use for assessing learning needs.
- Effective teachers think through likely misconceptions that may occur during instruction and monitor students for signs of these misconceptions.
- Clear, specific, and timely feedback given throughout the learning process supports student learning.
- Effective teachers give feedback in a manner that is supportive and encouraging to students.
- Effective teachers reteach material to students who did not achieve mastery, and they offer tutoring for students who need or seek additional help.

Key references: Berliner & Rosenshine, 1977; Blair, 2000; Brophy & Good, 1986; Cawelti, 1999a; Cotton, 2000; Covino & Iwanicki, 1996; Good & McCaslin, 1992; Johnson, 1997; Marzano, Pickering, & Pollock, 2001; Mason, Schroeter, Combs, & Washington, 1992; Mendro, 1998; Mitchell, 1998; Peart & Campbell, 1999; Porter & Brophy, 1988; Rosenshine & Stevens, 1986; Wang, Haertel, & Walberg, 1993a; Wang, Haertel, & Walberg, 1993b

Responding to the Range of Student Needs and Abilities in the Classroom

How best to differentiate instruction and individualize for the range of student needs and abilities in the classroom is an ongoing challenge. Effective teachers tend to recognize individual and group differences among their students and accommodate those differences in their instruction. They adapt instruction to meet student needs, which requires careful assessment and planning for all students in the classroom, as well as the ability to select from a range of strategies to find the optimal match to the context.

Successful teachers present information in such a way that the majority of the class is challenged, yet can be successful. They adapt the assignment to meet the needs of other students who are either higher or lower functioning or who simply need the material presented differently. They also take the time to teach study and organizational skills to students to provide them with the skills that many of their peers instinctively acquire and use.

The ability to improvise while teaching to meet the learning needs of all students is another sign of an effective teacher. Students of teachers who receive specialized training in working with a broad range of students, including culturally diverse students, gifted students, and students with special needs, perform (on average) more than one full grade level above their peers. These teachers understand and use "scaffolding" approaches to instruction that allow students to receive the help they need and to work at their own pace. For gifted learners, curriculum compacting can be used so that a student is able to master the objectives and move on to investigations and applications of greater interest to that student. Effective teachers use all available resources, including the school content area specialists, other students, siblings, parents, classroom volunteers, tutors, community members, and before- and after-school meeting times to meet the needs of students.

Studies of student achievement and of perceptions of teacher effectiveness have emphasized the importance of appropriate differentiation in instruction, including the following findings:

• Students are most engaged and achieve most successfully when instruction is appropriately suited to their achievement levels and needs.

• Students of teachers who participate in staff development training for implementing instruction for special populations tend to have students with higher learning outcomes.

• Effective teachers use a variety of grouping strategies, including cooperative grouping, flexible grouping, and ability grouping with differentiation to support student learning.

• Instructional differentiation requires careful monitoring and assessment of student progress, as well as proper management of activities and behavior in the classroom; placing students into groups based on ability without tailoring instruction to the different groups is insufficient to support academic success.

• Effective teachers know and understand their students as individuals in terms of their abilities, achievement, learning styles, and needs.

• Studies of student achievement have demonstrated that effective teachers demonstrate effectiveness with the full range of student abilities in their classrooms.

Key references: Bain & Jacobs, 1990; Blair, 2000; Brookhart & Loadman, 1992; Brophy & Good, 1986; Cawelti, 1999a; Cotton, 1999; Cotton, 2000; Covino & Iwanicki, 1996; Darling-Hammond, 2000; Education Review Office, 1998; Johnson, 1997; Kulik & Kulik, 1992; Mitchell, 1998; Molnar et al., 1999; Shellard & Protheroe, 2000; Wright, Horn, & Sanders, 1997

Figure 6.1
Key References: Monitoring Student Progress and Potential

Reference	Homework	Monitoring Student Progress	Responding to Student Needs & Abilities
Bain & Jacobs, 1990			●
Berliner & Rosenshine, 1977		●	
Blair, 2000			●
Brookhart & Loadman, 1992			●
Brophy & Good, 1986		●	●
Cawelti, 1999a	●	●	●
Cawelti, 1999b	●		
Cotton, 1999			●
Cotton, 2000		●	●
Covino & Iwanicki, 1996	●	●	●
Darling-Hammond, 2000			●
Education Review Office, 1998			●
Education USA Special Report, no date	●		
Good & McCaslin, 1992		●	
Johnson, 1997		●	●
Kulik & Kulik, 1992			●
Marzano, Pickering, & Pollock, 2001		●	
Mason, Schroeter, Combs, & Washington, 1992	●	●	
Mendro, 1998		●	
Mitchell, 1998		●	●
Molnar et al., 1999			●
Peart & Campbell, 1999		●	
Porter & Brophy, 1988		●	
Rosenshine & Stevens, 1986		●	

Figure 6.1 *continued*
Key References: Monitoring Student Progress and Potential

Reference	Homework	Monitoring Student Progress	Responding to Student Needs & Abilities
Senge, Cambron-McCabe, Lucas, Smith, Dutton, & Kleiner, 2000	●		
Shellard & Protheroe, 2000			●
Walberg, 1984	●		
Walberg, 1994	●		
Wang, Haertel, & Walberg, 1993a		●	
Wang, Haertel, & Walberg, 1993b		●	
Wenglinsky, 2000	●		
Wright, Horn, & Sanders, 1997			●

7

Effective Teaching: What Does It All Mean?

Think for a moment about your favorite teacher. Picture the teacher's appearance. Make a mental list of what made that teacher so special that years after leaving elementary, middle, high school, or college, you can still remember the teacher's name. Now, compare your mental list to what you have read in this book. How many effective teacher characteristics can you identify in your memory of your favorite teacher?

We are inherently drawn to teachers who are effective for us. Like the student in Chapter 2 who saw some of herself in her middle school science teacher, we recognized something in that special teacher. That something, those qualities, still resonate with us years after leaving that effective teacher's classroom. In research and in real life, we cherish many portraits of effective teachers. As is evident from this book and the research upon which it is based, as educators we have long searched for an answer to the fundamental question: What makes an effective teacher? Answers to this question are far from simple.

Effective teaching is the result of a combination of many factors, including aspects of the teacher's background and ways of interacting with others, as well as specific teaching practices. Moreover, the answers are complex because the question is complex. To discover what makes an effective teacher, we must understand what is meant by the word *effective*, understanding that the definition of this term has multiple layers and implications within the teaching profession.

Effective Teaching: A Summary

Based on the assumption that elements from all the categories identified in this book must be combined to achieve teaching effectiveness, the research results included in this text might be summarized under three overarching statements describing the effective teacher:

- The effective teacher recognizes complexity.
- The effective teacher communicates clearly.
- The effective teacher serves conscientiously.

Recognizing Complexity

Teaching is an extraordinarily complex undertaking. To illustrate, just think about how we teach a child to read or an older student to understand algebraic equations. In either case, teaching—at least successful teaching—is the process of teaching complex disciplines and processes to complex pupils. Teaching is the ability to transfer knowledge so that the learners acquire—even own—the knowledge and skills for themselves.

To succeed, the effective teacher must have sufficient knowledge of content, of pedagogy, of context, and of students to appreciate the intricacies that are bound up in the teaching-and-learning process. This deep understanding of complexity can help prevent the teacher from trivializing content and underestimating the work it takes to prepare lessons. An understanding of complexity is also reflected in the effort it takes to implement the lessons with students.

The effective teacher also recognizes each student as a unique individual, understanding that each one brings her own set of experiences and perspectives to the classroom. Moreover, the effective teacher recognizes that a class is a dynamic and multifaceted entity, made up of a myriad of personalities, with a personality all its own.

All these understandings contribute to a teacher's interactions with students, plans and practices for managing the environment, and preparation and differentiation for student learning needs. In a word, the effective teacher understands and can successfully navigate *complexity*.

Recognizing and understanding for a teacher is like getting into the driver's seat of a 5-speed, stick-shift automobile. The ineffective driver manages to get the car in gear, but cuts the engine off at every stop sign. The effective driver, like the effective teacher, adeptly and simultaneously handles multiple tasks and multiple meanings without losing sight of the goal of moving toward a specific destination.

Communicating Clearly

Communication is a key to success in any profession that requires interaction among people and within an organization. The teacher's job requires clear articulation of expectations, encouragement, and caring, as well as content knowledge. Moreover, the communication of content in teaching is far more than just talking about objectives. Effective communication in teaching requires that a teacher have a clear understanding of the subject matter and of how to share that material with students in a way that they come to own and understand it deeply. Beyond directly teaching content knowledge and skills, effective teachers also must be adept at facilitating students' own search for knowledge.

The teacher's affective characteristics are often a primary concern to the students. Therefore, the teacher must constantly communicate a climate of support and encouragement to ensure that students are engaged in the two-way teaching and learning process. Furthermore, effective management and student learning are clearly related to communication of expectations. Ultimately, being an effective communicator is about repackaging and delivering a message so that someone can receive, respond, adapt, and use the information successfully.

Serving Conscientiously

A final overarching construct that emerges from the review of effective teaching research is the teacher's willingness to dedicate time and energy to the profession. Working hard is important; but even better is working both hard and smart.

The effective teacher is concerned with his own continuous learning process and reflects on all the elements of performance in an effort to continuously improve. The effective teacher cares about students, and ensures that students recognize this caring and feel supported and encouraged. He cares about the classroom and strives to ensure an organized and positive learning environment. The importance of conscientious reflection and involvement in all aspects of teaching cannot be overemphasized in defining the effective teacher.

Improving Teacher Effectiveness

So where do we go from here? To improve teacher effectiveness, we need to consider all aspects of the profession—from preservice and inservice training to recruitment and retention of high-quality teachers. Many behaviors and characteristics found in effective teachers can be cultivated among novices through awareness brought about by observing other teachers, receiving peer feedback, cultivating collegial relationships, and participating in lifelong learning experiences.

• For those already in the field, high-quality professional development activities are necessary tools for improving teacher effectiveness. These activities must be collegial, challenging, and socially oriented, because learning itself entails these characteristics. Additionally, professional development training must be tailored to the individual teachers within a particular school to support both the individual and organizational needs as they exist within a particular context. In essence, teacher effectiveness is not an end product; rather, it is an ongoing, deliberate process. Teacher success is a lifelong pursuit.

One Size Doesn't Fit All

Qualities of Effective Teachers attempts to grasp the elusive concept of teaching effectiveness by summarizing research results in these major categories:
- Prerequisites of effective teaching
- The teacher as a person
- Classroom management and the learning environment
- The teaching-and-learning process, itself

Specific elements within each of these categories have been found to be important in the work of effective teachers, as demonstrated through the research summaries within each chapter.

Clearly, a teacher's success is not based on any one element or any single source. Rather, teaching effectiveness draws on a multitude of skills and attributes in different combinations and in different contexts to produce the results that define effectiveness. For example, a teacher whose effectiveness is marked by the use of a range of teaching strategies likely has had solid educational preparation through coursework and professional development. Additionally, this teacher can actually employ good instructional strategies because her classroom is well managed, thus, providing sufficient time to employ the strategies.

Part of an effective teacher's good rapport with students is based on maintaining appropriate roles, which suggests clarity in behavioral expectations and consistency in response to disciplinary situations. Thus, the effective teacher demonstrates behaviors and characteristics related to all four major categories delineated in this book to achieve her goals of promoting a positive classroom climate and student learning. Nonetheless, while this book attempts to provide practical, insightful guidance regarding what is effective teaching, a critically important point should not be lost: one size does *not* fit all teachers.

There is no single formula for classroom success. We can identify attributes, background characteristics, and behaviors that contribute to success, but these are, in the final analysis, a general guide and not a prescription. Each teacher, in a unique classroom, and in a personal and unique way, must continuously strive to achieve.

Effective Teaching: The Ultimate Proof

In one study of effective teaching, school board members, principals, and teachers were asked to answer the question, What is the make up of an effective teacher? Each group focused on what was important from their respective viewpoint, and they concurred on three important points:

- Knowledge and caring are important effectiveness attributes.
- Communication and classroom management are vital to the success of teaching.
- Process and mastery are important products of teaching.

What these school board members, administrators, and teachers were saying is that teachers' backgrounds and teaching processes are important; however, those characteristics alone are not enough to define effective teaching. The ultimate proof of teacher effectiveness is student results.

The ability to identify effective teachers and to cultivate effective teaching results in students gaining more during the time spent in the classroom. If a student walks through a teacher's classroom 180 or 190 times, she should be better in a tangible, measurable way for the experience. The student should be able to read better, compute math more accurately, demonstrate a better understanding of her place in the world, or show other worthy achievements. In other words, measuring teacher success merely by teaching processes is not enough; outcomes count.

Simply put, teacher success equals student success. The one clear, abiding hallmark of effective teaching is student learning. As Joe Carroll, a former teacher and educational researcher, so aptly stated, ". . . nothing, absolutely nothing has happened in education until it has happened to a student."

●   ●   ●

Reflecting back on the outstanding teacher you thought of at the beginning of the chapter, think about how that teacher was able to meet your learning needs within the classroom. Consider how the teacher communicated in such a way that the concepts made sense. Now imagine what it took for that favorite teacher to create a positive experience in which you were challenged to achieve. That is an effective teacher.

2

Teacher Effectiveness: Resources You Can Use

Part 2 of *Qualities of Effective Teachers* contains resources that can be used to apply the content and concepts presented in Part 1. Divided into three major sections, Part 2 provides skills checklists, detailed lists of teacher responsibilities and associated teacher behaviors, and an annotated bibliography.

Section I: Teacher Skills Assessment Checklists

The Teacher Skills Assessment Checklists are based on a synthesis of the research presented throughout this book. The checklists are designed to identify key indicators of effectiveness in a teacher's practice. Each effectiveness quality identified in a checklist includes multiple indicators of success. The checklists also provide a continuum for rating relative strengths and weaknesses, ranging from ineffective to master.

The checklists can be used for self-assessment by the teacher to review and reflect on the components identified as important for effective teaching. Additionally, supervisors and peers can use the skills checklists in their assessment of a

teacher's ability. The checklists are intended to support identification of strengths and weaknesses in order that professional growth can be stimulated and professional development opportunities tailored to specific teacher needs.

Section II: Teacher Responsibilities and Teacher Behaviors

The information in this section is designed primarily to assist administrators and peer coaches in identifying key components of effectiveness as they visit classrooms and observe teachers in action. In essence, Section II is intended to facilitate a type of action research focused on behaviors teachers exhibit in their daily work. For some teachers the guidance that can emerge from feedback on the classroom qualities may be the impetus to refine a strategy or add something new to their toolkit of skills and techniques.

Section III: Annotated Bibliography

For the reader who would like to know more about specific aspects of the teacher effectiveness research, a selection of noteworthy resources are summarized in an annotated format. The short annotations are presented in a straightforward, compact, and uniform format for ease in referencing and using the information. The matrix (p. 96) preceding the annotated bibliography is a reference designed to connect the annotations with chapters 1–6 of the book. Additionally, a complete list of all references used in *Qualities of Effective Teachers* is provided at the end of Part 2 (pp. 118–123).

Section I:
Teacher Skills Assessment Checklists

The Teacher Skills Assessment Checklists are based on a synthesis of the research presented throughout *Qualities of Effective Teachers*. The checklists are designed to help identify key indicators of effectiveness in a teacher's practice. Each effectiveness quality identified in a checklist includes multiple indicators of success. The checklists also provide a continuum for rating relative strengths and weaknesses, ranging from ineffective to master.

The checklists can be used for self-assessment by the teacher to review and reflect on the components identified as important for effective teaching. Additionally, supervisors and peers can use the skills checklists as part of their assessment of another teacher's ability. The checklists are intended to support identification of strengths and weaknesses so that professional growth can be stimulated and professional development opportunities tailored to specific teacher needs.

Key to the Teacher Skills Checklists

MASTER: Exhibits the quality such that others would be able to use the teacher as an expert for how to work with students. The teacher not only has a sense of the quality, but demonstrates an understanding of the essence of the quality.

PROFESSIONAL: A teacher who exhibits the quality most of the time

APPRENTICE: The teacher demonstrates the quality to the degree necessary to make the classroom function. May lack fluidness of use, but the result is still effective.

INEFFECTIVE: A teacher who would benefit from more work on the quality in terms of working with a teacher at the professional or master level or taking classes.

NOT OBSERVED: The observer has not seen evidence, either through demonstration or observation, of the quality.

Checklist 1—Teacher Skills Checklist
The Teacher as a Person

Quality	Indicators	Not Observed	Ineffective	Apprentice	Professional	Master
Caring	• Exhibits active listening • Shows concern for students' emotional and physical well-being • Displays interest in and concern about the students' lives outside school • Creates a supportive and warm classroom climate					
Fairness and Respect	• Responds to misbehavior on an individual level • Prevents situations in which a student loses peer respect • Treats students equally • Creates situations for all students to succeed • Shows respect to all students					
Interactions with Students	• Maintains professional role while being friendly • Gives students responsibility • Knows students' interests both in and out of school • Values what students say • Interacts in fun, playful manner; jokes when appropriate					
Enthusiasm	• Shows joy for the content material • Takes pleasure in teaching • Demonstrates involvement in learning activities outside school					
Motivation	• Maintains high-quality work • Returns student work in a timely manner • Provides students with meaningful feedback					

Checklist 1 *continued*
The Teacher as a Person

Quality	Indicators	Not Observed	Ineffective	Apprentice	Professional	Master
Dedication to Teaching	• Possesses a positive attitude about life and teaching • Spends time outside school preparing • Participates in collegial activities • Accepts responsibility for student outcomes • Seeks professional development • Finds, implements, and shares new instructional strategies					
Reflective Practice	• Knows areas of personal strengths and weaknesses • Uses reflection to improve teaching • Sets high expectations for personal classroom performance • Demonstrates high efficacy					

Checklist II—Teacher Skills Checklist
The Teacher as Classroom Manager and Organizer

Quality	Indicators	Not Observed	Ineffective	Apprentice	Professional	Master
Classroom Management	• Uses consistent and proactive discipline • Establishes routines for all daily tasks and needs • Orchestrates smooth transitions and continuity of classroom momentum • Balances variety and challenge in student activities • Multitasks • Is aware of all activities in the classroom • Anticipates potential problems • Uses space, proximity, or movement around the classroom for nearness to trouble spots and to encourage attention					
Organization	• Handles routine tasks promptly, efficiently, and consistently • Prepares materials in advance; ready to use • Organizes classroom space efficiently					
Disciplining Students	• Interprets and responds to inappropriate behavior promptly • Implements rules of behavior fairly and consistently • Reinforces and reiterates expectations for positive behavior • Uses appropriate disciplinary measures					

Checklist III—Teacher Skills Checklist
Organizing for Instruction

Quality	Indicators	Not Observed	Ineffective	Apprentice	Professional	Master
Importance of Instruction	• Focuses classroom time on teaching and learning • Links instruction to real-life situations of the students					
Time Allocation	• Follows a consistent schedule and maintains procedures and routines • Handles administrative tasks quickly and efficiently • Prepares materials in advance • Maintains momentum within and across lessons • Limits disruption and interruptions					
Teachers' Expectations	• Sets clearly articulated high expectations for self and students • Orients the classroom experience toward improvement and growth • Stresses student responsibility and accountability					
Instruction Plans	• Carefully links learning objectives and activities • Organizes content for effective presentation • Explores student understanding by asking questions • Considers student attention span and learning styles when designing lessons • Develops objectives, questions, and activities that reflect higher and lower level cognitive skills as appropriate for the content and the students					

Checklist IV—Teacher Skills Checklist
Implementing Instruction

Quality	Indicators	Not Observed	Ineffective	Apprentice	Professional	Master
Instructional Strategies	• Employs different techniques and instructional strategies, such as hands-on learning • Stresses meaningful conceptualization, emphasizing the student's own knowledge of the world					
Content & Expectations	• Sets overall high expectations toward improvement and growth in the classroom • Gives clear examples and offers guided practice • Stresses student responsibility and accountability in meeting expectations • Teaches metacognitive strategies to support reflection on learning progress					
Complexity	• Is concerned with having students learn and demonstrate understanding of meaning rather than memorization • Holds reading as a priority • Stresses meaningful conceptualization, emphasizing the student's knowledge of the world • Emphasizes higher order thinking skills in math					
Questioning	• Questioning reflects type of content, goals of lesson • Varies question type to maintain interest and momentum • Prepares questions in advance • Uses wait time during questioning					
Student Engagement	• Attentive to lesson momentum, appropriate questioning, clarity of explanation • Varies instructional strategies, types of assignments, and activities • Leads, directs, and paces student activities					

Checklist V—Teacher Skills Checklist
The Teacher Teaching: Monitoring Student Progress and Potential

Quality	Indicators	Not Observed	Ineffective	Apprentice	Professional	Master
Homework	• Clearly explains homework • Relates homework to the content under study and to student capacity • Grades, comments on, and discusses homework in class					
Monitoring Student Progress	• Targets questions to lesson objectives • Thinks through likely misconceptions that may occur during instruction and monitors students for these misconceptions • Gives clear, specific, and timely feedback • Re-teaches students who did not achieve mastery and offers tutoring to students who seek additional help					
Responding to Student Needs & Abilities	• Suits instruction to students' achievement levels and needs • Participates in staff development training • Uses a variety of grouping strategies • Monitors and assesses student progress • Knows and understands students as individuals in terms of ability, achievement, learning styles, and needs					

Section II:
Teacher Responsibilities and Behaviors

The teacher responsibilities and teacher behaviors, or qualities, are designed primarily to assist administrators and peer coaches in identifying key components of effectiveness as they visit classrooms and observe teachers in action. In essence, they are intended to facilitate a type of action research focused on behaviors that teachers exhibit in their daily work. For some teachers, the guidance that can emerge from feedback on the classroom qualities may be the impetus to refine a strategy or add something new to their toolkit of skills and techniques.

The positive and negative behaviors exhibited by teachers determine, to a great extent, their effectiveness in the classroom and, ultimately, the impact they have on student achievement. Several specific characteristics of teacher responsibilities and behaviors that contribute directly to effective teaching are listed for each of the following categories:

- The teacher as a person
- Classroom management and organization
- Organizing and orienting for instruction
- Implementing instruction
- Monitoring student progress and potential
- Professionalism

Red flags signaling ineffective teaching are presented at the end of each section. Both positive and negative characteristics are based on a plethora of research-based studies that address the concept of improving the educational system for both students and teachers. These qualities are general for any content area or grade level. Subject-specific qualities presented for the four content areas typically found in all schools include

- English
- History and Social Studies

- Mathematics
- Science

The lists are provided as a vehicle to promote teacher effectiveness.

The Teacher as a Person

The teacher is the representative of the content and the school. How a teacher presents himself makes an impression on administrators, colleagues, parents, and students. Often a student links the preference for a particular subject to a teacher and the way the subject was taught. A teacher who exudes enthusiasm and competence for a content area may transfer those feelings to the students. In addition, how the teacher relates to the pupils has an impact on the students' experience in the class. The teacher's personality is one of the first sets of characteristics to look for in an effective teacher. Many aspects of effective teaching can be cultivated, but it is difficult to effect change in an individual's personality.

Positive Qualities

- Assumes ownership for the classroom and the students' success
- Uses personal experiences as examples in teaching
- Understands feelings of students
- Communicates clearly
- Admits to mistakes and corrects them immediately
- Thinks about and reflects on practice
- Displays a sense of humor
- Dresses appropriately for the position
- Maintains confidential trust and respect
- Is structured, yet flexible and spontaneous
- Is responsive to situations and students' needs
- Enjoys teaching and expects students to enjoy learning
- Looks for the win-win solution in conflict situations
- Listens attentively to student questions and comments
- Responds to students with respect, even in difficult situations
- Communicates high expectations consistently

- Conducts one-on-one conversations with students
- Treats students equally and fairly
- Has positive dialogue and interactions with students outside the classroom
- Invests time with single students or small groups of students outside the classroom
- Maintains a professional manner at all times
- Addresses students by name
- Speaks in an appropriate tone and volume
- Works actively with students

Red Flags of Ineffective Teaching

- Believes that teaching is just a job
- Arrives late to school and class on a regular basis
- Has classroom discipline problems
- Is not sensitive to a student's culture or heritage
- Expresses bias (positive or negative) with regard to students
- Works on paperwork during class rather than working with students
- Has parents complaining about what is going on in the classroom
- Uses inappropriate language
- Demeans or ridicules students
- Exhibits defensive behavior for no apparent reason
- Is confrontational with students
- Lacks conflict resolution skills
- Does not accept responsibility for what occurs in the classroom

Classroom Management and Organization

A classroom reveals telltale signs of its user's style. Typically, a well-organized classroom has various instructional organizers, such as rules, posted on walls. Books and supplies are organized so that often needed ones are easily accessible. The furniture arrangement and classroom displays often reveal how the teacher uses the space. Once the students enter, the details of a classroom at work are evident. The teacher's plan for the environment, both the organization of the classroom and of students, allows the classroom to run itself amid the buzz of student and teacher interaction.

Positive Qualities

- Positions chairs in groups or around tables to promote interaction
- Manages classroom procedures to facilitate smooth transitions, instructional groups, procurement of materials and supplies, and supervision of volunteers and paraprofessionals in the classroom
- Manages student behavior through clear expectations and firm and consistent responses to student actions
- Maintains a physical environment where instructional materials and equipment are in good repair
- Covers walls with student work, student made signs, memos, and calendars of student events
- Has students welcome visitors and observers and explain activities
- Emphasizes students addressing one another in a positive and respectful manner
- Encourages interactions and allows low hum of conversations about activities or tasks
- Maximizes the physical aspect of the environment
- Manages emergency situations as they occur
- Maintains acceptable personal work space
- Establishes routines for the running of the classroom and the handling of routine student needs (e.g., bathroom visits, pencil sharpening, and throwing away trash)
- Provides positive reinforcement and feedback
- Disciplines students with dignity and respect
- Shows evidence of established student routines for responsibilities and student leadership
- Exhibits consistency in management style
- Posts classroom and school rules
- Posts appropriate safety procedures

Red Flags of Ineffective Teaching

- Arranges desks and chairs in rows facing forward (without regrouping)
- Displays inconsistencies in enforcing class, school, and district rules
- Is not prepared with responses to common issues (bathroom visits, pencil sharpening, and disruptions)
- Uses strictly commercial posters to decorate walls

- Lists rules and consequences for negative behaviors (teacher formulated)
- Ranks student progress on charts for all to view
- Emphasizes facts and correct answers
- Assigns one task to be completed by all students
- Does not post or is not clear about expectations of students
- Does not display school or classroom rules
- Allows student disengagement from learning
- Is unavailable outside of class for students
- Complains inappropriately about all the administrative details that must be done before class begins
- Maintains an unsafe environment or equipment
- Students have no specific routines or responsibilities
- Keeps an unclean or disorderly classroom
- Uses many discipline referrals
- Makes up rules and consequences or punishment according to mood; unpredictable
- Does not start class immediately, takes roll and dallies

Organizing and Orienting for Instruction

Some teachers plan at home, and others work after school, crafting unit plans that incorporate various objectives. Regardless where or how teachers plan and organize for instruction, the evidence of effective work is seen in the classroom. An observer in the classroom of an effective teacher can quickly understand the work by viewing the daily lesson objectives and activities posted. Further, the teacher is able to share what the class will be doing to follow-up the lesson of the day. In many schools, teachers are required to submit weekly lesson plans; these plans typically note accommodations for different learning styles or needs, and the variety of instructional approaches that will be used. It is important to note, however, that a lesson plan is not an end-all; it is merely a description of what should be occurring in the classroom. Thus, a good plan doesn't guarantee high-quality instruction, but a poor plan most certainly contributes to ineffective instruction.

Positive Qualities
- Lesson plans are written for every school day
- Students know the daily plan because an agenda of objectives and activities is given
- Student assessment and diagnostic data are available
- Assessment data and pretest results are included in the preparation of lesson plans
- Student work samples are available and considered when writing lesson plans
- Lesson plans are aligned with division curriculum guides
- Teacher-developed assessments are aligned with curriculum guides
- State learning objectives are incorporated into lesson plans
- Lesson plans have clearly stated objectives
- Lesson plans include use of available materials
- Lesson plans include activities and strategies to engage students of various ability levels
- Lesson plans address different learning modalities and styles
- Lesson plans include required accommodations for students with special needs
- State standards are posted in classroom
- Lesson plans include pacing information
- Lesson plans for a substitute or an emergency are located in an easily accessible area of the classroom containing all necessary information

Red Flags of Ineffective Teaching
- No (or very few) lesson plans are available
- Student assessment and diagnostic data are not available
- No connection between assessment data and lesson plans is evident
- No differentiated instruction is provided
- Lesson plans are not aligned with local or district curriculum guides
- State learning objectives are not incorporated into lesson plans
- Activities that are unrelated to the learning objective are selected
- No plans for or anticipation of potential problems
- Lesson plans mainly consist of text or worksheets
- Students are not engaged in learning
- Lesson plans do not address different learning styles of students
- Lesson plans do not reflect accommodations for students with special needs

- State standards are not posted in the classroom
- Information on pacing is not discernible in lesson plans
- Lesson plans are disjointed
- Lesson plans are short and do not allow for smooth transitions between activities
- Poor or inconsistent student achievement is the prevalent pattern
- Emergency lesson plans are not available
- Materials for substitutes are not available (attendance rolls, class procedures, lesson plans, fire and tornado drill evacuation route maps)

Implementing Instruction

Effective teaching combines the essence of good classroom management, organization, effective planning, and the teacher's personal characteristics. The classroom presentation of the material to the students and the provision of experiences for the students to make authentic connections to the material are vital. The effective teacher facilitates the classroom like a symphony conductor who brings out the best performance from each musician to make a beautiful sound. In the case of the classroom, each student is achieving instructional goals in a positive classroom environment that is supportive, challenging, and nurturing of those goals. The best lesson plan is of little use if the classroom management component is lacking or the teacher lacks rapport with the students. Implementing instruction is like opening night at the theater where all the behind-the-scenes work is hidden and only the magic is seen by the audience. Effective teachers seem to achieve classroom magic effortlessly. The trained observer, on the other hand, is likely to feel great empathy and appreciation for the carefully orchestrated art of teaching.

Positive Qualities
- Uses student questions to guide the lesson
- Uses pre-assessments to guide instruction
- Develops elements of an effective lesson
- Uses established routines to capture more class time (e.g., students have roles to play, such as passing out materials so the teacher need not stop the momentum of the lesson)
- Incorporates higher-order thinking strategies
- Uses a variety of activities and strategies to engage students

- Monitors student engagement in all activities and strategies
- Has high numbers of students actively engaged in the class continuously
- Adjusts the delivery and pacing of the lesson in response to student cues
- Effectively uses the entire classroom (e.g., teacher movement throughout the room)
- Student-centered classroom rather than teacher-centered classroom
- Provides feedback (verbal, nonverbal, and written)
- Designs and bases assignments on objectives
- Assists students in planning for homework assignments

Red Flags of Ineffective Teaching

- Experiences student behavior problems
- Has unengaged students (e.g., bored, off-task, asleep)
- Has poor student performance in class and on assessments
- Gives vague instructions for seatwork, projects, and activities
- Unresponsive to student cues that the delivery of instruction is ineffective
- Lacks variety in instructional methods used
- Has difficulty individualizing instruction
- Uses outdated material or terminology
- Fails to implement needed changes pointed out by peers or supervisors
- Tells students to "know the material"
- Does not apply current strategies or best practices
- Uses poor examples of or improper English
- Transitions slowly between activities or lessons

Monitoring Student Progress and Potential

Effective teachers have a sense of how each student is doing in the classes that they teach. They use a variety of formal and informal measures to monitor and assess their pupils' mastery of a concept or skill. When a student is having difficulty, the teacher targets the knowledge or skill that is troubling the student, and provides remediation as necessary to fill in that gap. Communication with all parties vested in the success of the student is important since parents and instructional teams are also interested in monitoring the student's progress. Monitoring of student progress and potential need not be solely the responsibility of the teacher; indeed, an effective teacher facilitates students' understanding of how to assess their own performance, that is, assists them in metacognition. However, ultimate accountability does lie with each teacher, so documenting a student's progress and performance needs to be accomplished. An effective teacher who has observed and worked with a student has a sense of the potential that student possesses, encourages the student to excel, and provides the push to motivate the student to make a sustained effort when needed.

Positive Qualities

- Enables students to track their own performances
- Grades homework
- Gives oral and written feedback
- Documents student progress and achievement
- Makes instructional decisions based on student achievement data analysis
- Circulates in the room to assist students and provide praise
- Gives pretests and graphs results
- Considers multiple assessments to determine whether a student has mastered a skill
- Keeps a log of parent communication
- Uses student intervention plans and maintains records of the plan's implementation
- Records team conference or teacher conference with students
- Gives assessments on a regular basis
- Makes use of a variety of assessments
- Uses rubrics for student assignments, products, and projects
- Practices differentiated instruction based on assessment analysis
- Exercises testing accommodations for special-needs students
- Maintains copies of all correspondence (written, e-mail) concerning student progress
- Holds teacher-parent-student conferences and meetings
- Produces class newsletters
- Invites parents and guests to special class events
- Maintains class Web page featuring student work, homework assignments
- Communicates with informal progress reports

• Uses appropriate and clear language in communications
• Participates in Individualized Education Program (IEP) meetings for special-needs students

Red Flags of Ineffective Teaching

• Does not monitor student progress or allow for questions
• Infrequently analyzes or lacks appropriate data
• Infrequently or fails to monitor student progress
• Does not keep a communication log
• Does not record conferences with students or parents and guardians
• Uses extremes in grading—high failure rates or unrealistically high percentage of excellent grades
• Fails to reteach after assessments to correct gaps in student learning
• Offers little or no variety of assessments
• Ignores testing accommodations for special-needs students
• Does not document or holds few parent communications (communication may include conferences, phone calls, e-mail, newsletters, Web sites)
• Uses vague, technical, or inappropriate language in communications
• Does not participate in or attend IEP meetings for students with special needs

Professionalism

Teachers have been portrayed in a variety of ways in the media, ranging from detrimental images to beloved masters of their craft who inspire students to excel. Effective teachers can be seen, heard, and sensed. The effective teacher engages in dialogue with students, colleagues, parents, and administrators and consistently demonstrates respect, accessibility, and expertise. Effective teachers are easily identified through their adept use of questioning and instruction given in the classroom. Finally, an observer who knows from all sources that this person truly makes a difference in the classroom can sense the presence of an effective teacher. The true teacher is a master of teaching.

Positive Qualities

• Practices honest two-way communication between teacher and administrators
• Communicates with families of students

- Maintains accurate records
- Reflects on teaching, personally and with peers
- Attends grade-level meetings; is a team player
- Attends and participates in faculty and other school committee meetings
- Focuses on students
- Performs assigned duties
- Implements school and school district goals and policies
- Acts "globally" around the school for the benefit of the whole school
- Volunteers to assist others
- Seeks community involvement
- Seeks leadership roles on school committees and teams
- Contacts central office personnel for technical support when needed
- Treats colleagues with respect and collegiality
- Works collaboratively with faculty and staff
- Attends professional development opportunities (e.g., conferences, graduate classes, workshops)
- Maintains current teaching certification
- Submits required reports on time and accurately
- Writes constructive, grammatically correct communications
- Writes appropriately for the intended audience
- No testing irregularities found that are within the control of the teacher
- Submits lesson plans and assessment documents on time
- Submits grades on time
- Maintains a calendar of report deadlines
- Keeps an accurate and complete grade book

Red Flags of Ineffective Teaching

- Gives negative feedback routinely at meetings
- Displays unwillingness to contribute to the mission and vision of the school
- Refuses to meet with parents and guardians or colleagues outside of contract hours
- Resents or is threatened by other adults visiting the classroom
- Does the minimum required to maintain certification or emergency certification status
- Submits reports late

- Submits grades late
- Writes inaccurate or unclear reports
- Does not update grade book or it is inaccurate

Subject Specific Qualities

Most teachers have been in an unfamiliar situation where they were not certain of what would be considered normal versus questionable. For example, while a chemical fume hood would look out of place in a history classroom, it is a common element in a chemistry classroom. The following subject specific qualities and red flags are shared to equip the reader with some indicators of what may be observed in effective and ineffective teachers' rooms.

English and Language Arts

An effective English teacher has a classroom that is text-rich and integrates the elements of the English language through writing, reading, and oral expression, including listening. The teacher is well read in the subject area and works diligently to convey enthusiasm for the subject. The teacher encourages the reading of great works of literature for class projects and for pleasure, maintains writing portfolios, provides opportunities for discussion, and gives plenty of feedback. In today's changing technological classrooms, software programs may be used to help enhance reading and writing instruction as well as research skills. The effective teacher's classroom integrates all key components of the English curriculum.

To enhance oral language in students, the teacher may
- Provide instruction in listening
- Model good listening behaviors
- Give instruction in speaking skills and verbal and nonverbal messages
- Provide activities for the preparation, practice, and presentation of formal speeches
- Demonstrate and practice the adaptation of oral communication strategies to match the needs of the situation and setting
- Offer opportunities to participate in role-plays, interviews, and impromptu speeches
- Lead discussion groups
- Give instruction in dialect, pronunciation, and articulation

• Use vocal elements in oral presentations: pitch, volume, rate, quality, animation, and pause

• Give instruction on how to use media for research, analysis, and evaluation of media messages

The teacher uses strategies in reading instruction, including
• Read-alouds
• Independent reading
• Dyad reading (paired reading)
• Library visits to promote use of the media center and facilitate book choice
• Classroom libraries
• Providing blocks of time for students to read
• Cause-and-effect frame
• Sequence of events
• Compare and contrast matrix
• Proposition and support outline
• Debriefing
• Discussion web
• Word wall
• Think-pair-share
• Literature circles
• Reader's workshop

Writing instruction may include these types of activities
• POWER writing (prewriting, organizing, writing, editing, rewriting)
• Peer-reviews and constructive criticism
• In-class writing and publishing
• Writer's workshop
• Journals
• Use of technology to facilitate the writing process
• Writing in different forms (technical, persuasive, research, expository, narrative, and poetry)
• Grammar instruction
• Outlining
• Note-taking (e.g., Cornell notes)

History and Social Studies

The effective teacher empowers students to think about history and the implications of past choices, in order to guide thinking about the future or to find patterns within history. Students are taught a blend of essential facts and skills that enable them to access knowledge and make interpretations of history. The effective history or social studies teacher usually has an area of historical expertise that is evident in discussions and interactions with students on that period in history. Teachers use their own understanding of how history works to teach students to construct their own personal bank of tools to critically examine current news and past events. The effective teacher finds ways to make the events of old become relevant to the students of today.

The teacher uses a variety of preteaching strategies including
- K-W-L charts (Know, Want to Know, Learned)
- Learning logs
- Timelines
- Anticipation guides
- Graphic organizers

The teacher uses a variety of classroom practices, such as
- Simulations
- Debates
- Independent research projects
- Socratic seminar
- Internet and technology based activities
- Historical archives and primary document analysis
- Current events
- Mapping (globes, wall maps, flat maps, computer maps, and sketched maps)

The teacher may use a variety of assessment strategies
- Cloze read activities
- Multimedia presentations
- Reaction papers
- Historical interpretation
- Rubrics
- Teacher-made tests, both objective and essay

Mathematics

An effective mathematics teacher has the ability to facilitate students' ability to understand, analyze, and solve problems. The teacher presents real-world applications of the math concepts to make the application real for the students. The teacher facilitates students thinking beyond the paper and the pencil to how mathematics is evident and applied to everyday life. The room probably is filled with manipulatives and decorated with math-related posters and 3-D constructions. The chalkboard tray holds oversized tools of the ones students use, such as protractors and compasses. The teacher uses the tools to break down the process and provide meaning for the class. If a student is having difficulty, the teacher is able to diagnose and remediate the gap in prior knowledge or identify where the student has misunderstood the process and gets the child back on track. Students are asked to compute problems, write about solutions, and discuss mathematics. Mathematics is not just numbers and symbols; it is a language for understanding.

The mathematics teacher uses a variety of tools and manipulatives to teach, including
- Various papers (grid, dot, patty, and notebook)
- Calculators (4-function, scientific, and graphing)
- Measurement tools (angle ruler, balance, compass, protractor, ruler, and thermometer)
- Mathematical software programs and spreadsheets
- Commercial manipulatives (algebra tiles, cubes, Cusinaire rods, decimal blocks, fraction circles, Geo boards, Hands-on Algebra, and tangrams)
- Common materials (spinners, coins, dice, and yarn)
- Chalkboards or white boards that have grids
- Overhead calculator and transparent tiles

The effective mathematics teacher uses a variety of approaches to teaching the content, including
- Application problems using real-life data
- 3-D constructions
- Reading and writing story problems
- Using visuals in problems

- Mental mathematics
- Estimation
- Discussing mathematical concepts
- Talking through how to do the problem by students
- Tessellations
- Examining musical patterns in algebra
- Considering angles and proportions in art when studying measurement
- Venn diagrams

Science

Scientific discoveries are constantly adding to and changing the body of science knowledge. Effective teachers engage students in experimentation and discussion of the findings. They are aware of changes and highlight new and older discoveries with students as, together, they investigate and develop an understanding of science.

The science classroom has safety as a focus with the following items displayed or easily available
- Posted safety rules
- Available protective materials (lab aprons and goggles)
- Fire extinguisher or fire blanket in rooms using flammable materials
- Classroom shut-off valves, if present, are labeled
- Chemicals are stored with MSDS sheets (materials safety data sheets)
- Marked disposal bin for broken glass

The science teacher uses a variety of techniques to facilitate the learning of the curriculum objectives
- Cooperative learning groups
- Computer simulations
- Laboratory investigations and experiments
- Lab write-ups
- Hands-on activities
- Demonstrations
- Reading scientific articles and journals

The science classroom contains a variety of equipment, including
- Beakers
- Graduated cylinders
- Flasks
- Rulers, compasses, and protractors
- Balances
- CBL (computer-based laboratory) probes
- Graphing calculators and scientific calculators
- Plant grow light
- Dissection tools

A teacher is not simply effective because of the presence of qualities. Likewise, red flags do not necessarily signal an ineffective teacher, just a behavior that needs improvement. Just as teachers must differentiate for student needs, additional qualities and red flags may be applicable to your unique situation. Teachers are effective because of how various personal and professional factors combine and are executed in a classroom.

Section III:
Annotated Bibliography

For the reader who would like to know more about specific aspects of the teacher effectiveness research, a selection of noteworthy resources are summarized in an annotated format. The annotations are presented in a straightforward, compact, and uniform format for ease in referencing and using the information. The matrix that precedes the annotated bibliography is a guide designed to connect the annotations with chapters 1–6. Additionally, a complete list of all references used in *Qualities of Effective Teachers* is provided in References.

Annotation Matrix for Selected References

Reference	Prerequisites	The Person	Management & Organization	Organizing for Instruction	Implementing Instruction	Monitoring Progress and Potential
Cawelti, G. (1999a)				●	●	●
Cawelti, G. (1999b)		●		●	●	●
Cotton, K. (2000)		●	●	●	●	●
Cunningham, P. M., & Allington, R. I.				●	●	
Darling-Hammond, L. (2000)	●	●		●	●	●
Darling-Hammond, L., Berry, B. & Thoreson, A.	●					
Emmer, E. T., Evertson, C. M., & Anderson, L. M.		●	●	●	●	
Ferguson, P. & Womack, S. T.	●					
Fetler, M.	●					
Goldhaber, D. D., & Brewer, D. J.	●					
Good, T. L., & Brophy, J. E.		●	●	●	●	
Hanushek, E.	●		●			
Hawk, P. P., Coble, C. R., & Swanson, M.	●					
Haycock, K.	●					
Johnson, B. L.	●	●	●	●	●	●
Marzano, R. J., Pickering, D., & McTighe, J.		●	●	●	●	●
Mason, D. A., Schroeter, D. D., Combs, R. K., & Washington, K.	●		●	●	●	●
McBer, H.		●				
Miller, J. W., McKenna, M. C., & McKenna, B. A.	●			●		
Monk, D. H., & King, J. A.	●	●				
NASSP Bulletin	●	●			●	
Peart, N. A., & Campbell, F. A.	●	●		●	●	●
Rowan, B., Chiang, F. S., & Miller, R. J.	●	●				
Shellard, E., & Protheroe, N.					●	
Stronge, J. H., & Tucker, P. D.				●		
Wang, M. C., Haertel, G. D., & Walberg, H. J. (1993b)			●	●	●	●

CAWELTI, G., editor. 1999. *Handbook of Research on Improving Student Achievement: The Schooling Practices That Matter Most.* Publication Information: Educational Research Service. Type of Publication: Handbook.

Keywords: Organizing for Instruction, Implementing Instruction, Monitoring Progress and Potential.

Summary: This research-based compendium of classroom practices for enhancing student achievement was compiled for use by teachers, principals, other instructional leaders, and policy makers. In addition to providing information on specific educational practices, the book contains feedback from users of the first edition of *Handbook of Research on Improving Student Achievement*. The handbook discusses the productive use of this information in six broad categories: (1) Teacher and staff development— The *Handbook* is a useful tool to validate the instructional practices that teachers are already employing. (2) Curriculum development and improvement—School districts use the *Handbook* to strengthen weaknesses that are identified by standardized tests. (3) Teacher evaluation process—The *Handbook* can be used as a resource by principals when observing teachers. (4) Development activities and a reference for principals and other administrators—Information from the *Handbook* is useful for administrators in preparing presentations for association meetings. (5) School improvement and planning activities—Districts will find the *Handbook* useful in systematic curriculum review. (6) Higher education programs—College and university professors will be able to use the *Handbook* as a graduate level textbook.

The *Handbook* is also a resource for the specific disciplines in K–12 classrooms. It addresses specific practices for use in the arts, foreign language, health education, language arts, mathematics, oral communications, physical education, science, and social studies.

CAWELTI, G. 1999. *Portraits of Six Benchmark Schools: Diverse Approaches to Improving Student Achievement.* Publication Information: Published by the Educational Research Service. Type of Publication: Monograph.

Keywords: The Person, Organizing for Instruction, Implementing Instruction, Monitoring Progress and Potential

Summary: Six schools from around the country are profiled as models for their approaches to meeting the needs of challenging students. Although the schools have varying approaches to creating high standards for student achievement, they have specific factors in common. The common factors include a focus on standards, teamwork, the principal as an instructional leader, changes to the student's instructional life, and dedicated teachers. In all six schools, the teachers' foundational commitment to student success is instrumental in the quality of the approaches taken by schools. On a daily basis, the teachers implement strategies to promote student success. Common denominators of these benchmark schools include teachers committed to the daily task of preparing students; high standards; an environment to ensure success; and unpredicted achievement at high levels based on student characteristics. In addition, the model schools link their programs to state-established standards and develop high-quality staff development practices. Parental support is strong and includes the monitoring of assignments by parents. For students who require additional assistance, summer programs are available to provide the support they need.

Each of the six profiled schools is unique in its approach to meet the needs of the student population. Strong leadership is vital to give direction, and the teachers are exemplary in their dedication to be accountable in order to effect change.

COTTON, K. 2000. *The Schooling Practices That Matter Most.* Publication Information: Northwest Regional Educational Laboratory. Type of Publication: Booklet.

Keywords: The Person, The Symphony Conductor, Organizing for Instruction, Implementing Instruction, Monitoring Progress and Potential.

Summary: In this booklet, written for classroom teachers, the author outlines the contextual and instructional factors drawn from the long list of known effective educational practices that he feels "enable virtually all students to learn successfully." The author states that he omitted factors, such as school size and socioeconomic status, that contribute to student learning since educators can only affect them minimally. The scope of this booklet is limited to those factors that can be addressed by teachers.

Cotton identifies these ten contextual factors: (1) academically heterogeneous class assignments; (2) flexible in-class grouping; (3) maximized learning time; (4) monitoring student progress; (5) parent and community involvement; (6) primary focus on learning; (7) safe and orderly school environment; (8) small class size; (9) strong administrative leadership; (10) supportive classroom climate.

Cotton identifies five instructional attributes: (1) careful orientation to lessons; (2) clear and focused instruction; (3) effective questioning techniques; (4) feedback and reinforcement; (5) review and researching as needed.

Cotton also explains that all these "critical attributes" do not need to be present for a student to learn well. The families of some students may provide enough experiences and support that can effectively compensate for an attribute lacking in a particular school. Individual students may have enough innate ability that they learn well in less than ideal conditions. The author maintains that all of these attributes need to be present for all students to learn.

CUNNINGHAM, P., & ALLINGTON, R. 1999. *Classrooms That Work: They Can All Read and Write.* Publication Information: Addison-Wesley. Type of Publication: Book
Keywords: Organizing for Instruction, Implementing Instruction, Monitoring Progress and Potential.
Summary: In an examination of successful reading and writing strategies for primary and intermediate school students, educators historically have faced various obstacles in their efforts to develop literacy in their students. The authors describe these problems and present specific approaches by which to overcome illiteracy. Of primary importance is the need for authentic writing and reading activities to be central to the curriculum and the school day if students are to become literate. Specific strategies are successful in guiding and supporting reading and writing for all students and for those who have particular difficulty learning to read. Activities, such as phonics, are presented that increase students' decoding and spelling fluency by teaching them to pronounce, spell, and look for patterns in words. Both the development of knowledge specific to the disciplines of science and social studies and the promotion of the abilities of reading, writing, and vocabulary in learning these disciplines are examined. Techniques are presented that enable educators to integrate, throughout the day and week, the components critical to learning in kindergarten, primary, and intermediate classrooms. In addition, larger school and social issues, such as class size and community involvement, impact literacy.

DARLING-HAMMOND, L. 2000. **Teacher Quality and Student Achievement: A Review of State Policy Evidence.** Publication Information: *Educational Policy Analysis Archive,* 8 (1), 35 pages. Available online from http://epaa.asu/epaa.asu.edu/epaa/v8n1/. Type of Publication: Online journal.
Keywords: Prerequisites, The Person, Organizing for Instruction, Implementing Instruction, Monitoring Progress and Potential
Summary: The 50-state study of policies for teacher education, licensing, hiring, and professional development indicate a relationship between teacher quality and student achievement. The 1993–1994 Schools and Staffing Surveys (SASS) and the National Assessment of Educational Progress (NAEP) results, along with case studies and policy

surveys, provide the data. The results indicate a correlation between teacher preparation and certification to student reading and mathematics achievement before and after controlling for language and poverty. Criteria for teacher preparation range from requirements for a bachelor's degree in states with high student achievement to requirements for only 6 weeks of student teaching in other states. Since the 1980s when the United States began investing in teacher preparation in reading, students have compared favorably with students in other countries. In the Third International Mathematics and Science Study (TIMSS) of 25 nations, U.S. students ranked 18th in mathematics and 17th in physics with 50 percent of the country's physics teachers uncertified or with no minor in the field.

The results of Darling-Hammond's study indicate that teachers certified or degreed in their teaching field correlate positively with higher student outcomes in reading and mathematics. Students in poverty and of non-English-speaking status are more likely to have uncertified teachers. Class size and pupil-teacher ratios do not seem to correlate to student achievement. The teacher's verbal ability, content knowledge, licensing exam scores, and professional development do seem to affect student achievement positively.

DARLING-HAMMOND, L., BERRY, B., & THORESON, A. Spring 2001. **Does Teacher Certification Matter? Evaluating the Evidence.** Publication Information: *Educational Evaluation and Policy Analysis*, (23)1, 57–77. Type of Publication: Journal.
Keywords: Prerequisites.

Summary: The authors present alternate conclusions to those reached by Goldhaber and Brewer, who propose from their research that states eliminate teacher certification requirements. According to Darling-Hammond, the data upon which their proposal was based included 24 math and 34 science teachers, a minute percentage of the total sample of 3,469 teachers. From Goldhaber's data, Darling-Hammond and coauthors conclude that certified teachers have a greater influence on student achievement than teachers with only a degree in their teaching field. This suggests that the preparation necessitated by state certification requirements is likely to increase subject matter competence. In addition, emergency and temporary certification status is nonrenewable by most standards after one to two years. In most states teachers who hold these types of credentials are fully qualified educators who can be classified in one of the following categories: certified in another state; returning after a hiatus from teaching; fully qualified in another field or in their teaching field except for completion of one course or test.

The authors reinterpret the data as follows. Students of experienced, certified teachers had significantly higher achievement than students of less experienced teachers with non-standard certification. An education degree is a major factor contributing to higher achievement along with years of teaching experience. Degrees in the field and in education have a positive influence on student achievement. Students of experienced teachers with standard certification have significantly higher achievement in math and science than students of less experienced teachers with non-standard certification. Critical to the issue of certification is the vast variability in standard and alternative teacher preparation programs.

EMMER, E. T., EVERTSON, C. M., & ANDERSON, L. M. May 1980. **Effective Classroom Management at the Beginning of the School Year.** Publication Information: *The Elementary School Journal, 80* (5), 219–231. Type of Publication: Journal.
Keywords: The Person, The Symphony Conductor, Organizing for Instruction, Implementing Instruction.
Summary: The study examines how effective and less effective teachers differ in behavior management, instruction, student concerns, and constraints. The study considers personality characteristics of 27 third grade teachers who were observed throughout the year with a focus on their initial strategies to start the year. Based on the observations, teacher interviews, and factors to establish comparable classrooms, the teachers were divided into two groups where the only difference was effectiveness. Seven teachers were included in the effective managers group, and seven teachers were included in the less effective group.

Less effective teachers tended to issue general criticisms such as "some children are too noisy" rather than addressing specific students. They had difficulty employing individualized instruction while other students engaged in off-task behavior. Instructions for seatwork were vague, and no monitoring was done to evaluate student understanding of expectations. They did not anticipate or plan for problems and were distracted from the class when problems impeded classroom operations.

The study concluded that more effective teachers spend maximum contact time with students the first day. They reinforce rules by explaining and reminding students; are good monitors of behavior and promptly stop inappropriate behavior; anticipate and work out procedures to address student needs. Effective teachers give clear, detailed instructions; anticipate student attention spans when designing lessons; anticipate and compensate for constraints such as a lack of supplies. These teachers have higher levels of student engagement and lower levels of off-task behaviors, and have higher ratings for listening and expressing feelings. Both groups of teachers in the study treated students equitably.

Ferguson, P., & Womack, S. T. January-February 1993. **The Impact of Subject Matter and Education Coursework on Teaching Performance**. Publication Information: *Journal of Teacher Education, 44* (1), 55–63. Type of Publication: Journal.
Keywords: Prerequisites.
Summary: The three-year study focuses on the graduates of Arkansas Tech University's teacher education program to evaluate the effectiveness of the university's program and to see to what extent coursework can be used to predict performance of the student teachers. Cooperating teachers, content specialists, student teaching supervisors, school of education student teaching supervisors, and the student teachers' evaluations on a 107 Likert-response item survey were used. Data from the four sources were collected for 266 students.

The results of the study indicated that coursework is the strongest predictor of teaching performance. Grade point average (GPA) and National Teacher Exam (NTE) specialty scores account for less than 4 percent of the variance in teacher performance. Increased coursework in the content area at the expense of pedagogical coursework will be counterproductive. Raising the GPA requirements above 2.5 for acceptance into teacher education programs will unnecessarily reject 63 percent of the participants in the study. Teacher education makes a difference in teaching performance.

The studies cited in the literature review reinforce the researchers' findings that subject matter preparation is important, but not sufficient by itself. The impact of teacher education is documented and shows a positive relationship between teacher education coursework and student achievement. In addition, the literature review indicates that not only did alternatively prepared teachers have more difficulty in day-to-day teaching than traditionally prepared teachers, but also that certified teachers are more effective than teachers with less formal training.

Fetler, M. March 25, 1999. **High School Staff Characteristics and Mathematics Test Results.** Publication Information: *Educational Policy Analysis Archives, 7* (9), 14 pages. Available online from http://epaa.asu.edu/epaa/v7n9.html. Type of Publication: Online Journal.

Keywords: Prerequisites.

Summary: In a California study, mathematics teachers with majors and minors in the subject were found to have students with higher test scores. This study was conducted to determine if the shortage in qualified math teachers results in lower test scores in high school mathematics. The Stanford Achievement Test (Stanford 9) and the annual state survey Professional Assignment Information Form results are used to determine how teachers' educational level and years of service affect student achievement. The issues of teacher preparation and experience are addressed after factoring out the impact of poverty. In this study of mathematics teachers, 10.5 percent had emergency permits, and 60 percent had been teaching 10 or more years.

Student test scores increased from grades 9–11, as a factor of student attrition and selective testing, as high-performing students elected to take upper-level mathematics courses. Schools with higher levels of poverty tended to have fewer well-prepared teachers and lower test scores. Teacher experience and preparation were significantly related to achievement when poverty was factored out. The more experienced and educated the staff, the higher the student achievement test scores will be. Schools with higher percentages of teachers on emergency permits tend to have lower test scores. The researcher suggested that the shortage of qualified mathematics teachers lowers student achievement scores.

The authors also suggested strategies for recruiting qualified teachers including staff development for unqualified teachers, increasing undergraduate requirements for college mathematics, and establishing a uniform assessment of the subject matter knowledge required to teach high school math successfully.

GOLDHABER, D. D., & BREWER, D. J. Summer 2000. **Does Teacher Certification Matter? High School Teacher Certification Status and Student Achievement.** Publication Information: *Educational Evaluation and Policy Analysis, 22* (2), 129–145. Type of Publication: Journal.

Keywords: Prerequisites.

Summary: This study examines the impact of teacher certification and state-by-state differences in teacher licensure requirements on student performance. The researchers test whether students of teachers possessing emergency, probationary, or private school certification have lower scores than students of teachers with standard certification. Of the teachers, 86 percent had standard certification in math, and 82 percent had standard certification in science. In a follow-up survey of seniors, studied in the National Educational Longitudinal Study of 1988, the following results are found:

- Students with teachers with standard or private school certification in mathematics show a 7–10 point gain in math test scores in 10th and 12th grades.
- Students who perform poorly in math in a previous grade are more likely to be assigned in 12th grade to a teacher without standard certification.
- Teachers with higher scores on a state certification exam have students with higher scores on math examinations.
- Math teachers with increased college coursework in mathematics have higher performing students.

No mention is made in the study as to the high school math levels that these teachers teach. No evidence is found that supports the belief that standard certified teachers outperform those teachers with emergency certifications. The authors speculate that school divisions may have more carefully screened these emergency certified teachers for ability and content knowledge. However, students whose teachers are teaching outside their field in math perform more poorly than students whose teachers have standard certifications in math.

GOOD, T. L., & BROPHY, J. E. 1997. **Increasing Teacher Awareness Through Observation**. Publication Information: *Looking in Classrooms*, chapter 2. Type of Publication: Textbook.

Keywords: The Person, The Symphony Conductor, Organizing for Instruction, Implementing Instruction.

Summary: Teachers receive a great deal of information throughout the course of the day and must make spontaneous decisions. Often they are unaware of classroom events because the interactions are rapid; teachers are sensitive to different stimuli; they are not taught to monitor and study their instructional behavior; and feedback to teachers about their own classroom behavior is rare. The reality is that teachers are very busy preparing lessons, interacting with students, and providing feedback. The chapter considers the benefits of increasing teachers' awareness of classroom interactions and indicates areas for improvement.

- Interpret and respond to student behavior immediately
- Focus on giving meaning to instruction, model techniques for acquiring information from reading and provide opportunities to apply the skill

- Call on all students, not just the most capable; give frequent praise
- Balance attention given to each gender during particular subjects
- Allocate time based on what is being accomplished instructionally and maximize interactive instructional time
  - Vary assignments and opportunities for the learner
  - Give all students, regardless of ability, equal amounts of time to respond to questions

To increase effectiveness, teachers may benefit from observing their own teaching through the use of technology or reflections of observers. The authors suggest that in reviewing videotapes, trained consultants are a valuable resource to help the teacher identify what to look for in the lesson.

HANUSHEK, E. 1971. **Teacher Characteristics and Gains in Student Achievement: Estimation Using Micro Data.** Publication Information: *American Economic Review,* 61 (2), 280–288. Type of Publication: Journal.

Keywords: Prerequisites, The Symphony Conductor.

Summary: Various factors, including characteristics of K–3 teachers, were evaluated for their effect on student achievement in a California school with large Mexican-American and Caucasian populations. The teacher characteristics included the level of education, teaching experience, and verbal facility, which was defined as intelligence and communication skills. Data used in the study include student Stanford Achievement Test scores, teacher surveys, and scores from a verbal facility test given to teachers.

The analysis indicates that the teacher makes a significant difference in the performance of white students, but does not affect the achievement of Mexican-American students, who progressed at a slower rate regardless of the teacher.

It was also shown that third graders with a teacher with recent educational experiences showed 0.2 to 0.3 years of additional gains in reading achievement. Verbal ability significantly affects achievement for a specific population of white children but does not affect the achievement of the others. Teaching experience and graduate degrees do not contribute to gains in student achievement scores except for a specific white population. Language may be a barrier for the Mexican-American students in this school district. More time spent on discipline negatively affects achievement.

HAWK, P. P., COBLE, C. R., & SWANSON, M. May-June 1985 **Certification: It Does**
     Matter. Publication Information: *Journal of Teacher Education, 36* (3), 13–15.
     Type of Publication: Journal.
Keywords: Prerequisites.
Summary: The study investigated the differences between certified and uncertified
mathematics teachers in middle and high school in the areas of student achievement,
content knowledge, and instructional presentation skills. Noncertified teachers were
characterized as those who were not certified in the area of mathematics, but who did
possess state certification in another field. The study matched 18 certified and 18
noncertified teachers in the same school who teach the same mathematics course to 826
students of similar ability; however, the teachers were not matched by years of experience. The pretest scores of these students on the Stanford Achievement Test for general
math and the Stanford Test of Academic Skills for algebra did not differ significantly. To
consider professional skills, trained observers conducted classroom observations. The
teachers took the Descriptive Tests of Mathematics Skills to measure their mathematical
knowledge. Five months later, the students were given the same Stanford test as a
posttest to assess student achievement.

     The study found that student achievement was greater for students taught by teach-
ers certified in their field. Certified teachers scored significantly higher on instructional
presentation, suggesting that those who are more knowledgeable in their field are more
successful in presenting material to students. In algebra, certified teachers scored significantly higher on content knowledge. Teacher demographics such as years of teaching
experience or the type of degree earned did not significantly affect student achievement
or teacher performance.

     The results suggest that the factors of content knowledge and instructional strategies
for teachers teaching in their field combine to increase student achievement.

HAYCOCK, K. Spring 2000. **No More Settling for Less.** Publication Information:
     Thinking K–16, 4 (1), 3–12. Type of Publication: Journal.
Keywords: Prerequisites.
Summary: Certification, strong content background, classroom experience, and cumu-
lative effects of teacher quality were considered in a study of the distribution of qualified
teachers in the schools of children of color and lower socioeconomic status.

     The results indicate a disparity in the number of qualified teachers among ethnic
groups and socioeconomic status. High school students in high poverty (greater than 75

percent) and/or high minority (greater than 90 percent) schools are twice as likely to have noncertified teachers as students in low poverty (less than 10 percent) and/or low minority (less than 10 percent) schools. Approximately 23 percent of teachers lack certification in their subject areas. Teachers of mathematics are more likely not to be certified in their teaching field than any other core content area teacher. Students with teachers scoring higher on mathematics and verbal skill tests achieve at higher levels than students with lower scoring teachers. Schools with high concentrations of minority and poor students were more likely to have inexperienced, unlicensed, or alternatively licensed teachers.

Reducing class size tended to increase the possibility of placing an uncertified reading teacher in a California classroom from 1 percent to 12 percent. Differences within schools were found in honors and advanced placement classes. Teachers of these classes are more likely to be certified and to have more years of teaching experience. The classes tended to have disproportionate numbers of Asian, white, and upper-income students.

Suggestions to alleviate the situation include raising standards for teacher licensure, for professional development, and for university teacher preparation programs in order to ensure qualified teachers in all classrooms.

JOHNSON, B. L. 1977. **An Organizational Analysis of Multiple Perspectives of Effective Teaching: Implications for Teacher Evaluation.** Publication Information: *Journal of Personnel Evaluation in Education, 11,* 69–87. Type of Publication: Journal.

Keywords: Prerequisites, The Person, The Symphony Conductor, Organizing for Instruction, Implementing Instruction, Monitoring Progress and Potential.

Summary: Urban, suburban, and rural school board members, principals, and teachers from elementary, middle, and secondary schools were interviewed to determine their concepts of effective teaching and to reflect on the effect of the educator's role on teacher evaluation policy. Their descriptions of effective teaching were categorized as teacher as person, teaching process, and teaching product.

Teachers provided the most descriptors of effective teaching, followed by principals and school board members. Board members emphasized product while the principals and teachers focused on process and person, using descriptors such as instructional strategies, identification of lesson objectives, monitoring and assessing students, student-centeredness, positive learning environment, and flexibility of instruction. All three groups recognized the importance of

- Teacher as person—knowledge and caring
- Teaching process—classroom control and communication
- Product—on-task behavior and process/learning/mastery

Only teachers included teacher outcomes in their descriptors. The greatest level of consensus within a group was among teachers, which may have been attributable to the common experience of the teacher training programs that many completed.

Descriptors that maximize the commonalities and are specific enough to warrant teacher acceptance may have implications for construction of a teacher evaluation model. As a result of the study the author defined effective teaching: "Effective teaching involves a two-way communicative process initiated by a teacher who is well versed in the subject matter, caring, and able to establish and maintain classroom control. In such a setting students are continually attentive and progress in their learning."

MARZANO, R. J., PICKERING, D., & McTIGHE, J. 1993. *Assessing Student Outcomes: Performance Assessment Using the Dimensions of Learning Model:* Introduction. Publication Information: *Assessing Student Outcomes: Performance Assessment Using the Dimensions of Learning Model*, Association for Supervision and Curriculum Development. Type of Publication: Book.

Keywords: The Person, The Symphony Conductor, Organizing for Instruction, Implementing Instruction, Monitoring Progress and Potential.

Summary: Dimensions of Learning, an instructional framework based on learning theory and research, is designed to help teachers become more effective in planning curriculum and instruction and in teaching to performance assessment. The theory focuses on five dimensions of learning or types of thinking that are vital for learning to occur.

- Dimension 1: Positive Attitudes and Perceptions About Learning. Learning increases when students feel comfortable in a classroom environment perceived as safe and orderly.

- Dimension 2: Acquiring and Integrating Knowledge. Instructional strategies should enable students to relate new knowledge to prior knowledge. As connections are made, information will be stored in long-term memory.

- Dimension 3: Extending and Refining Knowledge. Appropriate activities that extend and refine knowledge will enable the teacher to integrate the teaching of content and cognitive skills.

• Dimension 4: Using Knowledge Meaningfully. Instruction that enables students to apply information in meaningful ways significantly enhances learning. The five types of tasks that contribute to meaningful application of knowledge are (1) decision-making, (2) investigation, (3) experimental inquiry, (4) problem solving, and (5) invention.

   • Dimension 5: Productive Habits of Mind. Developing students' minds to be self-disciplined and to think critically and creatively will enable students to become self-motivated, lifelong learners.

The five dimensions are intertwined and cannot be implemented piecemeal. Incorporation of these types of thinking in development and delivery of curriculum will strengthen the link between instruction and learning and assessment.

MASON, D. A., SCHROETER, D. D., COMBS, R. K., & WASHINGTON, K. May 1992. **Assigning Average-Achieving Eighth Graders to Advanced Mathematics Classes in an Urban Junior High.** Publication Information: *The Elementary School Journal*, 92 (5), 587–599. Type of Publication: Journal.

Keywords: Prerequisites, The Symphony Conductor, Organizing for Instruction, Implementing Instruction, Monitoring Progress and Potential.

Summary: Average-achieving 8th grade students were placed in a pre-algebra class for high-achieving students. Traditionally they would have been placed in general mathematics classes. Thirty-four average ability students took the pre-algebra course with a highly effective teacher with a master's degree in mathematics who regularly took advanced coursework and workshops to enhance teaching skills. The study attributed the high achievement of these students to the following:
   • The teacher
   • Use of expectation theory and communication of teacher confidence in student ability to succeed with appropriate effort.
   • Workshops on active teaching
   • Use of techniques identified by the National Council of Teachers of Mathematics such as an integrative approach to problem solving
   • Application of word problems to the students' experiences
   • Cooperative learning techniques
   • Opportunities for tutoring from the teacher on an as-needed basis

The program saw a gradual increase in student scores on the Comprehensive Assessment Program Achievement Series Test during the three years of implementation. High achieving students scored significantly higher than average-achieving students; however, several students in the average-achieving group scored higher than the high achieving students. The higher achieving students earned higher grades in the class. Follow-up of the examination of high school records showed that average-achieving students who took pre-algebra as 8th graders enrolled more often in advanced math classes than their general math cohorts. The on-grade level students, who returned to the general mathematics curriculum in 9th grade, earned higher grades than their cohorts in the general math program.

McBer, H. June, 2000. **Research into Teacher Effectiveness: A Model of Teacher Effectiveness.** Publication Information: Research Report #216, Department for Education and Employment, England. Type of Publication: Research Report.

Keywords: The Person.

Summary: From research on the attributes of effective teaching and their major effect on student achievement, the author describes three characteristics of effective teaching under the control of teachers: teaching skills; professional characteristics; classroom climate. Teaching skills and professional characteristics—skills teachers bring into the classroom—interact to create a classroom climate conducive to learning. No prescribed combination of skills and characteristics creates a particular classroom environment; instead, effective teachers contribute their individual combinations of skills and characteristics in a multiplicity of ways to create successful learning environments.

Effective teachers have extensive content knowledge and possess a bank of appropriate teaching strategies, which they apply to their knowledge of the ways in which students learn. Since effective teachers significantly influence student progress, these three characteristics form a foundation for professional development programs and underscore teacher impact on raising school standards. The article analyzes and discusses the characteristics and the various levels of each one to create a model of teacher effectiveness. The teachers' descriptions were based on the following items:

• Professionalism—challenge and support, confidence, creating trust, respect for others.

• Thinking—analytical thinking, conceptual thinking.

• Planning and setting expectations—drive for improvement, information seeking, initiative.

• Leading—flexibility, holding people accountable, managing pupils, passion for learning.

• Relating to others—impact and influence, team working, understanding others.

MILLER, J. E., McKENNA, M. C., & McKENNA, B. A. May 1998. **A Comparison of Alternatively and Traditionally Prepared Teachers.** Publication Information: *Journal of Teacher Education*, 49 (3), 165–176. Type of Publication: Journal.
Keywords: Prerequisites, Organizing for Instruction.
Summary: The study compares a traditional certification program with an alternative certification program. The 82 teachers in the study were matched by three years of experience and teaching assignment according to grade level, subject, and school. The investigation was divided into three studies.
Study 1: Teacher Performance

No significant differences were found between the two groups in the area of pupil interaction or effective lessons.
Study 2: Student Achievement

5th or 6th grade students in the teacher's self-contained classrooms for the entire year were assessed using pretest and posttest scores earned on achievement tests. There were no significant differences on the pretest or posttest scores using the *Iowa Test of Basic Skills.*
Study 3: Teacher Perception of Teaching Abilities

Content analysis of teacher interviews found that neither group felt well prepared to start teaching. While traditionally certified teachers attribute their feelings of unease to lack of teaching experience, the alternatively certified teachers attribute their lack of behavior management and instructional preparation skills to the gaps in their educational preparation.

The alternative program utilized in this study gives individuals with bachelor's degrees condensed coursework in pedagogy and a strong mentoring component with ongoing coursework during the first year of teaching. The study concluded that, after three years, there were no discernable differences in teacher effectiveness between traditionally prepared teachers and those prepared in the alternative program.

MONK, D. H., & KING, J. A. 1994. **Multilevel Teacher Resource Effects on Pupil Performance in Secondary Mathematics and Science: The Case of Teacher Subject-Matter Preparation.** Publication Information: *Choices and Consequences: Contemporary Policy Issues in Education*, chapter 2. Type of Publication: Book.
Keywords: Prerequisites, The Person.

Summary: This study examined the effect on academic achievement of the subject-matter knowledge of secondary math and science teachers. A survey determined the number of subject-related courses taken by teachers, and items from the National Assessment of Educational Progress (NAEP) measured student performance.

• An effective teacher influences a student's willingness to focus on subject matter while an ineffective teacher discourages student interest.

• Two students with comparable SES and mathematics pretest scores enrolled in different types of mathematics courses showed different gain scores with the student in the more advanced course showing higher gains.

• The positive effect for students in advanced courses was not as great as the negative effect for students in remedial courses. However, these low-pretest students were positively affected by placement in advanced courses.

• Teacher subject matter preparation was related more strongly to positive effects for high pretest students in the sophomore year of a two-year sequence. In the second year the low-pretest students showed stronger gains, possibly due to increased subject matter coverage in math.

• In the sophomore year of students with low pretest scores, teacher experience showed positive effects. These gains could be the result of increased coverage of curriculum or of the quality of teaching.

• Students with high pretest scores in both mathematics and science were more likely to be assigned to teachers with more subject-matter preparation than students with low scores on the pretest.

NATIONAL ASSOCIATION OF SECONDARY SCHOOL PRINCIPALS. 1997. **Students Say: What Makes a Good Teacher?** Publication Information: *NASSP Bulletin,* May/June 1997, 15–17. Type of Publication: Journal Article.
Keywords: Prerequisites, The Person, Implementing Instruction.
Summary: This brief article outlines some of the results of a 1996 survey of almost 1,000 students between the ages of 13 and 17 who were asked to identify characteristics of best and worst teachers. The students responded that the number one characteristic of good teachers is their sense of humor. The number one characteristic of their worst teachers was that they are "dull and boring."

The following lists of the top five characteristics of the best and the worst teachers are a result of student responses to the survey. Top five characteristics of best teachers: have a sense of humor; make the class interesting; have knowledge of their subjects;

explain things clearly; spend time helping students. Top five characteristics of worst teachers: are dull/have a boring class; do not explain things clearly; show favoritism toward students; have a poor attitude; expect too much from students.

PEART, N. A., & CAMPBELL, F. A. July 1999. **At-Risk Students' Perceptions of Teacher Effectiveness.** Publication Information: *Journal for a Just and Caring Education*, 5 (3), 269–284. Type of Publication: Journal Article.

Keywords: Prerequisites, The Person, The Symphony Conductor, Organizing for Instruction, Implementing Instruction, Monitoring Progress and Potential.

Summary: Teacher effectiveness was ranked fourth in factors affecting achievement of African American students, accompanied by cultural differences, minority status, and poverty. Forty-seven African American adults were interviewed about teacher characteristics that facilitate or inhibit school success. Four areas were identified as important for teachers to address in order to promote student achievement. (1) **Interpersonal skills:** A positive student-teacher relationship is developed by showing interest in students and demonstrating caring, concern, and empathy for them. One-on-one instruction is vital as well as teacher self-disclosure and availability. (2) **Instructional methods:** The ability to communicate the material effectively with genuine enthusiasm is essential. The teacher must have command of the content and employ a bank of effective strategies for teaching it. (3) **Motivational leader:** The teacher who sets high standards for academic success, maintains an orderly environment, and encourages students to take responsibility for their learning should also assign appropriate challenges and offer reinforcement and encouragement. (4) **Racial impartiality:** Equitable treatment of all students is imperative. In addition, school activities must be inclusive of various cultures.

Academic success of at-risk students is enhanced if a personal connection that communicates respect and caring exists between the teacher and the student. The establishment of high academic expectations and a teacher's ability to enable students to meet the standards are important factors for positive perceptions of teacher effectiveness among African Americans.

ROWAN, B., CHIANG, F., & MILLER, R. 1997. **Using Research on Employees' Performance to Study the Effects of Teachers on Students' Achievement.** Publication Information: *Sociology of Education, 70*, 256–284. Type of Publication: Journal Article.

Keywords: Prerequisites, The Person.

Summary: This article reports on a study that used the general perceptions about employees' performance to investigate the impact of teachers on student achievement. The study hypothesized that a teacher's effect on student achievement can be attributed to the variables of teacher ability, motivation, and work situation. Unlike previous research, this study examines the combined effect of these three variables on student achievement.

The study sample, consisting of 5,381 students at 382 public schools and 28 Catholic schools, was limited to students who had taken both the 8th and 10th grade National Education Longitudinal Study of 1988 (NELS) mathematics tests. The study controls for a large number of variables including prior student achievement and students' opportunities to learn the content tested on the NELS mathematics test.

The study's findings suggest that although the effect size was small, the authors consider that there is "preliminary support for the broad hypothesis that teaching performance is a function" of these three dimensions. The authors attribute the small effect size and uneven results across the variables to unreliability in measurement.

The study suggests the effect of teacher ability on student achievement varies depending on context of the ability. Highly talented and motivated teachers have the greatest effect on student achievement. Talent was defined by three measures of teacher ability: content knowledge; training in the field; and use of instructional strategies. Teacher motivation was characterized by high expectations of self and of students.

SHELLARD, E., & PROTHEROE, N. 2000. **Effective Teaching: How Do We Know It When We See It?** Publication Information: *The Informed Educator Series*, Educational Research Service, Stock # IE-0405. Type of Publication: Monograph.

Keywords: Implementing Instruction.

Summary: Specific teacher behaviors are the keys to creating engaged classroom environments with a focus on learning that produce high-performing students. The monograph states that these productive behaviors can be taught; and, in order to identify them, four case studies are examined. The major productive behaviors found in each study are as follows:

Study 1: Planning for Instruction. High-performing teachers thoroughly plan and organize for instruction.

Study 2: Combining Instructional Strategies. In the SAGE Program, characterized by small class size, rigorous academics, appropriate staff development, and community partnerships, higher performing teachers use a combination of teacher-directed and student-directed instruction, individualized instruction for specific needs, and ongoing assessment.

Study 3: Differentiation of Instruction. High performing teachers emphasize critical thinking skills, individualized instruction to meet specific needs, and employment of appropriate teaching strategies and techniques for differing student populations. In this case study, teachers who use hands-on activities increased NAEP scores in science and math.

Study 4: Interactive Teaching Style. Teachers who were interactive rather than didactic and spent a minimum of time reviewing past information have higher achieving students. High-quality staff development was a major factor for those teachers who utilize interactive teaching methods.

The overview of the four studies indicates six behavioral characteristics of effective teachers: (1) more time spent on academic tasks and strong classroom management; (2) clear learning goals; (3) students as active learners; (4) individualized instruction to accommodate individual differences; (5) combination of skills-based and higher-level instruction; and (6) supportive and collaborative classroom climate.

A vital component for effective teaching is staff development that includes both modeling of the behaviors by master teachers and opportunities for observation and practice on the part of the teachers who desire to improve their classroom performance.

STRONGE, J. H., & TUCKER, P. D. 2001. *Teacher Evaluation and Student Achievement*. Publication Information: National Education Association. Type of Publication: Book.

Keywords: Organizing for Instruction.

Summary: Teachers are the most influential factor on student achievement, according to various research studies. Both the University of Texas study and Sanders' value-added research found increases in achievement among students placed with high performing, experienced teachers. In research conducted by Bob Munro, students with high performing teachers experienced the positive effects for three years, while students with low performing teachers experienced the negative effects for three years. The book examines four examples of assessment systems that use student achievement as a measure of teacher effectiveness: Assessing Teacher Performance through Comparative Student Gain Scores; Assessing Teacher Performance through Repeated Measures of Student Gains; Assessing Teacher Performance with Student Work; Assessing Teacher Performance in a Standards-based Environment.

Although student assessment measures can be used inappropriately as an indicator of teacher effectiveness, these measures are extremely valuable tools for improving student achievement. To reduce bias and maximize the appropriate use of achievement measures for teacher evaluation systems, several practices are proposed.

- Use student learning as only one component of multiple data sources.
- Consider the context in which teaching and learning occur.
- Use measures of student growth rather than a single, fixed achievement standard.
- Compare learning gains from one point to another for the same group of students, not different groups of students.
- Recognize that gain scores have pitfalls that must be avoided.
- Use a time frame that allows for patterns of student learning to be well documented.
- Use fair and valid measures of student learning.
- Select student assessment measures that are most closely aligned with existing curriculum.

Wang, M. C., Haertel, G. D., & Walberg, H. J. December 1993/January 1994. **What Helps Students Learn?** Publication Information: *Educational Leadership*, 51 (4), 74–79. Type of Publication: Journal.
Keywords: The Symphony Conductor, Organizing for Instruction, Implementing Instruction, Monitoring Progress and Potential.
Summary: This meta-analysis of 331 sources results in 11,000 statistical findings that show consensus on the significant influences on learning. Direct influences, such as time spent teaching a specific topic, have more effect on student learning than indirect influences such as policies. The findings are grouped into 28 categories and ranked by scholars. Of these categories, classroom management was determined to have the greatest impact on learning. However, when the categories are regrouped into six areas of influence, the weighting of the categories shows that student aptitude, classroom instruction and climate, and out-of-school contexts are approximately equal in their influence on learning.

Student aptitude is most influential in learning. This includes metacognitive and cognitive processes, social and behavioral attributes, motivational and affective attributes, and to a lesser degree the influence of psychomotor skills and student demographics.

Classroom instruction and climate include the influences of social interactions between the teacher and student, quality of instruction, and the climate of the classroom environment.

Out-of-school contexts consider the home environment, community influences, and how time is spent outside of school. The instructional program design and the school organization affect learning to a lesser degree. The characteristics of individual states and districts have the least effect on learning since they are quite removed from the actual classroom environment. By aligning classroom practices with state and district policies and the other areas of influence, a more effective route to reform can be established.

References

Archer, J. (1998). *Students' fortunes rest with assigned teacher.* Retrieved November 29, 2000 from the World Wide Web: http://www.edweek.org/ew/1998/23dallas.h17.

Ashton, P., & Crocker, L. (1987). Systematic study of planned variations: The essential focus of teacher education reform. *Journal of Teacher Education, 38,* 2–8.

Bain, H. P., & Jacobs, R. (1990, September). The case for smaller classes and better teachers. *Streamlined Seminar—National Association of Elementary School Principals, 9* (1).

Berendt, P. R., & Koski, B. (1999). No shortcuts to success. *Educational Leadership, 56* (6), 45–47.

Berliner, D. C. (1986). In pursuit of the expert pedagogue. *Educational Researcher, 15* (7), 5–13.

Berliner, D. C. & Rosenshine, B. V. (1977). The acquisition of knowledge in the classroom. In R. C. Anderson, R. J. Spiro, & W. E. Montague (Eds.), *Schooling and the acquisition of knowledge* (pp. 375–396). Mahwah, NJ: Lawrence Erlbaum Associates.

Blair, J. (2000). ETS study links effective teaching methods to test-score gains. *Education Week, 20* (8), 24.

Bloom, B. S. (1984). The search for methods of group instruction as effective as one-to-one tutoring. *Educational Leadership, 41* (8), 4–17.

Borich, G. D. (2000). *Effective teaching methods* (4th ed.). Upper Saddle River, NJ: Merrill.

Brookhart, S. M., & Loadman, W. E. (1992). Teacher assessment and validity: What do we want to know? *Journal of Personnel Evaluation in Education, 5,* 347–357.

Brophy, J., & Good, T. L. (1986). Teacher behavior and student achievement. In M. C. Wittrock (Ed.), *Handbook of research on teaching* (3rd ed.) (pp. 328–371). New York: Macmillan.

Carlsen, W. S. (1987). *Why do you ask? The effects of science teacher subject matter knowledge on teacher questioning and classroom discourse.* Paper presented at the annual meeting of the American Educational Research Association, Washington, DC.

Carlsen, W. S. & Wilson, S. M. (1988, April). *Responding to student questions: The effects of teacher subject matter knowledge and experience on teacher discourse strategies.* Paper presented at the annual meeting of the American Educational Research Association, Washington, DC.

Carroll, J. M. (1994). *The Copernican Plan Evaluated: The Evoluation of a Revolution.* Topsfield, VA: Copernican Associates, Ltd.

Cawelti, G. (Ed.). (1999a). *Handbook of research on improving student achievement* (2nd ed.). Arlington, VA: Educational Research Service.

Cawelti, G. (1999b). *Portraits of six benchmarks schools: Diverse approaches to improving student achievement.* Arlington, VA: Educational Research Service.

Collinson, V., Killeavy, M., & Stephenson, H. J. (1999). Exemplary teachers: Practicing an ethic of care in England, Ireland, and the United States. *Journal for a Just and Caring Education, 5* (4), 349–366.

Cotton, K. (1999). *Research you can use to improve results.* Portland, OR: Northwest Regional Educational Laboratory & Alexandria, VA: Association for Supervision and Curriculum Development.

Cotton, K. (2000). *The schooling practices that matter most.* Portland, OR: Northwest Regional Educational Laboratory & Alexandria, VA: Association for Supervision and Curriculum Development.

Covino, E. A., & Iwanicki, E. (1996). Experienced teachers: Their constructs on effective teaching. *Journal of Personnel Evaluation in Education, 11,* 325–363.

Cruickshank, D. R., & Haefele, D. (2001). Good teachers, plural. *Educational Leadership, 58* (5), 26–30.

Cunningham, P. M., & Allington, R. I. (1999). *Classrooms that work: They can all read and write.* New York: Addison-Wesley.

Darling-Hammond, L. (1996). What matters most: A competent teacher for every child. *Phi Delta Kappan, 78* (3), 193–200.

Darling-Hammond, L. (2000). *Teacher quality and student achievement: A review of state policy evidence.* Retrieved March 21, 2000 from the World Wide Web: http://epaa.asu.edu/epaa/v8n1/.

Darling-Hammond, L. (2001). The challenge of staffing our schools. *Educational Leadership, 58* (8), 12–17.

Darling-Hammond, L., Berry, B., & Thoreson, A. (2001). Does teacher certification matter? Evaluating the evidence. *Educational Evaluation and Policy Analysis, 23,* 1, 57–77.

Demmon-Berger, D. (1986). *Effective teaching: Observations from research.* Arlington, VA: American Association of School Administrators.

Doyle, W. (1986). Classroom organization and management. In M.C. Wittrock (Ed.), *Handbook of research on teaching* (3rd ed., pp. 392–431). New York: Macmillan.

Dozier, T., & Bertotti, C. (2000). *Eliminating barriers to quality teaching.* Retrieved on August 22, 2000 from the World Wide Web. Available: http://www.ed.gov/teacherquality/awareness.html.

Druva, C., & Anderson, R. D. (1983). Science teacher characteristics by teacher behavior and by student outcome: A meta-analysis of research. *Journal of Research in Science Teaching, 20,* 467–479.

Educational Review Office. (1998). *The Capable Teacher.* Retrieved online at http://www.ero.govt.nz/Publications/eers1998/98no2hl.htm.

Education USA Special Report. (n.d.). *Good teachers: What to look for.* A Publication of The National School Public Relations Association.

Emmer, E. T., Evertson, C. M., & Anderson, L. M. (1980). Effective classroom management at the beginning of the school year. *The Elementary School Journal, 80* (5), 219–231.

Evertson, C. M., Hawley, W. D., & Zlotnik, M. (1985). Making a difference in educational quality through teacher education. *Journal of Teacher Education, 36* (3), 2–10.

Ferguson, P., & Womack, S. T. (1993). The impact of subject matter and education coursework on teaching performance. *Journal of Teacher Education, 44* (1), 55–63.

Fetler, M. (1999). High school staff characteristics and mathematics test results. *Educational Policy Analysis Archives, 7* (9). Retrieved online at http://epaa.asu.edu/epaa/v7n9.html.

Goldhaber, D. D., & Brewer, D. J. (2000). Does teacher certification matter? High school certification status and students achievement. *Educational Evaluation and Policy Analysis, 22* (2), 129–145.

Good, T. L., & Brophy, J. E. (1997). *Looking in classrooms* (7th ed.). New York: Addison-Wesley.

Good, T. L., & McCaslin, M. M. (1992). Teacher licensure and certification. In M.C. Alkin (Ed.), *Encyclopedia of educational research* (6th ed., pp. 1352–1388). New York: Macmillan.

Hansen, J., & Feldhusen, J. F. (1994). Comparison of trained and untrained teachers of gifted students. *Gifted Child Quarterly, 38,* 115–123.

Hanushek, E. (1971). Teacher characteristics and gains in student achievement: Estimation using micro data. *American Economic Review, 61* (2), 280–288.

Hawk, P. P., Coble, C. R., & Swanson, M. (1985). Certification: It does matter. *Journal of Teacher Education, 36* (3), 13–15.

Haycock, K. (2000). No more settling for less. *Thinking K–16, 4* (1), 3–12.

Holt-Reynolds, D. (1999). Good readers, good teachers? Subject matter expertise as a challenge in learning to teach. *Harvard Educational Review, 69* (1), 29–50.

Ingersoll, R. M. (2001). The realities of out-of-field teaching. *Educational Leadership, 58* (8), 42–45.

Johnson, B. L. (1997). An organizational analysis of multiple perspectives of effective teaching: Implications for teacher evaluation. *Journal of Personnel Evaluation in Education, 11,* 69–87.

Kerrins, J. A., & Cushing, K. S. (1998). *Taking a second look: Expert and novice differences when observing the same classroom teaching segment a second time.* Paper presented at the Annual Meeting of the American Educational Research Association, San Diego, CA.

Kohn, A. (1996). What to look for in a classroom. *Educational Leadership, 54* (1), 54–55.

Kounin, J. (1970). *Discipline and group management in classrooms.* New York: Holt, Rinehart, & Winston.

Kulik, J. A., & Kulik, C. L. C. (1992). Meta-analytic findings on grouping programs. *Gifted Child Quarterly, 36,* 73–77.

Lilly, M. S. (1992). Research on teacher licensure and state approval of teacher education programs. *Teacher Education and Special Education, 15,* 149–160.

Marzano, R. J., Pickering, D., & McTighe, J. (1993). *Assessing student outcomes: Performance assessment using the dimensions of learning model.* Alexandria, VA: Association for Supervision and Curriculum Development.

Marzano, R. J., Pickering, D. J., & Pollock, J. E. (2001). *Classroom instruction that works.* Alexandria, VA: Association for Supervision and Curriculum Development.

Mason, D. A., Schroeter, D. D., Combs, R. K., & Washington, K. (1992). Assigning average-achieving eighth graders to advanced mathematics classes in an urban junior high. *The Elementary School Journal, 92* (5), 587–599.

Mathews, J. (1999, April 20). A call for education change. *The Washington Post* (p. A2).

McBer, H. (2000). *Research into teacher effectiveness: A model of teacher effectiveness* (Research Report #216). Nottingham, England: Department for Education and Employment.

Mendro, R. L. (1998). Student achievement and school and teacher accountability. *Journal of Personnel Evaluation in Education, 12,* 257–267.

Miller, J. W., McKenna, M. C., & McKenna, B. A. (1998). A comparison of alternatively and traditionally prepared teachers. *Journal of Teacher Education, 49* (3), 165–176.

Mitchell, R. D. (1998). World class teachers: When top teachers earn National Board Certification, schools—and students—reap the benefits. *The American School Board Journal, 185* (9) 27–29.

Molnar, A., Smith, P., Zahorik, J., Palmer, A., Halbach, A., & Ehrle, K. (1999). Evaluating the SAGE program: A pilot program in targeted pupil-teacher reduction in Wisconsin. *Educational Evaluation and Policy Analysis, 21* (2), 165–178.

Monk, D. H. & King, J. A. (1994). Multilevel teacher resource effects on pupil performance in secondary mathematics and science: The case of teacher subject matter preparation. In E. G. Ehrenberg (Ed.), *Choices and Consequences: Contemporary Policy Issues in Education* (pp. 29–58). Ithaca, NY: ILR Press.

Murnane, R. J. (1985, June). *Do effective teachers have common characteristics? Interpreting the quantitative research evidence.* Paper presented at the National Research Council Conference on Teacher Quality in Science and Mathematics, Washington, DC.

National Association of Secondary School Principals (NASSP). (1997). Students say: What makes a good teacher? *Schools in the Middle, 6* (5), 15–17.

National Board for Professional Teaching Standards. (n.d.). *What teachers should know and be able to do.* Retrieved on September 4, 1999 from the World Wide Web: http://www.nbpts.org/nbpts/standards.

National Center for Educational Statistics. (1992). *Adult literacy in America.* Washington, DC.: United States Department of Education.

Neilsen, L. (1999). To be a good teacher: Growing beyond the garden path. *The Reading Teacher, 44,* 152–153.

Olson, L. (1997). *Research notes: Bad news about bad teaching.* Retrieved November 21, 2000 from the World Wide Web: http://www.edweek.org/ew/vol-16/19ideas.h16.

Palmer, P. J. (1990). Good teaching: A matter of living the mystery. *Change,* January/February, 11–16.

Peart, N. A., & Campbell, F. A. (1999). At-risk students' perceptions of teacher effectiveness. *Journal for a Just and Caring Education, 5* (3), 269–284.

Porter, A., & Brophy, J. (1988). Synthesis of research on good teaching: Insights from the work of the institute for research on teaching. *Educational Leadership, 45* (8), 74–85.

Price, J. (2000). The effect of portfolio assessment on student achievement. In *What matters most: Improving student achievement. A report connecting findings of the National Teacher Policy Institute to recommendations of the National Commission on Teaching and America's Future* (pp. 49–51). New York: The Teacher's Network-Impact II.

Rosenshine, B., & Stevens, R. (1986). Teaching functions. In M.C. Wittrock (ed.), *Handbook of research on teaching* (3rd ed., pp. 376–391). New York: Macmillan.

Rowan, B., Chiang, F. S., & Miller, R. J. (1997). Using research on employees' performance to study the effects of teachers on student achievement. *Sociology of Education, 70,* 256–284.

Schalock, D., Schalock, M., & Myton, D. (1998). Effectiveness—along with quality—should be the focus. *Phi Delta Kappan, 79* (6), 468–470.

Scherer, M. (2001). Improving the quality of the teaching force: A conversation with David C. Berliner. *Educational Leadership, 58* (8), 6–10.

Senge, P., Cambron-McCabe, N., Lucus, T., Smith, B., Dutton, J., &, Kleiner, A. (2000). *Schools that learn: A fifth discipline fieldbook for educators, parents, and everyone who cares about education.* New York: Doubleday.

Shellard, E., & Protheroe, N. (2000). Effective teaching: How do we know it when we see it? *The Informed Educator Series.* Arlington, VA: Educational Research Service.

Shulman, L. S. (1987). Knowledge and teaching: Foundations of the new reform. *Harvard Educational Review, 57*(93), 1–22.

Southern Regional Education Board. (1999). *Getting beyond talk: Staff leadership needed to improve teacher quality.* Atlanta, GA: Educational Benchmark 2000 Series.

Strauss, R. P., & Sawyer, E. A. (1986). Some new evidence on teacher and student competencies. *Economics of Education Review, 5,* 41–48.

Stronge, J. H., & Tucker, P. D. (2000). *Teacher evaluation and student achievement.* Washington, DC: National Education Association.

Summers, A. A., & Wolfe, B. L. (1975, February). *Which school resources help learning? Efficiency and equality in Philadelphia Public Schools.* (ERIC Document Reproduction Service No. ED 102–716).

Taylor, B. M., Pearson, P. D., Clark, K. F., & Walpole, S. (1999). Center for the improvement of early reading achievement: Effective schools/accomplished teachers. *The Reading Teacher, 53* (2), 156–159.

Teddlie, C., & Stringfield, S. (1993). *Schools make a difference: Lessons learned from a ten-year study of school effects.* New York: Teachers College Press.

Tell, C. (2001). Appreciating good teaching: A conversation with Lee Shulman. *Educational Leadership, 58* (5), 6–11.

Thomas B. Fordham Foundation. (1999). *The teachers we need and how to get more of them.* Retrieved Aug. 26, 2001 from the World Wide Web. Available: http://www.edexcellence.net/library/teacher.html.

Thomas, J. A., & Montomery, P. (1998). On becoming a good teacher: Reflective practice with regard to children's voices. *Journal of Teacher Education, 49* (5), 372–380.

Tobin, K. (1980). The effect of an extended teacher wait-time on science achievement. *Journal of Research in Science Teaching, 17,* 469–475.

Tobin, K., & Capie, W. (1982). Relationships between classroom process variables and middle school science achievement. *Journal of Experimental Psychology, 74,* 441–454.

Traina, R. P. (1999). What makes a good teacher? *Education Week, 18* (19), 34.

Tschannen-Moran, M., Hoy, A. W., & Hoy, W. K. (1998). Teacher efficacy: Its meaning and measure. *Review of Educational Research, 68* (2), 202–248.

Virshup, A. (1997, November 9). Grading teachers. *The Washington Post Magazine: A Special Issue About Education,* 14–17, 31–34.

Walberg, H. J. (1984). Improving the productivity of America's schools. *Educational Leadership, 41* (8), 19–27.

Walberg, H. J. (1994). Homework. In M.C. Wittrock (Ed.), *Handbook of research on teaching.* New York: Macmillan.

Walker, M. H. (1998). 3 basics for better student output. *Education Digest,* May, 15–18.

Wang, M., Haertel, G. D., & Walberg, H. (1993a). Toward a knowledge base for school learning. *Review of Educational Research, 63* (3), 249–294.

Wang, M., Haertel, G. D., & Walberg, H. (1993b). What helps students learn? *Educational Leadership, 51* (4), 74–79.

Wenglinsky, H. (2000). *How teaching matters: Bringing the classroom back into discussions of teacher quality.* Princeton, NJ: Millikan Family Foundation and Educational Testing Service.

Wise, A. E. (2000, Winter). Teacher quality for the new millennium. *The State Education Standard,* 28–30.

Wong, H. K., & Wong, R. T. (1998). *The first days of school: How to be an effective teacher.* Mountain View, CA: Harry W. Wong Publications, Inc.

Wright, S. P., Horn, S. P., & Sanders, W. L. (1997). Teacher and classroom context effects on student achievement: Implications for teacher evaluation. *Journals of Personnel Evaluation in Education, 11,* 57–67.

Yamaguchi, B. J., Strawser, S., & Higgins, K. (1997). Children who are homeless: Implications for educators. *Intervention in School and Clinic, 33,* 90–97.

Index

About the Author

James H. Stronge is Heritage Professor in Educational Policy, Planning, and Leadership at the College of William and Mary in Williamsburg, Virginia. One of his primary research interests is educational personnel evaluation. Stronge has worked with several school districts and other educational organizations to design and develop evaluation systems for teachers, administrators, and support personnel. He is the author or co-author of numerous articles, books, and technical reports on teacher, administrator, and support personnel evaluation. Stronge is the author or editor of several publications, including *Evaluating Professional Support Personnel in Education* (Sage Publications), *Evaluation Handbook for Professional Support Personnel* (Center for Research on Educational Accountability and Teacher Evaluation), *Evaluating Teaching: A Guide to Current Thinking and Best Practice* (Corwin Press), and *Teacher Evaluation and Student Achievement* (National Education Association). Stronge also served as director of the Evaluating Professional Support Personnel project conducted by the Center for Research on Educational Accountability and Teacher Evaluation (CREATE). Currently, he is Associate Editor of the *Journal of Personnel Evaluation in Education*. Stronge's doctorate in the area of educational administration and planning was received from the University of Alabama. He has been a teacher, counselor, and district-level administrator.

Stronge may be reached at (757) 221-2339 or by e-mail at jhstro@wm.edu. His mailing address is The College of William and Mary-SOE, P.O. Box 8795, Williamsburg, VA 23187-8795 USA.

Related ASCD Resources

ASCD stock numbers are noted in parentheses. Although only a few products are listed, ASCD offers numerous publications for teachers, teachers-in-training, and supervisors of teachers.

Networks

Visit the ASCD Web site (www.ascd.org) and click on About ASCD. Under the header of Your Partnership with ASCD, click on Networks for information about professional educators who have formed groups around topics, such as "Affective Factors in Learning," "Mentoring Leadership and Resources," and "Performance Assessment for Leadership." Look in the Network Directory for current facilitators' addresses and phone numbers.

Print Products

A Better Beginning: Supporting and Mentoring New Teachers by Marge Scherer (#199236)

Classroom Instruction That Works: Research-Based Strategies for Increasing Student Achievement by Robert J. Marzano, Debra J. Pickering, and Jane E. Pollock (#101010)

Enhancing Professional Practice: A Framework for Teaching by Charlotte Danielson (#196074)

A Handbook for Classroom Instruction That Works by Robert J. Marzano, Jennifer S. Norford, Diane E. Paynter, Debra J. Pickering, and Barbara B. Gaddy (#101041)

How to Help Beginning Teachers Succeed, 2nd ed., by Stephen P. Gordon and Susan Maxey (#100217)

Teacher Evaluation/Teacher Portfolios ASCD Electronic Topic Pack (#197202)

A Teacher's Guide to Working with Paraeducators and Other Classroom Aides by Jill Morgan and Betty Y. Ashbaker (#100236)

Videotapes

The Teacher Series (series: two sets of 3 tapes each) (#401088, #401089)

For additional resources, visit us on the World Wide Web (http://www.ascd.org), send an e-mail message to member@ascd.org, call the ASCD Service Center (1-800-933-ASCD or 703-578-9600, then press 2), send a fax to 703-575-5400, or write to Information Services, ASCD, 1703 N. Beauregard St., Alexandria, VA 22311-1714 USA.

Writing Arguments

A Rhetoric with Readings

Tenth Edition

John D. Ramage
Arizona State University

John C. Bean
Seattle University

June Johnson
Seattle University

Boston   Columbus   Hoboken   Indianapolis   New York   San Francisco
Amsterdam   Cape Town   Dubai   London   Madrid   Milan   Munich   Paris   Montréal   Toronto
Delhi   Mexico City   São Paulo   Sydney   Hong Kong   Seoul   Singapore   Taipei   Tokyo

Senior Acquisitions Editor: Brad Potthoff
Program Manager: Anne Shure
Development Editor: Kassi Radomski
Product Marketing Manager: Ali Arnold
Field Marketing Manager: Mark Robinson
Executive Digital Producer: Stefanie A. Snajder
Content Specialist: Erin Jenkins
Project Manager: Savoula Amanatidis
Project Coordination, Text Design, and Page Makeup: Integra
Program Design Lead and Cover Designer: Barbara Atkinson
Cover Images: *Clockwise from top left:* Drill rig set up for winter drilling in Wyoming

(Tom Grundy/Shutterstock); Urban teenagers using multimedia devices (Csondy, Getty); American Female Soldier in combat uniform saluting a flag at sunset (Steve Cukrov/Shutterstock); Working bees on honey cells (Kotomiti Okuma/Shutterstock).

Photo Research: QBS Learning
Senior Manufacturing Buyer: Roy L. Pickering, Jr.
Printer and Binder: R. R. Donnelley and Sons Company–Crawfordsville
Cover Printer: Lehigh-Phoenix Color Corporation–Hagerstown
Text Font: 10.5/12 Minion Pro

Acknowledgments of third-party content appear on pages 562–566, which constitute an extension of this copyright page.

PEARSON, ALWAYS LEARNING, and MyWritingLab are exclusive trademarks in the United States and/or other countries, of Pearson Education, Inc., or its affiliates.

Unless otherwise indicated herein, any third-party trademarks that may appear in this work are the property of their respective owners and any references to third-party trademarks, logos, or other trade dress are for demonstrative or descriptive purposes only. Such references are not intended to imply any sponsorship, endorsement, authorization, or promotion of Pearson's products by the owners of such marks, or any relationship between the owner and Pearson Education, Inc., or its affiliates, authors, licensees, or distributors.

Library of Congress Cataloging-in-Publication Data
Ramage, John D.
   Writing arguments: a rhetoric with readings / John D. Ramage, John C. Bean, June Johnson.
     pages cm
   Includes bibliographical references and index.
   ISBN 978-0-321-90673-1 (student edition)
   1. English language—Rhetoric.   2. Persuasion (Rhetoric)   3. College readers.   4. Report writing.
   I. Bean, John C.   II. Johnson, June   III. Title.
   PE1431.R33 2014
   808'.0427—dc23

                                 2014018668

10 9 8 7 6 5 4 3 2 1—DOC—18 17 16 15

Complete Edition
ISBN-10:   0-321-90673-X
ISBN-13: 978-0-321-90673-1

Brief Edition
ISBN-10:   0-321-96427-6
ISBN-13: 978-0-321-96427-4

Concise Edition
ISBN-10:   0-321-96428-4
ISBN-13: 978-0-321-96428-1

PEARSON

www.pearsonhighered.com

Brief Contents

Detailed Contents

Appendix   Informal Fallacies   397

Part Six   An Anthology of Arguments   405

The Future of Food and Farming   406

Preface

Through nine editions, *Writing Arguments* has established itself as a leading college textbook in argumentation. By focusing on argument as dialogue in search of solutions to problems instead of as pro-con debate with winners and losers, *Writing Arguments* treats argument as a process of inquiry as well as a means of persuasion. Users and reviewers have consistently praised the book for teaching the critical thinking skills needed for *writing* arguments: how to analyze the occasion for an argument; how to ground an argument in the values and beliefs of the targeted audience; how to develop and elaborate an argument; and how to respond sensitively to objections and alternative views. We are pleased that in this tenth edition, we have made many improvements while retaining the text's signature strengths.

What's New in the Tenth Edition?

Based on our continuing research into argumentation theory and pedagogy, as well as on the advice of users, we have made significant improvements in the tenth edition that increase the text's flexibility for teachers and its appeal to students. We have made the following major changes:

- **An updated, revised, and streamlined Chapter 2 on "Argument as Inquiry" now focused on the "living wage" controversy.** The previous edition's inquiry topic about immigration has been replaced by the issue of raising the minimum wage for fast-food workers or retail store clerks. Chapter 2 now has all new student examples, visual arguments, and professional readings focussed on minimum wage, including a new annotated student exploratory essay that models the process of rhetorical reading and dialogic thinking.
- **Expanded treatment of evidence.** A revised and expanded Chapter 5 explains with greater clarity the kinds of evidence that can be used in argument and shows students how to analyze evidence rhetorically. A new section shows students how to evaluate evidence encountered in secondary sources by tracing it back to its primary sources.
- **Expanded treatment of Rogerian communication and other means of engaging alternative views.** In Chapter 7, we expand our treatment of Rogerian argument by reframing it as Rogerian communication, which focuses more on mutual listening, negotiation, and growth than on persuasion. Chapter 7 now contains an additional student example of Rogerian communication addressing the issue of charter schools. In addition, we have strengthened our explanation of how classical argument treats opposing views. A new annotated student essay using a rebuttal strategy shows how classical argument can appeal successfully to neutral, undecided, or mildly resistant audiences.
- **Streamlined organization of each chapter now keyed to learning outcomes.** Each chapter now begins with newly formulated learning outcomes. Each main heading in a rhetoric chapter is linked to a respective outcome, enhancing the explanatory power of the outcomes and helping students learn the high-level take-away points and concepts in each chapter

- **New "For Writing and Discussion" activities.** The class discussion activities in this edition now include two types. The first—identified as "For Class Discussion"—helps teachers incorporate small-group discussion tasks that enhance learning of course concepts and skills. The second type—identified as "For Writing and Discussion"—is new to this edition. Each of these activities begins with an "individual task" that can be assigned as homework in advance of class. These tasks are intended as informal, low-stakes write-to-learn activities that motivate reading of the chapter and help students build their own argumentative skills. Each chapter contains at least one of these "For Writing and Discussion" activities.
- **Seven new student model essays, many of which are annotated.** New student model arguments, including many newly annotated models, help demonstrate argument strategies in practice. Showing how other students have developed various types of arguments makes argument concepts and strategies easier for students to grasp and use themselves. New student essays address timely and relevant issues such as raising the minimum wage, evaluating charter schools, analyzing the ethics of downloading films from a person-to-person torrent site on the Web, critiquing a school culture that makes minorities "invisible," opposing women in combat roles, and evaluating the effect of social media on today's college students.
- **Seven new professional readings throughout the rhetoric section in the text.** New readings about issues such as a living wage, the use of dietary supplements among athletes, the "amateur" status of college athletes, the impact of adult cellphone use on children, and therapeutic cloning have been chosen for their illustrative power and student interest.
- **New visual examples throughout the text.** New images, editorial cartoons, and graphics throughout the text highlight current issues such as living wage, climate change, bullying, sexual trafficking, date rape, rainwater conservation, fracking, and gender or racial stereotypes.
- **A thoroughly updated and revised anthology.** The anthology in the tenth edition features newly updated units as well as one new unit.
  - A new unit on food and farming explores controversies over labelling genetically modified foods and the educational, nutritional, and social value of school gardens.
  - An updated unit on digital literacies explores the effects of communications technologies and social media on the way we think, read, and write as well as on our values and social relationships and online identities. The unit also explores the controversy over selfies and shows how social media have been employed to fight gender violence.
  - An updated unit on education continues its focus on the value of a college education. A new sequence of arguments examines the benefits and drawbacks of Massive Open Online Courses (MOOCs), including their effect on teaching, student learning, and society's commitment to educate its citizens.
  - The unit on immigration has been updated to reflect the latest controversies over the social and economic benefits of immigrants and the humanitarian crisis over undocumented children at the border.
  - An updated unit on sustainability now presents a range of arguments on the technological, economic, and political challenges of converting to renewable energy sources and on the controversy over fracking.

- An updated unit on the Millennial generation includes the difficulties of entering the workforce, the need to live with parents longer than planned, choosing to delay marriage, and more.

What Hasn't Changed? The Distinguishing Features of *Writing Arguments*

Building on earlier success, we have preserved the signature features of earlier editions praised by students, instructors, and reviewers:

- **Focus throughout on writing arguments.** Grounded in composition theory, this text combines explanations of argument with exploratory writing activities, sequenced writing assignments, and class-tested discussion tasks with the aim of helping students produce their own strong arguments. The text emphasizes the critical thinking that underlies effective arguments, particularly the skills of critical reading, of active questioning and listening, of believing and doubting, and of developing effective reasons and evidence to support claims.
- **Emphasis on argument as a rhetorical act.** Analyzing audience, understanding the real-world occasions for argument, and appreciating the context and genre of arguments are all treated as equally important rhetorical considerations. Focusing on both the reading and the writing of arguments, the text emphasizes the critical thinking that underlies effective arguments, particularly the skills of critical reading, of rhetorical analysis, of believing and doubting, of empathic listening, of active questioning, and of negotiating ambiguity and seeking synthesis.
- **Integration of four different approaches to argument.** This text uses
  - the Toulmin system as a means of inventing and analyzing arguments;
  - the enthymeme as a logical structure rooted in the beliefs and values of the audience;
  - the classical concepts of *logos, pathos,* and *ethos* as persuasive appeals; and
  - stasis theory (called claim types) as an aid to inventing and structuring arguments through the understanding of generic argumentative moves associated with different categories of claims.
- **Generous treatment of the research process.** Coverage includes guidance for finding sources, reading and evaluating them rhetorically, taking notes, integrating source material, and citing sources using two academic citation systems: MLA and APA.
- **Well-sequenced writing assignments.** The text provides a variety of sequenced writing assignments that include:
  - an argument summary
  - a researched, exploratory essay
  - a "supporting-reasons" argument
  - a classical argument
  - a delayed-thesis argument or Rogerian letter
  - a rhetorical analysis of a written argument
  - a rhetorical analysis of a visual argument
  - an advocacy ad
  - a short argument incorporating quantitative data

- an editorial cartoon
- a definition argument
- a causal argument
- an evaluation or ethical argument
- a proposal argument
- an advocacy poster
- a speech with PowerPoint slides

Part Six, the anthology, provides writing assignments focusing on problems related to each topical unit. Instructors can also design anthology assignments requiring argument analysis.

- **"For Writing and Discussion," "For Class Discussion," and "Examining Visual Arguments" exercises.** These class-tested informal activities, which teach critical thinking and build argumentative skills, are designed to produce active class discussion and debate. All "For Class Discussion" exercises can be used either for whole-class discussions or for collaborative group tasks.
- **Effective and engaging student and professional arguments.** The tenth edition contains 54 written arguments and 55 visual arguments drawn from public and academic arenas as well as 16 student essays and 2 student visual arguments to illustrate argumentative strategies and stimulate discussion, analysis, and debate.

Our Approaches to Argumentation

Our interest in argumentation grows out of our interest in the relationship between writing and thinking. When writing arguments, writers are forced to lay bare their thinking processes in an unparalleled way, grappling with the complex interplay between inquiry and persuasion, between issue and audience. In an effort to engage students in the kinds of critical thinking that argument demands, we draw on four major approaches to argumentation:

1. **The enthymeme as a rhetorical and logical structure.** This concept, especially useful for beginning writers, helps students "nutshell" an argument as a claim with one or more supporting *because* clauses. It also helps them see how real-world arguments are rooted in assumptions granted by the audience rather than in universal and unchanging principles.

2. **The three classical types of appeal—*logos, ethos*, and *pathos*.** These concepts help students place their arguments in a rhetorical context focusing on audience-based appeals; they also help students create an effective voice and style.

3. **Toulmin's system of analyzing arguments.** Toulmin's system helps students see the complete, implicit structure that underlies an enthymeme and develop appropriate grounds and backing to support an argument's reasons and warrants. It also highlights the rhetorical, social, and dialectical nature of argument.

4. **Stasis theory concerning types of claims.** This approach stresses the heuristic value of learning different patterns of support for different types of claims and often leads students to make surprisingly rich and full arguments.

Throughout the text these approaches are integrated and synthesized into generative tools for both producing and analyzing arguments.

Structure of the Text

Writing Arguments provides a sound pedagogical framework for the teaching of argument while giving instructors the flexibility to use what they need. Part One begins with an overview of argument and a chapter on reading arguments and exploring issues. Part Two examines the elements of writing arguments: the enthymeme (a claim with reasons); the rhetorical appeals of *logos, ethos,* and *pathos;* Toulmin's system for analyzing arguments; the use of evidence; acknowledging and responding to alternative views; and using delayed-thesis and Rogerian approaches. In Part Three, the focus shifts to analyzing written and visual arguments. Part Four provides a deeper understanding of definition, resemblance, causal, evaluation, and proposal arguments. Part Five shows students how to use sources in support of an argument by evaluating, integrating, citing, and documenting them properly. An appendix on logical fallacies is a handy section where all the major informal fallacies are treated at once for easy reference.

Part Six, the anthology, provides a rich and varied selection of professional arguments arranged into seven high-interest units including the value of higher education, digital literacies, current food issues, Millennials in the workplace, immigration, choices for a sustainable world, and a collection of classic arguments. The anthology selections are grouped by topic rather than by issue question to encourage students to see that any conversation of alternative views gives rise to numerous embedded and intertwined issues. Many of the issues raised in the anthology are first raised in the rhetoric (Parts One through Five) so that students' interest in the anthology topics will already be piqued.

Resources for Instructors and Students

Now Available for Composition   MyWritingLab™

Integrated solutions for writing. *MyWritingLab* is an online homework, tutorial, and assessment program that provides engaging experiences for today's instructors and students. New features designed specifically for composition instructors and their course needs include a new writing space for students, customizable rubrics for assessing and grading student writing, multimedia instruction on all aspects of composition, and advanced reporting to improve the ability to analyze class performance.

Adaptive learning. *MyWritingLab* offers pre-assessments and personalized remediation so students see improved results and instructors spend less time in class reviewing the basics. Visit www.mywritinglab.com for more information.

eTextbooks

Pearson eText gives students access to *Writing Arguments*, Tenth Edition, whenever and wherever they can access the Internet. The eText pages look exactly like the printed text, and include powerful interactive and customization functions. Users can create notes, highlight text in different colors, create bookmarks, zoom, click hyperlinked words and phrases to view definitions, and view as a single page or as two pages. Pearson eText also links students to associated media files, enabling them to view videos as they read the text, and offers a full-text search and the ability to save and export notes. The Pearson eText also includes embedded URLs in the chapter text with active links to the Internet.

The Pearson eText app is a great companion to Pearson's eText browser-based book reader. It allows existing subscribers who view their Pearson eText titles on a Mac or PC to additionally access their titles in a bookshelf on the iPad or an Android tablet either online or via download.

Instructor's Manual

The *Instructor's Manual*, Tenth Edition, includes the following features:

- Discussion of planning decisions an instructor must make in designing an argument course: for example, how to use readings; how much to emphasize Toulmin or claim type theory; how much time to build into the course for invention, peer review of drafts, and other writing instruction; and how to select and sequence assignments.
- For new instructors, a helpful discussion of how to sequence writing assignments and how to use a variety of collaborative tasks in the classroom to promote active learning and critical thinking.
- Four detailed syllabi that support a variety of course structures and emphases.
- An independent, highly teachable introductory lesson on the Toulmin schema and an additional exercise giving students practice using Toulmin to generate argument frames.
- Chapter-by-chapter teaching tips, responses to the For Class Discussion exercises, and sample quizzes.
- Suggestions for encouraging students to explore how visual arguments mold public thinking about issues and controversies.
- Helpful suggestions for using the exercises in Part Four on critiquing readings. By focusing on rhetorical context as well as on the strengths and weaknesses of these arguments, our suggestions will help students connect their reading of arguments to their writing of arguments.
- A list of anthology readings that employ each claim type, either as a major claim or as a substantial portion of the argument.
- An analysis of anthology readings that points out striking connections among readings, suggesting how the readings participate in larger societal argumentative conversations, but that also connects the anthology to the rhetoric portion of the text. Using a bulleted, quick-reference format, each analysis briefly discusses (1) the core of the argument, (2) the major or dominant claims of the argument, (3) the argument's use of evidence and argumentative strategies, (4) the appeals to *ethos* and *pathos* in the argument, and (5) the argument's genre.

Acknowledgments

We are happy for this opportunity to give public thanks to the scholars, teachers, and students who have influenced our approach to composition and argument. For this edition, we owe special thanks to those who helped us revise the anthology of *Writing Arguments*. Hilary Hawley, our colleague at Seattle University, researched and wrote the apparatus for many of the Anthology units. Her experience teaching argument and the public controversies over food appear in the new unit featuring controversies over GMO food and school gardens. We also thank Sarah Bean for her research on the anthology, her keen awareness of social justice issues, and her empathic perspective on Millennials.

We are particularly grateful to our talented students—Trudie Makens, Lauren Shinozuka, Monica Allen, Alex Mullen, Lorena Mendoza-Flores, and Ivan Snook—who contributed to this edition their timely arguments built from their intellectual curiosity, ideas, personal experience, and research. We also thank Janie Bube for her environmental advocacy poster and Trey Tice for his film criticism. Additionally, we are grateful to all our students whom we have been privileged to teach in our writing classes and to our other students who have enabled us to include their arguments in this text. Their insights and growth as writers have inspired our ongoing study of rhetoric and argumentation.

We thank too the many users of our texts who have given us encouragement about our successes and offered helpful suggestions for improvements. Particularly we thank the following scholars and teachers who reviewed this revision of *Writing Arguments* in its various stages:

Alicia Alexander, Cape Fear Community College; Elijah Coleman, Washington State University; Shannon Collins, Owensboro Community and Technical College; Veronda Hutchinson, Johnston Community College; A. Abby Knoblauch, Kansas State University; Beth Lewis, Moberly Area Community College; Layne Neeper, Morehead State University; Jessie Nixon, University of Alaska Anchorage; Thomas Riddle, Guilford Technical Community College; Dixie A. Shaw-Tillmon, The University of Texas San Antonio; Janice R. Showler, Holy Family University; Coreen Wees, Iowa Western Community College; and Stephen H. Wells, Community College of Allegheny County.

We thank our editor, Brad Potthoff for his publishing knowledge and cordial leadership. We also give special, heartfelt thanks to our two development editors, Kassi Radomski and Marion Castellucci, who shepherded this project through every stage, giving us timely insight, collaborative feedback, and professional support. We also thank Martha Beyerlein, our production editor, who has worked with us for years and patiently ushered us into the paperless stages of text preparation.

As always we thank our families who ultimately make this work possible. John Bean thanks his wife, Kit, also a professional composition teacher, and his children Matthew, Andrew, Stephen, and Sarah, all of whom have grown to adulthood since he first began writing textbooks. Our lively conversations at family dinners, which now include spouses, partners, and grandchildren, have kept him engaged in arguments that matter about how to create a just, humane, and sustainable world. June Johnson thanks her husband, Kenneth Bube, a mathematics professor and researcher, and her daughter, Janie Bube, now a student contributor to this text. Ken and Janie have played major roles in the ongoing family analysis of argumentation in the public sphere on wide-ranging subjects. Janie's knowledge of environmental issues and Kenneth's of mathematical thinking, online education, energy resources, and technology have broadened June's understanding of argument hotspots. They have also enabled her to meet the demands and challenges of continuing to infuse new ideas and material into this text in each revision.

John C. Bean
June Johnson

PART ONE
Overview of Argument

1 Argument: An Introduction

2 Argument as Inquiry: Reading and Exploring

Across the country, protests like this one in front of a Burger King in Boston are raising awareness of the poverty-level wages of fast-food workers, who are not represented by unions and who often depend on public assistance such as food stamps to get by every month. While protestors argue for a minimum wage of $15 per hour, opponents argue that raising the minimum wage would increase food prices and reduce the number of jobs. If you were making a brochure or poster in favor of an increased minimum wage for fast-food workers, how effective would this realistic, low-keyed photo be in raising sympathy for the cause? Chapters 2 and 7 explore the issue of a living wage for unskilled workers.

Argument: An Introduction

At the outset of a book on argument, you might expect us to provide a simple definition of argument. Instead, we're going to explain why no universally accepted definition is possible. Over the centuries, philosophers and rhetoricians have disagreed about the meaning of the term and about the goals that arguers should set for themselves. This opening chapter introduces you to some of these controversies.

We begin by showing some common misconceptions about argument while also explaining how arguments can be either implicit or explicit. We then proceed to three defining features of argument: it requires writers or speakers to justify their claims; it is both a product and a process; and it combines elements of truth seeking and persuasion. Finally, we explore more fully the relationship between truth seeking and persuasion by asking questions about the nature of "truth" that arguments seek.

What Do We Mean by Argument?

1.1 To explain common misconceptions about the meaning of argument

Let's begin by examining the inadequacies of two popular images of argument—fight and debate.

Argument Is Not a Fight or a Quarrel

To many, the word *argument* connotes anger and hostility, as when we say, "I just got in a huge argument with my roommate," or "My mother and I argue all the time." What we picture here is heated disagreement, rising pulse rates, and an urge to slam doors. Argument imagined as fight conjures images of shouting talk-show guests, flaming bloggers, or fist-banging speakers.

But to our way of thinking, argument doesn't imply anger. In fact, arguing is often pleasurable. It is a creative and productive activity that engages us at high levels of inquiry and critical thinking, often in conversation with people we like and respect. For your primary image of argument, we invite you to think not of a shouting match on cable news but of a small group of reasonable people seeking the best solution to a problem. We will return to this image throughout the chapter.

Argument Is Not Pro-Con Debate

Another popular image of argument is debate—a presidential debate, perhaps, or a high school or college debate tournament. According to one popular dictionary, *debate* is "a formal contest of argumentation in which two opposing teams defend and attack a given proposition." Although formal debate can develop critical thinking, its weakness is that it can turn argument into a game of winners and losers rather than a process of cooperative inquiry.

For an illustration of this weakness, consider one of our former students, a champion high school debater who spent his senior year debating the issue of prison reform. Throughout the year he argued for and against propositions such as "The United States should build more prisons" and "Innovative alternatives to prison should replace prison sentences for most crimes." We asked him, "What do you personally think is the best way to reform prisons?" He replied, "I don't know. I haven't thought about what I would actually choose."

Here was a bright, articulate student who had studied prisons extensively for a year. Yet nothing in the atmosphere of pro-con debate had engaged him in truth-seeking inquiry. He could argue for and against a proposition, but he hadn't experienced the wrenching process of clarifying his own values and taking a personal stand. As we explain throughout this text, argument entails a desire for truth; it aims to find the best solutions to complex problems. We don't mean that arguers don't passionately support their own points of view or expose weaknesses in views they find faulty. Instead, we mean that their goal isn't to win a game but to find and promote the best belief or course of action.

Arguments Can Be Explicit or Implicit

Before proceeding to some defining features of argument, we should note also that arguments can be either explicit or implicit. An *explicit* argument directly states its controversial claim and supports it with reasons and evidence. An *implicit* argument, in contrast, may not look like an argument at all. It may be a bumper sticker, a billboard, a poster, a photograph, a cartoon, a vanity license plate, a slogan on a T-shirt, an advertisement, a poem, or a song lyric. But like an explicit argument, it persuades its audience toward a certain point of view.

Consider the striking photograph in Figure 1.1—a baby wearing a bib labeled "POISON." This photograph enters a conversation about the safety of toys and other baby products sold in the United States. In recent years, fears about toy safety have

FIGURE 1.1 An implicit argument against phthalates

come mostly from two sources: the discovery that many toys imported from China contained lead paint and the discovery that a substance used to make plastics pliable and soft—called *phthalates* (pronounced "thalates")—may be harmful. Phthalates have been shown to interfere with hormone production in rat fetuses and, based on other rodent studies, may produce some kinds of cancers and other ailments. Because many baby products contain phthalates—bibs, edges of cribs, rubber duckies, and any number of other soft, rubbery toys—parents worry that babies can ingest phthalates by chewing on these toys.

The photograph of the baby and bib makes the argumentative claim that baby products are poisonous; the photograph implicitly urges viewers to take action against phthalates. But this photograph is just one voice in a surprisingly complex conversation. Is the bib in fact poisonous? Such questions were debated during a recent campaign to ban the sale of toys containing phthalates in California. A legislative initiative sparked intense lobbying from both child-advocacy groups and representatives of the toy industry. At issue were a number of scientific questions about the risk posed by phthalates. To what extent do studies on rats apply to humans? How much exposure to phthalates should be considered dangerous? (Experiments on rats used large amounts of phthalates—amounts that, according to many scientists, far exceed anything a baby could absorb by chewing on a toy.) Also at issue is the level of health risks a free market society should be willing to tolerate. The European Union, operating on the "precautionary principle," and citing evidence that such toys *might* be dangerous, has banned toys containing phthalates. The U.S. government sets less strict standards than does the European Union. A federal agency generally doesn't ban a substance unless it has been *proven* harmful to humans, not merely suspected of being harmful. In defense of free markets, the toy and chemical industries accused opponents of phthalates of using "junk science" to produce scary but inaccurate data.

Our point in summarizing the toxic toy controversy is to demonstrate the persuasive roles of both implicit and explicit arguments.

In contrast to the implicit argument made in Figure 1.1, consider the following explicit argument posted by student writer Juan Lucas on a blog site. As an explicit argument, it states its claim directly and supports it with reasons and evidence.

An Argument Against Banning Phthalates

(BLOG POST BY STUDENT JUAN LUCAS)

The campaign to ban phthalates from children's toys uses scare tactics that aren't grounded in good science. The anti-phthalate campaign shocks us with photos of baby bibs labeled "poison." It arouses fear by linking phthalates to possible cancers or abnormalities in hormone production. In contrast, the scientific literature about phthalates is much more guarded and cautious. Political pressure has already led to a 2009 federal ban on phthalates used in toys that can be put in a baby's mouth, such as bottle nipples and teething rings. But based on the scientific evidence, I argue that further banning of phthalates from children's toys is a mistake.

Despite the warnings from the anti-phthalates campaign, the federal Consumer Product Safety Commission, after extensive tests and review of the scientific literature, says that the level of phthalates absorbed from toys is too low to be harmful. No scientific study has yet demonstrated harm to humans. Moreover, humans are exposed to phthalates daily, especially from food packaging, plastic bottles, shower curtains, personal care products, and elsewhere. Banning phthalates in children's toys wouldn't significantly reduce human exposure to phthalates from other sources.

Banning substances on emotional rather than scientific grounds has its own negative consequences. If we try to ban all potentially harmful substances before they have been proven harmful, we will be less watchful against scientifically proven dangers such as lead, coal dust, sulfur dioxide, or mercury in fish. We should place phthalates in the same category as other possible-but-not-proven threats that are part of living in the industrial world: artificial sweeteners, electromagnetic waves, non-organic foods (because of possible pesticide residue), GMO corn and soy beans, and radon in our walls. We should demand rigorous testing of all these threats, but not try to ban them until evidence-based science proves their harmfulness.

We should also keep in mind the impact of too much regulation on people's jobs and the economy in general. The toy industry, a vibrant and important one in our economy (just ask Santa Claus), provides thousands of jobs, and is already highly regulated with safety standards. The use of phthalates, in fact, might make many toys safer by making them softer and less brittle. Ensuring toy safety through strong testing and regulation is absolutely necessary. But let's base our regulations on good science.

■ ■ ■ **FOR WRITING AND DISCUSSION** **Implicit and Explicit Arguments**   My**Writing**Lab™

Any argument, whether implicit or explicit, tries to influence the audience's stance on an issue, moving the audience toward the arguer's claim. Arguments work on us psychologically as well as cognitively, triggering emotions as well as thoughts and ideas. Each of the implicit arguments in Figures 1.2–1.4 makes a claim on its audience, trying to get viewers to adopt its position, perspective, belief, or point of view on an issue.

FIGURE 1.2 Poster related to the GMO controversy

FIGURE 1.3 Photograph of protestors at a New York State Occupy Wall Street Rally

"Do you John promise that your schedule, please put your iPhone away, will never be more important than your times together?"

FIGURE 1.4 Cartoon on social etiquette and digital media

Individual task: For each argument, answer the following questions:

1. What conversation does this argument join? What is the issue or controversy? What is at stake? (Sometimes "insider knowledge" might be required to understand the argument. In such cases, explain to an outsider the needed background information or cultural context.)
2. What is the argument's claim? That is, what value, perspective, belief, or position does the argument ask its viewers to adopt?
3. What is an opposing or alternative view? What views is the argument pushing against?
4. Convert the implicit argument into an explicit argument by stating its claim and supporting reasons in words. How do implicit and explicit arguments work differently on the brains or hearts of the audience?

Group task: Working in pairs or as a whole class, share your answers with classmates.

The Defining Features of Argument

1.2 To describe defining features of argument

We turn now to examine arguments in more detail. (Unless we say otherwise, by *argument* we mean explicit arguments that attempt to supply reasons and evidence to support their claims.) This section examines three defining features of such arguments.

Argument Requires Justification of Its Claims

To begin defining argument, let's turn to a humble but universal site of disagreement: the conflict between a parent and a teenager over rules. In what way and in what circumstances do such conflicts constitute arguments?

Consider the following dialogue:

YOUNG PERSON (*racing for the front door while putting coat on*):   Bye. See you later.

PARENT: Whoa! What time are you planning on coming home?

YOUNG PERSON (*coolly, hand still on doorknob*):   I'm sure we discussed this earlier. I'll be home around 2 A.M. (*The second sentence, spoken very rapidly, is barely audible.*)

PARENT (*mouth tightening*):   We did *not* discuss this earlier and you're *not* staying out till two in the morning. You'll be home at twelve.

At this point in the exchange, we have a quarrel, not an argument. Quarrelers exchange antagonistic assertions without any attempt to support them rationally. If the dialogue never gets past the "Yes-you-will/No-I-won't" stage, it either remains a quarrel or degenerates into a fight.

Let us say, however, that the dialogue takes the following turn:

YOUNG PERSON (*tragically*):   But I'm *sixteen years old!*

Now we're moving toward argument. Not, to be sure, a particularly well-developed or cogent one, but an argument all the same. It's now an argument because one of the quarrelers has offered a reason for her assertion. Her choice of curfew is satisfactory, she says, *because* she is sixteen years old, an argument that depends on the unstated assumption that sixteen-year-olds are old enough to make decisions about such matters.

The parent can now respond in one of several ways that will either advance the argument or turn it back into a quarrel. The parent can simply invoke parental authority ("I don't care—you're still coming home at twelve"), in which case argument ceases. Or the parent can provide a reason for his or her view ("You will be home at twelve because your dad and I pay the bills around here!"), in which case the argument takes a new turn.

So far we've established two necessary conditions that must be met before we're willing to call something an argument: (1) a set of two or more conflicting assertions and (2) the attempt to resolve the conflict through an appeal to reason.

But good argument demands more than meeting these two formal requirements. For the argument to be effective, an arguer is obligated to clarify and support the reasons presented. For example, "But I'm sixteen years old!" is not yet a clear support for the assertion "I should be allowed to set my own curfew." On the surface, Young Person's argument seems absurd. Her parent, of all people, knows precisely how old she is. What makes it an argument is that behind her claim lies an unstated assumption—all sixteen-year-olds are old enough to set their own curfews. What Young Person needs to do now is to support that assumption.* In doing so, she must anticipate the sorts of questions the assumption will raise in the mind of her parent: What is the legal status of sixteen-year-olds? How psychologically mature, as opposed to chronologically mature, is Young Person? What is the actual track record of Young Person in being responsible? and so forth. Each of these questions will force Young Person to reexamine and clarify her assumptions about the proper degree of autonomy for sixteen-year-olds. And her responses to those questions should in turn force the parent to reexamine his or her assumptions about the dependence of sixteen-year-olds on parental guidance and wisdom. (Likewise, the parent will need to show why "paying the bills around here" automatically gives the right to set Young Person's curfew.)

As the argument continues, Young Person and Parent may shift to a different line of reasoning. For example, Young Person might say: "I should be allowed to stay out until 2 A.M. because all my friends get to stay out that late." (Here the unstated assumption is that the rules in this family ought to be based on the rules in other families.) The parent might in turn respond, "But I certainly never stayed out that late when I was your age"—an argument assuming that the rules in this family should follow the rules of an earlier generation.

As Young Person and Parent listen to each other's points of view (and begin realizing why their initial arguments have not persuaded their intended audience), both parties find themselves in the uncomfortable position of having to examine their own beliefs and to justify assumptions that they have taken for granted. Here we encounter one of the earliest meanings of the term *to argue,* which is "to clarify." As an arguer begins to clarify her own position on an issue, she also begins to clarify her audience's position. Such clarification helps the arguer see how she might accommodate her audience's views, perhaps by adjusting her own position or by developing reasons that appeal to her audience's values. Thus Young Person might suggest an argument like this:

> I should be allowed to stay out until two on a trial basis because I need enough freedom to demonstrate my maturity and show you I won't get into trouble.

The assumption underlying this argument is that it is good to give teenagers freedom to demonstrate their maturity. Because this reason is likely to appeal to her parent's own values (the parent wants to see his or her daughter grow in maturity) and because it is tempered by the qualifier "on a trial basis" (which reduces some of the threat of Young Person's initial demands), it may prompt productive discussion.

Whether or not Young Person and Parent can work out a best solution, the preceding scenario illustrates how argument leads people to clarify their reasons and provide justifications that can be examined rationally. The scenario also illustrates two specific aspects of argument that we will explore in detail in the next sections: (1) Argument is both a process and a product. (2) Argument combines truth seeking and persuasion.

---

*Later in this text we will call the assumption underlying a line of reasoning its *warrant* (see Chapter 4).

Argument Is Both a Process and a Product

As the preceding scenario revealed, argument can be viewed as a *process* in which two or more parties seek the best solution to a question or problem. Argument can also be viewed as a *product,* each product being any person's contribution to the conversation at a given moment. In an informal discussion, the products are usually short, whatever time a person uses during his or her turns in the conversation. Under more formal settings, an orally delivered product might be a short, impromptu speech (say, during an open-mike discussion of a campus issue) or a longer, carefully prepared formal speech (as in a PowerPoint presentation at a business meeting or an argument at a public hearing for or against a proposed city project).

Similar conversations occur in writing. Roughly analogous to a small-group discussion is an exchange of the kind that occurs regularly online through informal chat groups or more formal blog sites. In an online discussion, participants have more thinking time to shape their messages than they do in a real-time oral discussion. Nevertheless, messages are usually short and informal, making it possible over the course of several days to see participants' ideas shift and evolve as conversants modify their initial views in response to others' views.

Roughly equivalent to a formal speech would be a formal written argument, which may take the form of an academic argument for a college course; a grant proposal; an online posting; a guest column for the op-ed* section of a newspaper; a legal brief; a letter to a member of Congress; or an article for an organizational newsletter, popular magazine, or professional journal. In each of these instances, the written argument (a product) enters a conversation (a process)—in this case, a conversation of readers, many of whom will carry on the conversation by writing their own responses or by discussing the writer's views with others. The goal of the community of writers and readers is to find the best solution to the problem or issue under discussion.

Argument Combines Truth Seeking and Persuasion

In thinking about argument as a product, the writer will find herself continually moving back and forth between truth seeking and persuasion—that is, between questions about the subject matter (What is the best solution to this problem?) and about audience (What do my readers already believe or value? What reasons and evidence will most persuade them?). Back and forth she'll weave, alternately absorbed in the subject of her argument and in the audience for that argument.

Neither of the two focuses is ever completely out of mind, but their relative importance shifts during different phases of the development of a paper. Moreover, different rhetorical situations place different emphases on truth seeking versus persuasion.

Op-ed stands for "opposite-editorial." It is the generic name in journalism for a signed argument that voices the writer's opinion on an issue, as opposed to a news story that is supposed to report events objectively, uncolored by the writer's personal views. Op-ed pieces appear in the editorial-opinion section of newspapers, which generally features editorials by the resident staff, opinion pieces by syndicated columnists, and letters to the editor from readers. The term *op-ed* is often extended to syndicated columns appearing in newsmagazines, advocacy Web sites, and online news services.

Truth Seeking   **Persuasion**

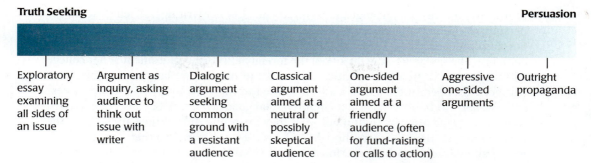

FIGURE 1.5 Continuum of arguments from truth seeking to persuasion

We could thus place arguments on a kind of continuum that measures the degree of attention a writer gives to subject matter versus audience. (See Figure 1.5.) At the far truth-seeking end of the continuum might be an exploratory piece that lays out several alternative approaches to a problem and weighs the strengths and weaknesses of each with no concern for persuasion. At the other end of the continuum would be outright propaganda, such as a political campaign advertisement that reduces a complex issue to sound bites and distorts an opponent's position through out-of-context quotations or misleading use of data. (At its most blatant, propaganda obliterates truth seeking; it will do anything, including the knowing use of bogus evidence, distorted assertions, and outright lies, to win over an audience.) In the middle ranges of the continuum, writers shift their focuses back and forth between truth seeking and persuasion but with varying degrees of emphasis.

As an example of a writer focusing primarily on truth seeking, consider the case of Kathleen, who, in her college argument course, addressed the definitional question "Is American Sign Language (ASL) a 'foreign language' for purposes of meeting the university's foreign language requirement?" Kathleen had taken two years of ASL at a community college. When she transferred to a four-year college, the chair of the foreign languages department at her new college would not allow her ASL proficiency to count for the foreign language requirement. ASL isn't a "language," the chair said summarily. "It's not equivalent to learning French, German, or Japanese."

Kathleen disagreed, so she immersed herself in developing her argument. While doing research, she focused almost entirely on subject matter, searching for what linguists, neurologists, cognitive psychologists, and sociologists had said about the language of deaf people. Immersed in her subject matter, she was only tacitly concerned with her audience, whom she thought of primarily as her classmates and the professor of her argument class—people who were friendly to her views and interested in her experiences with the deaf community. She wrote a well-documented paper, citing several scholarly articles, that made a good case to her classmates (and the professor) that ASL is indeed a distinct language.

Proud of the big red A the professor had placed on her paper, Kathleen decided for a subsequent assignment to write a second paper on ASL—but this time aiming it directly at the chair of foreign languages and petitioning him to accept her ASL proficiency for the foreign language requirement. Now her writing task fell closer to the persuasive end of our continuum. Kathleen once again immersed herself in research, but this time focused not on subject matter (whether ASL is a distinct language) but on audience. She researched the history of the foreign language requirement at her college and discovered some of the politics behind it (an old foreign language requirement had been dropped in the 1970s and reinstituted in the 1990s, partly—a math professor told her—to boost enrollments in foreign language courses). She also interviewed foreign language teachers to find out what they knew and didn't know about ASL. She discovered that many teachers thought ASL was "easy to learn," so that accepting ASL would allow students a Mickey Mouse way to avoid the rigors of a "real" foreign language class. Additionally, she learned that foreign language teachers valued immersing students in a foreign culture; in fact, the foreign language requirement was part of her college's effort to create a multicultural curriculum.

This new understanding of her target audience helped Kathleen reconceptualize her argument. Her claim that ASL is a real language (the subject of her first paper) became only one section of her second paper, much condensed and abridged. She added sections showing the difficulty of learning ASL (to counter her audience's belief that learning ASL is easy), showing how the deaf community forms a distinct culture with its own customs and literature (to show how ASL would meet the goals of multiculturalism), and showing that the number of transfer students with ASL credits would be negligibly small (to allay fears that accepting ASL would threaten enrollments in language classes). She ended her argument with an appeal to her college's public emphasis (declared boldly in its mission statement) on eradicating social injustice and reaching out to the oppressed. She described the isolation of deaf people in a world where almost no hearing people learn ASL, and she argued that the deaf community on her campus could be integrated more fully into campus life if more students could "talk" with them. Thus the ideas included in her new argument—the reasons selected, the evidence used, the arrangement and tone—all were determined by her primary focus on persuasion.

Our point, then, is that all along the continuum, writers attempt both to seek truth and to persuade, but not necessarily with equal balance. Kathleen could not have written her second paper, aimed specifically at persuading the chair of foreign languages, if she hadn't first immersed herself in truth-seeking research that convinced her that ASL is indeed a distinct language. Nor are we saying that her second argument was better than her first. Both fulfilled their purposes and met the needs of their intended audiences. Both involved truth seeking and persuasion, but the first focused primarily on subject matter whereas the second focused primarily on audience.

Argument and the Problem of Truth

1.3 To understand the relationship of argument to the problem of truth

The tension that we have just examined between truth seeking and persuasion raises an ancient issue in the field of argument: Is the arguer's first obligation to truth or to winning the argument? And just what is the nature of the truth to which arguers are supposed to be obligated?

In Plato's famous dialogues from ancient Greek philosophy, these questions were at the heart of Socrates' disagreement with the Sophists. The Sophists were professional rhetoricians who specialized in training orators to win arguments. Socrates, who valued truth seeking over persuasion and believed that truth could be discovered through philosophic inquiry, opposed the Sophists. For Socrates, Truth resided in the ideal world of forms, and through philosophic rigor humans could transcend the changing, shadowlike world of everyday reality to perceive the world of universals where Truth, Beauty, and Goodness resided. Through his method of questioning his interlocutors, Socrates would gradually peel away layer after layer of false views until Truth was revealed. The good person's duty, Socrates believed, was not to win an argument but to pursue this higher Truth. Socrates distrusted rhetoricians because they were interested only in the temporal power and wealth that came from persuading audiences to the orator's views.

Let's apply Socrates' disagreement with the Sophists to a modern instance. Suppose your community is divided over the issue of raising environmental standards versus keeping open a job-producing factory that doesn't meet new guidelines for waste discharge. The Sophists would train you to argue any side of this issue on behalf of any lobbying group willing to pay for your services. If, however, you followed the spirit of Socrates, you would be inspired to listen to all sides of the dispute, peel away false arguments, discover the Truth through reasonable inquiry, and commit yourself to a Right Course of Action.

But what is the nature of Truth or Right Action in a dispute between jobs and the environment? The Sophists believed that truth was determined by those in power; thus they could enter an argument unconstrained by any transcendent beliefs or assumptions. When Socrates talked about justice and virtue, the Sophists could reply contemptuously that these were fictitious concepts invented by the weak to protect themselves from the strong. Over the years, the Sophists' relativist beliefs became so repugnant to people that the term *sophistry* became synonymous with trickery in argument.

However, in recent years the Sophists' critique of a transcendent Universal Truth has been taken seriously by many philosophers, sociologists, and other thinkers who doubt Socrates' confident belief that arguments, properly conducted, necessarily arrive at a single Truth. For these thinkers, as for the Sophists, there are often different degrees of truth and different kinds of truths for different situations or cultures. From this perspective, when we consider questions of interpretation or value, we can never demonstrate that a belief or assumption is true—not through scientific observation, not through reason, and not through religious revelation. We get our beliefs, according to these contemporary thinkers, from the shared assumptions of our particular cultures. We are condemned (or liberated) to live in a pluralistic, multicultural world with competing visions of truth.

If we accept this pluralistic view of the world, do we then endorse the Sophists' radical relativism, freeing us to argue any side of any issue? Or do we doggedly pursue some modern equivalent of Socrates' truth?

Our own sympathies are with Socrates, but we admit to a view of truth that is more tentative, cautious, and conflicted than his. For us, truth seeking does not mean finding the "Right Answer" to a disputed question, but neither does it mean a valueless relativism in which all answers are equally good. For us, truth seeking means taking responsibility for determining the "best answer" or "best solution" to the question for the good of the whole community when taking into consideration the interests of all stakeholders. It means making hard decisions in the face of uncertainty. This more tentative view of truth means that you cannot use argument to "prove" your claim, but only to make a reasonable case for your claim. One contemporary philosopher says that argument can hope only to "increase adherence" to ideas, not absolutely convince an audience of the necessary truth of ideas. Even though you can't be certain, in a Socratic sense, that your solution to the problem is the best one available, you must ethically take responsibility for the consequences of your claim and you must seek justice for stakeholders beyond yourself. You must, in other words, forge a personal stance based on your examination of all the evidence and your articulation of values that you can make public and defend.

To seek truth, then, means to seek the best or most just solution to a problem while observing all available evidence, listening with an open mind to the views of all stakeholders, clarifying and attempting to justify your own values and assumptions, and taking responsibility for your argument. It follows that truth seeking often means delaying closure on an issue, acknowledging the pressure of alternative views, and being willing to change one's mind. Seen in this way, learning to argue effectively has the deepest sort of social value: It helps communities settle conflicts in a rational and humane way by finding, through the dialectic exchange of ideas, the best solutions to problems without resorting to violence or to other assertions of raw power.

■ ■ ■   **FOR CLASS DISCUSSION**   **Role-Playing Arguments**

On any given day, the media provides evidence of the complexity of living in a pluralistic culture. Issues that could be readily decided in a completely homogeneous culture raise questions in a society that has fewer shared assumptions. Choose one of the following cases as the subject for a "simulation game" in which class members present the points of view of the people involved.

Case 1: Political Asylum for German Family Seeking Right to Homeschool Their Children

In 2010 an Evangelical Christian family from Germany, Uwe and Hannelore Romeike and their five children, moved to the United States seeking asylum from political persecution. At the U.S. immigration hearings, the couple argued that if they remained in Germany their decision to homeschool their children would result in fines, possible arrest, and even forced separation from their children. German law forbids homeschooling on the grounds that failure to attend recognized schools will create "parallel societies" whose members will fail to integrate into Germany's open and pluralistic culture. In early 2011, a U.S. federal immigration judge granted political asylum to the family, denouncing the German government's policy against homeschooling. He called it "utterly repellent to everything we believe as Americans." However, in 2013 the Sixth Circuit Court unanimously overturned the original decision and revoked the family's status as political refugees. Stating that the United States cannot give political asylum to every victim of perceived unfairness in another country's laws, the court declared that Germany's ban on homeschooling did not constitute political persecution. The decision led to international debate about the role of homeschooling in a pluralistic society and about the definition of political persecution. In the United States, the Homeschooling Legal Defense Association urged that the case be heard by the United States Supreme Court and sponsored a petition drive supporting the Romeike family.

Your task: Imagine a public hearing on this issue where all stakeholders are invited to present their points of view. The U.S. Immigration Web site offers the following definition of refugee status:

> Refugee status or asylum may be granted to people who have been persecuted or fear they will be persecuted on account of race, religion, nationality, and/or membership in a particular social group or political opinion

Your goal isn't to make your own decision about this case but to bring to imaginative life all the points of view in the controversy. Hold a mock public hearing in which classmates play the following roles: (a) An American parent advocating homeschooling; (b) an American teacher's union representative opposing homeschooling; (c) an attorney arguing that the Romeike family meets the criteria for "refugee status"; (d) an attorney arguing that the Romeike family does not meet the criteria for refugee status; (e) a German citizen supporting the German law against homeschooling; (f) a Romeike parent arguing that they would be persecuted if they returned to Germany; (g) other roles that your class thinks are relevant to this case.

Case 2: HPV Vaccines for Sixth Grade Girls (and Boys)

In 2007 the pharmaceutical company Merke developed a vaccine against the sexually transmitted HPV virus (human papillomavirus), some strains of which can cause cervical cancer as well as genital warts. They launched an extensive television campaign promoting the vaccine (which would bring substantial profits to Merke) and advised that girls should get the vaccine before they reached puberty. Following recommendations from doctors and medical researchers, several states passed laws mandating that the HPV vaccine be included for girls among the other vaccinations required of all children for entry into the sixth or seventh grades (depending on the state). These laws sparked public debate about the benefits versus potential adverse effects of vaccines, and about the state's versus parents' role in determining what vaccines a child should get.

Your task: Imagine a public hearing addressing what your state's laws should be concerning HPV vaccinations for pre-pubescent children. Your goal isn't to make your own decision about this case but to bring to imaginative life all the points of view in the controversy. Hold a mock hearing in which classmates play the following roles: (a) a cancer specialist who supports mandatory HPV vaccination for girls; (b) a public health specialist who also supports expanding the requirement to include boys; (c) a skeptical person concerned about the potential adverse effects of vaccines in general; (d) a religiously conservative parent who believes in abstinence and monogamy and opposes the cultural message of the HPV vaccination.

Conclusion

In this chapter we have explored some of the complexities of argument, showing you why we believe that argument is a matter not of fist banging or of win-lose debate but of finding, through a process of rational inquiry, the best solution to a problem or issue. Good argument requires justification of its claim, is both a process and product, and combines truth seeking with persuasion. We particularly want to emphasize its truth-seeking dimension. We suggest that when you enter an argument you seek out a wide range of views, that you especially welcome views different from your own, that you treat these views respectfully, and that you see them as intelligent and rationally defensible. Although like the Sophists you can use the skills of argument to support any side of any issue, we hope you won't. We hope that, like Socrates, you will use argument for truth seeking and that you will consequently find yourself, on at least some occasions, changing your position on an issue while writing a rough draft (a sure sign that the process of arguing has complicated your views).

At the deepest level, we believe that the skills of reason and inquiry developed through writing arguments can help you get a clearer sense of who you are. If our culture sets you adrift in pluralism, argument can help you take a stand, to say, "These things I believe." In this text we will not pretend to tell you what position to take on any given issue. But as a responsible being, you will often need to take a stand, to define yourself, to say, "Here are the reasons that choice A is better than choice B, not just for me but for you also." If this text helps you base your commitments and actions on reasonable grounds, then it will have been successful.

MyWritingLab™

Visit Ch. 1 Argument: An Introduction in *MyWritingLab* to complete the For Writing and Discussion and to test your understanding of the chapter objectives.

Argument as Inquiry
Reading and Exploring

What you will learn in this chapter:

2.1 To find issues to explore
2.2 To read sources rhetorically by analyzing a text's genre, purpose, and degree of advocacy
2.3 To read to believe an argument's claims
2.4 To read to doubt an argument's claims
2.5 To delay closure by thinking dialectically

In the previous chapter we explained that argument focuses on both truth seeking and persuasion. In this chapter, we focus on inquiry (truth seeking) as the entry point into argumentative conversations. Unfortunately, in today's wired environment these conversations often preclude truth seeking. They are carried on within isolated echo chambers of like-minded participants who believe they already possess the truth. We can observe these echo chambers on politically homogenous Web sites, on cable news channels, or on talk-show debates where participants shout at each other with no interest in listening to alternative views. This reductive trend has elicited the concern of cultural critics, journalists, rhetoricians, scholars, and citizens. Journalist Matt Miller recently posed the questions, "Is it possible in America today to convince anyone of anything he doesn't already believe? . . . [A]re there enough places where this mingling of minds occurs to sustain a democracy?"*

We believe this "mingling of minds" is essential if we are to understand argument as a search for the best solutions to problems. To do so means to position ourselves as inquirers as well as persuaders. In this chapter we approach argument as an exploratory process in which participants try to suspend judgment and delay closure by engaging thoughtfully with alternative points of view, truly listening to other perspectives, examining their own values and assumptions, and perhaps even changing their views. We value the insight of rhetorician Wayne Booth, who proposes that when we enter an

---

*Matt Miller, "Is Persuasion Dead?" *New York Times* 4 June 2005, A29.

argumentative conversation, we should not ask first "How can I change your mind?" but rather "When should I change my mind?"*

In this chapter, we present some practical strategies for reading and exploring arguments in an open-minded and intellectually responsible way. To illustrate argument as inquiry, we will show you how one student, Trudie Makens, explored the problem of whether fast-food workers and other low-wage laborers should be paid a "living wage" of $15 per hour.

Finding Issues to Explore

2.1 To find issues to explore

Your engagement with a controversial issue might be sparked by personal experience, by conversations with others, or by something you listen to, see, or read. Sometimes you will be confused about the issue, unable to take a stand. At other times, you will have a visceral gut reaction that causes you to take an immediate position, even though you haven't thought through the issue in depth. At the start of the arguing process, the confused or puzzled position is often the stronger one because it promotes inquiry as truth seeking. If you start with a firm stand, you might be less disposed to uncover your issue's complexity and let your position evolve. In this section we examine some strategies you can use to find issues worth exploring.

Do Some Initial Brainstorming

As a first step, make an inventory of issues that interest you. Many of the ideas you develop may become subject matter for arguments that you will write later in this course. The chart on page 19 will help you generate a productive list.

Once you've made a list, add to it as new ideas strike you and return to it each time you are given a new argumentative assignment.

Be Open to the Issues All around You

We are surrounded by argumentative issues. You'll start noticing them everywhere once you get attuned to them. You will be invited into argumentative conversations by posters, bumper stickers, blog sites, newspaper editorial pages, magazine articles, the sports section, movie reviews, song lyrics, and so forth. When you read or listen, watch for "hot spots"—passages or moments that evoke strong agreement, disagreement, or confusion. As an illustration of how arguments are all around us, try the following exercise on the issue of a living wage for low wage workers.

---

*Wayne Booth raised these questions in a featured session with Peter Elbow titled "Blind Skepticism vs. the Rhetoric of Assent: Implications for Rhetoric, Argument, and Teaching," presented at the CCCC annual convention, Chicago, Illinois, March 2002.

Brainstorming Issues to Explore

What You Can Do	How It Works
Make an inventory of the communities to which you belong. Consider classroom communities; clubs and organizations; residence hall, apartment, neighborhood, or family communities; church/synagogue or work communities; communities related to your hobbies or avocations; your city, state, region, nation, and world communities.	Because arguments arise out of disagreements within communities, you can often think of issues for argument by beginning with a list of the communities to which you belong.
Identify controversies within those communities. Think both big and small: ■ Big issue in world community: What is the best way to prevent destruction of rain forests? ■ Small issue in residence hall community: Should quiet hours be enforced?	To stimulate thinking, use prompts such as these: ■ People in this community frequently disagree about _____ . ■ Within my work community, Person X believes _____ ; however, this view troubles me because _____ . ■ In a recent residence hall meeting, I didn't know where I stood on _____ . ■ The situation at _____ could be improved if _____ .
Narrow your list to a handful of problematic issues for which you don't have a position; share it with classmates. Identify a few issues that you would like to explore more deeply. When you share with classmates, add their issues to yours.	Sharing your list with classmates stimulates more thinking and encourages conversations. The more you explore your views with others, the more ideas you will develop. Good writing grows out of good talking.
Brainstorm a network of related issues. Any given issue is always embedded in a network of other issues. To see how open-ended and fluid an argumentative conversation can be, try connecting one of your issues to a network of other issues including subissues and side issues.	Brainstorm questions that compel you to look at an issue in a variety of ways. For example, if you explored the controversy over whether toys with phthalates should be banned (see Chapter 1), you might generate questions such as these about related issues: ■ How dangerous are phthalates? ■ Is the testing that has been done on rats adequate or accurate for determining the effects on humans? ■ Is the European "precautionary principle" a good principle for the United States to follow? ■ To what extent are controversies over phthalates similar to controversies over steroids, genetically modified foods, nitrites in cured meat, or mercury in dental fillings?

FIGURE 2.1 Full-page ad opposed to raising the minimum wage for fast-food workers

■ ■ ■   **FOR CLASS DISCUSSION**   **Responding to Visual Arguments about a Living Wage**

Suppose, in your initial search for a controversial issue, you encounter visual texts related to raising the minimum wage for fast-food workers: photos of protestors, newspaper ads, cartoons, graphics, and other forms of visual arguments (see protest photo on page 1 and Figures 2.1–2.3). Working individually or in small groups, generate exploratory responses to these questions:

1. What claim is each of these visual texts making?
2. What background information about the problems of minimum-wage workers do these visual texts assume?
3. What network of issues do these visual texts suggest?
4. What puzzling questions do these visual texts raise for you?

FIGURE 2.2   Political cartoon on minimum wage

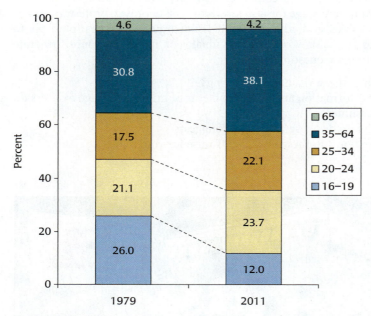

Percentage of Low-Wage Workers By Age Group, 1979 and 2011

FIGURE 2.3 Graph offering employment statistics relevant to minimum wage controversy

Adapted from Schmitt, John, and Janelle Jones, "Low-Wage Workers Are Older and Better Educated than Ever." Center for Economic and Policy Research. April 2012.

Explore Ideas by Freewriting

Freewriting is useful at any stage of the writing process. When you freewrite, you put fingers to keyboard (or pen to paper) and write rapidly *nonstop,* usually five to ten minutes at a stretch, without worrying about structure, grammar, or correctness. Your goal is to generate as many ideas as possible without stopping to edit your work. If you can't think of anything to say, write "relax" or "I'm stuck" over and over until new ideas emerge. Here is how Trudie Makens did a freewrite in response to the protest photo on page 1.

Trudie's Freewrite

Working in the food and service industry as a busser, I relate to the man in the picture holding the sign reading "Stand with Fast Food Workers." It's hard to live off of minimum wage, and if it weren't for my tips, I wouldn't be able to pay some of my bills. And that is with help from my parents since I am a college student. I can't imagine what it would be like for full-time workers in the fast-food industry where orders are taken via counter. I remember when I worked counter service jobs, as a barista and at a dumpling café, no one ever tipped. They didn't feel like they needed too since it was not formal wait service.

My work, and my coworkers' work, was not valued. What some people don't realize is that whether you are working at McDonalds or in an upscale restaurant, you are still working hard to provide good service. If anything, it is harder to work jobs like McDonalds where customers are dismissive and don't value the service they are receiving. Think, relax. Why do people not value the work of fast-food and counter service workers? Because it is considered unskilled labor? A lot of the people I have worked with didn't have the time or money to go to college because they were burdened with the financial strains of having children or caring for sick or elderly relatives. I remember my coworker Maria who was always stressed out because she couldn't pay her rent and had a child to support. A living wage would help people who haven't been lucky enough to inherit wealth to pull themselves out of poverty. And it wouldn't hurt corporations like McDonalds to live with a little less profit.

Explore Ideas by Idea Mapping

Another good technique for exploring ideas is *idea mapping*. When you make an idea map, draw a circle in the center of a page and write some trigger idea (a broad topic, a question, or working thesis statement) in the center of the circle. Then record your ideas on branches and subbranches extending from the center circle. As long as you pursue one train of thought, keep recording your ideas on that branch. But when that line of thinking gives out, start a new branch. Often your thoughts will jump back and forth between branches. That's a major advantage of "picturing" your thoughts; you can see them as part of an emerging design rather than as strings of unrelated ideas.

Idea maps usually generate more ideas, though less well-developed ones, than freewrites. Figure 2.4 shows an idea map that student Trudie Makens created on the issue of minimum wage after class discussion of the visual texts in Figures 2.1–2.3.

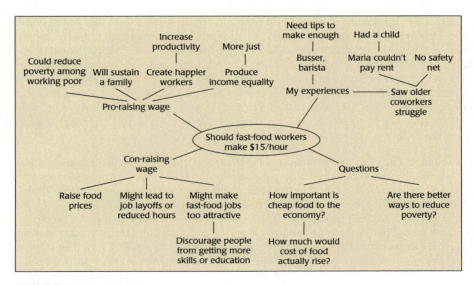

FIGURE 2.4 Trudie's idea map

Explore Ideas by Playing the Believing and Doubting Game

The believing and doubting game, a critical thinking strategy developed by rhetorician Peter Elbow that systematically stretches your thinking, is an excellent way to imagine views different from your own and to anticipate responses to those views.

- **As a believer, your role is to be wholly sympathetic to an idea.** You must listen carefully to the idea and suspend all disbelief. You must identify all the ways in which the idea may appeal to different audiences and all the reasons for believing the idea. The believing game can be difficult, even frightening, if you are asked to believe an idea that strikes you as false or threatening.
- **As a doubter, your role is to be judgmental and critical, finding fault with an idea.** The doubting game is the opposite of the believing game. You do your best to find counterexamples and inconsistencies that undermine the idea you are examining. Again, it can be threatening to doubt ideas that you instinctively want to believe.

When you play the believing and doubting game with an assertion, simply write two different chunks, one chunk arguing for the assertion (the believing game) and one chunk opposing it (the doubting game). Freewrite both chunks, letting your ideas flow without censoring. Or, alternatively, make an idea map with believing and doubting branches. Here is how student writer Trudie Makens played the believing and doubting game with the assertion "Fast-food workers should be paid $15 per hour."

Trudie's Believing and Doubting Game

Believing: I doubt anyone strives to become a full-time fast-food worker, but many people become stuck in those jobs and can't advance because they don't have a college education or because there are no better jobs available. Sometimes the workers are college students, so an increase in minimum pay would help them not accrue so much debt and perhaps have more time to study because they wouldn't have to work so many hours. But the real benefit would come to the uneducated, unskilled fast-food worker whose financial situation has led him or her to the fast-food job. The current minimum wage is barely livable. If the fast-food worker were to receive $15 per hour, there is far more of a chance for them to support themselves and their family comfortably without the stress of poverty. Even if the full-time fast-food worker does not go on to get more skills or go to college, it becomes more likely their children will be able to go to college if the fast-food worker is receiving a higher wage. Thus, the cycle of poverty as it is inherited generationally is, at least mildly, disrupted.

Doubting: If a $15 per hour minimum wage were to be implemented, the fast-food corporations would have to find ways to compensate for the profit loss. The most obvious way would be to raise food prices. If prices were to rise, fast food would no longer be affordable. This could have damaging and reversing effects on the working class who may rely on cheap fast food. Another problem is that the $15 per hour minimum wage may encourage workers to stay put in their jobs and not strive for a career. The student worker may no longer see the benefit of going into debt to get a degree and be satisfied with their current fast-food job. The effect of more desirable fast-food jobs may put pressure on other companies to raise the hourly wage of their entry-level positions. The rise in wage may, again, have the ripple effect of higher-priced products, thus reducing sales and forcing these companies to lay off some workers. No matter what scenario is dreamt up, it would seem that raising the minimum wage to $15 per hour, even if just for fast-food workers, might have damaging effects on the economy that would diminish any benefits or advantages that theoretically come from receiving a higher wage.

Although Trudie sees the injustice of paying low wages to fast-food workers, she also sees that paying such workers $15 per hour might raise the cost of food, reduce the number of jobs available, or have other negative consequences. Playing the believing and doubting game has helped her articulate her dilemma and see the issue in more complex terms.

■ ■ ■ **FOR WRITING AND DISCUSSION**   **Playing the Believing and Doubting Game**   MyWritingLab™

Individual task: Choose one or more of the following controversial claims and play the believing and doubting game with it, through either freewriting or idea mapping.

1. A student should report a fellow student who is cheating on an exam or plagiarizing an essay.
2. Federal law should forbid the purchase of assault weapons or high-capacity magazines.
3. Athletes should be allowed to take steroids and human growth hormone under a doctor's supervision.
4. Illegal immigrants already living in the United States should be granted amnesty and placed on a fast track to U.S. citizenship.

Group task: Working in pairs, in small groups, or as a whole class, share your results with classmates.   ■ ■ ■

Reading Texts Rhetorically

2.2 To read sources rhetorically by analyzing a text's genre, purpose, and degree of advocacy

Once you become engaged with an issue, you will typically research it to understand the various voices in the conversation, the points of disagreement, the uses of evidence and counter-evidence, and the underlying assumptions and beliefs of different stakeholders. When you find these sources yourself, you will need the skills of library, database, and Web research taught in Part Five of this text. Often, however, the sources you read may be supplied for you in an anthology, textbook, course pack, or course Web site. In this section, we focus on the skills of reading sources rhetorically by analyzing their genre, their author's purpose and intended audience, and the text's degree of advocacy. In later chapters, we discuss rhetorical reading in more depth: Chapter 5 teaches the concept of "angle of vision" based on the way an argumentative text selects and frames evidence; Chapter 8 teaches you how to write a rhetorical analysis of a text; and finally Chapters 15–17 teach the skills of research writing from a rhetorical perspective.

Genres of Argument

To situate an argument rhetorically, you should know something about its genre. A *genre* is a recurring type or pattern of argument such as a letter to the editor, a political cartoon, or the home page of an advocacy Web site. Genres are often categorized by recurring features, formats, and styles. The genre of any given argument helps determine its length, tone, sentence complexity, level of informality or formality, use of visuals, kinds of evidence, and the presence or absence of documentation.

When you read arguments reprinted in a textbook such as this one, you lose clues about the argument's original genre. (You should therefore note the information about genre provided in our introductions to readings.) Likewise, you can lose clues about genre when you download articles from the Internet or from licensed databases such as LexisNexis or ProQuest. (See Chapter 15 for explanations of these research tools.) When you do your own research, you therefore need to be aware of the original genre of the text you are reading—to know, for example, whether the piece was originally a newspaper editorial, a blog, a peer-reviewed scholarly article, or something else.

In the following chart we identify most of the genres of argument through which readers and writers carry on the conversations of a democracy.

Genres of Argument

Genre	Explanation and Examples	Stylistic Features
Personal correspondence	■ Letters or e-mail messages ■ Often sent to specific decision makers (complaint letter, request for an action)	■ Style can range from a formal business letter to an informal note
Letters to the editor	■ Published in newspapers and some magazines ■ Provide a forum for citizens to voice views on public issues	■ Very short (fewer than three hundred words) and time sensitive ■ Can be summaries of longer arguments, but often focus in "sound bite" style on one point
Newspaper editorials and op-ed pieces	■ Published on the editorial or op-ed ("opposite-editorial") pages ■ Editorials promote views of the newspaper owners/editors ■ Op-ed pieces, usually written by professional columnists or guest writers, range in bias from ultraconservative to socialist (see pages 343–345 in Chapter 15) ■ Often written in response to political events or social problems in the news	■ Usually short (500–1,000 words) ■ Vary from explicit thesis-driven arguments to implicit arguments with stylistic flair ■ Have a journalistic style (short paragraphs) without detailed evidence ■ Sources usually not documented

Genre	Explanation and Examples	Stylistic Features
Blogs and postings to chat rooms and electronic bulletin boards	■ Web-published commentaries, usually on specific topics and often intended to influence public opinion ■ Blogs (Web logs) are gaining influence as alternative commentaries to the established media	■ Often blend styles of journalism, personal narrative, and formal argument ■ Often difficult to determine identity and credentials of blogger
Articles in public affairs or niche magazines	■ Reflect a wide range of perspectives ■ Usually written by staff writers or freelancers ■ Appear in public affairs magazines such as *National Review* or *The Progressive* or in niche magazines for special-interest groups such as *Rolling Stone* (popular culture), *Minority Business Entrepreneur* (business), or *The Advocate* (gay and lesbian issues) ■ Often reflect the political point of view of the magazine	■ Often provide hyperlinks to related sites on the Web ■ Frequently include narrative elements rather than explicit thesis-and-reasons organization ■ Often provide well-researched coverage of various perspectives on a public issue
Articles in scholarly journals	■ Peer-reviewed articles published by nonprofit academic journals subsidized by universities or scholarly societies ■ Characterized by scrupulous attention to completeness and accuracy in treatment of data	■ Usually employ a formal academic style ■ Include academic documentation and bibliographies ■ May reflect the biases, methods, and strategies associated with a specific school of thought or theory within a discipline
Legal briefs and court decisions	■ Written by attorneys or judges ■ "Friend-of-the-court" briefs are often published by stakeholders to influence appeals courts ■ Court decisions explain the reasoning of justices on civic cases (and often include minority opinions)	■ Usually written in legalese, but use a logical reasons-and-evidence structure ■ Friend-of-the-court briefs are sometimes aimed at popular audiences

(Continued)

Genre	Explanation and Examples	Stylistic Features
Organizational white papers	■ In-house documents or PowerPoint presentations aimed at influencing organizational policy or decisions or giving informed advice to clients ■ Sometimes written for external audiences to influence public opinion favorable to the organization ■ External white papers are often posted on Web sites or sent to legislators	■ Usually desktop or Web published ■ Often include graphics and other visuals ■ Vary in style from the dully bureaucratic (satirized in *Dilbert* cartoons) to the cogent and persuasive
Public affairs advocacy advertisements	■ Published as posters, fliers, Web pages, or paid advertisements ■ Condensed verbal/visual arguments aimed at influencing public opinion ■ Often have explicit bias and ignore alternative views	■ Use succinct "sound bite" style ■ Employ document design, bulleted lists, and visual elements (graphics, photographs, or drawings) for rhetorical effect
Advocacy Web sites	■ Usually identified by the extension ".org" in the Web site address ■ Often created by well-financed advocacy groups such as the NRA (National Rifle Association) or PETA (People for the Ethical Treatment of Animals) ■ Reflect the bias of the site owner ■ For further discussion of reading and evaluating Web sites, see Chapter 15, page 355	■ Often contain many layers with hyperlinks to other sites ■ Use visuals and verbal text to create an immediate visceral response favorable to the site owner's views ■ Ethically responsible sites announce their bias and purpose in an "About Us" or "Mission Statement" link on the home page
Visual arguments	■ Political cartoons, usually drawn by syndicated cartoonists ■ Other visual arguments (photographs, drawings, graphics, ads), usually accompanied by verbal text	■ Make strong emotional appeals, often reducing complex issues to one powerful perspective (see Chapter 9)

Genre	Explanation and Examples	Stylistic Features
Speeches and PowerPoint presentations	▪ Political speeches, keynote speeches at professional meetings, informal speeches at hearings, interviews, business presentations ▪ Often made available via transcription in newspapers or on Web sites ▪ In business or government settings, often accompanied by PowerPoint slides	▪ Usually organized clearly with highlighted claim, supporting reasons, and transitions ▪ Accompanying PowerPoint slides designed to highlight structure, display evidence in graphics, mark key points, and sometimes provide humor
Documentary films	▪ Formerly nonfiction reporting, documentary films now range widely from efforts to document reality objectively to efforts to persuade viewers to adopt the filmmaker's perspective or take action ▪ Usually cost less to produce than commercial films and lack special effects ▪ Cover topics such as art, science, and economic, political, environmental, and military crises	▪ Often use extended visual arguments, combined with interviews and voice-overs, to influence as well as inform viewers ▪ The filmmaker's angle of vision may dominate, or his or her perspective and values may be more subtle

Authorial Purpose and Audience

A democratic society depends on the lively exchange of ideas—people with stakes in issues and different perspectives advocating for their positions. In reconstructing the rhetorical context of an argument, consider how any given writer is spurred to write by a motivating occasion and by the desire to change the views of a particular audience. Individuals often write arguments addressing personal or workplace issues. For public issues, the following list identifies the wide range of writers, as well as cartoonists, filmmakers, and others, who are apt to produce arguments.

- **Lobbyists and advocacy groups.** Lobbyists and advocacy groups commit themselves to a cause, often with passion, and produce avidly partisan arguments aimed at persuading voters, legislators, government agencies, and other decision makers. They often maintain advocacy Web sites, buy advertising space in newspapers and magazines, and lobby legislators face-to-face.

- **Legislators, political candidates, and government officials.** Whenever new laws, regulations, or government policies are proposed, staffers do research and write white papers recommending positions on an issue. Often these are available on the Web.

- **Business professionals, labor union leaders, and bankers.** Business spokespeople often try to influence public opinion in ways that support corporate or business interests, whereas labor union officials support wage structures favorable to union members. Typically businesspeople produce "corporate image" advertisements, send white papers to legislators, or write op-ed pieces that frame issues from a business perspective, whereas labor unions produce arguments favorable to workers.

- **Lawyers and judges.** Many controversial issues are entangled in legal matters. Lawyers write briefs supporting their clients' cases. Sometimes lawyers or legal experts not directly connected to a case, particularly law professors, file "friend-of-the-court" briefs aimed at influencing the decision of judges. Finally, judges write court opinions explaining their decisions on a case.

- **Media commentators.** Many controversial issues are in the news and attract the attention of media commentators (journalists, editorial writers, syndicated columnists, bloggers, political cartoonists) who write articles and blogs or op-ed pieces on the issue or produce editorial cartoons, filtering their arguments through the perspective of their own political views.

- **Professional freelance or staff writers.** Some of the most thoughtful analyses of public issues are composed by freelance or staff writers for public forum magazines such as *Atlantic Monthly*, *The Nation*, *Ms.*, *The National Review*, *The New Yorker*, or for online news sites or blogs such as *The Daily Kos* or *Little Green Footballs*. These can range from in-depth background pieces to arguments with a highly persuasive aim.

- **Think tanks.** Because today many political, economic, and social issues are very complex, policy makers and commentators often rely on research institutions or think tanks to supply statistical studies and in-depth investigation of problems. These think tanks range across the political spectrum, from conservative (the Hoover Institute, the Heritage Foundation) or libertarian (the Cato Institute) to the centrist or liberal (the Brookings Institution, the Pew Foundation, the Economic Policy Institute). They usually maintain many-layered Web sites that include background on research writers, recent publications, and archives of past publications, including policy statements and white papers.

- **Scholars and academics.** College professors play a public role through their scholarly research, contributing data, studies, and analyses to public debates. Scholarly research differs substantially from advocacy argument in its systematic attempt to arrive at the best answers to questions based on the full examination of relevant data. Scholarly research is usually published in refereed academic journals rather than in popular magazines.

- **Independent and commercial filmmakers.** Testifying to the growing popularity of film and its power to involve people in issues, documentary filmmakers often reflect on issues of the day, and commercial filmmakers often embed arguments within their dramatic storytelling. The global film industry is adding international perspectives as well.

■ **Citizens and students.** Engaged citizens influence social policy through letters, contributions to advocacy Web sites, guest editorials for newspapers, blogs, and speeches in public forums. Students also write for university communities, present their work at undergraduate research conferences, and influence public opinion by writing to political leaders and decision makers.

Determining Degree of Advocacy

As you read any given source connected to your issue, try to determine whether it is a background piece that provides the context for an issue, an overview article that tries to summarize the various positions in the controversy, or an argument that supports a position. If it is an argument, also try to determine its degree of advocacy along the continuum from "truth seeking" to "persuasion" shown in Figure 1.5 (page 11). It is important to know, for example, whether a blog that you are reading appears on Daily Kos (a liberal blog site) or on Little Green Footballs (a conservative blog site). Particularly pay attention to how an argument selects and frames evidence—a rhetorical reading skill that we cover in depth in Chapter 5, pages 95–101.

The background we have just provided about the genres of argument, a writer's purpose and audience, and a text's degree of advocacy will help you situate arguments in their rhetorical context. When you encounter any argumentative text, whether reprinted in a textbook or retrieved through your own library and Web research, use the following guide questions to help you read the text rhetorically. This same skill is covered in more depth in Chapter 8, pages 154–159.

Questions for Reading Texts Rhetorically

1. What genre of argument is this? How do the conventions of that genre help determine the depth, complexity, and even appearance of the argument?
2. Who is the author? What are the author's credentials and what is his or her investment in the issue?
3. What audience is he or she writing for?
4. What motivating occasion prompted the writing? The motivating occasion could be a current event, a crisis, pending legislation, a recently published alternative view, or another ongoing problem.
5. What is the author's purpose? The purpose could range from strong advocacy to inquiring truth seeker (analogous to the continuum from persuasion to truth seeking discussed in Chapter 1, page 11).
6. What information about the publication or source (magazine, newspaper, advocacy Web site) helps explain the writer's perspective or the structure and style of the argument?

7. What is the writer's angle of vision? By angle of vision, we mean the filter, lens, or selective seeing through which the writer is approaching the issue. What is left out from this argument? What does this author not see? (Chapter 5, pages 95–101, discusses how angle of vision operates in the selection and framing of evidence.)

This rhetorical knowledge becomes important in helping you select a diversity of voices and genres of argument when you are exploring an issue. Note how Trudie Makens makes use of her awareness of rhetorical context in her exploratory paper on pages 44–50.

■ ■ ■ **FOR CLASS DISCUSSION**   **Placing Readings in Their Rhetorical Context**

Find two recent arguments on the subject of minimum wage* or on another subject specified by your instructor. Your arguments should (1) represent different genres and (2) represent different kinds of arguers (syndicated newspaper columnists, bloggers, freelance magazine writers, scholars, and so forth). You can find your arguments in any of these places:

- In magazines: news commentary/public affairs magazines or niche magazines
- On the Web: on Web sites for think tanks, advocacy organizations, or blogs
- In newspapers: local, regional, or national

For each argument, answer the "Questions for Reading Texts Rhetorically" on page 31. Then share your findings with classmates.

■ ■ ■

Reading to Believe an Argument's Claims

2.3 To read to believe an argument's claims

A powerful strategy for reading an argument rhetorically is to follow the spirit of the believing and doubting game, beginning with "believing." When you read to believe an argument, you practice what psychologist Carl Rogers calls *empathic listening*. Empathic listening requires that you see the world through the author's eyes, temporarily adopt the author's beliefs and values, and suspend your scepticism and biases in order to hear what the author is saying.

To illustrate what we mean by reading to believe, we will continue with our example of raising the minimum wage, a highly controversial issue. The following article, "The Pay Is Too Damn Low," is by James Surowiecki, an American journalist who writes the "Financial Page" column in *The New Yorker*, a magazine with a liberal perspective. This article appeared in *The New Yorker* in August 2013. Please read this article carefully in preparation for the exercises and examples that follow.

---

*For help on how to find articles through Web or licensed database searches, see Chapter 15.

The Pay Is Too Damn Low

JAMES SUROWIECKI

A few weeks ago, Washington, D.C., passed a living-wage bill designed to make Walmart pay its workers a minimum of $12.50 an hour. Then President Obama called on Congress to raise the federal minimum wage (which is currently $7.25 an hour). McDonald's was widely derided for releasing a budget to help its employees plan financially, since that only underscored how brutally hard it is to live on a McDonald's wage. And last week fast-food workers across the country staged walkouts, calling for an increase in their pay to fifteen dollars an hour. Low-wage earners have long been the hardest workers to organize and the easiest to ignore. Now they're front-page news.

The workers' grievances are simple: low wages, few (if any) benefits, and little full-time work. In inflation-adjusted terms, the minimum wage, though higher than it was a decade ago, is still well below its 1968 peak (when it was worth about $10.70 an hour in today's dollars), and it's still poverty-level pay. To make matters worse, most fast-food and retail work is part time, and the weak job market has eroded what little bargaining power low-wage workers had: their earnings actually fell between 2009 and last year, according to the National Employment Law Project.

Still, the reason this has become a big political issue is not that the jobs have changed; it's that the people doing the jobs have. Historically, low-wage work tended to be done either by the young or by women looking for part-time jobs to supplement family income. As the historian Bethany Moreton has shown, Walmart in its early days sought explicitly to hire underemployed married women. Fast-food workforces, meanwhile, were dominated by teenagers. Now, though, plenty of family breadwinners are stuck in these jobs. That's because, over the past three decades, the U.S. economy has done a poor job of creating good middle-class jobs; five of the six fastest-growing job categories today pay less than the median wage. That's why, as a recent study by the economists John Schmitt and Janelle Jones has shown, low-wage workers are older and better educated than ever. More important, more of them are relying on their paychecks not for pin money or to pay for Friday-night dates but, rather, to support families. Forty years ago, there was no expectation that fast-food or discount-retail jobs would provide a living wage, because these were not jobs that, in the main, adult heads of household did. Today, low-wage workers provide 46 percent of their family's income. It is that change which is driving the demand for higher pay.

The situation is the result of a tectonic shift in the American economy. In 1960, the country's biggest employer, General Motors, was also its most profitable company and one of its best-paying. It had high profit margins and real pricing power, even as it was paying its workers union wages. And it was not alone: firms such as Ford, Standard Oil, and Bethlehem Steel employed huge numbers of well-paid workers while earning big profits. Today, the country's biggest employers are retailers and fast-food chains, almost all of which have built their businesses on low pay—they've striven to keep wages down and unions out—and low prices.

5   This complicates things, in part because of the nature of these businesses. They make plenty of money, but most have slim profit margins: Walmart and Target earn between three and four cents on the dollar; a typical McDonald's franchise restaurant earns around six cents on the dollar before taxes, according to an analysis from Janney Capital Markets. In fact, the combined profits of all the major retailers, restaurant chains, and supermarkets in the Fortune 500 are smaller than the profits of

Apple alone. Yet Apple employs just 76,000 people, while the retailers, supermarkets, and restaurant chains employ 5.6 million. The grim truth of those numbers is that low wages are a big part of why these companies are able to stay profitable while offering low prices. Congress is currently considering a bill increasing the minimum wage to $10.10 over the next three years. That's an increase that the companies can easily tolerate, and it would make a significant difference in the lives of low-wage workers. But that's still a long way from turning these jobs into the kind of employment that can support a middle-class family. If you want to accomplish that, you have to change the entire way these companies do business. Above all, you have to get consumers to accept significantly higher, and steadily rising, prices. After decades in which we've grown used to cheap stuff, that won't be easy.

Realistically, then, a higher minimum wage can be only part of the solution. We also need to expand the earned-income tax credit and strengthen the social-insurance system, including child care and health care (the advent of Obamacare will help in this regard). Fast-food jobs in Germany and the Netherlands aren't much better-paid than in the United States, but a stronger safety net makes workers much better off. We also need many more of the "middle-class jobs" we're always hearing about. A recent McKinsey report suggested that the government should invest almost a trillion dollars over the next five years in repairing and upgrading the national infrastructure, which seems like a good place to start. And we really need the economy as a whole to grow faster, because that would both increase the supply of good jobs and improve the bargaining power of low-wage workers. As Jared Bernstein, an economist at the Center for Budget and Policy Priorities told me, "The best friend that low-wage workers have is a strong economy and a tight job market." It isn't enough to make bad jobs better. We need to create better jobs.

Summary Writing as a Way of Reading to Believe

One way to show that you have listened well to an article is to summarize its argument in your own words. A summary (also called an *abstract,* a *précis,* or a *synopsis*) presents only a text's major points and eliminates supporting details. Writers often incorporate summaries of other writers' views into their own arguments, either to support their own views or to represent alternative views that they intend to oppose. (When opposing someone else's argument, writers often follow the template "Although X contends that [summary of X's argument], I argue that _____.") Summaries can be any length, depending on the writer's purpose, but usually they range from several sentences to one or two paragraphs. To maintain your own credibility, your summary should be as neutral and fair to that piece as possible.

To help you write an effective summary, we recommend the following steps:

Step 1: *Read the argument for general meaning.* Don't judge it. Put your objections aside; just follow the writer's meaning, trying to see the issue from the writer's perspective. Try to adopt the writer's values and belief system. Walk in the writer's shoes.

Step 2: *Reread the article slowly, writing brief* does *and* says *statements for each paragraph (or group of closely connected paragraphs).* A *does* statement identifies a paragraph's function, such as "summarizes an opposing view," "introduces a supporting reason," "gives an example," or "uses statistics to support the previous point."

A *says* statement summarizes a paragraph's content. Your challenge in writing *says* statements is to identify the main idea in each paragraph and translate that idea into your own words, most likely condensing it at the same time. This process may be easier with an academic article that uses long, developed paragraphs headed by clear topic sentences than with more informal, journalistic articles that use shorter, less developed paragraphs. What follows are *does* and *says* statements for the first three paragraphs of Surowiecki's article:

Does/Says Analysis of Surowiecki's Article

Paragraph 1: *Does:* Gives examples of recent news stories about protests of low-wage workers. *Says:* Hard-to-organize, low-wage earners are now in the news demanding an increase in the minimum wage.

Paragraph 2: *Does:* Provides details about the workers' grievances. *Says*: A weakening job market combined with low wages, lack of benefits, and mainly part-time hours keeps low-wage workers at poverty levels.

Paragraph 3: *Does:* Explains the changing demographics of those who hold low-wage jobs. *Says*: In the past, minimum-wage jobs were held primarily by teenagers or by women desiring part-time work to supplement family incomes, but today many primary breadwinners depend on minimum-wage jobs to support a family.

■ ■ ■ **FOR CLASS DISCUSSION** **Writing *Does/Says* Statements**

Working individually or in small groups, write *does* and *says* statements for the remaining paragraphs of Surowiecki's article.

Step 3: *Examine your* does *and* says *statements to determine the major sections of the argument.* Create a list of the major points (and subpoints) that must appear in a summary in order to represent that argument accurately. If you are visually oriented, you may prefer to make a diagram, flowchart, or scratch outline of the sections of Surowiecki's argument.

Step 4: *Turn your list, outline, flowchart, or diagram into a prose summary.* Typically, writers do this in one of two ways. Some start by joining all their *says* statements into a lengthy paragraph-by-paragraph summary and then prune it and streamline it. They combine ideas into sentences and then revise those sentences to make them clearer and more tightly structured. Others start with a one-sentence summary of the argument's thesis and major supporting reasons and then flesh it out with more supporting ideas. Your goal is to be as neutral and objective as possible by keeping your own response to the writer's ideas out of your summary. To be fair to the writer, you also need to cover all the writer's main points and give them the same emphasis as in the original article.

Step 5: *Revise your summary until it is the desired length and is sufficiently clear, concise, and complete.* Your goal is to spend your words wisely, making every word count. In a summary of several hundred words, you will often need transitions to indicate structure and create a coherent flow of ideas: "Surowiecki's second point is that...," or "Surowiecki concludes by...." However, don't waste words with meaningless transitions such as "Surowiecki goes on to say...." When you incorporate a summary into your own essay, you must distinguish that author's views from your own by using *attributive tags* (expressions such as "Surowiecki asserts" or "according to Surowiecki"). You must also put any directly borrowed wording in quotation marks. Finally, you must cite the original author using appropriate conventions for documenting sources.

What follows are two summaries of Surowiecki's article—a one-paragraph version and a one-sentence version—by student writer Trudie Makens. Trudie's one-paragraph version illustrates the MLA documentation system, in which page numbers for direct quotations are placed in parentheses after the quotation and complete bibliographic information is placed in a Works Cited list at the end of the paper. See Chapter 17 for a complete explanation of the MLA and APA documentation systems.

Trudie's One-Paragraph Summary of Surowiecki's Argument

In his *New Yorker* article "The Pay Is Too Damn Low," James Surowiecki analyzes the grievances of workers at fast-food franchises, Walmart, or Target. In the past, it didn't matter that these jobs were low-pay, part-time, and without benefits because they were held mainly by teenagers or married women seeking to supplement a husband's wages. But today, says Surowiecki, a growing number of primary breadwinners rely on these poverty-level wages to support families. The problem stems from a "tectonic shift in the American economy" (26). While in 1960, "firms such as Ford, Standard Oil, and Bethlehem Steel employed huge numbers of well-paid workers while earning big profits" (26), nowadays America's biggest employers are fast-food and retail companies with low profit margins. These companies depend on low-wage workers to keep prices cheap for the American consumer. Paying living wages to workers would completely change the business model, resulting in steadily rising prices. According to Surowiecki raising the minimum wage is only one tool for fighting poverty. America also needs to create a social insurance system like that of Germany or the Netherlands. Surowiecki calls for an increase in earned income tax credit, universal health insurance, affordable child care, and investment of almost a trillion dollars in infrastructure to create good middle-class jobs.

Work Cited

Surowiecki, James. "The Pay Is Too Damn Low." *New Yorker* 12 Aug. 2013: 35. Rpt. in *Writing Arguments: A Rhetoric with Readings.* John D. Ramage, John C. Bean, and June Johnson. 10th ed. New York: Pearson Education, 2016. 32–34. Print.

Trudie's One-Sentence Summary of Surowiecki's Argument

In his *New Yorker* article, "The Pay Is Too Damn Low," James Surowiecki argues that raising the minimum wage is only a partial solution to the problem of poverty and needs to be supplemented with a European-style social security network including an increase in earned income tax credit, universal health insurance, affordable child care, and investment of almost a trillion dollars in infrastructure to create good middle-class jobs.

Practicing Believing: Willing Your Own Belief in the Writer's Views

Although writing an accurate summary of an argument shows that you have listened to it effectively and understood it, summary writing by itself doesn't mean that you have actively tried to enter the writer's worldview. Before we turn in the next section to doubting an argument, we want to stress the importance of believing it. Rhetorician Peter Elbow reminds us that before we critique a text, we should try to "dwell with" and "dwell in" the writer's ideas—play the believing game—in order to "earn" our right to criticize.* He asserts, and we agree, that this use of the believing game to engage with strange, threatening, or unfamiliar views can lead to a deeper understanding and may provide a new vantage point on our own knowledge, assumptions, and values. To believe a writer and dwell with his or her ideas, find places in the text that resonate positively for you, look for values and beliefs you hold in common (however few), and search for personal experiences and values that affirm his or her argument.

Reading to Doubt

2.4 To read to doubt an argument's claims

After willing yourself to believe an argument, will yourself to doubt it. Turn your mental energies toward raising objections, asking questions, expressing skepticism, and withholding your assent. When you read as a doubter, you question the writer's logic, the writer's evidence and assumptions, and the writer's strategies for developing the argument. You also think about what is *not* in the argument by noting what the author has glossed over, left unexplained, or left out entirely. You add a new layer of marginal notes, articulating what is bothering you, demanding proof, doubting evidence, challenging the author's assumptions and values, and so forth. Writing your own notes helps you read a text actively, bringing your own voice into conversation with the author.

■ ■ ■ **FOR CLASS DISCUSSION** **Raising Doubts about Surowiecki's Argument**

Return now to Surowiecki's article and read it skeptically. Raise questions, offer objections, and express doubts. Then, working as a class or in small groups, list all the doubts you have about Surowiecki's argument.

■ ■ ■

Now that you have doubted Surowiecki's article, compare your questions and doubts to some raised by student writer Trudie Makens.

Trudie's Doubts about Surowiecki's Article

■ In his second paragraph, Surowiecki outlines three workers' grievances: "low wages, few (if any) benefits, and little full-time work." But increasing the minimum wage addresses only one of the grievances. A higher minimum wage might make it less likely for a worker to receive benefits or obtain full-time rather than part-time work. Moreover, with a higher wage, large companies may try to maintain profits by cutting jobs.

---

*Peter Elbow, "Bringing the Rhetoric of Assent and the Believing Game Together—Into the Classroom," *College English,* 67.4 (March 2005), 389.

- Surowiecki asserts that large retailers and fast-food companies would absorb the cost of a higher minimum wage by raising prices on consumer goods. But if low-wage workers are also consumers, won't higher prices on previously cheap products defeat the benefits of a higher wage?
- Though he ends his article by calling for a multifaceted solution to poverty, he does so without offering a way to accomplish this goal. Where would the money come from in order to expand the earned income tax credit, strengthen the United States' current social insurance system, or invest in infrastructure? Further, how would the United States effectively implement and sustain these nationwide social programs without upsetting the already delicate economy?
- In his article Surowiecki mentions several studies, but there is no way to tell if these are widely respected studies or controversial ones. Would other studies, for example, conclude that low-wage workers today are responsible for 46 percent of their family's income?

These are only some of the objections that might be raised against Surowiecki's argument. The point here is that doubting as well as believing is a key part of the exploratory process and purpose. *Believing* takes you into the views of others so that you can expand your views and perhaps see them differently and modify or even change them. *Doubting* helps protect you from becoming overpowered by others' arguments and teaches you to stand back, consider, and weigh points carefully. It also leads you to new questions and points you might want to explore further.

Thinking Dialectically

2.5 To delay closure by thinking dialectically

This chapter's final strategy—thinking dialectically to bring texts into conversation with each other—encompasses all the previous strategies and can have a powerful effect on your growth as a thinker and arguer. The term *dialectic* is associated with the German philosopher Georg Wilhelm Friedrich Hegel, who postulated that each thesis prompts an opposing thesis (which he calls an "antithesis") and that the conflict between these views can lead thinkers to a new claim (a "synthesis") that incorporates aspects of both views. Dialectic thinking is the philosophical underpinning of the believing and doubting game, pushing us toward new and better ideas. As Peter Elbow puts it, "Because it's so hard to let go of an idea we are holding (or more to the point, an idea that's holding us), our best hope for leverage in learning to doubt such ideas is *to take on different ideas*."*

This is why expert thinkers actively seek out alternative views—not to shout them down but to listen to them. If you were an arbitrator, you wouldn't settle a dispute between A and B on the basis of A's testimony only. You would also insist on hearing B's side of the story (and perhaps also C's and D's if they are stakeholders in the dispute). Dialectic thinking means playing ideas against each other, creating a tension that forces you to keep expanding your perspective. It helps you achieve the "mingling of minds" that we discussed in the introduction to this chapter.

---

*Peter Elbow, "Bringing the Rhetoric of Assent and the Believing Game Together—Into the Classroom," *College English* 67.4 (March 2005), 390.

As you listen to differing views, try to identify sources of disagreement among arguers, which often fall into two categories: (1) disagreement about the facts of the case and (2) disagreement about underlying values, beliefs, or assumptions. We saw these disagreements in Chapter 1 in the conversation about phthalates in children's toys. At the level of facts, disputants disagreed about the amount of phthalates a baby might ingest when chewing a rubber toy or about the quantity of ingested phthalates needed to be harmful. At the level of values, disputants disagreed on the amount of risk that must be present in a free market economy before a government agency should ban a substance. As you try to determine your own position on an issue, consider what research you might have to do to resolve questions of fact; also try to articulate your own underlying values, beliefs, and assumptions.

As you consider multiple points of view on an issue, try using the following questions to promote dialectic thinking:

Questions to Promote Dialectic Thinking

1. What would writer A say to writer B?
2. After I read writer A, I thought _____; however, after I read writer B, my thinking on this issue had changed in these ways: _____.
3. To what extent do writer A and writer B disagree about facts and interpretations of facts?
4. To what extent do writer A and writer B disagree about underlying beliefs, assumptions, and values?
5. Can I find any areas of agreement, including shared values and beliefs, between writer A and writer B?
6. What new, significant questions do these texts raise for me?
7. After I have wrestled with the ideas in these two texts, what are my current views on this issue?

Responding to questions like these—either through class discussion or through exploratory writing—can help you work your way into a public controversy. Earlier in this chapter you read James Surowiecki's article expressing liberal support for raising the minimum wage and enacting other government measures to help the poor. Now consider an article expressing a quite different point of view, an opinion piece written by Michael Saltsman, the research director at the Employment Policies Institute—a pro-business, free market think tank opposed to raising the minimum wage. It appeared in *The Huffington Post* on April 26, 2013. We ask you to read the article and then use the preceding questions to stimulate dialectic thinking about Surowiecki versus Saltsman.

■ ■ ■   **FOR WRITING AND DISCUSSION**   Practicing Dialectic Thinking with Two Articles   **MyWritingLab**™

Individual task: Freewrite your responses to the preceding questions, in which Surowiecki is writer A and Saltsman is writer B. **Group task:** Working as a whole class or in small groups, share your responses to the two articles, guided by the dialectic questions.   ■ ■ ■

To Help the Poor, Move Beyond "Minimum" Gestures

MICHAEL SALTSMAN

Actor and director Ben Affleck made news this week with the announcement that he'll spend five days living on just $1.50—the U.S.-dollar daily equivalent of extreme poverty, according to the Global Poverty Project.

Affleck's heart is in the right place, but his actions won't provide a measurable benefit for people who actually live in poverty. On that score, Affleck's actions are not unlike a series of recently-introduced proposals to raise the federal minimum wage—well-intentioned but ultimately empty gestures that will do little to raise poor families out of poverty.

For poverty-reducing policies to benefit the poor, the benefits first have to be properly targeted to people living in poverty. On this count, a higher minimum wage fails miserably. Census Bureau data shows that over 60 percent of people living below the poverty line don't work. They don't need a raise—they need a job.

Among those who do earn the minimum wage, a majority actually don't live in poverty. According to a forthcoming Employment Policies Institute analysis of Census Bureau data, over half of those covered by President Obama's $9 proposal live in households with income at least twice the poverty level—and one-third are in households with an income three times or greater than the poverty level.

5   That's because nearly 60 percent of affected employees aren't single earners, according to the EPI report—they're living in households where a parent or a spouse often earns an income far above the minimum. (The average family income of this group is $50,789.) By contrast, we found that only nine percent of people covered by President Obama's $9 minimum wage are single parents with children.

It's for reasons like these that the majority of academic research shows little connection between a higher minimum wage and reductions in poverty. For instance, economists from American and Cornell Universities examined data from the 28 states that raised their minimum wages between 2003 and 2007, and found no associated reductions in poverty.

Of course, poor targeting isn't the only problem. The vast majority of economic research—including 85 percent of the most credible studies from the last two decades—finds that job loss for the least-skilled employees follows on the heels of minimum wage hikes.

That's why better-targeted policies like the Earned Income Tax Credit (EITC) deserve the support of politicians and public figures who want to do something about poverty. It's been empirically proven to boost employment and incomes, without the unintended consequences of a wage hike. Accounting for the EITC, the full-time hourly wage for many minimum wage earners is already above the $9 figure that President Obama has proposed.

Three Ways to Foster Dialectic Thinking

In this concluding section, we suggest three ways to stimulate and sustain the process of dialectic thinking: Effective discussions in class, over coffee, or online; a reading log in which you make texts speak to each other; or a formal exploratory essay. We'll look briefly at each in turn.

Effective Discussions   Good, rich talk is one of the most powerful ways to stimulate dialectic thinking and foster a "mingling of minds." The key is to keep these discussions from being shouting matches or bully pulpits for those who like to dominate the air-time. Discussions are most productive if people are willing to express different points of view or to role-play those views for the purpose of advancing the conversation. Try Rogerian listening, in which you summarize someone else's position before you offer your own, different position. (See Chapter 7 for more explanation of Rogerian listening.) Probe deeply to discover whether disagreements are primarily about facts and evidence or about underlying values and beliefs. Be respectful of others' views, but don't hesitate to point out where you see problems or weaknesses. Good discussions can occur in class, in late-night coffee shops, or in online chat rooms or on discussion boards.

Reading Logs   In our classes, we require students to keep reading logs or journals in which they use freewriting and idea mapping to explore their ideas as they encounter multiple perspectives on an issue. One part of a journal or reading log should include summaries of each article you read. Another part should focus on your own dialectic thinking as you interact with your sources while you are reading them. Adapt the questions for promoting dialectic thinking on page 39.

A Formal Exploratory Essay   A formal exploratory essay tells the story of an intellectual journey. It is both a way of promoting dialectical thinking and a way of narrating one's struggle to negotiate multiple views. The keys to writing successful exploratory essays are: (1) choosing an issue to explore on which you don't yet have an answer or position (or on which you are open to changing your mind); (2) wrestling with an issue or problem by resisting quick, simple answers and by exploring diverse perspectives; and (3) letting your thinking evolve and your own stance on the issue grow out of this exploration.

Exploratory essays can be powerful thinking and writing experiences in their own right, but they can also be a valuable precursor to a formal argument. Many instructors assign a formal exploratory paper as the first stage of a course research project—what we might call a "thesis-seeking" stage. (The second stage is a formal argument that converts your exploratory thinking into a hierarchically organized argument using reasons and evidence to support your claim.) Although often used as part of a research project, exploratory essays can also be low-stakes reflective pieces narrating the evolution of a writer's thinking during a class discussion.

An exploratory essay includes these thinking moves and parts:

- The essay is opened and driven by the writer's issue question or research problem—not a thesis.
- The introduction to the essay presents the question and shows why it interests the writer, why it is significant, and why it is problematic rather than clear-cut or easy to resolve.

- The body of the essay shows the writer's inquiry process. It demonstrates how the writer has kept the question open, sincerely wrestled with different views on the question, accepted uncertainty and ambiguity, and possibly redefined the question in the midst of his or her reading and reflection on multiple perspectives.
- The body of the essay includes summaries of the different views or sources that the writer explored and often includes believing and doubting responses to them.
- In the essay's conclusion, the writer may clarify his or her thinking and discover a thesis to be developed and supported in a subsequent argument. But the conclusion can also remain open because the writer may not have discovered his or her own position on the issue and may acknowledge the need or desire for more exploration.

One of the writing assignment options for this chapter is a formal exploratory paper. Trudie Makens's exploratory essay on pages 44–50 shows how she explored different voices in the controversy over raising the minimum wage to $15 per hour.

Conclusion

This chapter has focused on inquiry as a way to enrich your reading and writing of arguments. This chapter has offered five main strategies for deep reading: (1) Use a variety of questions and prompts to find an issue to explore; (2) read sources rhetorically by placing them in their rhetorical context; (3) read as a believer; (4) read as a doubter; and (5) think dialectically. This chapter has also shown you how to summarize an article and incorporate summaries into your own writing, using attributive tags to distinguish the ideas you are summarizing from your own. It has explained why a reading's rhetorical context (purpose, audience, and genre) must be considered in any thoughtful response to an argument. Finally, it has emphasized the importance of dialectic thinking and has offered the exploratory essay as a way to encourage wrestling with multiple perspectives rather than seeking early closure.

WRITING ASSIGNMENT   **An Argument Summary or a Formal Exploratory Essay**   MyWritingLab™

Option 1: **An Argument Summary** Write a 250-word summary of an argument selected by your instructor. Then write a one-sentence summary of the same argument. Use as models Trudie Makens's summaries of James Surowiecki's argument on raising the minimum wage (page 36).

Option 2: **A Formal Exploratory Essay** Write an exploratory essay in which you narrate in first-person, chronological order the evolution through time of your thinking about an issue or problem. Rather than state a thesis or claim, begin with a question or problem. Then describe your inquiry process as you worked your way through sources or different views. Follow the guidelines for an exploratory paper shown on page 43. When you cite the sources you have considered, be sure to use attributive tags so that the reader can distinguish between your own ideas and those of the sources you have summarized. If you use research sources, use MLA documentation for citing ideas and quotations and for creating a Works Cited at the end (see Chapter 17).

Organization Plan for an Exploratory Essay

Introduction (one to several paragraphs)	• Establish that your question is complex, problematic, and significant. • Show why you are interested in it. • Present relevant background on your issue. Begin with your question or build up to it, using it to end your introductory section.
Body section 1: First view or source	• Introduce your first source and show why you started with it. • Provide rhetorical context and information about it. • Summarize the source's content and argument. • Offer your response to this source, including both believing and doubting points. • Talk about what this source contributes to your understanding of your question: What did you learn? What value does this source have for you? What is missing from this source that you want to consider? Where do you want to go from here?
Body section 2: Second view or source	• Repeat the process with a new source selected to advance the inquiry. • Explain why you selected this source (to find an alternative view, pursue a subquestion, find more data, and so forth). • Summarize the source's argument. • Respond to the source's ideas. Look for points of agreement and disagreement with other sources. • Show how your cumulative reading of sources is shaping your thinking or leading to more questions.
Body sections 3, 4, 5, etc.	• Continue exploring views or sources.
Conclusion	• Wrap up your intellectual journey and explain where you are now in your thinking and how your understanding of your problem has changed. • Present your current answer to your question based on all that you have learned so far, or explain why you still can't answer your question, or explain what research you might pursue further.

Explanation and Organization

An exploratory essay could grow out of class discussion, course readings, field work and interviews, or simply the writer's role-playing of alternative views. In all cases, the purpose of an exploratory paper is not to state and defend a thesis. Instead, its purpose is to think dialectically about multiple perspectives, narrating the evolution through time of the writer's thought process. Many students are inspired by the open, "behind-the-scenes" feel of an exploratory essay. They enjoy taking readers on the same intellectual and emotional journey they have just traveled. A typical organization plan for an exploratory essay is shown on page 43. ■

Reading

What follows is Trudie Makens's exploratory essay on the subject of raising the minimum wage. Her research begins with the articles by Surowiecki and Saltsman that you have already read and discussed. She then moves off in her own direction.

Title as question indicates an exploratory purpose.

Should Fast-Food Workers Be Paid $15 per Hour?

TRUDIE MAKENS (STUDENT)

Introduction identifies the issue, explains the writer's interest in it, and acknowledges its complexity.

Having worked as a busser in a pizza restaurant, a part-time barista, and a server at a dumpling cafe, I was immediately attracted to our class discussions of minimum wage, sparked by recent protests of fast-food workers demanding pay of $15 per hour. My first job as a barista exposed me to the harsh reality of living on today's existing minimum wage as I witnessed my coworker Maria lose her home because she couldn't pay rent and support her kids at the same time. As a single mother of two, Maria had to bounce from relative to relative putting a strain on her family relations, her image of herself as an able provider, and her children. I am lucky because, as a student, I am blessed to have my family operate as a safety net for me. If I am ever short on a bill or get sick or hurt, my parents will assist me financially. Many of the individuals I have worked with do not have that same safety net. These individuals are often older and have children or are beginning a family. Understanding the hardships of minimum-wage jobs, I entered our class discussions in support of the $15/hour demand because this pay rate would give workers a living wage. However, despite my personal affinities with these workers, I also understood that raising the minimum wage might have negative consequences for our economy. I wanted to explore this issue in more depth so I decided to pose my research question as "Should fast-food workers be paid a living wage of $15 per hour?"

My exploration began with an article that our instructor assigned to the whole class: "The Pay Is Too Damn Low" by James Surowiecki from *The New Yorker*. In the past, according to Surowiecki, it didn't matter that jobs at Walmart, Target, or fast-food franchises were low-pay, part-time, and without benefits because they were held mainly by teenagers or married women seeking to supplement a husband's wages. But today, says Surowiecki, a growing number of primary breadwinners rely on these poverty-level wages to support families. The problem stems from a "tectonic shift in the American economy." (35) While in 1960, "firms such as Ford, Standard Oil, and Bethlehem Steel employed huge numbers of well-paid workers while earning big profits," (35) nowadays America's biggest employers are fast-food and retail companies with low profit margins. While Surowiecki acknowledges that these retail companies and food franchises depend on low-wage workers to keep prices cheap for the American consumer, he still supports increasing the minimum wage but sees it as only one tool for fighting poverty. He argues that America also needs to create a European-style safety net system and calls for an increase in earned income tax credit, universal health insurance, affordable child care, and investment of almost a trillion dollars in infrastructure to create good middle-class jobs.

Surowiecki's concluding remarks about a safety net system resonated with me. I understood that what protected me from a financial crisis was my family acting like a safety net. The government, Surowiecki argues, should perform the same function for low-wage earners through such programs as childcare and health care. He points to Germany and the Netherlands, arguing the stronger safety net put in place for workers by these European governments provides a better economic and social situation for low-wage workers, even though they are paid around the same amount as United States low-wage workers. Surowiecki also addressed some of my concerns regarding the economic consequences of implementing a living wage. Even though some low-wage jobs might be eliminated and food costs might go up, government investment in infrastructure might create more high-paying, middle-class jobs, resulting in a net benefit. But I still wasn't convinced or completely satisfied. How exactly would the government raise the money for a redesigned social insurance system? Would the country accept the needed higher taxes? While Surowiecki had convinced me that the government had

---

Margin annotations:

Writer states her research question.

Writer identifies her first source.

Writer summarizes the article.

Writer shows how this article has advanced her thinking by strengthening her previous mention of "safety nets."

Writer includes doubting points by identifying problems not resolved in first source.

an important role to play in creating the conditions for a living wage, I still was unclear on how the government could effectively do so without detrimentally upsetting the economy.

Writer shows rhetorical thinking by purposely seeking an argument from a business perspective; she identifies conservative credentials of author and summarizes his argument.

Writer summarizes second source.

I wanted to know more about raising the minimum wage from the business perspective, so I Googled "living wage" and found an anti-minimum wage article from Michael Saltsman, the research director of the Employment Policy Institute. The opinion piece was published online in *The Huffington Post* and entitled, "To Help the Poor, Move Beyond 'Minimum' Gestures." I also found a full-page ad from the same conservative institute depicting a robot doing the work of a fast-food employee. Saltsman believes that despite the good intentions of living wage proponents a higher federal minimum wage will do more harm than good. Within his piece, Saltsman equates the symbolic value of Ben Affleck's pledge to live five days on $1.50, "the U.S.-dollar equivalent of extreme poverty," to proposals for a higher federal minimum wage. Both, according to Saltsman, are "ultimately empty gestures" that do little to lift families out of poverty. What the poor need, Saltsman asserts, is "not a raise" but a job. Saltsman claims that over "60% of people living below the poverty line don't work" and those who do earn a minimum wage don't live in poverty households. Even if a member of the working poor were to receive a living wage, Saltsman argues, "job loss for the least-skilled employees follows on the heels of a minimum wage hike." What helps to reduce poverty, according to Saltsman, is not a higher minimum wage but the Earned Income Tax Credit, "empirically proven to boost employment and incomes" and thus providing "a measurable difference for the poor."

Writer includes both believing and doubting points.

5   Prior to reading Saltsman, I had not fully considered the potential that workers would be laid off because it would be cheaper for businesses to use robots or other automation than to employ higher-wage workers. Though Saltsman got me thinking about the dangers of job displacement, I wasn't convinced by his argument that an increased minimum wage would primarily benefit people who didn't need it such as teenagers or second earners in an already middle-class family. I could see that an increased minimum wage wouldn't help the 60 percent of the poor who were unemployed, but I also realized that the Earned Income Tax Credit wouldn't help the unemployed either because it goes only to poor people who report income. (I Googled "earned income tax credit" just to make sure I understood how it works by giving a boost of income to poor but working tax filers.) Though Saltsman persuaded me to consider the negative economic consequences of a living wage, I wasn't convinced the living wage was entirely ineffective. I thought back to Surowiecki who, unlike Saltsman, saw a living wage as one component in a larger solution to reduce poverty. Both recommended an expanded

Writer shows dialectic thinking by comparing and contrasting views of first two sources.

Earned Income Tax Credit, but Surowiecki went further and also encouraged a stronger social-insurance system in addition to a higher minimum wage. Neither article persuaded me the living wage was either fully beneficial or fully injurious. To clarify my position, I needed to do more research.

I wanted another economist's perspective, so I typed in "economic impact and living wage" into ProQuest, an interdisciplinary research database. One of the articles that caught my attention was "Living Wage: Some Gain, Neediest Lose Out." The article was an interview with labor economist Richard Toikka by author Charles Oliver featured in *Investor's Business Daily,* a conservative financial newspaper focused on stock and bond investments. In the interview, Oliver prompts Toikka to discuss the unintended consequences of a higher minimum wage. Toikka asserts that in order to absorb the cost of a higher wage, companies seek to hire higher-skilled workers who require less training, and thus cost the company less money. With a higher wage offered, Toikka argues, more high-skilled workers, such as college students, seek these jobs, increasing "the competition low skilled workers face." Thus an increased minimum wage reduces the number of low-skilled jobs available. Toikka also makes the same argument as Saltsman, concluding that the benefits of a higher wage don't go towards the families who need it, but instead to second-earners who aren't living below the poverty line. Toikka cites a survey among labor economists asked to rate the efficiency of anti-poverty measures, and "69% said living wages weren't at all efficient in meeting the needs of poor families." The more efficient way to combat poverty, Toikka argues, is not a living wage but an expansion of the Earned Income Tax Credit.

Putting Toikka in conversation with Saltsman, I began to understand and heed the warnings of both economists. Though well-intentioned, increasing the minimum wage by itself is not apt to reduce poverty and would ultimately injure the poor rather than helping. If a living wage does lead to heightened competition and employers slashing jobs, then perhaps a living wage is ineffective and therefore should be abandoned in favor of the Earned Income Tax Credit. So far, all the articles agreed the Earned Income Tax Credit was a good way to reduce poverty, even though it too benefits only those with jobs. Even so, I couldn't help but think that abandoning a living wage was a concession to a flawed economic system that doesn't value the working poor or the impoverished unemployed enough. I thought back to Surowiecki when he praised Germany and the Netherlands for providing a strong social insurance system that served as a safety net for those in low-wage jobs. If Europe can ensure dignity and security to its citizens, then why

---

Writer again seeks sources purposefully; she shows how she found the source and places it in rhetorical context.

Writer summarizes the article.

Writer shows how the pro-business sources have complicated her initial tentative position.

Writer uses believing and doubting strategies to think dialectically, looking for a synthesis.

can't the United States? Although 69 percent of labor economists say that a living wage is an inefficient way to alleviate poverty, we don't know what they would say if the government also invested in infrastructure to create well-paying jobs. Right now, it seems from my readings, that the current market doesn't value low-wage workers. What is valued in our economy is capital, profit, and cheap goods, all of which come at the expense of millions of workers. Is the structure of the economy where wealth is unequally distributed and workers are exploited really inevitable? Or is it an economic trend that can be reversed? I wanted to believe the latter, so I returned to ProQuest to find another article addressing the economic impact of a living wage but from a pro-labor perspective.

Writer purposefully seeks a different perspective.

Writer identifies next source and places it in rhetorical context.

Writer summarizes the article.

In my search, I found an article entitled "The Task Rabbit Economy," authored by Robert Kuttner and published in the progressive magazine *The American Prospect*. Kuttner begins by describing a successful San Francisco company whose Web site matches people who have an odd job they need done with people who will do the work for a fee. The company, named the Task Rabbit, is like an online temp agency that operates by having would-be workers bid against each other, driving the price down for their labor. Kuttner argues that Task Rabbit's business model, which produces cheap labor, is analogous to our current economy, where workers have lost "bargaining power" and work has become casual and unstable (46). Kuttner argues that this low-wage economy has produced less economic growth, less prosperity, and more unemployment than earlier eras when there was more job stability and higher wages. According to Kuttner, the claim made by labor economists that a higher minimum wage leaves low-skilled workers without a job ignores how an unregulated labor market has allowed corporations to "weaken labor...and extract abnormal profits" (47). Kuttner draws on the economy of Sweden to provide an example where a living wage, full employment, and a "deliberate effort to narrow wage gaps" has been implemented effectively (48). What's more, Kuttner addresses the concern of rising prices by citing a Demos study that found raising wages so retail workers "earned at least $25,000 a year" only cost large retailers "1 percent of the $2.17 trillion annual sales" (52). Kuttner closes out his article by emphasizing that "organized labor" is what will change the labor market, using both collective bargaining and "political force" (55).

Writer shows how this source has advanced and solidified her own thinking.

Kuttner's article moved me in a way that Toikka and Saltsman's pieces could not. Instead of accepting an economic system where low-wage workers are exploited for stockholder profits and cheap goods, Kuttner criticizes the labor market for its failure to value workers. Kuttner acknowledges that a higher minimum wage will upset the present economy, but he argues that the present economic system isn't inevitable but the result of large employers choosing to value capital over people without strong governmental policies protecting labor and the poor. Moreover, Kuttner's article illuminates the inefficiency of our economy. The studies Kuttner references reveal that the United States was better off in the years after World War II, when jobs were stable, plentiful, and paid a living wage. Most of all, I appreciated Kuttner's concluding call to action, and his assurance that such action will not lead to economic suicide but create the "dynamic, supple, and innovative" economy our nation strives for. According to Kuttner, we can choose to allow the market to continue unregulated, or, through organizing workers, we can push towards policies that value people—their rights, health, and dignity. As I read Kuttner, I wondered what current labor movements are in existence today and the progress they are making in their fight to gain rights and a living wage. I, again, turned to ProQuest.

My search handed me a long list of results, but I found one article that provided a relevant look into a labor campaign organized by Walmart sales associates. Titled "Job Insecurity," the article was written by Kevin Clarke and published in the Catholic magazine *America*. Clarke begins by introducing William Fletcher, a twenty-three-year-old retail sales associate at Walmart. According to Fletcher, he loves his job and "working with the public" but, he says, he and other employees constantly struggle with "low wages, chaotic scheduling, and insensitive management" (11). Both Fletcher and Clarke wonder why being a retail sales associate for Walmart warrants not receiving enough to "have a home, have health insurance, have all the basic things in life" (11). In order to improve his working conditions, Fletcher joined Organization United for Respect at Walmart, or OUR Walmart. OUR Walmart, Clarke states, is "part of an emerging labor phenomenon of non-union activism against Walmart and other powerful, profitable U.S. corporations that maintain large, low paid work forces" (12). Walmart, according to both Fletcher and Clarke, is a trend-setting company. If labor conditions improve at Walmart, other companies could follow suit. The organization draws from the tactics of "community organizing and the civil rights movement" (12). Unfortunately, Clarke states, Walmart management continues to thwart protests or walkouts. Despite obstacles, OUR Walmart persists, marking a major moment in the contemporary labor movement. The article ends with Clarke's appeal to the Catholic social justice tradition of solidarity with the poor. He notes that Walmart sales associates depend on government support programs such as food stamps and housing assistance. He reminds his readers that our continual search for the cheapest goods

Writer again shows purposeful search for next source.

Writer identifies next source and places it in rhetorical context.

10

makes us partially guilty for the exploitation of workers. He urges us to shop conscientiously and thoughtfully (14).

Writer pulls together the results of her dialectic thinking, which has resulted in a synthesis.

I reached the end of the article feeling shocked. In lieu of everything I read from Kuttner, I was amazed that Walmart could dismiss the demands of OUR Walmart. Clarke states the owners of Walmart, the Walton family, possess "48% of Walmart stock and [are] the richest family on earth, with over $107 billion in net worth" (14). Hearing numbers like these confirmed my forming conviction that the unregulated labor market dangerously exploits workers in order to gain cheap labor, cheap goods, and bloated profits. What's more, Walmart actively tries to scare workers from organizing—threatening to take away their jobs. Though there is much more to read and learn about the growing labor movement in the United States, Clarke's article, as well as Surowiecki, Saltsman, Toikka, and Kuttner's pieces, allowed me to round out my position on a higher minimum wage. As I end my exploratory paper, I understand that a living wage is possible and should be provided to service workers as a basic human right. But it also needs to be supplemented with the kinds of social insurance systems stressed by Surowiecki and Kuttner.

Final sentences reveal synthesis that goes beyond original leanings in first paragraph.

Works Cited

Writer compiles an MLA-formatted "Works Cited" page that lists alphabetically all the sources discussed in the paper.

Clarke, Kevin. "Job Insecurity." *America* 18 Feb. 2013: 11-14. *ProQuest*. Web. 8 Jan. 2014.

Kuttner, Robert. "The Task Rabbit Economy." *American Prospect* 24 Sept. 2013: 45-55. *ProQuest*. Web. 10 Jan. 2014.

Oliver, Charles. "Living Wage: Some Gain, Neediest Lose Out." *Investor's Business Daily* 5 Sept. 2000. *ProQuest*. Web. 10 Jan. 2014.

Saltsman, Michael. "To Help the Poor Move Beyond 'Minimum' Gestures." *Huffington Post.* 26 Apr. 2013. Web. 13 Jan. 2014.

Surowiecki, James. "The Pay Is Too Damn Low." *New Yorker* 12 Aug. 2013: 35. *ProQuest*. Web. 5 Jan. 2014.

MyWritingLab™

Visit Ch. 2 Argument as Inquiry: Reading and Exploring in *MyWritingLab* to complete the For Writing and Discussion and Writing Assignments and to test your understanding of the chapter objectives.

PART TWO
Writing an Argument

This still from the *Tomb Raider* video game series features main character Lara Croft engaged in one of her typical combats with humans, beasts, or supernatural creatures. Lara, an adventurer and archaeologist, represents both a sexualized and an empowered woman. Women and violent video games are the focus of student Carmen Tieu's argument developed in Chapters 3–5; however, Carmen explores gender roles from the perspective of a woman playing a "male" video game, *Halo*.

The Core of an Argument

A Claim with Reasons

What you will learn in this chapter:

3.1 To describe the key elements of classical argument
3.2 To explain the rhetorical appeals
3.3 To distinguish between issue and information questions and between genuine and pseudo-arguments
3.4 To describe the basic frame of an argument

In Part One we explained that argument combines truth seeking with persuasion. Part One, by highlighting the importance of exploration and inquiry, emphasizes the truth-seeking dimension of argument. The suggested writing assignments in Part One included a variety of exploratory tasks: freewriting, playing the believing and doubting game, and writing a formal exploratory essay. In Part Two we show you how to convert your exploratory ideas into a thesis-governed classical argument that uses effective reasons and evidence to support its claims. Each chapter in Part Two focuses on a key skill or idea needed for responsible and effective persuasion.

The Classical Structure of Argument

3.1 To describe the key elements of classical argument

Classical argument is patterned after the persuasive speeches of ancient Greek and Roman orators. In traditional Latin terminology, the main parts of a persuasive speech are the *exordium,* in which the speaker gets the audience's attention; the *narratio,* which provides needed background; the *propositio,* which is the speaker's claim or thesis; the *partitio,* which forecasts the main parts of the speech; the *confirmatio,* which presents the speaker's arguments supporting the claim; the *confutatio,* which summarizes and rebuts opposing views; and the *peroratio,* which concludes the speech by summing up the argument, calling for action, and leaving a strong, lasting impression. (Of course, you don't need to remember these tongue-twisting Latin terms. We cite them only to assure you that in writing a classical argument, you are joining a time-honored tradition that links back to the origins of democracy.)

Let's go over the same territory again using more contemporary terms. We provide an organization plan below showing the structure of a classical argument, which shows these typical sections:

■ **The introduction.** Writers of classical argument typically begin by connecting the audience to the issue by showing how it arises out of a current event or by using an illustrative story, memorable scene, or startling statistic—something that grabs the audience's attention. They continue the introduction by focusing the issue—often by stating it directly as a question or by briefly summarizing opposing views—and providing needed background and context. They conclude the introduction by presenting their claim (thesis statement) and forecasting the argument's structure.

(continued)

Organization Plan for an Argument with a Classical Structure

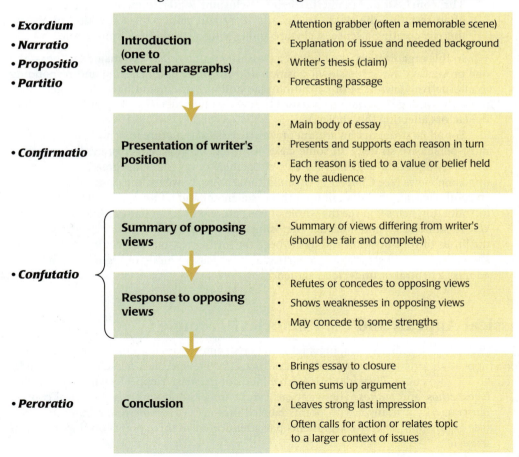

• *Exordium* • *Narratio* • *Propositio* • *Partitio*	**Introduction (one to several paragraphs)**	• Attention grabber (often a memorable scene) • Explanation of issue and needed background • Writer's thesis (claim) • Forecasting passage
• *Confirmatio*	**Presentation of writer's position**	• Main body of essay • Presents and supports each reason in turn • Each reason is tied to a value or belief held by the audience
• *Confutatio*	**Summary of opposing views**	• Summary of views differing from writer's (should be fair and complete)
	Response to opposing views	• Refutes or concedes to opposing views • Shows weaknesses in opposing views • May concede to some strengths
• *Peroratio*	**Conclusion**	• Brings essay to closure • Often sums up argument • Leaves strong last impression • Often calls for action or relates topic to a larger context of issues

- **The presentation of the writer's position.** The presentation of the writer's own position is usually the longest part of a classical argument. Here writers present the reasons and evidence supporting their claims, typically choosing reasons that tie into their audience's values, beliefs, and assumptions. Usually each reason is developed in its own paragraph or sequence of paragraphs. When a paragraph introduces a new reason, writers state the reason directly and then support it with evidence or a chain of ideas. Along the way, writers guide their readers with appropriate transitions.

- **The summary and critique of alternative views.** When summarizing and responding to opposing views, writers have several options. If there are several opposing arguments, writers may summarize all of them together and then compose a single response, or they may summarize and respond to each argument in turn. As we will explain in Chapter 7, writers may respond to opposing views either by refuting them or by conceding to their strengths and shifting to a different field of values.

- **The conclusion.** Finally, in their conclusion, writers sum up their argument, often restating the stakes in the argument and calling for some kind of action, thereby creating a sense of closure and leaving a strong final impression.

In this organization, the body of a classical argument has two major sections—the one presenting the writer's own position and the other summarizing and responding to alternative views. The organization plan and our discussion have the writer's own position coming first, but it is possible to reverse that order. (In Chapter 7 we consider the factors affecting this choice.)

For all its strengths, an argument with a classical structure may not always be your most persuasive strategy. In some cases, you may be more effective by delaying your thesis, by ignoring alternative views altogether, or by showing great sympathy for opposing views (see Chapter 7). Even in these cases, however, the classical structure is a useful planning tool. Its call for a thesis statement and a forecasting statement in the introduction helps you see the whole of your argument in miniature. And by requiring you to summarize and consider opposing views, the classical structure alerts you to the limits of your position and to the need for further reasons and evidence. As we will show, the classical structure is a particularly persuasive mode of argument when you address a neutral or undecided audience.

Classical Appeals and the Rhetorical Triangle

3.2 To explain the rhetorical appeals | Besides developing a template or structure for an argument, classical rhetoricians analyzed the ways that effective speeches persuaded their audiences. They identified three kinds of persuasive appeals, which they called *logos, ethos,* and *pathos.* These appeals can be understood within a rhetorical context illustrated by a triangle with points labeled *message, writer or speaker,* and *audience* (see Figure 3.1). Effective arguments pay attention to all three points on this *rhetorical triangle.*

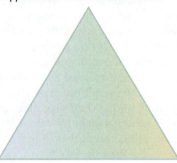

Message
LOGOS: *How can I make the argument*
internally consistent and logical?
How can I find the best reasons and
support them with the best evidence?

Audience
PATHOS: *How can I make the reader*
open to my message? How can I best
appeal to my reader's values and
interests? How can I engage my
reader emotionally and imaginatively?

Writer or Speaker
ETHOS: *How can I present myself*
effectively? How can I enhance my
credibility and trustworthiness?

FIGURE 3.1 The rhetorical triangle

As Figure 3.1 shows, each point on the triangle corresponds to one of the three persuasive appeals:

- *Logos* (Greek for "word") focuses attention on the quality of the message—that is, on the internal consistency and clarity of the argument itself and on the logic of its reasons and support. The impact of logos on an audience is referred to as its logical appeal.

- *Ethos* (Greek for "character") focuses attention on the writer's (or speaker's) character as it is projected in the message. It refers to the credibility of the writer. *Ethos* is often conveyed through the writer's investment in his or her claim, through the fairness with which the writer considers alternative views, through the tone and style of the message, and even through the message's professional appearance on paper or screen, including correct grammar, flawless proofreading, and appropriate formats for citations and bibliography. In some cases, *ethos* is also a function of the writer's reputation for honesty and expertise independent of the message. The impact of *ethos* on an audience is referred to as the *ethical appeal* or *appeal from credibility*.

- *Pathos* (Greek for "suffering" or "experience") focuses attention on the values and beliefs of the intended audience. It is often associated with emotional appeal. But *pathos* appeals more specifically to an audience's imaginative sympathies—their capacity to feel and see what the writer feels and sees. Thus, when we turn the abstractions of logical discourse into a tangible and immediate story, we are making a pathetic appeal. Whereas appeals to *logos* and *ethos* can further an audience's intellectual assent to our claim, appeals to *pathos* engage the imagination and feelings, moving the audience to a deeper appreciation of the argument's significance.

A related rhetorical concept, connected to the appeals of *logos, ethos,* and *pathos,* is that of *kairos,* from the Greek word for "right time," "season," or "opportunity." This concept suggests that for an argument to be persuasive, its timing must be effectively chosen and its tone and structure in right proportion or measure. You may have had the experience of composing an argumentative e-mail and then hesitating before clicking the "send" button. Is this the right moment to send this message? Is my audience ready to hear what I'm saying? Would my argument be more effective if I waited for a couple of days? If I send this message now, should I change its tone and content? This attentiveness to the unfolding of time is what is meant by *kairos.* We will return to this concept in Chapter 6, when we consider *ethos* and *pathos* in more depth.

Given this background on the classical appeals, let's turn now to *logos*—the logic and structure of arguments.

Issue Questions as the Origins of Argument

3.3 To distinguish between issue and information questions and between genuine and pseudo-arguments

At the heart of any argument is an issue, which we can define as a controversial topic area such as "the labeling of genetically modified foods" or "racial profiling," that gives rise to differing points of view and conflicting claims. A writer can usually focus an issue by asking an issue question that invites at least two alternative answers. Within any complex issue—for example, the issue of abortion—there are usually a number of separate issue questions: Should abortions be legal? Should the federal government authorize Medicaid payments for abortions? When does a fetus become a human being (at conception? at three months? at quickening? at birth?)? What are the effects of legalizing abortion? (One person might stress that legalized abortion leads to greater freedom for women. Another person might respond that it lessens a society's respect for human life.)

Difference between an Issue Question and an Information Question

Of course, not all questions are issue questions that can be answered reasonably in two or more differing ways; thus not all questions can lead to effective arguments. Rhetoricians have traditionally distinguished between *explication,* which is writing that sets out to inform or explain, and *argumentation,* which sets out to change a reader's mind. On the surface, at least, this seems like a useful distinction. If a reader is interested in a writer's question mainly to gain new knowledge about a subject, then the writer's essay could be considered explication rather than argument. According to this view, the following questions about teenage pregnancy might be called information questions rather than issue questions:

How does the teenage pregnancy rate in the United States compare with the rate in Sweden? If the rates are different, why?

Although both questions seem to call for information rather than for argument, we believe that the second one would be an issue question if reasonable people disagreed on the answer. Thus, different writers might agree that the teenage pregnancy rate in the United States is seven times higher than the rate in Sweden. But they might disagree about why. One writer might emphasize Sweden's practical, secular sex-education courses, leading to more consistent use of contraceptives among Swedish teenagers. Another writer might point to the higher use of oral contraceptives among teenage girls in Sweden (partly a result of Sweden's generous national health program) and to less reliance on condoms for preventing pregnancy. Another might argue that moral decay in the United States or a breakdown of the traditional family is at fault. Thus, underneath the surface of what looks like a simple explication of the "truth" is really a controversy.

How to Identify an Issue Question

You can generally tell whether a question is an issue question or an information question by examining your purpose in relationship to your audience. If your relationship to your audience is that of teacher to learner, so that your audience hopes to gain new information, knowledge, or understanding that you possess, then your question is probably an information question. But if your relationship to your audience is that of advocate to decision maker or jury, so that your audience needs to make up its mind on something and is weighing different points of view, then the question you address is an issue question.

Often the same question can be an information question in one context and an issue question in another. Let's look at the following examples:

- **How does a diesel engine work?** (This is probably an information question, because reasonable people who know about diesel engines will probably agree on how they work. This question would be posed by an audience of new learners.)
- **Why is a diesel engine more fuel efficient than a gasoline engine?** (This also seems to be an information question, because all experts will probably agree on the answer. Once again, the audience seems to be new learners, perhaps students in an automotive class.)
- **What is the most cost-effective way to produce diesel fuel from crude oil?** (This could be an information question if experts agree and you are addressing new learners. But if you are addressing engineers and one engineer says process X is the most cost-effective and another argues for process Y, then the question is an issue question.)
- **Should the present highway tax on diesel fuel be increased?** (This is certainly an issue question. One person says yes; another says no; another offers a compromise.)

■ ■ ■   **FOR CLASS DISCUSSION**   Information Questions versus Issue Questions

Working as a class or in small groups, try to decide which of the following questions are information questions and which are issue questions. Many of them could be either, depending on the rhetorical context. For such questions, create hypothetical contexts to show your reasoning.

1. What percentage of public schools in the United States are failing?
2. Which causes more traffic accidents, drunk driving or texting while driving?
3. What is the effect on children of playing first-person-shooter games?
4. Is genetically modified corn safe for human consumption?
5. Should people get rid of their land lines and have only cell phones?

Difference between a Genuine Argument and a Pseudo-Argument

Although every argument features an issue question with alternative answers, not every dispute over answers is a rational argument. Rational arguments require two additional factors: (1) reasonable participants who operate within the conventions of reasonable behavior and (2) potentially sharable assumptions that can serve as a starting place or foundation for the argument. Lacking one or both of these conditions, disagreements remain stalled at the level of pseudo-arguments.

Pseudo-Arguments: Committed Believers and Fanatical Skeptics

A reasonable argument assumes the possibility of growth and change; disputants may modify their views as they acknowledge strengths in an alternative view or weaknesses in their own. Such growth becomes impossible—and argument degenerates to pseudo-argument—when disputants are fanatically committed to their positions. Consider the case of the fanatical believer and the fanatical skeptic.

From one perspective, committed believers are admirable persons, guided by unwavering values and beliefs. Committed believers stand on solid rock, unwilling to compromise their principles or bend to the prevailing winds. But from another perspective, committed believers can seem rigidly fixed, incapable of growth or change. When committed believers from two clashing belief systems try to engage in dialogue with each other, a truth-seeking exchange of views becomes difficult. They talk past each other; dialogue is replaced by monologue from within isolated silos. Once committed believers push each other's buttons on global warming, guns, health care, taxes, religion, or some other issue, each disputant resorts to an endless replaying of the same prepackaged arguments. Disagreeing with a committed believer is like ordering the surf to quiet down. The only response is another crashing wave.

In contrast to the committed believer, the fanatical skeptic dismisses the possibility of ever believing anything. Skeptics often demand proof where no proof is possible. So what if the sun has risen every day of recorded history? That's no proof that it will rise tomorrow. Short of absolute proof, which never exists, fanatical skeptics accept nothing. In a world where the most we can hope for is increased audience adherence to our ideas, the skeptic demands an ironclad, logical demonstration of our claim's rightness.

A Closer Look at Pseudo-Arguments: The Lack of Shared Assumptions

As we have seen, rational argument degenerates to pseudo-argument when there is no possibility for listening, learning, growth, or change. In this section, we look more closely at a frequent cause of pseudo-arguments: lack of shared assumptions.

Shared Assumptions and the Problem of Ideology   As our discussion of committed believers suggests, reasonable argument is difficult when the disputants have differing "ideologies," which is an academic word for belief systems or worldviews. We all have our own ideologies. We all look at the world through a lens shaped by our life's experiences. Our beliefs and values are shaped by our family background, our friends, our culture, our particular time in history, our race or ethnicity, our gender or sexual orientation, our social class, our religion, our education, and so forth. Because we tend to think that our particular lens for looking at the world is natural and universal rather than specific to ourselves, we must be aware that persons who disagree with us may not share our deepest assumptions and beliefs. To participate in rational argument, we and our audience must seek shared assumptions—certain principles or values or beliefs that can serve as common ground.

The failure to find shared assumptions often leads to pseudo-arguments, particularly if one disputant makes assumptions that the other disputant cannot accept. Such pseudo-arguments often occur in disputes arising from politics or religion. For example, consider differences within the Christian community over how to interpret the Bible. Some Christian groups choose a straightforward, literal interpretation of the Bible as God's inerrant word, while other groups read some passages metaphorically or mythically and focus on the paradoxes, historical contexts, and interpretive complexities of the Bible; still other Christian groups read it as an ethical call for social justice. Members of these different Christian groups may not be able to argue rationally about, say, evolution or gay marriage because they have very different ways of reading Biblical passages and invoking the authority of the Bible. Similarly, within other religious traditions, believers may also differ about the meaning and applicability of their sacred texts to scientific issues and social problems.

Similar disagreements about assumptions occur in the political arena as well. (See the discussions of "angle of vision" and "degree of advocacy" in Chapter 15, page 346.) Our point is that certain religious or political beliefs or texts cannot be evoked for evidence or authority when an audience does not assume the belief's truth or does not agree on the way that a given text should be read or interpreted.

Shared Assumptions and the Problem of Personal Opinions   Lack of shared assumptions also dooms arguments about purely personal opinions—for example, someone's claim that opera is boring or that pizza is better than nachos. Of course, a pizza-versus-nachos argument might be possible if the disputants assume a shared criterion about nutrition. For example, a nutritionist could argue that pizza is better than nachos because pizza provides more balanced nutrients per calorie. But if one of the disputants responds, "Nah, nachos are better than pizza because nachos taste better," then he makes a different assumption—"My sense of taste is better than your sense of taste." This is a wholly personal standard, an assumption that others are unable to share.

■ ■ ■   **FOR WRITING AND DISCUSSION**   **Reasonable Arguments versus Pseudo-Arguments**   **MyWritingLab**™

The following questions can all be answered in alternative ways. However, not all of them will lead to reasonable arguments. Your goal is to show your understanding of the difference between reasonable arguments and pseudo-arguments.

Individual task: Which of the following questions will lead to reasonable arguments and which will lead only to pseudo-arguments? Imagining someone who disagrees with you, explain why you think the question is arguable (or not) in a short written passage.

1. Are the *Star Wars* films good science fiction?
2. Is it ethically justifiable to capture dolphins or orca whales and train them for human entertainment?
3. Should cities subsidize professional sports venues?
4. Is this abstract oil painting created by a monkey smearing paint on a canvas a true work of art?
5. Are nose rings and tongue studs attractive?

Group task: Working in pairs, small groups, or as a whole class, share your reasoning about these questions with classmates.   ■ ■ ■

Frame of an Argument: A Claim Supported by Reasons

3.4 To describe the basic frame of an argument

We said earlier that an argument originates in an *issue question,* which by definition is any question that provokes disagreement about the best answer. When you write an argument, your task is to take a position on the issue and to support it with reasons and evidence. The *claim* of your essay is the position you want your audience to accept. To put it another way, your claim is your essay's *thesis statement,* a one-sentence summary answer to your issue question. Your task, then, is to make a claim and support it with reasons.

What Is a Reason?

A *reason* (also called a *premise*) is a claim used to support another claim. In speaking or writing, a reason is usually linked to the claim with connecting words such as *because, since, for, so, thus, consequently,* and *therefore,* indicating that the claim follows logically from the reason.

Let us take an example of a controversial issue that frequently gets reported in the news—the public debate over keeping large sea mammals such as dolphins, porpoises, and orcas (killer whales) in captivity in marine parks where they entertain large crowds with their performances. This issue has many dimensions, including safety concerns for both the animals and their human trainers, as well as moral, scientific, legal, and economic concerns. Recent popular documentary films have heightened the public's awareness of the dangers of captivity to both the animals and the humans who work with them. *The Cove* (2009) exposes the gory dolphin hunts in Japan in which dolphins are killed en masse by fishermen and some are captured for display in shows around the world. *Blackfish* (2012) tells the history of the orca Tilicum who, in 2010, killed his trainer, Dawn Blancheau, at SeaWorld in Orlando, Florida. Recently a flurry of legal efforts to release the captive orca Lolita back into the wild has joined the larger battle among advocacy, governmental, scientific, and commercial groups over wild animals in captivity. In one of our recent classes, students heatedly debated the ethics of capturing wild dolphins and training them to perform in marine parks. Another student cited the personal experience of his sister's internship at SeaWorld San Diego where she worked on sea mammal rescue and rehabilitation, one of the projects of the marine park. In response, another student mentioned the millions of dollars these marine parks make on their dolphin and orca shows as well as on the stuffed animals, toys, magnets, T-shirts, and hundreds of other lucrative marine park souvenirs. Here are the frameworks the class developed for two alternative positions on this issue:

One View

CLAIM: The public should not support marine parks.

REASON 1:   Marine parks stressfully separate dolphins and orcas from their natural habitat.

REASON 2:   The education these parks claim to offer about marine mammals is just a series of artificial, exploitive tricks taught through behavior modification.

REASON 3:   The motive behind these parks is big business profit.

REASON 4:   Marine parks encourage artificial breeding programs and inhumane hunts and captures.

REASON 5:   Marine parks promote an attitude of human dominance over animals.

Alternative View

CLAIM: The public should continue to enjoy marine parks.

REASON 1:   These parks observe accreditation standards for animal welfare, health, and nutrition.

REASON 2:   These marine parks enable scientists and veterinarians to study animal behavior in ways not possible with field studies in the wild.

REASON 3:   These marine parks provide environmental education and memorable entertainment.

REASON 4:   Marine parks use some of their profits to support research, conservation, and rescue and rehabilitation programs.

REASON 5:   In their training of dolphins and orcas, these marine parks reinforce natural behaviors, exercise the animals' intelligence, and promote beneficial bonding with humans.

Formulating a list of reasons in this way breaks your argumentative task into a series of subtasks. It gives you a frame for building your argument in parts. In the previous example, the frame for the argument opposing commercial use of sea mammals suggests five different lines of reasoning a writer might pursue. A writer might use all five reasons or select only two or three, depending on which reasons would most persuade the intended audience. Each line of reasoning would be developed in its own separate section of the argument. For example, you might begin one section of your argument with the following sentence: "The public should not support marine parks because they teach dolphins and orcas clownish tricks and artificial behaviors, which they pass off as 'education about these animals.'" You would then provide examples of the tricks and stunts that dolphins and orcas are taught, explain how these contrast with their natural behaviors, and offer examples of erroneous facts or information about these animals supplied by these programs. You might also need to support the underlying assumption that it is good to acquire *real knowledge* about sea mammals in the wild. (How one articulates and supports the underlying assumptions of an argument will be developed in Chapter 4 when we discuss warrants and backing.) You would then proceed in the same way for each separate section of your argument.

To summarize our point in this section, the frame of an argument consists of the claim (the thesis statement of the essay), which is supported by one or more reasons, which are in turn supported by evidence or sequences of further reasons.

■ ■ ■ **FOR CLASS DISCUSSION**   **Using Images to Support an Argument**

In Chapter 1, we talked about implicit and explicit arguments and introduced you to some visual arguments. This exercise asks you to consider how images can shape or enhance an argument. Imagine that your task is to argue why a nonprofit group in your city should (or should not) offer as a fund-raising prize a trip to SeaWorld in Orlando, Florida, San Antonio, Texas, or San Diego, California. Examine the photographs of orcas in Figures 3.2 and 3.3 and describe the implicit argument that each photo seems to make about these whales. How might one or both of these photos be used to support an argument for or against the prize trip to SeaWorld? What reasons for going (or not going) to SeaWorld are implied by each photo? Briefly sketch out your argument for your group and explain your choice of photograph to support your position.

■ ■ ■

Expressing Reasons in *Because* Clauses

Chances are that when you were a child, the word *because* contained magical explanatory powers. Somehow *because* seemed decisive. It persuaded people to accept your view of the world; it changed people's minds. Later, as you got older, you discovered that *because* only introduced your arguments and that it was the reasons following *because* that made the difference. Still, *because* introduced you to the powers potentially residing in the adult world of logic.

FIGURE 3.2 Orca performance at a marine park

FIGURE 3.3 Jumping orcas

Of course, there are many other ways to express the logical connection between a reason and a claim. Our language is rich in ways of stating *because* relationships:

- The public should not support marine parks because these parks stressfully separate dolphins and orcas from their natural habitat.
- Marine parks stressfully separate dolphins and orcas from their natural habitat. Therefore the public should not support them.
- Marine parks stressfully separate dolphins and orcas from their natural habitat, so the public should not support them.
- One reason that the public should not support marine animal parks is that they stressfully separate dolphins and orcas from their natural habitat.
- My argument that the public should not support marine animal parks is based mainly on the grounds that they stressfully separate dolphins and orcas from their natural habitat.

Even though logical relationships can be stated in various ways, writing out one or more *because* clauses seems to be the most succinct and manageable way to clarify an argument for oneself. We therefore suggest that sometime in the writing process, you create a *working thesis statement* that summarizes your main reasons as because clauses attached to your claim.* Just when you compose your own working thesis statement depends largely on your writing process. Some writers like to plan out their whole argument from the start and often compose their working thesis statements with *because* clauses before they write their rough drafts. Others discover their arguments as they write. And sometimes it is a combination of both. For these writers, an extended working thesis statement is something they might write halfway through the composing process as a way of ordering their argument when various branches seem to be growing out of control. Or they might compose a working thesis statement at the very end as a way of checking the unity of the final product.

Whenever you write your extended thesis statement, the act of doing so can be simultaneously frustrating and thought provoking. Composing *because* clauses can be a powerful discovery tool, causing you to think of many different kinds of arguments to support your claim. But it is often difficult to wrestle your ideas into the *because* clause shape, which sometimes seems to be overly tidy for the complex network of ideas you are trying to work with. Nevertheless, trying to summarize your argument as a single claim with reasons should help you see more clearly what you have to do.

---

*A working thesis statement opposing the commercial use of captured dolphins and orcas might look like this: The public should not support marine parks because marine parks stressfully separate dolphins and orcas from their natural habitat; because they are mainly big businesses driven by profit; because they create inaccurate and incomplete educational information about dolphins and orcas; because they encourage inhumane breeding programs and hunts and captures; and because they promote an attitude of human dominance over animals. You might not put a bulky thesis statement like this into your essay; rather, a working thesis statement is a behind-the-scenes way of summarizing your argument so that you can see it whole and clear.

■ ■ ■   **FOR CLASS DISCUSSION**   Developing Claims and Reasons

Try this group exercise to help you see how writing *because* clauses can be a discovery procedure. Divide into small groups. Each group member should contribute an issue that he or she would like to explore. Discussing one person's issue at a time, help each member develop a claim supported by several reasons. Express each reason as a *because* clause. Then write out the working thesis statement for each person's argument by attaching the *because* clauses to the claim. Finally, try to create *because* clauses in support of an alternative claim for each issue. Recorders should select two or three working thesis statements from the group to present to the class as a whole.   ■ ■ ■

Conclusion

This chapter has introduced you to the structure of classical argument, to the rhetorical triangle (message, writer or speaker, and audience), and to the classical appeals of *logos, ethos*, and *pathos*. It has also shown how arguments originate in issue questions, how issue questions differ from information questions, and how arguments differ from pseudo-arguments. At the heart of this chapter we explained that the frame of an argument is a claim supported by reasons. As you generate reasons to support your own arguments, it is often helpful to articulate them as *because* clauses attached to the claim.

In the next chapter we will see how to support a reason by examining its logical structure, uncovering its unstated assumptions, and planning a strategy of development.

WRITING ASSIGNMENT   An Issue Question and Working Thesis Statements   MyWritingLab™

Decide on an issue and a claim for a classical argument that you would like to write. Write a one-sentence question that summarizes the controversial issue that your claim addresses. Then draft a working thesis statement for your proposed argument. Organize the thesis as a claim with bulleted *because* clauses for reasons. You should have at least two reasons, but it is okay to have three or four. Also include an opposing thesis statement—that is, a claim with *because* clauses for an alternative position on your issue.

Recall that in Part One we emphasized exploratory writing as a way of resisting closure and helping you wrestle with multiple perspectives. Now we ask you to begin a process of closure by developing a thesis statement that condenses your argument into a claim with supporting reasons. However, as we emphasize throughout this text, drafting itself is an exploratory process. Writers almost always discover new ideas when they write a first draft; as they take their writing project through multiple drafts, their views may change substantially. Often, in fact, honest writers can change positions on an issue by discovering that a counterargument is stronger than their own. So the working thesis statement that you submit for this assignment may evolve substantially once you begin to draft.

In this chapter, as well as in Chapters 4 and 5, we will follow the process of student writer Carmen Tieu as she constructs an argument on violent video games. During earlier exploratory writing, she wrote about a classroom incident in which her professor had described video game playing as gendered behavior (overwhelmingly male). The professor indicated his dislike for such games, pointing to their antisocial, dehumanizing values. In her freewrite, Carmen described her own enjoyment of violent video games—particularly first-person-shooter games—and explored the pleasure that she derived from beating boys at Halo 2. She knew that she wanted to write an argument on this issue. What follows is Carmen's submission for this assignment.

Carmen's Issue Question and Working Thesis Statements

Issue Question: Should girls be encouraged to play first-person-shooter video games?

My claim: First-person-shooter (FPS) video games are great activities for girls,

- because beating guys at their own game is empowering for girls
- because being skilled at FPS games frees girls from feminine stereotypes
- because they give girls a different way of bonding with males
- because they give girls new insights into a male subculture

Opposing claim: First-person-shooter games are a bad activity for anyone, especially girls,

- because they promote antisocial values such as indiscriminate killing
- because they amplify the bad, macho side of male stereotypes
- because they waste valuable time that could be spent on something constructive
- because FPS games could encourage women to see themselves as objects ■

MyWritingLab™

Visit Ch. 3 The Core of an Argument: A Claim with Reasons in *MyWritingLab* to complete the For Writing and Discussion and Writing Assignments and to test your understanding of the chapter objectives.

The Logical Structure of Arguments

What you will learn in this chapter:

4.1 To explain the logical structure of argument in terms of claim, reason, and assumption granted by the audience

4.2 To use the Toulmin system to describe an argument's logical structure

4.3 To use the Toulmin system to generate ideas for your argument and test it for completeness

In Chapter 3 you learned that the core of an argument is a claim supported by reasons and that these reasons can often be stated as *because* clauses attached to a claim. In the present chapter we examine the logical structure of arguments in more depth.

An Overview of *Logos*: What Do We Mean by the "Logical Structure" of an Argument?

4.1 To explain the logical structure of argument in terms of claim, reason, and assumption granted by the audience

As you will recall from our discussion of the rhetorical triangle, *logos* refers to the strength of an argument's support and its internal consistency. *Logos* is the argument's logical structure. But what do we mean by "logical structure"?

Formal Logic versus Real-World Logic

First of all, what we *don't* mean by logical structure is the kind of precise certainty you get in a philosophy class in formal logic. Logic classes deal with symbolic assertions that are universal and unchanging, such as "If all ps are qs and if r is a p, then r is a q." This statement is logically certain so long as p, q, and r are pure abstractions. But in the real world, p, q, and r turn into actual things, and the relationships among them suddenly become fuzzy. For example, p might be a class of actions called "Sexual Harassment," while q could be the class called "Actions That Justify Getting Fired from One's Job." If r is the class "Telling Off-Color Stories," then the logic of our p–q–r statement suggests that telling off-color stories (r) is an instance of sexual harassment (p), which in turn is an action justifying getting fired from one's job (q).

Now, most of us would agree that sexual harassment is a serious offense that might well justify getting fired. In turn, we might agree that telling off-color stories, if the jokes are sufficiently raunchy and are inflicted on an unwilling audience, constitutes sexual harassment. But few of us would want to say categorically that all people who tell off-color stories are harassing their listeners and ought to be fired. Most of us would want to know the particulars of the case before making a final judgment.

In the real world, then, it is difficult to say that *r*s are always *p*s or that every instance of a *p* results in *q*. That is why we discourage students from using the word *prove* in claims they write for arguments (as in "This paper will prove that euthanasia is wrong"). Real-world arguments seldom *prove* anything. They can only make a good case for something, a case that is more or less strong, more or less probable. Often the best you can hope for is to strengthen the resolve of those who agree with you or weaken the resistance of those who oppose you.

The Role of Assumptions

A key difference, then, between formal logic and real-world argument is that real-world arguments are not grounded in abstract, universal statements. Rather, as we shall see, they must be grounded in beliefs, assumptions, or values granted by the audience. A second important difference is that in real-world arguments, these beliefs, assumptions, or values are often unstated. So long as writer and audience share the same assumptions, it's fine to leave them unstated. But if these underlying assumptions aren't shared, the writer has a problem.

To illustrate the nature of this problem, consider one of the arguments we introduced in the last chapter.

> The public should not support marine parks because they stressfully separate dolphins and orcas from their natural habitat.

On the face of it, this is a plausible argument. But the argument is persuasive only if the audience agrees with the writer's assumption that it is wrong to separate wild animals from their natural habitats and social groups. What if you believed that confinement of wild animals is not always harmful or stressful to the animals, that the knowledge derived from the capture of wild animals enables humans to preserve the natural environment for these animals, and that the benefits to be gained from the captivity of a small number of wild animals outweigh the animals' loss of freedom? If this were the case, you might believe that marine parks have positive consequences so long as they strive to provide humane conditions for the animals, with minimal stress. If these were your beliefs, the argument wouldn't work for you because you would reject the underlying assumption. To persuade you with this line of reasoning, the writer would have to defend this assumption, showing why it is unwise or unethical to remove animals from their free and wild conditions.

The Core of an Argument: The Enthymeme

The previous core argument ("The public should not support marine parks because they stressfully separate dolphins and orcas from their natural habitat") is an incomplete logical structure called an *enthymeme*. Its persuasiveness depends on an underlying assumption or belief that the audience must accept. To complete the enthymeme and make it effective, the audience must willingly supply a missing premise—in this case, that it is wrong to separate wild animals from their natural environments. The Greek philosopher Aristotle showed how successful enthymemes root the speaker's argument in assumptions, beliefs, or values held by the audience. The word *enthymeme* comes from the Greek *en* (meaning "in") and *thumos* (meaning "mind"). Listeners or readers must have in mind an assumption, belief, or value that lets them willingly supply the missing premise. If the audience is unwilling to supply the missing premise, then the argument fails. Our point is that successful arguments depend both on what the arguer says and on what the audience already has "in mind."

To clarify the concept of "enthymeme," let's go over this same territory again, this time more slowly, examining what we mean by "incomplete logical structure." The sentence "The public should not support marine parks because they stressfully separate dolphins and orcas from their natural habitat" is an enthymeme. It combines a claim (the public should not support marine parks) with a reason expressed as a *because* clause (because they stressfully separate dolphins and orcas from their natural habitat). To render this enthymeme logically complete, the audience must willingly supply a missing assumption—that it is wrong to separate wild animals from their natural habitats. If your audience accepts this assumption, then you have a starting place on which to build an effective argument. If your audience doesn't accept this assumption, then you must supply another argument to support it, and so on until you find common ground with your audience.

To sum up:

1. Claims are supported with reasons. You can usually state a reason as a *because* clause attached to a claim (see Chapter 3).
2. A *because* clause attached to a claim is an incomplete logical structure called an enthymeme. To create a complete logical structure from an enthymeme, the underlying assumption (or assumptions) must be articulated.
3. To serve as an effective starting point for the argument, this underlying assumption should be a belief, value, or principle that the audience grants.

Let's illustrate this structure by putting the previous example into schematic form.

ENTHYMEME

CLAIM The public should not support marine parks

REASON because they stressfully separate dolphins and orcas from their natural habitat.

Audience must supply this assumption ———→

UNDERLYING ASSUMPTION

It is wrong to separate wild animals from their natural habitats.

The Power of Audience-Based Reasons

Aristotle's concept of the enthymeme focuses on the writer's need to create what we can now call "audience-based reasons" as opposed to "writer-based reasons." A reason that is persuasive to you might not be persuasive to your audience. Finding audience-based reasons means finding arguments effectively anchored within your audience's beliefs and values. To illustrate the difference between an audience-based reason and a writer-based reason, suppose that you are a vegetarian persuaded mainly by ethical arguments against causing needless suffering to animals. Suppose further that you wanted to persuade others to become vegetarians or at least to reduce their consumption of meat. Your "writer-based reason" for vegetarianism could be stated as follows:

> You should become a vegetarian because doing so will help reduce the needless suffering of animals.

The underlying assumption here is that it is wrong to cause the suffering of animals. This writer-based reason might also be an audience-based reason for persons who are wrestling with the moral dimension of animal suffering. But this assumption might not resonate with people who have made their own peace with eating meat. How might you use audience-based reasons to appeal to these meat-eaters? Here are two more possible enthymemes:

> You should become a vegetarian because doing so may help you lower your cholesterol.

> You should become a vegetarian because doing so will significantly lower your carbon footprint.

These arguments hook into the assumption that it is good to lower one's cholesterol (health values) or that it is good to lower one's carbon footprint (environmental values). All three of the arguments—whether based on ethics, health, or the environment—might further the practice of vegetarianism or at least reduce the amount of meat consumed, but they won't appeal equally to all audiences. From the perspective of logic alone, all three arguments are equally sound. But they will affect different audiences differently.

■ ■ ■   **FOR CLASS DISCUSSION**   **Identifying Underlying Assumptions and Choosing Audience-Based Reasons**

Part 1: Working individually or in small groups, identify the unstated assumption that the audience must supply in order to make the following enthymemes persuasive.

Example

Enthymeme: Rabbits make good pets because they are gentle.

Underlying assumption: Gentle animals make good pets.

1. We shouldn't elect Joe as committee chair because he is too bossy.
2. Airport screeners should use racial profiling because doing so will increase the odds of stopping terrorists.

3. Racial profiling should not be used by airport screeners because it violates a person's civil rights.
4. We should strengthen the Endangered Species Act because doing so will preserve genetic diversity on the planet.
5. The Endangered Species Act is too stringent because it severely damages the economy.

Part 2: In the following items, decide which of the two reasons offered would be more persuasive to the specified audience. How might the reason not chosen be effective for a different kind of audience? Be prepared to explain your reasoning.

1. Audience: people who advocate a pass/fail grading system on the grounds that the present grading system is too competitive
   a. We should keep the present grading system because it prepares people for the dog-eat-dog pressures of the business world.
   b. We should keep the present grading system because it tells students that certain standards of excellence must be met if individuals are to reach their full potential.
2. Audience: environmentalists
   a. We should support fracking for natural gas because doing so will help reduce our dependence on foreign sources of oil.
   b. We should support fracking for natural gas because doing so will provide a greener "bridge fuel" that will give us time to develop better renewable technologies.
3. Audience: conservative proponents of "family values"
   a. Same-sex marriages should be legalized because doing so will promote public acceptance of homosexuality.
   b. Same-sex marriages should be legalized because doing so will make it easier for gay people to establish and sustain long-term, stable relationships.

Adopting a Language for Describing Arguments: The Toulmin System

4.2 To use the Toulmin system to describe an argument's logical structure

Understanding a new field usually requires us to learn a new vocabulary. For example, if you were taking biology for the first time, you'd have to learn dozens and dozens of new terms. Luckily, the field of argument requires us to learn a mere handful of new terms. A particularly useful set of argument terms, one we'll be using occasionally throughout the rest of this text, comes from philosopher Stephen Toulmin. In the 1950s, Toulmin rejected the prevailing models of argument based on formal logic in favor of a very audience-based courtroom model.

Toulmin's courtroom model differs from formal logic in that it assumes that (1) all assertions and assumptions are contestable by "opposing counsel" and that (2) all final "verdicts" about the persuasiveness of the opposing arguments will be rendered by a neutral third party, a judge, or jury. As writers, keeping in mind the "opposing counsel" forces us to anticipate counterarguments and to question our assumptions. Keeping in mind the judge and jury reminds us to answer opposing arguments fully, without rancor, and to present positive reasons for supporting our case as well as negative reasons for disbelieving the opposing case. Above all else, Toulmin's model reminds us not to construct an argument that appeals only to those who already agree with us. In short, it helps arguers tailor arguments to their audiences.

The system we use for analyzing arguments combines Toulmin's language with Aristotle's concept of the enthymeme. It builds on the system you have already been practicing. We simply need to add a few key terms from Toulmin. The first term is Toulmin's *warrant,* the name we will now use for the underlying assumption that turns an enthymeme into a complete, logical structure as shown below.

Toulmin derives his term *warrant* from the concept of "warranty" or "guarantee." The warrant is the value, belief, or principle that the audience has to hold if the soundness of the argument is to be guaranteed or warranted. We sometimes make similar use of this word in ordinary language when we say, "That is an unwarranted conclusion," meaning one has leaped from information about a situation to a conclusion about that situation without any sort of general principle to justify or "warrant" that move. Thus the warrant—once accepted by the audience—"guarantees" the soundness of the argument.

ENTHYMEME

CLAIM The public should not support marine parks

REASON because they stressfully separate dolphins and orcas from their natural habitat.

Audience must supply this warrant ⟶

WARRANT

It is wrong to separate wild animals from their natural habitats.

But arguments need more than claims, reasons, and warrants. These are simply one-sentence statements—the frame of an argument, not a developed argument. To give body and weight to our arguments and make them convincing, we need what Toulmin calls *grounds* and *backing.* Let's start with grounds. Grounds are the supporting evidence that causes an audience to accept your reason. Grounds are facts, data, statistics, causal links, testimony, examples, anecdotes—the blood and muscle that flesh out the skeletal frame of your enthymeme. Toulmin suggests that grounds are "what you have to go on" in an argument—the stuff you can point to and present before a jury. Here is how grounds fit into our emerging argument schema:

ENTHYMEME

CLAIM The public should not support marine parks

REASON because they stressfully separate dolphins and orcas from their natural habitat.

Grounds support the reason → **GROUNDS**

Evidence and arguments showing stressful difference between dolphin and orca behavior in the wild and in captivity:

- In the wild, dolphins and orcas swim in pods, dolphins around forty miles a day, and orcas around sixty miles a day, in the open ocean whereas marine park tanks provide only a tiny fraction of that space.

- Evidence that separation from their family members and pods in their natural habitats creates emotional distress that can't be remedied by the presence of randomly selected other dolphins and orcas in these marine parks.

- Statistics that the stress caused by confinement and the echoes and noise of concrete pools, audiences, and music often results in the animals needing medication.

- Statistics that show that dolphins and orcas don't live as long in captivity as in their natural habitat.

In many cases, successful arguments require just these three components: a claim, a reason, and grounds. If the audience already accepts the unstated assumption behind the reason (the warrant), then the warrant can safely remain in the background, unstated and unexamined. But if there is a chance that the audience will question or doubt the warrant, then the writer needs to back it up by providing an argument in its support. *Backing* is the argument that supports the warrant. It may require no more than one or two sentences or as much as a major section in your argument. Its goal is to persuade the audience to accept the warrant. Here is how *backing* is added to our schema:

WARRANT

It is wrong to separate wild animals from their natural habitats.

Backing supports the warrant → **BACKING**

Arguments showing why it is unwise, unethical, or otherwise wrong to separate wild animals from their natural environments:

- Examples of wild animals (those in aquariums and zoos) that do not thrive in artificially constructed environments, that don't live long, or that suffer psychological stress from confinement

- An ecological argument about the beauty of animals in the wild and of the complexity of the natural webs of which animals are a part

- A philosophical argument that humans shouldn't treat animals as instruments for their own enjoyment or profit

Toulmin's system next asks us to imagine how a resistant audience would try to refute our argument. Specifically, the adversarial audience might challenge our reason and grounds by arguing that dolphins and orcas in captivity are not as stressed as we claim (evidence provided by veterinarians, caretakers, or animal trainers verifying that most sea mammals in captivity are in good health). Or the adversary might attack our warrant and backing by showing how the captivity of some wild animal might save the species from extinction or how animals are often saved from illness and predators by caring humans. An adversary might attack our philosophical or spiritual arguments by saying that the same reasoning, taken to its logical conclusion, would eliminate zoos and require all humans to become vegetarians or vegans. An adversary might even argue that dolphins and orcas enjoy being with humans and have the same capacity to be animal companions as dogs or horses.

In the case of the argument opposing dolphins in captivity, an adversary might offer one or more of the following rebuttals.

Writer must anticipate these attacks from skeptics

ENTHYMEME

CLAIM The public should not support marine parks

REASON because they stressfully separate dolphins and orcas from their natural habitat.

GROUNDS

Evidence and arguments showing stressful difference between dolphin behavior in the wild and in captivity:

- In the wild, dolphins swim in pods around forty miles a day in the open ocean whereas marine park tanks provide only a tiny fraction of that space.
- Evidence that the echoes from concrete pools, music of dolphin shows, and the applause and noise of audiences are stressful and harmful
- Statistics about the excessive number of performances or about the levels of stress hormones produced in dolphins

"POSSIBLE CONDITIONS OF REBUTTAL
A skeptic can attack the reason and grounds":

- Argument that these programs must observe strict accreditation standards for animal welfare, health, and education
- Marine parks exercise dophins' and orcas' intelligence and abilities and build on their natural behaviors.
- Many dolphins and orcas have been bred in captivity, so they aren't "wild."
- The education and entertainment provided by marine parks promote public concern for dolphins and orcas.

WARRANT

It is wrong to separate wild animals from their natural habitats.

BACKING

Arguments showing why it is unwise, unethical, or otherwise wrong to separate wild animals from their natural environments:

- Examples of wild animals (those in aquariums and zoos) that do not thrive in artificially constructed environments, that don't live long, or that suffer psychological stress from confinement
- An ecological argument about the beauty of animals in the wild and of the complexity of the natural webs of which animals are a part
- A philosophical argument that humans shouldn't treat animals as instruments for their own enjoyment or profit

"POSSIBLE CONDITIONS OF REBUTTAL
A skeptic can attack the warrant and backing."

- The natural habitat is not always the best environment for wild animals.
- Captivity may actually preserve some species.
- Scientists have been able to conduct valuable studies of dolphins and learn more about orcas in captivity, which would have been impossible in the wild.

As this example shows, adversarial readers can question an argument's reasons and grounds or its warrant and backing or sometimes both. Conditions of rebuttal remind writers to look at their arguments from the perspective of skeptics. The same principle can be illustrated in the following analysis of an argument that the minimum wage for fast-food workers should be raised to $15/hour.

ENTHYMEME

CLAIM The federal government should mandate a minimum living wage of $15/hour

REASON because such a wage will reduce poverty.

GROUNDS

- Statistical data showing that $15/hour will support a family of four at an above-poverty level

- Statistical data about the numbers of people affected by a higher minimum wage

---

CONDITIONS OF REBUTTAL ATTACKING GROUNDS

Raising minimum wage doesn't directly target the poor:

- Only about 20 percent of those receiving the minimum wage have incomes below the poverty line; the remaining 80 percent are often teenagers or second earners who come from families above the poverty line.

- Of those below the poverty line, 60 percent do not have jobs and would not benefit from a minimum wage. (The poor need jobs, not raises.)

- There are better ways to reduce poverty than increasing the minimum wage.

WARRANT

Policies that reduce poverty are good.

BACKING

Arguments showing how reducing the number of poor people reduces the ills associated with poverty.

- Data about crime rates in poor neighborhoods

- Data about poor education and health outcomes among poor people

- Data about the need for taxpayer assistance for those working at current minimum wage (food stamps, housing assistance)

CONDITIONS OF REBUTTAL ATTACKING WARRANT

Policies aimed at reducing poverty are good only if they don't bring harmful consequences that outweigh the good. Raising minimum wage brings many harmful consequences:

- Increases cost of goods to consumers

- Leads to fewer jobs as companies automate, hire fewer workers, or move to new locations

- Causes many small businesses to close their doors

Toulmin's final term, used to limit the force of a claim and indicate the degree of its probable truth, is *qualifier*. The qualifier reminds us that real-world arguments almost never prove a claim. We may say things such as *very likely, probably,* or *maybe* to indicate the strength of the claim we are willing to draw from our grounds and warrant. Thus if there are exceptions to your warrant or if your grounds are not very strong, you will have to qualify your claim. For example, you might say, "Except for limited cases of scientific research, dolphins and orcas should not be held in captivity," or "We should consider raising the minimum wage because doing so may be one possible way to reduce poverty." In our future displays of the Toulmin scheme we will omit the qualifiers, but you should always remember that no argument is 100 percent conclusive.

■ ■ ■   **FOR CLASS DISCUSSION**   Developing Enthymemes with the Toulmin Schema

Working individually or in small groups, imagine that you have to write arguments developing the five enthymemes listed in the For Class Discussion exercise on pages 70–71. Use the Toulmin schema to help you determine what you need to consider when developing each enthymeme. We suggest that you try a four-box diagram structure as a way of visualizing the schema. We have applied the Toulmin schema to the first enthymeme: "We shouldn't elect Joe as committee chair because he is too bossy."

ENTHYMEME

CLAIM We shouldn't elect Joe as committee chair
REASON because he is too bossy.

GROUNDS

Evidence of Joe's bossiness:

• Examples of the way he dominates meetings—doesn't call on people, talks too much

• Testimony about his bossiness from people who have served with him on committees

• Anecdotes about his abrasive style

CONDITIONS OF REBUTTAL
Attacking the reason and grounds

Evidence that Joe is not bossy or is only occasionally bossy:

• Counterevidence showing his collaborative style

• Testimony from people who have liked Joe as a leader and claim he isn't bossy; testimony about his cooperativeness and kindness

• Testimony that anecdotes about Joe's bossiness aren't typical

WARRANT

Bossy people make bad committee chairs.

BACKING

Problems caused by bossy committee chairs:

• Bossy people don't inspire cooperation and enthusiam.

• Bossy people make others angry.

• Bossy people tend to make bad decisions because they don't incorporate advice from others.

CONDITIONS OF REBUTTAL
Attacking the warrant and backing

• Arguments that bossiness can be a good trait

  • Sometimes bossy people make good chairpersons.

  • This committee needs a bossy person who can make decisions and get things done.

• Argument that Joe has other traits of good leadership that outweigh his bossiness

■ ■ ■

Using Toulmin's Schema to Plan and Test Your Argument

4.3 To use the Toulmin system to generate ideas for your argument and test it for completeness

So far we have seen that a claim, a reason, and a warrant form the frame for a line of reasoning in an argument. Most of the words in an argument, however, are devoted to grounds and backing.

Hypothetical Example: Cheerleaders as Athletes

For an illustration of how a writer can use the Toulmin schema to generate ideas for an argument, consider the following case. In April 2005, the Texas House of Representatives passed a bill banning "sexually suggestive" cheerleading. Across the nation, evening television show comedians poked fun at the bill, while newspaper editorialists debated its wisdom and constitutionality. In one of our classes, however, several students, including one who had earned a high school varsity letter in competitive cheerleading, defended the bill by contending that provocative dance moves hurt the athletic image of cheerleading. In the following example, which draws on ideas developed in class discussion, we create a hypothetical student writer (we'll call her Chandale) who argues in defense of the Texas bill. Chandale's argument is based on the following enthymeme:

> The bill banning suggestive dancing for high school cheerleaders is a good law because it promotes a view of female cheerleaders as athletes.

Chandale used the Toulmin schema to brainstorm ideas for developing her argument. Here are her notes:

Chandale's Planning Notes Using the Toulmin Schema

Enthymeme: The bill banning suggestive dancing for high school cheerleaders is a good law because it promotes a view of female cheerleaders as athletes.

Grounds: First, I've got to use evidence to show that cheerleaders are athletes.

- Cheerleaders at my high school are carefully chosen for their stamina and skill after exhausting two-week tryouts.
- We begin all practices with a mile run and an hour of warm-up exercises—we are also expected to work out on our own for at least an hour on weekends and on days without practice.
- We learned competitive routines and stunts consisting of lifts, tosses, flips, catches, and gymnastic moves. This requires athletic ability! We'd practice these stunts for hours each week.
- Throughout the year cheerleaders have to attend practices, camps, and workshops to learn new routines and stunts.
- Our squad competed in competitions around the state.
- Competitive cheerleading is a growing movement across the country—University of Maryland has made it a varsity sport for women.
- Skimpy uniforms and suggestive dance moves destroy this image by making women eye candy like the Dallas Cowboys cheerleaders.

Warrant: It is a good thing to view female cheerleaders as athletes.

Backing: Now I need to make the case that it is good to see cheerleaders as athletes rather than as eye candy.

- Athletic competition builds self-esteem, independence, and a powerful sense of achievement. It also contributes to health, strength, and conditioning.
- Competitive cheerleading is one of the few sports where teams are made up of both men and women. (Why is this good? Should I use this?)
- The suggestive dance moves turn women into sex objects whose function is to be gazed at by men, which suggests that women's value is based on their beauty and sex appeal.

- We are talking about HIGH SCHOOL cheerleading—it is a very bad early influence on girls to model themselves on Dallas Cowboys cheerleaders or sexy MTV videos of rock stars.
- Junior high girls want to do what senior high girls do—suggestive dance moves promote sexuality way too early.

Conditions of Rebuttal: Would anybody try to rebut my reasons and grounds that cheerleading is an athletic activity?

- No. I think it is obvious that cheerleading is an athletic activity once they see my evidence.
- However, they might not think of cheerleading as a sport. They might say that the University of Maryland just declared it a sport as a cheap way to meet Title IX federal rules to have more women's sports. I'll have to make sure that I show this is really a sport.
- They also might say that competitive cheerleading shouldn't be encouraged because it is too dangerous—lots of serious injuries, including paralysis, have been caused by mistakes in doing flips, lifts, and tosses. If I include this, maybe I could say that other sports are dangerous also, and it is in fact danger that makes this sport so exciting.

Would anyone doubt my warrant and backing that it is good to see female cheerleaders as athletes?

- Yes, all those people who laughed at the Texas legislature think that people are being too prudish and that banning suggestive dance moves violates free expression. I'll need to make my case that it is bad for young girls to see themselves as sex objects too early.

The information that Chandale lists under "grounds" is what she sees as the facts of the case—the hard data she will use as evidence to support her contention that cheerleading is an athletic activity. The paragraph that follows shows how this argument might look when placed in written form.

First Part of Chandale's Argument

Summarizes opposing view

States her claim

For grounds, uses personal experience details to show that cheerleading is an athletic activity

Although evening television show comedians have made fun of the Texas legislature's desire to ban "suggestive" dance moves from cheerleading routines, I applaud this bill because it promotes a healthy view of female cheerleaders as athletes rather than showgirls. I was lucky enough to attend a high school where cheerleading is a sport, and I earned a varsity letter as a cheerleader. To get on my high school's cheerleading squad, students have to go through an exhausting two-week tryout of workouts and instruction in the basic routines; then they are chosen based on their stamina and skill. Once on the squad, cheerleaders begin all practices with a mile run and an hour of grueling warm-up exercises, and they are expected to exercise on their own on weekends. As a result of this regimen, cheerleaders achieve and maintain a top level of physical fitness. In addition, to get on the squad, students must be able to do handstands, cartwheels, handsprings, high jumps, and the splits. Each year the squad builds up to its complex routines and stunts consisting of lifts, tosses, flips, catches, and gymnastic moves that only trained athletes can do. In tough competitions at the regional and state levels, the cheerleading squad demonstrates its athletic talent. This view of cheerleading as a competitive sport is also spreading to colleges. As reported recently in a number of newspapers, the University of Maryland has made cheerleading a varsity sport, and many other universities are following suit. Athletic performance of this caliber is a far cry from the sexy dancing that many high school girls often associate with cheerleading. By banning suggestive dancing in cheerleading routines, the Texas legislature creates an opportunity for schools to emphasize the athleticism of cheerleading.

Provides more grounds by showing emerging views of cheerleading as a competitive sport

As you can see, Chandale has plenty of evidence for arguing that competitive cheerleading is an athletic activity quite different from sexy dancing. But how effective is this argument as it stands? Is this all she needs? The Toulmin schema encourages writers to include—if needed for the intended audience—explicit support for their warrants as well as attention to conditions for rebuttal. Because the overwhelming national response to the Texas law was ridicule at the perceived prudishness of the legislators, Chandale decides to expand her argument as follows:

Continuation of Chandale's Argument

Supplies warrant: It is good to see cheerleaders as athletic and bad to see them as sex objects

This emphasis on cheerleaders as athletes rather than sexy dancers is good for girls. The erotic dance moves that many high school cheerleaders now incorporate into their routines show that they are emulating the Dallas Cowboys cheerleaders or pop stars on MTV. Our already sexually saturated culture (think of the suggestive clothing marketed to little girls) pushes girls and women to measure their value by their beauty and sex appeal. It would be far healthier, both physically and psychologically, if high school cheerleaders were identified as athletes. For women and men both, competitive cheerleading can build self-esteem, pride in teamwork, and a powerful sense of achievement, as well as promote health, strength, and fitness.

Supplies backing: Shows benefits that come from seeing cheerleaders as athletes

Anticipates an objection

Responds to objection by supplying more evidence that cheerleading is a sport; in fact it is a dangerous sport

Sums up by returning to claim

Some people might object to competitive cheerleading by saying that cheerleading isn't really a sport. Some have accused the University of Maryland of making cheerleading a varsity sport only as a cheap way of meeting Title IX requirements. But anyone who has watched competitive cheerleading, and imagined what it would be like to be thrown high into the air, knows instinctively that this is a sport indeed. In fact, other persons might object to competitive cheerleading because it is too dangerous, with potential for very severe injuries, including paralysis. Obviously the sport is dangerous—but so are many sports, including football, gymnastics, diving, and trampoline. The danger and difficulty of the sport is part of its appeal. Part of what can make cheerleaders as athletes better role models for girls than cheerleaders as erotic dancers is the courage and training needed for success. Of course, the Texas legislators might not have had athleticism in mind when they banned suggestive dancing. They might only have been promoting their vision of morality. But at stake are the role models we set for young girls. I'll pick an athlete over a Dallas Cowboys cheerleader every time.

Our example suggests how a writer can use the Toulmin schema to generate ideas for an argument. For evidence, Chandale draws primarily on her personal experiences as a cheerleader/athlete and on her knowledge of popular culture. She also draws on her reading of several newspaper articles about the University of Maryland making cheerleading a varsity sport. (In an academic paper rather than a newspaper editorial, she would need to document these sources through formal citations.) Although many arguments depend on research, many can be supported wholly or in part by your own personal experiences, so don't neglect the wealth of evidence from your own life when searching for data. (A more detailed discussion of evidence in arguments occurs in Chapter 5.)

Extended Student Example: Girls and Violent Video Games

Let's look at one more example of how the Toulmin system can help you generate ideas for your argument. In this case we will look at a complete example from student writer Carmen Tieu, whose evolving argument about girls and violent video games was introduced in the last chapter. Carmen's assignment was to write a "supporting reasons" argument, which is a shortened form of the classical argument described on pages 53–54. It has all the features of a classical argument except for the requirement to summarize and rebut opposing views. In planning her argument, Carmen decided to use four lines of reasoning, as shown in her *because* clauses listed on page 66. She began by creating a basic Toulmin frame for each reason:

Carmen's Toulmin Frames

My claim: Playing first-person-shooter (FPS) video games is good for girls

1. **Reason**: because playing FPS lets girls beat guys at their own game. **Warrant:** It is good for girls to beat guys at their own game.
2. **Reason:** because playing FPS games frees girls from feminine stereotypes. **Warrant:** It is good for girls to be freed from feminine stereotypes.
3. **Reason:** because playing FPS games gives girls a different way of bonding with males. **Warrant:** It is good for girls to find a different way of bonding with boys.
4. **Reason:** because playing FPS games gives girls new insights into a male subculture. **Warrant:** It is good for girls to get new insights into a male subculture.

As Carmen began drafting her essay, she was confident she could support her first three lines of reasoning. For reason 1 she could use evidence (grounds) from personal experience to show how she learned to beat guys at video games. She could also support her warrant by showing how beating boys made her feel empowered. For reason 2, she decided that she primarily needed to support her warrant (backing). It is obvious that playing FPS games breaks feminine stereotypes. What she had to show was why it was good or valuable to be freed from feminine stereotypes. Reason 3, she felt, needed support for both the reason and the warrant. She had to show how these games gave her a different way of bonding with males (grounds) and then why this different way was a good thing (backing). Carmen felt that her reason 4 was the most complex. Here are her more detailed planning notes for reason 4:

Carmen's Planning Notes for Reason 4

Enthymeme: First-person-shooter (FPS) video games are great activities for girls because playing these games gives girls new insights into male subculture.

Grounds: I've got to show the insights into male subculture I gained.

- The guys who play these video games are intensely competitive.
    - They can play for hours without stopping—intense concentration.
    - They don't multitask—no small talk during the games; total focus on playing.
    - They take delight in winning at all costs—they boast with every kill; they call each other losers.
- They often seem homophobic or misogynist.
    - They put each other down by calling opponents "faggot" and "wussy," or other similar names that are totally obscene.
    - They associate victory with being macho.

Warrant: It is beneficial for a girl to get these insights into male subculture.

Backing: How can I show these benefits?

- It was a good learning experience to see how girls' way of bonding is very different from that of boys; girls tend to be nicer to each other rather than insulting each other. Although I enjoy winning at FPS games, as a girl I feel alienated from this male subculture.

- The game atmosphere tends to bring out these homophobic traits; guys don't talk this way as much when they are doing other things.
- This experience helped me see why men may progress faster than women in a competitive business environment—men seem programmed to crush each other and they devote enormous energy to the process.
- What else can I say? I need to think about this further.

Based on these planning notes, Carmen's composed argument went through several drafts. Here is her final version.

Title makes persuasive claim

Why Violent Video Games Are Good for Girls

CARMEN TIEU (STUDENT)

Attention-grabbing scene

It is ten o'clock P.M., game time. My entire family knows by now that when I am home on Saturday nights, ten P.M. is my gaming night when I play my favorite first-person-shooter games, usually *Halo 3,* on Xbox Live. Seated in my mobile chair in front of my family's 42-inch flat screen HDTV, I log onto Xbox Live. A small message in the bottom of the screen appears with the words "Kr1pL3r is online," alerting me that one of my male friends is online and already playing. As the game loads, I send Kr1pL3r a game invite, and he joins me in the pre-game room lobby.

Continues scene and provides more background

In the game room lobby, all the players who will be participating in the match are chatting aggressively with each other: "Oh man, we're gonna own you guys so bad." When a member of the opposing team notices my gamer tag, "embracingapathy," he begins to insult me by calling me various degrading, gay-associated names: "Embracing apa-what? Man, it sounds so emo. Are you some fag? I bet you want me so bad. You're gonna get owned!" Players always assume from my gamer tag that I am a gay male, never a female. The possibility that I am a girl is the last thing on their minds. Of course, they are right that girls seldom play first-person-shooter games. Girls are socialized into activities that promote togetherness and talk, not high-intensity competition involving fantasized shooting and killing. The violent nature of the games tends to repulse girls. Opponents of violent video games typically hold that these games are so graphically violent that they will influence players to become amoral and sadistic. Feminists also argue that violent video games often objectify women by portraying them as sexualized toys for men's gratification. Although I understand these objections, I argue that playing first-person-shooter games can actually be good for girls.

Sums up opposing views

States claim

States first reason

For grounds, uses personal narrative to show how she can beat guys

Briefly backs warrant by showing the good feeling of empowerment

States second reason

Details focus on backing for warrant: It is good for girls to be freed from feminine stereotypes

Provides third reason   5

Uses a narrative example for grounds; shows how FPS games give her a different way of bonding with males

First, playing FPS games gives girls the chance to beat guys at their own game. When I first began playing *Halo 2,* I was horrible. My male friends constantly put me down for my lack of skills, constantly telling me that I was awful, "but for a girl, you're good." But it didn't take much practice until I learned to operate the two joy sticks with precision and with quick instinctual reactions. While guys and girls can play many physical games together, such as basketball or touch football, guys will always have the advantage because on average they are taller, faster, and stronger than females. However, when it comes to video games, girls can compete equally because physical strength isn't required, just quick reaction time and manual dexterity—skills that women possess in abundance. The adrenaline rush that I receive from beating a bunch of testosterone-driven guys at something they supposedly excel at is empowering and exciting; I especially savor the look of horror on their faces when I completely destroy them.

Since female video gamers are so rare, playing shooter games allows girls to be freed from feminine stereotypes and increases their confidence. Culture generally portrays females as caring, nonviolent, and motherly beings who are not supposed to enjoy FPS games with their war themes and violent killings. I am in no way rejecting these traditional female values since I myself am a compassionate, tree-hugging vegan. But I also like to break these stereotypes. Playing video games offers a great way for females to break the social mold of only doing "girly" things and introduces them to something that males commonly enjoy. Playing video games with sexist males has also helped me become more outspoken. Psychologically, I can stand up to aggressive males because I know that I can beat them at their own game. The confidence I've gotten from excelling at shooter games may have even carried over into the academic arena because I am majoring in chemical engineering and have no fear whatsoever of intruding into the male-dominated territory of math and science. Knowing that I can beat all the guys in my engineering classes at *Halo* gives me that little extra confidence boost during exams and labs.

Another reason for girls to play FPS games is that it gives us a different way of bonding with guys. Once when I was discussing my latest *Halo 3* matches with one of my regular male friends, a guy whom I didn't know turned around and said, "You play *Halo*? Wow, you just earned my respect." Although I was annoyed that this guy apparently didn't respect women in general, it is apparent that guys will talk to me differently now that I can play video games. From a guy's perspective I can also appreciate why males find video games so addicting. You get joy from perfecting your skills so that your high-angle grenade kills become a thing of beauty. While all of these skills may seem trivial to some, the acknowledgment of my skills from other players leaves me with a perverse sense of pride in knowing that I played the game better than everyone else. Since I have started playing, I have also noticed that it is much easier to talk to males about lots of different subjects. Talking video games with guys is a great ice-breaker that leads to different kinds of friendships outside the realm of romance and dating.

Finally, playing violent video games can be valuable for girls because it gives them insights into a disturbing part of male subculture. When the testosterone starts kicking in, guys become blatantly homophobic and misogynistic. Any player, regardless of gender, who cannot play well (as measured by having a high number of kills and a low number of deaths) is made fun of by being called gay, a girl, or worse. Even when some guys finally meet a female player, they will also insult her by calling her a lesbian or an ugly fat chick that has no life. Their insults towards the girl will dramatically increase if she beats them because they feel so humiliated. In their eyes, playing worse than a girl is embarrassing because girls are supposed to be inept at FPS games. Whenever I play *Halo* better than my male friends, they often comment on how "it makes no sense that we're getting owned by Carmen."

When males act like such sexist jerks it causes one to question if they are always like this. My answer is no because I know, first hand, that when guys like that are having one-on-one conversations with a female, they show a softer side, and the macho side goes away. They don't talk about how girls should stay in the kitchen and make them dinner, but rather how they think it is cool that they share a fun, common interest with a girl. But when they are in a group of males their fake, offensive macho side comes out. I find this phenomenon troubling because it shows a real problem in the way boys are socialized. To be a real "man" around other guys, they have to put down women and gays in activities involving aggressive behavior where men are supposed to excel. But they don't become macho and aggressive in activities like reading and writing, which they think of as feminine. I've always known that guys are more physically aggressive than women, but until playing violent video games I had never realized how this aggression is related to misogyny and homophobia. Perhaps these traits aren't deeply ingrained in men but come out primarily in a competitive male environment. Whatever the cause, it is an ugly phenomenon, and I'm glad that I learned more about it. Beating guys at FPS games has made me a more confident woman while being more aware of gender differences in the way men and women are socialized. I joined the guys in playing *Halo,* but I didn't join their subculture of ridiculing women and gays.

The Thesis-Governed "Self-Announcing" Structure of Classical Argument

Like the complete classical argument explained on pages 70–71, Carmen's supporting-reasons argument has a thesis-governed structure in which she states her claim near the end of the introduction, begins body paragraphs with clearly stated reasons, and uses effective transitions throughout to keep her reader on track. This kind of tightly organized structure is sometimes called a *self-announcing* or *closed-form* structure because the writer states his or her claim before beginning the body of the argument and forecasts the structure that is to follow. In contrast, an *unfolding* or *open-form* structure often doesn't give away the writer's position until late in the essay. (We discuss delayed-thesis arguments in Chapter 7.) A general rule of thumb for arguments using more than one line of reasoning is to place your most important or interesting reason last, where it will have the greatest impact on your readers.

In writing a self-announcing argument, students often ask how much of the argument to summarize in the thesis statement. Consider Carmen's options:

■ She might announce only her claim:

Playing first-person-shooter games can be good for girls.

■ She might forecast a series of parallel reasons:

There are several reasons that playing first-person-shooter games can be good for girls.

■ She might forecast the actual number of reasons:

I will present four reasons that playing first-person-shooter games can be good for girls.

■ Or she might forecast the whole argument by including her *because* clauses with her claim:

Playing first-person-shooter games can be good for girls because it lets girls feel empowered by beating guys at their own game, because it frees girls from feminine stereotypes, because it gives girls a different way of bonding with males, and because it gives girls new insights into a male subculture.

This last thesis statement forecasts not only the claim, but also the supporting reasons that will serve as topic sentences for key paragraphs throughout the body of the paper.

No formula can tell you precisely how much of your argument to forecast in the introduction. However, these suggestions can guide you. In writing a self-announcing argument, forecast only what is needed for clarity. In short arguments, readers often need only your claim. In longer arguments, however, or in especially complex ones, readers appreciate your forecasting the complete structure of the argument (claim with reasons). Also, as we explain in later chapters, the directness of classical argument is not always the best way to reach all audiences. On many occasions more open-form or delayed-thesis approaches are more effective.

■ ■ ■ **FOR WRITING AND DISCUSSION** **Reasons, Warrants, and Conditions** MyWritingLab™
                                          of Rebuttal

Individual task:

1. Choose one of the following reasons. Then write a passage that provides grounds to support the reason. Use details from personal experience or imagine plausible, hypothetical details.
   a. For college students, Web surfing or checking social media can be harmful because it causes you to waste so much study time.
   b. Rap has a bad influence on teenagers because it celebrates angry violence.
   c. The university's decision to charge more for parking permits for solo drivers is a good environmental plan because it encourages students to use public transportation.
2. Now create an argument to support the warrant for the reason you chose in 1. The warrants for each of the arguments are stated below.
   a. Support this warrant: Wasting study time is harmful for college students.
   b. Support this warrant: It is bad to celebrate angry violence.
   c. Support this warrant: It is good for the environment to encourage students to use public transportation.

Group task: Working in pairs, small groups, or as a whole class, share your strategies ■ ■ ■ for supporting your chosen reason and warrant.

Conclusion

Chapters 3 and 4 have provided an anatomy of argument. They have shown that the core of an argument is a claim with reasons that usually can be summarized in one or more *because* clauses attached to the claim. Often, it is as important to articulate and support the underlying assumptions in your argument (warrants) as it is to support the stated reasons because a successful argument should be rooted in your audience's beliefs and values. In order to plan an audience-based argument strategy, arguers can use the Toulmin schema to help them discover grounds, warrants, and backing for their arguments and test them through conditions of rebuttal.

A Note on the Informal Fallacies

The Toulmin system explained in this chapter is a response to the problem of uncertainty or inconclusiveness in real-world arguments, where we have to deal with probability as opposed to the certainty of formal logic. In the real world, we seldom encounter arguments that are absolutely conclusive. We can say that an argument is more or less "persuasive" or "non-persuasive" to certain audiences but not that it proves its case conclusively.

Another response to the problem of conclusiveness is the class of reasoning problems known as the informal fallacies. (You have probably at least heard of some of them with their exotic, Latinate, or sometimes funny names—hasty generalization, *post hoc ergo propter hoc*, slippery slope, or poisoning the well.) They are called "informal" because, like the Toulmin system, they don't focus on the form of the syllogism. Although the fallacies are not useful for helping writers plan and test their own arguments, they can often help us name what is uncertain or illogically seductive in someone else's argument. They function as a kind of compendium of the ways that flawed arguments can nevertheless seem persuasive on the surface. To provide flexibility in the way that informal fallacies can be integrated into a course, we have placed them all together in a convenient appendix (pages 397–404). In this text we discuss selected fallacies at moments when they are illuminating and relevant to the material at hand.

WRITING ASSIGNMENT   **Plan of an Argument's Details**   MyWritingLab™

This assignment asks you to return to the working thesis statement that you created for the brief writing assignment in Chapter 3. From that thesis statement extract one of your enthymemes (your claim with one of your *because* clauses). Write out the warrant for your enthymeme. Then use the Toulmin schema to brainstorm the details you might use (grounds, backing, conditions of rebuttal) to convert your enthymeme into a fleshed-out argument. Use as your model Chandale's planning notes on pages 77–78 or Carmen's planning notes on pages 81–82. Note that this is a process-oriented brainstorming task aimed at helping you generate ideas for an argument in progress. You may end up changing your ideas substantially as you compose the actual argument. (An assignment to write a complete "supporting reasons" argument like Carmen's comes at the end of the next chapter on uses of evidence.) ■

MyWritingLab™

Visit Ch. 4 The Logical Structure of Arguments in *MyWritingLab* to complete the For Writing and Discussion and Writing Assignments and to test your understanding of the chapter objectives.

Using Evidence Effectively

5

What you will learn in this chapter:

5.1 To explain the different kinds of evidence

5.2 To make your evidence persuasive by using the STAR criteria and other strategies

5.3 To understand evidence rhetorically by explaining how the selection and framing of evidence reveals an angle of vision

In Chapters 3 and 4 we introduced you to the concept of *logos*—the logical structure of reasons and evidence in an argument—and showed you how an effective argument advances the writer's claim by linking its supporting reasons to one or more assumptions, beliefs, or values held by the intended audience. In this chapter, we turn to the uses of evidence in argument. By "evidence," we mean all the verifiable data and information a writer might use as support for an argument. In Toulmin's terms, evidence is part of the "grounds" or "backing" of an argument in support of reasons or warrants. By understanding evidence rhetorically, you will better understand how to use evidence ethically, responsibly, and persuasively in your own arguments.

Kinds of Evidence

5.1 To explain the different kinds of evidence

Writers have numerous options for the kinds of evidence they can use in an argument, including personal experience, observations, interviews, questionnaires, field or laboratory research, or findings derived from researching primary or secondary sources found in libraries, databases, or the World Wide Web. Carmen Tieu's argument in the last chapter is based on personal experience. More commonly, college arguments require library and Internet research—what professors call "information literacy." The skills and knowledge needed for information literacy are explained in Part Five, where we show you how to find and evaluate sources, incorporate them into your own argument, and cite and document them properly. This chapter focuses more basically on how evidence functions rhetorically in an argument and how it is selected and framed.

We will begin by categorizing different kinds of evidence, illustrating how each kind might be incorporated into an argument, and suggesting the strengths and limitations of each.

Data from Personal Experience

One powerful kind of evidence comes from personal experience:

Example	Strengths and Limitations
Despite recent criticism that Ritalin is overprescribed for hyperactivity and attention-deficit disorder, it can often seem like a miracle drug. My little brother is a perfect example. Before he was given Ritalin, he was a terror in school.... [Tell the "before" and "after" story of your little brother.]	■ Personal-experience examples help readers identify with writer; they show writer's personal connection to the issue. ■ Vivid stories capture the imagination and appeal to *pathos*. ■ Skeptics may sometimes argue that personal-experience examples are insufficient (writer is guilty of hasty generalization), not typical, or not adequately scientific or verifiable.

Data from Observation or Field Research

You can also develop evidence by personally observing a phenomenon or by doing your own field research:

Example	Strengths and Limitations
The intersection at Fifth and Montgomery is particularly dangerous because pedestrians almost never find a comfortable break in the heavy flow of cars. On April 29, I watched fifty-seven pedestrians cross the street. Not once did cars stop in both directions before the pedestrian stepped off the sidewalk onto the street. [Continue with observed data about danger.]	■ Field research gives the feeling of scientific credibility. ■ It increases typicality by expanding database beyond example of one person. ■ It enhances the *ethos* of the writer as personally invested and reasonable. ■ Skeptics may point to flaws in how observations were conducted, showing how data are insufficient, inaccurate, or nontypical.

Data from Interviews, Questionnaires, Surveys

You can also gather data by interviewing stakeholders in a controversy, creating questionnaires, or doing surveys. (See pages 347–348 for advice on how to conduct this kind of field research.)

Example	Strengths and Limitations
Another reason to ban laptops from classrooms is the extent to which laptop users disturb other students. In a questionnaire that I distributed to fifty students in my residence hall, a surprising 60 percent said that they are annoyed by fellow students checking Facebook, sending e-mail, paying their bills, or surfing the Web while pretending to take notes in class. Additionally, I interviewed five students who gave me specific examples of how these distractions interfere with learning. [Report the examples.]	■ Interviews, questionnaires, and surveys enhance the sufficiency and typicality of evidence by expanding the database beyond the experiences of one person. ■ Quantitative data from questionnaires and surveys often increase the scientific feel of the argument. ■ Surveys and questionnaires often uncover local or recent data not available in published research. ■ Interviews can provide engaging personal stories, thus enhancing *pathos*. ■ Skeptics can raise doubts about research methodology, questionnaire design, or typicality of interview subjects.

Data from Library or Internet Research   For many arguments, evidence is derived from reading, particularly from library or Internet research. Part Five of this text helps you conduct effective research and incorporate research sources into your arguments:

Example	Strengths and Limitations
The belief that a high-carbohydrate, low-fat diet is the best way to lose weight has been challenged by research conducted by Walter Willett and his colleagues in the department of nutrition at the Harvard School of Public Health. Willett's research suggests that complex carbohydrates such as pasta and potatoes spike glucose levels, increasing the risk of diabetes. Additionally, some fats—especially monounsaturated and polyunsaturated fats found in nuts, fish, and most vegetable oils—help lower "bad" cholesterol levels (45).*	■ Researched evidence is often powerful, especially when sources are respected by your audience; writers can spotlight source's credentials through attributive tags (see Chapter 16, pages 368–370). ■ Researched data may take the form of facts, examples, quotations, summaries of research studies, and so forth (see Chapters 15 and 16). ■ Skeptics might doubt the accuracy of facts, the credentials of a source, or the research design of a study. They might also cite studies with different results. ■ Skeptics might raise doubts about sufficiency, typicality, or relevance of your research data.

Testimony   Writers frequently use testimony when direct data are either unavailable or highly technical or complex. Testimonial evidence can come from research or from interviews:

---

*Parenthetical citations in this example and the next follow the MLA documentation system. See Chapter 17 for a full discussion of how to cite and document sources.

Example	Strengths and Limitations
Although the Swedish economist Bjorn Lomborg claims that acid rain is not a significant problem, many environmentalists disagree. According to David Bellamany, president of the Conservation Foundation, "Acid rain does kill forests and people around the world, and it's still doing so in the most polluted places, such as Russia" (qtd. in *BBC News*).	▪ By itself, testimony is generally less persuasive than direct data. ▪ Persuasiveness can be increased if source has impressive credentials, which the writer can state through attributive tags introducing the testimony (see Chapter 16, pages 368–370). ▪ Skeptics might undermine testimonial evidence by questioning credentials of source, showing source's bias, or quoting a countersource.

Statistical Data   Many contemporary arguments rely heavily on statistical data, often supplemented by graphics such as tables, pie charts, and graphs. (See Chapter 9 for a discussion of the use of graphics in argument.)

Example	Strengths and Limitations
Americans are delaying marriage at a surprising rate. In 1970, 85 percent of Americans between ages twenty-five and twenty-nine were married. In 2010, however, only 45 percent were married (U.S. Census Bureau).	▪ Statistics can give powerful snapshots of aggregate data from a wide database. ▪ They are often used in conjunction with graphics (see pages 200–206). ▪ They can be calculated and displayed in different ways to achieve different rhetorical effects, so the reader must be wary (see page 101). ▪ Skeptics might question statistical methods, research design, and interpretation of data.

Hypothetical Examples, Cases, and Scenarios   Arguments occasionally use hypothetical examples, cases, or scenarios, particularly to illustrate conjectured consequences of an event or to test philosophical hypotheses:

Example	Strengths and Limitations
Consider what might happen if we continue to use biotech soybeans that are resistant to herbicides. The resistant gene, through cross-pollination, might be transferred to an ordinary weed, creating an out-of-control superweed that herbicides couldn't kill. Such a superweed could be an ecological disaster.	▪ Scenarios have strong imaginative appeal. ▪ They are persuasive only if they seem plausible. ▪ A scenario narrative often conveys a sense of "inevitability" even if the actual scenario is unlikely; hence rhetorical effect may be illogical. ▪ Skeptics might show the implausibility of the scenario or offer an alternative scenario.

Reasoned Sequence of Ideas   Sometimes arguments are supported with a reasoned sequence of ideas rather than with concrete facts or other forms of empirical evidence. The writer's concern is to support a point through a logical progression of ideas. Such arguments are conceptual, supported by linked ideas, rather than evidential. This kind of support occurs frequently in arguments and is often intermingled with evidential support.

Example	Strengths and Limitations
Embryonic stem cell research, despite its promise in fighting diseases, may have negative social consequences. This research encourages us to place embryos in the category of mere cellular matter that can be manipulated at will. Currently we reduce animals to this category when we genetically alter them for human purposes, such as engineering pigs to grow more human-like heart valves for use in transplants. Using human embryos in the same way—as material that can be altered and destroyed at will—may benefit society materially, but this quest for greater knowledge and control involves a reclassifying of embryos that could potentially lead to a devaluing of human life.	■ These sequences are often used in causal arguments to show how causes are linked to effects or in definitional or values arguments to show links among ideas. ■ They have great power to clarify values and show the belief structure on which a claim is founded. ■ They can sketch out ideas and connections that would otherwise remain latent. ■ Their effectiveness depends on the audience's acceptance of each link in the sequence of ideas. ■ Skeptics might raise objections at any link in the sequence, often by pointing to different values or outlining different consequences.

The Persuasive Use of Evidence

5.2 To make your evidence persuasive by using the STAR criteria and other strategies

We turn now from kinds of evidence to strategies for making evidence as convincing and persuasive as possible. Consider a target audience of educated, reasonable, and careful readers who approach an issue with healthy skepticism, open-minded but cautious. What demands would such readers make on a writer's use of evidence? To begin to answer that question, let's look at some general principles for using evidence persuasively.

Apply the STAR Criteria to Evidence

Our open-minded but skeptical audience would first of all expect the evidence to meet what rhetorician Richard Fulkerson calls the STAR criteria:*

Sufficiency: Is there enough evidence?

Typicality: Is the chosen evidence representative and typical?

Accuracy: Is the evidence accurate and up-to-date?

Relevance: Is the evidence relevant to the claim?

Let's examine each in turn.

---

*Richard Fulkerson, *Teaching the Argument in Writing* (Urbana, IL: National Council of Teachers of English, 1996), 44–53. In this section, we are indebted to Fulkerson's discussion.

Sufficiency of Evidence   How much evidence you need is a function of your rhetorical context. In a court trial, opposing attorneys often agree to waive evidence for points that aren't in doubt in order to concentrate on contested points. The more a claim is contested or the more your audience is skeptical, the more evidence you may need to present. If you provide too little evidence, you may be accused of *hasty generalization* (see Appendix, page 401), a reasoning fallacy in which a person makes a sweeping conclusion based on only one or two instances. On the other hand, if you provide too much evidence your argument may become overly long and tedious. You can guard against having too little or too much evidence by appropriately qualifying the claim your evidence supports.

> **Strong claim:** Working full-time seriously harms a student's grade point average. (much data needed—probably a combination of examples and statistical studies)
>
> **Qualified claim**: Working full-time often harms a student's grade point average. (a few representative examples may be enough)

Typicality of Evidence   Whenever you select evidence, readers need to believe the evidence is typical and representative rather than extreme instances. Suppose that you want to argue that students can combine full-time work with full-time college and cite the case of your friend Pam, who pulled a straight-A grade point average while working forty hours per week as a night receptionist in a small hotel. Your audience might doubt the typicality of Pam's case since a night receptionist can often use work hours for studying. What about more typical jobs, they'll ask, where you can't study while you work?

Accuracy of Evidence   Evidence can't be used ethically unless it is accurate and up-to-date, and it can't be persuasive unless the audience believes in the credibility of the writer's sources. We'll develop this point more fully later in this section.

Relevance of Evidence   Finally, evidence will be persuasive only if the reader considers it relevant to what is at stake in the dispute. Consider the following student argument: "I deserve an A in this course because I worked exceptionally hard." The student then cites substantial evidence of how hard he worked—a log of study hours, copies of multiple drafts of papers, testimony from friends, and so forth. But what is at stake here is the underlying assumption (warrant) that grades should be based on effort, not quality of work. The student provides ample evidence to support the reason ("I worked exceptionally hard") but this evidence is irrelevant for the warrant ("People who work exceptionally hard deserve an A"). Although some instructors may give partial credit for effort, the criterion for grades is usually the quality of the student's performance, not the student's time spent studying.

Establish a Trustworthy Ethos

Besides supplying evidence that meets the STAR criteria, you can make your evidence more persuasive by being fair, honest, and open to uncertainty (the appeal to *ethos*—see Chapter 6, pages 106–107). To establish your readers' confidence, you must first tell them the source of your evidence. If your evidence comes from personal experience or observation, your prose needs to make that clear. If your evidence comes from others (say through interviews or library/Internet research), you must indicate these sources through attributive tags (phrases like "according to T. Alvarez" or "as stated by a recent EPA report"). For academic papers, you must also cite and document your sources using an appropriate style for in-text citations and concluding bibliography. (Part Five of this text explains how to find, use, and cite research sources.) Finally, you need to be fair in the way you select evidence from your research sources. For example, it is unethical to take quotations out of context or to write an unfair summary that over-simplifies or distorts a source author's intended meaning.

Be Mindful of a Source's Distance from Original Data

When you support an argument through library/Internet research, you often encounter sources that report evidence from a second- or third-hand perspective. You need to imagine where your source author found the information that you now want to use in your own argument. How might you trace the process that led from the original data to your source author's use of it? Let's take as an example a passage from James Surowiecki's article on the minimum wage reprinted in Chapter 2. Because this is a magazine article rather than an academic paper, it contains no footnotes or bibliography, but Surowiecki nevertheless uses attributive tags to identify his main sources. Here is a passage from page 33:

**Passage from "The Pay Is Too Damn Low"
by James Surowiecki**

Attributive tag
(cites this study as his
source)

Purported factual
statement that we are
examining

[O]ver the past three decades, the U.S. economy has done a poor job of creating good middle-class jobs; five of the six fastest-growing job categories today pay less than the median wage. That's why, as a recent study by the economists John Schmitt and Janelle Jones has shown, low-wage workers are older and better educated than ever. More important, more of them are relying on their paychecks not for pin money or to pay for Friday-night dates but, rather, to support families.

   Much of Surowiecki's argument for increasing the minimum wage depends on evidence that low-wage workers are "older and better educated than ever." But we might ask, How does Surowiecki know about the age and education of low-wage workers? Why should we trust him? Using an attributive tag, he identifies his source as a recent study by economists John Schmitt and Janelle Jones. We plugged these names into a Google search and quickly located the source: A white paper titled, "Low-wage Workers Are Older and Better Educated than Ever," dated April 2012, from the Center for Economic and Policy Research, which, according to its Web site, is a nonprofit, nonpartisan research center aimed at providing factual economic data for public policy makers.

So where did Schmitt and Jones get their data? They cite statistical tables compiled by the "Current Population Survey," which is a joint effort of the Census Bureau and Bureau of Labor Statistics. Based on these original data, Schmitt and Jones constructed two graphs showing shifts in distribution of low-wage workers by age and then by education from 1971 to 2011. One of these graphs, for example, shows that in 1979, 26 percent of low-wage jobs were held by teenagers, but by 2011 only 12 percent were teenagers. (You can see this graph in Chapter 2, Figure 2.3, page 22). Conversely, the second graph shows that in 1979 only 25 percent of low-wage job holders had completed at least some college, but by 2011, 43 percent had completed some college.

Let's summarize the process we have just traced: The original data came from government statistics collected by the Census Bureau and the Bureau of Labor Statistics. Schmitt and Jones then converted these data into detailed graphs. Surowiecki then summarized the message of the graphs into his single sentence. If you were then to cite Surowiecki as your source for this same information, you would be depending on a chain of trust stretching from the original data through Schmitt and Jones and Surowiecki to you. Of course, you can't be expected to trace all your research-gathered evidence back to the original data, but you need to imagine that it is possible to do so. Ideally, the closer you can get to the original data, the more trustworthy your evidence. Often, unfortunately, fact-checkers employed by news sources or nonprofit organizations discover that purportedly accurate information cannot be traced back to a credible original source. They might show that the information is not factual at all, that it is derived from flawed or discredited studies, that it has been distorted unfairly, or that sometimes it has even been invented in the service of propaganda. *Politifact.com*, a nationally respected fact-checker, uses a "truth-o-meter" to rank purported evidential statements along a scale from "True" to "False," with the most egregiously false statements earning their famous "Pants-on-Fire" award. To develop a respected *ethos*, you need to develop your own internal truth-o-meter by being aware of a source's distance from the original data and by occasionally tracing back a piece of evidence to its origins.

Rhetorical Understanding of Evidence

5.3 To understand evidence rhetorically by explaining how the selection and framing of evidence reveals an angle of vision

In the previous section we presented some principles for persuasive use of evidence. We now ask you to look more closely at the rhetorical context in which evidence operates.

Angle of Vision and the Selection and Framing of Evidence

When we enter the argumentative arena, we come as complex, whole persons, not as disembodied computers that reach claims through a value-free calculus. We enter with our own ideologies, beliefs, values, and guiding assumptions as formed by our particular lived lives. These differences help explain why one person's terrorist might be another person's freedom fighter or why a hand gun in a drawer might be one person's defense against intruders and another person's child accident waiting to happen. In writing about guns, a believer in Second Amendment rights is apt to cite evidence that having a gun can stop a violent intruder or prevent a rape. Conversely, proponents of gun control are apt to cite evidence about accidental deaths or suicides. In an argument, evidence is always selected to further the arguer's claim and is never simply an inert, neutral "fact."

These guiding beliefs and values work together to create a writer's "angle of vision." By this term we mean a perspective, bias, lens, filter, frame, or screen that helps determine what a writer sees or doesn't see. This angle of vision makes certain items stand out in a field of data and other items become invisible. It both determines and reveals the writer's view of which data are important and which are trivial, which are significant, and which can be ignored.

To illustrate how angle of vision creates this kind of selective seeing, consider how two hypothetical speakers might select different data about homeless people when presenting speeches to their city council. The first speaker argues that the city should increase its services to the homeless. The second asks the city to promote tourism more aggressively. Their differing angles of vision will cause the two speakers to select different data about homeless people and to frame these data in different ways. Because the first speaker wants to increase the council's sympathy for the homeless, she frames homeless people positively by telling the story of one homeless man's struggle to find shelter and nutritious food. Her speech focuses primarily on the low number of tax dollars devoted to helping the homeless. In contrast, the second speaker, using data about lost tourist income, might frame the homeless as "panhandlers" by telling the story of obnoxious, urine-soaked winos who pester shoppers for handouts. As arguers, both speakers want their audience to see the homeless from their own angles of vision. Consequently, lost tourist dollars don't show up at all in the first speaker's argument, whereas the story of a homeless man's night in the cold doesn't show up in the second speaker's argument. As this example shows, one goal writers have in selecting and framing evidence is to bring the reader's view of the subject into alignment with the writer's angle of vision. The writer selects and frames evidence to limit and control what the reader sees.

To help you better understand the concepts of selection and framing, we offer the following exercise based on different angles of vision regarding "festival seating" at rock concerts. Because of nationally reported injuries and near-death experiences resulting from stage diving and crowd surfing at rock concerts, many cities have tried to ban festival seating that allows for the spontaneous creation of mosh pits. Critics of mosh pits have pointed to the injuries caused by crowd surfing and to the ensuing law-suits against concert venues. Meanwhile, supporters cite the almost ecstatic enjoyment of crowd-surfing rock fans who seek out concerts with "festival seating."

Suppose that your city has scheduled a public hearing on a proposed ordinance to ban mosh pits at rock concerts. Among the possible data and evidence available to various speakers are the following:

- Some bands, such as Nine Inch Nails, specify festival seating that allows a mosh pit area.
- A female mosher writing on the Internet says: "I experience a shared energy that is like no other when I am in the pit with the crowd. It is like we are all a bunch of atoms bouncing off of each other. It's great. Hey, some people get that feeling from basketball games. I get mine from the mosh pit."

- A student conducted a survey of fifty students on her campus who had attended rock concerts in the last six months. Of the respondents, 80 percent thought that mosh pits should be allowed at concerts.
- Narrative comments on these questionnaires included the following:
  - Mosh pits are a passion for me. I get an amazing rush when crowd surfing.
  - I don't like to be in a mosh pit or do crowd surfing. But I love festival seating and like to watch the mosh pits. For me, mosh pits are part of the ambience of a concert.
  - I know a girl who was groped in a mosh pit, and she'll never do one again. But I have never had any problems.
  - Mosh pits are dangerous and stupid. I think they should be outlawed.
  - If you are afraid of mosh pits, just stay away. Nobody forces you to go into a mosh pit! It is ridiculous to ban them because they are totally voluntary. They should just post big signs saying, "City assumes no responsibility for accidents occurring in mosh pit area."
- On September 14, 2013, six people were taken to hospitals with injuries after a mosh pit broke out at the Riot Fest music festival in Chicago.
- According to a 2008 ABC news special, a company specializing in crowd management at rock festivals estimated that "10,000 people have been injured in and around mosh pits in the last decade." The company said further that "most injuries incurred from mosh pits aren't actually by the moshers but by innocent bystanders."
- In 2005, a blogger reported breaking his nose on an elbow; another described having his lip ring pulled out. Another blogger on the same site described having his lip nearly sliced off by the neck of a bass guitar. The injury required seventy-eight stitches. In May 2008, fifty people were treated at emergency rooms for mosh pit injuries acquired at a Bamboozle concert in New Jersey.
- Twenty-four concert deaths were recorded in 2001, most of them in the area closest to the stage where people are packed in.
- A twenty-one-year-old man suffered cardiac arrest at a Metallica concert in Indiana and is now in a permanent vegetative state. Because he was jammed into the mosh pit area, nobody noticed he was in distress.
- A teenage girl suffered brain damage and memory loss at a 1998 Pearl Jam concert in Rapid City, South Dakota. According to her attorney, she hadn't intended to body surf or enter the mosh pit but "got sucked in while she was standing at its fringe."
- The Web site Wikihow offers tips on staying safe in a mosh pit. According to the site, "While it may seem otherwise, moshing is by no means a way to hurt someone. Moshing is about releasing aggression, and having fun while enjoying some awesome music."

■ ■ ■   **FOR WRITING AND DISCUSSION**   Creating Contrasting Angles of Vision   MyWritingLab™

Individual task: Compose two short speeches, one supporting the proposed city ordinance to ban mosh pits and one opposing it. How you use these data is up to you, but be able to explain your reasoning in the way you select and frame your evidence.

Group task: Working in pairs or as a whole class, share your speeches with class-mates. Then, after you have shared examples of different speeches, explain the approaches that different classmates employed. What principle of selection was used? If arguers included evidence contrary to their positions, how did they handle it, respond to it, minimize its importance, or otherwise channel its rhetorical effect?

EXAMINING VISUAL ARGUMENTS   MyWritingLab™

Crowd surfing in a mosh pit

Angle of Vision

Angle of vision can be conveyed visually as well as verbally. These photos display different angles of vision toward mosh pits. Suppose you were writing a blog in support of festival seating and mosh pits. Which image would you include in your posting? Why? Suppose alternatively that you were blogging against mosh pits, perhaps urging local officials to outlaw them. Which image would you choose? Why?

Analyze the visual features of these photographs in order to explain how they are constructed to create alternative angles of vision on mosh pits.

An alternative view of a mosh pit

Rhetorical Strategies for Framing Evidence

What we hope you learned from the preceding exercises is that an arguer consciously selects evidence from a wide field of data and then frames these data through rhetorical strategies that emphasize some data, minimize others, and guide the reader's response. Now that you have a basic idea of what we mean by framing of evidence, here are some strategies writers can use to guide what the reader sees and feels.

Strategies for Framing Evidence

- **Controlling the space given to supporting versus contrary evidence:** Depending on their audience and purpose, writers can devote most of their space to supporting evidence and minimal space to contrary evidence (or omit it entirely). Thus people arguing in favor of mosh pits may have used lots of evidence supporting mosh pits, including enthusiastic quotations from concertgoers, while omitting (or summarizing very rapidly) the data about the dangers of mosh pits.

- **Emphasizing a detailed story versus presenting lots of facts and statistics:** Often, writers can choose to support a point with a memorable individual case or with aggregate data such as statistics or lists of facts. A memorable story can have a strongly persuasive effect. For example, to create a negative view of mosh pits, a writer might tell the heartrending story of a teenager suffering permanent brain damage from being dropped on a mosh pit floor. In contrast, a supporter of mosh pits might tell the story of a happy music lover turned on to the concert scene by the rush of crowd surfing. A different strategy is to use facts and statistics rather than case narratives—for example, data about the frequency of mosh pit accidents, financial consequences of lawsuits, and so forth. The single-narrative case often has a more powerful rhetorical effect, but it is always open to the charge that it is an insufficient or nonrepresentative example. Vivid anecdotes make for interesting reading, but by themselves they may not be compelling logically. In contrast, aggregate data, often used in scholarly studies, can provide more compelling, logical evidence but sometimes make the prose wonkish and dense.

- **Providing contextual and interpretive comments when presenting data:** When citing data, writers can add brief contextual or interpretive comments that act as lenses over the readers' eyes to help them see the data from the writer's perspective. Suppose you want to support mosh pits, but also want to admit that mosh pits are dangerous. You could make that danger seem irrelevant or inconsequential by saying: "It is true that occasional mosh pit accidents happen, just as accidents happen in any kind of recreational activity such as swimming or weekend softball games." The concluding phrase frames the danger of mosh pits by comparing it to other recreational accidents that don't require special laws or regulations. The implied argument is this: banning mosh pits because of an occasional accident would be as silly as banning recreational swimming because of occasional accidents.

■ **Putting contrary evidence in subordinate positions:** Just as a photographer can place a flower at the center of a photograph or in the background, a writer can place a piece of data in a subordinate or main clause of a sentence. Note how the structure of the following sentence minimizes emphasis on the rarity of mosh pit accidents: "Although mosh pit accidents are rare, the danger to the city of multi-million-dollar liability lawsuits means that the city should nevertheless ban them for reasons of fiscal prudence." The factual data that mosh pit accidents are rare is summarized briefly and tucked away in a subordinate *although* clause, while the writer's own position is elaborated in the main clause where it receives grammatical emphasis. A writer with a different angle of vision might say, "Although some cities may occasionally be threatened with a lawsuit, serious accidents resulting from mosh pits are so rare that cities shouldn't interfere with the desires of music fans to conduct concerts as they please."

■ **Choosing labels and names that guide the reader's response to data:** One of the most subtle ways to control your readers' response to data is to choose labels and names that prompt them to see the issue as you do. If you like mosh pits, you might refer to the seating arrangements in a concert venue as "festival seating, where concertgoers have the opportunity to create a free-flowing mosh pit." If you don't like mosh pits, you might refer to the seating arrangements as "an accident-inviting use of empty space where rowdies can crowd together, slam into each other, and occasionally punch and kick." The labels you choose, along with the connotations of the words you select, urge your reader to share your angle of vision.

■ **Using images (photographs, drawings) to guide the reader's response to data:** Another strategy for moving your audience toward your angle of vision is to include a photograph or drawing that portrays a contested issue from your perspective. Consider how the photographs on page 98 make arguments about mosh pits. Most people agree that the first photo supports a positive view of mosh pits. The crowd looks happy and relaxed (rather than rowdy or out of control), and the young woman lifted above the crowd smiles broadly, her body relaxed, her arms extended. In contrast, the second photo emphasizes muscular men (rather than a smiling and relaxed woman) and threatens danger rather than harmony. The crowd seems on the verge of turning ugly. (See Chapter 9 for a complete discussion of the use of visuals in argument.)

■ **Revealing the value system that determines the writer's selection and framing of data:** Ultimately, how a writer selects and frames evidence is linked to the system of values that organize his or her argument. If you favor mosh pits, you probably favor maximizing the pleasure of concertgoers, promoting individual choice, and letting moshers assume the risk of their own behavior. If you want to forbid mosh pits, you probably favor minimizing risks, protecting the city from lawsuits, and protecting individuals from the danger of their own out-of-control actions. Sometimes you can foster connections with your audience by openly addressing the underlying values that you hope your audience shares with you. You can often frame your selected data by stating explicitly the values that guide your argument.

Special Strategies for Framing Statistical Evidence

Numbers and statistical data can be framed in so many ways that this category of evidence deserves its own separate treatment. By recognizing how writers frame numbers to support the story they want to tell, you will always be aware that other stories are also possible. Ethical use of numbers means that you use reputable sources for your basic data, that you don't invent or intentionally distort numbers for your own purposes, and that you don't ignore alternative points of view. Here are some of the choices writers make when framing statistical data:

- **Raw numbers versus percentages.** You can alter the rhetorical effect of a statistic by choosing between raw numbers and percentages. In the summer of 2002, many American parents panicked over what seemed like an epidemic of child abductions. If you cited the raw number of these abductions reported in the national news, this number, although small, could seem scary. But if you computed the actual percentage of American children who were abducted, that percentage was so infinitesimally small as to seem insignificant. You can apply this framing option directly to the mosh pit case. To emphasize the danger of mosh pits, you can say that twenty-four deaths occurred at rock concerts in a given year. To minimize this statistic, you could compute the percentage of deaths by dividing this number by the total number of people who attended rock concerts during the year, certainly a number in the several millions. From the perspective of percentages, the death rate at concerts is extremely low.

- **Median versus mean.** Another way to alter the rhetorical effect of numbers is to choose between the median and the mean. The mean is the average of all numbers on a list. The median is the middle number when all the numbers are arranged sequentially from high to low. In 2006 the mean annual income for retired families in the United States was $41,928—not a wealthy amount but enough to live on comfortably if you owned your own home. However, the median income was only $27,798, a figure that gives a much more striking picture of income distribution among older Americans. This median figure means that half of all retired families in the United States had annual incomes of $27,798 or less. The much higher mean income indicates that many retired Americans are quite wealthy. This wealth raises the average of all incomes (the mean) but doesn't affect the median.

- **Unadjusted versus adjusted numbers.** Suppose your boss told you that you were getting a 5 percent raise. You might be happy—unless inflation rates were running at 6 percent. Economic data can be hard to interpret across time unless the dollar amounts are adjusted for inflation. This same problem occurs in other areas. For example, comparing grade point averages of college graduates in 1970 versus 2012 means little unless one can somehow compensate for grade inflation.

- **Base point for statistical comparisons.** Suppose you create a graph of global average temperatures from 1998 to the present. This graph, with 1998 as a base starting point, will suggest that the earth is cooling slightly, not heating up. However, if you begin the graph in 1980, the line, though fluctuating, rises steadily. (See graph on page 248). One's choice of the base point for a comparison often makes a significant rhetorical difference.

■ ■ ■   **FOR CLASS DISCUSSION**   **Using Strategies to Frame Statistical Evidence**

A proposal to build a publicly funded sports stadium in a major American city yielded a wide range of statistical arguments. All of the following statements are reasonably faithful to the same facts:

- The stadium would be paid for by raising the sales tax from 8.2 percent to 8.3 percent during a twenty-year period.
- The sales tax increase is one-tenth of 1 percent.
- This increase represents an average of $7.50 per person per year—about the price of a large special coffee drink and a pastry.
- This increase represents $750 per five-person family over the twenty-year period of the tax.
- For a family building a new home in this city, this tax will increase building costs by $200.
- This is a $250 million tax increase for city residents.

How would you describe the costs of the proposed ballpark if you opposed the proposal?

How would you describe the costs if you supported the proposal?   ■ ■ ■

Creating a Plan for Gathering Evidence

We conclude this chapter with a list of brainstorming questions that may help you think of possible sources for evidence in your own argument. As you begin contemplating an argument, you can use the following checklist to help you think of possible sources for evidence.

A Checklist for Brainstorming Sources of Evidence

- What personal experiences have you had with this issue? What details from your life or the lives of your friends, acquaintances, or relatives might serve as examples or other kinds of evidence?
- What observational studies would be relevant to this issue?
- What people could you interview to provide insights or expert knowledge on this issue?
- What questions about your issue could be addressed in a survey or questionnaire?
- What useful information on this issue might encyclopedias or specialized references in your university library provide? (See Chapter 15.)
- What evidence might you seek on this issue using licensed databases to search for relevant articles from magazines, newspapers, and scholarly journals? (See Chapter 15.)
- How might an Internet search engine help you research this issue? (See Chapter 15.)
- What evidence might you find on this issue from reliable statistical resources such as U.S. Census Bureau data, the Centers for Disease Control, or *Statistical Abstract of the United States*? (See Chapter 15.)

Conclusion

Effective use of evidence is an essential skill for arguers. In this chapter we showed you various kinds of evidence ranging from personal experience to library/Internet research. We then discussed ways you can make your evidence persuasive by applying the STAR criteria, developing a trustworthy *ethos*, and being mindful of a secondary source's distance from the original data. We next examined how a writer's angle of vision influences his or her selection and framing of evidence. Finally, we described framing strategies for emphasizing evidence, de-emphasizing it, and guiding your reader's response to it.

WRITING ASSIGNMENT   **A Supporting-Reasons Argument**   MyWritingLab™

Write an argument that uses at least two reasons to support your claim. Your argument should include all the features of a classical argument except that you can omit the section on summarizing and responding to opposing views, which we will cover in Chapter 7. This assignment builds on the brief writing assignments in Chapter 3 (create a thesis statement for an argument) and Chapter 4 (brainstorm support for one of your enthymemes using the Toulmin schema). Like a complete classical argument, a supporting-reasons argument has a thesis-governed structure in which you state your claim at the end of the introduction, begin body paragraphs with clearly stated reasons, and use effective transitions throughout to keep your reader on track. In developing your own argument, place your most important, persuasive, or interesting reason last, where it will have the greatest impact on your readers. A model for a supporting-reasons argument is Carmen Tieu's "Why Violent Video Games Are Good for Girls" on pages 82–84. ∎

MyWritingLab™

> Visit Ch. 5 Using Evidence Effectively in *MyWritingLab* to complete the For Writing and Discussion, Examining Visual Arguments, and Writing Assignments and to test your understanding of the chapter objectives.

Moving Your Audience

Ethos, Pathos, and Kairos

What you will learn in this chapter:

6.1 To explain how the classical appeals of *logos, ethos,* and *pathos* work together to move your audience

6.2 To create effective appeals to *ethos*

6.3 To create effective appeals to *pathos*

6.4 To be mindful of *kairos* or the "timeliness" of your argument

6.5 To explain how images make visual appeals to *logos, ethos, pathos,* and *kairos*

6.6 To explain how audience-based reasons appeal to *logos, ethos, pathos,* and *kairos*

In Chapters 4 and 5 we focused on *logos*—the logical structure of reasons and evidence in argument. Even though we have treated *logos* in its own chapters, an effective arguer's concern for *logos* is always connected to *ethos* and *pathos* (see the rhetorical triangle introduced in Chapter 3, page 55) and always considers the *kairos*, or timeliness of the argument. This chapter explains how arguers can create effective appeals from *ethos*, *pathos*, and *kairos*. It also explains the crucial role played by concrete language, examples, narrative stories, and use of images in enhancing ethical and emotional appeals. We conclude by showing how audience-based reasons enhance *logos* while also appealing to *ethos* and *pathos*.

Logos, Ethos, and *Pathos* as Persuasive Appeals: An Overview

6.1 To explain how the classical appeals of *logos, ethos,* and *pathos* work together to move your audience

At first, one may be tempted to think of *logos, ethos,* and *pathos* as "ingredients" in an essay, like spices you add to a casserole. But a more appropriate metaphor might be that of different lamps and filters used on theater spotlights to vary lighting effects on a stage. Thus if you switch on a *pathos* lamp (possibly through using more concrete language or vivid examples), the resulting image will engage the audience's sympathy and emotions more deeply. If you overlay an *ethos* filter (perhaps by adopting a different tone toward your audience), the projected image of the writer as a person will be subtly altered. If you switch on a *logos* lamp (by adding, say, more data for evidence), you will draw the reader's attention to the logical appeal of the argument. Depending on how you modulate the lamps and filters, you shape and color your readers' perception of you and your argument.

Our metaphor is imperfect, of course, but our point is that *logos, ethos,* and *pathos* work together to create an impact on the reader. Consider, for example, the different impacts of the following arguments, all having roughly the same logical appeal.

1. People should adopt a vegetarian diet because doing so will help prevent the cruelty to animals caused by factory farming.
2. If you are planning to eat chicken tonight, please consider how much that chicken suffered so that you could have a tender and juicy meal. Commercial growers cram the chickens so tightly together into cages that they never walk on their own legs, see sunshine, or flap their wings. In fact, their beaks must be cut off to keep them from pecking each other's eyes out. One way to prevent such suffering is for more and more people to become vegetarians.
3. People who eat meat are no better than sadists who torture other sentient creatures to enhance their own pleasure. Unless you enjoy sadistic tyranny over others, you have only one choice: become a vegetarian.
4. People committed to justice might consider the extent to which our love of eating meat requires the agony of animals. A visit to a modern chicken factory—where chickens live their entire lives in tiny, darkened coops without room to spread their wings—might raise doubts about our right to inflict such suffering on sentient creatures. Indeed, such a visit might persuade us that vegetarianism is a more just alternative.

Each argument has roughly the same logical core:

ENTHYMEME

CLAIM People should adopt a vegetarian diet

REASON because doing so will help prevent the cruelty to animals caused by factory farming.

GROUNDS

- Evidence of suffering in commercial chicken farms, where chickens are crammed together and lash out at one another

- Evidence that only widespread adoption of vegetarianism will end factory farming

WARRANT

If we have an alternative to making animals suffer, we should use it.

But the impact of each argument varies. The difference between arguments 1 and 2, most of our students report, is the greater emotional power of argument 2. Whereas argument 1 refers only to the abstraction "cruelty to animals," argument 2 paints a vivid picture of chickens with their beaks cut off to prevent their pecking each other blind. Argument 2 makes a stronger appeal to *pathos* (not necessarily a stronger argument), stirring feelings by appealing simultaneously to the heart and to the head.

The difference between arguments 1 and 3 concerns both *ethos* and *pathos*. Argument 3 appeals to the emotions through highly charged words such as *torture, sadists,* and *tyranny.* But argument 3 also draws attention to its writer, and most of our students report not liking that writer very much. His stance is self-righteous and insulting. In contrast, argument 4's author establishes a more positive *ethos*. He establishes rapport by assuming his audience is committed to justice and by qualifying his argument with the conditional term *might.* He also invites sympathy for the chickens' plight—an appeal to *pathos*—by offering a specific description of chickens crammed into tiny coops.

Which of these arguments is best? The answer depends on the intended audience. Arguments 1 and 4 seem aimed at receptive audiences reasonably open to exploration of the issue, whereas arguments 2 and 3 seem designed to shock complacent audiences or to rally a group of True Believers. Even argument 3, which is too abusive to be effective in most instances, might work as a rallying speech at a convention of animal liberation activists.

Our point thus far is that *logos, ethos,* and *pathos* are different aspects of the same whole, different lenses for intensifying or softening the light beam you project onto the screen. Every choice you make as a writer affects in some way each of the three appeals. The rest of this chapter examines these choices in more detail.

How to Create an Effective *Ethos*: The Appeal to Credibility

6.2 To create effective appeals to *ethos*

The ancient Greek and Roman rhetoricians recognized that an argument would be more persuasive if the audience trusted the speaker. Aristotle argued that such trust resides within the speech itself, not in the prior reputation of the speaker. In the speaker's manner and delivery, tone, word choice, and arrangement of reasons, in the sympathy with which he or she treats alternative views, the speaker creates a trustworthy persona. Aristotle called the impact of the speaker's credibility the appeal from *ethos*. How does a writer create credibility? We suggest four ways:

- **Be knowledgeable about your issue.** The first way to gain credibility is to *be* credible—that is, to argue from a strong base of knowledge, to have at hand the examples, personal experiences, statistics, and other empirical data needed to make a sound case. If you have done your homework, you will command the attention of most audiences.
- **Be fair.** Besides being knowledgeable about your issue, you need to demonstrate fairness and courtesy to alternative views. Because true argument can occur only where people may reasonably disagree with one another, your *ethos* will be

strengthened if you demonstrate that you understand and empathize with other points of view. There are times, of course, when you may appropriately scorn an opposing view. But these times are rare, and they mostly occur when you address audiences predisposed to your view. Demonstrating empathy to alternative views is generally the best strategy.

- **Build a bridge to your audience.** A third means of establishing credibility—building a bridge to your audience—has been treated at length in our earlier discussions of audience-based reasons. By grounding your argument in shared values and assumptions, you demonstrate your goodwill and enhance your image as a trustworthy person respectful of your audience's views. We mention audience-based reasons here to show how this aspect of *logos*—finding the reasons that are most rooted in the audience's values—also affects your *ethos* as a person respectful of your readers' views.

- **Demonstrate professionalism.** Finally, you can enhance your *ethos* by the professionalism revealed in your manuscript itself: Appropriate style, careful editing and proofreading, accurate documentation, and adherence to the genre conventions expected by your audience all contribute to the image of the person behind the writing. If your manuscript is sloppy, marred by spelling or grammatical errors, or inattentive to the tone and style of the expected genre, your own credibility will be damaged.

How to Create *Pathos*: The Appeal to Beliefs and Emotions

6.3 To create effective appeals to *pathos*

Before the federal government outlawed unsolicited telephone marketing, newspapers published flurries of articles complaining about annoying telemarketers. Within this context, a United Parcel Service worker, Bobbi Buchanan, wanted to create sympathy for telemarketers. She wrote a *New York Times* op-ed piece entitled "Don't Hang Up, That's My Mom Calling," which begins as follows:

> The next time an annoying sales call interrupts your dinner, think of my 71-year-old mother, LaVerne, who works as a part-time telemarketer to supplement her social security income. To those Americans who have signed up for the new national do-not-call list, my mother is a pest, a nuisance, an invader of privacy. To others, she's just another anonymous voice on the other end of the line. But to those who know her, she's someone struggling to make a buck, to feed herself and pay her utilities—someone who personifies the great American way.

The editorial continues with a heartwarming description of LaVerne. Buchanan's rhetorical aim is to transform the reader's anonymous, depersonalized image of telemarketers into the concrete image of her mother: a "hardworking, first generation American; the daughter of a Pittsburgh steelworker; survivor of the Great Depression; the widow of a World War II veteran; a mother of seven, grandmother of eight, great-grandmother of three…." The intended effect is to alter our view of telemarketers through the positive emotions triggered by our identification with LaVerne.

By urging readers to think of "my mother, LaVerne" instead of an anonymous telemarketer, Buchanan illustrates the power of *pathos,* an appeal to the reader's emotions. Arguers create pathetic appeals whenever they connect their claims to readers' values, thus triggering positive or negative emotions depending on whether these values are affirmed or transgressed. Pro-life proponents appeal to *pathos* when they graphically describe the dismemberment of a fetus during an abortion. Proponents of improved women's health and status in Africa do so when they describe the helplessness of wives forced to have unprotected sex with husbands likely infected with HIV. Opponents of oil exploration in the Arctic National Wildlife Refuge (ANWR) do so when they lovingly describe the calving grounds of caribou.

Are such appeals legitimate? Our answer is yes, if they intensify and deepen our response to an issue rather than divert our attention from it. Because understanding is a matter of feeling as well as perceiving, *pathos* can give access to nonlogical, but not necessarily nonrational, ways of knowing. *Pathos* helps us see what is deeply at stake in an issue, what matters to the whole person. Appeals to *pathos* help readers walk in the writer's shoes. That is why arguments are often improved through the use of stories that make issues come alive or sensory details that allow us to see, feel, and taste the reality of a problem.

Appeals to *pathos* become illegitimate, we believe, when they confuse an issue rather than clarify it. Consider the case of a student who argues that Professor Jones ought to raise his grade from a D to a C, lest he lose his scholarship and be forced to leave college, shattering the dreams of his dear old grandmother. To the extent that students' grades should be based on performance or effort, the student's image of the dear old grandmother is an illegitimate appeal to *pathos* because it diverts the reader from rational to irrational criteria. The weeping grandmother may provide a legitimate motive for the student to study harder but not for the professor to change a grade.

Although it is difficult to classify all the ways that writers can create appeals from *pathos,* we will focus on four strategies: concrete language; specific examples and illustrations; narratives; and connotations of words, metaphors, and analogies. Each of these strategies lends "presence" to an argument by creating immediacy and emotional impact.

Use Concrete Language

Concrete language—one of the chief ways that writers achieve voice—can increase the liveliness, interest level, and personality of a writer's prose. When used in argument, concrete language typically heightens *pathos.* For example, consider the differences between the first and second drafts of the following student argument:

First Draft

People who prefer driving a car to taking a bus think that taking the bus will increase the stress of the daily commute. Just the opposite is true. Not being able to find a parking spot when in a hurry to be at work or school can cause a person stress. Taking the bus gives a person time to read or sleep, etc. It could be used as a mental break.

Second Draft (Concrete Language Added)

Taking the bus can be more relaxing than driving a car. Having someone else behind the wheel gives people time to chat with friends or study for an exam. They can check Facebook and Twitter, send text messages, doze off, read the daily newspaper, or get lost in a novel rather than foam at the mouth looking for a parking space.

In this revision, specific details enliven the prose by creating images that trigger positive feelings. Who wouldn't want some free time to doze off or to get lost in a novel?

Use Specific Examples and Illustrations

Specific examples and illustrations serve two purposes in an argument. They provide evidence that supports your reasons; simultaneously, they give your argument presence and emotional resonance. Note the flatness of the following draft arguing for the value of multicultural studies in a university core curriculum:

First Draft

Another advantage of a multicultural education is that it will help us see our own culture in a broader perspective. If all we know is our own heritage, we might not be inclined to see anything bad about this heritage because we won't know anything else. But if we study other heritages, we can see the costs and benefits of our own heritage.

Now note the increase in "presence" when the writer adds a specific example:

Second Draft (Example Added)

Another advantage of multicultural education is that it raises questions about traditional Western values. For example, owning private property (such as buying your own home) is part of the American dream. However, in studying the beliefs of American Indians, students are confronted with a very different view of private property. When the U.S. government sought to buy land in the Pacific Northwest from Chief Sealth, he is alleged to have replied:

> The president in Washington sends words that he wishes to buy our land. But how can you buy or sell the sky? The land? The idea is strange to us. If we do not own the freshness of the air and the sparkle of the water, how can you buy them?[…] We are part of the earth and it is part of us.[…] This we know: The earth does not belong to man, man belongs to the earth.

Our class was shocked by the contrast between traditional Western views of property and Chief Sealth's views. One of our best class discussions was initiated by this quotation from Chief Sealth. Had we not been exposed to a view from another culture, we would have never been led to question the "rightness" of Western values.

The writer begins his revision by evoking a traditional Western view of private property, which he then questions by shifting to Chief Sealth's vision of land as open, endless, and unobtainable as the sky. Through the use of a specific example, the writer brings to life his previously abstract point about the benefit of multicultural education.

Use Narratives

A particularly powerful way to evoke *pathos* is to tell a story that either leads into your claim or embodies it implicitly and that appeals to your readers' feelings and imagination. Brief narratives—whether true or hypothetical—are particularly effective as opening attention grabbers for an argument. To illustrate how an introductory narrative (either a story or a brief scene) can create pathetic appeals, consider the following first paragraph to an argument opposing jet skis:

> I dove off the dock into the lake, and as I approached the surface I could see the sun shining through the water. As my head popped out, I located my cousin a few feet away in a rowboat waiting to escort me as I, a twelve-year-old girl, attempted to swim across the mile-wide, pristine lake and back to our dock. I made it, and that glorious summer day is one of my most precious memories. Today, however, no one would dare attempt that swim. Jet skis have taken over this small lake where I spent many summers with my grandparents. Dozens of whining jet skis crisscross the lake, ruining it for swimming, fishing, canoeing, rowboating, and even water-skiing. More stringent state laws are needed to control jet skiing because it interferes with other uses of lakes and is currently very dangerous.

This narrative makes a case for a particular point of view toward jet skis by winning our identification with the writer's experience. She invites us to relive that experience with her while she also taps into our own treasured memories of summer experiences that have been destroyed by change.

Opening narratives to evoke *pathos* can be powerfully effective, but they are also risky. If they are too private, too self-indulgent, too sentimental, or even too dramatic and forceful, they can backfire on you. If you have doubts about an opening narrative, read it to a sample audience before using it in your final draft.

Use Words, Metaphors, and Analogies with Appropriate Connotations

Another way of appealing to *pathos* is to select words, metaphors, or analogies with connotations that match your aim. We have already described this strategy in our discussion of the "framing" of evidence (Chapter 5, pages 99–100). By using words with particular connotations, a writer guides readers to see the issue through the writer's angle of vision. Thus if you want to create positive feelings about a recent city council decision, you can call it "bold and decisive"; if you want to create negative feelings, you can call it "short-sighted and autocratic." Similarly, writers can use favorable or unfavorable metaphors and analogies to evoke different imaginative or emotional responses. A tax bill might be viewed as a "potentially fatal poison pill" or as "unpleasant but necessary economic medicine." In each of these cases, the words create an emotional as well as intellectual response.

■ ■ ■ **FOR CLASS DISCUSSION** **Incorporating Appeals to** *Pathos*

Outside class, rewrite the introduction to one of your previous papers (or a current draft) to include more appeals to *pathos*. Use any of the strategies for giving your argument presence: concrete language, specific examples, narratives, metaphors, analogies, and connotative words. Bring both your original and your rewritten introductions to class. In pairs or in groups, discuss the comparative effectiveness of these introductions in trying to reach your intended audience. ■ ■ ■

Kairos: The Timeliness and Fitness of Arguments

6.4 To be mindful of *kairos* or the "timeliness" of your argument

To increase your argument's effectiveness, you need to consider not only its appeals to *logos, ethos,* and *pathos,* but also its *kairos*—that is, its timing, its appropriateness for the occasion. *Kairos* is one of those wonderful words adopted from another language (in this case, ancient Greek) that is impossible to define, yet powerful in what it represents. In Greek, *kairos* means "right time," "season," or "opportunity." It differs subtly from the ordinary Greek word for time, *chronos,* the root of our words "chronology" and "chronometer." You can measure *chronos* by looking at your watch, but you measure *kairos* by sensing the opportune time through psychological attentiveness to situation and meaning. To think *kairotically* is to be attuned to the total context of a situation in order to act in the right way at the right moment. By analogy, consider a skilled base runner who senses the right moment to steal second, a wise teacher who senses the right moment to praise or critique a student's performance, or a successful psychotherapist who senses the right moment to talk rather than listen in a counseling session. *Kairos* reminds us that a rhetorical situation is not stable and fixed, but evolves as events unfold or as audiences experience the psychological ebbs and flows of attention and care. Here are some examples that illustrate the range of insights contained by the term *kairos*:

■ If you write a letter to the editor of a newspaper or post a response to a blog, you usually have a one- or two-day window before a current event becomes "old news" and is no longer interesting. An out-of-date response will go unread, not because it is poorly written or argued but because it misses its *kairotic* moment. (Similar instances of lost timeliness occur in class discussions: On how many occasions have you wanted to contribute an idea to class discussion, but the professor doesn't acknowledge your raised hand? When you finally are called on, the *kairotic* moment has passed.)

■ Bobbi Buchanan's "Don't Hang Up, That's My Mom Calling," which we used to illustrate *pathos* (page 107), could have been written only during a brief historical period when telemarketing was being publicly debated. Moreover, it could have been written only late in that period, after numerous writers had attacked telemarketers. The piece was published in the *New York Times* because the editor received it at the right *kairotic* moment.

■   A sociology major is writing a senior capstone paper for graduation. The due date for the paper is fixed, so the timing of the paper isn't at issue. But *kairos* is still relevant. It urges the student to consider what is appropriate for such a paper. What is the "right way" to produce a sociology paper at this moment in the history of the discipline? Currently, what are leading-edge versus trailing-edge questions in sociology? What theorists are now in vogue? What research methods would most impress a judging committee? How would a good capstone paper written in 2015 differ from one written a decade earlier?

As you can see from these examples, *kairos* concerns a whole range of questions connected to the timing, fitness, appropriateness, and proportions of a message within an evolving rhetorical context. There are no rules to help you determine the *kairotic* moment for your argument, but being attuned to *kairos* will help you "read" your audience and rhetorical situation in a dynamic way.

Often you can establish the *kairos* of your argument in the opening sentences of your introduction. An introduction might mention a recent news event, political speech, legislative bill, or current societal problem that the audience may have experienced, thereby using awareness of *kairos* to connect with the audience's interests, knowledge, and experience. Elsewhere in your argument, attention to *kairos* can infuse currency and immediacy by establishing the stakes in the argument and enlist the audience's concern. For example, if you were going to argue that your university's policy on laptops in the classroom is too restrictive, you might enhance your argument by mentioning several recent editorials in your campus newspaper on this subject. If you were going to argue for increased urban gardening in your city, you might site a recent TED talk on successful experiments with urban gardening. If you are creating a text that includes images, you might also establish *kairos* through a photograph or cartoon that signals appropriate currency. Thinking about *kairos* helps you focus on the public conversation your argument is joining and on the interests, knowledge, and values of your audience.

■ ■ ■   **FOR CLASS DISCUSSION**   **Analyzing an Argument from the Perspectives of *Logos, Ethos, Pathos,* and *Kairos***

Your instructor will select an argument for analysis. Working in small groups or as a whole class, analyze the assigned argument first from the perspective of *kairos* and then from the perspectives of *logos, ethos,* and *pathos.*

1. As you analyze the argument from the perspective of *kairos,* consider the following questions:
    a. What is the motivating occasion for this argument? That is, what causes this writer to put pen to paper or fingers to keyboard?

b. What conversation is the writer joining? Who are the other voices in this conversation? What are these voices saying that compels the writer to add his or her own voice? How was the stage set to create the *kairotic* moment for this argument?

c. Who is the writer's intended audience and why?

d. What is the writer's purpose? Toward what view or action is the writer trying to persuade his or her audience?

e. To what extent can various features of the argument be explained by your understanding of its *kairotic* moment?

2. Now analyze the same argument for its appeals to *logos, ethos,* and *pathos*. How successful is this argument in achieving its writer's purpose?

Using Images to Appeal to *Logos, Ethos, Pathos,* and *Kairos*

6.5 To explain how images make visual appeals to *logos, ethos, pathos,* and *kairos*

One of the most powerful ways to move your audience is to use photos or other images that can appeal to *logos, ethos, pathos,* and *kairos* in one glance. (Chapter 9 focuses exclusively on visual rhetoric—the persuasive power of images.) Although many written arguments do not lend themselves to visual illustrations, we suggest that when you construct arguments you consider the potential of visual support. Imagine that your argument were to be delivered as a PowerPoint presentation or appear in a newspaper, in a magazine, or on a Web site where space would be provided for one or two visuals. What photographs or drawings might help persuade your audience toward your perspective?

When images work well, they make particularly powerful appeals to *pathos* analogous to the verbal strategies of concrete language, specific illustrations, narratives, and connotative words. The challenge in using visuals is to find material that is straightforward enough to be understood without elaborate explanations, that is timely and relevant, and that clearly adds impact to a specific part of your argument. As an example, suppose you are writing an argument supporting fund-raising efforts to help a third-world country that has recently experienced a natural catastrophe. To add a powerful appeal to *pathos,* you might consider incorporating into your argument the photograph shown in Figure 6.1 of the devastation and personal loss caused by typhoon Haiyan in the Philippines in 2013. A photograph such as this one can evoke a strong emotional and imaginative response as well as make viewers think.

FOR WRITING AND DISCUSSION **Analyzing Images as Appeals to *Pathos*** **MyWritingLab**™

Individual task: Use the following questions to analyze the photo in Figure 6.1.

1. How would you describe the emotional/imaginative impact of Figure 6.1? What details of the photo specifically create its appeal to *pathos*?

2. Many disaster-relief photos seek to convey the magnitude of the destruction and suffering, sometimes shockingly, by depicting destroyed buildings, mangled

FIGURE 6.1 Photo after Typhoon Haiyan in the Philippines

bodies, and images of human misery. How is your response to Figure 6.1 similar to or different from your response to commonly encountered close-up photographs of grief-stricken victims or to distance shots of widespread destruction? To what extent is Figure 6-1's story—told from the perspective of a child—different from the more typical photographs of destroyed buildings or anguished faces?

3. After searching the Web for other photos taken after typhoon Haiyan, write a rationale for why you would, or would not, choose this photo to accompany a proposal argument appealing for support for people in this region of the Philippines.

Group task: Share your individual analysis and rationale with others in your class.

EXAMINING VISUAL ARGUMENTS

MyWritingLab™

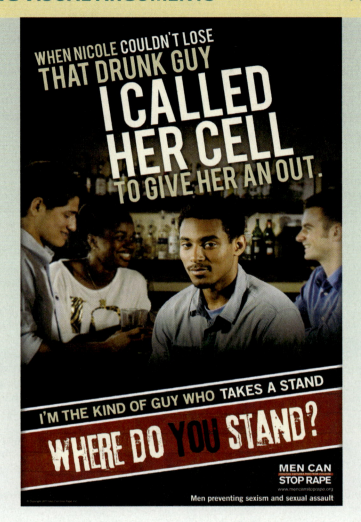

Logos, Ethos, Pathos, and *Kairos*

Efforts to combat sexual assault and the culture of date rape on campuses have figured prominently in public conversation recently, with discussions booming on the Web sites of newly formed organizations and stories of rallies on university campuses appearing on news sites. As this advocacy poster shows, the need to bolster bystander intervention is a critical piece in addressing this problem.

How does this advocacy poster attempt to move its audience? Analyze the poster's visual and verbal appeals to *logos, ethos, pathos,* and *kairos.*

How Audience-Based Reasons Appeal
To *Logos, Ethos, Pathos,* and *Kairos*

6.6 To explain how audience-based reasons appeal to *logos ethos, pathos,* and *kairos*

We conclude this chapter by returning to the concept of audience-based reasons that we introduced in Chapter 4. Audience-based reasons enhance *logos* because they build on underlying assumptions (warrants) that the audience is likely to accept. But they also enhance *ethos, pathos,* and *kairos* by helping the audience identify with the writer, by appealing to shared beliefs and values, and by conveying a shared sense of an issue's timeliness. To consider the needs of your audience, you can ask yourself the following questions:

Questions for Analyzing Your Audience

What to Ask	Why to Ask It
1. *Who is your audience?*	Your answer will help you think about audience-based reasons.
	▪ Are you writing to a single person, a committee, or the general readership of a newspaper, magazine, blog site, and so forth?
	▪ Are your readers academics, professionals, fellow students, general citizens, or people with specialized background and interests?
	▪ Can you expect your audience to be politically and culturally liberal, middle of the road, conservative, or all over the map? What about their religious views?
	▪ How do you picture your audience in terms of social class, ethnicity, gender, sexual orientation, age, and cultural identity?
	▪ To what extent does your audience share your own interests and cultural position? Are you writing to insiders or outsiders with regard to your own values and beliefs?
2. *How much does your audience know or care about your issue?*	Your answer can especially affect your introduction and conclusion:
	▪ Do your readers need background on your issue or are they already in the conversation?
	▪ If you are writing to specific decision makers, are they currently aware of the problem you are addressing? If not, how can you get their attention?
	▪ Does your audience care about your issue? If not, how can you get them to care?

What to Ask	Why to Ask It
3. *What is your audience's current attitude toward your issue?*	Your answer will help you decide the structure and tone of your argument.
	■ Are your readers already supportive of your position? Undecided? Skeptical? Strongly opposed? ■ What other points of view besides your own will your audience be weighing?
4. *What will be your audience's likely objections to your argument?*	Your answer will help determine the content of your argument and will alert you to extra research you may need.
	■ What weaknesses will audience members find? ■ What aspects of your position will be most threatening to them and why? ■ How are your basic assumptions, values, or beliefs different from your audience's?
5. *What values, beliefs, or assumptions about the world do you and your audience share?*	Your answer will help you find common ground with your audience.
	■ Despite different points of view on this issue, where can you find common links with your audience? ■ How might you use these links to build bridges to your audience?

To see how a concern for audience-based reasons can enhance *ethos* and *pathos,* suppose that you support racial profiling (rather than random selection) for determining who receives intensive screening at airports. Suppose further that you are writing a guest op-ed column for a liberal campus newspaper and imagine readers repulsed by the notion of racial profiling (as indeed you are repulsed too in most cases). It's important from the start that you understand and acknowledge the interests of those opposed to your position. The persons most likely targeted by racial profiling would be Middle Eastern males as well as black males with African passports, particularly those from African nations with large Islamic populations. These persons will be directly offended by racial profiling at airports. From the perspective of social justice, they can rightfully object to the racial stereotyping that lumps all people of Arabic, Semitic, or African appearance into the category "potential terrorists." Similarly, African Americans and Hispanics, who frequently experience racial profiling by police in U.S. cities, may object to further extension of this hated practice. Also, most political liberals, as well as many moderates and conservatives, may object to the racism inherent in selecting people for airport screening on the basis of ethnicity or country of origin.

What shared values might you use to build bridges to those opposed to racial profiling at airports? You need to develop a strategy to reduce your audience's fears and to link your reasons to their values. Your thinking might go something like this:

Problem: How can I create an argument rooted in shared values? How can I reduce fear that racial profiling in this situation endorses racism or will lead to further erosion of civil liberties?

Bridge-building goals: I must try to show that my argument's goal is to increase airline safety by preventing terrorism like that of 9/11/01. My argument must show my respect for Islam and for Arabic and Semitic peoples. I must also show my rejection of racial profiling as normal police practice.

Possible strategies:

- Stress the shared value of protecting innocent people from terrorism.
- Show how racial profiling significantly increases the efficiency of secondary searches. (If searches are performed at random, then we waste time and resources searching people who are statistically unlikely to be terrorists.)
- Argue that airport screeners must also use indicators other than race to select people for searches (for example, traits that might indicate a domestic terrorist).
- Show my respect for Islam.
- Show sympathy for people selected for searching via racial profiling and acknowledge that this practice would normally be despicable except for the extreme importance of airline security, which overrides personal liberties in this case.
- Show my rejection of racial profiling in situations other than airport screening— for example, stopping African Americans for traffic violations more often than whites and then searching their cars for drugs or stolen goods.
- Perhaps show my support of affirmative action, which is a kind of racial profiling in reverse.

These thinking notes allow you to develop the following plan for your argument.

- Airport screeners should use racial profiling rather than random selection to determine which people undergo intensive screening
  - because doing so will make more efficient use of airport screeners' time, increase the odds of finding terrorists, and thus lead to greater airline safety (*WARRANT: Increased airline safety is good;* or, at a deeper level, *The positive consequences of increasing airline safety through racial profiling outweigh the negative consequences.*)
  - because racial profiling in this specific case does not mean allowing it in everyday police activities nor does it imply disrespect for Islam or for Middle Eastern or African males (WARRANT: *Racial profiling is unacceptable in everyday police practices. It is wrong to show disrespect for Islam or Middle Eastern or African males.*)

As this plan shows, your strategy is to seek reasons whose warrants your audience will accept. First, you will argue that racial profiling will lead to greater airline safety, allowing you to stress that safe airlines benefit all passengers. Your concern is the lives of hundreds of passengers as well as others who might be killed in a terrorist attack. Second, you plan to reduce adversaries' resistance to your proposal by showing that the consequences aren't as severe as they might fear. Using racial profiling in airports would not justify using it in urban police work (a practice you find despicable) and it would not imply disrespect for Islam or Middle Eastern or African males. As this example shows, your focus on audience—on the search for audience-based reasons—shapes the actual invention of your argument from the start. It also encourages you to fuse concerns for *ethos* and *pathos* into your foundational planning for your argument as you think about how to reach your audience and how to establish yourself as sympathetic, fair, and concerned about social justice and the public good.

■ ■ ■ **FOR WRITING AND DISCUSSION**   Planning an Audience-Based   MyWritingLab™
                                         Argumentative Strategy

Individual task:

1. Choose one of the following cases and plan an audience-based argumentative strategy. Follow the thinking process used by the writer of the racial-profiling argument: (1) state several problems that the writer must solve to reach the audience, and (2) develop possible solutions to those problems.

   a. An argument for the right of software companies to continue making and selling violent video games: aim the argument at parents who oppose their children playing these games.

   b. An argument to reverse grade inflation by limiting the number of As and Bs a professor can give in a course: aim the argument at students who fear getting lower grades.

   c. An argument supporting the legalization of cocaine: aim the argument at readers of *Reader's Digest,* a conservative magazine that supports the current war on drugs.

Group task: Share your planning notes with other members of your class, and discuss how your sketched argument would make appeals to *ethos* and *pathos* as well as to *logos.* ■ ■ ■

Conclusion

In this chapter, we have explored ways that writers can strengthen the persuasiveness of their arguments by creating appeals to *ethos* and *pathos,* by being attentive to *kairos,* by thinking visually, and by building bridges to their readers through audience-based reasons. Arguments are more persuasive if readers trust the credibility of the writer and if the argument appeals to readers' hearts and imaginations as well as to their intellects. Attentiveness to *kairos* keeps the writer attuned to the dynamics of a rhetorical situation in order to create the right message at the right time. Sometimes images such as drawings or photographs may reinforce the argument by evoking strong emotional responses, thus enhancing *pathos.* Finally, all these appeals come together when the writer explicitly focuses on finding audience-based reasons.

WRITING ASSIGNMENT **Revising a Draft for *Ethos, Pathos,***   MyWritingLab™
                                          and Audience-Based Reasons

Part 1: Choose an argument that you have previously written or that you are currently drafting. Revise the argument with explicit focus on increasing its appeals to *logos, ethos, pathos,* and *kairos* via audience-based reasons and other strategies. Consider especially how you might improve *ethos* by building bridges to the audience or improve *pathos* through concrete language, specific examples, metaphors, or connotations of words. Finally, consider the extent to which your reasons are audience-based.

Or

Multimodal option: Imagine an argument that you have previously written or are currently drafting that could be enhanced with effective photographs or images. Revise your argument to include these images, perhaps creating a desktop published document that wraps text around visuals chosen to enhance *pathos.* Other multimodal possibilities include transforming your argument into a speech supported by Power-Point images (see Chapter 14, pages 333–334), into a poster argument (see Chapter 9, page 196 and Chapter 14, page 332), or even into a podcast that includes music.

Part 2: Attach to your revision or transformed project a reflective letter explaining the choices you made in revising your original argument or in transforming it using a multimodal approach. Describe for your instructor the changes or transformations you made and explain how or why your new version enhances your argument's effectiveness at moving its audience. ■

MyWritingLab™

Visit Ch. 6 Moving Your Audience: *Ethos, Pathos,* and *Kairos* in *MyWritingLab* to complete the For Writing and Discussion, Examining Visual Arguments, and Writing Assignments and to test your understanding of the chapter objectives.

Responding to Objections and Alternative Views

7

In the previous chapter we discussed strategies for moving your audience through appeals to *ethos, pathos,* and *kairos.* In this chapter we examine strategies for addressing opposing or alternative views—whether to omit them, refute them, concede to them, or incorporate them through compromise and conciliation—and we explain when a very different, collaborative approach would be appropriate, when your audience holds views that clash with yours.

One-Sided, Multisided, and Dialogic Arguments

7.1 To explain the differences between one-sided, multisided, and dialogic argument

Arguments are said to be one-sided, multisided, or dialogic:

- *A one-sided argument* presents only the writer's position on the issue without summarizing and responding to alternative viewpoints.
- *A multisided argument* presents the writer's position, but also summarizes and responds to possible objections and alternative views.
- *A dialogic argument* has a much stronger component of inquiry in which the writer presents herself as uncertain or searching, the audience is considered a partner in the dialogue, and the writer's purpose is to seek common ground, perhaps leading to a consensual solution to a problem. (See our discussion in Chapter 1 of argument as truth seeking versus persuasion, pages 10–12.)

121

One-sided and *multisided* arguments often take an adversarial stance in that the writer regards alternative views as flawed or wrong and supports her own claim with a strongly persuasive intent. Although multisided arguments can be adversarial, they can also be made to feel *dialogic*, depending on the way the writer introduces and responds to alternative views.

At issue, then, is the writer's treatment of alternative views. Does the writer omit them (a one-sided argument), summarize them in order to rebut them (an adversarial kind of multisided argument), or summarize them in order to acknowledge their validity, value, and force (a more dialogic kind of multisided argument)? Each of these approaches can be appropriate for certain occasions, depending on your purpose, your confidence in your own stance, and your audience's resistance to your views.

How can you determine the kind of argument that would be most effective in a given case? As a general rule, one-sided arguments occur commonly when an issue is not highly contested. If the issue is highly contested, then one-sided arguments tend to strengthen the convictions of those who are already in the writer's camp, but alienate those who aren't. In contrast, for those initially opposed to a writer's claim, a multisided argument shows that the writer has considered other views, and thus reduces some initial hostility. An especially interesting effect can occur with neutral or undecided audiences. In the short run, one-sided arguments are often persuasive to a neutral audience, but in the long run, multisided arguments have more staying power. Neutral audiences who have heard only one side of an issue tend to change their minds when they hear alternative arguments. By anticipating and rebutting opposing views, a multisided argument diminishes the surprise and force of subsequent counterarguments. If we move from neutral to highly resistant audiences, adversarial approaches—even multisided ones—are seldom effective because they increase hostility and harden the differences between writer and reader. In such cases, more dialogic approaches have the best chance of establishing common ground for inquiry and consensus.

In the rest of this chapter we will show you how your choice of writing one-sided, multisided, or dialogic arguments is a function of how you perceive your audience's resistance to your views, your level of confidence in your own views, and your purpose—to persuade your audience or open up dialogue.

Determining Your Audience's Resistance to Your Views

7.2 To determine the degree of your audience's resistance to your views in order to shape the content, structure, and tone of your argument

When you write an argument, you must always consider your audience's point of view. One way to imagine your relationship to your audience is to place it on a scale of resistance ranging from strong support of your position to strong opposition (see Figure 7.1). At the "Accord" end of this scale are like-minded people who basically agree with your position on the issue. At the "Resistance" end are those who strongly disagree with you, perhaps unconditionally, because their values, beliefs, or assumptions sharply differ from your own. Between "Accord" and "Resistance" lies a range of opinions. Close to your position will be those leaning in your direction but with less conviction than you have.

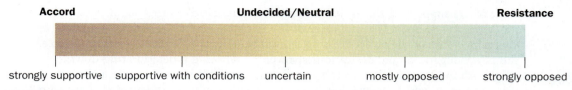

FIGURE 7.1 Scale of resistance

Close to the resistance position will be those basically opposed to your view but willing to listen to your argument and perhaps willing to acknowledge some of its strengths. In the middle are those undecided people who are still sorting out their feelings, seeking additional information, and weighing the strengths and weaknesses of alternative views.

Seldom, however, will you encounter an issue in which the range of disagreement follows a simple line from accord to resistance. Often resistant views fall into different categories so that no single line of argument appeals to all those whose views are different from your own. You thus have to identify not only your audience's resistance to your ideas but also the causes of that resistance.

Consider, for example, the issues surrounding publicly financed sports stadiums. In one city, a ballot initiative asked citizens to agree to an increase in sales taxes to build a new retractable-roof stadium for its baseball team. Supporters of the initiative faced a complex array of resisting views (see Figure 7.2). Opponents of the initiative could be placed into four categories. Some simply had no interest in sports, cared nothing about baseball, and saw no benefit in building a huge, publicly financed sports facility. Another group loved baseball and followed the home team passionately, but was philosophically opposed to subsidizing rich players and owners with taxpayer money. This group argued that the whole sports industry needed to be restructured so that stadiums were paid for out of sports revenues. Still another group was opposed to tax hikes in general. It focused on the principle of reducing the size of government and of using tax revenues only for essential services. Finally, another powerful group supported baseball and supported the notion of public funding of a new stadium but opposed the kind of retractable-roof stadium specified in the initiative. This group wanted an old-fashioned, open-air stadium like Baltimore's Camden Yards or Cleveland's Jacobs Field.

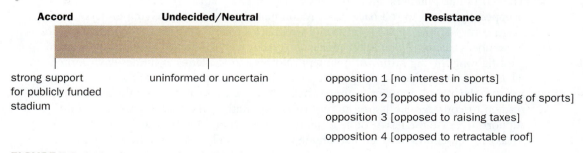

FIGURE 7.2 Scale of resistance, baseball stadium issue

Writers supporting the initiative found it impossible to address all of these resisting audiences at once. If a supporter of the initiative wanted to aim an argument at sports haters, he or she could stress the spinoff benefits of a new ballpark (for example, the new ballpark would attract tourist revenue, renovate a deteriorating downtown neighborhood, create jobs, make sports lovers more likely to vote for public subsidies of the arts, and so forth). But these arguments would be irrelevant to those who wanted an open-air stadium, who opposed tax hikes categorically, or who objected to public subsidy of millionaires.

The baseball stadium example illustrates the difficulty of adapting your argument to your audience's position on the scale of resistance. Yet doing so is important because you need a stable vision of your audience before you can determine an effective content, structure, and tone for your argument. As we showed in Chapter 4, effective content derives from choosing audience-based reasons that appeal to your audience's values, assumptions, and beliefs. As we show in the rest of this chapter, an effective structure and tone are often a function of where your audience falls on the scale of resistance. The next sections show how you can adjust your arguing strategy depending on whether your audience is supportive, neutral, or hostile.

Appealing to a Supportive Audience: One-Sided Argument

7.3 To use one-sided argument to appeal to supportive audiences

One-sided arguments commonly occur when an issue isn't highly contested and the writer's aim is merely to put forth a new or different point of view. When an issue is contested, however, one-sided arguments are used mainly to stir the passions of supporters—to convert belief into action by inspiring a party member to contribute to a senator's campaign or a bored office worker to sign up for a change-your-life weekend seminar.

Typically, appeals to a supportive audience are structured as one-sided arguments that either ignore opposing views or reduce them to "enemy" stereotypes. Filled with motivational language, these arguments list the benefits that will ensue from the reader's donations to the cause and the horrors just around the corner if the other side wins. One of the authors of this text received a fund-raising letter from an environmental lobbying group declaring, "It's crunch time for the polluters and their pals on Capitol Hill." The "corporate polluters" and "anti-environment politicians," the letter continues, have "stepped up efforts to roll back our environmental protections—relying on large campaign contributions, slick PR firms and well-heeled lobbyists to get the job done before November's election." This letter makes the reader feel like part of an in-group of good guys fighting the big business "polluters." Nothing in the letter examines environmental issues from business's perspective or attempts to examine alternative views fairly. Because the intended audience already believes in the cause, nothing in the letter invites readers to consider the issues more thoroughly. Rather, the letter's goal is to solidify support, increase the fervor of belief, and inspire action. Most appeal arguments make it easy to act, ending with an 800 phone number to call, a Web site to visit, an online petition to sign, or a congressperson's address to write to.

Appealing to a Neutral or Undecided Audience: Classical Argument

7.4 To use classical argument to appeal to neutral or undecided audiences, using refutation and concession

The in-group appeals that motivate an already supportive audience can repel a neutral or undecided audience. Because undecided audiences are like jurors weighing all sides of an issue, they distrust one-sided arguments that caricature other views. Generally the best strategy for appealing to undecided audiences is the classically structured argument described in Chapter 3 (pages 53–54).

What characterizes the classical argument is the writer's willingness to summarize opposing views fairly and to respond to them openly—either by trying to refute them or by conceding to their strengths and then shifting to a different field of values. Let's look at these strategies in more depth.

Summarizing Opposing Views

The first step toward responding to opposing views in a classical argument is to summarize them fairly. Follow the *principle of charity,* which obliges you to avoid loaded, biased, or "straw man" summaries that oversimplify or distort opposing arguments, making them easy to knock over.

Consider the difference between an unfair and a fair summary of an argument. In the following example, a hypothetical supporter of genetically engineered foods intends to refute the argument of organic-food advocate Lisa Turner, who opposes all forms of biotechnology.

Unfair Summary of Turner's Argument

In a biased article lacking scientific understanding of biotechnology, natural-foods huckster Lisa Turner parrots the health food industry's party line that genetically altered crops are Frankenstein's monsters run amok. She ignorantly claims that consumption of biotech foods will lead to worldwide destruction, disease, and death, ignoring the wealth of scientific literature showing that genetically modified foods are safe. Her misinformed attacks are scare tactics aimed at selling consumers on overpriced "health food" products to be purchased at boutique organic-food stores.

Fair Summary of Turner's Argument

In an article appearing in a nutrition magazine, health food advocate Lisa Turner warns readers that much of our food today is genetically modified using gene-level techniques that differ completely from ordinary crossbreeding. She argues that the potential, unforeseen, harmful consequences of genetic engineering offset the possible benefits of increasing the food supply, reducing the use of pesticides, and boosting the nutritional value of foods. Turner asserts that genetic engineering is imprecise, untested, unpredictable, irreversible, and also uncontrollable because of animals, insects, and winds.

In the unfair summary, the writer distorts and oversimplifies Turner's argument, creating a straw man argument that is easy to knock over because it doesn't make the opponent's best case. In contrast, the fair summary follows the "principle of charity," allowing the strength of the opposing view to come through clearly.

■ ■ ■ **FOR WRITING AND DISCUSSION** **Distinguishing Fair from Unfair Summaries**   MyWritingLab™

Individual task: Use the following questions to analyze the differences between the two summaries of Lisa Turner's article.

1. What makes the first summary unfair? How can you tell?
2. In the unfair summary, what strategies does the writer use to make the opposing view seem weak and flawed? In the fair summary, how is the opposing view made strong and clear?
3. In the unfair summary, how does the writer attack Turner's motives and credentials? This attack is sometimes called an *ad hominem* argument ("against the person"—see Appendix 1 for a definition of this reasoning fallacy) in that it attacks the arguer rather than the argument. How does the writer treat Turner differently in the fair summary?
4. Do you agree with our view that arguments are more persuasive if the writer summarizes opposing views fairly rather than unfairly? Why?

Group task: As a group, write a fair and an unfair summary of an argument that your instructor gives you, using the strategies you analyzed in the Turner examples.   ■ ■ ■

Refuting Opposing Views

Once you have summarized opposing views, you can either refute them or concede to their strengths. In refuting an opposing view, you attempt to convince readers that its argument is logically flawed, inadequately supported, or based on erroneous assumptions. In refuting an argument, you can rebut (1) the writer's stated reason and grounds, (2) the writer's warrant and backing, or (3) both. Put in less specialized language, you can rebut a writer's reasons and evidence or the writer's underlying assumptions. Suppose, for example, that you wanted to refute this argument:

> Students should limit the number of internships they take because internships are time-consuming.

We can clarify the structure of this argument by showing it in Toulmin terms:

ENTHYMEME

CLAIM: Students should limit the number of internships they take

REASON: because internships are time-consuming.

WARRANT

Time-consuming internships are bad for students.

One way to refute this argument is to rebut the stated reason that internships are time-consuming. Your rebuttal might go something like this:

I disagree that internships are time-consuming. In fact, organizations and businesses are usually very upfront, realistic, and flexible in the weekly hours that they ask of students. The examples that you cite of overly demanding internships are exceptions. Furthermore, these internships have since been retailored to students' schedules. [The writer could then provide examples of realistic, limited-time internships.]

Or you could concede that internships are time-consuming but rebut the argument's warrant that using time in these apprentice situations is bad for students:

> I agree that internships take sizable chunks of students' time, but investment in real-world work environments is a worthwhile use of students' time. Through this investment, students clarify their professional goals, log work experience, and gain references. Without interning in these work environments, students would miss important career preparation.

Let's now illustrate these strategies in a more complex situation. Consider the controversy inspired by a *New York Times Magazine* article titled "Recycling Is Garbage." Its author, John Tierney, argued that recycling is not environmentally sound and that it is cheaper to bury garbage in a landfill than to recycle it. Tierney argued that recycling wastes money; he provided evidence that "every time a sanitation department crew picks up a load of bottles and cans from the curb, New York City loses money." In Toulmin's terms, one of Tierney's arguments is structured as shown below.

A number of environmentalists responded angrily to Tierney's argument, challenging either his reason, his warrant, or both. Those refuting the reason offered counterevidence showing that recycling isn't as expensive as Tierney claimed. Those refuting the warrant said that even if the costs of recycling are higher than the costs of burying wastes in a landfill, recycling still benefits the environment by reducing the amount of virgin materials taken from nature. These critics, in effect, offered a new warrant: Conserving the world's resources is an important goal of garbage disposal.

ENTHYMEME

CLAIM Recycling is bad policy

REASON because it costs more to recycle material than to bury it in a landfill.

GROUNDS

- Evidence of the high cost of recycling [Tierney says it costs New York City $200 more per ton for recyclables than trash.]

WARRANT

We should dispose of garbage in the least expensive way.

Strategies for Rebutting Evidence

Whether you are rebutting an argument's reasons or its warrant, you will frequently need to question a writer's use of evidence. Here are some strategies you can use:

- **Deny the truth of the data.** Arguers can disagree about the facts of a case. If you have reasons to doubt a writer's facts, call them into question.

- **Cite counterexamples and countertestimony.** You can often rebut an argument based on examples or testimony by citing counterexamples or countertestimony that denies the conclusiveness of the original data.
- **Cast doubt on the representativeness or sufficiency of examples.** Examples are powerful only if they are believed to be representative and sufficient. Many environmentalists complained that John Tierney's attack on recycling was based too largely on data from New York City and that it didn't accurately take into account more positive experiences of other cities and states. When data from outside New York City were examined, the cost-effectiveness and positive environmental impact of recycling seemed more apparent.
- **Cast doubt on the relevance or recency of the examples, statistics, or testimony.** The best evidence is up-to-date. In a rapidly changing universe, data that are even a few years out-of-date are often ineffective. For example, as the demand for recycled goods increases, the cost of recycling will be reduced. Out-of-date statistics will skew any argument about the cost of recycling.
- **Question the credibility of an authority.** If an opposing argument is based on testimony, you can undermine its persuasiveness if you show that a person being cited lacks current or relevant expertise in the field. (This approach is different from the *ad hominem* fallacy discussed in the Appendix because it doesn't attack the personal character of the authority but only the authority's expertise on a specific matter.)
- **Question the accuracy or context of quotations.** Evidence based on testimony is frequently distorted by being either misquoted or taken out of context. Often scientists qualify their findings heavily, but these qualifications are omitted by the popular media. You can thus attack the use of a quotation by putting it in its original context or by restoring the qualifications in its original source.
- **Question the way statistical data were produced or interpreted.** Chapter 5 provides fuller treatment of how to question statistics. In general, you can rebut statistical evidence by calling into account how the data were gathered, treated mathematically, or interpreted. It can make a big difference, for example, whether you cite raw numbers or percentages or whether you choose large or small increments for the axes of graphs.

Conceding to Opposing Views

In writing a classical argument, a writer must sometimes concede to an opposing argument rather than refute it. Sometimes you encounter portions of an argument that you simply can't refute. For example, suppose that you are a libertarian who supports the legalization of hard drugs such as cocaine and heroin. Adversaries argue that legalizing hard drugs will increase the number of drug users and addicts. You might dispute the size of their numbers, but you reluctantly agree that they are right. Your strategy is thus not to refute the opposing argument but to concede to it by admitting that legalization of hard drugs will promote heroin and cocaine addiction. Having made that concession, your task is then to show that the benefits of drug legalization, such as a reduction in crime and the emptying out of America's prisons, still outweigh the costs you've just conceded.

As this example shows, the strategy of a concession argument is to switch from the field of values employed by the writer you disagree with to a different field of values more favorable to your position. You don't try to refute the writer's stated reason and grounds (by arguing that legalization will *not* lead to increased drug usage and addiction) or the writer's warrant (by arguing that increased drug use and addiction is not a problem). Rather, you shift the argument to a new field of values by introducing a new warrant, one that you think your audience can share (that the benefits of legalization outweigh the costs of increased addiction). To the extent that opponents of legalization share your desire to stop drug-related crime, shifting to this new field of values is a good strategy. Although it may seem that you weaken your own position by conceding to an opposing argument, you may actually strengthen it by increasing your credibility and gaining your audience's goodwill. Moreover, conceding to one part of an opposing argument doesn't mean that you won't refute other parts of that argument.

Example of a Student Essay Using Refutation Strategy

The following student essay, which grew out of Trudie's exploratory essay in Chapter 2, illustrates how a classical argument appealing to a neutral or even mildly resistant audience engages with alternative views. Note the use of both concession and rebuttal strategies.

Bringing Dignity to Workers: Make the Minimum Wage a Living Wage

TRUDIE MAKENS (STUDENT)

Uses personal example to illustrate problems of low-wage workers

Having worked as a busser in a pizza restaurant, a part-time barista, and a server at a dumpling cafe I have worked a number of minimum-wage jobs. My coworkers have ranged from students like myself to single parents and primary providers for their families. As a student, I have always had my parents as a safety net protecting me from financial hardship. However, my coworkers whose only income is their minimum wage endured financial hardships daily. I witnessed one of my coworkers, Maria, lose her home trying to balance supporting her two children and paying her rent. At work, Maria would describe her anxiety as she bounced from relative to relative, straining her family relations and image of herself as an able provider. Without a living wage or the government's providing social insurance programs to ensure financial security for all citizens, families like Maria's are locked into poverty. Raising the federal minimum wage to a livable standard is an important and necessary step to eradicate poverty and ensure dignified living for individuals and families.

Thesis statement

Yet some argue that a higher federal minimum wage will do more harm than good. Michael Saltsman, the research director of the

Forecasts rebuttal
of three opposing
views raised by
Saltsman

Summarizes Saltsman's
first objection to
minimum wage

Rebuts argument by
citing more recent
research

Summarizes Saltsman's
second objection

Concedes that higher
minimum wage won't
help jobless, but shifts
to other benefits that
Saltsman ignores

Summarizes
Saltsman's last
argument.

Rebuts this argument
by showing weak-
nesses in the Earned
Income Tax Credit
approach.

Uses conclusion to
summarize additional
measures (besides
higher minimum
wage) to combat
poverty.

Employment Policy Institute, elaborates the pro-business objections to a minimum wage in several op-ed pieces published in national print or online newspapers. Saltsman primarily makes three arguments against raising the minimum wage. Each of them, I contend, is weak or flawed.

First, Saltsman warns that raising the minimum wage will force businesses to cut jobs. In order to maintain profit and to keep prices low, Saltsman argues, businesses will pay for a higher wage by slashing the number of workers. Worse, businesses may cut entire departments in favor of automation such as having fast-food customers order their meals from computer touch screens. Saltsman's argument, however, depends on older studies that, according to University of California economist Michael Reich, are "fundamentally flawed" (Maclay). In a study published in 2010, Reich and his coauthors find that these earlier studies fail to account for all the critical variables besides wages that influence employment levels. By comparing employment levels between states with higher versus lower minimum-wage levels, Reich and his colleagues provide empirical evidence that raising the minimum wage produces no "adverse employment effects" (954).

Saltsman's second objection to a higher minimum wage is that it targets the wrong people and thus won't reduce overall poverty levels. According to Saltsman, a majority of people living in poverty are unemployed while a majority of minimum-wage workers are from households above the poverty line. Although Saltsman may be correct that a higher minimum-wage won't help a jobless person, he ignores the benefits of a living wage to the working poor who would be lifted out of poverty. Moreover, a higher minimum wage might itself stimulate jobs because minimum-wage workers with more money in their pockets are apt to spend it, increasing demand for goods.

5   Finally Saltsman argues that the minimum wage is less effective at reducing poverty than the Earned Income Tax Credit, which boosts the income of low-wage workers while not giving any income boost to work-ers who are already above the poverty level. However, the Earned Income Tax Credit, like the minimum wage, does nothing for the jobless poor. Moreover, the Earned Income Tax Credit puts the burden of poverty relief on taxpayers rather than employers and corporate shareholders, doing little to shift the economy in an equitable direction. We need both an increased minimum wage and the Earned Income Tax Credit.

It seems clear that to combat poverty, the United States needs a many-pronged effort with a hike in the minimum wage being only one of the prongs. Although a higher minimum wage will not by itself elim-inate poverty, it will certainly help. It needs to be combined with invest-ments in infrastructure to create jobs, with affordable higher education, with better job training, and with other safety-net systems such as those in place in Europe to give dignity to all citizens. Rather than our government and market system prioritizing corporations and profit, the rights and dignity of workers should be held foremost important. Raising the minimum wage to a living wage will help change the structure of a market system that often exploits workers.

Works Cited

Maclay, Kathleen. "Minimum Wage Hikes Don't Eliminate Jobs, Study Finds." *UC Berkeley News Center.* 1 Dec. 2010. Web. 23 Feb. 2014.

Reich, Michael, Arandrajit Dube, and William Lester. "Minimum Wage Effects across State Borders: Estimates Using Contiguous Counties." *Review of Economics and Statistics* 92.4 (2010): 945-64. *Irle.berkeley.edu.* UC Berkeley. Web. 23 Feb. 2014.

Saltsman, Michael. "The Wrong Way to Reduce Poverty." *USA Today.* 20 Sept. 2013. *Employment Policy Institute.* Web. 18 Feb. 2014.

—. "To Help the Poor, Move beyond Minimum Gestures." *Huffington Post.* 26 Apr. 2013. Web. 17 Feb. 2014.

■ ■ ■ **FOR WRITING AND CLASS DISCUSSION** **Refutation Strategies**

Individually or in groups, examine each of the following arguments, imagining how the claim and reason could be fleshed out with grounds and backing. Then attempt to refute each argument. Suggest ways to rebut the reason, or the warrant, or both, or to concede to the argument and then switch to a different field of values.

a. The criminal justice system should reduce sentences for low-level, nonviolent offenders because this change will save taxpayers' money.

b. Majoring in engineering is better than majoring in music because engineers make more money than musicians.

c. The SAT exam for college entrance should be not be required by colleges and universities because high school grades are a better predictor of student success than SAT scores.

d. The United States should build more nuclear reactors because nuclear reactors will provide substantial electrical energy without emitting greenhouse gases.

e. People should be allowed to own handguns because owning handguns helps them protect their homes against potentially violent intruders. ■ ■ ■

Appealing to a Resistant Audience: Dialogic Argument

7.5 To use dialogic, delayed-thesis argument to appeal to resistant audiences

We now turn to an approach to argument that envisions a less confrontational role for the writer and a more collaborative relationship between the writer and a resistant audience. This approach, often called dialogic argument, emphasizes an exploratory, "let's think this out together" structure and tone. In today's public sphere, dialogic argument could be particularly important because it resists the impulsive and superficial comments, often posted on online forums, with no regard for the audience. Syndicated columnist Frank Bruni asserts that Twitter and other social media promote a style of communication that fosters the online publishing of "unformed thoughts, half-baked wit or splenetic reactions" before people take time to deliberate about issues or consider their audience. Citing the research of social psychologist Jonathan Haidt, Bruni writes that "people are more likely to be moved by information that challenges their prejudices if they're prevented from responding to it straight away and it has time to sink in, to steep."* Dialogic argument offers both writers and audiences this calm thinking time to live with opposing views, consider reasons on different sides of an issue, and weigh the evidence.

Let's think about the instances when writers would want to enlist dialogic argument. Whereas classical argument is effective for neutral or undecided audiences, it is often less effective for audiences strongly opposed to the writer's views or for arguments that lean toward the inquiry end of the argument continuum. Because resistant audiences hold values, assumptions, or beliefs widely different from the writer's, they are often unswayed by classical argument, which attacks their worldview too directly. Writers, too, may recognize that progress toward communication on some values-laden issues may require them to take a more open, problem-solving approach. On issues such as abortion, gun control, certain environmental regulations, or the role of religion in the public sphere, the distance between a writer and a resistant audience can be so great that dialogue seems impossible. In these cases the writer's goal may be simply to open dialogue by seeking common ground—that is, by finding places where the writer and audience agree. For example, pro-choice and pro-life advocates may never agree on a woman's right to an abortion, but they may share common ground in wanting to reduce teenage pregnancy. There is room, in other words, for conversation, if not for agreement.

Because of these differences in basic beliefs and values, the goal of dialogic argument is seldom to convert resistant readers to the writer's position. The best a writer can hope for is to reduce somewhat the level of resistance, perhaps by increasing the reader's willingness to listen as preparation for future dialogue. In this section and the next, we introduce you to two strategies for reducing the resistance of hostile audiences—a dialogic argument with a delayed thesis and Rogerian communication, a listening and thinking strategy that can enlarge the writer's as well as the reader's view of a conflicted issue.

Creating a Dialogic Argument with a Delayed Thesis

Unlike a classical argument, a delayed-thesis argument assumes an exploratory approach to a subject. With some issues, you may want to convey that you are still thinking out your position, finding your way through a thicket of alternative views and the complexities of the issue. You yourself may be pulled in multiple directions and may have arrived at your position after pondering different views. In addition, your readers' resistance to your views means that they may be turned off if you forthrightly plunge into your claim and reasons. Under these rhetorical conditions, a delayed-thesis argument enables you to engage your audience in a dialogic exploration of the problem before you argue a thesis.

---

*Frank Bruni, "Tweet Less, Read More in 2014," *Seattle Times* 2 January 2014. A11.

Instead of declaring a claim and reasons early in the argument, you may work your way slowly to your claim, devoting a large part of the argument to examining different views and re-creating your own inquiry into the subject.

Let's look at an example of a delayed-thesis argument, examining its form and its emotional impact. (For another example of a delayed-thesis argument, see Ellen Goodman's commentary piece "Womb for Rent—for a Price" on pages 169–170.) The following op-ed piece by syndicated columnist Ross Douthat appeared in the *New York Times* during the public debates about building a Muslim community center near Ground Zero in lower Manhattan. Note how Douthat takes a nonthreatening tone and pulls readers into his exploration of the issue.

Islam in Two Americas*

ROSS DOUTHAT

Writer frames the controversy as a conflict of American identities, two divergent ways that the country thinks of itself.

There's an America where it doesn't matter what language you speak, what god you worship or how deep your New World roots run. An America where allegiance to the Constitution trumps ethnic differences, language barriers and religious divides. An America where the newest arrival to our shores is no less American than the ever-so-great granddaughter of the Pilgrims.

But there's another America as well, one that understands itself as a distinctive culture, rather than just a set of political propositions. This America speaks English, not Spanish or Chinese or Arabic. It looks back to a particular religious heritage: Protestantism originally, and then a Judeo-Christian consensus that accommodated Jews and Catholics as well.

Writer establishes the problem and its timeliness and invites his readers to contemplate it with him.

These two understandings of America, one constitutional and one cultural, have been in tension throughout our history. They're in tension in the controversy over the Islamic mosque and cultural center scheduled to go up two blocks from ground zero.

Writer explores the problem from several perspectives: first, the inclusive constitutional America, which defends the right of all religious groups to worship as they please.

The first America views the project as the consummate expression of our nation's high ideals. "This is America," President Barack Obama intoned last week, "and our commitment to religious freedom must be unshakeable." The construction of the mosque, Mayor Michael Bloomberg told New Yorkers, is as important a test of the principle of religious freedom "as we may see in our lifetimes."

5   The second America begs to differ. It sees the project as an affront to the memory of 9/11, and a sign of disrespect for the values of a country

---

Writer shows his awareness of the problem's complexity by exploring the second perspective, the melting-pot America, which emphasizes its Judeo-Christian heritage.

Writer keeps the problem open as he examines how these two identities functioned in American history.

Writer finally presents his own viewpoint, his thesis-claim that Muslims should not build a community center near Ground Zero.

He briefly develops his claim.

He argues that by not building near Ground Zero, American Muslims would signal their disassociation from Islamic terrorist groups and their respect for the national pain caused by 9/11.

He sums up his argument by restating his thesis-claim in larger terms that leave readers with his thinking.

where Islam has only recently become part of the public consciousness. And beneath these concerns lurks the darker suspicion that Islam in any form may be incompatible with the American way of life.

Both understandings of this country have wisdom to offer, and both have been necessary to the American experiment's success. During the great waves of 19th-century immigration, the insistence that new arrivals adapt to Anglo-Saxon culture was crucial to their swift assimilation.

The same was true in religion. The steady pressure to conform to American norms eventually persuaded the Mormons to abandon polygamy, smoothing their assimilation into the American mainstream. Nativist concerns about Catholicism's illiberal tendencies inspired American Catholics to prod their church toward a recognition of the virtues of democracy, making it possible for generations of immigrants to feel unambiguously Catholic and American.

So it is today with Islam. The first America is correct to insist on Muslims' absolute right to build and worship where they wish. But the second America is right to press for something more from Muslim Americans—particularly from figures like Feisal Abdul Rauf, the imam behind the mosque—than simple protestations of good faith.

Too often, American Muslim institutions have turned out to be entangled with ideas and groups that most Americans rightly consider beyond the pale. Too often, American Muslim leaders strike ambiguous notes when asked to disassociate themselves completely from illiberal causes.

10 For Muslim Americans to integrate fully into our national life, they'll need leaders who don't describe America as "an accessory to the crime" of 9/11 (as Rauf did shortly after the 2001 attacks), or duck questions about whether groups like Hamas count as terrorist organizations (as Rauf did in June). They'll need leaders whose antennas are sensitive enough to recognize that the quest for inter-religious dialogue is ill served by throwing up a high-profile mosque two blocks from the site of a mass murder committed in the name of Islam.

They'll need leaders, in other words, who understand that while the ideals of the first America protect the *e pluribus,* it's the demands the second America makes of new arrivals that help create the *unum.*

In this delayed-thesis argument, Ross Douthat, a conservative columnist writing for the liberal *New York Times,* asks readers to think with him about the fierce clash of views over building a Muslim community center near Ground Zero. Douthat wants to reach typical *New York Times* readers, who are apt to support the Muslim project based on their liberal views of tolerance and religious freedom. Douthat enters this public debate calmly, admits the legitimacy of different opposing views, and only toward the end of the argument states his own position.

If Douthat had chosen to write a classical argument, he would have declared his position in the first paragraph, perhaps with a thesis statement like this:

> Muslim Americans should not build their community center near Ground Zero because doing so represents disrespect for America's core cultural identity and insensitivity to Americans' national pain caused by Islamic terrorists.

With this thesis, readers would have no initial doubt where Douthat stands. However, this in-your-face thesis would activate the emotional objections of readers who support the Islamic community center and might prevent them from even reading the piece. In contrast, both liberal and conservative readers can get drawn into the building momentum of Douthat's delayed-thesis version and appreciate its subtlety and surprise.

Writing a Delayed-Thesis Argument

Clearly, where you place your claim can affect your argument's impact on its audience. We should note, however, that a delayed-thesis argument is not simply a classical argument turned upside down. Instead, it promotes dialogue with the audience rather than compels readers to accept the writer's views. It strives to enrich and complicate the discussion as well as present a view of an issue. It entails some risk to the writer because it leaves space only at the end of the argument for developing the writer's claim. However, it may lead the writer and readers to a deeper understanding of the issue, provide clarification, and promote further discussion. Although there is no set form, the organization plan below shows characteristic elements often found in delayed-thesis arguments.

Organization Plan for a Delayed-Thesis Argument

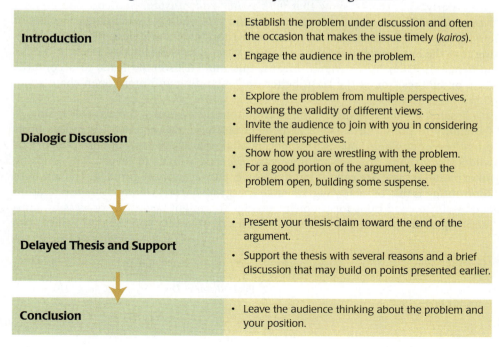

Introduction	• Establish the problem under discussion and often the occasion that makes the issue timely (*kairos*). • Engage the audience in the problem.
Dialogic Discussion	• Explore the problem from multiple perspectives, showing the validity of different views. • Invite the audience to join with you in considering different perspectives. • Show how you are wrestling with the problem. • For a good portion of the argument, keep the problem open, building some suspense.
Delayed Thesis and Support	• Present your thesis-claim toward the end of the argument. • Support the thesis with several reasons and a brief discussion that may build on points presented earlier.
Conclusion	• Leave the audience thinking about the problem and your position.

A More Open-Ended Approach: Rogerian Communication

7.6 To use Rogerian communication to open up new channels of understanding between you and an opposing audience

We now turn to a more complex kind of dialogic method: *Rogerian communication*. We use the term "communication" rather than "argument" because, as we will explain in more detail shortly, this strategy focuses on mutual listening and growth more than on persuasion. All dialogic arguments emphasize problem solving, collaborative thinking, and negotiation with a resistant audience. But Rogerian communication, besides delaying its thesis, works to change the writer as well as the reader. Rogerian communication is named after psychotherapist Carl Rogers, who developed a communication strategy for helping people resolve differences.* The Rogerian strategy emphasizes "empathic listening," which Rogers defined as the ability to see an issue sympathetically from another person's perspective or "frame of reference." He trained people to withhold judgment of another person's ideas until after they had listened attentively to the other person, understood that person's reasoning, appreciated that person's values, and respected that person's humanity—in short, walked in that person's shoes. What Carl Rogers understood is that traditional methods of argumentation are threatening. Because Rogerian communication stresses the psychological as well as the logical dimensions of argument, it is particularly effective when dealing with emotion-laden issues.

With Rogerian communication, the writer tries to reduce the sense of difference between writer and reader by releasing her tight hold on her own views. Particularly, she tries to show that *both writer and resistant audience share many basic values.* This search for common ground often has the psychological effect of enlarging, complicating, or deepening the writer's own worldview. By acknowledging that she has empathy for the audience's views, the writer makes it easier for the audience to listen to her views. Ideally, this mutual listening leads to a compromise or synthesis or, at the least, better understanding and more open channels of communication.

Essential to successful Rogerian communication, besides the art of listening, is the ability to point out areas of agreement between the writer's and reader's positions. For example, if you, as a supporter of alternative energy, oppose offshore or wilderness drilling and are arguing with someone who is in favor of maximizing oil exploration, you are caught in an impasse. However, if the problem you are both confronting is that of increasing available energy resources, you might reduce tension and establish conditions for problem solving. You might begin this process by summarizing your reader's position sympathetically, stressing your shared values. You

---

*See Carl Rogers's essay "Communication: Its Blocking and Its Facilitation" in his book *On Becoming a Person* (Boston: Houghton Mifflin, 1961), 329–37. For a fuller discussion of Rogerian argument, see Richard Young, Alton Becker, and Kenneth Pike, *Rhetoric: Discovery and Change* (New York: Harcourt Brave, 1972).

might say, for example, that you also value energy independence, that you appreciate recent advances in safe drilling technology, and that you are disturbed by people who deny our country's vast energy needs. You also agree that it is unrealistic to pretend that we can dispense with our oil needs overnight. Your effort to understand your audience's views and to build bridges between you and your audience will encourage dialogue and make it more likely that your audience will listen when you offer your perspective.

Rogers's communication strategies have been the subject of intense debate among scholars. On the one hand, some rhetoricians don't like the term "Rogerian *argument*," preferring instead "Rogerian *rhetoric*" or "Rogerian *communication*." These theorists say that Rogerian listening isn't a form of argument or persuasion at all. Rather, its goal is increased mutual understanding and enlarged perspectives on reality for both writer and audience. According to rhetorician Nathaniel Teich, Rogerian rhetoric seeks to foster discovery of others' perspectives and revision of both parties' worldviews.*

In contrast to this perspective, other scholars view Rogerian argument as a means of manipulating resistant audiences. According to this view, the best way to persuade a hostile audience is to adopt a nonthreatening tone and approach, treat the opponent views sympathetically, and then lure the opponent into accepting your views. The problem with this perspective is that it is purely instrumental and reduces Rogerian argument to a technique, a clever means to an end.

Our view of Rogerian communication forges a middle path between these two perspectives. Throughout this text, we emphasize that argument includes inquiry. (See particularly Chapters 1 and 2.) Here we treat Rogerian communication as dialogic inquiry in which the writer negotiates with the audience in a mutual search for provisional solutions.

Rogerian Communication as Growth for the Writer

One of the key features of Rogerian communication is the open relationship it establishes between the writer and the subject; it recasts argument as a process of growth for the writer. Because Rogerian communication asks the writer to listen to the opponent's views—views that the writer may find uncomfortable or threatening—it promotes inquiry and self-reflection, a more tentative and exploratory approach to the subject than the writer takes in classical argument or delayed-thesis argument. Rogerian communication urges writers to play Peter Elbow's "believing game," where the writer must try "to get inside the head of someone" who holds unwelcome ideas.[†]

---

*For one of the most thorough analyses of Carl Rogers's influence on rhetoric and composition, see Nathaniel Teich's scholarly anthology *Rogerian Perspectives: Collaborative Rhetoric for Oral and Written Communication* (Norwood, NJ: Ablex Publishing Corporation, 1992).

[†]For more suggestions on how to encourage empathic listening, see Elbow's "Bringing the Rhetoric of Assent and the Believing Game Together—and into the Classroom," *College English* 67.4 (March 2005), 389.

(See our discussion of the believing and doubting game in Chapter 2, pages 24–25.) This "dwelling in" unappealing ideas often compels writers to articulate their own values and to achieve a new understanding of them. Extending Elbow's strategy and emphasizing the connection between values and identity, rhetorician James Baumlin argues that Rogerian rhetoric creates "a realm of plural selves or identities" in the process of taking on "another's beliefs and worldview" through role-playing.* Rogerian communication thus promotes a writer's self-examination and exploration of multiple perspectives on a problem. This double process of exploration and reflection can in turn lead to a change of mind or at least a deeper understanding of a problem.

Rogerian Communication as Collaborative Negotiation

A second key feature of Rogerian communication is its altered argumentative purpose and attitude toward the audience. In the absence of the possibility of persuading a resistant audience to accept the writer's views, the writer seeks different goals through a relationship with the audience. These goals include reducing antagonism toward those with different beliefs, initiating small steps in understanding, cultivating mutual respect, and encouraging further problem solving—in short, nurturing conditions for future exchanges. The focus shifts from persuasion toward collaborative negotiation. Thus Rogerian communication particularly lends itself to rhetorical situations involving complex, emotionally volatile issues. Rogerian communication is appropriate whenever writers are seeking to open up dialogue with a resistant audience and are themselves willing to work toward a synthesis of views.

Writing Rogerian Communication

A major thrust of Rogerian communication is building bridges between writer and audience. Because Rogers's principles originated as a communication strategy between two parties in conversation, Rogerian communication most commonly takes the form of a letter or an open letter directed to a specific person or group. For example, the audience for a Rogerian letter might be a particular person whom the writer already knows, a speaker the writer has recently heard, or the author of an article that the writer has recently read. In all these cases, the writer is disturbed by the audience's views and hopes to open up dialogue. Rogerian communication will most likely include the features shown in the chart on the next page, although not necessarily in any set form.

---

*For more discussion of the relationship between role-playing, understanding, and identity, see James S. Baumlin's "Persuasion, Rogerian Rhetoric, and Imaginative Play," *Rhetoric Society Quarterly* 17.1 (Winter 1987), 36.

Organization Plan for Rogerian Communication

Introduction	• Address the audience and identify the problem that you and your audience want to solve. • Possibly, show the timeliness (*kairos*) of the problem. • Try to establish a friendly or cordial relationship with the audience. • Possibly include information that shows your familiarity with the audience.
Summary of the Audience's Views	• Summarize the audience's views in a fair and neutral way that the audience would accept. • Show that you understand the audience's position. • Also show an understanding of, and respect for, the audience's values and beliefs; the goal of this "saying back" (Rogers's term) is to summarize these views in a way that will be entirely acceptable to the audience.
Common Ground	• Identify common ground you share with your audience. • Demonstrate your growth through empathic consideration of views that you would otherwise find threatening or unwelcome. • Show understanding of the audience's views by "indwelling" with them and perhaps by extending them to other situations through new examples. • Show how your views have been enlarged by empathic listening to the audience's ideas.
Contribution of New Points to the Negotiation	• Respectfully propose your own way of looking at this issue. • Through a respectful and inquiring tone, encourage the audience to listen and work with you to solve the problem.
Conclusion	• Possibly propose a synthesis of the two positions, discuss how both parties gain from an enlarged vision, or invite the audience to ongoing negotiation.

In the following example of a Rogerian letter, student writer Colleen Fontana responds to an article written by Robert A. Levy, a senior fellow for constitutional studies at the Cato Institute, a libertarian think tank. In this open letter, Colleen conducts a collaborative discussion directed toward solving the problem of gun violence.* Annotations in the margins indicate how Colleen is practicing Rogerian principles.

An Open Letter to Robert Levy in Response to His Article "They Never Learn"

COLLEEN FONTANA (STUDENT)

Dear Robert Levy,

Writer addresses the audience.

My recent interest in preventing gun violence led me to find your article "They Never Learn" in *The American Spectator* about the mass shooting at Virginia Tech in 2007. I was struck by the similarities between that incident and the recent shooting in Tucson, Arizona, where a young man gunned down U.S. Representative Gabrielle Giffords and nineteen others in a supermarket parking lot. Although your article came several years before this Arizona incident, we can see that gun violence remains an enduring issue. I have long struggled with the question of how we can reduce gun-related violence without detracting from an individual's right to own a gun. Your article shed new light on this question for me.

Writer identifies the problem, shows its current timeliness (kairos), and establishes a cordial relationship with the audience.

Your article stresses the need for something different from our nation's current gun policies. You assert that the solution lies not in stricter gun control policies, but rather in "liberalized laws." According to you, Mr. Levy, it was primarily the existence of anti-gun laws on the Virginia Tech campus that prevented an armed citizen from saving the victims of the 2007 shooting. You comment that "gun control does not work. It just prevents weaker people from defending themselves against stronger predators." Your article gives detailed examples of studies that have substantiated that stricter gun laws have not resulted in lower murder rates. You also cite evidence that fewer crimes are likely to happen if the victim brandishes a gun, even if he or she never fires it. According to your article, stricter gun laws are doing nothing to help society, and your solution lies in relaxed laws, allowing more responsible citizens to carry concealed weapons.

In neutral, fair terms, the writer summarizes the audience's previous argument, the article to which she is responding.

Living on a college campus myself, I identify immediately with your concern for preventing school shootings. I appreciate that you are

---

*We are indebted to Doug Brent for his insight that Rogerian arguments can often be addressed to the author of an article that a reader finds disturbing. See "Rogerian Rhetoric: Ethical Growth Through Alternative Forms of Argumentation." In *Argument Revisited; Argument Redefined,* eds. Barbara Emmel, Paula Resch, and Deborah Tenney (Thousand Oaks, CA: Sage, 1996), 81.

Common ground:
Writer identifies common values that she shares with her audience; she demonstrates empathic listening; she imagines instances where the audience's values make the most sense.

concerned with the safety of the students and the public, and I agree that there exists a need for greater safety on school campuses. I also agree that current gun laws are not effective, as is shown by the number of gun-related deaths that happen annually. Even though such laws exist, they are not likely to stop "crazed fanatics undeterred by laws against murder," as you say, from committing certain crimes. I particularly agree with you when you discuss the right of self-defense. I struggle with laws that forbid carrying a gun because I believe in the right of self-defense. As you mentioned in your article, instances do occur in which civilians carrying guns have the ability to save themselves and others. Although I have not experienced this situation personally, I have read of brave acts of self-defense and intervention. For example, my research turned up an article by John Pierce on Minneapolis' Examiner.com, "It Takes a Gun to Stop a Gunman." In this article Pierce describes an occurrence in Richmond, Virginia, in July of 2009 where a store owner and several customers were saved from an armed robber by a civilian in the store who happened to be carrying a firearm. Even though Pierce is a long-time gun rights advocate and an NRA-certified instructor, the points he brought up were striking. If that civilian hadn't been carrying a gun in that store on that day, then everyone in the store might have been killed by the robber. This realization resonates with me. I imagine myself in that store, and I know I would have been quite grateful that he was carrying a weapon that saved my life. Reading this story has forced me to think of the responsibility many gun-owning citizens must feel—a responsibility to protect not only themselves but those around them as well. A similar event happened recently in New York where a person attempting to rob a jewelry shop was shot by the owner in an act of self-defense. His neighbors regard him as a hero (Kilgannon).

Writer moves respectfully to presenting her own questions and differing perspectives on the problem. Note her tone of negotiation and her willingness to engage in further discussion.

While I agree with you that self-defense is an important right and that armed citizens can sometimes prevent the death of innocent people, I wonder whether the possibility of allowing more guns in public through liberalized gun laws is the best solution. Is there a chance more guns in the hands of more people would foster a more danger-prone climate both from accidents and from sudden fits of rage? I was surprised to learn in a recent *New York Times* article by Charles M. Blow that for every ten people in America there are nine guns. Among major nations, according to a U.N. study, we have both the highest ratio of guns to people and the highest incidence of violence. If liberalizing gun ownership will lead to even more guns, then my concern is that there will be a higher chance of children finding a loaded gun in a parent's bed stand or of deaths caused by gang warfare or from momentary rage in an escalating fight between neighbors. Such danger could also exist on school campuses if guns were allowed. On a campus where drinking nurtures the party scene, I worry that rowdy people waving a gun perhaps as a joke might turn a party into a tragedy. Do you have any ideas, Mr. Levy, for reducing gun accidents or irresponsible use of firearms if they are widely available?

5   I found your point about owning a firearm for self-defense really thought provoking. But even if Virginia Tech had allowed guns on campus, what are the odds that an armed student or teacher would have been at the right place at the right time with an actual chance of shooting the gunman? Only in the movies are good guys and heroes *always* on the spot and capable of taking the right action to protect potential victims. Although I can really see your point about using handguns for self-defense, I don't think self-defense can be used as a justification for assault weapons or automatic weapons with large clips. If guns were freely allowed on campuses, perhaps massacres such as Virginia Tech might occur more often. Or is there a way to allow people to carry concealed handguns on campus but still to forbid rifles, shotguns, or other weapons more useful for massacres than for self-defense?

Writer expresses a second concern, one that Levy did not mention: assault weapons.

After reading your article I have more understanding of the arguments in favor of guns, and I continue to ponder the ethical and practical issues of gun control versus the right to self-defense. You have underscored for me the importance of our continuing to seek means of preventing these terrible massacres from happening in our nation's schools. You have also opened my eyes to the fact that no amount of enforcement of gun laws can deter determined people from using guns to harm others. I am not sure, however, that your proposal to eliminate gun control laws is the best solution, and I am hoping that you might be willing to consider some of my reasons for fearing guns, especially assault weapons and automatic weapons that can be fired like machine guns. Perhaps we could both agree that pursuing responsible gun ownership is a step in the right direction so that we reduce the number of accidents, keep guns away from children, and reduce access to guns capable of unleashing mass murder. I am hopeful that with our common concern over the current ineffectiveness of gun laws and the desire for safety in our schools, we can find a reasonable solution while still preserving the human right of self-defense.

Writer concludes her letter with a reiteration of the mutual concerns she shares with her audience; she acknowledges how her perspectives have been widened by Levy's views; she seeks to keep the channel of communication open; and she expresses interest in further problem solving.

Sincerely,

Colleen Fontana

Works Cited

Blow, Charles M. "Obama's Gun Play." *New York Times.* New York Times, 21 Jan. 2011. Web. 21 Mar. 2011.

Kilgannon, Cory. "After Shooting, Merchant Is Hero of Arthur Avenue." *New York Times.* New York Times, 12 Feb. 2011. Web. 21 Mar. 2011.

Levy, Robert A. "They Never Learn." *American Spectator.* American Spectator, 25 Apr. 2007. Web. 13 Mar. 2011.

Pierce, John. "It Takes a Gun to Stop a Gunman." *Examiner.com.* Clarity Digital Group, 15 July 2009. Web. 15 Mar. 2011.

■ ■ ■ **FOR WRITING AND DISCUSSION** **Listening Empathically and Searching for Common Ground** MyWritingLab™

The heated national debate over immigration reform is highlighted in the photos shown in Figures 7.3–7.6. One of the most contentious parts of the immigration debate concerns deportation of illegals by the U.S. Immigration and Customs Enforcement. Intended to be enforced primarily on illegal immigrants guilty of crimes, this practice has swept up many illegals who have been peacefully raising families and working in the United States, often for many years. Illegals are often

FIGURE 7.3 Demonstrators in Tacoma, Washington, protest immigrant deportations as inhumane

FIGURE 7.4 Demonstrators in Phoenix support Arizona's tough law against illegal immigration

FIGURE 7.5 A rally on Capitol Hill opposes immigration reform with amnesty

FIGURE 7.6 Demonstrators urge executive support of immigrant family unity

detained in harsh prison-like conditions before they are deported. Another part of the immigration debate focuses on illegal immigrants' impact on American jobs. Usually, stakeholders who believe illegal immigrants are displacing American workers also oppose creating a path to citizenship for illegals. The photos portray protestors taking strong, emotional stands on the problem of illegal immigration and the treatment of illegal immigrants.

Individual task: Among the photos, choose one that represents the position on immigration with which you most disagree. Then imagine that you are conducting a Rogerian discussion with the people in the photo and follow these thinking and writing steps:

1. What are your own views about how the United States should handle the problem of 11 million illegal immigrants in the country? In what ways have you benefitted from the presence of illegal workers? Should the government try to establish a path to citizenship for them? Evict them from the country? Deport only those who have a criminal record? Explore your own values.
2. Write a summary of the views you think the people in your chosen photo hold. Write your summary in fair, neutral language that indicates your understanding and that would make your summary acceptable to the people you oppose.
3. Then write a common-grounds paragraph in which you go beyond summary to show your respectful understanding of the values held by these people. Consider how these views might be valid. Demonstrate your empathy, and add an example of your own that shows how your views and those of the people in the photo could intersect.

Group task: As you share your summaries and common-grounds paragraphs with members of your class, role-play being the people in the photo with whom the writer is trying to seek common values and a basis for collaborative problem solving. From your assumed role, comment on how well the writer has understood and identified with your views and values.

Conclusion

This chapter explains strategies for addressing alternative views. When intending to engage supportive audiences in a cause, writers often compose one-sided arguments. Neutral or undecided audiences generally respond most favorably to classical argument, which uses strong reasons in support of its claim while openly summarizing alternative views and responding to them through rebuttal or concession. Strongly resistant audiences typically respond most favorably to dialogic strategies, such as delayed-thesis or Rogerian communication, which seeks common ground with an audience, aims at reducing hostility, and takes a more inquiring or conciliatory stance. Rogerian communication, especially, envisions both writer and reader undergoing mutual change.

WRITING ASSIGNMENT   A Classical Argument or a Rogerian Letter   MyWritingLab™

Option 1: A Classical Argument Write a classical argument following the explanations in Chapter 3, pages 52–54, and using the guidelines for developing such an argument throughout Chapters 3–7. Depending on your instructor's preferences, this argument could be on a new issue, or it could be a final stage of an argument in progress throughout Part Two. This assignment expands the supporting-reasons assignment from Chapter 5 by adding sections that summarize opposing views and respond to them through refutation or concession. For an example of a classical argument, see "The Dangers of Digital Distraction" by Lauren Shinozuka (pages 145–148). Note how Lauren uses research to show that she is joining a larger public conversation on her generation's use of digital technology.

Option 2: A Rogerian Letter Write a Rogerian letter addressed to a specific person, either someone you know, someone you have heard deliver a speech, or the author of an article that has disturbed you. As you generate ideas for your letter, take stock of what you know about your audience and summarize his or her views in a way that your audience would find satisfactory. As you explore what your audience values and believes in, also explore how your own values differ. Where do you agree with your audience? Under what conditions would you find your audience's values acceptable? Follow the suggestions in the chart that explains the elements of a Rogerian letter on page 139 for determining a purpose and structure for your letter. Depending on the distance between your views and your audience's, your goal may be simply to encourage your audience to be willing to consider your perspective. For examples of Rogerian communication, see Colleen Fontana's "Open Letter to Robert Levy" on pages 140–142 and Monica Allen's "An Open Letter to Christopher Eide in Response to His Article 'High-Performing Charter Schools Can Close the Opportunity Gap'" on pages 149–152. Your instructor may ask you to attach a reflective response in which you describe how your experience of writing this Rogerian letter differed from your experience of writing classical arguments. ■

READINGS

Our first student essay illustrates a classical argument. This essay grew out of Lauren's own wrestling with her immersion in social media. She decided to persuade her peers to see the problem her way with the goal that they will join her in new awareness and new habits.

The Dangers of Digital Distractedness

LAUREN SHINOZUKA (STUDENT)

We are the Net Generation, the Facebook Generation—digital natives. Cultural critics praise us for our digital skills, our facility with multimedia, and our ability to interact electronically with others through collaboration and co-creation. But at what cost? If we are honest, the following anti-social scene is familiar. You are sitting at a table with friends, and then you hear various pings and look up to see every one of your friends with squinted eyes, checking social media apps and text messages, scrolling away on their phones and furiously punching a reply. What kind of togetherness is this? We seem to feel some urgency or need to know what the world wants from us in that moment, prompting us to check our smartphones every six and a half minutes a day. Rather than being skillfully technologically interactive, I argue that our behavior represents dependence, even addiction, that has deep, pervasive consequences. It harms us by promoting an unproductive habit of multitasking, by dehumanizing our relationships, and by encouraging a distorted self-image.

I can hear my peers immediately rejecting these claims as too extreme and too critical, and I acknowledge that a good case can be made for our digital savvy and the benefits that brings. Armed with smartphones and laptops, we believe we are masters of technology because we can access so much information easily and immediately. Thanks to our cell phones, all of our friends are only a mere click or swipe away for starting a conversation or sending an invitation to meet up. I also have to admit that our digital knowledge gives us on-the-job advantages. At my part-time job at a high-end retail store, I constantly use a mobile point-of-sale system to ring up customers for fast and easy "on-the-spot checkout," receiving compliments for my competence. With my comfort with the company's technology, I can troubleshoot easily and help other employees. Because technology facilitates much of what we do and keeps us plugged into the rest of the world, I recognize that it can be difficult to see the negative aspects of our relationship to digital technology, but it is time for serious self-examination.

In college, we tell ourselves that multitasking with technology helps us use our time wisely, but in actuality we become even less productive. I notice that while I study, I feel the need to stop every five or ten minutes to check my phone, or log on to a Web site and allow myself to get distracted before going back to my task. These momentary distractions eat away at my time; when I sit down to write a paper at 9 P.M. I am often startled to find that it is suddenly 12 A.M. and I have less than a page written. We Millennials think we are so cutting edge with our multitasking, yet we get little done with our time. We submerge ourselves into a technological bubble consisting of laptops and music and cell phones, convinced that by arming ourselves with these tools, we can really do it all. In actuality, as writer John Hamilton explains in his report for National Public Radio, our brains cannot "focus on more than one thing at a time." Hamilton cites MIT neuroscientist Earl Miller who says that our minds are "not paying attention to...two things simultaneously, but switching between them very rapidly"; thus, multitasking in itself is a myth. Furthermore, as we continue to overload our brains with multiple tasks, we also begin to reshape our thought processes. Technology—the Internet in particular—helps us avoid the hard work of concentration and contemplation. In the article "Is Google Making Us Stupid?" nonfiction business and technology writer Nicholas Carr describes this way we take in and distribute information as a "swiftly moving stream of particles." We skim rather than read; we rapidly switch tasks rather than truly multitask. I recognize this superficial way of operating in the world in my own behavior. I often turn to Google for an immediate answer to a question I have: Who's the current Speaker of the House? How many ounces are in a cup? Then I click on the first link I see, and more often than not, I see the little subheading that states, "You've visited this page X times." I realize my mental instincts tell me that it's much easier to Google an answer multiple times rather than just *learn* the information. Because I constantly overindulge in my technology, I have engrained the habits of skimming streams of information, constantly bouncing from one task to another, but never stopping to bask in its depths.

Our obsession with technology and social media not only reshapes the way we think, but also fosters a type of false superficial friendship with people we barely know, dehumanizing the kinds of relationships we have. Since coming to college, I've had hundreds of new Facebook friends and dozens of new followers on Twitter. To be fair, a number of these people are truly my good friends, but most of these "friendships" came from a one-time meeting at a party or a class I had with them during my sophomore year. Although some will insist on the vital role social media plays in keeping them connected to distant family and friends, we need to address more directly the extent and pervasive effects of our more common arbitrary cyber friendships. Last summer, while I taught a program at a local elementary school, I would occasionally post a Facebook status of something funny that happened that day, or a picture of my class. Back home later for a short vacation, I ran into a girl from high school whom I hadn't seen in four years and barely knew then. When we stopped to chat, she asked me all about my summer program, and commented that all my students were so cute! After our chat, I left feeling perturbed and uneasy. Immediately, I thought she was so "creepy," but I realized that ultimately I chose to share my life with the rest of the world. Speaking about these digital relationships, Sherry Turkle, MIT professor and author of *Alone Together: Why We Expect More from Technology and Less from Each Other,* labels our behavior "a Goldilocks effect": "we can't get enough of one another if we can use technology to keep one another at distances we can control: not too close, not too far, just right" ("The Flight from Conversation"). That moment when my distant "friend" reached out to me about my summer felt so disturbing because she crossed that Goldilocks line through a personal face-to-face conversation. I am embarrassed to say that I was comfortable only when she was one of the masses; I didn't want to engage in a true interpersonal connection.

5   This lack of intimacy through false relationships leads to the creation of a distorted identity. We begin to form a social identity through our conscious decisions of what we choose to share with the rest of the digital world. We want to post pretty pictures that will garner us a number of "likes," and we want to tweet something witty or profound so others will retweet us. When I began to reevaluate my own social media identity, I found that I consciously try to word my Facebook status in order for people to find it funny, and I'm obsessed with editing my pictures with the right filters to achieve that hipster artist effect. I realized that I was interpreting my own life experiences in such a way that I would seem interesting or entertaining to all of my "friends," as if I were performing for an audience I was trying to please. That image of myself is dishonest: It conveys the person I want people to think I am, not the real me.

We see this willful self-distortion in a growing trend called "catfishing": an Internet phenomenon where one person creates a false online identity to engage in a romantic relationship with another person physically far removed. The "catfisher" uses fake pictures of attractive people and an image of talent to create a different person. Coined by a documentary of the same name, *Catfish*, a reality show spin-off, features these long-distance lovers traveling across the country for a chance to meet who really is on the other side of the screen. Often that person's appearance and even gender and motives are strikingly at odds with the self-portrayal. While it is easy for us to judge negatively these extreme cases of catfishing, Molly McHugh, writer for *Digital Trends*, points out what she calls the "slippery slope of catfishdom." These cases may seem extreme, but to an extent, all of us who embrace social media are indeed "catfish" as well. We succumb to what McHugh calls the "aspirational beast" of social media, bending the truth online to some degree in order to portray the self that we want to be. With our growing reliance on social media and technology, the tendency for our romantic relationships to blend into our digital selves becomes even more prevalent. When we continue to mix this intimate, personal self with the demands and desires of social media, we produce tragic, ill-formed identities that no longer resemble our true selves.

Of course, we may draw a sharp distinction between our own digital dependence and the growing number of young users who are actual technological addicts. (According to Carolyn Gregoire's *Huffington Post* article, there is now an inpatient Internet rehabilitation center designed specifically for true addicts.) However, our own participation in the more wide-spread digital craze remains a serious problem too. Yet by taking the first step of making the unconscious conscious, I believe we can combat the digital damage in our lives. I have begun by taking several steps. I purposefully put my phone across the table so I physically need to get up to check it; I only let myself binge-check all my social media apps just before going to bed rather than ten times a day, and I have stopped trying to take pictures of every pretty meal I consume or sunset I see because I know that those are my own special moments, not some glamorous, envious image I want to project. I have begun to avoid friends who find their phones more interesting than the immediate world around them, and this new company has made it easier to break away from my own addiction. I am trying to rehumanize my friendships, and I am finding solace in deep reading once more without the distractions of cell phone vibrations. I invite members of my generation to join me, so we can be together, no longer alone together.

Works Cited

Carr, Nicholas. "Is Google Making Us Stupid?" *Atlantic.* The Atlantic, 1 July 2008. Web. 25 Feb. 2014.

Gregoire, Carolyn. "Welcome to Internet Rehab." *Huffington Post*. Huffington Post, 25 Sept. 2013. Web. 4 Mar. 2014.

Hamilton, John. "Think You're Multitasking? Think Again." *Nat'l Public Radio*. Nat'l Public Radio, 2 Oct. 2008. Web. 10 Feb. 2014.

McHugh, Molly. "It's Catfishing Season! How to Tell Lovers from Liars Online, and More." *Digital Trends.* Digital Trends, 23 Aug. 2013. Web. 25 Feb. 2014.

Turkle, Sherry. "The Flight from Conversation." *New York Times*. New York Times, 21 Apr. 2012. Web. 25 Feb. 2014.

To illustrate a conciliatory or Rogerian approach to an issue, we show you student writer Monica Allen's Rogerian letter written for this assignment. Monica's letter grew out of her research on charter schools and educational reform in preparation for writing her own proposal argument later. In this Rogerian letter, she listens carefully to a proponent of charter schools whose views were very different from her own. Monica writes in the hope of opening up a deeper problem-solving conversation.

An Open Letter to Christopher Eide in Response to His Article "High-Performing Charter Schools Can Close the Opportunity Gap"

MONICA ALLEN (STUDENT)

Dear Mr. Eide,

I want to thank you for your article "High-Performing Charter Schools Can Close the Opportunity Gap," which contributes to the national conversation about the role of charter schools in education reform. Like you, I am concerned about whether publically run, privately funded charter schools can provide innovative new approaches to increase the quality of education for minority and economically disadvantaged students. I have been wrestling with the claims that charter schools can help reduce this troubling opportunity gap. Your helpful article has deepened my understanding of charter schools and has given me much to think about.

Your article proposes legislation specifically designed to create high-performing, effective charter schools. What is most exciting in your article is your suggestion that this legislation has the potential to close the opportunity gap. Citing the Stanford Center for Research on Education (CREDO) study and national charter efforts like the Knowledge is Power Program (KIPP), which focus on achievement gains in particular for low-income students in some charter schools, you believe that increased charter education will enable our nation to better educate academically underserved students. Ultimately, you want to look beyond the inconsistent results charter schools have historically shown nationwide and urge our state to focus its charter school innovation on improving opportunities for its students suffering most from the opportunity gap.

Your encouraging article speaks to the belief I share with you that the highest priority in educational innovation needs to be closing the opportunity gap. As education researcher Sean Reardon has shown in "The Widening Income Achievement Gap," the differences in opportunities and outcomes between low- and high-income background students have continued to widen throughout the past three decades. Clearly, we are in desperate need of more and better educational improvement. I share your concern that charter schools, focusing on the wrong objectives, could become a force that widens, rather than narrows, the opportunity gap. I particularly appreciate your commitment to concentrating reform efforts where they are needed most—with students from low-income backgrounds who are disproportionately left behind in traditional public schools. As an English Language Learning tutor and teacher, I am encouraged that the CREDO study you cite indicates that some charter schools produce better gains for ELL students than do traditional public schools. I am grateful that you advocate for underserved students, such as English Language Learners, and am now much more interested in understanding the charter movement because of your conviction that it can address our most pressing educational issue.

Your article also answers some of my prior concerns about charter schools, making me more open to charter education. In particular, I have been wary of the inconsistent performance of charter schools nationwide, and so I appreciate that you support rigorous legislation to hold charter schools accountable to the highest standards possible. Your article also helped dispel some of my concerns that charter schools tend to serve disproportionately higher income students and thereby segregate our schools into high-income charters and low-income traditional public schools. It led me to do more research about charter schools' student demographics and to find that there are many examples of charters serving primarily low-income groups of students. Finally, I appreciated your article's urgency. I, too, believe that the needs of disproportionally poorly educated, low-income students today make this issue a pressing one that calls for immediate action.

5   Because your article awakened me to the social benefits that charter schools can provide, I'd like to share with you four reservations in the hopes that, together, people like us who hold different perspectives on charter schools can learn from one another and better close our education opportunity gap.

First, I share your belief that charter schools offer needed opportunities to be education laboratories—places whose freedom from bureaucracy enables them to test out new strategies that can inform widespread practices. However, are charter schools really experimental? Adamant charter school supporter and Columbia University researcher Priscilla Wohlstetter writes that despite her belief in the prospects of charter schools generally, "most [charter schools] do little to tap the potential of unique, innovative strategies. For all the hype, charters typically borrow familiar classroom strategies (back-to-basics, project-based learning, college prep) from private and traditional public schools." I share Wohlstetter's concern that while the education laboratory concept has popularized charter schools, research demonstrates they have not functioned as such in our education system. Though I am encouraged by your commitment to highly regulated charter schools, I am unsure whether state legislation that only regulates based on the test results of charter school students really ensures that charters deliver what they intend to. Perhaps we should explore other means to measure innovation to ensure that the investment of public funds in charter schools results in gains for the education system as a whole, in part by demonstrating that charter schools can teach us how to teach better. That would be a partnership between public and charter education that I believe we all hope to see.

A second question I have is whether charter schools will make innovative learning more accessible to students who are traditionally underserved. While the CREDO study you cite shows some promising results, Jean Allen, head of the Center for Education Reform, has questioned the conclusiveness of the data (Sanchez). Indeed, researchers across the board believe that the jury is very much still out on the question of whether charter school students really learn as much as traditional public school students, which is why the National Alliance for Public Charter Schools and Harvard University just started afresh with a comprehensive study last fall. I am concerned that we may be implementing a system that has yet to be effectively tested. I do think the anecdotal evidence you cite about KIPP schools is extremely exciting and deserves public attention, because KIPP schools serve a majority of low-income student populations *and* are outperforming traditional public schools near them. But shouldn't we also consider that KIPP schools rely heavily on significant private donations and are unique among charters in this way? To me, it makes sense that KIPP schools outperform other local schools when their operating budgets are 30–50 percent higher (Di Carlo). Could we agree that this income disparity and school funding as a significant predictor of student success calls for more investigation?

I also have a third, more fundamental question with respect to charter schools. I wonder whether in the enthusiasm to innovate our schools, we will lose sight of that which makes American education innovative at its core—its commitment to democratic education. I am concerned that charter schools focusing on low-income student bodies might contribute to the non-democratic socio-economic and ethnic segregation of our schools. I believe that the segregation of schools into the haves and have-nots is one of the largest issues facing our national education system. Could charter schools that concentrate on serving low-income and traditionally underserved ethnic groups unintentionally widen the gap? Along with education activist and writer Jonathan Kozol (Cody), I fear that charter schools with names like "Black Success Academy" and "The African-American Academy for Leadership and Enterprise" divert attention from what really needs to be attended to—the de-segregating of our already divided schools and our school funding on lines of race and socio-economic status. While I, like you, want us to do everything we can immediately to improve the chances for underserved students, I am most interested in focusing our efforts on equalizing our schools' demographics and budgets. How can charters and traditional public schools work together to do this?

Finally, Mr. Eide, I also wonder whether privatizing education will ultimately be in the best interest of students on the low spectrum of the opportunity gap. Public education promises public responsibility to educate each of its students for successful vocational and civic lives. Right now, you and I both know that the American public has not been living up to that responsibility. How can we do better? I am concerned that privatizing education removes not only the public investment in education (namely, tax dollars) from public hands, but diminishes our sense of responsibility and capacity to be a nation that educates all its citizens. I wonder whether, in the long run, the students who stand to lose the most from the public's loss of responsibility to educate all are those who are the most vulnerable. How can charter and traditional schools work together to build public confidence in the civic power of education?

10   Because my own home state will soon be instituting new charter schools, I am thankful for having read your article. Clearly, people who hold different views about

the potential of charter schools have much to learn from one another. I hope to see my home state pioneer cutting-edge methods for charter school regulation and to build relationships between charter and public school communities so that the existence of charter schools in our state has a large-scale impact. I am very glad to have read your article and to know that many advocates of charter schools are committed to equalizing opportunity in education.

Regards,

Monica Allen

Works Cited

Cody, Anthony. "Confronting the Inequality Juggernaut: A Q&A with Jonathan Kozol." *Education Week: Teacher*. Web. 22 Feb. 2014.

Di Carlo, Matthew. "Controversial Consensus on KIPP Charter Schools." *Albert Shanker Institute*. 12 Mar. 2013. Web. 22 Feb. 2014.

Eide, Christopher. "High-Performing Charter Schools Can Close the Opportunity Gap." *Seattle Times*. 11 July 2012. Web. 23 Feb. 2014.

Reardon, Sean F. "The Widening Income Achievement Gap." *Educational Leadership* 70.8 (2013): 10-16. Print.

Sanchez, Claudio. "The Charter School vs. Public School Debate Continues." *NPR Education*. 16 July 2013. Web. 13 Feb. 2014.

Wohlstetter, Priscilla. "The Debate Must Move On: Charter Schools Are Here to Stay." *WYNC: School Book*. 9 Dec. 2013. Web. 17 Feb. 2014.

MyWritingLab™

Visit Ch. 7 Responding to Objections and Alternative Views in *MyWritingLab* to complete the For Writing and Discussion and Writing Assignments and to test your understanding of the chapter objectives.

PART THREE
Analyzing Arguments

Increasingly, countries are employing hydraulic fracturing (called fracking), which extracts natural gas from deeply buried shale, to meet their energy needs. Burning natural gas is cleaner than burning gasoline, oil, and coal and emits less carbon dioxide. However, each fracking site uses millions of gallons of water, leaves contaminated waste water, and often emits methane. Also environmentalists fear that fracking may contaminate aquifers. This photo depicts anti-fracking views in a protest near Manchester, England, in January 2014. To what extent does the garb of the protestors make effective appeals to *logos* and *pathos* to turn viewers against fracking?

Analyzing Arguments Rhetorically

What you will learn in this chapter:

8.1 To explain what it means to *think rhetorically* about texts

8.2 To conduct a rhetorical analysis of a specific text

In Part Two of this book, we explained thinking and writing strategies for composing your own arguments. Now in Part Three we show you how to use your new rhetorical knowledge to conduct in-depth analyses of other people's arguments. To analyze an argument rhetorically means to examine closely how it is composed and what makes it effective or ineffective for its targeted audience. A rhetorical analysis identifies the text under scrutiny, summarizes its main ideas, presents some key points about the text's rhetorical strategies for persuading its audience, and elaborates on these points.

Becoming skilled at analyzing arguments rhetorically will have multiple payoffs for you. Rhetorical analyses are common assignments in courses in critical thinking and argument. Additionally, thinking rhetorically about texts is crucial for writing the "literature review" section of research assignments across the disciplines. Furthermore, rhetorical analysis also plays a major role in constructing your own arguments, especially in your decisions about reputable evidence and in sections where you summarize and respond to opposing views. This chapter focuses on the rhetorical analysis of written arguments, and the next one (Chapter 9) equips you to analyze visual arguments.

Thinking Rhetorically about a Text

8.1 To explain what it means to *think rhetorically* about texts

Before we turn directly to rhetorical analysis of specific texts, let's focus on the key word *rhetoric*. In popular usage, *rhetoric* often means empty or deceptive language, as in, "Well, that's just rhetoric." Another related meaning of *rhetoric* is decorative or artificial language. The Greek Stoic philosopher Epictetus likened rhetoric to hairdressers fixing hair*—a view that sees rhetoric as superficial decoration.

---

*Chaim Perelman, "The New Rhetoric: A Theory of Practical Reasoning." In *Professing the New Rhetorics: A Sourcebook,* eds. Theresa Enos and Stuart C. Brown (Englewood Cliffs, NJ: Prentice Hall, 1994), 149.

Most contemporary rhetoricians, however, adopt the larger view of rhetoric articulated by Greek philosopher Aristotle: the art of determining what will be persuasive in every situation. Contemporary rhetorician Donald C. Bryant has described rhetoric in action as "the function of adjusting ideas to people and of people to ideas."* Focusing on this foundational meaning of rhetoric, this chapter shows you how to analyze a writer's motivation, purpose, and rhetorical choices for persuading a targeted audience. This chapter draws primarily on rhetorical concepts with which you are already familiar: audience-based reasons, the STAR criteria for evidence, and the classical appeals of *logos, ethos,* and *pathos.*

Questions for Rhetorical Analysis

Conducting a rhetorical analysis asks you to bring to bear on an argument your knowledge of argument and your repertoire of reading strategies. The chart of questions for analysis on pages 155–157 can help you examine an argument in depth. Although a rhetorical analysis will not include answers to all of these questions, using some of these questions in your thinking stages can give you a thorough understanding of the argument while helping you generate insights for your own rhetorical analysis essay.

Questions for Rhetorical Analysis

What to Focus On	Questions to Ask	Applying These Questions
The *kairotic* moment and writer's motivating occasion	■ What motivated the writer to produce this piece? ■ What social, cultural, political, legal, or economic conversations does this argument join?	■ Is the writer responding to a bill pending in Congress, a speech by a political leader, or a local event that provoked controversy? ■ Is the writer addressing cultural trends such as the impact of science or technology on values?
Rhetorical context: Writer's purpose and audience	■ What is the writer's purpose? ■ Who is the intended audience? ■ What assumptions, values, and beliefs would readers have to hold to find this argument persuasive? ■ How well does the text suit its particular audience and purpose?	■ Is the writer trying to change readers' views by offering a new interpretation of a phenomenon, calling readers to action, or trying to muster votes or inspire further investigations? ■ Does the audience share a political or religious orientation with the writer?

(Continued)

---

*Donald C. Bryant, "Rhetoric: Its Functions and Its Scope." In *Professing the New Rhetorics: A Sourcebook,* eds. Theresa Enos and Stuart C. Brown (Englewood Cliffs, NJ: Prentice Hall, 1994), 282.

What to Focus On	Questions to Ask	Applying These Questions
Rhetorical context: Writer's identity and angle of vision	■ Who is the writer and what is his or her profession, background, and expertise? ■ How does the writer's personal history, education, gender, ethnicity, age, class, sexual orientation, and political leaning influence the angle of vision? ■ What is emphasized and what is omitted in this text? ■ How much does the writer's angle of vision dominate the text?	■ Is the writer a scholar, researcher, scientist, policy maker, politician, professional journalist, or citizen blogger? ■ Is the writer affiliated with conservative or liberal, religious or lay publications? ■ Is the writer advocating a stance or adopting a more inquiry-based mode? ■ What points of view and pieces of evidence are "not seen" by this writer?
Rhetorical context: Genre	■ What is the argument's original genre? ■ What is the original medium of publication? How does the genre and the argument's place of publication influence its content, structure, and style?	■ How popular or scholarly, informal or formal is this genre? ■ Does the genre allow for in-depth or only sketchy coverage of an issue? ■ (See Chapter 2, pages 26–29, for detailed explanations of genre.)
***Logos* of the argument**	■ What is the argument's claim, either explicitly stated or implied? ■ What are the main reasons in support of the claim? Are the reasons audience-based? ■ How effective is the writer's use of evidence? How is the argument supported and developed? ■ How well has the argument recognized and responded to alternative views?	■ Is the core of the argument clear and soundly developed? Or do readers have to unearth or reconstruct the argument? ■ Is the argument one-sided, multisided, or dialogic? ■ Does the argument depend on assumptions the audience may not share? ■ What evidence does the writer employ? Does this evidence meet the STAR criteria? (See pages 92–93.)
***Ethos* of the argument**	■ What *ethos* does the writer project? ■ How does the writer try to seem credible and trustworthy to the intended audience? ■ How knowledgeable does the writer seem in recognizing opposing or alternative views and how fairly does the writer respond to them?	■ If you are impressed or won over by this writer, what has earned your respect? ■ If you are filled with doubts or skepticism, what has caused you to question this writer? ■ How important is the character of the writer in this argument?

What to Focus On	Questions to Ask	Applying These Questions
Pathos of the argument	■ How effective is the writer in using audience-based reasons? ■ How does the writer use concrete language, word choice, narrative, examples, and analogies to tap readers' emotions, values, and imaginations?	■ What examples, connotative language, and uses of narrative or analogy stand out for you in this argument? ■ Does this argument rely heavily on appeals to *pathos*? Or is it more brainy and logical?
Writer's style	■ How do the writer's language choices and sentence length and complexity contribute to the impact of the argument? ■ How well does the writer's tone (attitude toward the subject) suit the argument?	■ How readable is this argument? ■ Is the argument formal, scholarly, journalistic, informal, or casual? ■ Is the tone serious, mocking, humorous, exhortational, confessional, urgent, or something else?
Design and visual elements	■ How do design elements—layout, font sizes and styles, and use of color—influence the effect of the argument? (See Chapter 9 for a detailed discussion of these elements.) ■ How do graphics and images contribute to the persuasiveness of the argument?	■ Do design features contribute to the logical or the emotional/imaginative appeals of the argument? ■ How would this argument benefit from visuals and graphics or some different document design?
Overall persuasiveness of the argument	■ What features of this argument contribute most to making it persuasive or not persuasive for its target audience and for you yourself? ■ How would this argument be received by different audiences? ■ What features contribute to the rhetorical complexity of this argument? ■ What is particularly memorable, disturbing, or problematic about this argument? ■ What does this argument contribute to its *kairotic* moment and the argumentative controversy of which it is a part?	■ For example, are appeals to *pathos* legitimate and suitable? Does the quality and quantity of the evidence help build a strong case or fall short? ■ What specifically would count as a strength for the target audience? ■ If you differ from the target audience, how do you differ and where does the argument derail for you? ■ What gaps, contradictions, or unanswered questions are you left with? ■ How does this argument indicate that it is engaged in a public conversation? How does it "talk" to other arguments you have read on this issue?

■ ■ ■ **FOR WRITING AND DISCUSSION** Practicing Rhetorical Analysis   MyWritingLab™

In the following exercise, consider the strategies used by two different writers to persuade their audiences to act to stop climate change. The first is from the opening paragraphs of an editorial in the magazine *Creation Care: A Christian Environmental Quarterly*. The second is from the Web site of the Sierra Club, an environmental action group.

Individual task: Read the following passages carefully, and then write out your exploratory answers to the questions that follow. Refer to the chart "Questions for Rhetorical Analysis" on pages 155–157 to help you in your examination of how the key features of these texts contribute to their impact on readers.

Passage 1

As I sit down to write this column, one thing keeps coming to me over and over: "Now is the time; now is the time."

In the New Testament the word used for this type of time is *kairos*. It means "right or opportune moment." It is contrasted with *chronos,* or chronological time as measured in seconds, days, months, or years. In the New Testament *kairos* is usually associated with decisive action that brings about deliverance or salvation.

The reason the phrase, "Now is the time" kept coming to me over and over is that I was thinking of how to describe our current climate change moment.

The world has been plodding along in chronological time on the problem of climate change since around 1988. No more.

Simply put: the problem of climate change has entered *kairos* time; its *kairos* moment has arrived. How long will it endure? Until the time of decisive action to bring about deliverance comes—or, more ominously, until the time when the opportunity for decisive action has passed us by. Which will we choose? Because we do have a choice.

—Rev. Jim Ball, Ph.D., "It's *Kairos* Time for Climate Change: Time to Act," *Creation Care: A Christian Environmental Quarterly* (Summer 2008), 28.

Passage 2

[Another action that Americans must take to combat global warming is to transition] to a clean energy economy in a just and equitable way. Global warming is among the greatest challenges of our time, but also presents extraordinary opportunities to harness home-grown clean energy sources and encourage technological innovation. These bold shifts toward a clean energy future can create hundreds of thousands of new jobs and generate billions of dollars in capital investment. But in order to maximize these benefits across all sectors of our society, comprehensive global warming legislation must auction emission allowances to polluters and use these public assets for public benefit programs.

Such programs include financial assistance to help low and moderate-income consumers and workers offset higher energy costs as well as programs that assist with adaptation efforts in communities vulnerable to the effects of climate change. Revenue generated from emissions allowances should also aid the expansion of renewable and efficient energy technologies that quickly, cleanly, cheaply, and safely reduce our dependence on fossil fuels and curb global warming. Lastly, it is absolutely vital that comprehensive global warming legislation not preempt state authority to cut greenhouse gas emissions more aggressively than mandated by federal legislation.

—Sierra Club, "Global Warming Policy Solutions," 2008, http://www.sierraclub.org/

1. How do the strategies of persuasion differ in these two passages? Explain these differences in terms of targeted audience, original genre, writer's purpose, and writer's angle of vision.
2. How would you describe the relationship between *logos* and *pathos* in each text?
3. How would you describe the writer's style in each?
4. How effective would either argument be for readers outside the intended audience?

Group task: Share your responses to the above questions with class members. Explain your points with specific examples from the texts.

Conducting a Rhetorical Analysis

8.2 To conduct a rhetorical analysis of a specific text

To illustrate rhetorical analysis (both in this section and in the student example at the end of the chapter), we will analyze two articles on reproductive technology, a subject that continues to generate arguments in the public sphere. By *reproductive technology* we mean scientific advances in the treatment of infertility such as egg and sperm donation, artificial insemination, in vitro fertilization, and surrogate motherhood. Our first article, from over a decade ago, springs from the early and increasing popularity of these technological options. Our second article—to be used in our later student example—responds to the recent globalization of this technology.

At this point, please read our first article, "Egg Heads" by Kathryn Jean Lopez, and then proceed to the discussion questions that follow. Lopez's article was originally published in the September 1, 1998, issue of the biweekly conservative news commentary magazine *National Review*.

Egg Heads

KATHRYN JEAN LOPEZ

Filling the waiting room to capacity and spilling over into a nearby conference room, a group of young women listen closely and follow the instructions: Complete the forms and return them, with the clipboard, to the receptionist. It's all just as in any medical office. Then they move downstairs, where the doctor briefs them. "Everything will be pretty much normal," she explains. "Women complain of skin irritation in the local area of injection and bloating. You also might be a little emotional. But, basically, it's really bad PMS."

This is not just another medical office. On a steamy night in July, these girls in their twenties are attending an orientation session for potential egg donors at a New Jersey fertility clinic specializing in in-vitro fertilization. Within the walls of IVF

New Jersey and at least two hundred other clinics throughout the United States, young women answer the call to give "the gift of life" to infertile couples. Egg donation is a quietly expanding industry, changing the way we look at the family, young women's bodies, and human life itself.

It is not a pleasant way to make money. Unlike sperm donation, which is over in less than an hour, egg donation takes the donor some 56 hours and includes a battery of tests, ultrasound, self-administered injections, and retrieval. Once a donor is accepted into a program, she is given hormones to stimulate the ovaries, changing the number of eggs matured from the usual one per month up to as many as fifty. A doctor then surgically removes the eggs from the donor's ovary and fertilizes them with the designated sperm.

Although most programs require potential donors to undergo a series of medical tests and counseling, there is little indication that most of the young women know what they are getting themselves into. They risk bleeding, infection, and scarring. When too many eggs are matured in one cycle, it can damage the ovaries and leave the donor with weeks of abdominal pain. (At worst, complications may leave her dead.) Longer term, the possibility of early menopause raises the prospect of future regret. There is also some evidence of a connection between the fertility drugs used in the process and ovarian cancer.

5   But it's good money—and getting better. New York's Brooklyn IVF raised its "donor compensation" from $2,500 to $5,000 per cycle earlier this year in order to keep pace with St. Barnabas Medical Center in nearby Livingston, New Jersey. It's a bidding war. "It's obvious why we had to do it," says Susan Lobel, Brooklyn IVF's assistant director. Most New York–area IVF programs have followed suit.

Some infertile couples and independent brokers are offering even more for "reproductive material." The International Fertility Center in Indianapolis, Indiana, for instance, places ads in the *Daily Princetonian* offering Princeton girls as much as $35,000 per cycle. The National Fertility Registry, which, like many egg brokerages, features an online catalogue for couples to browse in, advertises $35,000 to $50,000 for Ivy League eggs. While donors are normally paid a flat fee per cycle, there have been reports of higher payments to donors who produce more eggs.

College girls are the perfect donors. Younger eggs are likelier to be healthy, and the girls themselves frequently need money—college girls have long been susceptible to classified ads offering to pay them for acting as guinea pigs in medical research. One 1998 graduate of the University of Colorado set up her own website to market her eggs. She had watched a television show on egg donation and figured it "seemed like a good thing to do"—especially since she had spent her money during the past year to help secure a country-music record deal. "Egg donation would help me with my school and music expenses while helping an infertile couple with a family." Classified ads scattered throughout cyberspace feature similar offers.

The market for "reproductive material" has been developing for a long time. It was twenty years ago this summer that the first test-tube baby, Louise Brown, was born. By 1995, when the latest tally was taken by the Centers for Disease Control, 15 percent of mothers in this country had made use of some form of assisted-reproduction technology in conceiving their children. (More recently, women past menopause have begun to make use of this technology.) In 1991 the American Society for Reproductive Medicine was aware of 63 IVF programs offering egg donation. That number had jumped to 189 by 1995 (the latest year for which numbers are available).

Defenders argue that it's only right that women are "compensated" for the inconvenience of egg donation. Brooklyn IVF's Dr. Lobel argues, "If it is unethical to accept payment for loving your neighbor, then we'll have to stop paying babysitters." As long as donors know the risks, says Glenn McGee of the

University of Pennsylvania's Center for Bioethics, this transaction is only "a slightly macabre version of adoption."

Not everyone is enthusiastic about the "progress." Egg donation "represents another rather large step into turning procreation into manufacturing," says the University of Chicago's Leon Kass. "It's the dehumanization of procreation." And as in manufacturing, there is quality control. "People don't want to say the word any more, but there is a strong eugenics issue inherent in the notion that you can have the best eggs your money can buy," observes sociology professor Barbara Katz Rothman of the City University of New York.

10   The demand side of the market comes mostly from career-minded baby-boomers, the frontierswomen of feminism, who thought they could "have it all." Indeed they *can* have it all—with a little help from some younger eggs. (Ironically, feminists are also among its strongest critics; *The Nation*'s Katha Pollitt has pointed out that in egg donation and surrogacy, once you remove the "delusion that they are making babies for other women," all you have left is "reproductive prostitution.")

Unfortunately, the future looks bright for the egg market. Earlier this year, a woman in Atlanta gave birth to twins after she was implanted with frozen donor eggs. The same technology has also been successful in Italy. This is just what the egg market needed, since it avoids the necessity of coordinating donors' cycles with recipients' cycles. Soon, not only will infertile couples be able to choose from a wider variety of donor offerings, but in some cases donors won't even be needed. Young women will be able to freeze their own eggs and have them thawed and fertilized once they are ready for the intrusion of children in their lives.

There are human ovaries sitting in a freezer in Fairfax, Virginia. The Genetics and IVF Institute offers to cut out and remove young women's ovaries and cryopreserve the egg-containing tissue for future implantation. Although the technology was originally designed to give the hope of fertility to young women undergoing treatment for cancer, it is now starting to attract the healthy. "Women can wait to have children until they are well established in their careers and getting a little bored, sometime in their forties or fifties," explains Professor Rothman. "Basically, motherhood is being reduced to a good leisure-time activity."

Early this summer, headlines were made in Britain, where the payment of egg donors is forbidden, when an infertile couple traveled to a California clinic where the woman could be inseminated with an experimental hybrid egg. The egg was a combination of the recipient's and a donor's eggs. The clinic in question gets its eggs from a Beverly Hills brokerage, the Center for Surrogate Parenting and Egg Donation, run by Karen Synesiou and Bill Handel, a radio shock-jock in Los Angeles. Miss Synesiou recently told the London *Sunday Times* that she is "interested in redefining the family. That's why I came to work here."

The redefinition is already well under way. Consider the case of Jaycee Buzzanca. After John and Luanne Buzzanca had tried for years to have a child, an embryo was created for them, using sperm and an egg from anonymous donors, and implanted in a surrogate mother. In March 1995, one month before the baby was born, John filed for divorce. Luanne wanted child support from John, but he refused—after all, he's not the father. Luanne argued that John is Jaycee's father legally. At this point the surrogate mother, who had agreed to carry a baby for a stable two-parent household, decided to sue for custody.

15   Jaycee was dubbed "Nobody's Child" by the media when a California judge ruled that John was not the legal father nor Luanne the legal mother (neither one was genetically related to Jaycee, and Luanne had not even borne her). Enter Erin Davidson, the egg donor, who claims the egg was used without her permission. Not to be left out, the sperm donor jumped into the ring, saying that his sperm was used without his permission, a claim he later dropped. In March of this year, an appeals

court gave Luanne custody and decided that John is the legal father, making him responsible for child support. By contracting for a medical procedure resulting in the birth of a child, the court ruled, a couple incurs "the legal status of parenthood." (John lost an appeal in May.) For Jaycee's first three years on earth, these people have been wrangling over who her parents are.

In another case, William Kane left his girlfriend, Deborah Hect, 15 vials of sperm before he killed himself in a Las Vegas hotel in 1991. His two adult children (represented by their mother, his ex-wife) contested Miss Hect's claim of ownership. A settlement agreement on Kane's will was eventually reached, giving his children 80 percent of his estate and Miss Hect 20 percent. Hence she was allowed three vials of his sperm. When she did not succeed in conceiving on the first two tries, she filed a petition for the other 12 vials. She won, and the judge who ruled in her favor wrote, "Neither this court nor the decedent's adult children possess reason or right to prevent Hect from implementing decedent's pre-eminent interest in realizing his 'fundamental right' to procreate with the woman of his choice." One day, donors may not even have to have lived. Researchers are experimenting with using aborted female fetuses as a source of donor eggs.

And the market continues to zip along. For overseas couples looking for donor eggs, Bill Handel has the scenario worked out. The couple would mail him frozen sperm of their choice (presumably from the recipient husband); his clinic would use it to fertilize donor eggs, chosen from its catalogue of offerings, and reply back within a month with a frozen embryo ready for implantation. (Although the sperm does not yet arrive by mail, Handel has sent out embryos to at least one hundred international customers.) As for the young women at the New Jersey clinic, they are visibly upset by one aspect of the egg-donation process: they can't have sexual intercourse for several weeks after the retrieval. For making babies, of course, it's already obsolete.

■ ■ ■ **FOR CLASS DISCUSSION** **Identifying Rhetorical Features**

Working in groups or as a whole class, develop responses to the following questions:

1. How does Lopez appeal to *logos*? What is her main claim and what are her reasons?
2. What does she use for evidence? What ideas would you have to include in a short summary?
3. What appeals to *pathos* does Lopez make in this argument? How well are these suited to the conservative readers of the *National Review*?
4. How would you characterize Lopez's *ethos*? Does she seem knowledgeable and credible? Does she seem fair to stakeholders in this controversy?
5. Choose an additional focus from the "Questions for Rhetorical Analysis" on pages 155–157 to apply to "Egg Heads." How does this question expand your understanding of Lopez's argument?
6. What strikes you as problematic, memorable, or disturbing in this argument? ■ ■ ■

Our Own Rhetorical Analysis of "Egg Heads"

Now that you have identified some of the rhetorical features of "Egg Heads," we offer our own notes for a rhetorical analysis of this argument.

Rhetorical Context   As we began our analysis, we reconstructed the rhetorical context in which "Egg Heads" was published. In the late 1990s, a furious debate about egg donation rippled through college and public newspapers, popular journalism, Web sites, and scholarly commentary. This debate had been kicked off by several couples placing ads in the newspapers of the country's most prestigious colleges, offering up to $50,000 for the eggs of brilliant, attractive, athletic college women. Coinciding with these consumer demands, advances in reproductive technology provided an increasing number of complex techniques to surmount the problem of infertility, including fertilizing eggs in petri dishes and implanting them into women through surgical procedures. These procedures could use either a couple's own eggs and sperm or donated eggs and sperm. All these social and medical factors created the *kairotic* moment for Lopez's article and motivated her to protest the increasing use of these procedures. (Egg donation, surrogate motherhood, and the potential dehumanizing of commercial reproduction continue to be troubling and unresolved controversies across many genres, as you will see when you read Ellen Goodman's op-ed piece at the end of this chapter and student Zachary Stumps's rhetorical analysis of it.)

Genre and Writer   When we considered the genre and writer of this article and its site of publication, we noted that this article appeared in the *National Review*, which describes itself as "America's most widely read and influential magazine and Web site for Republican/conservative news, commentary, and opinion." It reaches "an affluent, educated, and highly responsive audience of corporate and government leaders, the financial elite, educators, journalists, community and association leaders, as well as engaged activists all across America" (http://www.nationalreview.com). According to our Internet search, Kathryn Jean Lopez is known nationally for her conservative journalistic writing on social and political issues. Currently the editor-at-large of *National Review Online*, she has also published in the *Wall Street Journal,* the *New York Post*, and the *Washington Times*. This information told us that in her article "Egg Heads," Lopez is definitely on home territory, aiming her article at a conservative audience.

Logos   Turning to the *logos* of Lopez's argument, we decided that the logical structure of Lopez's argument is clear throughout the article. Her claim is that egg donation and its associated reproductive advances have harmful, long-reaching consequences for society. Basically, she argues that egg donation and reproductive technology represent bad scientific developments for society because they are potentially harmful to the long-range health of egg donors and because they lead to an unnatural dehumanizing of human sexuality. She states a version of this last point at the end of the second paragraph: "Egg donation is a quietly expanding industry, changing the way we look at the family, young women's bodies, and human life itself " (page 160).

The body of her article elaborates on each of these reasons. In developing her reason that egg donation endangers egg donors, Lopez lists the risks but doesn't supply supporting evidence about the frequency of these problems: damage to the ovaries, persistent pain, early menopause, possible ovarian cancer, and even death. She supports her claim about "the expanding industry" by showing how the procedures have become commercialized. To show the popularity of these procedures as well as their commercial value, she quotes a variety of experts such as directors of in vitro clinics, fertility centers, bioethicists, and the American Society for Reproductive Medicine. She also cleverly bolsters her own case by showing that even liberal cultural critics agree with her views about the big ethical questions raised by the reproductive-technology business. In addition to quoting experts, Lopez has sprinkled impressive numbers and vivid examples throughout the body of her argument that give her argument momentum as it progresses from the potential harm to young egg donors to a number of case studies that depict increasingly disturbing ethical problems.

Pathos   Much of the impact of this argument, we noted, comes from Lopez's appeals to *pathos*. By describing in detail the waiting rooms for egg donors at fertility clinics, Lopez relies heavily on pathetic appeals to move her audience to see the physical and social dangers of egg donation. She conveys the growing commercialism of reproductive technology by giving readers an inside look at the egg-donation process as these young college women embark on the multistep process of donating their eggs. These young women, she suggests in her title "Egg Heads," are largely unaware of the potential physical dangers to themselves and of the ethical implications and consequences of their acts. She asserts that they are driven largely by the desire for money. Lopez also appeals to *pathos* in her choice of emotionally loaded and often cynical language, which creates an angle of vision opposing reproductive technology: "turning procreation into manufacturing"; "reproductive prostitution"; "the intrusion of children in their lives"; "motherhood…reduced to a good leisure-time activity"; "aborted female fetuses as a source of donor eggs"; and intercourse as an "obsolete" way to make babies (pages 160–162).

Audience   Despite Lopez's success at spotlighting serious medical and ethical questions, her lack of attention to alternative views and the alarmism of her language caused us to wonder: Who might find this argument persuasive and who would challenge it? What is noticeably missing from her argument—and apparently from her worldview—is the perspective of infertile couples hoping for a baby. Pursuing our question, we decided that a provocative feature of this argument—one worthy of deeper analysis—is the disparity between how well this argument is suited to its target audience and yet how unpersuasive it is for readers who do not share the assumptions, values, and beliefs of this primary audience.

To Lopez's credit, she has attuned her reasons to the values and concerns of her conservative readers of the *National Review*, who believe in traditional families, gender differences, and gender roles. Opposed to feminism as they understand it, this audience sanctions careers for women only if women put their families first. Lopez's choice of evidence and her orchestration of it are intended to play to her audience's fears that science has uncontrollably fallen into the hands of those who have little regard for the sanctity of the family or traditional motherhood. For example, in playing strongly to the values of her conservative readers, Lopez belabors the physical, social, and ethical dangers of egg donation, mentioning worst-case scenarios; however, these appeals to *pathos* will most likely strike other readers who do some investigating into reproductive technology as overblown. She emphasizes the commercialism of the process as her argument moves from college girls as egg donors to a number of sensationalist case studies that depict intensifying ethical ambiguity. In other words, both the *logos* and the *pathos* of her argument skillfully focus on details that tap her target audience's values and beliefs and feed that audience's fears and revulsion.

Use of Evidence   For a broader or skeptical audience, the alarmism of Lopez's appeals to *pathos,* her use of atypical evidence, and her distortion of the facts weaken the *logos* and *ethos* of her argument. First, Lopez's use of evidence fails to measure up to the STAR criteria (that evidence should be sufficient, typical, accurate, and relevant). She characterizes all egg donors as young women seeking money. But she provides little evidence that egg donors are only out to make a buck. She also paints these young women as shortsighted, uninformed, and foolish. Lopez weakens her *ethos* by not considering the young women who have researched the process and who may be motivated, at least in part, by compassion for couples who can't conceive on their own. Lopez also misrepresents the people who are using egg donation, placing them all into two groups: (1) wealthy couples eugenically seeking designer babies with preordered special traits and (2) feminist career women. She directs much of her criticism toward this latter group: "The demand side of the market comes mostly from career-minded baby-boomers, the frontierswomen of feminism, who thought they could 'have it all'" (page 161). However, readers who do a little research on their own, as we did, will learn that infertility affects one in seven couples; that it is often a male and a female problem, sometimes caused by an incompatibility between the husband's and the wife's reproductive material; and that most couples who take the big step of investing in these expensive efforts to have a baby have been trying to get pregnant for a number of years. Rather than being casual about having children, they are often deeply desirous of children and depressed about their inability to conceive. In addition, far from being the sure thing and quick fix that Lopez suggests, reproductive technology has a success rate of only 50 percent overall and involves a huge investment of time, money, and physical discomfort for women receiving donor eggs.

Another way that Lopez violates the STAR criteria is her choice of extreme cases. For readers outside her target audience, her argument appears riddled with straw man and slippery-slope fallacies. (See the Appendix, "Informal Fallacies," pages 397–404.) Her examples become more bizarre as her tone becomes more hysterical. Here are some specific instances of extreme, atypical cases:

- her focus on career women casually and selfishly using the service of young egg donors
- the notorious case of Jaycee Buzzanca, dubbed "Nobody's Child" because her adoptive parents who commissioned her creation divorced before she was born
- the legal contest between a dead man's teen girlfriend and his ex-wife and adult children over his vials of sperm
- the idea of taking eggs from aborted female fetuses

By keeping invisible the vast majority of ordinary couples who go to fertility clinics out of last-hope desperation, Lopez uses extreme cases to create a "brave new world" intended to evoke a vehement rejection of these reproductive advances. These skeptical readers would offer the alternative view of the sad, ordinary couples of all ages sitting week after week in fertility clinics, hoping to conceive a child through the "miracle" of these reproductive advances and grateful to the young women who have contributed their eggs.

Concluding Points   In short, we concluded that Lopez's angle of vision, although effectively in sync with her conservative readers of the *National Review,* exaggerates and distorts her case against these reproductive advances. Lopez's traditional values and slanting of the evidence undermine her *ethos,* limit the value of this argument for a wider audience, and compel that audience to seek out alternative sources for a more complete view of egg donation.

Conclusion

To analyze a text rhetorically means to determine how it works: what effect it has on readers and how it achieves or fails to achieve its persuasiveness. Assignments involving rhetorical analysis are present in courses across the curriculum, and analyzing texts rhetorically is a major step in constructing your own arguments. In this chapter, we showed you how to apply your understanding of argument concepts, such as the influence of genre and appeals to *logos, ethos,* and *pathos,* to the examination of the strength of verbal texts. We conclude with a student's rhetorical analysis written for the assignment in this chapter.

WRITING ASSIGNMENT **A Rhetorical Analysis**   MyWritingLab™

Write a thesis-driven rhetorical analysis essay in which you examine the rhetorical effectiveness of an argument specified by your instructor. Unless otherwise stated, direct your analysis to an audience of your classmates. In your introduction, establish the argumentative conversation to which this argument is contributing. Briefly summarize the argument and present your thesis highlighting two or more rhetorical features of the argument that you find central to the effectiveness or ineffectiveness of this argument. To develop and support your own points, you will need to include textual evidence in the form of examples or short quotations from the argument. Use attributive tags to distinguish your ideas from those of the writer of the argument. Use MLA documentation to cite points and quotations in your essay and in a Works Cited list at the end. Use your rhetorical analysis to share your interpretation of this argument's important features with your audience. Zachary Stumps's analysis of Ellen Goodman's "Womb for Rent" on pages 171–174 is an example of this assignment.

Generating Ideas for Your Rhetorical Analysis

To develop ideas for your essay, you might follow these steps:

Step	How to Do It
Familiarize yourself with the article you are analyzing.	Read your article several times. Divide it into sections to understand its structure.
Place the article in its rhetorical context.	Follow the strategies in Chapter 2 and use the "Questions for Rhetorical Analysis" on pages 155–157.
Summarize the article.	Follow the steps in Chapter 2 on pages 34–36. You may want to produce a longer summary of 150–200 words as well as a short, one-sentence summary.
Reread the article, identifying "hot spots."	Note hot spots in the article—points that impress you, disturb you, confuse you, or puzzle you.
Use the "Questions for Rhetorical Analysis" on pages 157–159.	Choose several of these questions and freewrite responses to them.
From your notes and freewriting, identify the focus for your analysis.	Choose several features of the article that you find particularly important and that you want to discuss in depth in your essay. Identify points that will bring something new to your readers and that will help them see this article with new understanding. You may want to list your ideas and then look for ways to group them together around main points.
Write a thesis statement for your essay.	Articulate your important points in one or two sentences, setting up these points clearly for your audience.

In finding a meaningful focus for your rhetorical analysis essay, you will need to create a focusing thesis statement that avoids wishy-washy formulas such as, "This argument has some strengths and some weaknesses." To avoid a vapid thesis statement, focus on the complexity of the argument, the writer's strategies for persuading the target audience, and the features that might impede its persuasiveness for skeptics. These thesis statements articulate how their writers see the inner workings of these arguments as well as the arguments' contributions to their public conversations.

> Lopez's angle of vision, although effectively in sync with her conservative readers of the *National Review*, exaggerates and distorts her case against these reproductive advances, weakening her *ethos* and the value of her argument for a wider audience. [This is the thesis we would use if we were writing a stand-alone essay on Lopez.]

In his *New Yorker* article "The Pay Is Too Damn Low," Surowiecki adopts an angle of vision empathic to low-wage workers rather than owners; by linking an increase in minimum wage with other liberal causes such as universal health care, investment in infrastructure, and establishing European-style safety nets, Surowiecki appeals to his liberal audience but may alienate the business community by under-representing economic arguments opposing the minimum wage.

To make your rhetorical analysis of your article persuasive, you will need to develop each of the points stated or implied in your thesis statement using textual evidence, including short quotations. Your essay should show how you have listened carefully to the argument you are analyzing, summarized it fairly, and probed it deeply.

Organizing Your Rhetorical Analysis

The organization plan below provides a possible structure for your rhetorical analysis. ■

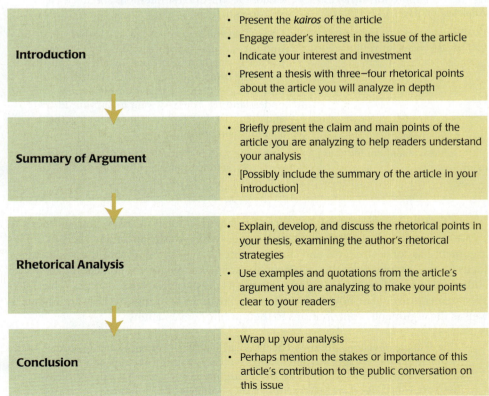

Organization Plan for a Rhetorical Analysis of an Argument

Introduction
- Present the *kairos* of the article
- Engage reader's interest in the issue of the article
- Indicate your interest and investment
- Present a thesis with three–four rhetorical points about the article you will analyze in depth

Summary of Argument
- Briefly present the claim and main points of the article you are analyzing to help readers understand your analysis
- [Possibly include the summary of the article in your introduction]

Rhetorical Analysis
- Explain, develop, and discuss the rhetorical points in your thesis, examining the author's rhetorical strategies
- Use examples and quotations from the article's argument you are analyzing to make your points clear to your readers

Conclusion
- Wrap up your analysis
- Perhaps mention the stakes or importance of this article's contribution to the public conversation on this issue

READINGS

Our first reading is by Pulitzer Prize–winning columnist, author, and speaker Ellen Goodman. This op-ed piece is analyzed rhetorically by student Zachary Stumps in our second reading.

Womb for Rent

ELLEN GOODMAN

By now we all have a story about a job outsourced beyond our reach in the global economy. My own favorite is about the California publisher who hired two reporters in India to cover the Pasadena city government. Really.

There are times as well when the offshoring of jobs takes on a quite literal meaning. When the labor we are talking about is, well, labor.

In the last few months we've had a full nursery of international stories about surrogate mothers. Hundreds of couples are crossing borders in search of lower-cost ways to fill the family business. In turn, there's a new coterie of international workers who are gestating for a living.

Many of the stories about the globalization of baby production begin in India, where the government seems to regard this

as, literally, a growth industry. In the little town of Anand, dubbed "The Cradle of the World," 45 women were recently on the books of a local clinic. For the production and delivery of a child, they will earn $5,000 to $7,000, a decade's worth of women's wages in rural India.

But even in America, some 5 women, including Army wives, are supplementing their income by contracting out their wombs. They have become surrogate mothers for wealthy couples from European countries that ban the practice.

This globalization of baby-making comes at the peculiar intersection of a high reproductive technology and a low-tech work force. The biotech business was created in the same petri dish as Baby Louise, the first IVF baby. But since then, we've seen

conception outsourced to egg donors and sperm donors. We've had motherhood divided into its parts from genetic mother to gestational mother to birth mother and now contract mother.

We've also seen the growth of an international economy. Frozen sperm is flown from one continent to another. And patients have become medical tourists, searching for cheaper health care whether it's a new hip in Thailand or an IVF treatment in South Africa that comes with a photo safari thrown in for the same price. Why not then rent a foreign womb?

I don't make light of infertility. The primal desire to have a child underlies this multinational Creation, Inc. On one side, couples who choose surrogacy want a baby with at least half their own genes. On the other side, surrogate mothers, who are rarely implanted with their own eggs, can believe that the child they bear and deliver is not really theirs.

As one woman put it, "We give them a baby and they give us much-needed money. It's good for them and for us." A surrogate in Anand used the money to buy a heart operation for her son. Another raised a dowry for her daughter. And before we talk about the "exploitation" of the pregnant woman, consider her alternative in Anand: a job crushing glass in a factory for $25 a month.

10   Nevertheless, there is—and there should be—something uncomfortable about a free market approach to baby-making. It's easier to accept surrogacy when it's a gift from one woman to another. But we rarely see a rich woman become a surrogate for a poor family. Indeed, in Third World countries, some women sign these contracts with a fingerprint because they are illiterate.

For that matter, we have not yet had stories about the contract workers for whom pregnancy was a dangerous occupation, but we will. What obligation does a family that simply contracted for a child have to its birth mother? What control do—should—contractors have over their "employees'" lives while incubating "their" children? What will we tell the offspring of this international trade?

"National boundaries are coming down," says bioethicist Lori Andrews, "but we can't stop human emotions. We are expanding families and don't even have terms to deal with it."

It's the commercialism that is troubling. Some things we cannot sell no matter how good "the deal." We cannot, for example, sell ourselves into slavery. We cannot sell our children. But the surrogacy business comes perilously close to both of these deals. And international surrogacy tips the scales.

So, these borders we are crossing are not just geographic ones. They are ethical ones. Today the global economy sends everyone in search of the cheaper deal as if that were the single common good. But in the biological search, humanity is sacrificed to the economy and the person becomes the product. And, step by step, we come to a stunning place in our ancient creation story. It's called the marketplace.

Critiquing "Womb for Rent"

MyWritingLab™

1. What is Goodman's main claim and what are her reasons? In other words, what ideas would you have to include in a short summary?
2. What appeals to *pathos* does Goodman make in this argument? How do these appeals function in the argument?
3. Choose an additional focus from the "Questions for Rhetorical Analysis" to apply to "Womb for Rent" How does this question affect your perspective of Goodman's argument?
4. What strikes you as problematic, memorable, or disturbing in this argument?

Our second reading shows how student writer Zachary Stumps analyzed the Ellen Goodman article.

A Rhetorical Analysis of Ellen Goodman's "Womb for Rent"

ZACHARY STUMPS (STUDENT)

Introduction provides context and poses issue to be addressed.

   With her op-ed piece "Womb for Rent," published in the *Seattle Times* (and earlier in the *Washington Post*), syndicated columnist Ellen Goodman enters the murky debate about reproductive technology gone global. Since Americans are outsourcing everything else, "Why not then rent a foreign womb?" (169) she asks. Goodman, a Pulitzer Prize–winning columnist for the Washington Post Writers Group, is known for helping readers understand the "tumult of social change and its impact on families," and for shattering "the mold of men writing exclusively about politics" ("Ellen Goodman"). This op-ed piece continues her tradition of examining social change from the perspective of family issues.

Provides background on Goodman

   Goodman launches her short piece by asserting that one of the most recent and consequential "jobs" to be outsourced is having babies. She explains how the "globalization of baby production" (169) is thriving because it brings together the reproductive desires of people in developed countries and the bodily resources of women in developing countries such as India. Briefly tracing how both reproductive technology and medical tourism have taken advantage of global possibilities, Goodman acknowledges that the thousands of dollars Indian women earn by carrying the babies of foreign couples represent a much larger income than these women could earn in any other available jobs.

Summarizes the op-ed piece

   After appearing to legitimize this global exchange, however, Goodman shifts to her ethical concerns by raising some moral questions that she says are not being addressed in this trade. She concludes with a full statement of her claim that this global surrogacy is encroaching on human respect and dignity, exploiting business-based science, and turning babies into products.

Thesis paragraph

   In this piece, Goodman's delay of her thesis has several rhetorical benefits: it gives Goodman space to present the perspective of poor women, enhanced by her appeals to *pathos,* and it invites readers to join her journey into the complex contexts of this issue; however, this strategy is also risky because it limits the development of her own argument.

Develops first point in thesis: use of pathos in exploring perspective of poor women

5   Instead of presenting her thesis up front, Goodman devotes much of the first part of her argument to looking at this issue from the perspective of foreign surrogate mothers. Using the strategies of *pathos*

to evoke sympathy for these women, she creates a compassionate and progressive-minded argument that highlights the benefits to foreign surrogate mothers. She cites factual evidence showing that the average job for a woman in Anand, India, yields a tiny "$25 a month" gotten through the hard work of "crushing glass in a factory" (170), compared to the "$5,000 to $7,000" made carrying a baby to term (169). To carry a baby to term for a foreign couple represents "a decade's worth of women's wages in rural India" (169). Deepening readers' understanding of these women, Goodman cites one woman who used her earnings to finance her son's heart operation and another who paid for her daughter's dowry. In her fair presentation of these women, Goodman both builds her own positive *ethos* and adds a dialogic dimension to her argument by helping readers walk in the shoes of otherwise impoverished surrogate mothers.

Develops second point in thesis: the complex contexts of this issue—outsourcing and medical tourism

The second rhetorical benefit of Goodman's delayed thesis is that she invites readers to explore this complex issue of global surrogacy with her before she declares her own view. To help readers understand and think through this issue, she relates it to two other familiar global topics: outsourcing and medical tourism. First, she introduces foreign surrogacy as one of the latest forms of outsourcing: "This globalization of baby-making comes at the peculiar intersection of a high reproductive technology and a low-tech work force" (169). Presenting these women as workers, she explains that women in India are getting paid for "the production and delivery of a child" (269) that is analogous to the production and delivery of sneakers or bicycle parts. Goodman also sets this phenomenon in the context of global medical tourism. If people can pursue lower-cost treatment for illnesses and health conditions in other countries, why shouldn't an infertile couple seeking to start a family not also have such access to these more affordable and newly available means? This reasoning provides a foundation for readers to begin understanding the many layers of the issue.

Shows how the delayed-thesis structure creates two perspectives in conflict

The result of Goodman's delayed-thesis strategy is that the first two-thirds of this piece seem to justify outsourcing surrogate motherhood. Only after reading the whole op-ed piece can readers see clearly that Goodman has been dropping hints about her view all along through her choice of words. Although she clearly sees how outsourcing surrogacy can help poor women economically, her use of market language such as "production," "delivery," and "labor" carry a double meaning. On first reading of this op-ed piece, readers don't know if Goodman's punning is meant to be catchy and entertaining or serves another purpose. This other purpose becomes clear in the last third of the article when Goodman forthrightly asserts her criticism of the commercialism of the global marketplace that promotes worldwide searching for a "cheaper deal": "humanity is sacrificed to the economy and the person becomes the product" (170). This is a bold and big claim, but does the final third of her article support it?

In the final five paragraphs of this op-ed piece, Goodman begins to develop the rational basis of her argument; however, the brevity of the op-ed genre and her choice not to state her view openly initially have left Goodman with little space to develop her own claim. The result is that she presents some profound ideas very quickly. Some of the ethically complex ideas she introduces but doesn't explore much are these:

- The idea that there are ethical limits on what can be "sold."
- The idea that surrogate motherhood might be a "dangerous occupation."
- The idea that children born from this "international trade" may be confused about their identities.

Goodman simply has not left herself enough space to develop these issues and perhaps leaves readers with questions rather than with changed views. I am particularly struck by several questions. Why have European countries banned surrogacy in developing countries and why has the United States not banned this practice? Does Goodman intend to argue that the United States should follow Europe's lead? She could explore more how this business of finding illiterate women to bear children for the wealthy continues to exploit third-world citizens much as sex tourism exploits women in the very same countries. It seems to perpetuate a tendency for the developed world to regard developing countries as a poor place of lawlessness where practices outlawed in the rest of the world (e.g., child prostitution, slave-like working conditions) are somehow tolerable. Goodman could have developed her argument more to state explicitly that a woman who accepts payment for bearing a baby becomes an indentured servant to the family. Yet another way to think of this issue is to see that the old saying of "a bun in the oven" is more literal than metaphoric when a woman uses her womb as a factory to produce children, a body business not too dissimilar to the commercialism of prostitution. Goodman only teases readers by mentioning these complex problems without producing an argument.

10   Still, although Goodman does not expand her criticism of outsourced surrogate motherhood or explore the issues of human dignity and rights, this argument does introduce the debate on surrogacy in the global marketplace, raise awareness, and begin

Restates the third point in his thesis: lack of space limits development of Goodman's argument

Discusses examples of ideas raised by Goodman but not developed

Conclusion

to direct the conversation toward a productive end of seeking a responsible, healthy, and ethical future. Her op-ed piece lures readers into contemplating deep, perplexing ethical and economic problems and lays a foundation for readers to create an informed view of this issue.

Works Cited

Uses MLA format to list sources cited in the essay

"Ellen Goodman." *Postwritersgroup.com*. Washington Post Writer's Group, 2008. Web. 19 May 2008.

Goodman, Ellen. "Womb for Rent." *Washington Post* 11 Apr. 2008: B6. Rpt. in *Writing Arguments*. John D. Ramage, John C. Bean, and June Johnson. 10th ed. New York: Pearson Education, 2016. 169-170. Print.

MyWritingLab™

Visit Ch. 8 Analyzing Arguments Rhetorically in *MyWritingLab* to complete the For Writing and Discussion, Critiquing, and Writing Assignments and to test your understanding of the chapter objectives.

Analyzing Visual Arguments

9

What you will learn in this chapter:

9.1 To explain the elements of design in visual arguments

9.2 To analyze the compositional features of photographs and drawings rhetorically

9.3 To explain the genres of visual argument

9.4 To construct your own visual argument

9.5 To use information graphics rhetorically in arguments

To see how images can make powerful arguments, consider the rhetorical persuasiveness of the "polar bear" marching in a small town parade (Figure 9.1). Sponsored by local environmentalists advocating action against climate change, the polar bear uses arguments from *logos* (drawing on audience knowledge

FIGURE 9.1 A visual argument about climate change

that climate change threatens polar bears), *pathos* (evoking the bears' vulnerability), and *ethos* (conveying the commitment of the citizens group). Delighting children and adults alike, the bear creates a memorable environmental argument.

When an image such as the parade photograph is joined with words, the resulting text is often called a "multimodal argument." The word *multimodal* combines the concept of "multi" (more than one) and "modality" (a channel, medium, or mode of communication). Multimodal arguments published on the Web might take the form of videos, podcasts, blogs, and advocacy Web pages with arguments blending texts and images, all of which make complex rhetorical appeals to viewers. In static print texts, the visual element of a multimodal text might be an image, drawing, or graph, but it might also include purposeful uses of fonts, type size, and document design. This chapter focuses on the visual component of such multimodal texts.

Understanding Design Elements in Visual Argument

9.1 To explain the elements of design in visual arguments

To understand how visual images can produce an argument, you need to understand the design elements that work together to create a visual text. In this section we'll explain and illustrate the four basic components of visual design: use of type, use of space and layout, use of color, and use of images and graphics.

Use of Type

Type is an important visual element of written arguments. Variations in type, such as size, boldface, italics, or all caps, can direct a reader's attention to an argument's structure and highlight main points. In arguments designed specifically for visual impact, such as posters or advocacy advertisements, type is often used in eye-catching and meaningful ways. In choosing type, you need to consider the typeface or font style, the size of the type, and formatting options. The main typefaces or fonts are classified as serif, sans serif, and specialty type. Serif type has little extensions on the letters. (This text is set in serif type.) Sans serif type lacks these extensions. Specialty type includes script fonts and special symbols. In addition to font style, type comes in different sizes. It is measured in points, with 1 point equal to $\frac{1}{72}$ of an inch. Most text-based arguments consisting mainly of body text are written in 10- to 12-point type, whereas more image-based arguments may use a mixture of type sizes that interacts with the images for persuasive effect. Type can also be formatted using bold, italics, underlining, or shading for emphasis. Table 9.1 shows examples of type styles, as well as their typical uses.

The following basic principles for choosing type for visual arguments can help you to achieve your overall goals of readability, visual appeal, and suitability.

Principles for Choosing Type for Visual Arguments

1. If you are creating a poster or advocacy advertisement, you will need to decide how much of your argument will be displayed in words and how much in images. For the text portions, choose *display type* (sans serif) or specialty fonts for titles, headings, and slogans, and *body* or *text type* (serif) for longer passages of text.

TABLE 9.1   Examples and Uses of Type Fonts

Font Style	Font Name	Example	Use
Serif fonts	Times New Roman Courier New Bookman Old Style	Use type wisely. Use type wisely. Use type wisely.	Easy to read; good for long documents, good for *body type*, or the main verbal parts of a document
Sans serif fonts	Arial Century Gothic	Use type wisely. Use type wisely.	Tiring to read for long stretches; good for *display type* such as headings, titles, and slogans
Specialty fonts	*Zapf Chancery* Onyx MT	*Use type wisely.* Use type wisely.	Difficult to read for long stretches; effective when used sparingly for playful or decorative effect

2. Make type functional and appealing by using only two or three font styles per document.
3. Use consistent patterns of type (similar type styles, sizes, and formats) to indicate relationships among similar items or different levels of importance.
4. Choose type to project a specific impression (a structured combination of serif and sans serif type to create a formal, serious, or businesslike impression; sans serif and specialty type to create a casual, informal, or playful impression, and so forth).

Besides these general principles, rhetorical considerations of genre and audience expectations should govern decisions about type. Text-based arguments in scholarly publications generally use plain, conservative fonts with little variation, whereas text-based arguments in popular magazines may use more variations in font style and size, especially in headings and opening leads. Visual arguments such as posters, fliers, and advocacy ads exploit the aesthetic potential of type.

Use of Space or Layout

A second component of visual design is layout, which is critical for creating the visual appeal of an argument and for conveying meaning. Even visual arguments that are mainly textual should use space very purposefully. By spacing and layout we mean all of the following points:

- Page size and type of paper
- Proportion of text to white space
- Proportion of text to image(s) and graphics
- Arrangement of text on page (space, margins, columns, size of paragraphs, spaces between paragraphs, justification of margins)

- Use of highlighting elements such as bulleted lists, tables, sidebars, and boxes
- Use of headings and other means of breaking text into visual elements

In arguments that don't use visuals directly, the writer's primary visual concern is document design, in which the writer tries to meet the conventions of a genre and the expectations of the intended audience. For example, Julee Christianson's researched argument on pages 266–271 is designed to meet the document conventions of the American Psychological Association (APA). Note the use of a plain, conventional typeface (for easy reading); double spacing and one-inch margins (to leave room for editorial marking and notations); and special title page, headers, and page number locations (to meet expectations of readers familiar with APA documents, which all look exactly the same).

But in moving from verbal-only arguments to visual arguments that use visual elements for direct persuasive effect—for example, posters, fliers, or advocacy ads—creative use of layout is vital. Here are some ideas to help you think about the layout of a visual argument.

Principles for Laying Out Parts of a Visual Text

1. Choose a layout that avoids clutter and confusion by limiting how much text and how many visual items you put on a page.
2. Focus on creating coherence and meaning with layout.
3. Develop an ordering or structuring principle that clarifies the relationships among the parts.
4. Use layout and spacing to indicate the importance of items and to emphasize key ideas. Because Western readers read from left to right and top to bottom, top and center are positions that readily draw readers' eyes.

An Analysis of a Visual Argument Using Type and Spatial Elements

To illustrate the persuasive power of type and layout, we ask you to consider Figure 9.2, which shows a public affairs ad sponsored by the Ad Council and an advocacy organization, StopBulllying.gov. This advocacy piece, which is part of an ongoing campaign to curtail bullying among young people, is aimed at parents, urging them to encourage their children to be active in opposing bullying.

This ad demonstrates how use of type can create powerful visual and verbal rhetorical effects to convey its argument. The ad's creators chose to use lettering—not an image—to illustrate bullying. The type style, presentation of the letters, and words themselves create a strange effect—simultaneously personal and impersonal—that draws viewers into the ad more than an image would. The type style and font make strong appeals to *pathos* through the blend of the shocking abusive language and disturbing lettering style. The words "dumb," "piece," and "trash" are all harshly derogatory. The direct address to the viewer in the word "you" conveys that bullying is an attack, sometimes verbal, and often physical. Note how the blurring of the message in the large bold type makes a visual statement about the act of bullying and about both perception and psychological damage. These large, heavy, blurred letters convey multiple messages.

FIGURE 9.2 Anti-bullying public affairs ad

Bullying can be crude and forceful, but it is often carried on covertly where authority figures cannot see or stop it. The lettering itself bullies the viewers while at the same time reinforcing the idea that not everyone is aware of bullying. The blurring of these letters also suggests that bullying harmfully washes out the personhood of victims. In addition, the ad makes it look as though these dark letters have smudged and stained the yellow background, suggesting that bullying harms the social environment.

The layout of this ad also contributes to the *logos* and *ethos* of the ad. The shock of reading the bold message propels readers to the black sidebar in the lower right side of the ad, where the message in smaller type interprets and explains the message of the blurred letters. The text speaks directly to parents' unawareness of the hostility of their kids' environment and makes an urgent appeal to parental responsibility. While the lettering and layout convey the causal reasons behind the need for action, the message in the smaller letters states the proposal claim: Instruct your kids how to be more than passive observers of bullying: "Teach your kids to be more than a bystander." In addition to delivering a strong message, this ad conveys a positive *ethos* by demonstrating knowledge of the problem and directing readers to authoritative sources of information that will help in engaging with this serious social issue.

Use of Color

A third important element of visual design is use of color, which can contribute significantly to the visual appeal of an argument and move readers emotionally and imaginatively. In considering color in visual arguments, writers are especially controlled by genre conventions. For example, academic arguments use color minimally, whereas popular magazines often use color lavishly. The appeal of colors to an audience and the associations that colors have for an audience are also important. For instance, the psychedelic colors of 1960s rock concert posters would probably not be effective in poster arguments directed toward conservative voters. Color choices in visual arguments often have crucial importance, including the choice of making an image black-and-white when color is possible. As you will see in our discussions of color throughout this chapter, makers of visual arguments need to decide whether color will be primarily decorative (using colors to create visual appeal), functional (for example, using colors to indicate relationships), realistic (using colors like a documentary photo), aesthetic (for example, using colors that are soothing, exciting, or disturbing), or some intentional combination of these.

Use of Images and Graphics

The fourth design element includes images and graphics, which can powerfully condense information into striking and memorable visuals; clarify ideas; and add depth, liveliness, and emotion to your arguments. A major point to keep in mind when using images is that a few simple images may be more powerful than complicated and numerous images. Other key considerations are (1) how you intend an image to work in your argument (for example, to convey an idea, illustrate a point, or evoke an emotional response) and (2) how you will establish the relationship between the image or graphic and the verbal text. Because using images and graphics effectively is especially challenging, we devote the rest of this chapter to explaining how images and graphics can be incorporated into visual arguments. We treat the use of photographs and drawings in the next main section and the use of quantitative graphics in the final section.

An Analysis of a Visual Argument Using All the Design Components

Before we discuss the use of images and graphics in detail, we would like to illustrate how all four of the design components—use of type, layout, color, and images— can reinforce and support each other to achieve a rhetorical effect. Consider the

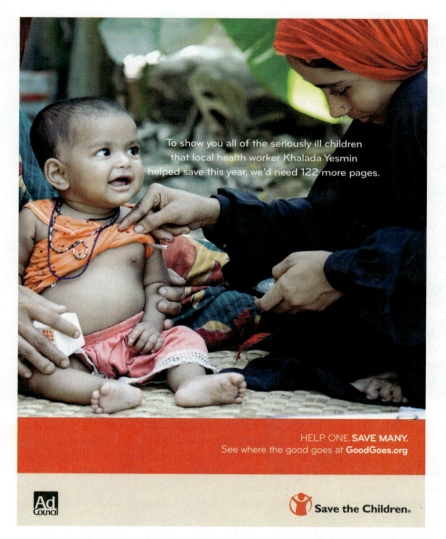

FIGURE 9.3 Save the Children advocacy ad

"Save the Children" advocacy ad from an April 2011 edition of *Newsweek* (Figure 9.3). This advocacy ad highlights the design features of image, color, and layout, with type used to interpret and reinforce the message delivered by the other features. The layout of the page highlights the connection between the adorable baby on the left side of the page and the female health care worker on the right. The "story" of the ad is told in unobtrusive text (in small white font), which leads the readers' eyes from the baby's face to the heart of the health worker. Interestingly from a design perspective, a third figure, probably the baby's mother, is just partly visible in the form of hands holding the baby. The text itself celebrates the effectiveness of this local health healer, identified by name: "To show you all of the seriously ill children that local health worker Khalada Yesmin helped save this year, we'd need 122 more pages." At the bottom of the page, text conveys the call to action in the form of memorable tag lines "HELP ONE. SAVE MANY"; and "See where the good goes at GoodGoes.org."

This advocacy ad works on readers by blending three themes—the universal appeal of babies; the beneficial effects of educating local workers, particularly women; and the symbolic meaning of helping/healing hands—to convey how those of us in the developed world can provide aid that empowers people in developing countries to help themselves. These themes are portrayed through various visual strategies. In this ad, a baby, the health worker, and a third figure outside the frame of the photo (probably the baby's mother) sit on a woven mat, inside a structure. (Information on the Web site for "Save the Children" and the clothing of the people suggest that this scene takes place in Bangladesh.) The use of bright colors, creating a feeling of warmth and love, the arrangement of the figures, and the close-up shots of the baby and health worker draw viewers into the scene. The close-up, slightly low-angle shot accentuates faces, hands, feet, and traditional clothing. The blurred background suggests palm trees and the doorway to a house. The building is, most likely, the home of the mother and baby, which the health worker is visiting on her rounds. The baby, wearing an orange-beaded blouse or smock, pink shorts or skirt, and a necklace of purple beads, sits and smiles alertly at the health worker, in dark clothing and a red headscarf, who is engrossed in taking the baby's temperature. She seems to be holding the thermometer under the baby's arm with one hand and holding a watch with the other. Her focus on her task conveys her expertise; she knows what she is doing, an idea reinforced by the caption, which tells us that this health worker, Khalada Yesmin, "has helped 122 sick children this year." This caption and the prominence of hands in this photo—Khalada Yesmin's hands, the baby's hand, and the mother's hands supporting the baby—accentuate the idea of direct, grassroots aid that is improving the lives of mothers and children in a community through compassion and knowledge. The slogans at the bottom of the ad "Help one. Save many" and "See where the good goes" extend this network of help to viewers of the ad. If we contribute money to the training and medical supplies of health workers like Khalada Yesmin, we will help expand the web of aid.

In choosing to make this ad portray a positive, upbeat scene of medical success, instead of portraying scenes of pneumonia, malaria, malnutrition, or other diseases that the "seriously ill" children mentioned suffer from, the designers of this ad gave a memorable embodiment to the ideas in the words "help," "save," and "good." Perhaps most importantly, unlike some global ads, this one empowers people in the developing world. Rather than depict them as victims or helpless people in backward countries, this ad shows them—through the image of Khalada Yesmin and the eagerness of the people she is helping—as primary agents in the improvements in their lives. Rather than take control and rush in to solve problems, viewers in developed countries are invited to contribute to this success, figuratively lending a hand through financial support.

◼ ◼ ◼ FOR WRITING AND DISCUSSION Analyzing an Advocacy Ad   MyWritingLab™

Individual Task: Using your knowledge of type, layout, color, and image, write a paragraph that analyzes the Buzzed Driving ad sponsored by the Ad Council and the National Highway and Traffic Safety Administration (Figure 9.4). The following questions can guide your response:

1. What story does this ad tell? What is the core argument of this ad?
2. How does this ad use type, layout, image, and color for persuasive effect?
   - Layout and Image: Does the image convey an idea, illustrate a point, or evoke an emotional response? Why do you think the ad makers chose to give spatial preference to the image?

FIGURE 9.4 Advocacy ad against drunk driving

- Color: Is the use of color in this ad decorative, realistic, aesthetic, or some combination of these? How does the use of color contribute to the message of the ad?
- Type: What is the relationship between the image and the type? Look at the words and ideas in each line of type. What is the effect of using different font sizes?

3. How does this ad appeal to *logos, ethos,* and *pathos*?

Group Task: Working in pairs or as a whole class, share your analysis of this advocacy ad. Consider alternative designs for ads warning against driving under the influence of alcohol. What other images, layouts, use of type, and color might be effective in conveying the same message as this ad?

The Compositional Features of Photographs and Drawings

9.2 To analyze the compositional features of photographs and drawings rhetorically

Now that we have introduced you to the four major elements of visual design—type, layout, color, and images—we turn to an in-depth discussion of photographic images and drawings. Used with great shrewdness in product advertisements, photos and drawings can be employed with equal shrewdness in posters, fliers, advocacy ads, and Web sites. When an image is created specifically for an argument, almost nothing is left to chance. Although such images are often made to seem spontaneous and "natural," they are almost always composed; designers consciously select the details of staging and composition as well as manipulate camera techniques (filters, camera angle, lighting) and digital or chemical development techniques (airbrushing, merging of images). Even news photography can have a composed feel. For example, public officials often try to control the effect of photographs by creating "photo ops" (photographing opportunities), wherein reporters are allowed to photograph an event only during certain times and from certain angles. Political photographs appearing in newspapers are often press releases officially approved by the politician's staff. To analyze a photograph or drawing, or to create visual images for your own arguments, you need to think both about the composition of the image and about the camera's relationship to the subject. Because drawings produce a perspective on a scene analogous to that of a camera, design considerations for photographs can be applied to drawings as well. The following list of questions can guide your analysis of any persuasive image.

- **Type of photograph or drawing**: Is the image documentary-like (representing a real event), fiction-like (intending to tell a story or dramatize a scene), or conceptual (illustrating or symbolizing an idea or theme)? The photos of the protest for higher wages for fast-food workers on page 1 and of the anti-fracking march on page 153 are documentary photos capturing real events in action. In contrast, the cartoonish drawing of the fly in the health poster in

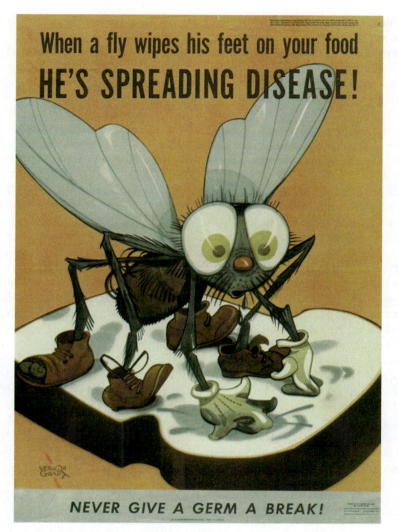

FIGURE 9.5 Health poster from the War Department in World War II

Figure 9.5 is both a fictional narrative telling a story and a conceptual drawing illustrating a concept.

- **Distance from the subject**: Is the image a close-up, medium shot, or long shot? Close-ups tend to increase the intensity of the image and suggest the importance of the subject; long shots tend to blend the subject into the background. In the baby photograph opposing phthalates in children's toys (Chapter 1, page 4), the effect of the baby wearing a "poison" bib is intensified by the close-up shot without background. In contrast, the medium shot of the boy holding the toy he has found in the wreckage caused by Typhoon Haiyan (Chapter 6, page 114) focuses on both the boy and his surroundings. While the photo captures the magnitude of the disaster, it also shows the child's interests and his attempt to recover some of his past life.

- **Orientation of the image and camera angle**: Is the camera (or artist) positioned in front of or behind the subject? Is it positioned below the subject, looking up (a low-angle shot)? Or is it above the subject, looking down (a high-angle shot)? Front-view shots, for example, the photo of the fracking protestor (page 153), tend to emphasize the persons being photographed. In contrast, rear-view shots often emphasize the scene or setting. A low-angle perspective tends to make the subject look superior and powerful, whereas a high-angle perspective can reduce the size—and by implication, the importance—of the subject. A level angle tends to imply equality. The low-angle perspective of Katniss Everdeen, the main character of *The Hunger Games,* (page 193) accentuates her heroic stature.

- **Point of view:** Does the camera or artist stand outside the scene and create an objective effect? Or is the camera or artist inside the scene as if the photographer or artist is an actor in the scene, creating a subjective effect?

- **Use of color:** Is the image in color or in black and white? Is this choice determined by the restrictions of the medium, (such as images designed to run in black and white in newspapers) or is it the conscious choice of the photographer or artist? Are the colors realistic or muted? Have special filters been used (a photo made to look old through the use of brown tints)? Are bright colors intended to be catchy and attractive or dominant or disturbing?

- **Compositional special effects:** Is the entire image clear and realistic? Is any portion of it blurred? Is it blended with other realistic or nonrealistic images (a car ad that blends a city and a desert; a body lotion ad that merges a woman and a cactus)? Is the image an imitation of some other famous image such as a classic painting (as in parodies)? The story of the polar bear in the Nissan Leaf ad in Figures 9.6–9.11 and the photo of the young girls trying out the Nerf Rebelle bows in Figure 9.17 make visual associations with popular stories.

- **Juxtaposition of images:** Are several different images juxtaposed, suggesting relationships between them? Juxtaposition can suggest sequential or causal relationships or can metaphorically transfer the identity of a nearby image or background to the subject (as when a bath soap is associated with a meadow). This technique is frequently used in public relations to shape viewers' perceptions of political figures, as when political figures are photographed with American flags or patriotic monuments.

- **Manipulation of images:** Are staged images made to appear real, natural, or documentary-like? Are images altered with airbrushing? Are images actually composites of a number of images (for instance, using images of different women's bodies to create one perfect model in an ad or film)? Are images cropped for emphasis? What is left out? Are images downsized or enlarged?

- **Settings, furnishings, props:** Is the photo or drawing an outdoor or indoor scene? What is in the background and foreground? What furnishings and props, such as furniture, objects in a room, pets, and landscape features, help create the scene? What social associations of class, race, and gender are attached to these settings and props?

FIGURE 9.6 Nissan Leaf ad: Glacier melting and calving ice bergs

FIGURE 9.7 Nissan Leaf ad: Polar bear floating on shrinking sea ice

FIGURE 9.8 Nissan Leaf ad: Polar bear walking on railroad tracks

FIGURE 9.9 Nissan Leaf ad: Polar bear walking along a highway

FIGURE 9.10 Nissan Leaf ad: Polar bear walking through a suburb

FIGURE 9.11 Nissan Leaf ad: Polar bear hugging car owner

■ **Characters, roles, actions:** Does the photo or drawing tell a story? Are the people in the scene models? Are the models instrumental (acting out real-life roles) or are they decorative (extra and included for visual or sex appeal)? What are the facial expressions, gestures, and poses of the people? What are the spatial relationships of the figures? (Who is in the foreground, center, and background? Who is large and prominent?) What social relationships are implied by these poses and positions? In the "Save the Children" advocacy ad shown in Figure 9.3, the pose of the health worker and the baby—the health worker intently treating the baby and the baby happily trusting the health worker—tells the story of successful health care.

■ **Presentation of images:** Are images separated from each other in a larger composition or connected to each other? Are the images large in proportion to verbal text? How are images labeled? How does the text relate to the image(s)? Does the image illustrate the text? Does the text explain or comment on the image?

An Analysis of a Visual Argument Using Images

To show you how images can be analyzed, let's examine the advertisement for Nissan's new electric car, the Nissan Leaf. Stills for this television ad are shown in Figures 9.6–9.11. You can see the whole one-minute ad on YouTube, where the fluid sequence of frames gives the full effect. With this ad's debut during a National Football League broadcast in fall 2010, Nissan boldly entered the global controversy over global warming and climate change, casting the iconic polar bear and the Nissan Leaf owner as heroes in a dramatic narrative intended to portray environmental consciousness and responsible consumerism.

This ad links a series of images in a suspenseful story of a long journey culminating in a dramatic encounter. The ad begins with frames of dripping ice melt and a crumbling glacier crashing into the ocean. The next frame shows a polar bear lying on a small floating island of ice, succeeded by a long view of calved icebergs, fragments of the glacier. The camera follows the polar bear swimming, with views of its powerful body above and below the water, until it arrives on land. From there, the polar bear takes a long journey: walking through northern forests; sheltering in a concrete culvert under a train trestle; walking along a train track; padding along a country highway, where it growls at a passing diesel truck; sitting and observing the brilliant lights of a big city at night; traveling across a massive suspension bridge into the city; walking through the city; and finally, walking down a suburban street. In the final frames, a bright blue Nissan Leaf sits in the wide driveway of a comfortable suburban home. Suddenly, the polar bear appears from behind the Nissan Leaf and surprises its owner, who has just come out of his house dressed in a sports coat and carrying a briefcase, presumably heading out for his commute to his white-collar job. As the bear rises on its hind legs, towering above the man, the astonished owner is met not by an attack but by a bear hug: the bear's thank-you for the driver's act of environmental responsibility in buying this electric car. The final frame includes the only text of the ad, which invites viewers to check out the features of the Nissan Leaf on the Web site. A musical soundtrack accompanies the images, with the only other sounds the honk of the truck and the growl of the bear in response. Noticeably absent from this ad is any specific information about the car itself, such as its five-passenger carrying capacity, its zero emissions, and its hundred-mile distance per charge.

The ad uses visual narrative to convey both a causal and an ethical argument. Through vivid, memorable scenes—the glacier calving, the bear afloat, the bear swimming—the ad taps viewers' knowledge of recent scientific accounts of the increased rate of glacial melting and the vanishing sea ice. The ad argues that these events are real, immediate, and threatening. By implication, it argues that the high volume of carbon dioxide emissions from gasoline-powered vehicles—in other words, human actions—has caused this increased rate of melting and destruction of polar bears' habitat. It asks viewers to fill in the links in the causal chain: large amounts of carbon dioxide emissions from internal combustion engines in cars and trucks have contributed to an increase in temperatures, which has sped up the rate at which glaciers and sea ice are melting. This increased rate of melting has in turn decreased the number of seals who usually live on the sea ice and thus reduced the food supply of polar bears. The ad reminds viewers that polar bears are endangered and need human aid. The ad's ethical argument is that humans can help polar bears and the environment by buying electric Nissan Leafs.

The ad's effect is enhanced by its positive *ethos* and its powerful appeals to *pathos*. By making these causal links through bold images and a memorable story, Nissan has staked its claim as a leader in producing alternative-fuel vehicles. In our view, the ad makes brilliant use of visual images, drawing on the most famous environmental icons in the global warming debate: the melting glacier and the polar bear. (See the photograph of the parade polar bear at the beginning of this chapter on page 175.) While news reports of declining polar bear populations arouse concern in some people, numbers can be vague and abstract. Many more people will be stirred by the heroic character of the lone bear making a long journey. This visual narrative taps viewers' familiarity with other animal stories, often featured on Animal Planet and the Discovery Channel, that blend environmental education and entertainment. But the Nissan ad pushes further by creatively drawing on Disney-like, anthropomorphic movies in which a wild creature becomes a friend of humans. Any Inuit will testify that polar bears are intimidating and dangerous, but this ad constructs an environmental fantasy, eliciting viewers' compassion for the heroic bear. It creates a kind of inverted "call of the wild" narrative: Instead of a captured or domesticated animal finding its way back to its wilderness home, this wild creature, endowed with knowledge and filled with gratitude, courageously finds its way to civilization on a mission to thank the Nissan Leaf owner. The ad cultivates warm feelings toward the bear through juxtaposing its isolation against the background of our technologically transformed and urbanized environment—the diesel truck; the concrete culvert; the impressive bridge; the vast, illuminated city; the well-cultivated suburban neighborhood. The ad enhances the character of the bear by showing it take time to watch a delicately flitting butterfly and exchange a glance with a raccoon, a wild creature at home in the city. As viewers are engrossed with the travels of this bear, they wonder, "Where is it going? What will happen?" The genius of the ad is that it casts the bear as an ambassador of the threatened environment and makes viewers care about the bear.

It also converts the Nissan Leaf owner into an environmental hero. The implied ethical argument is that the right moral action is to drive a Nissan Leaf and thus save the environment. Viewers, identifying with the awestruck Nissan owner, will feel, "I want to be an environmental hero, too."

In this sense, the ad follows a problem-solution scenario. Nissan has skillfully enlisted the main symbols of global warming in the service of promoting its new electric car. It has, of course, greatly oversimplified an environmental problem and skirted major issues such as the problem of producing the electricity necessary to charge the Nissan Leaf, the environmental costs of producing the cars themselves, and the drop-in-the-bucket effect of replacing only a tiny portion of gasoline cars with electric vehicles. However, the ad works by suppressing these concerns and implying instead that the individual consumer can make a substantial difference in saving the environment.

■ ■ ■ **FOR CLASS DISCUSSION** **Analyzing Photos and Drawings Rhetorically**

Working individually or in groups, imagine that you have been asked to compose a flier advertising a self-defense workshop for women on your university campus. This workshop will include some basic self-defense moves and some fundamentals of martial arts and blocking. Your task is to choose one of the four photos or images in Figures 9.12–9.15 for the poster. Your goal is to get students to notice your poster, appreciate what is at stake in the workshops, and become motivated to sign up. What image might best encourage women to attend? What image might encourage men to urge their female friends or girlfriends to attend?

1. Study the four photos in Figures 9.12 through 9.15, and then answer the following questions:
   a. What camera techniques and composition features do you see in each photo or image? Consider all the composition features described on pages 184–186 and 188 for each image.
   b. What do you think is the dominant impression of each photo? In other words, what is each photo's implicit argument?
2. Once you have analyzed the images, decide which is the most striking or memorable and try to reach consensus about your choice for a rhetorically effective poster.
3. Sometimes designers and ad creators choose cartoonish images to deliver their arguments. You might examine the Chipotle Scarecrow ad that aired during the 2014 Super Bowl (on YouTube), some other cartoon image in an ad, or the War Department's health poster in Figure 9.5 on page 185.
   a. What are the compositional features in this cartoon drawing or ad?
   b. How would you state the argument made by this image?
   c. How does the use of cartoon images affect the *logos*, *ethos*, and *pathos* of the argument?
   d. Why do you think cartoon images were chosen?

FIGURE 9.12 Photo of girl practicing boxing moves

FIGURE 9.13 Photo of a guy in a hoodie

FIGURE 9.14 Drawing of a girl booting a guy

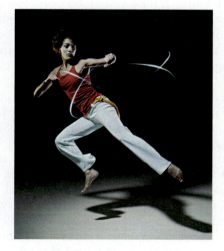

FIGURE 9.15 Photo of woman executing a martial arts move

The Genres of Visual Argument

9.3 To explain the genres of visual argument

We have already mentioned that verbal arguments today are frequently accompanied by photographs or drawings that contribute to the text's persuasive appeal. For example, a verbal argument promoting U.N. action to help AIDS victims in Africa might be accompanied by a photograph of a dying mother and child. However, some genres of argument are dominated by visual elements. In these genres, the visual design carries most of the argumentative weight; verbal text is used primarily for labeling, for focusing the argument's claim, or for commenting on the images. In this section we describe specifically these highly visual genres of argument.

Posters and Fliers

To persuade audiences, an arguer might create a poster designed for placement on walls or kiosks or a flier to be passed out on street corners. Posters dramatically attract and direct viewers' attention toward a subject or issue. They often seek to rally supporters to a strong stance on an issue, and call people to action. For example, during World War II, posters asked Americans to invest in war bonds and urged women to join the workforce in order to free men for active combat. During the Vietnam War, famous posters used slogans such as "Make Love, Not War" or "Girls say yes to boys who say no" to increase national resistance to the war.

The hallmark of an effective poster is the way it focuses and encodes a complex meaning in a verbal-visual text, often with one or more striking images. These images are often symbolic—for example, using children to symbolize family and home, a soaring bird to symbolize freedom, or three firefighters raising the American flag over the World Trade Center rubble on September 11, 2001, to symbolize American heroism, patriotism, and resistance to terrorism. These symbols derive potency from the values they share with their target audience. Posters tend to use words sparingly, either as slogans or as short, memorable directives. This terse verbal text augments the message encoded in an eye-catching, dominant image.

As an example of a contemporary poster, consider the poster on page 193 urging people to see the second *Hunger Games* film, *Catching Fire*. This poster for this popular culture film shows actress Jennifer Lawrence as lead character Katniss Everdeen aiming her weapon of choice, her bow. She is framed by a large version of her mockingjay pin (a symbol from District 12, her home) and a ring of fire. Readers who know Susan Collins's dystopian novels and/or the films know that Katniss appeared in a costume with special-effect flames in the first film and that her defiant spirit sparks the rebellion against the Capital and its repressive government. The impact of the poster is intensified by the angry reds and dark colors and by the centrality and size of the image of Katniss (Jennifer Lawrence) that dominates the poster. The tagline at the top of the poster "Remember who the enemy is" intimates the plotline of the film and calls all potential rebels to be discerning and ready for courageous and risky acts of solidarity.

Fliers and brochures often use visual elements similar to those in posters. An image might be the top and center attraction of a flier or the main focus of the front cover of a brochure. However, unlike posters, fliers and brochures offer additional space for verbal arguments, which often present the writer's claim supported with bulleted lists of reasons. Sometimes pertinent data and statistics, along with testimony from supporters, are placed in boxes or sidebars.

FIGURE 9.16 Poster for *The Hunger Games: Catching Fire*

Public Affairs Advocacy Advertisements

Public affairs advocacy advertisements share with posters an emphasis on visual elements, but they are designed specifically for publication in newspapers and magazines or Web sites and, in their persuasive strategies, are directly analogous to product advertisements. Public affairs advocacy ads are usually sponsored by a corporation or an advocacy organization, often are part of a particular campaign with a theme, and have a more immediate and defined target audience than posters. Designed as condensed arguments aimed at influencing public opinion on civic issues, these ads are characterized by their brevity, audience-based appeals, and succinct, "sound bite" style. Often, in order to sketch out their claim and reasons clearly and concisely, they employ headings and subheadings, bulleted lists, different sizes and styles of type, and a clever, pleasing layout on the page. They usually have an attention-getting slogan or headline such as "MORE KIDS ARE GETTING BRAIN CANCER. WHY?" or "STOP THE TAX REVOLT JUGGERNAUT!" And they usually include a call to action, whether it be a donation, a letter of protest to legislators, or an invitation to join the advocacy group.

The balance between verbal and visual elements in an advocacy advertisement varies. Some advocacy ads are verbal only, with visual concerns focused on document design (for example, an "open letter" from the president of a corporation appearing as a full-page newspaper ad). Other advocacy ads are primarily visual, using images and other design elements with the same shrewdness as advertisements. We looked closely at advocacy ads in this chapter when we examined the StopBullying.gov ad (Figure 9.2) and the Save the Children ad (Figure 9.3). These use text and images in different ways to present their messages.

As another example of a public affairs advocacy ad, consider the ad in Chapter 14, page 305, that attempts to counter the influence of the pro-life movement's growing campaign against abortion. As you can see, this ad is dominated by one stark image: a question mark formed by the hook of a coat hanger. The shape of the hook draws the reader's eye to the concentrated type centered below it. The hook carries most of the weight of the argument. Simple, bold, and harsh, the image of the hanger, tapping readers' cultural knowledge, evokes the dangerous scenario of illegal abortions performed crudely by nonmedical people in the dark backstreets of cities. The ad wants viewers to think of the dangerous last resorts that desperate women would have to turn to if they could not obtain abortions legally. The hanger itself creates a visual pun: As a question mark, it conveys the ad's dilemma about what will happen if abortions are made illegal. As a coat hanger, it provides the ad's frightening answer to the printed question— desperate women will return to backstreet abortionists who use coat hangers as tools.

■ ■ ■ **FOR CLASS DISCUSSION** Analyzing Posters Rhetorically

Working individually or in groups, examine the images mentioned here to conduct a rhetorical analysis of them.

1. Some visual arguments gain influence and function by way of intertextuality. By this term, analysts mean the way that a viewer's reading of an image depends on familiarity with a network of "connected" images. Note the social influences

FIGURE 9.17 Photo of young girls with toy bows imitating Katniss Everdeen

and the layering of intertextuality in the photo in Figure 9.17 and the poster for *Catching Fire* on page 193. Readers, viewers, and critics have commented on the mythic qualities of heroine Katniss Everdeen, who as huntress, survivor, and rebel, resembles a Greek goddess, managing her hazardous world largely through her boldness, character, and physical prowess. The novels and films of Susan Collins's *The Hunger Games* have had far-ranging social effects, particularly on the behavior and interests of young girls. Examine the poster for *Catching Fire* on page 193 and the photo of young girls, trying out toymaker Hasbro's new Nerf Rebelle Heartbreaker Exclusive Golden Edge Bow in Figure 9.17. Compare the photo of the young girls with the poster for the film.

a. Analyze the ways that the young girls in the photo reflect the influence of Katniss Everdeen as a role model.

b. What vision of the feminine does the huntress image in the poster exemplify?

2. Examine the poster shown in Figure 9.18 on page 196 that shows a photo of an attractive girl behind the line "HEATHER'S LIFE ENDED TOO SOON." This poster, which appears on the TxtResponsibly.org Web site, reaches out to young drivers and their parents, using both images and text.

a. What visual features of this poster immediately attract your eyes? What principles for effective use of type, layout, color, and image does this ad exemplify?

b. What is the core argument of this ad?

c. Why did Heather's parents choose a large photo of her? How does that photo work with the other photo of a completely mangled car?

d. How does the frankness of the text and the size and use of color of the lettering combine to convey the message of the ad?

e. How would you design a poster warning against texting while driving? Consider questions about its use of type, layout, and image; about the core of its argument; and about its appeals to *ethos, pathos,* and *kairos.*

FIGURE 9.18 Poster argument warning against texting while driving

Cartoons

An especially charged kind of visual argument is the editorial or political cartoon and its extended forms, the comic strip and the graphic novel. Here we focus on political cartoons, which are often mini-narratives portraying an issue dramatically, compactly, and humorously, through images and a few well-chosen words that dramatize conflicts and problems. Using caricature, exaggeration, and distortion, a cartoonist distills an issue down to an image that boldly reveals the creator's perspective on the issue. The purpose of political cartoons is usually satire, or, as one famous cartoonist says, "afflicting the comfortable and comforting the afflicted."* Because they are so condensed and are often connected to current affairs, political cartoons are particularly dependent on the audience's background knowledge of cultural and political events. When political cartoons work well, through their perceptive combination of images and words, they flash a brilliant, clarifying light on a perspective or open a new lens on an issue, often giving readers a shock of insight.

As an illustration, note the cartoon by Milt Priggee in Figure 9.19, which was posted on the cartoon Web site index www.caglecartoons.com. The setting of the cartoon envisions a humorous blend of prehistoric and contemporary times. This cartoon responds to the recent scientific discussions of the creation and development

FIGURE 9.19 Tweeting and evolution cartoon

---

*"The Truth Told in Jest: Interview: Martin Rowson." *Morning Star.* Morning Star Online, 31 July 2007 Web. 6 June 2011.

of the universe and the aging of the Earth. (Note the mention of dark matter, which is a kind of energy-mass concept from physics and astronomy.) However, the main story of the cartoon connects the dinosaur characters with the behavior of people today who go about walking and tweeting, oblivious to anything around them, including dangerous environments. Thus, the cartoon links discussions of evolution to discussions of the contemporary obsession with cell phones and forms of social media.

■ ■ ■ **FOR CLASS DISCUSSION**   **Analyzing Cartoons**

Cartoons can provide insight into how the public is lining up on issues. Choose a current issue such as health care reform, use of drones, dependence on foreign oil, income inequality, or identity theft. Then, using an online cartoon index such as Daryl Cagle's Professional Cartoonists Index (www.cagle.com) or a Web search of your own, find several cartoons that capture different perspectives on your issue.

1. What is the mini-narrative, the main claim, and the use of caricature, exaggeration, or distortion in each?
2. How is *kairos*, or timeliness, important to each cartoon?

Web Pages

So far we have only hinted at the influence of the World Wide Web in accelerating the use of visual images in argument. Multimodal Web pages, with their hypertext design, exhibit the Web's complex mix of text and image, a mix that has changed the way many writers think of argument. The home page of an advocacy site, for example, often has many features of a poster argument, with hypertext links to galleries of images on the one hand and to verbal arguments on the other. These verbal arguments themselves often contain photographs, drawings, and graphics. The strategies discussed in this chapter for analyzing and interpreting visual texts also apply to Web pages.

Because the Web is such an important tool in research, we have placed our main discussion of Web sites in Chapter 15, pages 354–356. On these pages you will find our explanations for reading, analyzing, and evaluating Web sites.

Constructing Your Own Visual Argument

9.4 To construct your own visual argument

The most common visual arguments you are likely to create are posters, fliers, and public affairs advocacy ads. You may also decide that in longer verbal arguments, the use of visuals or graphics could clarify your points while adding visual variety to your paper. The following guidelines will help you apply your understanding of visual elements to the construction of your own visual arguments.

Guidelines for Creating Visual Arguments

1. **Genre:** Determine where this visual argument is going to appear (on a bulletin board, passed out as a flier, imagined as a one-page magazine or newspaper spread, or as a Web page).
2. **Audience-based appeals:** Determine who your target audience is.
   - What values and background knowledge of your issue can you assume that your audience has?
   - What specifically do you want your audience to think or do after reading your visual argument?
   - If you are promoting a specific course of action (sign a petition, send money, vote for or against a bill, attend a meeting), how can you make that request clear and direct?
3. **Core of your argument:** Determine what clear claim and reasons will form the core of your argument; decide whether this claim and these reasons will be explicitly stated or implicit in your visuals and slogans.
   - How much verbal text will you use?
   - If the core of your argument will be largely implicit, how can you still make it readily apparent and clear for your audience?
4. **Visual design:** What visual design and layout will grab your audience's attention and be persuasive?
   - How can font sizes and styles, layout, and color be used in this argument to create a strong impression?
   - What balance and harmony can you create between the visual and verbal elements of your argument? Will your verbal elements be a slogan, express the core of the argument, or summarize and comment on the image(s)?
5. **Use of images:** If your argument lends itself to images, what photo or drawing would support your claim or have emotional appeal? (If you want to use more than one image, be careful that you don't clutter your page and confuse your message. Simplicity and clarity are important.)
   - What image would be memorable and meaningful to your audience? Would a photo image or a drawing be more effective?
   - Will your image(s) be used to provide evidence for your claim or illustrate a main idea, evoke emotions, or enhance your credibility and authority?

■ ■ ■   **FOR CLASS DISCUSSION**   **Developing Ideas for an Advocacy Ad or Poster Argument**

This exercise asks you to do the thinking and planning for an advocacy ad or poster argument to be displayed on your college or university campus. Working individually, in small groups, or as a whole class, choose an issue that is controversial on your campus (or in your town or city), and follow the Guidelines for Creating Visual Arguments on page 199, above to envision the view you want to advocate on that issue. What might the core of your argument be? Who is your target audience? Are you representing a group, club, or other organization? What image(s) might be effective in attracting and moving this audience? Possible issues might be commuter parking; poor conditions in the computer lab; student reluctance to use the counseling center; problems with dorm life; financial aid programs, or intramural sports; ways to improve orientation programs for new students, work-study programs, or travel-abroad opportunities; or new initiatives such as study groups for the big lecture courses or new service-learning opportunities.

Using Information Graphics in Arguments

9.5 To use information graphics rhetorically in arguments

Besides images in the form of photographs and drawings, writers often use quantitative graphics to support arguments using numbers. In Chapter 5 we introduced you to the use of quantitative data in arguments. We discussed the persuasiveness of numbers and showed you ways to use them responsibly in your arguments. With the availability of spreadsheet and presentation programs, today's writers often create and import quantitative graphics into their documents. These visuals—such as tables, pie charts, and line or bar graphs—can have great rhetorical power by making numbers tell a story at a glance. In this section, we'll show you how quantitative graphics can make numbers speak. We'll also show you how to analyze graphics, incorporate them into your text, and reference them effectively.

How Tables Contain a Variety of Stories

Data used in arguments usually have their origins in raw numbers collected from surveys, questionnaires, observational studies, scientific experiments, and so forth. Through a series of calculations, the numbers are combined, sorted, and arranged in a meaningful fashion, often in detailed tables. Some of the tables published by the U.S. Census Bureau, for example, contain dozens of pages. The more dense the table, the more their use is restricted to statistical experts who pore over the data to analyze their meanings. More useful to the general public are midlevel tables contained on one or two pages that report data at a higher level of abstraction.

Consider, for example, Table 9.2, published by the U.S. Census Bureau and based on the 2010 census. This table shows the marital status of people age 15 and older, broken into gender and age groupings, in March 2010. It also provides comparative data on the "never married" percentage of the population in March 2010 and March 1970.

Take a few moments to peruse the table and be certain you know how to read it. You read tables in two directions: from top to bottom and from left to right. Always begin with the title, which tells you what the table contains and includes elements from both the vertical and the horizontal dimensions of the table. In this case the vertical dimension presents demographic categories for people "15 years old and over" for both sexes, for males, and for females. Each of these gender categories is subdivided into age categories. The horizontal dimension provides information about "marital status." Seven of the columns give total numbers (reported in thousands)

TABLE 9.2 Marital Status of People 15 Years and Over by Age and Sex: March 1970 and March 2010 (Numbers in thousands, except for percentages)

Characteristic	Total	Married spouse present	Married spouse absent	Separated	Divorced	Widowed	Never married	Percent never married	March 1970 percent never married
Both Sexes									
Total 15 years old and over	242,047	120,768	3,415	5,539	23,742	14,341	74,243	30.7	24.9
15 to 19 years old	21,079	178	109	151	60	22	20,559	97.5	93.9
20 to 24 years old	21,142	2,655	202	309	195	17	17,765	84.0	44.5
25 to 29 years old	21,445	7,793	406	594	766	60	11,826	55.1	14.7
30 to 34 years old	19,623	10,896	337	632	1,447	72	6,239	31.8	7.8
35 to 44 years old	40,435	25,729	733	1,331	4,697	345	7,599	18.8	5.9
45 to 54 years old	44,373	28,619	703	1,295	6,951	1,080	5,725	12.9	6.1
55 to 64 years old	35,381	23,621	463	763	5,750	1,923	2,861	8.1	7.2
65 years old and over	38,569	21,276	461	465	3,875	10,823	1,668	4.3	7.6
Males									
Total 15 years old and over	117,686	60,384	1,789	2,352	9,981	2,974	40,206	34.2	28.1
15 to 19 years old	10,713	61	55	62	30	8	10,498	98.0	97.4
20 to 24 years old	10,677	946	86	123	49	3	9,469	88.7	54.7
25 to 29 years old	10,926	3,343	220	224	318	21	6,800	62.2	19.1
30 to 34 years old	9,759	5,143	188	246	593	28	3,561	36.5	9.4
35 to 44 years old	20,066	12,614	392	578	1,998	81	4,402	21.9	6.7
45 to 54 years old	21,779	14,280	367	539	3,063	284	3,246	14.9	7.5
55 to 64 years old	16,980	11,958	244	343	2,465	424	1,545	9.1	7.8
65 years old and over	16,786	12,039	237	237	1,464	2,124	685	4.1	7.5
Females									
Total 15 years old and over	124,361	60,384	1,626	3,187	13,760	11,368	34,037	27.4	22.1
15 to 19 years old	10,365	118	55	90	30	13	10,061	97.1	90.3
20 to 24 years old	10,465	1,708	116	185	146	14	8,296	79.3	35.8
25 to 29 years old	10,519	4,451	186	370	448	39	5,026	47.8	10.5
30 to 34 years old	9,864	5,753	150	386	854	44	2,678	27.1	6.2
35 to 44 years old	20,369	13,115	341	753	2,698	264	3,198	15.7	5.2
45 to 54 years old	22,594	14,339	337	756	3,889	794	2,479	11.0	4.9
55 to 64 years old	18,401	11,663	220	420	3,284	1,499	1,315	7.1	6.8
65 years old and over	21,783	9,238	224	227	2,412	8,700	983	4.5	7.7

for March 2010. The eighth column gives the "percent never married" for March 2010, while the last column gives the "percent never married" for March 1970. To make sure you know how to read the table, pick a couple of rows at random and say to yourself what each number means. For example, the first row under "Both sexes" gives total figures for the entire population of the United States age 15 and older. In March 2010 there were 242,047,000 people age 15 and older (remember that the numbers are presented in thousands). Of these, 120,768,000 were married and living with their spouses. As you continue across the columns, you'll see that 3,415,000 people were married but not living with their spouses (a spouse may be stationed overseas or in prison; or a married couple may be maintaining a "commuter marriage" with separate households in different cities). Continuing across the columns, you'll see that 5,539,000 people were separated from their spouses, 23,742,000 were divorced, and 14,341,000 were widowed, and an additional 74,243,000 were never married. In the next-to-last column, the number of never-married people is converted to a percentage: 30.7 percent. Finally, the last column shows the percentage of never-married people in 1970: 24.9 percent. These last two columns show us that the number of unmarried people in the United States rose 5.8 percentage points since 1970.

Now that you know how to read the table, examine it carefully to see the kinds of stories it tells. What does the table show you, for example, about the percentage of married people age 25–29 in 1970 versus 2010? What does it show about different age-related patterns of marriage in males and females? By showing you that Americans are waiting much later in life to get married, a table like this initiates many causal questions for analysis and argument. What happened in American culture between 1970 and 2010 to explain the startling difference in the percentage of married people within, say, the 20–24 age bracket? In 2010 only 16 percent of people in this age bracket were married (we converted "unmarried" to "married" by subtracting 84 from 100). However, in 1970, 55.5 percent of people in this age bracket were married.

Using a Graph to Tell a Story

Table 9.2, as we have seen, tells the story of how Americans are postponing marriage. However, one has to tease out the story from the dense columns of numbers. To focus on a key story and make it powerfully immediate, you can create a graph.

Bar Graphs   Suppose you are writing an argument in which you want to show that the percentage of married women in the 20–29 age bracket has dropped significantly since 1970. You could tell this story through a bar graph (Figure 9.20).

Bar graphs use bars of varying length, extending either horizontally or vertically, to contrast two or more quantities. As with any graphic presentation, you must create a comprehensive title. In the case of bar graphs, titles tell readers what is being compared to what. Most bar graphs also have "legends," which explain what the different features on the graph represent. Bars are typically distinguished from each other by use of different colors, shades, or patterns of crosshatching. The special power of bar graphs is that they can help readers make quick comparisons.

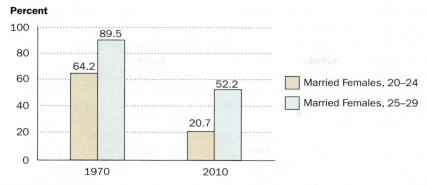

FIGURE 9.20 Percentage of married females ages 20–29, 1970 and 2010

Source: U.S. Census Bureau, *Current Population Survey,* March 2010.

Pie Charts   Another vivid kind of graph is a pie chart or circle graph, which depicts different percentages of a total (the pie) in the form of slices. Pie charts are a favorite way of depicting the way parts of a whole are divided up. Suppose, for example, that you wanted your readers to notice the high percentage of widows among women age 65 and older. To do so, you could create a pie chart (Figure 9.21) based on the data in the last row of Table 9.2. As you can see, a pie chart shows at a glance how the whole of something is divided into segments. However, the effectiveness of pie charts diminishes as you add more slices. In most cases, you'll begin to confuse readers if you include more than five or six slices.

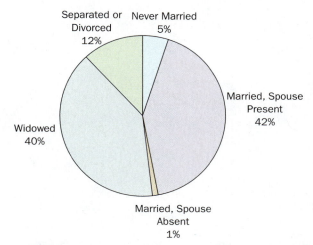

FIGURE 9.21 Marital status of females age 65 and older, 2010

Source: U.S. Census Bureau, *Current Population Survey,* March 2010.

Line Graphs   Another powerful quantitative graphic is a line graph, which converts numerical data into a series of points on a grid and connects them to create flat, rising, or falling lines. The result gives us a picture of the relationship between the variables represented on the horizontal and vertical axes.

Suppose you wanted to tell the story of the rising number of separated/divorced women in the U.S. population. Using Table 9.2, you can calculate the percentage of separated/divorced females in 2010 by adding the number of separated females (3,187,000) and the number of divorced females (13,760,000) and dividing that sum by the total number of females (124,361,000). The result is 13.6 percent. You can make the same calculations for 2000, 1990, 1980, and 1970 by looking at U.S. census data from those years (available on the Web or in your library). The resulting line graph is shown in Figure 9.22.

To determine what this graph is telling you, you need to clarify what's represented on the two axes. By convention, the horizontal axis of a graph contains the predictable, known variable, which has no surprises—what researchers call the "independent variable." In this case the horizontal axis represents the years 1970–2010 arranged predictably in chronological order. The vertical axis contains the unpredictable variable, which forms the graph's story—what researchers call the "dependent variable"—in this case, the percentage of separated or divorced females. The ascending curve tells the story at a glance.

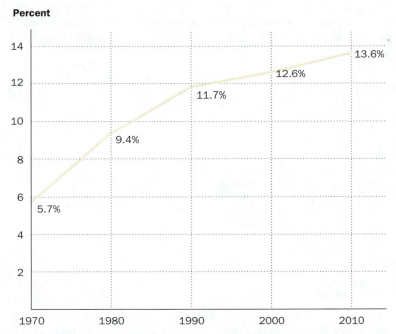

FIGURE 9.22 Percentage of females age 15 and older who were separated or divorced, 1970–2010

Source: U.S. Census Bureau, *Current Population Survey,* March 2010.

Note that with line graphs, the steepness of the slope (and hence the rhetorical effect) can be manipulated by the intervals chosen for the vertical axis. Figure 9.22 shows vertical intervals of 2 percent. The slope could be made less dramatic by choosing intervals of, say, 10 percent and more dramatic by choosing intervals of 1 percent.

Incorporating Graphics into Your Argument

Today, writers working with quantitative data usually use graphing software that automatically creates tables, graphs, or charts from data entered into the cells of a spreadsheet. For college papers, some instructors may allow you to make your graphs with pencil and ruler and paste them into your document.

Designing the Graphic   When you design your graphic, your goal is to have a specific rhetorical effect on your readers, not to demonstrate all the bells and whistles available on your software. Adding extraneous data to the graph or chart or using such features as a three-dimensional effect can often distract from the story you are trying to tell. Keep the graphic as uncluttered and simple as possible and design it so that it reinforces the point you are making.

Numbering, Labeling, and Titling the Graphic   In newspapers and popular magazines, writers often include graphics in boxes or sidebars without specifically referring to them in the text itself. However, in academic and professional workplace writing, graphics are always labeled, numbered, titled, and referred to directly in the text. By convention, tables are listed as "Tables," whereas line graphs, bar graphs, pie charts, or any other kinds of drawings or photographs are labeled as "Figures." Suppose you create a document that includes four graphics—a table, a bar graph, a pie chart, and a photograph. The table would be labeled as Table 1. The rest would be labeled as Figure 1, Figure 2, and Figure 3.

In addition to numbering and labeling, every graphic needs a comprehensive title that explains fully what information is being displayed. Look back over the tables and figures in this chapter and compare their titles to the information in the graphics. In a line graph showing changes over time, for example, a typical title will identify the information on both the horizontal and vertical axes and the years covered. Bar graphs also have a "legend" explaining how the bars are coded if necessary. When you import the graphic into your own text, be consistent in where you place the title—either above the graphic or below it.

Referencing the Graphic in Your Text   Academic and professional writers follow a referencing convention called *independent redundancy*. The general rule is this: The graphic should be understandable without the text; the text should be understandable without the graphic; the text should repeat the most important information in the graphic. An example is shown in Figure 9.23.

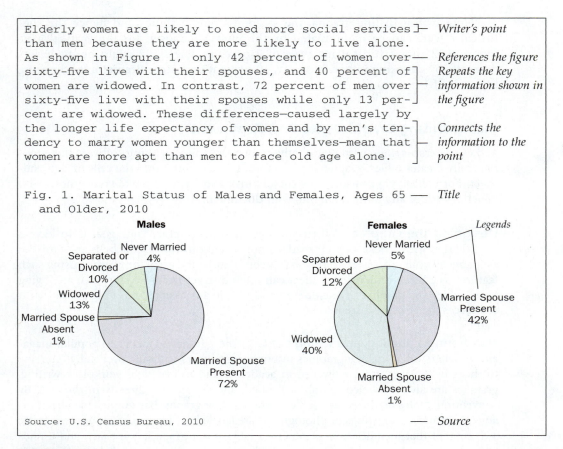

Elderly women are likely to need more social services]— *Writer's point*
than men because they are more likely to live alone.
As shown in Figure 1, only 42 percent of women over —— *References the figure*
sixty-five live with their spouses, and 40 percent of]   *Repeats the key*
women are widowed. In contrast, 72 percent of men over   *information shown in*
sixty-five live with their spouses while only 13 per-]   *the figure*
cent are widowed. These differences—caused largely by
the longer life expectancy of women and by men's ten-]   *Connects the*
dency to marry women younger than themselves—mean that   *information to the*
women are more apt than men to face old age alone.]   *point*

Fig. 1. Marital Status of Males and Females, Ages 65 —— *Title*
and Older, 2010

Males   **Females**   *Legends*

Never Married   Never Married
Separated or   4%   Separated or   5%
Divorced   Divorced
10%   12%
                                                          Married Spouse
Widowed   Present
13%   42%
Married Spouse
Absent
1%   Widowed
                                 40%
Married Spouse
Present   Married Spouse
72%   Absent
                                 1%

Source: U.S. Census Bureau, 2010   —— *Source*

FIGURE 9.23 Example of a student text with a referenced graph

Conclusion

In this chapter we have explained the challenge and power of using visuals in arguments. We have examined the components of visual design—use of type, layout, color, and images—and have shown how these components can be used for persuasive effect in arguments. We have also described the argumentative genres that depend on effective use of visuals—posters and fliers, advocacy advertisements, cartoons, and Web pages—and invited you to produce your own visual argument. Finally, we showed you that graphics can tell a numeric story in a highly focused and dramatic way. Particularly, we explained the functions of tables, bar graphs, pie charts, and line graphs, and showed you how to reference graphics and incorporate them into your own prose.

WRITING ASSIGNMENT   A Visual Argument Rhetorical Analysis, a Visual Argument, or a Microtheme Using Quantitative Data   MyWritingLab™

Option 1: **Writing a Rhetorical Analysis of a Visual Argument** Write a thesis-driven rhetorical analysis essay in which you examine the rhetorical effectiveness of a visual argument, either one of the visual arguments in this text or one specified by your instructor. Unless otherwise stated, direct your analysis to an audience of your class-mates. In your introduction, establish the argumentative conversation to which this argument is contributing. Briefly summarize the argument and describe the visual text. Present your thesis, highlighting two or more rhetorical features of the argument—such as the way the argument appeals to *logos, ethos,* and *pathos*—that you find central to the effectiveness or ineffectiveness of this argument. To develop and support your own points, you will need to include visual features and details (such as color, design, camera angle, framing, and special effects) as well as short quotations from any verbal parts of the argument.

Option 2: **Multimodal Assignment: A Public Affairs Advocacy Ad or a Poster Argument** Working with the idea of an advocacy ad or poster argument that you explored in For Class Discussion on page 199, use the visual design principles through-out the chapter, the guidelines presented on page 199, your understanding of visual argument and the genre of poster arguments, and your own creativity to produce a visual argument that can be displayed on your campus or in your town or city. Try out the draft of your advocacy ad or poster argument on people who are part of your target audience. Based on these individuals' suggestions for improving the clarity and impact of this visual argument, prepare a final version of your poster argument.

Option 3: **Multimodal Assignment: Intertextual Visual Argument** Often, visual arguments rely on what scholars call "intertextual associations." By "intertextual" (literally "between texts"), we mean that an image gets its power by drawing on ideas or emotions associated with other images that are part of our cultural background. An example is the photo of the young girls shooting bows (Figure 9.17), in which interpreting the intensity in the girls' faces depends on our cultural knowledge of *The Hunger Games.* Examples of frequently used intertextual images include the Statue of Liberty, the Uncle Sam "I Want You" recruitment poster, Adam and Eve in the garden with an apple or snake, Rosie the Riveter, the raising of the flag on Iwo Jima, and the Rodin sculpture *The Thinker.* Intertextual associations can also be drawn from fairy tales, legends, societal trends, or popular culture. For this assignment, create an idea for a poster or bumper sticker that would depend on an intertextual association for its persuasive effect. Think of an idea or behavior that you would like to promote and then link your persuasive purpose to an image from history, popular culture, or fairy tales that would speak to your audience and enliven your message. Finally, write a short reflection explaining the challenge of creating an intertextual visual argument. Possible ideas for an intertextual visual argument might include silencing cell phones in public places, buying local food, voting for a certain candidate, changing a school policy, supporting or criticizing skateboarders, admiring or mocking video game players, opposing Facebook addiction, defending an art form you value, supporting or criticizing car drivers who are angry at bikers, attacking employers' fixation on dress codes, and so forth.

Option 4: **Multimodal Assignment: Cartoon** Choose a controversial issue important to you and create a single-frame political cartoon that presents your perspective on the issue in a memorable way. Use the cartoon strategies of mini-narrative, caricature, exaggeration, distortion, and the interaction between image and text.

Option 5: **A Microtheme Using a Quantitative Graphic** Write a microtheme that tells a story based on data you select from Table 9.2 or from some other table provided by your instructor or located by you. Include in your microtheme at least one quantitative graphic (table, line graph, bar graph, pie chart), which should be labeled and referenced according to standard conventions. Use as a model the short piece shown in Figure 9.23 on page 206. ■

MyWritingLab™

Visit Ch. 9 Analyzing Visual Arguments in *MyWritingLab* to complete the For Writing and Discussion and Writing Assignments and to test your understanding of the chapter objectives.

PART FOUR
Arguments in Depth
Types of Claims

This advertisement for Nicolites is one voice in the public controversy over e-cigarettes. The ad claims that e-cigarettes are safer than regular cigarettes but chooses to use the word "smoking" rather than the more sanitized word "vaping." The vapor from an e-cigarette usually includes nicotine (and may have added flavors) but not the tar from cigarettes. However, as the discussion in Chapter 10 on pages 213–215 shows, the safety, healthfulness, and advisability of e-cigarettes are hotly debated issues. Using strategies from Chapter 9 on analyzing visual texts, how do the words and images in this ad work together to make positive claims about e-cigarettes?

An Introduction to the Types of Claims

What you will learn in this chapter:

10.1 To identify different claim types and show how each type has characteristic patterns of development

10.2 To use strategies based on claim types to help focus an argument, generate ideas for it, and structure it persuasively

10.3 To be mindful of how different claim types work together in hybrid arguments

In Parts One, Two, and Three of this text, we showed how argument entails both inquiry and persuasion. We explained strategies for creating a compelling structure of reasons and evidence for your arguments (*logos*), for linking your arguments to the beliefs and values of your audience (*pathos*), and for establishing your credibility and trustfulness (*ethos*). We also explained how to do a rhetorical analysis of both verbal and visual texts.

Now in Part Four we examine arguments in depth by explaining five types of claims, each type having its own characteristic patterns of development and support. Because almost all arguments use one or more of these types of claims as "moves" or building blocks, knowing how to develop each claim type will advance your skills in argument. The claims we examine in Part Four are related to an ancient rhetorical concept called *stasis,* from a Greek term meaning "stand," as in "to take a stand on something." There are many competing theories of stasis, so no two rhetoricians discuss stasis in exactly the same way. In Part Four, we present a version of stasis theory based on five types of claims. Studying these claim types will increase your flexibility and sophistication as an arguer.

The Types of Claims and Their Typical Patterns of Development

10.1 To identify different claim types and show how each type has characteristic patterns of development

To appreciate what a study of claim types can do, imagine one of those heated but frustrating arguments in which the question at issue keeps shifting. Everyone talks at cross-purposes, each speaker's point unconnected to the previous speaker's. Suppose your heated discussion is about the use of steroids. You might get such a discussion back on track if one person says: "Hold it for a moment. What are we actually arguing about here? Are we arguing about whether steroids are a health risk or whether steroids should be banned from sports? These are two different issues. We can't debate both at once." Whether she recognizes it or not, this person is applying the concept of claim types to get the argument focused.

To understand how claim types work, let's return to the concept of stasis. A stasis is an issue or question that focuses a point of disagreement. You and your audience may agree on the answer to question A and so have nothing to argue about. Likewise you may agree on the answer to question B. But on question C you disagree. Question C constitutes a stasis where you and your audience diverge. It is the place where disagreement begins, where as an arguer you take a stand against another view. Thus you and your audience may agree that steroids, if used carefully under a physician's supervision, pose few long-term health risks but still disagree on whether steroids should be banned from sports. This last issue constitutes a stasis, the point where you and your audience part company.

Rhetoricians have discovered that the kinds of questions that divide people have classifiable patterns. In this text we identify five broad types of claims—each type originating in a different kind of question. The following chart gives you a quick overview of these five types of claims, each of which is developed in more detail in subsequent chapters in Part Four. It also shows you a typical structure for each type of argument. Note that the first three claim types concern questions of truth or reality, whereas the last two concern questions of value. You'll appreciate the significance of this distinction as this chapter progresses.

Claims about Reality, Truth, or the Way Things Are

Claim Type and Generic Question	Examples of Issue Questions	Typical Methods for Structuring an Argument
Definitional arguments: *In what category does this thing belong?* (Chapter 11)	▪ Is solitary confinement cruel and unusual punishment? ▪ Is a skilled video game player an athlete?	▪ Create a definition that establishes criteria for the category. ▪ Use examples to show how the contested case meets the criteria.
Resemblance arguments: *To what is this thing similar?* (Chapter 11)	▪ Is opposition to gay marriage like opposition to interracial marriage? ▪ Is investing in the stock market like gambling?	▪ Let the analogy or precedent itself create the desired rhetorical effect. [or] ▪ Elaborate on the relevant similarities between the given case and the analogy or precedent.

(continued)

Claim Type and Generic Question	Examples of Issue Questions	Typical Methods for Structuring an Argument
Causal arguments: *What are the causes or consequences of this phenomenon?* (Chapter 12)	▪ What are the causes of bee colony collapse disorder? ▪ What might be the consequences of raising the minimum wage?	▪ Explain the links in a causal chain going from cause to effect or summarize experimental studies showing cause or consequence.
Evaluation and ethical arguments: *What is the worth or value of this thing?* (Chapter 13)	▪ Is talk therapy a good approach for treating anxiety? ▪ Is it ethical to use reproductive technology to make "designer babies"?	▪ Establish the criteria for a "good" or "ethical" member of this class or category. ▪ Use examples to show how the contested case meets the criteria.
Proposal arguments: *What action should we take?* (Chapter 14)	▪ Should colleges abolish the SAT and ACT for admissions? ▪ Should the federal government enact a carbon tax?	▪ Make the problem vivid. ▪ Explain your solution. ▪ Justify your solution by showing how it is motivated by principle, by good consequences, or by resemblance to a previous action the audience approves.

■ ■ ■ **FOR CLASS DISCUSSION** **Identifying Types of Claims**

Working as a class or in small groups, read the following questions and decide which claim type is represented by each. Sometimes there might be several different ways to classify a claim, so if the question fits two categories, explain your reasoning.

1. Should the president be authorized to employ weaponized drones to kill terrorists?
2. Is taking Adderall to increase concentration for an exam a form of cheating?
3. What would be the economic consequences of a carbon tax aimed at reducing carbon emissions?
4. Is burning the American flag an act of free speech?
5. Were the terrorist attacks of September 11, 2001, more like Pearl Harbor (an act of war) or more like an earthquake (a natural disaster)?
6. How effective is acupuncture in reducing morning sickness?
7. Is acupuncture quackery or real medicine?
8. Should universities ban the use of calculators in calculus exams?
9. Does the rodeo sport of riding bucking horses or bulls constitute cruelty to animals?
10. Why are couples who live together before marriage more likely to divorce than couples who don't live together before marriage?

Using Claim Types to Focus an Argument and Generate Ideas: An Example

10.2 To use strategies based on claim types to help focus an argument, generate ideas for it, and structure it persuasively

Having provided an overview of the types of claims, we now show you some of the benefits of this knowledge. First of all, understanding claim types will help you focus an argument by asking you to determine what's at stake between you and your audience. Where do you and your audience agree and disagree? What are the questions at issue? Second, it will help you generate ideas for your argument by suggesting the kinds of reasons, examples, and evidence you'll need.

To illustrate, let's take the recent public controversy about e-cigarettes, which use a battery-powered heating element to vaporize the liquid in a small cartridge. The user inhales the vapor (an act often called "vaping"). Cartridges can be purchased containing various amounts of nicotine or no nicotine at all; flavored liquids (such as apple cinnamon or peach cobbler) are also available. Although there is debate about whether the vapors from e-cigarettes are harmful, everyone agrees that the nicotine-laced liquid itself is poisonous if ingested in its liquid form. In the absence of federal regulations, many states and cities have enacted their own laws about e-cigarettes, often treating them exactly as if they were real cigarettes—banning them from bars, restaurants, and other public places, forbidding their sale to minors, and restricting the ways they can be advertised.

Let's now take the hypothetical case of a city debating a policy on e-cigarettes. Imagine three different writers. Writer 1 wants to ban e-cigarettes, making them subject to the same restrictions as real cigarettes. Writer 2 wants to promote e-cigarettes as a preferred alternative to real cigarettes. Writer 3, a libertarian opposed to the nanny state, wants no restrictions on e-cigarettes other than forbidding sale of nicotine cartridges to minors and making sure that the liquid-containing cartridges are childproof. Let's consider how familiarity with claim types can help each writer generate ideas for his or her argument.

Writer 1: Ban E-Cigarettes

Writer 1, who believes that e-cigarettes are harmful, imagines a somewhat live-and-let-live audience inclined to take no action against e-cigarettes. Her goal is to portray e-cigarettes negatively in order to persuade this audience that e-cigarettes should be banned.

- **Definition argument:** Because regular cigarettes are already banned in public places, Writer 1 wants to place e-cigarettes in the same category as real cigarettes. For part of her argument she can use a definitional strategy, showing that e-cigarettes and regular cigarettes belong in the same category in that they both deliver nicotine extracted from tobacco leaves. She can argue that the differences between e-cigarettes and regular cigarettes, such as one producing smoke and the other vapor, are superficial. What makes them the same is the delivery of nicotine.

- **Resemblance argument:** Using a resemblance strategy, Writer 1 can also show how e-cigarettes are designed to look like regular cigarettes and make smoking look cool again. You can blow "smoke" rings with the exhaled vapor, just as you can with real tobacco smoke.

■ **Causal argument:** To increase her negative portrayal of e-cigarettes, Writer 1 can also use a causal strategy. She can argue that e-cigarettes will hook children and teenagers on real cigarettes. She can show how the creation of flavored vapors such as "bubble gum" or "pancake" seem marketed to children and how the availability of cartridges that combine flavored vapors with nicotine give Big Tobacco a new way to create the next generation of nicotine addicts.

■ **Evaluation argument:** Here Writer 1 will have to summarize and rebut counter-views that e-cigarettes are a good replacement for regular cigarettes. Supporters will say the e-cigarettes are better than regular cigarettes because they produce fewer carcinogens and are thus safer. Writer 1 will need to argue that the negative aspects of e-cigarettes—nicotine addiction and the enticement of children toward smoking—outweigh the increased safety. She can also argue that the propellant ingredients in the cartridges have not yet been proven safe, and she can refer to research showing the liquid itself is extremely poisonous if ingested directly.

■ **Proposal argument:** The city council should ban e-cigarettes.

This example shows that writers often need to argue issues of reality and truth in order to make claims about values. In this particular case, Writer 1's proposal claim to ban e-cigarettes is based on reasons that are themselves derived from definition, resemblance, and cause: "E-cigarettes should be banned because they contain the same tobacco-derived nicotine as real cigarettes (definition), because they are advertised to make smoking look cool again (resemblance), and because they will hook kids on smoking (cause)."

Writer 2: Promote E-Cigarettes as a Preferred Alternative to Real Cigarettes

Writer 2 shares with his audience a belief that cigarettes are harmful and that smoking should be banned. However, he wants to emphasize the benefits of e-cigarettes to people who already smoke. Like Writer 1, he can use the five claim types to generate strategies for his argument.

■ **Definition argument:** To portray e-cigarettes more positively, Writer 2 can make the definitional claim that e-cigarettes are **not** the same as real cigarettes and thus belong in a different category. He can argue that the essential trait of real cigarettes is cancer-causing tar derived from the combustion of tobacco leaves. It is the danger of the tar, not the nicotine, that caused the anti-smoking movement in the first place, especially the danger of secondhand smoke to others. By arguing that the delivery of nicotine is a superficial rather than essential criterion for defining cigarettes, he can show that the absence of tar and secondhand smoke makes e-cigarettes essentially different from real cigarettes.

■ **Resemblance argument:** Using this strategy, Writer 2 can show that although e-cigarettes are essentially different from real cigarettes, the two have pleasing similarities. Vaping provides the same physical and social pleasures as does smoking, but without the harm to self and others.

- **Causal argument:** Writer 2 can also portray e-cigarettes positively through the causal argument that they can save the lives of current smokers by converting them from a dangerous to less dangerous way of getting nicotine. Without condoning nicotine addiction, Writer 2 can point to the positive health consequences of getting a nicotine hit without the carcinogens. Writer 2 can also argue that e-cigarettes can help people stop smoking because they can gradually reduce the nicotine content in the cartridges they purchase.
- **Evaluation argument:** Here Writer 2 can claim that e-cigarettes are better than real cigarettes by arguing that the health benefits of no smoke and tar outweigh the addiction to nicotine, which in itself causes little health risk.
- **Proposal argument:** E-cigarettes should be promoted as a safe alternative to real cigarettes.

Writer 3: Place No Restrictions on E-Cigarettes

Writer 3 is a libertarian who dislikes nanny-state restrictions on our individual freedoms. She wants to argue that the only restrictions on e-cigarettes should be federally mandated childproofing of the cartridges, truth-in-labeling about what is contained in the cartridges, and prevention of sales of nicotine-containing cartridges to minors.

- **Definition argument:** Writer 3, like Writer 2, can argue that e-cigarettes are in a different category from regular cigarettes. They present no proven dangers either to self or to others through secondhand smoke.
- **Resemblance argument:** To celebrate the libertarian endorsement of individual freedom, Writer 3 can show the resemblance between taking a pleasurable hit on an e-cigarette with other pleasures frowned upon by the nanny state—drinking sugary sodas, buying a Big Mac, or owning a muscle car.
- **Causal argument:** Whereas Writer 2 argues that e-cigarettes are safer than regular cigarettes, Writer 3 can argue that nobody has demonstrated any firsthand or secondhand health hazards for e-cigarettes. She can make the additional causal argument that government wants to treat e-cigarettes like regular cigarettes so that they can tax them heavily to produce sin-tax revenue. She can also argue that nanny-state regulations lead to increased loss of personal freedoms and the shutting down of markets for free enterprise.
- **Evaluation argument:** Writer 3 can argue that people should be free to make their own evaluations of e-cigarettes.
- **Proposal argument:** For consenting adults, the city should place no restrictions on e-cigarettes.

Hybrid Arguments: How Claim Types Work Together in Arguments

10.3 To be mindful of how different claim types work together in hybrid arguments

As the e-cigarette example shows, hybrid arguments can be built from different claim types. A writer might develop a proposal argument with a causal subargument in one section, a resemblance subargument in another section, and an evaluation subargument in still another section. Although the overarching proposal argument follows the typical structure of a proposal, each of the subsections follows a typical structure for its own claim type.

Some Examples of Hybrid Arguments

The following examples show how these combinations of claim types can play out in actual arguments. (For more examples of these kinds of hybrid arguments, see Chapter 14, pages 312–313, where we explain how lower-order claims about reality and truth can support higher-order claims about values.)

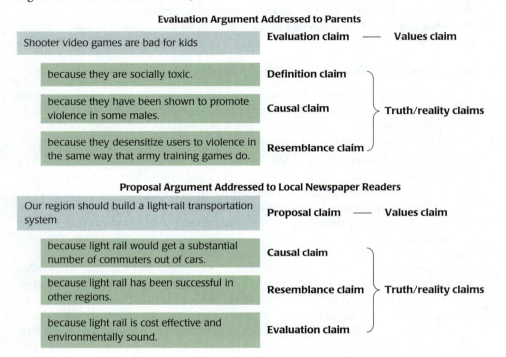

Evaluation Argument Addressed to Parents

Shooter video games are bad for kids — **Evaluation claim** —— **Values claim**

because they are socially toxic. — **Definition claim**

because they have been shown to promote violence in some males. — **Causal claim**

because they desensitize users to violence in the same way that army training games do. — **Resemblance claim**

} **Truth/reality claims**

Proposal Argument Addressed to Local Newspaper Readers

Our region should build a light-rail transportation system — **Proposal claim** —— **Values claim**

because light rail would get a substantial number of commuters out of cars. — **Causal claim**

because light rail has been successful in other regions. — **Resemblance claim**

because light rail is cost effective and environmentally sound. — **Evaluation claim**

} **Truth/reality claims**

■ ■ ■   **FOR WRITING AND DISCUSSION   Exploring Different Claim Types and Audiences**   MyWritingLab™

Individual task: Choose one of the following issues and role-play one of the suggested authorial purposes. Write out your exploratory ideas for how you might use several of the claim types to develop your argument (definition, resemblance, cause, evaluation, proposal). Use as your models our example arguments about e-cigarettes. Imagine an audience skeptical of your chosen position.

1. Carbon footprint: You want (do not want) the Environmental Protection Agency to regulate the amount of carbon dioxide that can be emitted from power plants.
2. Gun restrictions: You want (do not want) the federal government to ban assault rifles and high-volume ammunition cartridges.
3. Diet: You want your classmates to adopt (or not adopt) the paleo diet.

4. Minimum wage: You want (do not want) your city or state to adopt as its minimum wage a living wage of $15/hour.

5. Some other issue that you think will be reasonably familiar to your classmates.

Group task: Share with classmates your initial efforts to use the claim types to help generate ideas. What worked for you and what didn't? Where was it useful to think of the category that something belonged in (definition)? For example, is carbon dioxide a "pollutant," a "poison," or a "harmless and natural chemical compound"? Where was it helpful to think about resemblance? Is a paleo diet like a caveman's diet? How about cause? What will be the consequences of raising the minimum wage? How did your thinking about issues of truth or reality help develop evaluation or proposal claims?

An Extended Example of a Hybrid Argument

As the previous examples illustrate, different claim types often serve as building blocks for larger arguments. We ask you now to consider a more extended example. Read the following argument from *Outside Magazine* aimed at enthusiasts of outdoor sports such as hiking, camping, mountain climbing, skiing, biking, and distance running. The magazine's readers are often health-conscious consumers of multivitamins and other diet supplements such as minerals, fish oils, herbals, botanicals, enzymes, antioxidants, amino acids, and other substances often taken as tablets, capsules, powders, energy drinks, or energy bars. In this startling article the writer uses recent scientific studies to make the evaluation claim that these supplements are either "useless" or "worse than useless." Notice how this overall evaluation claim is supported by claims from definition, resemblance, and cause.

Your Daily Multivitamin May Be Hurting You

ALEX HUTCHINSON

*Introduces the **evaluation** issue "Are supplements good/bad?"*

In JUNE, at this year's European College of Sport Science conference in Barcelona, Mari Carmen Gomez-Cabrera, a physiologist at the University of Valencia and one of the world's leading experts on antioxidants, was debating the merits of supplements with two top researchers. For more than 90 minutes they went back and forth, parsing the accumulated evidence in front of a packed auditorium. Finally, Gomez-Cabrera landed on a provocative question that summarized her position.

*Restates **evaluation** issue with implied claim: Supplements are either useless or worse than useless.*

The debate, she explained, isn't whether supplements are good or bad for athletes. Rather, it's "are they useless, or are they worse than useless?"

The question may come as a shock to the more than half of Americans who take some sort of dietary supplement—a vast catch-all term that includes everything from vitamins and minerals to herbal remedies to exotic performance boosters like deer-antler spray

Further develops **evaluation claim:** Supplements are bad because they make unproven claims and because they may come with hazardous side effects.

and glutamine. It's no surprise that the purported muscle-building supplements make unproven claims and may come with hazardous side effects. But in the past few years, Gomez-Cabrera and a growing number of researchers have come to believe that even respectable mainstream supplements such as vitamins C and E suffer from the same basic flaw: few apparent benefits and increasing evidence of negative effects. For example, in July's issue of the *Journal of Physiology,* researchers discovered that resveratrol, an antioxidant in red wine, actually limited the positive effects of cardiovascular exercise—like an increased VO2 max—when taken daily in high concentrations. In July, scientists at the Fred Hutchinson Cancer Research Center found that men with high levels of the omega-3 fatty acid DHA in their blood, often from fish-oil supplements, had a significantly greater risk of prostate cancer.

Uses **causal arguments** to illustrate bad side effects

Definition claim: Supplements belong to one of two categories: (1) safe but don't work or (2) work but have bad side effects

According to Pieter Cohen, a professor at Harvard Medical School, there are really only two types of sports supplements: those that are safe but don't work, and those that might work but have side effects, especially at higher than normal levels. "If any supplement, no matter how beneficial, has a pharmaceutical effect, it's also got a downside," he says. "There's no way to get around that basic principle."

Develops **definition** argument by showing how supplements fit first category of being safe but useless

5   Most supplements stay firmly in the first category. Taking a daily multivitamin, Cohen emphasizes, won't harm you, but it usually won't help either, which is why major health organizations such as the American Heart Association and the American College of Sports Medicine don't recommend supplements to healthy people.

It's not that vitamins and minerals aren't important. If you don't get enough vitamin C, you can get scurvy; without enough iron, you can become anemic; and if you live far enough north to see Russia from your backyard, you may need some extra vitamin D. But all three of these substances have also been linked to negative effects at high doses. Same goes for prolonged use of other common supplements such as vitamin E and calcium. In short, unless tests have shown that you're low in a particular vitamin or mineral, there's no evidence to suggest that you should take a daily supplement.

Causal argument showing bad side effects (places supplements in second category of being harmful)

That rule also applies if you're an athlete who takes supplements because, say, you assume your training requires an antioxidant boost to speed recovery. Gomez-Cabrera and her colleagues at the University of Valencia have shown that antioxidant supplements suppress the oxidative stress that signals your body to adapt and get stronger. The result: regular use of something seemingly innocuous such as vitamin C can actually block gains in endurance-boosting mitochondria.

Causal argument showing still more bad side effects

Causal argument from psychology showing different bad effect: People who take supplements feel they are healthier and thus actually act in less healthy ways.

The balance between risk and return also works in subtler ways, as Wen-Bin Chiou, a psychologist at National Sun Yatsen University in Taiwan, has shown in a series of experiments on a phenomenon called the licensing effect. As part of a battery of tests, subjects were asked to take a pill; half were told the pill was a multivitamin, while the other half were told it was a placebo. In truth, they were all placebos.

In subsequent tests, the subjects who thought they'd taken a vitamin consistently behaved in less healthy ways. When asked to try out a pedometer, they were more likely to choose a shorter walking route; at lunch, they chose less healthy food. In follow-up studies, Chiou has also discovered that smokers who think they've been given a vitamin smoke more, and people who are given a weight-loss supplement are less likely to stick to their diet.

Brief **resemblance** argument: Taking a vitamin is NOT like eating spinach or going to the gym.

The same thing happens when you go to the gym or eat a plate of spinach. The difference is that exercise and vegetables have real benefits, so you've still got a chance to come out ahead. If you take a pill with no benefits, the best you can do is break even.

Conclusion

Which brings us back to Gomez-Cabrera in Barcelona. She, of all people, has enormous respect for the powers of micronutrients such as antioxidants—she has devoted her life to studying them. "But if you eat enough fruits and vegetables, five servings a day," she says, "I don't think you need anything else." And if you're not eating like that, then taking a pill isn't a solution. In fact, it may be part of the problem.

As this editorial demonstrates, awareness of different kinds of claims can help you increase your flexibility and effectiveness as an arguer. In the following chapters in Part Four, we discuss each of the claim types in more detail, showing how they work and how you can develop skills and strategies for supporting each type of claim.

MyWritingLab™

Visit Ch. 10 An Introduction to the Types of Claims in *MyWritingLab* to complete the For Writing and Discussion and to test your understanding of the chapter objectives.

Definition and Resemblance Arguments

11

What you will learn in this chapter:

11.1 To explain what is at stake in arguments about definition and resemblance

11.2 To explain four types of categorical arguments

11.3 To explain the criteria-match structure of categorical arguments based on definition

11.4 To use criteria-match reasoning to generate ideas for your own definition argument

Arguments about definition or resemblance concern disputes about what category something belongs to, either directly by definition or indirectly or metaphorically through comparison or resemblance. They are among the most common argument types you will encounter.

Case 1 Are Global Warming Skeptics Like The Outlier Frog In This Cartoon?

This cartoon by award-wining political cartoonist (as well as children's book author) Pat Bagley makes two overlapping resemblance arguments. First, it argues that global warming happens slowly, like a heating pot of water. Second, it argues that the Republican Science Committee, comprised of global warming skeptics, selects its evidence from outlier sources, analogous to the outlier frog in this cartoon. This striking visual analogy makes a resemblance argument against the objectivity of the GOP Science Committee.

Case 2   Is a Frozen Embryo a Person or Property?

An infertile couple conceived several embryos in a test tube and then froze the fertilized embryos for future use. During the couple's divorce, they disagreed about the disposition of the embryos. The woman wanted to use the frozen embryos to try to get pregnant, and the man wanted to destroy them. When the courts were asked to decide what should be done with the embryos, several questions of definition arose: Should the frozen embryos be categorized as "persons," thus becoming analogous to children in custody disputes? Or should they be divided up as "property," with the man getting half and the woman getting the other half? Or should a new legal category be created for them that regards them as more than property but less than actual persons? The judge decided that frozen embryos "are not, strictly speaking, either 'persons' or 'property,' but occupy an interim category that entitles them to special respect because of their potential for human life."*

What Is at Stake in an Argument about Definition and Resemblance?

11.1 To explain what is at stake in arguments about definition and resemblance

Definition and resemblance arguments occur whenever a community disagrees about the category a particular person, thing, act, or phenomenon should be placed in or identified with. Here are some examples:

Issues Involving Categories

Question	Does this specific phenomenon …	… belong to (or is it similar to) this category?
Is atmospheric carbon dioxide a pollutant?	Atmospheric carbon dioxide	Pollutant
Is LASIK surgery for nearsightedness "medically necessary" surgery or "cosmetic" surgery?	LASIK surgery for nearsightedness	Medically necessary surgery (or cosmetic surgery)
Is women's obsession with thinness today similar in effect to women's footbinding in ancient China?	Women's obsession with thinness	Footbinding in ancient China

Much is at stake when we place things into categories because the category that something belongs to can have real consequences. Naming the category that something belongs to makes an implicit mini-argument.

---

*See Vincent F. Stempel, "Procreative Rights in Assisted Reproductive Technology: Why the Angst?" *Albany Law Review* 62 (1999), 1187.

Consequences Resulting from Categorical Claims

To appreciate the consequences of categorical claims, consider the competing categories proposed for whales in the international controversy over commercial whaling. What category does a whale belong to? Some arguers might say that "whales are sacred animals," implying that their intelligence, beauty, grace, and power mean they should never be killed. Others might argue that "whales are a renewable food resource" like tuna, crabs, cattle, and chickens. This category implies that we can harvest whales for food the same way we harvest tuna for tuna fish sandwiches or cows for beef. Still others might argue that "whales are an endangered species"—a category that argues for the preservation of whale stocks but not necessarily for a ban on controlled hunting of individual whales. Each of these whaling arguments places whales in a separate, different category that implicitly urges the reader to adopt that category's perspective on whaling.

Significant consequences can also result from resemblance claims. Consider the way that media analysts tried to make sense of the September 11, 2001, terrorist attacks on the World Trade Center and the Pentagon by comparing them to different kinds of previous events. Some commentators said, "The September 11 attacks are like Timothy McVeigh's bombing of the Alfred P. Murrah Federal Building in Oklahoma City in 1995"—an argument that framed the terrorists as criminals who must be brought to justice. Others said, "The September 11 attacks are like the 1941 Japanese attack on Pearl Harbor"—an argument suggesting that the United States should declare war on some as-yet-to-be-defined enemy. Still others said, "The September 11 attacks are like an occasionally disastrous earthquake or an epidemic," arguing that terrorists will exist as long as the right conditions breed them and that it is useless to fight them using the strategies of conventional war. Under this analogy, the "war on terror" is a metaphorical war like the "war on poverty" or the "war against cancer." Clearly, each of these resemblance claims had high-stakes consequences. In 2001, the Pearl Harbor claim prevailed, and the United States went to war, first in Afghanistan and then in Iraq. Many critics of these wars continue to say that war is an inappropriate strategy for fighting the "disease of terrorism."

The Rule of Justice: Things in the Same Category Should Be Treated the Same Way

As you can see, the category we place something into—either directly through definition or indirectly through comparison—can have significant implications for people's actions or beliefs. To ensure fairness, philosophers refer to the rule of justice, which states that "beings in the same essential category should be treated in the same way." For example, the problem of how the courts should treat the users or sellers of marijuana depends on the category marijuana belongs to. Marijuana might be placed in the same category as tobacco and alcohol, in which case the possession and sale of marijuana would be legal but subject to regulation and taxes. Or marijuana could be placed in the same category as meth, cocaine, and heroin; in this case, it would be an illegal drug subject to criminal prosecution. Some states have placed marijuana in the same category as penicillin and insulin, making it a legal drug so long as it is obtained from a licensed dispensary with a doctor's prescription. Many states are not happy with any of these categories and are trying to define marijuana in some fourth way. Or to take a more homely example, suppose your professor says that absence from an exam can be excused for emergencies only. How would you define "emergency"? Clearly if you broke your leg on the morning of an exam, you would be excused. But is attending your grandmother's funeral or your best friend's wedding an "emergency"? How about missing an exam because your car wouldn't start? Although your interests might be best served by a broad definition of emergency, your professor might prefer a narrow definition, which would permit fewer exemptions.

The rule of justice becomes especially hard to apply when we consider contested cases marked by growth or slow change through time. At what point does a child become an adult? When does a binge drinker become an alcoholic, an Internet poker player a compulsive gambler, or a fetus a human person? Although we may be able arbitrarily to choose a particular point and declare that "adult" means someone at least eighteen years old or that "human person" means a fetus at conception, or at three months, or at birth, in the everyday world the distinction between child and adult, between fetus and person, between Friday-night poker playing and compulsive gambling seems an evolution, not a sudden and definitive step. Nevertheless, our language requires an abrupt shift between categories. In short, applying the rule of justice often requires us to adopt a digital approach to reality (switches are either on or off, either a fetus is a human person or it is not), whereas our sense of life is more analogical (there are numerous gradations between on and off; there are countless shades of gray between black and white).

As we can see from the preceding examples, the promise of language to structure what psychologist William James called "the buzz and confusion of the world" into an orderly set of categories turns out to be elusive. In most category debates, an argument, not a quick trip to the dictionary, is required to settle the matter.

■ ■ ■ **FOR CLASS DISCUSSION** **Applying the Rule of Justice**

Suppose your landlord decides to institute a "no pets" rule. The rule of justice requires that all pets have to go—not just your neighbor's barking dog, but also Mrs. Brown's cat, the kids' hamster downstairs, and your own pet tarantula. That is, all these animals have to go, unless you can argue that some of them are not "pets" for purposes of the landlord's "no pets" rule.

1. Working in small groups or as a whole class, define pets by establishing the criteria an animal would have to meet to be included in the category "pets." Consider your landlord's "no pets" rule as the cultural context for your definition.

2. Based on your criteria, which of the following animals is definitely a pet that would have to be removed from the apartment? Based on your criteria, which animals could you exclude from the "no pets" rule? How would you make your argument to your landlord?
   - a German shepherd
   - a small housecat
   - a tiny, well-trained lapdog
   - a gerbil in a cage
   - a canary
   - a tank of tropical fish
   - a tarantula

Types of Categorical Arguments

11.2 To explain four types of categorical arguments

Categorical arguments assert that a disputed phenomenon is (or is not) either a member of a certain category or is like a certain category. Such arguments can be divided into four kinds:

1. **Simple categorical arguments,** in which there is no dispute about the definition of the category.
2. **Definition arguments,** in which there is a dispute about the boundaries of the category and hence of its definition.
3. **Resemblance arguments by analogy**, in which the writer uses metaphor or other figurative language to link the phenomenon to a certain category.
4. **Resemblance arguments by precedent**, in which the arguer claims that one phenomenon or situation is similar to another phenomenon or situation.

Let's look at each in turn.

Simple Categorical Arguments

A categorical argument can be said to be "simple" if there is no disagreement about the definition of the category into which a person, event, or phenomenon is placed. For example, if you make the claim that "Joe is bossy," you are placing him in the category of "bossy people." In this case, you assume that you and the audience agree on what "bossy" means. Your dispute is simply whether Joe meets the criteria for "bossy." To support your claim, you would provide examples of his bossiness (his poor listening skills, his shouting at people, his making decisions without asking the committee). Similarly, if you want to make the simple categorical claim that "low-carb diets are dangerous," you would need to provide evidence of this danger (scientific studies, testimony from doctors, anecdotes, and so forth). The dispute in this case is about low-carb diets, not about the definition of "dangerous." To rebut a simple categorical claim, you would provide counterevidence to show that the person, event, or phenomenon does not meet the criteria for the category.

■ ■ ■ **FOR CLASS DISCUSSION** **Supporting and Rebutting Simple Categorical Claims**

Working individually or in small groups, consider how you would support the following simple categorical claims. What examples or other data would convince readers that the specified case fits within the named category? Then discuss ways you might rebut each claim.

1. Bottled water is environmentally unfriendly. [That is, bottled water belongs in the category of "environmentally unfriendly substances."]
2. Macklemore is a pure rapper.
3. Americans today are obsessed with their appearance. [That is, Americans belong in the category of "people obsessed with their appearance."]
4. Competitive cheerleading is physically risky.
5. Dinosaurs were warm blooded.

Definition Arguments

Simple categorical arguments morph into definition arguments whenever stakeholders disagree about the boundaries of a category. In the previous exercise, suppose that you had said about Macklemore, "Well, that depends on how you define 'pure rapper.'" The need to define the term "pure rapper" adds a new layer of complexity to your arguments about Macklemore. You are disputing not only specifics about Macklemore but also the definition of "pure rapper" itself.

Full-blown definition arguments occur, then, when the disputants don't agree on the definition of the category into which a person, event, or phenomenon is placed. Consider, for example, the environmental controversy over the definition of *wetland*. Section 404 of the federal Clean Water Act provides for federal protection of wetlands, but it leaves the task of defining *wetland* to administrative agencies and the courts. Currently, about 5 percent of the land surface of the contiguous forty-eight states is potentially affected by the wetlands provision, and 75 percent of this land is privately owned. Efforts to define *wetland* have created a battleground between pro-environment and pro-development or property rights groups. Farmers, homeowners, and developers often want a narrow definition of wetlands so that more property is available for commercial or private use. Environmentalists favor a broad definition in order to protect different habitat types and maintain the environmental safeguards that wetlands provide (control of water pollution, spawning grounds for aquatic species, floodwater containment, and so forth).

The problem is that defining *wetland* is tricky. For example, one federal regulation defines a wetland as any area that has a saturated ground surface for twenty-one consecutive days during the year. But how would you apply this law to a pine flatwood ecosystem that was wet for ten days this year but thirty days last year? And how should the courts react to lawsuits claiming that the regulation itself is either too broad or too narrow? One can see why the wetlands controversy provides hefty incomes for lawyers and congressional lobbyists.

As we will explain in more detail later in this chapter, definition arguments require a "criteria-match" structure in which the arguer must first define the category term by specifying the criteria that must be met for something to be placed in that category. The writer then shows that the disputed person, event, or phenomenon matches those criteria.

Resemblance Argument Using Analogy

Whereas definition arguments claim that a particular phenomenon belongs to a certain category, resemblance arguments simply compare one thing to another. A common kind of resemblance argument uses analogies—imaginative kinds of comparisons often with subtle persuasive effects. If you don't like your new boss, you can say that she's like a Marine drill sergeant or the cowardly captain of a sinking ship. Each of these analogies suggests a different category in which to place your boss, clarifying the nature of your dislike while conveying an emotional charge. The arguer's intention is to transfer the audience's understanding of (or feelings about) the second thing back to the first. The risk of resemblance arguments is that the differences between the two things being compared are often so significant that the argument collapses under close examination.

Sometimes, as in the "My boss is like a Marine drill sergeant" example, arguers use short, undeveloped analogies for quick rhetorical effect. At other times, arguers develop extended analogies that carry a substantial portion of the argument. As an example of an extended analogy, consider the following excerpt from a professor's argument opposing a proposal to require a writing proficiency exam for graduation. In the following portion of his argument, the professor compares development of writing skills to the development of physical fitness.

> A writing proficiency exam gives the wrong symbolic messages about writing. It suggests that writing is simply a skill, rather than an active way of thinking and learning. It suggests that once a student demonstrates proficiency then he or she doesn't need to do any more writing.
>
> Imagine two universities concerned with the physical fitness of their students. One university requires a junior-level physical fitness exam in which students must run a mile in less than 10 minutes, a fitness level it considers minimally competent. Students at this university see the physical fitness exam as a one-time hurdle. As many as 70 percent of them can pass the exam with no practice; another 10–20 percent need a few months' training; and a few hopeless couch potatoes must go through exhaustive remediation. After passing the exam, any student can settle back into a routine of TV and potato chips having been certified as "physically fit."
>
> The second university, however, believing in true physical fitness for its students, is not interested in minimal competency. Consequently, it creates programs in which its students must take one credit physical fitness course each term for the entire four years of the undergraduate curriculum. There is little doubt which university will have the most physically fit students. At the second university, fitness becomes a way of life with everyone developing his or her full potential. Similarly, if we want to improve our students' writing abilities, we should require writing in every course throughout the curriculum.

Thus analogies have the power to get an audience's attention like virtually no other persuasive strategy. But seldom are they sufficient in themselves to provide full understanding. At some point, with every analogy, you need to ask yourself, "How far can I legitimately go with this? At what point are the similarities between the two things I am comparing going to be overwhelmed by their dissimilarities?" Analogies are useful attention-getting devices, but they can conceal and distort as well as clarify.

■ ■ ■   **FOR CLASS DISCUSSION** **Developing Analogies**

The following exercise will help you clarify how analogies function in the context of arguments. Working individually or in small groups, think of two analogies for each of the following topics. One analogy should urge readers toward a positive view of the topic; the other should urge a negative view. Write each of your analogies in the following one-sentence format:

_____ is like _____: A, B, C … (in which the first term is the contested topic being discussed; the second term is the analogy; and A, B, and C are the points of comparison).

Example

Topic: Cramming for an exam

Negative analogy: Cramming for an exam is like pumping iron for ten hours straight to prepare for a weight-lifting contest: exhausting and counterproductive.

Positive analogy: Cramming for an exam is like carbohydrate loading before a big race: it gives your brain a full supply of facts and concepts, all fresh in your mind.

1. Checking social media constantly
2. Using racial profiling for airport security
3. Using steroids to increase athletic performance
4. Paying college athletes
5. Eating at fast-food restaurants

Resemblance Arguments Using Precedent

Another kind of resemblance argument uses precedent for its persuasive force. An argument by precedent tries to show that a current situation is like a past situation and that therefore a similar action or decision should be taken or reached. You can refute a precedence argument by showing that the present situation differs substantially from the past situation.

Precedence arguments are very common. For example, during the debate about health care reform in the first year of Barack Obama's presidency, supporters of a single-payer, "Medicare-for-all" system pointed to Canada as a successful precedent. Supporters said that since a single-payer system was successful in Canada, it would also be successful in the United States. But opponents also used the Canadian precedent to attack a single-payer system. They pointed to problems in the Canadian system as a reason to reject a Medicare-for-all system in the United States.

A good example of an extended precedence argument can be found in an article entitled "The Perils of Ignoring History: Big Tobacco Played Dirty and Millions Died. How Similar Is Big Food?"* The authors' goal is to place "Big Food" in the same category as "Big Tobacco." The authors argue that the food-processing industry is trying to avoid government regulations by employing the same "dirty tricks" used earlier by Big Tobacco. The authors show how Big Tobacco hired lobbyists to fight regulation, how it created clever advertising to make cigarette smoking seem cool, and how it sponsored its own research to cast doubt on data linking nicotine to lung cancer or asthma to secondhand smoke. The researchers argue that Big Food is now doing the same thing. Through lobbying efforts, coordinated lawsuits, and public relations campaigns, Big Food resists labeling ingredients in food products, casts doubt on scientific evidence about possible carcinogens in processed foods, and uses advertising to create a local, "family farm" image for Big Food. The researchers use this precedence argument to call for stricter government oversight of Big Food.

---

*Kelly D. Brownell and Kenneth E. Warner, "The Perils of Ignoring History: Big Tobacco Played Dirty and Millions Died. How Similar Is Big Food?" *The Milbank Quarterly* 87.1 (2009), 259–294.

■ ■ ■   **FOR CLASS DISCUSSION**   **Using Claims of Precedent**

Consider the following claims of precedent, and evaluate how effective you think each precedent might be in establishing the claim. How would you develop the argument? How would you cast doubt on it?

1. To increase alumni giving to our university, we should put more funding into our football program. When University X went to postseason bowls for three years in a row, alumni donations to building programs and academics increased by 30 percent. We can expect the same increases here.
2. Postwar democracy can be created successfully in Afghanistan because it was created successfully in Germany and Japan following World War II.
3. Euthanasia laws work successfully in the Netherlands. Therefore they will work successfully in the United States.

■ ■ ■

EXAMINING VISUAL ARGUMENTS   MyWritingLab™

Claim about Category (Definition)

This cartoon, by political cartoonist Randy Bish of the *Pittsburgh Tribune Review*, creates a visual pun that makes a categorical argument against heroin. How does Bish's rendering of the letter "r" make a categorical claim? What is that claim? How effective do you find this cartoon in highlighting the seductive danger of heroin addiction?

The Criteria-Match Structure of Definition Arguments

11.3 To explain the criteria-match structure of categorical arguments based on definition

Of the four types of categorical arguments explained in the previous section, definition arguments require the fullest range of argumentative skills. For the rest of this chapter, we'll explain more fully the argumentative moves required to write your own definition argument.

Overview of Criteria-Match Structure

Definition arguments usually have a two-part structure—(1) a definition part that tries to establish the boundaries of the category and (2) a match part that argues whether a given case meets that definition. To describe this structure, we use the term *criteria-match*. Here are two examples:

> **Definition issue:** In a divorce proceeding, is a frozen embryo a "person" rather than "property"?
>
> **Criteria part:** What criteria must be met for something to be a "person"?
>
> **Match part:** Does a frozen embryo meet these criteria?
>
> **Definition issue:** Is this thirty-acre parcel of land near Swan Lake a "wetland"?
>
> **Criteria part:** What criteria must be met for something to be a wetland?
>
> **Match part:** Does this parcel of land meet these criteria?

To show how a definition issue can be developed into a claim with supporting reasons, let's look more closely at a third example:

> **Definition issue:** For purposes of my feeling good about buying my next pair of running shoes, is the Hercules Shoe Company a socially responsible company?
>
> **Criteria part:** What criteria must be met for a company to be deemed "socially responsible"?
>
> **Match part:** Does the Hercules Shoe Company meet these criteria?

Let's suppose you work for a consumer information group that wishes to encourage patronage of socially responsible companies while boycotting irresponsible ones. Your group's first task is to define *socially responsible company*. After much discussion and research, your group establishes three criteria that a company must meet to be considered socially responsible:

> *Your definition:* A company is socially responsible if it (1) avoids polluting the environment, (2) sells goods or services that contribute to the well-being of the community, and (3) treats its workers justly.

The criteria section of your argument would explain and illustrate these criteria.

The match part of the argument would then try to persuade readers that a specific company does or does not meet the criteria. A typical thesis statement might be as follows:

> *Your thesis statement:* Although the Hercules Shoe Company is nonpolluting and provides a socially useful product, it is not a socially responsible company because it treats workers unjustly.

Toulmin Framework for a Definition Argument

Here is how the core of the preceding Hercules definition argument could be displayed in Toulmin terms. Note how the reason and grounds constitute the match argument while the warrant and backing constitute the criterion argument.

Toulmin Analysis of the Hercules Shoe Company Argument

ENTHYMEME

CLAIM The Hercules Shoe Company is not a socially responsible company

REASON because it treats workers unjustly.

GROUNDS

Evidence of unjust treatment:

- Evidence that the company manufactures its shoes in East Asian sweatshops

- Evidence of the inhumane conditions in these shops

- Evidence of hardships imposed on displaced American workers

CONDITIONS OF REBUTTAL
Attacking reasons and grounds

- Possible counter evidence that the shops maintain humane working conditions

- Possible questioning of statistical data about hardships on displaced workers

WARRANT

Socially responsible companies treat workers justly.

BACKING

- Arguments showing that just treatment of workers is right in principle and also benefits society

- Arguments that capitalism helps society as a whole only if workers achieve a reasonable standard of living, have time for leisure, and are not exploited

CONDITIONS OF REBUTTAL
Attacking warrant and backing

Justice needs to be considered from an emerging nation's standpoint:

- The wages paid workers are low by American standards but are above average by East Asian standards.

- Displacement of American workers is part of the necessary adjustment of adapting to a global economy and does not mean that a company is unjust.

As this Toulmin schema illustrates, the warrant and backing constitute the criteria section of the argument by stating and defending "just treatment of workers" as a criterion for a socially responsible company. The reason and grounds constitute the match section of the argument by arguing that the Hercules Shoe Company does not treat its workers justly. How much emphasis you need to place on justifying each criterion and supporting each match depends on your audience's initial beliefs. The conditions of rebuttal help you imagine alternative views and see places where opposing views need to be acknowledged and rebutted.

■ ■ ■ **FOR CLASS DISCUSSION** Identifying Criteria and Match Issues

Consider the following definition claims. Working individually or in small groups, identify the criteria issue and the match issue for each of the following claims.

> **Definition issue:** A Honda assembled in Ohio is (is not) an American-made car.
>
> **Criteria part:** What criteria have to be met before a car can be called "American made"?
>
> **Match part:** Does a Honda assembled in Ohio meet these criteria?

1. American Sign Language is (is not) a "foreign language" for purposes of a college graduation requirement.
2. The violence in *Grand Theft Auto* is (is not) constitutionally protected free speech.
3. Bungee jumping from a crane is (is not) a "carnival amusement ride" subject to state safety inspections.
4. For purposes of a state sales tax on "candy," a Twinkie is (is not) candy.
5. A skilled video game player is (is not) a true athlete.

■ ■ ■

Creating Criteria Using Aristotelian Definition

When creating criteria for a category, you can often follow the pattern of *Aristotelian definition.* The Aristotelian definitional strategy, regularly used in dictionaries, defines a term by placing it within the next larger class or category and then showing the specific attributes that distinguish the term from other terms within the same category. For example, according to a legal dictionary, *robbery* is "the felonious taking of property" (next larger category) that differs from other acts of theft because it seizes property "through violence or intimidation." Legal dictionaries often provide specific examples to show the boundaries of the term. Here is one example:

> There is no robbery unless force or fear is used to overcome resistance. Thus, surreptitiously picking a man's pocket or snatching something from him without resistance on his part is *larceny,* but not robbery.

Many states specify degrees of robbery with increasingly heavy penalties. For example, *armed robbery* involves the use of a weapon to threaten the victim. In all cases, *robbery* is distinguished from the lesser crime of *larceny,* in which no force or intimidation is involved.

As you can see, an Aristotelian definition of a term identifies specific attributes or criteria that enable you to distinguish it from other members of the next larger class. We created an Aristotelian definition in our example about socially responsible companies. A socially responsible company, we said, is any company (next larger class) that meets three criteria: (1) it doesn't pollute the environment; (2) it creates goods or services that promote the well-being of the community; and (3) it treats its workers justly.

In constructing Aristotelian definitions, you may find it useful to employ the concept of accidental, necessary, and sufficient criteria.

■ An *accidental criterion* is a usual but not essential feature of a concept. For example, armed robbers frequently wear masks, but wearing a mask is an accidental criterion because it has no bearing on the definition of *robbery*. In our example about socially responsible companies, "makes regular contributions to charities" might be an accidental criterion; most socially responsible companies contribute to charities, but some do not. And many socially irresponsible companies also contribute to charities—often as a public relations ploy.

- A *necessary criterion* is an attribute that *must* be present for something to belong to the category being defined. To be guilty of robbery rather than larceny, a thief must have used direct force or intimidation. The use of force is thus a necessary criterion for robbery. However, for a robbery to occur, another criterion must also be met: the robber must also take property from the victim.

- *Sufficient criteria* are all the criteria that must be present for something to belong to the category being defined. Together, the use of force plus the taking of property are *sufficient criteria* for an act to be classified as robbery.

Consider again our defining criteria for a "socially responsible" company: (1) the company must avoid polluting the environment; (2) the company must create goods or services that contribute to the well-being of the community; and (3) the company must treat its workers justly. In this definition, each criterion is necessary, but none of the criteria alone is sufficient. In other words, to be defined as socially responsible, a company must meet all three criteria at once, as the word *and* signals. It is not enough for a company to be nonpolluting (a necessary but not sufficient criterion); if that company makes a shoddy product or treats its workers unjustly, it fails to meet the other necessary criteria and can't be deemed socially responsible. Because no one criterion by itself is sufficient, all three criteria together must be met before a company can be deemed socially responsible.

In contrast, consider the following definition of *sexual harassment* as established by the U.S. Equal Employment Opportunity Commission in its 1980 guidelines:

> Unwelcome sexual advances, requests for sexual favors, and other verbal or physical conduct of a sexual nature constitute sexual harassment when (1) submission to such conduct is made either explicitly or implicitly a term or condition of an individual's employment, (2) submission to or rejection of such conduct by an individual is used as the basis for employment decisions affecting such individual, or (3) such conduct has the purpose or effect of unreasonably interfering with an individual's work performance or creating an intimidating, hostile, or offensive working environment.*

Here each of these criteria is sufficient, but none is necessary. In other words, an act constitutes sexual harassment if any one of the three criteria is satisfied, as the word *or* indicates.

■ ■ ■   **FOR CLASS DISCUSSION**   **Working with Criteria**

Working individually or in small groups, try to determine whether each of the following is a necessary criterion, a sufficient criterion, an accidental criterion, or no criterion for defining the indicated concept. Be prepared to explain your reasoning and to account for differences in points of view.

---

*Quoted in Stephanie Riger, "Gender Dilemmas in Sexual Harassment Policies and Procedures," *American Psychologist* 46 (May 1991), 497–505.

Criterion	Concept to Be Defined
Presence of gills	Fish
Profane and obscene language	R-rated movie
Line endings that form a rhyming pattern	Poem
Disciplining a child by spanking	Child abuse
Diet that excludes meat	Vegetarian
Killing another human being	Murder
Good sex life	Happy marriage

Creating Criteria Using an Operational Definition

In some rhetorical situations, particularly those arising in the physical and social sciences, writers need precise, *operational definitions* that can be measured empirically and are not subject to problems of context and conflicting values and beliefs. A social scientist studying the effects of television on aggression in children needs a precise, measurable definition of *aggression*. Typically, the scientist might measure "aggression" by counting the number of blows a child gives to an inflatable bobo doll over a fifteen-minute period when other play options are available. In our wetlands example, a federal authority created an operational definition of *wetland*: a wetland is a parcel of land that has a saturated ground surface for twenty-one consecutive days during the year.

Such operational definitions are useful because they are precisely measurable, but they are also limited because they omit criteria that may be unmeasurable but important. Thus, we might ask whether it is adequate to define an *honors student* as someone with a 3.8 GPA or higher or a *successful sex-education program* as one that results in a 25 percent reduction in teenage pregnancies. What important aspects of an honors student or a successful sex-education program are not considered in these operational definitions?

Conducting the Match Part of a Definition Argument

In conducting a match argument, you need to supply examples and other evidence showing that your contested case does (does not) meet the criteria you established in your definition. In essence, you support the match part of your argument in much the same way you would support a simple categorical claim.

For example, if you were developing the argument that the Hercules Shoe Company is not socially responsible because it treats its workers unjustly, your match section would provide evidence of this injustice. You might supply data about the percentage of shoes produced in East Asia, about the low wages paid these workers, and about the working conditions in these factories. You might also describe the suffering of displaced American workers when Hercules closed its American factories and moved operations to Asia, where the labor is nonunion and cheap. The match section should also summarize and respond to opposing views.

Idea-Generating Strategies for Creating Your Own Criteria-Match Argument

11.4 To use criteria-match reasoning to generate ideas for your own definition argument

In constructing criteria to define your contested term, you can either research how others have defined your term or make your own definitions. If you use the first strategy, you turn to standard or specialized dictionaries, judicial opinions, or expert testimony to establish a definition based on the authority of others. The second strategy is to use your own critical thinking to make your own definition, thereby defining the contested term yourself. This section explains these approaches in more detail.

Strategy 1: Research How Others Have Defined the Term

When you take this approach, you search for authoritative definitions acceptable to your audience yet favorable to your case. When the state of Washington tried to initiate a new sales tax on candy, lawyers and legislators wrestled with a definition. They finally created the following statute available to the public on a government Web site:

What Is the Definition of Candy?

"Candy" is a preparation of sugar, honey, or other natural or artificial sweeteners combined with chocolate, fruits, nuts, or other ingredients or flavorings in the form of bars, drops, or pieces. Candy does not require refrigeration, and does not include flour as an ingredient.

> "Natural or artificial sweeteners" include, but are not limited to, high fructose corn syrup, dextrose, invert sugar, sucrose, fructose, sucralose, saccharin, aspartame, stevia, fruit juice concentrates, molasses, evaporated cane juice, and rice syrup.
>
> "Flour" includes any flour made from a grain, such as wheat flour, rice flour, and corn flour.
>
> Items that require "refrigeration," either before or after opening, are not candy. For example, popsicles, ice cream bars, and fruits in sweetened syrups are not candy.

This definition made it easy for state officials to exclude from the "candy tax" any snack food that contained flour. Thus Twinkies, Fruit Loops cereal, and chocolate-covered pretzels were exempt from the tax. But considerable debate occurred over cough drops and halvah (a traditional dessert in India and Mediterranean countries). The state decided to exclude cough drops if the package contained a "drug facts" panel and a list of active ingredients. (Such cough drops were then classified as "over-the-counter drugs.") The state ruled that nut-butter halvah was taxable but that flour-based halvah was not taxable; even so, many kinds of halvah didn't fit neatly into these two categories.

Turning to established definitions is thus a first step for many definition arguments. Common sources of these definitions are specialized dictionaries such as *Black's Law Dictionary*, which form a standard part of the reference holdings of any library. Other sources of specialized definitions are state and federal appellate court decisions, legislative and administrative statutes, and scholarly articles examining a given definition conflict. Lawyers use this research strategy exhaustively in preparing court briefs. They begin by looking at the actual text of laws as passed by legislatures or written by administrative authorities. Then they look at all the court cases in which the laws have been tested and examine the ways courts have refined legal definitions and applied them to specific cases. Using these refined definitions, lawyers then apply them to their own case at hand.

If your research uncovers definitions that seem ambiguous or otherwise unfavorable to your case, you can sometimes appeal to the "original intentions" of those who defined the term. For example, if a scientist is dissatisfied with definitions of *wetlands* based on consecutive days of saturated ground surface, she might proceed as follows: "The original intention of Congress in passing the Clean Water Act was to preserve the environment." What Congress intended, she could then claim, was to prevent development of those wetland areas that provide crucial habitat for wildlife or that inhibit water pollution. She could then propose an alternative definition based on criteria other than consecutive days of ground saturation.

Strategy 2: Create Your Own Extended Definition*

Often, however, you need to create your own definition of the contested term. An effective strategy is to establish initial criteria for your contested term by thinking of hypothetical cases that obviously fit the category you are trying to define and then by altering one or more variables until the hypothetical case obviously doesn't fit the category. You can then test and refine your criteria by applying them to borderline cases. For example, suppose you work at a homeless agency where you overhear street people discuss an incident that strikes you as potential "police brutality." You wonder whether you should write to your local paper to bring attention to the incident.

A Possible Case of Police Brutality

Two police officers confront an inebriated homeless man who is shouting obscenities on a street corner. The officers tell the man to quiet down and move on, but he keeps shouting obscenities. When the officers attempt to put the man into the police car, he resists and takes a wild swing at one of the officers. As eyewitnesses later testified, this officer shouted obscenities back at the drunk man, pinned his arms behind his back in order to handcuff him, and lifted him forcefully by the arms. The man screamed in pain and was later discovered to have a dislocated shoulder. Is this officer guilty of police brutality?

To your way of thinking, this officer seems guilty: An inebriated man is too unco-ordinated to be a threat in a fight, and two police officers ought to be able to arrest

---

*The defining strategies and collaborative exercises in this section are based on the work of George Hillocks and his research associates at the University of Chicago. See George Hillocks Jr., Elizabeth A. Kahn, and Larry R. Johannessen, "Teaching Defining Strategies as a Mode of Inquiry: Some Effects on Student Writing," *Research in the Teaching of English* 17 (October 1983), 275–84. See also Larry R. Johannessen, Elizabeth A. Kahn, and Carolyn Calhoun Walter, *Designing and Sequencing Prewriting Activities* (Urbana, IL: NCTE, 1982).

him without dislocating his shoulder. But a friend argues that because the man took a swing at the officer, the police were justified in using force. The dislocated shoulder was simply an accidental result of using justified force.

To make your case, you need to develop a definition of "police brutality." You can begin by creating a hypothetical case that is obviously an instance of "police brutality":

A Clear Case of Police Brutality

A police officer confronts a drunk man shouting obscenities and begins hitting him in the face with his police baton. *[This is an obvious incidence of police brutality because the officer intentionally tries to hurt the drunk man without justification; hitting him with the baton is not necessary for making an arrest or getting the man into the police car.]*

You could then vary the hypothetical case until it is clearly *not* an instance of police brutality.

Cases That Are Clearly Not Police Brutality

Case 1: The police officer handcuffs the drunk man, who, in being helped into the police car, accidentally slips on the curb and dislocates his arm while falling. *[Here the injury occurs accidentally; the police officer does not act intentionally and is not negligent.]*

Case 2: The police officer confronts an armed robber fleeing from a scene and tackles him from behind, wrestling the gun away from him. In this struggle, the officer pins the robber's arm behind his back with such force that the robber's shoulder is dislocated. *[Here aggressive use of force is justified because the robber was armed, dangerous, and resisting arrest.]*

Using these hypothetical cases, you decide that the defining criteria for police brutality are (1) *intention* and (2) use of *excessive force*—that is, force beyond what was required by the immediate situation. After more contemplation, you are convinced that the officer was guilty of police brutality and have a clearer idea of how to make your argument. Here is how you might write the "match" part of your argument:

Match Argument Using Your Definition

If we define police brutality as the *intentional* use of *excessive* force, then the police officer is guilty. His action was intentional because he was purposefully responding to the homeless man's drunken swing and was angry enough to be shouting obscenities back at the drunk (according to eyewitnesses). Second, he used excessive force in applying the handcuffs. A drunk man taking a wild swing hardly poses a serious danger to two police officers. Putting handcuffs on the drunk may have been justified, but lifting the man's arm violently enough to dislocate a shoulder indicates excessive force. The officer lifted the man's arms violently not because he needed to but because he was angry, and acting out of anger is no justification for that violence. In fact, we can charge police officers with "police brutality" precisely to protect us from being victims of police anger. It is the job of the court system to punish us, not the police's job. Because this officer acted intentionally and applied excessive force out of anger, he should be charged with police brutality.

The strategy we have demonstrated—developing criteria by imagining hypothetical cases that clearly do and do not belong to the contested category—gives you a systematic procedure for developing your own definition for your argument.

■ ■ ■   **FOR WRITING AND DISCUSSION**   **Developing a Definition**   **MyWritingLab**™

Individual task:

1. Suppose you want to define the concept of courage. In each of the following cases, decide whether the person in question is acting courageously or not. In each instance explain your reasoning.

   a. A neighbor rushes into a burning house to rescue a child from certain death and emerges, coughing and choking, with the child in his arms. Is the neighbor courageous?

   b. A firefighter rushes into a burning house to rescue a child from certain death and emerges with the child in her arms. The firefighter is wearing protective clothing and a gas mask. When a newspaper reporter calls her courageous, she says, "Hey, this is my job." Is the firefighter courageous?

   c. A teenager rushes into a burning house to recover a memento given to him by his girlfriend, the first love of his life. Is the teenager courageous?

   d. A parent rushes into a burning house to save a trapped child. The fire marshal tells the parent to wait because there is no chance that the child can be reached from the first floor. The fire marshal wants to try cutting a hole in the roof to reach the child. The parent rushes into the house anyway and is burned to death. Was the parent courageous?

2. Now formulate your own definition of a "courageous act." "An act would be considered courageous if it meets the following criteria: [you specify]."

3. Finally, apply your definition to the following case: An extreme sport enthusiast sets a record for a hang gliding descent from a certain state's highest cliff. Is this record-setting descent a courageous act? Write a paragraph in which you argue that the descent is or is not courageous.

Group task: Share the results from the individual task on courage. Then make up your own series of controversial cases, like those given previously for "courage," for one or more of the following concepts:

a. cruelty to animals

b. child abuse

c. true athlete

d. sexual harassment

e. free speech protected by the First Amendment

Finally, using the strategy of making up hypothetical cases that do and do not belong to each category, construct a definition of your chosen concept.

■ ■ ■

WRITING ASSIGNMENT A Definition Argument   MyWritingLab™

The assignment for this chapter focuses on definition disputes about categories. Write an essay in which you argue that a borderline or contested case fits (or does not fit) within a given category. In the opening of your essay, introduce the borderline case you will examine and pose your definition question. In the first part of your argument, define the boundaries of your category (criteria) by reporting a definition used by others or by developing your own extended definition. In the second part of your argument (the match), show how your borderline case meets (or doesn't meet) your definition criteria.

Exploring Ideas

Ideally, in writing this argument you will join an ongoing conversation about a definition issue that interests you. What cultural and social issues that concern you involve disputed definitions? In the public arena, you are likely to find numerous examples simply by looking through news stories—for example, the disputes about the definition of "torture" in interrogating terrorist suspects or about "freedom of religion" in debates about religious organizations having to pay for contraception in employees' health insurance. Often you can frame your own definition issues even if they aren't currently in the news. Is using TiVo to avoid TV commercials a form of theft? Is flag burning protected free speech? Is solitary confinement "cruel and unusual punishment"? Is Wal-Mart a socially responsible company? Are voter ID laws racist?

If you have trouble discovering a local or national issue that interests you, you can create fascinating definition controversies among your classmates by asking whether certain borderline cases are "true" or "real" examples of some category: Are highly skilled video game players (race car drivers, synchronized swimmers, marbles players) true athletes? Is a gourmet chef (skilled furniture maker, tagger) a true artist? Is a chiropractor (acupuncturist, naturopathic physician) a "real doctor"? Working as a whole class or in small groups inside or outside class, create an argumentative discussion on one or more of these issues. Listen to the various voices in the controversy, and then write out your own argument.

You can also stimulate definition controversies by brainstorming borderline cases for such terms as *courage* (Is mountain climbing an act of courage?), *cruelty to animals* (Are rodeos [zoos, catch-and-release trout fishing, use of animals for medical research] guilty of cruelty to animals?), or *war crime* (Was the American firebombing of Tokyo in World War II a war crime?).

As you explore your definition issue, try to determine how others have defined your category. If no stable definition emerges from your search, create your own definition by deciding what criteria must be met for a contested case to fit within your category. Try using the strategy for creating criteria that we discussed on pages 235–237 with reference to police brutality. Once you have determined your criteria, freewrite for five or ten minutes, exploring whether your contested case meets each of the criteria.

Identifying Your Audience and Determining What's at Stake

Before drafting your argument, identify your targeted audience and determine what's at stake. Consider your responses to the following questions:

- What audience are you targeting? What background do they need to understand your issue? How much do they already care about it?
- Before they read your argument, what stance on your issue do you imagine them holding? What change do you want to bring about in their views?

Organization Plan 1: Definition Argument with Criteria and Match in Separate Sections

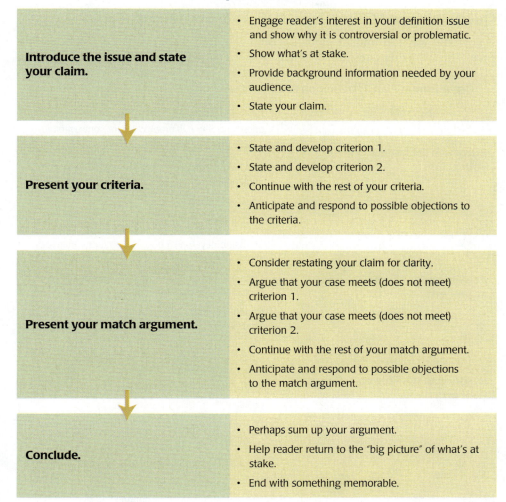

Introduce the issue and state your claim.

- Engage reader's interest in your definition issue and show why it is controversial or problematic.
- Show what's at stake.
- Provide background information needed by your audience.
- State your claim.

Present your criteria.

- State and develop criterion 1.
- State and develop criterion 2.
- Continue with the rest of your criteria.
- Anticipate and respond to possible objections to the criteria.

Present your match argument.

- Consider restating your claim for clarity.
- Argue that your case meets (does not meet) criterion 1.
- Argue that your case meets (does not meet) criterion 2.
- Continue with the rest of your match argument.
- Anticipate and respond to possible objections to the match argument.

Conclude.

- Perhaps sum up your argument.
- Help reader return to the "big picture" of what's at stake.
- End with something memorable.

- What will they find new or surprising about your argument?
- What objections might they raise? What counterarguments or alternative points of view will you need to address?
- Why does your argument matter? Who might be threatened or made uncomfortable by your views? What is at stake?

Organizing a Definition Argument

As you compose a first draft of your essay, you may find it helpful to know typical structures for definition arguments. There are two basic approaches, as shown in Organization Plans 1 and 2. You can either discuss the criteria and the match separately or interweave the discussion.

Questioning and Critiquing a Definition Argument

A powerful way to stimulate global revision of a draft is to role-play a skeptical audience. The following questions will help you strengthen your own argument or rebut

Organization Plan 2: Definition Argument with Criteria and Match Interwoven

Introduce the issue and state your claim.	• Engage reader's interest in your definition issue and show why it is problematic or controversial. • Show what's at stake. • Provide background information needed by your audience. • State your claim.
Present series of criterion-match arguments.	• State and develop criterion 1 and argue that your case meets (does not meet) the criterion. • State and develop criterion 2 and argue that your case meets (does not meet) the criterion. • Continue with the rest of your criterion-match arguments.
Respond to possible objections to your argument.	• Anticipate and summarize possible objections. • Respond to the objections through rebuttal or concession.
Conclude.	• Perhaps sum up your argument. • Help reader return to the "big picture" of what's at stake. • End with something memorable.

the definition arguments of others. In critiquing a definition argument, you need to appreciate its criteria-match structure because you can question your criteria argument, your match argument, or both.

Questioning Your Criteria

- Could a skeptic claim that your criteria are not the right ones? Could he or she offer different criteria or point out missing criteria?
- Could a skeptic point out possible bad consequences of accepting your criteria?
- Could a skeptic cite unusual circumstances that weaken your criteria?
- Could a skeptic point out bias or slant in your definition?

Questioning Your Match

- Could a skeptic argue that your examples or data don't meet the STAR criteria (see Chapter 5, pages 92–93) for evidence?
- Could a skeptic point out counterexamples or alternative data that cast doubt on your argument?
- Could a skeptic reframe the way you have viewed your borderline case? ■

READINGS

Our first reading, by student writer Arthur Knopf, grew out of his research into agricultural subsidies and the nutritional content of foods. It was written for the assignment on page 238.

Is Milk a Health Food?

ARTHUR KNOPF (STUDENT)

If asked to name a typical health food, most of us would put milk high on our lists. We've all seen the "Got Milk?" ads with their milk-mustached celebrities or the dairy product campaigns entitled "Milk, It Does a Body Good" or "Body By Milk." These ads, featuring well known athletes or trim celebrities, argue visually that milk helps you grow fit and strong. But if you define "health food" based on science rather than on marketing claims, and if you include in your definition of health food concerns for the planet as well as for individual bodies, then milk might not fit the category of health food at all.

My first criterion for a "health food" is that the food should have a scientifically supported health benefit with minimal risks. Based on the food pyramid from the United States Department of Agriculture (USDA), milk at first glance seems to fit this criterion. On the *MyPyramid* Web site the dairy group (milk, yogurt, cheese) is one of the essential components of a healthy diet (United States). All elements of the milk group provide calcium, which is important for healthy bones and the prevention of osteoporosis. Dairy products also provide important vitamins. But the Web site entry under the dairy group specifies in a footnote, "Choose fat-free or low-fat milk, yogurt, and cheese." One cup of whole milk, according to the Web site, contains 70 more calories than a cup of skim milk (147 calories compared to 83). The extra 70 calories are potentially harmful saturated fats and sugar, linked to heart disease and obesity. We can say then that "nonfat milk" fits my first criterion for a health food, but that the rest of the milk group may not.

So how do dairy products in general get listed as essential ingredients on the food pyramid rather than just low-fat milk or yogurt? The answer to this question brings us to my second criterion for a health food: Potentially unhealthy aspects of the food should be widely disclosed, not hidden by marketing. Because we are bombarded daily by conflicting nutrition claims, many people turn to the U.S. government for neutral, unbiased information. But the place of dairy products on the USDA food pyramid may be itself a result of marketing. The USDA's mandate isn't directly to promote health, but to promote agriculture and to help farmers flourish economically. In recommending three servings of dairy products per day, the food pyramid serves the interests of dairy farmers by promoting the whole class of dairy products, not just skim milk. According to the Environmental Working Group's Farm Subsidies Database, the USDA spent

$4.8 billion in dairy subsidies between 1995 and 2009 ("Dairy Program Subsidies"). All these policies invest public dollars to create a steady consumption of dairy products and fundamentally depend on the premise that dairy products are good for us.

As we have seen, skim milk may be good for us but dairy products in general are more problematic. When the fat in whole milk is removed to make skim milk, it is not thrown away. It is used to make high-calorie, high-fat products like cheese and ice cream. Revealing its true ambivalence to public nutrition, the USDA warns against saturated fats in its food pyramid site while simultaneously working with companies like Domino's Pizza to increase the amount of cheese in their products. According to the *New York Times* (Moss), the USDA helped Domino's create a pizza with 40 percent more cheese and paid for a $12 million ad campaign to promote it. The *New York Times* further writes that Americans now consume almost three times as much cheese as we did in 1970. At a time of a national obesity epidemic, the promotion of dairy products either directly or indirectly introduces high-calorie, high-saturated fat foods into our diet while making many persons think they are eating healthfully.

5   Finally, I would like to suggest a third criterion for health food. A true health food should be good not only for our bodies but also for the earth. Milk, as it is currently produced in the United States, clearly does not meet this criterion. According to environmental writer Jim Motavalli, both "the front and rear ends of a cow" compete with coal plant smokestacks and vehicle tail pipes as "iconic" causes of global warming and environmental degradation (27). Drawing on statistical sources from both the United Nations and the USDA, Motavalli states that livestock in the United States consume 90 percent of the soy crop and more than 70 percent of the corn and grain crops—foods that could otherwise be used for people and could be grown in a more environmentally friendly way. Not only do cattle consume much of the world's grain supply, the need to clear space for grazing contributes to the destruction of rain forests. The other end of the cow, says Motavalli, is equally destructive. While chewing their cuds, cows directly emit methane gas (according to Motavalli, methane has a greenhouse effect 23 times more potent than carbon dioxide) and the concentration of their manure in factory farm sludge ponds produces ammonia, nitrous oxide, and additional methane. According to Motavalli, cows produce a staggering amount of manure ("five tons of waste for every U.S. citizen" [27]), producing 18 percent of the world's greenhouse gases—more than all of the world's cars, trains, and planes (27). Motavalli also cites additional health risks posed by cows, including dangers of disease from unsafe processing of manure and from antibiotic-resistant bacteria (half of the world's antibiotics are given to cattle instead of humans [28]).

In sum, there is no doubt that skim milk, along with low-fat yogurt and cheese, is a vital source of bone-building calcium and belongs on our list of health foods. But for most people, "milk" evokes dairy products in general, all of which we tend to associate with health. What we don't picture is the extra sugar and saturated fat in whole milk and cheese nor the environmental dangers of the dairy and livestock industries in general. From the perspective of the earth, perhaps dairy products should not be considered a health food at all.

Works Cited

"Dairy Program Subsidies." Farm Subsidies Database. Environmental Working Group, Jan. 2009. Web. 21 Jan. 2011.

Moss, Michael. "While Warning about Fat, U.S. Pushes Cheese Sales." *New York Times*. New York Times, 6 Nov. 2010. Web. 2 Jan. 2011.

Motavalli, Jim. "The Meat of the Matter: Our Livestock Industry Creates More Greenhouse Gas than Transportation Does." *Environmental Magazine* July-Aug. 2008: 26-33. Academic Search Complete. Web. 11 Jan. 2011.

United States. Dept. of Agriculture. *MyPyramid.gov: Steps to a Healthier You.* Jan. 2011. Web. 20 Jan. 2011.

Critiquing "Is Milk a Health Food?"

MyWritingLab™

1. Identify the following features of Arthur's essay: (1) his implied definition of "health food"; (2) his criteria for determining whether a borderline case is a health food; (3) his "match" arguments showing whether milk fits each of the criteria.
2. Do you agree with Arthur's criterion that a true health food ought to be good for the planet as well as good for the body?
3. Based on Arthur's argument, do you think the inclusion of dairy products in the USDA's recommendations for a healthy diet is still justified? Visit the USDA's new nutrition Web site, www.choosemyplate.gov. Would you suggest changes to these USDA recommendations? If so, what and why?

The second reading, by student Alex Mullen, was also written for the definition assignment on page 238. Alex's argument was stimulated by class discussions of property ownership in digital environments.

A Pirate But Not a Thief: What Does "Stealing" Mean in a Digital Environment?

ALEX MULLEN (STUDENT)

I am a pirate. In the eyes of the law, I could face serious punishment in fines, up to thousands of dollars, or jail time for my crime. Legally, it matters very little that my crime is one perpetrated by millions of people every year (you yourself may be guilty of it) or that there are far worse offenders out there. But before we get out the noose and head for the yardarm, I think I ought to describe my crime. In my History of Film class we were asked to watch Jean Renoir's *La Grande Illusion*. Now, if you've spent any time searching for 1930s foreign films you will undoubtedly know what a pain it is to find them, and of the twenty or so films we watched for my class a grand total of three were available on streaming sites such as Netflix, Hulu, and YouTube. While there were several copies of this particular film at my

University Library, all had been checked out. I planned to make a journey to the fabled Scarecrow Video (one of the largest rental libraries in the United States), but time was running low at this point. Finally, I broke down and used a person-to-person torrent site to download the film illegally. In the end all the trouble was worthwhile, as *La Grande Illusion* remains one of the greatest films I have ever seen. After watching it several times and writing a brief paper, I deleted the film from my computer. Although I feel that my action was justifiable, many people think what I did was no better than shoplifting and that I am guilty of theft. As a film lover and aspiring filmmaker, I am conflicted on the issue of online piracy. Nevertheless, I contend that what I did wasn't stealing because I deprived no one of either property or profit.

Let's take a step back from online piracy and focus simply on what stealing is in its most basic form. In my mind, stealing is the unlawful taking of another's property or profits without permission. It is the underlying assumption about what makes stealing wrong that needs to be considered. In the case of property, stealing is wrong not because the thief has the property but because the original owner has been deprived of it. The owner's loss causes the wrong, not the thief's gain. To give an example in very simple terms, if you have a phone case and I make a copy of that case (as is quite possible with a 3D printer), you still possess the original case, so no harm has been done to you the owner. However, suppose that you made your living by selling these phone cases. If I made exact duplicates with my 3-D printer and then sold these cases to others, then you could be deprived of profits that might otherwise have been received. Again, the wrong comes from the creator's loss and not the thief's gain.

Now let's focus on my particular example of online piracy. While I concede that piracy has the distinct potential to be stealing, I reject the accusation that all piracy is stealing. Based on the first part of my definition of stealing, my downloading *La Grande Illusion* deprived no consumer or creator of his or her copy of the film. This is why accusations that compare online piracy to shoplifting are false. In the case of shoplifting the owner/creator has one fewer piece of merchandise to make a profit on; with online piracy such loss does not occur because the original copy still exists.

However, the second part of my definition, which focuses on profits, still remains to be examined. Perhaps by downloading the film I have deprived the creators/owners of profits they would normally receive. Let me begin by saying that I never intended to purchase *La Grande Illusion*. While intention does not often register in legal matters, it does have a bearing on the type and degree of wrongdoing. Film industry lawyers often argue that every time a film is pirated the rightful owner is deprived of money because the pirate would have otherwise purchased the film. This claim, however, is fallacious because there is no way to show that these potential consumers would have purchased the film (I certainly wouldn't have). So while we may agree that some of these people would have purchased the film, it would be inaccurate to claim that in all cases piracy directly deprives creators of profit. I argue that what I did in the case of *La Grande Illusion* was more like borrowing than theft. Borrowing a film from a library (or renting it from a video store) has the same basic effect on the owner/creator as online piracy.

That is, a library or video store purchases a copy and then loans it or rents to others. Thus, many persons may not purchase a copy from the owner/creator because they can use this single public or commercial copy. Yet we do not consider borrowing or renting stealing even though it can have the same economic ramification as piracy. To go a step further, any time I borrow a film from a friend I cause the same outcome so reprehensible in online piracy. In my case, instead of borrowing *La Grande Illusion* from an institution or business, I borrowed it from another individual via the Internet.

5   There is, of course, the counterargument that I could have rented the film from Scarecrow and thus stole profit from this film rental store much loved by film buffs. While it is true that I did not benefit Scarecrow with my patronage (a fact that I partially regret because I do try to support Scarecrow as often as possible), it would be inaccurate to say that I stole from Scarecrow. I am under no obligation to supply them with profits. When I pay money to a rental organization I am not paying for the film; I am paying for the service of being able to use their copy of the film for 24 hours. Had I purchased the film directly from the filmmaker, I would do the same harm to Scarecrow. Thus my not utilizing Scarecrow to obtain *La Grande Illusion* is not theft.

While I understand why the film industry (and also the music industry) views downloading from file-sharing torrent sites as piracy, their motives focus on preserving profits and blur the distinctions among "buying," "renting," and "borrowing." If I owned a DVD version of a movie and loaned it to a friend, no one would object. But if I make the same movie available to a friend via a torrent or file-sharing site, I become a pirate subject to huge fines. The intention is the same, only the format changes. The problem stems from the hazy concept of "ownership" in a digital environment where physical copies are replaced by digital copies. Certainly, we pay to possess digital copies of films, music, and video games, but is this really the same as physical ownership? After all I can lend, rent, or even sell a physical DVD, but such actions are impossible with digital copies without committing piracy. Our consumption of media is evolving rapidly, and while undoubtedly there will always be those who exploit these changes for personal gain, I feel we need to realize that our understanding of ownership, stealing, and illegal use must evolve along with these changes.

Critiquing "A Pirate But Not a Thief: What Does 'Stealing' Mean in a Digital Environment?"

MyWritingLab™

1. Identify the following features of Alex's essay: (1) his definition of "stealing"; (2) his examples to illustrate the definition; (3) his "match" argument showing whether his downloading of the film fits each of the criteria; and (4) his summary of and responses to objections and opposing views.
2. Do you agree with Alex's contention that his downloading the film was an act of "borrowing" rather than "stealing"?
3. What do you see as the major strengths of Alex's argument? How about weaknesses?
4. Do you think that the laws about online piracy should be changed? At what point does online piracy clearly become "stealing"?

Our last reading is an editorial from the *Los Angeles Times* on the day following a controversial decision by the Chicago director of the National Labor Relations Board that gave scholarship-receiving football players at Northwestern University the right to unionize. The decision turns on whether to place football players in the category of "student athlete" or in the category of "paid employee." The editorial illustrates how often definition issues play a role in public controversies.

College Football—Yes, It's a Job

LOS ANGELES TIMES EDITORIAL BOARD

University officials and the NCAA have been reluctant to acknowledge that top-tier college football programs are run these days less as athletic programs than as businesses. But a labor administrator's decision Wednesday that Northwestern University's scholarship football players are, in fact, employees with the right to unionize should get their attention.

This issue has been bubbling for decades as major sports programs evolved from important but ancillary parts of a college's mission into powerful businesses enriched by multimillion-dollar TV contracts and merchandising revenue, all built on the labor of student-athletes who received no compensation beyond scholarships. That might be a workable relationship when the players are truly students whose main focus is on academics. But as the ruling by Peter Sung Ohr, the National Labor Relations Board's Chicago director, makes clear, scholarship players at Northwestern University are on campus first and foremost to play revenue-generating football. And that, he says, makes them employees.

The logic is clear. The players are accepted first as members of the football team, then as students, Ohr found. Players devote well over 40 hours a week to the team, overwhelming the amount of time they devote to academics. And players sign scholarship "tenders" that define conditions under which they will receive free tuition, room and board, and other support. If players fail to meet the conditions, they lose their scholarships. That, Ohr says, makes them workers. Significantly, Ohr found that non-scholarship players are not workers because they receive no compensation.

It's unclear whether the ruling will apply to other private colleges, such as USC, because Ohr's decision turns on specific circumstances at Northwestern. (The NLRB does not have jurisdiction over public universities such as UCLA.) It's also unclear whether the ruling will survive the anticipated appeals, because, among other issues, the players are not receiving direct wages but grants-in-kind.

What is clear is that the collegiate athletic system generates billions of dollars through the work of people who, if they get paid at all, receive nothing more than free college. No small thing, that, but hardly equitable given the economic scope of top-tier college athletics. This ruling could—and should—force universities and the NCAA to end what has become an exploitative system and make athletic programs subsidiary to the core mission: education.

Critiquing "College Football—Yes It's a Job"   MyWritingLab™

1. What is the implied definition of "employee" in this editorial?
2. How does the editorial make its "match" argument—that is, what evidence is used to support the case that scholarship football players are employees?
3. What is at stake in this argument?

Causal Arguments

12

What you will learn in this chapter:

12.1 To explain and illustrate kinds of causal arguments.
12.2 To explain how different causal mechanisms function in cause/consequence arguments.
12.3 To understand key causal terms and the need to avoid inductive fallacies in causal arguments.
12.4 To write your own cause or consequence argument.

We encounter causal issues all the time. What has caused the declining birth rate among teens in the United States? Why has the dance exercise called Zumba become popular globally? Why are American teens shopping less at traditional teenage clothing stores such as Abercrombie & Fitch and American Eagle Outfitters? Why are white teenage girls seven times as likely to smoke as African American teenage girls? Why do couples who live together before marriage have a higher divorce rate than those who don't? In addition to asking causal questions like these, we pose consequence questions as well: What might be the consequences of installing stricter proof-of-citizenship requirements for voting? What might be the social and economic consequences of establishing public preschool programs? What might be the consequences—expected or unexpected—of expanding commercial use of drones? Often arguments about causes and consequences have important stakes because they shape our view of reality and influence government policies and individual decisions. This chapter explains how to wrestle responsibly with cause/consequence issues to produce effective causal arguments.

Case 1   What Causes Global Warming?

One of the early clues linking global warming to atmospheric carbon dioxide (CO_2) came from side-by-side comparisons of graphs plotting atmospheric carbon dioxide and global temperatures over time. These graphs show that increases in global temperature parallel increases in the percentage of carbon dioxide in the atmosphere. However, the graphs show only a correlation, or link, between increased carbon dioxide and higher average temperature. To argue that an increase in CO_2 could cause global warming, scientists needed to explain the links in a causal chain. They could do so by comparing the earth to a greenhouse. Carbon dioxide, like glass in a greenhouse, lets some of the earth's heat radiate into space but also reflects some of it back to the earth. The higher the concentration of carbon dioxide, the more heat is reflected back to the earth.

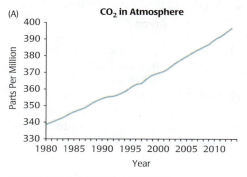

(A)

CO₂ in Atmosphere

Source: Data from Dr. Pieter Tans, NOAA/ESRL

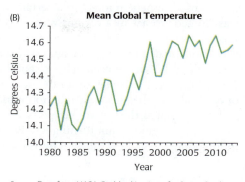

(B)

Mean Global Temperature

Source: Data from NASA Goddard Institute for Space Studies Surface Temperature Analysis

---

Case 2   What Has Caused the Change in the Rate of Teen Pregnancies in the United State in the Last Five Years?

Although the United States still has the highest rate of teen pregnancies among developed countries, studies show a decline in teen pregnancies since the early 1990s. What has caused this decline? Some economists point to the recession as a major cause, claiming that as the job market has tightened, teens are afraid of not being able to get jobs when encumbered with babies. Other sources emphasize the role of parents in cautioning teens about irresponsible choices concerning sexual behavior and reproduction. A quite different explanation comes from a recent study by the National Bureau of Economic Research analyzing the impact of media images on viewers. This study has found a correlation between the decline in teen pregnancies and the watching of the MTV docudrama *16 and Pregnant* (premiered in 2009) and its spinoff *Teen Moms*. While Parents Television Council and other critics argue that these shows sensationalize and glamorize the lives of the teen moms, researchers, using Nielsen ratings and geographic data on viewership and data from Google Trends and Twitter, found that watching these shows "led to more searches and tweets regarding birth control and abortion, and ultimately led to a 5.7 percent reduction in teen births in the eighteen months" after *16 and Pregnant* first aired.* This study broadens social thinking on the use of reality TV and social media in promoting safe sex, as well as its potential value in addressing other social and health causes.

An Overview of Causal Arguments

12.1 To explain and illustrate kinds of causal arguments.

Typically, causal arguments try to show how one event brings about another. When causal investigation focuses on material objects—for example, one billiard ball striking another—the notion of causality

---

*Melissa S. Kearney and Phillip B. Levine. "Media Influences on Social Outcomes: The Impact of MTV's *16 and Pregnant* on Teen Childbearing," NBER Working Paper No. 19795, National Bureau of Economic Research, January 2014.

appears fairly straightforward. But when humans become the focus of a causal argument, the nature of causality becomes more vexing. If we say that something happened that "caused" a person to act in a certain way, what do we mean? Do we mean that she was "forced" to act in a certain way, thereby negating her free will (as in, an undiagnosed brain tumor caused her to act erratically), or do we mean more simply that she was "motivated" to act in a certain way (as in, her anger at her parents caused her to act erratically)? When we argue about causality in human beings, we must guard against confusing these two senses of "cause" or assuming that human behavior can be predicted or controlled in the same way that nonhuman behavior can. A rock dropped from a roof will always fall at thirty-two feet per second squared, and a rat zapped for turning left in a maze will always quit turning left. But if we raise interest rates, will consumers save more money? If so, how much? This is the sort of question we debate endlessly.

Kinds of Causal Arguments

Arguments about causality can take a variety of forms. Here are three typical kinds:

- **Speculations about possible causes.** Sometimes arguers speculate about possible causes of a phenomenon. For example, whenever a shooter opens fire on innocent bystanders (as in the 2012 Sandy Hook Elementary School massacre or the 2011 attempted assassination of Arizona Representative Gabrielle Giffords in a Tucson parking lot), social scientists, police investigators, and media commentators begin analyzing the causes. One of the most heavily debated shooting incidents occurred in 1999 at Columbine High School in Littleton, Colorado, when two male students opened fire on their classmates, killing thirteen people, wounding twenty-three others, and then shooting themselves. Figure 12.1 illustrates some of the proposed

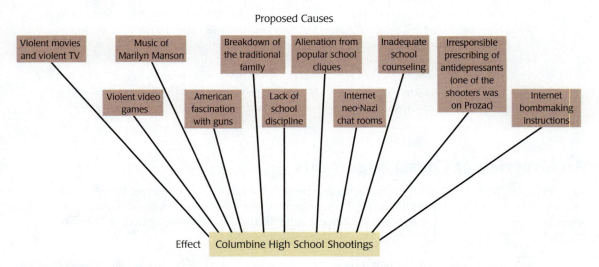

FIGURE 12.1 Speculation about possible causes: Columbine High School massacre

theories for the Columbine shootings. What was at stake was not only our desire to understand the sociocultural sources of school violence but also our desire to institute policies to prevent future school shootings. If a primary cause is the availability of guns, then we might push for more stringent gun control laws. But if the primary cause is the disintegration of the traditional family, the shooters' alienation from high school cliques, or the dangerous side effects of Prozac, then we might seek different solutions.

- **Arguments for an unexpected or surprising cause.** Besides sorting out possible causes of a phenomenon, sometimes arguers try to persuade readers to see the plausibility of an unexpected or surprising cause. This was the strategy used by syndicated columnist John Leo, who wanted readers to consider the role of violent video games as a contributing cause to the Columbine massacre.* After suggesting that the Littleton killings were partly choreographed on video game models, Leo suggested the causal chain shown in Figure 12.2.

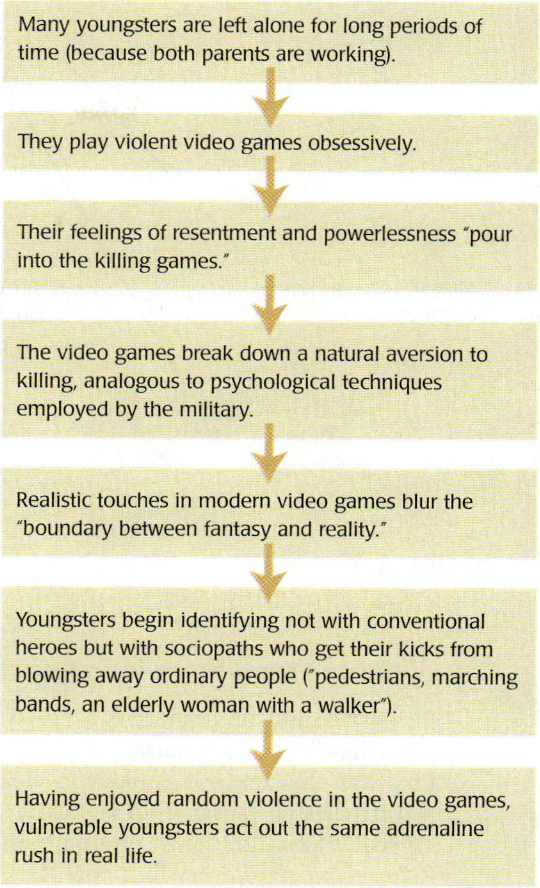

- **Predictions of consequences.** Still another frequently encountered kind of causal argument predicts the consequences of current, planned, or proposed actions or events. Consequence arguments have high stakes because we often judge actions on whether their benefits outweigh their costs. As we will see in Chapter 14, proposal arguments usually require writers to predict the consequences of a proposed action, do a cost/benefit analysis, and persuade readers that no unforeseen negative consequences will result. Just as a phenomenon can have multiple causes, it can also have multiple consequences. Figure 12.3 shows the consequence arguments considered by environmentalists who propose eliminating several dams on the Snake River in order to save salmon runs.

Many youngsters are left alone for long periods of time (because both parents are working).

↓

They play violent video games obsessively.

↓

Their feelings of resentment and powerlessness "pour into the killing games."

↓

The video games break down a natural aversion to killing, analogous to psychological techniques employed by the military.

↓

Realistic touches in modern video games blur the "boundary between fantasy and reality."

↓

Youngsters begin identifying not with conventional heroes but with sociopaths who get their kicks from blowing away ordinary people ("pedestrians, marching bands, an elderly woman with a walker").

↓

Having enjoyed random violence in the video games, vulnerable youngsters act out the same adrenaline rush in real life.

FIGURE 12.2 Argument for a surprising cause: Role of violent video games in the Columbine massacre

---

*John Leo, "Kill-for-Kicks Video Games Desensitizing Our Children," *Seattle Times* 27 April 1999, B4.

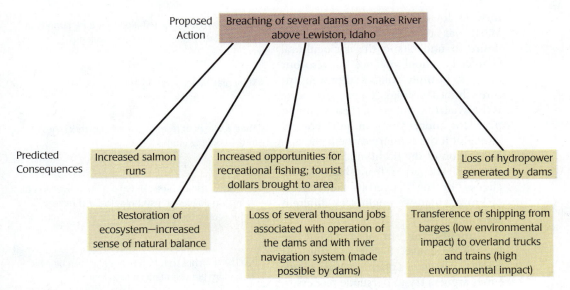

FIGURE 12.3 Predictions of consequences: Breaching dams on the Snake River

Toulmin Framework for a Causal Argument

Because causal arguments can involve lengthy or complex causal chains, they are often harder to summarize in *because* clauses than are other kinds of arguments. Likewise, they are not as likely to yield quick analysis through the Toulmin schema. Nevertheless, a causal argument can usually be stated as a claim with *because* clauses. Typically, a *because* clause pinpoints one or two key elements in the causal chain rather than summarizes every link. John Leo's argument linking the Columbine massacre to violent video games could be summarized in the following claim with a *because* clause:

> Violent video games may have been a contributing cause to the Littleton massacre because playing these games can make random, sociopathic violence seem pleasurable.

Once stated as an enthymeme, the argument can be analyzed using Toulmin's schema. It is easiest to apply Toulmin's schema to causal arguments if you think of the grounds as the observable phenomena at any point in the causal chain and the warrants as the shareable assumptions about causality that join links together.

Toulmin Analysis of the Violent Video Games Argument

ENTHYMEME

CLAIM Violent video games may have been a contributing cause to the Columbine school shooting

REASON because playing these games can make random, sociopathic violence seem pleasurable.

Qualifiers

GROUNDS

- Evidence that the killers, like many young people, played violent video games
- Evidence that the games are violent
- Evidence that the games involve random, sociopathic violence (not good guys versus bad guys) such as killing ordinary people—marching bands, little old ladies, etc.
- Evidence that young people derive pleasure from these games

CONDITIONS OF REBUTTAL
Attacking the reason and grounds

- Perhaps the killers didn't play violent video games.
- Perhaps the video games are no more violent than traditional kids' games such as cops and robbers.
- Perhaps the video games do not feature sociopathic killing.

WARRANT

If young people derive pleasure from random, sociopathic killing in video games, they can transfer this pleasure to real life, thus leading to the Columbine shooting.

BACKING

- Testimony from psychologists
- Evidence that violent video games desensitize people to violence
- Analogy to military training in which video games are used to "make killing a reflex action"
- Evidence that the distinction between fantasy and reality becomes especially blurred for unstable young people

CONDITIONS OF REBUTTAL
Attacking the warrant and backing

- Perhaps kids are fully capable of distinguishing fantasy from reality.
- Perhaps the games are just fun with no transference to real life.
- Perhaps the games are substantially different from military training games.

■ ■ ■ **FOR WRITING AND DISCUSSION** **Developing Causal Chains**   MyWritingLab™

Individual task:

1. Create a causal chain to show how the item on the left could help lead to the item on the right.

a. Invention of the automobile	Changes in sexual mores
b. Popularity of cell phones	Reduction in size and importance of phone directories
c. Growth of social media around the world	The increase in social activism and political uprisings such as Arab Spring
d. Millennials' desire for an urban lifestyle	Redesign of cities
e. Development of way to prevent rejections in transplant operations	Liberalization of euthanasia laws

2. For each of your causal chains, compose a claim with an attached *because* clause summarizing one or two key links in the causal chain—for example, "Millennials' desire for an urban lifestyle is spurring the redesign of cities because Millennials' car- and house-free habits are prompting developers to build new high-density urban communities that offer easy access to work and pleasure."

Group task: Share your causal claim and *because* clause links with your other class members.   ■ ■ ■

Two Methods for Arguing that One Event Causes Another

12.2 To explain how different causal mechanisms function in cause/consequence arguments.

One of the first things you need to do when preparing a causal argument is to note exactly what sort of causal relationship you are dealing with—a onetime phenomenon, a recurring phenomenon, or a puzzling trend. Here are some examples.

Kind of Phenomenon	Examples
Onetime phenomenon	■ Mysterious disappearance of Malaysia Airlines Flight 370 in March 2014 ■ Firing of a popular teacher at your university ■ 2007 collapse of a freeway bridge in Minneapolis
Recurring phenomenon	■ Eating disorders ■ Road rage ■ Tendency of Chevy Cobalt engines to shut off unexpectedly
Puzzling trend	■ Increase in the number of events counted as Olympic sports ■ Declining audience for TV news ■ Declining populations of both bats and honeybees

With recurring phenomena or with trends, one has the luxury of being able to study multiple cases, often over time. You can interview people, make repeated observations, or study the conditions in which the puzzling phenomenon occurs. But with a onetime occurrence, one's approach is more like that of a detective than a scientist. Because one can't repeat the event with different variables, one must rely only on the immediate evidence at hand, which can quickly disappear. Having briefly stated these words of caution, let's turn now to two main ways that you can argue that one event causes another.

First Method: Explain the Causal Mechanism Directly

The most convincing kind of causal argument identifies every link in the causal chain, showing how an initiating cause leads step by step to an observed effect. A causes B, which causes C, which causes D. In some cases, all you have to do is fill in the missing links. In other cases—when your assumptions about how one step leads to the next may seem questionable to your audience—you have to argue for the causal connection with more vigor.

A careful spelling out of each step in the causal chain is the technique used by science writer Robert S. Devine in the following passage from his article "The Trouble with Dams." Although the benefits of dams are widely understood (they produce pollution-free electricity while providing flood control, irrigation, barge transportation, and recreational boating), the negative effects are less commonly known and understood. In this article, Devine tries to persuade readers that dams have serious negative consequences. In the following passage, he explains how dams reduce salmon flows by slowing the migration of smolts (newly hatched, young salmon) to the sea.

Causal Argument Describing a Causal Chain

Such transformations lie at the heart of the ongoing environmental harm done by dams. Rivers are rivers because they flow, and the nature of their flows defines much of their character. When dams alter flows, they alter the essence of rivers.

Consider the erstwhile river behind Lower Granite (a dam on Idaho's Snake River). Although I was there in the springtime, when I looked at the water it was moving too slowly to merit the word "flow"—and Lower Granite Lake isn't even one of the region's enormous storage reservoirs, which bring currents to a virtual halt. In the past, spring snowmelt sent powerful currents down the Snake during April and May. Nowadays hydropower operators of the Columbia and Snake systems store the runoff behind the dams and release it during the winter, when demand—and the price—for electricity rises. Over the ages, however, many populations of salmon have adapted to the spring surge. The smolts used the strong flows to migrate, drifting downstream with the current. During the journey smolts' bodies undergo physiological changes that require them to reach salt water quickly. Before dams backed up the Snake, smolts coming down from Idaho got to the sea in six to twenty days; now it takes from sixty to ninety days, and few of the young salmon reach salt water in time. The emasculated current is the single largest reason that the number of wild adult salmon migrating up the Snake each year has crashed from predevelopment runs of 100,000–200,000 to what was projected to be 150–750 this year.*

---

*Robert S. Devine, "The Trouble with Dams," *Atlantic* (August 1995), 64–75. The example quotation is from page 70.

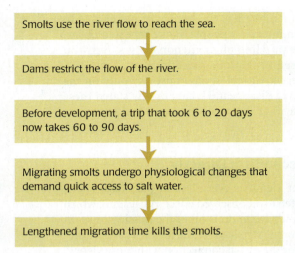

Smolts use the river flow to reach the sea.

Dams restrict the flow of the river.

Before development, a trip that took 6 to 20 days now takes 60 to 90 days.

Migrating smolts undergo physiological changes that demand quick access to salt water.

Lengthened migration time kills the smolts.

This tightly constructed passage connects various causal chains to explain the decline of salmon runs.

Describing each link in the causal chain—and making each link seem as plausible as possible—is the most persuasive means of convincing readers that a specific cause leads to a specific effect.

Second Method: Infer Causal Links Using Inductive Reasoning

If we can't explain a causal link directly, we often employ a reasoning strategy called *induction*. Through induction we infer a general conclusion based on a limited number of specific cases. For example, if on several occasions you got a headache after drinking red wine but not after drinking white wine, you would be likely to conclude inductively that red wine causes you to get headaches, although you can't explain directly how it does so. However, because there are almost always numerous variables involved, inductive reasoning gives only probable truths, not certain ones.

Three Ways of Thinking Inductively   When your brain thinks inductively, it sorts through data looking for patterns of similarity and difference. In this section we explain three ways of thinking inductively: looking for a common element, looking for a single difference, and looking for correlations.

1. **Look for a common element.** One kind of inductive thinking places you on a search for a common element that can explain recurrences of the same phenomenon. For example, psychologists attempting to understand the causes of anorexia have discovered that many anorexics (but not all) come from perfectionist, highly work-oriented homes that emphasize duty and responsibility. This common element is thus a suspected causal factor leading to anorexia.

2. **Look for a single difference.** Another approach is to look for a single difference that may explain the appearance of a new phenomenon. When infant death rates in the state of Washington shot up in July and August 1986, one event making these two months different stood out: increased radioactive fallout over Washington from the April Chernobyl nuclear meltdown in Ukraine. This single difference led some researchers to suspect radiation as a possible cause of the increase in infant deaths.

3. **Look for correlations.** Still another method of induction is correlation, which means that two events or phenomena tend to occur together but doesn't imply that one causes the other. For example, there is a correlation between nearsightedness and intelligence. (That is, in a given sample of nearsighted people and people with normal eyesight, the nearsighted group will have a somewhat higher mean IQ score.) But the direction of causality isn't clear. It could be that high intelligence causes people to read more, thus ruining their eyes (high intelligence causes nearsightedness). Or it could

be that nearsightedness causes people to read more, thus raising their intelligence (nearsightedness causes high intelligence). Or it could be that some unknown phenomenon, perhaps a gene, is related to both nearsightedness and intelligence. So keep in mind that correlation is not causation—it simply suggests possible causation.

■ ■ ■ **FOR CLASS DISCUSSION**   **Developing Plausible Causal Chains Based on Correlations**

Working individually or in small groups, develop plausible causal chains that may explain the relationship between the following pairs of phenomena:

a. A person who registers a low stress level on an electrochemical stress meter — does daily meditation

b. A binge drinker at college parties — has increased risk of becoming a perpetrator or victim of sexual violence

c. A person who grew up in a house with two bathrooms — is likely to have higher SAT scores than a person who grew up in a one-bathroom home

d. A person who takes prescription pain medicine — is more likely to develop dependency on heroin and opiates

e. A member of the National Rifle Association — supports the death penalty

■ ■ ■

EXAMINING VISUAL ARGUMENTS

MyWritingLab™

A Causal Claim

This billboard is part of a Texas campaign to fight sex trafficking. How do both the text and image in this billboard suggest links in a causal chain? Although this ad oversimplifies the complex issue of human trafficking, and some would say it represents only one view of sex workers, how do both the words and the choice of images make powerful appeals to both *logos* and *pathos*?

Key Terms and Inductive Fallacies in Causal Arguments

12.3 To understand key causal terms and the need to avoid inductive fallacies in causal arguments.

Because causal arguments are often easier to conduct if writer and reader share a few specialized terms and concepts, this section explains key terms in causal reasoning and offers ways to avoid inductive fallacies.

A Glossary of Key Terms

- **The problem of oversimplified cause.** One of the great temptations is to look for *the* cause of something, as if a phenomenon had only one cause rather than multiple causes. For example, in recent years the number of persons in the United States sending out Christmas cards has declined substantially. Many commentators attribute the decline to the increasing use of Facebook, which keeps old friends in touch year-round, eliminating the need for holiday "family letters." But there may be other causes also, such as a decline in the number of nuclear families, fewer networks of long-term friends, or generational shifts away from older traditions. When you make a causal argument, be especially careful how you use words such as *all, most, some, the,* or *in part.* For example, to say that *all* the decline in Christmas cards is caused by Facebook is to make a universal statement about Facebook as *the* cause. An argument will be stronger and more accurate if the arguer makes a less sweeping statement: *Some of the cause for the decline in Christmas cards can be attributed to Facebook.* Arguers sometimes deliberately mix up these quantifiers to misrepresent and dismiss opposing views.

- **Immediate and remote causes.** Every causal chain extends backward indefinitely into the past. An immediate cause is the closest in time to the event being examined. Consider the causes for the release of nuclear contaminants around the Fukushima nuclear power plant following the 2011 earthquake off the coast of Japan. The immediate cause was loss of power to the water pumps that cooled the reactor's fuel rods, causing the rods to overheat and partially melt. A slightly less immediate cause (several days earlier) was the earthquake-produced tsunami that had swept away the diesel fuel tanks needed to run the backup generators. These immediate causes can be contrasted with a remote cause—in this case, a late-1960s design decision that used backup diesel generators to power the water pumps in case of an electrical power loss to the reactor facility. Still more remote causes were the economic and regulatory systems in the late 1960s that led to this particular design.

- **Precipitating and contributing causes.** These terms are similar to *immediate* and *remote* causes but don't designate a temporal link going into the past. Rather, they refer to a main cause emerging out of a background of subsidiary causes. If, for example, a husband and wife decide to separate, the *precipitating cause* may be a stormy fight over money, after which one of the partners (or both) says, "I've had enough." In contrast, *contributing causes* would be all the background factors that are dooming the marriage—preoccupation with their careers, disagreement about priorities, in-law problems, and so forth. Note that contributing causes and the precipitating cause all coexist at the same time.

■ **Constraints.** Sometimes an effect occurs because some stabilizing factor—a *constraint*—is removed. In other words, the presence of a constraint may keep a certain effect from occurring. For example, in the marriage we have been discussing, the presence of children in the home may be a constraint against divorce; as soon as the children graduate from high school and leave home, the marriage may well dissolve.

■ **Necessary and sufficient causes.** A *necessary cause* is one that has to be present for a given effect to occur. For example, fertility drugs are necessary to cause the conception of septuplets. Every couple who has septuplets must have used fertility drugs. In contrast, a *sufficient cause* is one that always produces or guarantees a given effect. Smoking more than a pack of cigarettes per day is sufficient to raise the cost of one's life insurance policy. This statement means that if you are a smoker, no matter how healthy you appear to be, life insurance companies will always place you in a higher risk bracket and charge you a higher premium. In some cases, a single cause can be both necessary and sufficient. For example, lack of ascorbic acid is both a necessary and a sufficient cause of scurvy. (Think of those old-time sailors who didn't eat fruit for months.) It is a necessary cause because you can't get scurvy any other way except through absence of ascorbic acid; it is a sufficient cause because the absence of ascorbic acid always causes scurvy.

Avoiding Common Inductive Fallacies that Can Lead to Wrong Conclusions

Largely because of its power, informal induction can often lead to wrong conclusions. You should be aware of two common fallacies of inductive reasoning that can tempt you into erroneous assumptions about causality. (Both fallacies are treated more fully in the Appendix.)

■ *Post hoc* **fallacy:** The *post hoc, ergo propter hoc* fallacy ("after this, therefore because of this") mistakes sequence for cause. Just because event A regularly precedes event B doesn't mean that event A causes event B. The same reasoning that tells us that flipping a switch causes the light to go on can make us believe that low levels of radioactive fallout from the Chernobyl nuclear disaster caused a sudden rise in infant death rates in the state of Washington. The nuclear disaster clearly preceded the rise in death rates. But did it clearly *cause* it? Our point is that precedence alone is no proof of causality and that we are guilty of this fallacy whenever we are swayed to believe that one thing causes another just because it comes first.

■ **Hasty generalization:** The *hasty generalization* fallacy occurs when you make a generalization based on too few cases or too little consideration of alternative explanations: You flip the switch, but the lightbulb doesn't go on. You conclude—too hastily—that the lightbulb has burned out. (Perhaps the power has gone off or the switch is broken.) How many trials does it take before you can make a justified generalization rather than a hasty generalization? It is difficult to say for sure.

Both the *post hoc* fallacy and the hasty generalization fallacy remind us that induction requires a leap from individual cases to a general principle and that it is always possible to leap too soon.

■ ■ ■   **FOR CLASS DISCUSSION** **Brainstorming Causes and Constraints**

The terms in the preceding glossary can be effective brainstorming tools for thinking of possible causes of an event. For the following events, try to think of as many causes as possible by brainstorming possible *immediate causes, remote causes, precipitating causes, contributing causes,* and *constraints*:

1. Working individually, make a list of different kinds of causes/constraints for one of the following:
   a. Your decision to attend your present college
   b. An important event in your life or your family (a job change, a major move, etc.)
   c. A personal opinion you hold that is not widely shared
2. Working as a group, make a list of different kinds of causes/constraints for one of the following:
   a. Why women's fashion and beauty magazines are the most frequently purchased magazines in college bookstores
   b. Why American students consistently score below Asian and European students in academic achievement
   c. Why large supermarket chains are selling more organic food

■ ■ ■

WRITING ASSIGNMENT **A Causal Argument**   MyWritingLab™

12.4 To write your own cause or consequence argument.

Choose an issue about the causes or consequences of a trend, event, or other phenomenon. Write an argument that persuades an audience to accept your explanation of the causes or consequences of your chosen phenomenon. Within your essay you should examine alternative hypotheses or opposing views and explain your reasons for rejecting them. You can imagine your issue either as a puzzle or as a disagreement. If a puzzle, your task will be to create a convincing case for an audience that doesn't have an answer to your causal question already in mind. If a disagreement, your task will be more overtly persuasive because your goal will be to change your audience's views.

Exploring Ideas

Arguments about causes and consequences abound in public, professional, or personal life, so you shouldn't have difficulty finding a causal issue worth investigating and arguing.

In response to a public controversy over why there are fewer women than men on science and math faculties, student writer Julee Christianson argued that culture, not biology, is the primary cause (see pages 265–272). Student writer Carlos

Macias, puzzled by the ease with which college students are issued credit cards, wrote a researched argument disentangling the factors leading young people to bury themselves in debt (see pages 274–277). Other students have focused on causal issues such as these: Why do kids join gangs? What are the consequences of mandatory drug testing (written by a student who has to take amphetamines for narcolepsy)? What has happened since 1970 to cause young people to delay getting married? (This question was initiated by the student's interest in the statistical table in Chapter 9, page 201.)

If you have trouble finding a causal issue to write about, you can often create provocative controversies among your classmates through the following strategies:

- **Make a list of unusual likes and dislikes.** Think about unusual things that people like or dislike. You could summarize the conventional explanations that people give for an unusual pleasure or aversion and then argue for a surprising or unexpected cause. What attracts people to extreme sports? How do you explain the popularity of the paleo diet or of *The Hunger Games*?
- **Make a list of puzzling events or trends.** Another strategy is to make a list of puzzling phenomena and then try to explain their causes. Start with onetime events (a curriculum change at your school, the sudden popularity of a new app). Then list puzzling recurring events (failure of knowledgeable teenagers to practice safe sex). Finally, list some recent trends (growth of naturopathic medicine, increased interest in tattoos). Engage classmates in discussions of one or more of the items on your list. Look for places of disagreement as entry points into the conversation.
- **Brainstorm consequences of a recent or proposed action.** Arguments about consequences are among the most interesting and important of causal disputes. If you can argue for an unanticipated consequence of a real or proposed action, whether good or bad, you can contribute importantly to the conversation. What might be the consequences, for example, of placing "green taxes" on coal-produced electricity; of legalizing marijuana; of overturning *Roe v. Wade*; or of requiring national public service for all young adults?

Identifying Your Audience and Determining What's at Stake

Before drafting your argument, identify your targeted audience and determine what's at stake. Consider your responses to the following questions:

- What audience are you targeting? What background do they need to understand your issue? How much do they already care about it?
- Before they read your argument, what stance on your issue do you imagine them holding? What change do you want to bring about in their views?
- What will they find new or surprising about your argument?
- What objections might they raise? What counterarguments or alternative points of view will you need to address?
- Why does your argument matter? Who might be threatened or made uncomfortable by your views? What is at stake?

Organizing a Causal Argument

At the outset, it is useful to know some of the standard ways that a causal argument can be organized. Later, you may decide on a different organizational pattern, but the standard ways shown in Organization Plans 1, 2, and 3 on pages 263–264 will help you get started.

Plans 2 and 3 are similar in that they examine numerous possible causes or consequences. Plan 2, however, tries to establish the relative importance of each cause or consequence, whereas Plan 3 aims at rejecting the causes or consequences normally assumed by the audience and argues for an unexpected, surprising cause or consequence. Plan 3 can also be used when your purpose is to change your audience's mind about a cause or consequence.

Questioning and Critiquing a Causal Argument

Knowing how to question and critique a causal argument will help you anticipate opposing views in order to strengthen your own. It will also help you rebut another person's causal argument. Here are some useful questions to ask:

- When you explain the links in a causal chain, can a skeptic point out weaknesses in any of the links?
- If you speculate about the causes of a phenomenon, could a skeptic argue for different causes or arrange your causes in a different order of importance?
- If you argue for a surprising cause or a surprising consequence of a phenomenon, could a skeptic point out alternative explanations that would undercut your argument?
- If your argument depends on inferences from data, could a skeptic question the way the data were gathered or interpreted? Could a skeptic claim that the data weren't relevant (for example, research done with lab animals might not apply to humans)?
- If your causal argument depends on a correlation between one phenomenon and another, could a skeptic argue that the direction of causality should be reversed or that an unidentified, third phenomenon is the real cause? ■

Organization Plan 1: Argument Explaining Links in a Causal Chain

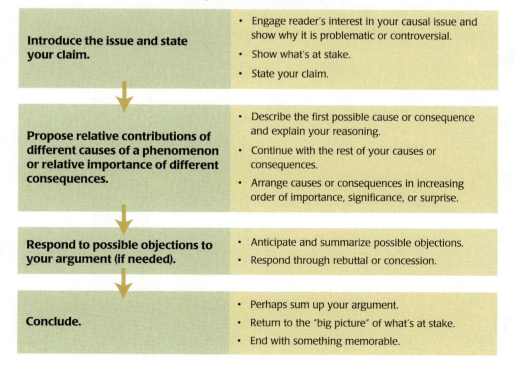

Introduce the issue and state your claim.

- Engage reader's interest in your causal issue and show why it is controversial or problematic.
- Show what's at stake.
- State your claim.

Explain the links in the chain going from cause to effect.

- Explain the links and their connections in order.
- Anticipate and respond to possible objections if needed.

Conclude.

- Perhaps sum up your argument.
- Return to the "big picture" of what's at stake.
- End with something memorable.

Organization Plan 2: Argument Proposing Multiple Causes or Consequences of a Phenomenon

Introduce the issue and state your claim.

- Engage reader's interest in your causal issue and show why it is problematic or controversial.
- Show what's at stake.
- State your claim.

Propose relative contributions of different causes of a phenomenon or relative importance of different consequences.

- Describe the first possible cause or consequence and explain your reasoning.
- Continue with the rest of your causes or consequences.
- Arrange causes or consequences in increasing order of importance, significance, or surprise.

Respond to possible objections to your argument (if needed).

- Anticipate and summarize possible objections.
- Respond through rebuttal or concession.

Conclude.

- Perhaps sum up your argument.
- Return to the "big picture" of what's at stake.
- End with something memorable.

Organization Plan 3: Argument Proposing a Surprising Causes or Consequence

Introduce the issue and state your claim.	• Engage reader's interest in your causal issue and show why it is problematic or controversial. • Show what's at stake. • State your claim.
Reject commonly assumed causes or consequences.	• Describe the first commonly assumed cause or consequence and show why you don't think the explanation is adequate. • Continue with the rest of your commonly assumed causes or consequences.
Argue for your surprising cause or consequence.	• Describe your surprising cause or consequence. • Explain your causal reasoning. • Anticipate and respond to possible objections if needed.
Conclude.	• Perhaps sum up your argument. • Return to the "big picture" of what's at stake. • End with something memorable.

READINGS

Our first reading, by student Julee Christianson, was written in response to the assignment in this chapter. Julee was entering an intense public debate about the underrepresentation of women on prestigious math and science faculties, a controversy initiated by Lawrence Summers, then president of Harvard, who suggested the possibility of a genetic cause for this phenomenon. A furious reaction ensued. The Web site of the Women in Science and Engineering Leadership Institute has extensive coverage of the controversy, including Summers's original speech.

Julee's argument illustrates the format and documentation system for a paper following the guidelines of the American Psychological Association (APA). For further discussion of the APA documentation system, see pages 389–396.

APA

Why Lawrence Summers Was Wrong: Culture Rather Than Biology
Explains the Underrepresentation of Women in Science and Mathematics
Julee Christianson
December 8, 2008

WHY LAWRENCE SUMMERS WAS WRONG   2

Why Lawrence Summers Was Wrong: Culture Rather

Than Biology Explains the Underrepresentation of

Women in Science and Mathematics

In 2005, Harvard University's president, Lawrence H. Summers, gave a controversial speech that suggested that the underrepresentation of women in tenured positions in math and science departments is partly caused by biological differences. In his address, Summers proposed three hypotheses explaining why women shy away from math and science careers. First, he gave a "high-powered job hypothesis" that stated that women naturally want to start a family and therefore will not have the time or desire to commit to the high-stress workload required for research in math and science. His second hypothesis was that genetic differences between the sexes cause more males than females to have high aptitude for math and science. Lastly, he mentioned the hypothesis that women are underrepresented because of discrimination, but he dismissed discrimination as an insignificant factor. It was Summers's second hypothesis about biological differences that started a heated national debate. The academic world seems split over this nature/nurture issue. Although there is some evidence that biology plays a role in determining math ability, I argue that culture plays a much larger role, both in the way that women are socialized and in the continued existence of male discrimination against women in male-dominated fields.

Evidence supporting the role of biology in determining math ability is effectively presented by Steven Pinker (2005), a Harvard psychologist who agrees with Summers. In his article "The Science of Difference: Sex Ed," Pinker focuses extensively on Summers's argument. According to Pinker, "in many traits, men show greater variance than women, and are disproportionately found at both the low and high ends of the distribution" (p. 16). He explains that males and females have similar average scores on math tests but that there are more males than females in the top and the bottom percentiles. This greater variance means that there are disproportionately more male than female math geniuses (and math dunces) and thus more male than female candidates for top math and science positions at major research universities. Pinker explains this greater variance through evolutionary biology: men can pass on their genes to dozens of offspring, whereas women can pass on their genes to only a few. Pinker also argues that men and women have different brain structures that result in different kinds of thinking. For example, Pinker cites research that shows that on average men are better at mental rotation of figures and mathematical word problems,

APA

while women are better at remembering locations, doing mathematical calculations, reading faces, spelling, and using language. Not only do males and females think differently, but they release different hormones. These hormones help shape gender because males release more testosterone and females more estrogen, meaning that men are more aggressive and apt to take risks, while women "are more solicitous to their children" (p. 16). One example Pinker uses to support his biological hypothesis is the case of males born with abnormal genitals and raised as females. These children have more testosterone than normal female children, and many times they show characteristically male interests and behavior. Pinker uses these cases as evidence that no matter how a child is raised, the child's biology determines the child's interests.

Although Pinker demonstrates that biology plays some role in determining math aptitude, he almost completely ignores the much larger role of discrimination and socialization in shaping the career paths of women. According to an editorial from *Nature Neuroscience* (2005), "[t]he evidence to support [Summers's] hypothesis of 'innate difference' turns out to be quite slim" ("Separating," p. 253). The editorial reports that intercultural studies of the variance between boys' and girls' scores on math tests show significant differences between countries. For example, in Iceland girls outscore boys on math tests. The editorial also says that aptitude tests are not very good at predicting the future success of students and that the "SATs tend to underpredict female and over-predict male academic performance" (p. 253). The editorial doesn't deny that men and women's brains work differently, but states that the differences are too small to be blamed for the underrepresentation of women in math and science careers.

If biology doesn't explain the low number of women choosing math and science careers, then what is the cause? Many believe the cause is culture, especially the gender roles children are taught at a very young age. One such believer is Deborah L. Rhode (1997), an attorney and social scientist who specializes in ethics and gender, law, and public policy. Rhode describes the different gender roles females and males are expected to follow from a very young age. Gender roles are portrayed in children's books and television shows. These gender roles are represented by male characters as heroes and problem solvers, while the female characters are distressed damsels. Another example of gender roles is that only a very small number of these shows and books portray working mothers or stay-at-home fathers. Rhodes also discusses how movies and popular music, especially rap and heavy metal, encourage violence and objectify women. As girls grow up, they face more and more gender stereotypes, from toys to

WHY LAWRENCE SUMMERS WAS WRONG   4

magazines. Parents give their boys interactive, problem-solving toys such as chemistry sets and telescopes, while girls are left with dolls. Although more organizations such as the Girl Scouts of America, who sponsor the Web site Girls Go Tech.org, are trying to interest girls in science and math and advertise careers in those fields to girls, the societal forces working against this encouragement are also still pervasive. For example, magazines for teenage girls encourage attracting male attention and the importance of looks, while being smart and successful is considered unattractive. Because adolescents face so many gender stereotypes, it is no wonder that these stereotypes shape the career paths they choose later in life. The gender roles engraved in our adolescents' minds cause discrimination against women later in life. Once women are socialized to see themselves as dependent and not as smart as males, it becomes very difficult to break away from these gender stereotypes. With gender bias so apparent in our society, it is hard for females to have high enough self-confidence to continue to compete with males in many fields.

The effect of socialization begins at a very early age. One study (Clearfield & Nelson, 2006) shows how parents unconsciously send gendered messages to their infants and toddlers. This study examined differences in mothers' speech patterns and play behaviors based on the gender of infants ranging from six months to fourteen months. Although there was no difference in the actual play behavior of male and female infants, the researchers discovered interesting differences in the way mothers interacted with daughters versus sons. Mothers of daughters tended to ask their daughters more questions, encouraging social interaction, whereas mothers of sons were less verbal, encouraging their sons to be more independent. The researchers concluded that "the mothers in our study may have been teaching their infants about gender roles through modeling and reinforcement.... Thus girls may acquire the knowledge that they are 'supposed' to engage in higher levels of interaction with other people and display more verbal behavior than boys.... In contrast, the boys were reinforced for exploring on their own" (p. 136).

One of the strongest arguments against the biological hypothesis comes from a transgendered Stanford neurobiologist, Ben A. Barres (2006), who has been a scientist first as a woman and then as a man. In his article "Does Gender Matter?" Barres states that "there is little evidence that gender differences in [mathematical] abilities exist, are innate or are even relevant to the lack of advancement of women in science" (p. 134). Barres provides much anecdotal evidence of the way women are discriminated against

APA

WHY LAWRENCE SUMMERS WAS WRONG   5

in this male-dominated field. Barres notes that simply putting a male name rather than a female name on an article or résumé increases its perceived value. He also describes research showing that men and women do equally well in gender-blind academic competitions but that men win disproportionately in contests where gender is revealed.

As Barres says, "The bar is unconsciously raised so high for women and minority candidates that few emerge as winners" (p. 134). In one study reported by Barres, women applying for a research grant needed more than twice the productivity of men in order to be considered equally competent. As a female-to-male transgendered person, Barres has personally experienced discrimination when trying to succeed in the science and math fields. When in college, Barres was told that her boyfriend must have done her homework, and she later lost a prestigious fellowship competition to a male even though she was told her application was stronger and she had published "six high-impact papers," while the man that won published only one. Barres even notices subtle differences, such as the fact that he can now finish a sentence without being interrupted by a male.

Barres urges women to stand up publicly against discrimination. One woman he particularly admires as a strong female role model is MIT biologist Nancy Hopkins, who sued the MIT administration for discrimination based on the lesser amount of lab space allocated to female scientists. The evidence from this study was so strong that even the president of MIT publicly admitted that discrimination was a problem (p. 134). Barres wants more women to follow Hopkins's lead. He believes that women often don't realize they are being discriminated against because they have faith that the world is equal. Barres explains this tendency as a "denial of personal disadvantage" (p. 134). Very few women will admit to seeing or experiencing discrimination. Until discrimination and sexism are addressed, women will continue to be oppressed.

As a society, we should not accept Lawrence Summers's hypothesis that biological differences are the reason women are not found in high-prestige tenured jobs in math and science. In fact, in another generation the gap between men and women in math and science might completely disappear. In 2003–2004, women received close to one-third of all doctorates in mathematics, up from 15 percent of doctorates in the early 1980s (American Mathematical Society, 2005). Although more recent data are not yet available, the signs point to a steadily increasing number of women entering the fields of math, science, and engineering. Blaming biology for the lack of women in these fields and refusing to fault our culture is taking the easy way out. Our culture can change.

WHY LAWRENCE SUMMERS WAS WRONG   6

References

American Mathematical Society. (2005, July 6). *Women in mathematics: Study shows gains.* Retrieved from http://www/ams.org/news?news_id=489

Barres, B. A. (2006). Does gender matter? *Nature, 44*(7), 133–136. doi:10.1038/442133a

Clearfield, M. W., & Nelson, N. M. (2006). Sex differences in mothers' speech and play behavior with 6-, 9-, and 14-month-old infants. *Sex Roles, 54*(1–2), 127–137. doi:.10.1007/s11199-005-8874-1

Pinker, S. (2005, February 14). The science of difference: Sex ed. *New R*epublic. *232,* 15–17.

Rhode, D. L. (1997). *Speaking of sex: The denial of gender inequality.* Cambridge, MA: Harvard University Press.

Separating science from stereotype [Editorial]. (2005). *Nature Neuroscience, 8*(3) 253. doi:10.1038/nn0305-253

Summers, L. H. (2005, January 14). Remarks at NBER conference on diversifying the science and engineering workforce. Retrieved from http://designintelligences .wordpress.com/lawrence-h-summers-remarks-at-nber-conference/

APA

Critiquing "Why Lawrence Summers Was Wrong"

1. The controversy sparked by Harvard president Lawrence Summers's remarks was a highly politicized version of the classic nature/nurture problem. Liberal commentators claimed that women were underrepresented in science because of cultural practices that discouraged young girls from becoming interested in math and science and that blocked female Ph.D.s from advancing in their scientific careers. In contrast, conservative commentators—praising Summers's courage for raising a politically incorrect subject—took the "nature" side of this argument by citing studies pointing to innate cognitive differences between human males and females. How would you characterize Christianson's position in this controversy?
2. How does Christianson handle opposing views in her essay?
3. Do you regard Christianson's essay as a valuable contribution to the controversy over the reasons for the low numbers of women in math and science? Why or why not?
4. How would you characterize Christianson's *ethos* as a student writer in this piece? Does her *ethos* help convince you that her argument is sound? Explain.

Our second reading, by linguist Deborah Fallows, published in the column Wordplay in *The Atlantic* in summer 2013 warns of surprising consequences of a common social phenomenon—multitasking with cell phones.

Papa, Don't Text: The Perils of Distracted Parenting

DEBORAH FALLOWS

Last summer, as my baby grandson and I strolled through the same neighborhood his father and I had strolled through 30 years earlier, I saw that something vital had changed. Back then, adults pushing babies in strollers talked with those babies about whatever came across their path. But these days, most adults engage instead in one-sided conversations on their cellphones, or else text in complete silence.

As a linguist, I wondered whether the time adults spend with their mobile devices might be affecting the way children learn language. Since the technology hasn't been ubiquitous for long, research on this question is scarce. But other research on the effects of adult-child conversation makes a strong case for putting cellphones away when you're around children.

For a study published in the journal *Pediatrics* in 2009, researchers outfitted young children with small digital recorders, which captured the language each child heard and produced. The researchers could then identify and count the two-sided exchanges, or conversational "turns," between children and adults. Subjects were also tested on a range of linguistic measures, from the earliest preverbal behaviors, to nascent phonology and grammar skills, to preliteracy and the integration of complex parts of language.

The children exposed to more conversational give-and-take scored higher at every stage of language proficiency. In essence, the children made greater linguistic strides when adults talked *with* them than when they were simply in the presence of language or even when adults talked *to* them. We learned long ago that children's language abilities and eventual academic success are linked to the sheer volume of words they are exposed to early on. Now we have additional evidence that the quality of linguistic exposure, not just its quantity, matters.

5 Two other studies, reported in the *Proceedings of the National Academy of Sciences* in 2003, looked at the effects of parent-child interactions on very early stages of language production and perception. In one, babbling infants and their mothers were tracked during on-the-floor playtime. Mothers in one group were directed to respond to their babies' vocalizations with smiles and touches, and by moving closer. Mothers in the other group were not cued to respond in the same way. The study found that babies whose moms interacted with them in sync with their babbling soon began to vocalize more, with more complex sounds, and articulated more accurately than the other children.

In the other study, 9-month-old babies, who are in the late stages of locking in to the sound system of their native language, were exposed to mini lessons in Mandarin, to see if they could still learn to discern the sounds of a foreign language. One group of babies was taught by real live Chinese speakers. Another group got lessons from electronic versions of the adults, who appeared either on TV or on audiotape. Infants with live teachers learned to discern the sounds of Mandarin, while those in the group with electronic instruction did not.

These studies suggest that social interaction is important to early language learning. Of course, everyone learns to talk. But how ironic is it that, in this era when child-rearing is the focus of unprecedented imagination, invention, sophistication, and expense, something as simple and pleasurable as conversing with our children can be overlooked? As Dimitri Christakis, one of the authors of the *Pediatrics* paper, put it to me, "You can only do one thing at a time: talk to the baby or talk on the phone."

Critiquing "Papa, Don't Text"

MyWritingLab™

1. According to Deborah Fallows's causal claim in this argument, what is likely to be a serious consequence of adults' texting and cell phone habits?
2. What links and reasoning does Fallows use to develop her causal argument?
3. How does Fallows enlist her professional knowledge as evidence to support her causal claim?
4. What features of this argument—think of its new take on the problem of multi-tasking, for instance—both speak particularly to the readers of *The Atlantic* and convey the stakes and urgency of her argument?

Our final causal argument, by student writer Carlos Macias, examines the phenomenon of credit card debt among college students. Note how Macias intermixes personal experiences and research data in order to make his case.

"The Credit Card Company Made Me Do It!"—The Credit Card Industry's Role in Causing Student Debt

CARLOS MACIAS (STUDENT)

One day on spring break this year, I strolled into a Gap store. I found several items that I decided to buy. As I was checking out, the cute female clerk around my age, with perfect hair and makeup, asked if I wanted to open a GapCard to save 10 percent on all purchases I made at Gap, Banana Republic, and Old Navy that day. She said I would also earn points toward Gap gift certificates in the future. Since I shop at the Gap often enough, I decided to take her up on her offer. I filled out the form she handed me, and within seconds I—a jobless, indebted-from-student-loans, full-time college student with no substantial assets or income whatsoever—was offered a card with a $1000 credit line. Surprised by the speed at which I was approved and the amount that I was approved for, I decided to proceed to both Banana Republic and Old Navy that day to see if there was anything else I might be interested in getting (there was). By the end of the day, I had rung up nearly $200 in purchases.

I know my $200 shopping spree on credit is nothing compared to some of the horror stories I have heard from friends. One of my friends, a college sophomore, is carrying $2000 on a couple of different cards, a situation that is not unusual at all. According to a May 2005 study by Nellie Mae, students with credit cards carry average balances of just under $3000 by the time they are seniors (2). The problem is that most students don't have the income to pay off their balances, so they become hooked into paying high interest rates and fees that enrich banks while exploiting students who have not yet learned how to exercise control on their spending habits.

Who is to blame for this situation? Many people might blame the students themselves, citing the importance of individual responsibility and proclaiming that no one forces students to use credit cards. But I put most of the blame directly on the credit card companies. Credit cards are enormously profitable; according to a *New York Times* article, the industry made $30 billion in pretax profits in 2003 alone (McGeehan). Hooking college students on credit cards is essential for this profit, not only because companies make a lot of money off the students themselves, but because hooking students on cards creates a habit that lasts a lifetime. Credit card companies' predatory lending practices—such as using exploitive advertising, using credit scoring to determine creditworthiness, disguising the real cost of credit, and taking advantage of U.S. government deregulation—are causing many unwitting college students to accumulate high levels of credit card debt.

First of all, credit card companies bombard students with highly sophisticated advertising. College students, typically, are in an odd "in-between" stage where they are not necessarily teens anymore, provided for by their parents, but neither are they fully adults, able to provide entirely for themselves. Many students feel the pressures from family, peers and themselves to assume adult roles in terms of their dress and jobs, not relying on Mom or Dad for help. Card companies know about these pressures. Moreover, college students are easy to target because they are concentrated on campuses and generally consume the same media. I probably get several mailings a month offering me a preapproved credit card. These advertisements are filled with happy campus scenes featuring students wearing just the right clothes, carrying their books in just the right backpack, playing music on their iPods or opening their laptop computers. They also appeal to students' desire to feel like responsible adults by emphasizing little emergencies that college students can relate to such as car breakdowns on a road trip. These advertisements illustrate a point made by a team of researchers in an article entitled "Credit Cards as Lifestyle Facilitators": The authors explain how credit card companies want consumers to view credit cards as "lifestyle facilitators" that enable "lifestyle building" and "lifestyle signaling" (Bernthal, Crockett, and Rose). Credit cards make it easy for students to live the lifestyle pictured in the credit card ads.

5   Another contributing cause of high credit card debt for college students is the method that credit card companies use to grant credit—through credit scoring that does not consider income. It was credit scoring that allowed me to get that quadruple-digit credit line at the Gap while already living in the red. The application I filled out never asked my income. Instead, the personal information I listed was used to pull up my credit score, which is based on records of outstanding debts and payment history. Credit scoring allows banks to grant credit cards based on a person's record of responsibility in paying bills rather than on income. According to finance guru Suze Orman, "Your FICO [credit] score is a great tool to size up how good you will be handling a new loan or credit card" (21). Admittedly, credit scoring has made the lending process as a whole much fairer, giving individuals such as minorities and women the chance to qualify for credit even if they have minimal incomes. But when credit card companies use credit scoring to determine college students' creditworthiness, many students are unprepared to handle a credit line that greatly exceeds their ability to pay based on income. In fact, the Center for Responsible Lending, a consumer advocacy organization in North Carolina, lobbied Congress in September 2003 to require credit card companies to secure proof of adequate income for college-age customers before approving credit card applications ("Credit Card Policy Recommendations"). If Congress passed such legislation, credit card companies would not be able to as easily take advantage of college students who have not yet learned how to exercise control on their spending habits. They would have to offer students credit lines commensurate to their incomes. No wonder these companies vehemently opposed this legislation.

Yet another contributing cause of high levels of credit card debt is the high cost of having this debt, which credit card companies are especially talented at disguising. As credit card debt increases, card companies compound unpaid interest, adding it to the balance that must be repaid. If this balance is not repaid, they charge interest on unpaid interest. They add exorbitant fees for small slip-ups like making a late payment or exceeding the credit limit. While these costs are listed on statements when first added to the balance, they quickly vanish into the "New Balance" number on all subsequent statements, as if these fees were simply past purchases that have yet to be repaid. As the balance continues to grow, banks spike interest rates even higher. In his 2004 article "Soaring Interest Is Compounding Credit Card Pain for Millions," Patrick McGeehan describes a "new era of consumer credit, in which thousands of Americans are paying millions of dollars each month in fees that they did not expect...lenders are doubling or tripling interest rates with little warning or explanation." These rate hikes are usually tucked into the pages of fine print that come with credit cards, which many consumers are unable to fully read, let alone understand. Usually, a credit card company will offer a very low "teaser rate" that expires after several months. While this industry practice is commonly understood by consumers, many do not understand that credit card companies usually reserve the right to raise the rate at any time for almost any reason, causing debt levels to rise further.

Admittedly, while individual consumers must be held accountable for any debt they accumulate and should understand compound and variable interest and fees, students' ignorance is welcomed by the credit card industry. In order to completely understand how the credit card industry has caused college students to amass high amounts of credit card debt, it is necessary to explain how this vicious monster was let loose during banking deregulation over the past 30 years. In 1978, the Supreme Court opened the floodgates by ruling that the federal government could not set a cap on interest rates that banks charged for credit cards; that was to be left to the states. With Uncle Sam no longer protecting consumers, Delaware and South Dakota passed laws that removed caps on interest rates, in order to woo credit card companies to conduct nationwide business there (McGeehan). Since then, the credit card industry has become one of the most profitable industries ever. Credit card companies were given another sweet deal from the U.S. Supreme Court in 1996, when the Court deregulated fees. Since then, the average late fee has risen from $10 or less, to $39 (McGeehan). While a lot of these fees and finance charges are avoidable if the student pays the balance in full, on time, every month, for college students who carry balances for whatever reason, these charges are tacked on, further adding to the principal on which they pay a high rate of compounded interest. (Seventy-nine percent of the students surveyed in the Nellie Mae study said that they regularly carried a balance on their cards [8].) Moreover, the U.S. government has refused to step in to regulate the practice of universal default, where a credit card company can raise the rate they charge if a consumer is late on an unrelated bill, like a utility payment. Even for someone who pays his or her bills in full, on time, 99 percent of the time, one bill-paying slip-up can cause an avalanche of fees and frustration, thanks to the credit card industry.

Credit card companies exploit college students' lack of financial savvy and security. It is no secret that most full-time college students are not independently wealthy; many have limited means. So why are these companies so willing to issue cards to poor college students? Profits, of course! If they made credit cards less available to struggling consumers such as college students, consumers would have a more difficult time racking up huge balances, plain and simple. It's funny that Citibank, one of the largest, most profitable credit card companies in the world, proudly exclaims "Live richly" in its advertisements. At the rate that it and other card companies collect interest and fees from their customers, a more appropriate slogan would be "Live poorly."

Works Cited

Bernthal, Matthew J., David Crockett, and Randall L. Rose. "Credit Cards as Lifestyle Facilitators." *Journal of Consumer Research* 32.1 (2005): 130–45. *Research Library Complete.* Web. 18 June 2005.

"Credit Card Policy Recommendations." *Center for Responsible Lending.* Center for Responsible Lending, Sept. 2003. Web. 18 June 2005.

McGeehan, Patrick. "Soaring Interest Is Compounding Credit Card Pain for Millions." *New York Times.* New York Times, 21 Nov. 2004. Web. 3 July 2005.

Nellie Mae. "Undergraduate Students and Credit Cards in 2004: An Analysis of Usage Rates and Trends." *Nellie Mae.* SLM Corporation, May 2005. Web. 3 July 2005.

Orman, Suze. *The Money Book for the Young, Fabulous and Broke.* New York: Riverhead, 2005. Print.

Critiquing "The Credit Card Company Made Me Do It!"   MyWritingLab™

1. How effective is Macias's argument that the predatory practices of banks and credit card companies are the primary cause of credit card debt among college students?
2. Suppose that you wanted to join this conversation by offering a counterview with a thesis something like this: "Although Macias is partially correct that banks and credit card companies play a role in producing credit card debt among college students, he underestimates other important factors." What would you emphasize as the causes of credit card debt? How would you make your case?

MyWritingLab™

Visit Ch. 12 Causal Arguments in *MyWritingLab* to complete the For Writing and Discussion, Examining Visual Arguments, Critiquing, and Writing Assignments and to test your understanding of the chapter objectives.

Evaluation and Ethical Arguments

13

What you will learn in this chapter:

13.1 To explain and illustrate the difference between categorical and ethical evaluation arguments

13.2 To conduct a categorical evaluation argument using a criteria-match strategy

13.3 To conduct an ethical evaluation argument using principles or consequences

13.4 To be mindful of common problems encountered in evaluation arguments

13.5 To write your own categorical or ethical evaluation argument

---

In our roles as citizens and professionals, we are continually expected to make evaluations and to persuade others to accept them. In this chapter, you will learn to conduct two kinds of evaluation arguments: categorical and ethical. Both have clarifying power to help us make difficult choices about good or bad, right or wrong.

Case 1   How Should We Evaluate the Film *District 9?*

In the film *District 9* (2009), directed by South African Neill Blomkamp and produced by Peter Jackson, a spaceship has stalled out over Johannesburg, South Africa, where it has hovered for several decades. Its starving alien passengers, derogatorily called "The Prawns" for their appearance, have been placed in what has become a crowded, militarized prison ghetto called District 9. As the film begins, South Africans have grown disgusted with and intolerantly fearful of the growing alien population, while corporate powers seek these aliens' technologically advanced bio-weapons. As this poster suggests—based on its "No Humans Allowed" sign, its ominous "You are not welcome here" slogan, and its barbed wire perimeter—the film includes graphic echoes of the racism of apartheid and disturbing depiction of xenophobia, abusive corporate powers, and mistreatment of refugees (the aliens). Nominated for numerous awards, *District 9* has sparked heated evaluation arguments about whether it is a good or a flawed film. Part of the debate focuses on what evaluative criteria to use—a decision that depends on the category into which the film should be placed. Should it be evaluated as a science fiction film, as a corporate espionage thriller, or as a commentary on global social justice? Some critics, for example, have argued that *District 9* is not a great science fiction film, but it is a deeply provocative and moving commentary on social justice.

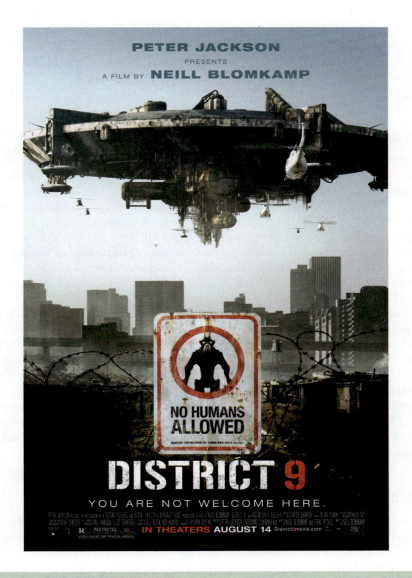

Case 2   What Is a "Good Organ" for a Transplant? How Can an Ill Person Ethically Find an Organ Donor?

In the United States some 87,000 sick people have been waiting as long as six years for an organ transplant, with a portion of these dying before they can find a donor. The problem of organ shortages raises two kinds of evaluation issues. First, doctors are reevaluating the criteria by which they judge a "good" organ—that is, a good lung, kidney, or liver suitable for transplanting. Formerly, people who were elderly or obese or who had engaged in risky behaviors or experienced heart failure or other medical conditions were not considered sources of good organs. Now doctors are reconsidering these sources as well as exploring the use of organs from pigs. Second, the shortage of organs for donation has raised numerous ethical issues: Is it ethical for people to bypass the national waiting list for organs by advertising on billboards and Web sites in search of a volunteer donor? Is it morally right for people to sell their organs? Is it right for patients and families to buy organs or in any way remunerate living organ donors? Some states are passing laws that allow some financial compensation to living organ donors.

An Overview of Categorical and Ethical Evaluation Arguments

13.1 To explain and illustrate the difference between categorical and ethical evaluation arguments

In this chapter we explain strategies for conducting two different kinds of evaluation arguments. First, we examine categorical evaluations of the kind "Is this thing a good member of its class?"[*] (Is Ramon a good leader?) In such an evaluation, the writer determines the extent to which a given something possesses the qualities or standards of its category or class. What are the traits of good leaders? Does Ramon possess these traits? Second, we examine ethical arguments of the kind "Is this action right (wrong)?" (Was it right or wrong to drop atomic bombs on Hiroshima and Nagasaki in World War II?) In these arguments, the writer evaluates a given act from the perspective of some system of morality or ethics.

To see the difference between the two kinds of evaluations, consider the case of terrorists. From a nonethical standpoint, you could make a categorical evaluation by saying that certain people are "good terrorists" in that they fully realize the purpose of the class "terrorist": they cause great anguish and damage with a minimum of resources, and they bring much attention to their cause. In other words, they are good at what they do—terrorism. However, if we want to condemn terrorism on ethical grounds, we have to construct an ethical argument that terrorism is wrong. The ethical question is not whether a person fulfills the purposes of the class "terrorist," but whether it is wrong for such a class to exist. In the rest of this chapter we will explain categorical evaluations and ethical evaluations in more detail.

Constructing a Categorical Evaluation Argument

13.2 To conduct a categorical evaluation argument using a criteria-match strategy

A categorical evaluation uses a criteria-match structure similar to the structure we examined in definition arguments (see Chapter 11).

Criteria-Match Structure of Categorical Evaluations

A typical claim-with-reasons frame for an evaluation argument has the following criteria-match structure:

> This thing/phenomenon is/is not a good member of its class because it meets (fails to meet) criteria A, B, and C.

---

[*]In addition to the term *good*, a number of other evaluative terms involve the same kind of thinking—*effective, successful, workable, excellent, valuable,* and so forth.

Claim: This thing/phenomenon is (is not) a good member of its class.

Criteria: The criteria for being a good member of this class are A, B, and C.

Match: The thing/phenomenon meets (fails to meet) criteria A, B, and C.

The main conceptual difference between an evaluation argument and a definition argument is the nature of the contested category. In a definition argument, one argues whether a particular thing belongs within a certain category. (Is this swampy area a *wetland*?) In an evaluation argument, we know what category something belongs to. For example, we know that this 2008 Chevy Cobalt is a *used car*. For an evaluation argument, the question is whether this 2008 Chevy Cobalt is a *good used car*. Or, to place the question within a rhetorical context, is this 2008 Chevy Cobalt a *good used car for me to buy for college*?

To illustrate the criteria-match structure of an evaluation argument, let's ask whether hydraulic fracturing (commonly called fracking) is a good means for extracting natural gas from shale formations. Supporters of fracking might say, "yes," because it meets three major criteria:

- It is technologically efficient at extracting huge supplies of otherwise untappable natural gas.
- It is cost effective.
- It is environmentally safe.

Opponents might make two counterarguments: First, they might claim that fracking is not environmentally safe. (Safety is still a crucial criterion. Opponents argue that fracking doesn't meet this criterion.) Second, they might argue that fracking, by producing lots of relatively cheap natural gas, removes the urgency from efforts to convert to renewable energy such as solar and wind. Thus it might be cost effective (criterion 2) in the short run, but disastrous in the long run. Page 282 provides a Toulmin analysis of how proponents of fracking might develop their third reason: "Fracking is environmentally safe."

Developing Your Criteria

To help you develop your criteria, we suggest a three-step thinking process:

1. Place the thing you are evaluating in the smallest relevant category so that you don't compare apples to oranges.
2. Develop criteria for your evaluation based on the purpose or function of this category.
3. Determine the relative weight of your criteria.

Let's look at each of these steps in turn.

Step 1: Place the Thing You Are Evaluating in the Smallest Relevant Category

Placing your contested thing in the smallest category is a crucial first step. Suppose, for example, that you want one of your professors to write you a letter of recommendation for a summer job. The professor will need to know what kind of summer job. Are you

TOULMIN ANALYSIS OF THE FRACKING ARGUMENT SUPPORTING ENVIRONMENTAL SAFETY

ENTHYMEME

CLAIM Fracking is a good method for extracting natural gas from shale formations

REASON because it is environmentally safe.

GROUNDS

- Descriptions of safety measures employed by industry
- Descriptions of local, state, and federal regulations aimed at insuring safety
- Summaries of peer-reviewed studies and government studies showing the safety of fracking
- Refutation of anecdotal scare stories told by environmentalists

CONDITIONS OF REBUTTAL

Attacking the reason and grounds

Arguments that fracking is not environmentally safe

- Studies pointing to possible dangers such as contamination of aquifers, earthquakes, flaring of methane, and so forth
- Arguments that local, state, and federal regulations are too loose and unenforced
- Statistics about environmental costs in doing the fracking (huge amounts of required water, recovering contaminated water, use of carbon fuels to run the machinery, and so forth)

WARRANT

Environmental safety is an important criterion for evaluating a method of drilling for natural gas

BACKING

Arguments that safety must be a prime consideration of any business plan. One major accident could undermine public support of fracking. [Backing tries to counter the arguments of environmentalists that business interests put profit ahead of safety.]

CONDITIONS OF REBUTTAL

Attacking the warrant and backing

- Environmentalists will endorse the warrant, but may say that even if fracking is safe, it undermines the urgency of finding alternative energy sources.
- Business interests might want to loosen an insistence on absolute safety by acknowledging that some accidents are inevitable.

applying to become a camp counselor, a law office intern, a retail sales clerk, or a tour guide at a wild animal park in your state? Each of these jobs has different criteria for excellence. Or to take a different example, suppose that you want to evaluate e-mail as a medium of correspondence. To create a stable context for your evaluation, you need to place e-mail in its smallest relevant category. You may choose to evaluate e-mail as a medium for business communication (by contrasting e-mail with direct personal contact, phone conversations, or postal mail), as a medium for staying in touch with high school friends (in contrast, say, to text messaging or Facebook), or as a medium for carrying on a long-distance romance (in contrast, say, to old-fashioned "love letters"). Again, criteria will vary across these different categories.

By placing your contested thing in the smallest relevant class, you avoid the apples-and-oranges problem. That is, to give a fair evaluation of a perfectly good apple, you need to judge it under the class "apple" and not under the next larger class, "fruit," or a neighboring class such as "orange." And to be even more precise, you may wish to evaluate your apple in the class "eating apple" as opposed to "pie apple" because the latter class is supposed to be tarter and the former class juicier and sweeter.

Step 2: Develop Criteria for Your Evaluation Based on the Purpose or Functions of This Category

Suppose that the summer job you are applying for is tour guide at a wild animal park in your state. The functions of a tour guide are to drive the tour buses, make people feel welcome, give them interesting information about the wild animals in the park, make their visit pleasant, and so forth. Criteria for a good tour guide would thus include reliability and responsibility, a friendly demeanor, good speaking skills, and knowledge of the kinds of animals in the wild animal park. In our e-mail example, suppose that you want to evaluate e-mail as a medium for business communication. The purpose of this class is to provide a quick and reliable means of communication that increases efficiency, minimizes misunderstandings, protects the confidentiality of internal communications, and so forth. Based on these purposes, you might establish the following criteria:

A good medium for business communication:

- Is easy to use, quick, and reliable
- Increases employee efficiency
- Prevents misunderstandings
- Maintains confidentiality where needed

Step 3: Determine the relative weight of your criteria

In some evaluations all the criteria are equally important. However, sometimes a phenomenon to be evaluated is strong in one criterion but weak in another—a situation that forces the evaluator to decide which criterion takes precedence. For example, the supervisor interviewing candidates for tour guide at the wild animal park may find one candidate who is very knowledgeable about the wildlife but doesn't have good speaking skills. The supervisor would need to decide which of these two criteria gets more weight.

Making Your Match Argument

Once you've established and weighed your criteria, you'll need to use examples and other evidence to show that the thing being evaluated meets or does not meet the criteria. For example, your professor could argue that you would be a good wildlife park tour guide because you have strong interpersonal skills (based on your work on a college orientation committee), that you have good speaking skills (based on a speech you gave in the professor's class), and that you have quite a bit of knowledge about animals and ecology (based on your major in environmental science).

In our e-mail example, you might establish the following working thesis:

Despite its being easy to learn, quick, and reliable, e-mail is often not an effective medium for business communication because it reduces worker efficiency, leads to frequent misunderstandings, and often lacks confidentiality.

EXAMINING VISUAL ARGUMENTS

MyWritingLab™

An Evaluation Claim

This photograph of Stephen Colbert and Jon Stewart of *The Colbert Report* and *The Daily Show* was taken at the October 30, 2010 "Rally to Restore Sanity 'or Fear,'" on the Washington D.C. National Mall, an event that drew thousands of people. The event followed by two months the "Restoring Honor Rally" led by conservative Fox News talk show celebrity Glenn Beck on August 28, 2010. Political commentators debated whether the Colbert and Stewart rally was simply a satirical entertainment mocking the Beck rally or whether it was serious political activism supporting the liberal left. If your goal was to portray this event as serious political activism, would this photograph be a good image to accompany your argument? What criteria would you establish for selecting a photograph to support your argument that Colbert and Stewart are effective political activists and not simply entertainers?

You could develop your last three points as follows:

- **E-mail reduces worker efficiency.** You can use personal anecdotes and research data to show how checking e-mail is addictive and how it eats into worker time (one research article says that the average worker devotes ten minutes of every working hour to reading and responding to e-mail).
- **E-mail leads to misunderstandings.** Because an e-mail message is often composed rapidly without revision, e-mail can cause people to state ideas imprecisely, to write something they would never say face-to-face, or to convey an unintended tone. You could give a personal example of a high-consequence misunderstanding caused by e-mail.
- **E-mail often lacks confidentiality.** You could provide anecdotal or research evidence of cases in which a person clicked on the "reply to all" button rather than the "reply" button, sending a message intended for one person to a whole group of people. Also, people sometimes forward e-mails without the sender's permission. Finally, e-mail messages are archived forever, so that messages that you thought were deleted may show up years later in a lawsuit.

As these examples illustrate, the key to a successful match argument is to use sufficient examples and other evidence to show how your contested phenomenon meets or does not meet each of your criteria.

■ ■ ■ **FOR CLASS DISCUSSION** Developing Criteria and Match Arguments

The following small-group exercise can be accomplished in one or two class hours. It gives you a good model of the process you can go through in order to write your own categorical evaluation.

1. Choose a specific controversial person, thing, or event to evaluate. To help you think of ideas, try brainstorming controversial members of the following categories: *people* (athletes, political leaders, musicians); *technology* (new car features, phone apps); *media* (a social network, a TV program, a radio station); *government and world affairs* (an economic policy, a Supreme Court decision); *the arts* (a film, a book); *your college or university* (food service, an administrative policy); *the world of work* (a job, a company operation, a dress policy); or any other categories of your choice.

2. Place your controversial person or thing within the smallest relevant class, thus providing a rhetorical context for your argument and showing what is at stake. Do you want to evaluate Harvey's Hamburger Haven in the broad category of *restaurants,* in the narrow category of *hamburger joints,* or in a different narrow category such as *late-night study places*?

3. Make a list of the purpose or function of that class, and then list the criteria that a good member of that class would need to have in order to accomplish the purpose or function. (What is the purpose or function of a hamburger joint versus a late-night study place? What criteria for excellence can you derive from these purposes or functions?)

4. If necessary, rank your criteria from most to least important. (For a late-night study place, what is more important: good ambience, Wi-Fi availability, good coffee, or convenient location?)

5. Provide examples and other evidence to show how your contested something matches or does not match each of your criteria. (As a late-night study place, Carol's Coffee Closet beats out Harvey's Hamburger Haven. Although Harvey's Hamburger Haven has the most convenient location, Carol's Coffee Closet has Wi-Fi, an ambience conducive to studying, and excellent coffee.)

Constructing an Ethical Evaluation Argument

13.3 To conduct an ethical evaluation argument using principles or consequences

A second kind of evaluation argument focuses on moral or ethical issues, which can often merge or overlap with categorical evaluations. For example, many apparently straightforward categorical evaluations can turn out to have an ethical dimension. Consider again the criteria for buying a car. Most people would base their evaluations on cost, safety, comfort, and so forth. But some people may feel morally obligated to buy the most fuel-efficient car, to buy an American car, or not to buy a car from a manufacturer whose labor policies they find morally repugnant. Depending on how large a role ethical considerations play in the evaluation, we may choose to call this an ethical argument based on moral considerations rather than a categorical evaluation based on the purposes of a class or category.

When we are faced with an ethical issue, we must move from arguments of good or bad to arguments of right or wrong. The terms *right* and *wrong* are clearly different from the terms *good* and *bad* when the latter terms mean, simply, "effective" (meets purposes of class, as in "This is a good laptop") or "ineffective" (fails to meet purposes of class, as in "This is a bad cookbook"). But *right* and *wrong* often also differ from what seems to be a moral use of the terms *good* and *bad*. We may say, for example, that sunshine is good because it brings pleasure and that cancer is bad because it brings pain and death, but that is not quite the same thing as saying that sunshine is "right" and cancer is "wrong." It is the problem of "right" and "wrong" that ethical arguments confront.

There are many schools of ethical thought—too many to cover in this brief overview—so we'll limit ourselves to two major systems: arguments from consequences and arguments from principles.

Consequences as the Base of Ethics

Perhaps the best-known example of evaluating acts according to their ethical consequences is utilitarianism, a down-to-earth philosophy that grew out of nineteenth-century British philosophers' concern to demystify ethics and make it work in the practical world. Jeremy Bentham, the originator of utilitarianism, developed the goal of the greatest good for the greatest number, or "greatest happiness," by which he meant the most pleasure for the least pain. John Stuart Mill, another British philosopher, built on Bentham's utilitarianism by using predicted consequences to determine the morality of a proposed action.

Mill's consequentialist approach allows you readily to assess a wide range of acts. You can apply the principle of utility—which says that an action is morally right if it produces a greater net value (benefits minus costs) than any available alternative action—to virtually any situation, and it will help you reach a decision. Obviously, however, it's not always easy to make the calculations called for by this approach because, like any prediction of the future, an estimate of consequences is conjectural. In particular, it's often very hard to assess the long-term consequences of any action. Too often, utilitarianism seduces us into a short-term analysis of a moral problem simply because long-term consequences are difficult to predict.

Principles as the Base of Ethics

Any ethical system based on principles will ultimately rest on moral tenets that we are duty bound to uphold, no matter what the consequences. Sometimes the moral tenets come from religious faith—for example, the Ten Commandments. At other times, however, the principles are derived from philosophical reasoning, as in the case of German philosopher Immanuel Kant. Kant held that no one should ever use another person as a means to his own ends and that everyone should always act as if his acts are the basis of universal law. In other words, Kant held that we are duty bound to respect other people's sanctity and to act in the same way that we would want all other people to act. The great advantage of such a system is its clarity and precision. We are never overwhelmed by a multiplicity of contradictory and difficult-to-quantify consequences; we simply make sure we are following (or not violating) the principles of our ethical system and proceed accordingly.

Example Ethical Arguments Examining Capital Punishment

To show you how to conduct an ethical argument, let's now apply these two strategies to the example of capital punishment. In general, you can conduct an ethical evaluation by using the frame for either a principles-based argument or a consequences-based argument or a combination of both.

Principles-Based Frame: An act is right (wrong) because it follows (violates) principles A, B, and C.

Consequences-Based Frame: An act is right (wrong) because it will lead to consequences A, B, and C, which are good (bad).

A principles-based argument looks at capital punishment through the lens of one or more guiding principles. Kant's principle that we are duty bound not to violate the sanctity of other human lives could lead to arguments opposing capital punishment. One might argue as follows:

Principles-based argument opposing capital punishment: The death penalty is wrong because it violates the principle of the sanctity of human life.

You could support this principle either by summarizing Kant's argument that one should not violate the selfhood of another person or by pointing to certain religious systems such as Judeo-Christian ethics, where one is told, "Vengeance is mine, saith the Lord" or "Thou shalt not kill." To develop this argument further, you might examine two exceptions in which principles-based ethicists may allow killing—self-defense and war—and show how capital punishment does not fall into either category.

Principles-based arguments can also be developed to support capital punishment. You may be surprised to learn that Kant himself—despite his arguments for the sanctity of life—supported capital punishment. To make such an argument, Kant evoked a different principle about the suitability of the punishment to the crime:

> There is no sameness of kind between death and remaining alive even under the most miserable conditions, and consequently there is no equality between the crime and the retribution unless the criminal is judicially condemned and put to death.

Stated as an enthymeme, Kant's argument is as follows:

> *Principles-based argument supporting capital punishment:* Capital punishment is right because it follows the principle that punishments should be proportionate to the crime.

In developing this argument, Kant's burden would be to show why the principle of proportionate retribution outweighs the principle of the supreme worth of the individual. Our point is that a principles-based argument can be made both for and against capital punishment. The arguer's duty is to make clear what principle is being evoked and then to show why this principle is more important than opposing principles.

Unlike a principles-based argument, which appeals to certain guiding maxims or rules, a consequences-based argument looks at the consequences of a decision and measures the positive benefits against the negative costs. Here is the frame that an arguer might use to oppose capital punishment on the basis of negative consequences:

> *Consequences-based argument opposing capital punishment:* Capital punishment is wrong because it leads to the following negative consequences:
>
> ■ The possibility of executing an innocent person
> ■ The possibility that a murderer who may repent and be redeemed is denied that chance
> ■ The excessive legal and political costs of trials and appeals
> ■ The unfair distribution of executions so that one's chances of being put to death are much greater if one is a minority or is poor

To develop this argument, the reader would need to provide facts, statistics, and other evidence to support each of the stated reasons.

A different arguer might use a consequences-based approach to support capital punishment:

> *Consequences-based argument supporting capital punishment:* Capital punishment is right because it leads to the following positive consequences:
>
> ■ It may deter violent crime and slow down the rate of murder.
> ■ It saves the cost of lifelong imprisonment.

■ It stops criminals who are menaces to society from committing more murders.

■ It helps grieving families reach closure and sends a message to victims' families that society recognizes their pain.

It should be evident, then, that adopting an ethical system doesn't lead to automatic answers to one's ethical dilemmas. A system offers a way of proceeding—a way of conducting an argument—but it doesn't relieve you of personal responsibility for thinking through your values and taking a stand. When you face an ethical dilemma, we encourage you to consider both the relevant principles and the possible consequences the dilemma entails. In many arguments, you can use both principles-based and consequences-based reasoning as long as irreconcilable contradictions don't present themselves.

■ ■ ■ **FOR WRITING AND DISCUSSION: Developing an Ethical Argument** MyWritingLab™

Individual task: Develop a frame for an ethical argument (based on principles, consequences, or both) for or against any two of the following actions. Use the previous examples on capital punishment as a model.

1. Eating meat
2. Using public transportation instead of owning a car
3. Legalizing assisted suicide for the terminally ill
4. Selling organs
5. Allowing concealed weapons on college campuses

Group task: Share your arguments with classmates   ■ ■ ■

Common Problems in Making Evaluation Arguments

13.4 To be mindful of common problems encountered in evaluation arguments

When conducting evaluation arguments (whether categorical or ethical), writers can bump up against recurring problems that are unique to evaluation. In some cases these problems complicate the establishment of criteria; in other cases they complicate the match argument. Let's look briefly at some of these common problems.

■ **The problem of standards—what is commonplace versus what is ideal:** In various forms, we experience the dilemma of the commonplace versus the ideal all the time. Is it fair to get a ticket for going seventy miles per hour on a sixty-five-mile-per-hour freeway when most of the drivers go seventy miles per hour or faster? (Does what is *commonplace*—going seventy—override what is *ideal*—obeying the law?) Is it better for high schools to pass out free contraceptives to students because students are having sex anyway (what's *commonplace*), or is it better not to pass them out in order to support abstinence (what's *ideal*)?

■ **The problem of mitigating circumstances:** This problem occurs when an arguer claims that unusual circumstances should alter our usual standards of judgment. Ordinarily, it is fair for a teacher to reduce a grade if you turn in a paper late. But what if you were up all night taking care of a crying baby? Does that count as a *mitigating circumstance* to waive the ordinary criterion? When you argue for mitigating circumstances, you will likely assume an especially heavy burden of proof. People assume the rightness of usual standards of judgment unless there are compelling arguments for abnormal circumstances.

■ **The problem of choosing between two goods or two bads:** Often an evaluation issue forces us between a rock and a hard place. Should we cut pay or cut people? Put our parents in a nursing home or let them stay at home, where they have become a danger to themselves? In such cases one has to weigh conflicting criteria, knowing that the choices are too much alike—either both bad or both good.

■ **The problem of seductive empirical measures:** The need to make high-stakes evaluations has led many people to seek quantifiable criteria that can be weighed mathematically. Thus we use grade point averages to select scholarship winners, student evaluation scores to decide merit pay for teachers, and combined scores of judges to evaluate figure skaters. In some cases, empirical measures can be quite acceptable, but they are often dangerous because they discount important non-quantifiable traits. The problem with empirical measures is that they seduce us into believing that complex judgments can be made mathematically, thus rescuing us from the messiness of alternative points of view and conflicting criteria.

■ **The problem of cost:** A final problem in evaluation arguments is cost. Something may be the best possible member of its class, but if it costs too much, we have to go for second or third best. We can avoid this problem somewhat by placing items into different classes on the basis of cost. For example, a Mercedes will exceed a Kia on almost any criterion, but if we can't afford more than a Kia, the comparison is pointless. It is better to compare a Mercedes to a Lexus and a Kia to an equivalent Ford. Whether costs are expressed in dollars, personal discomfort, moral repugnance, or some other terms, our final evaluation of an item must take cost into account.

WRITING ASSIGNMENT An Evaluation or Ethical Argument

MyWritingLab™

13.5 To write your own categorical or ethical evaluation argument

Write an argument in which you try to change your readers' minds about the value, worth, or ethics of something. Choose a phenomenon to be evaluated that is controversial so that your readers are likely at first to disagree with your evaluation or at least to be surprised by it. Somewhere in your essay you should summarize alternative views and either refute them or concede to them (see Chapter 7).

Exploring Ideas

Evaluation issues are all around us. Think of disagreements about the value of a person, thing, action, or phenomenon within the various communities to which you belong—your dorm, home, or apartment community; your school community, including clubs or organizations; your academic community, including classes you are currently taking; your work community; and your city, state, national, and world communities. Once you have settled on a controversial thing to be evaluated, place it in its smallest relevant category, determine the purposes of that category, and develop your criteria. If you are making an ethical evaluation, consider your argument from the perspective of both principles and consequences.

Identifying Your Audience and Determining What's at Stake

Before drafting your argument, identify your targeted audience and determine what's at stake. Consider your responses to the following questions:

- What audience are you targeting? What background do they need to understand your issue? How much do they already care about it?
- Before they read your evaluation argument, what stance on your issue do you imagine them holding? What change do you want to bring about in their view?
- What will they find new or surprising about your argument?
- What objections might they raise? What counterarguments or alternative points of view will you need to address?
- Why does your evaluation matter? Who might be threatened or made uncomfortable by your views? What is at stake?

Organizing an Evaluation Argument

As you write a draft, you may find useful the following prototypical structures for evaluation arguments shown in Organization Plans 1 and 2 on pages 292 and 293. Of course, you can always alter these plans if another structure better fits your material.

Questioning and Critiquing a Categorical Evaluation Argument

Here is a list of questions you can use to critique a categorical evaluation argument:

Will a skeptic accept my criteria? Many evaluative arguments are weak because the writers have simply assumed that readers will accept their criteria. Whenever your audience's acceptance of your criteria is in doubt, you will need to argue for your criteria explicitly.

Will a skeptic accept my general weighting of criteria? Another vulnerable spot in an evaluation argument is the relative weight of the criteria. How much anyone weights a given criterion is usually a function of his or her own interests relative to your contested something. You should always ask whether some particular group might have good reasons for weighting the criteria differently.

Organization Plan 1: Criteria and Match in Separate Sections

Introduce the issue and state your claim.	• Engage reader's interest in your evaluation issue and show why it is controversial or problematic. • Show what's at stake. • Provide background information needed by your audience. • State your claim.
Present your criteria.	• State and develop criterion 1. • State and develop criterion 2. • Continue with the rest of your criteria. • Anticipate and respond to possible objections to the criteria.
Present your match argument.	• Consider restating your claim for clarity. • Argue that your case meets (does not meet) criterion 1. • Argue that your case meets (does not meet) criterion 2. • Continue with the rest of your match argument. • Anticipate and respond to possible objections to the match argument.
Conclude.	• Perhaps sum up your argument. • Help reader return to the "big picture" of what's at stake. • End with something memorable.

Will a skeptic accept my criteria but reject my match argument? The other major way of testing an evaluation argument is to anticipate how readers may object to your stated reasons and grounds. Will readers challenge you by showing that you have cherry-picked your examples and evidence? Will they provide counterexamples and counterevidence?

Organization Plan 2: Criteria and Match Interwoven

Introduce the issue and state your claim.	• Engage reader's interest in your evaluation issue and show why it is controversial or problematic. • Show what's at stake. • Provide background information needed by your audience. • State your claim.
Present series of criterion-match arguments.	• State and develop criterion 1 and argue that your case meets (does not meet) the criterion. • State and develop criterion 2 and argue that your case meets (does not meet) the criterion. • Continue with the rest of your criterion-match arguments.
Respond to possible objections to your argument.	• Anticipate and summarize possible objections. • Respond to the objections through rebuttal or concession.
Conclude.	• Perhaps sum up your argument. • Help reader return to the "big picture" of what's at stake. • End with something memorable.

Critiquing an Ethical Argument

Ethical arguments can be critiqued through appeals to consequences or principles. If an argument appeals primarily to principles, it can be vulnerable to a simple cost analysis. What are the costs of adhering to this principle? There will undoubtedly be some, or else there would be no real argument. If the argument is based strictly on consequences, we should ask whether it violates any rules or principles, particularly such commandments as the Golden Rule—"Do unto others as you would have others do unto you"—which most members of our audience adhere to. By failing to mention these alternative ways of thinking about ethical issues, we undercut not only our argument but our credibility as well. ■

READINGS

Our first reading, by student writer Lorena Mendoza-Flores, critiques her former high school for the way it marginalizes Hispanic students. Lorena, a physics major in college, has changed the name of her high school and chosen not to reveal her home state.

Silenced and Invisible: Problems of Hispanic Students at Valley High School

LORENA MENDOZA-FLORES (STUDENT)

Every year, thousands of Mexican families come to the United States in order to escape economic hardships in Mexico and hope for better schools for their children. While many American schools try to accommodate immigrant non-native speakers, many immigrant families, according to case study interviews, have increasingly negative perceptions of these attempts (Roessingh). There are action plans to bridge the gap between disadvantaged and advantaged students, yet Hispanic ESL (English as a Second Language) youth continue to perform considerably below that of other students (Good, Masewicz, and Vogel). These problems pose the question: what is wrong with the way our schools treat Hispanic immigrants? Perhaps we could gain some understanding if we looked at a specific school—my own Valley High School in an agricultural region of [name of state]. Valley High School is a perfect example of a school with a growing Hispanic population, well-intentioned teachers, and hopes for their success that simply fall through. The failures at my school include inadequate ESL training for teachers, inadequate counseling for immigrant students, poor multicultural training for all teachers, and failure to value Hispanic identity and provide support for transitioning families.

Despite the fact that the Valley School District has 52 percent Hispanic students, a large percentage of whom have Spanish as their first language and parents who only speak Spanish, the staff at Valley High School is overwhelmingly white with only one Hispanic teacher and only three or four teachers who speak Spanish. Even with a large number of ESL students, Valley High School has not hired teachers who are adequately trained in ESL. There is only one ESL teacher, who is responsible for all the ESL students. They are assigned to regular classes and then go to the ESL classrooms for what is supposed to be extra support. When I've gone into the ESL classroom, I've found students surfing random sites online and the teacher, also the yearbook advisor, working on pages for the annual. Because I was senior editor of the yearbook, he was very open to talking to me about his students, always complaining that they didn't work hard enough even though I could see they weren't being given meaningful work. I was frustrated because it was obvious that the ESL classroom did not engage either the students or the teacher. The students' language progress remained stagnant, while the expectations of standardized testing became increasingly more demanding, dooming ESL students to failure.

Another problem is inadequate counseling for Hispanic students and inadequate methods of assessing their progress so they can be placed in the right classes. When immigrant students need help, teachers often recruit other students to address their needs. As a student mentor, I was called upon a few times to speak with students about their performance in class. In one particular situation, the math teacher called me in to talk to a student who had decided to drop out. The teacher was visibly concerned for the student's welfare but didn't have any means for understanding or addressing the student's issues. The student told me that he did not feel like he belonged at school. The lack of adequate counseling sent the message that immigrant students were not worth fighting for to stay in our school.

Additionally, when students enter the school, their skills in other coursework are not taken into consideration. All ESL students are placed in the basic Math and English courses and while they might move down, sometimes as far as being placed in special education classes, they're never moved up. A student's aptitude in math or science may never get recognized in the four years that he or she is in high school because the ESL students move as a single group and take just about all coursework together. Their status as ESL students becomes the sole determinant of their identity as a student within the school system, and they are not given the same considerations and levels of attention required to grow and develop academically. Personally, I have fallen victim to our school's overlooking of student progress. When I entered the Valley School District in 8th grade, I had already taken several years of algebra and tested far above other students in my grade. At my previous school in another district, I had surpassed the school's highest level of math. In fact, my 5th–7th grade math instructor had to find advanced online material for me so that I could keep progressing. Entering the Valley School District, however, I regressed two years. Even though I communicated to both my math teacher and the counselor that I was being placed too low and that the nearby high school had several higher-level courses, I was kept in the same class. The next year, I was shocked to see that two 8th grade white students were in my 9th grade geometry class; the system had catered to them while it had denied to me an acknowledgement of the same earned achievement. I felt dismissed because I was Hispanic.

5   A third problem is that outside of the ESL classroom, in the regular classroom settings, teachers are often untrained in how to create safe multicultural dialogue. One time in sociology my teacher asked the class why the Hispanic students were performing so much worse than white students. I tried to explain that our support was inadequate. I stated that since most Hispanic students came from immigrant backgrounds, our parents weren't able to help us maneuver through the school system. In doing our homework, we had no one to turn to, and if the instructions were unclear, we did not have access to a resource such as an English speaking parent, something that many white students and faculty never even thought about when

considering this gap in performance. When I started talking about these things, white students around the room started becoming upset. They argued that they were hard workers and didn't have their parents do their homework for them. Obviously, my point was not to dismiss their efforts but to emphasize that these are two different worlds we're living in. Coming from an immigrant background, I and my fellow Hispanic students undoubtedly had more obstacles to overcome every step of the way. What was most troubling about this situation was that at no point did my sociology teacher step up and defend the validity of my arguments. Teachers need to know how to facilitate these multicultural clashes by helping make injustices more visible rather than marginalizing someone for bringing up uncomfortable issues.

Finally, Valley High School does little to honor cultural identity or reach out to immigrant families. My senior year I was president of the International Club (the only club at our school that had lots of immigrant student participation). Without my consent, or that of the members, my advisor began a transition to convert the International Club into the InterAct club affiliated with the community's Rotaract Club (part of Rotary). While this new connection with the Rotary would provide more funding, the only club that was primarily made up of Hispanic members was now being taken over by one sponsored by an all-white organization. In this transition, our advisor had pre-elected leaders to move it forward (also all white). By the time I graduated, the transition was well under way. In fact, on Cinco de Mayo, International Club's major event every year, our club members realized that our advisor didn't think this event was worth our time. As the only Mexican teacher, this advisor did not even advocate for the desires of our community. Ultimately, she turned her back on the members, and the following year InterAct became a primarily white club just like every other club at school.

The loss of a club supporting Hispanic students is matched by failure to create a welcoming environment for Hispanic parents and families. When immigrant parents come to the school, they have to wait around until they can find a translator if they want to speak to a teacher or administrator. Usually this interpreter is another student, creating awkward moments for parents who don't want to discuss their children's problems in front of another student. The school occasionally does try to reach out to Hispanic parents by holding Hispanic Nights where all the events are held in Spanish. However, all the other school events are held only in English. Considering that the school population is more than half Hispanic, the absence of any interpreters makes it clear the school thinks of itself as white. In addition, there are no translators at larger school events such as academic award nights or sporting banquets. As a result, immigrant parents and families feel isolated from the school and unwelcomed.

Debate remains over the exact or best procedures for helping immigrant ESL students successfully integrate into schools, but what is not debated is that these students deserve equal opportunities to learn and grow. Just as any other student, immigrant students should meet the demanding academic standards needed for higher education, but first they must have adequate support. It is essential that schools support educational reforms that address the problem areas apparent at Valley High School. Particularly, schools need to hire qualified ESL instructors, provide adequate counseling for immigrant students, enable teachers to develop multicultural sensitivity and skills at handling ethnic conflict, and provide outreach to immigrant families while valuing their culture.

Works Cited

Good, Mary Ellen; Masewicz, Sophia; Vogel, Linda. "Latino English Language Learners: Bridging Achievement and Cultural Gaps between Schools and Families." *Journal of Latinos & Education* 9.4 (2010): 321-39. *Education Research Complete.* Web. 15 Feb. 2014.
Roessingh, Hetty. "The Teacher Is the Key: Building Trust in ESL High School Programs." *Canadian Modern Language Review* 62.4 (2006): 563-90. *Education Research Complete.* Web. 17 Feb. 2014.

Critiquing "Silenced and Invisible: Problems of Hispanic Students at Valley High School"

MyWritingLab™

1. What criteria does Lorena Mendoza-Flores use to evaluate her high school's treatment of Hispanic students?
2. For evidence, Lorena uses primarily personal experiences, anecdotes, and observations. How effective do you find this evidence in developing the match part of her argument?
3. If Lorena were to identify the real name of her former high school and send the argument directly to the principal and to the city newspaper, how do you think it would be received?
4. How effectively does Lorena make appeals to *logos, ethos*, and *pathos?*

Our second reading, by student writer Christopher Moore, grew out of class discussions about what constitutes a "good news medium" and about whether today's college students are informed about the news.

Information Plus Satire: Why *The Daily Show* and *The Colbert Report* Are Good Sources of News for Young People

CHRISTOPHER MOORE (STUDENT)

Media commentators often complain that college-age students, along with much of the older population, are uninformed about the news. Fewer people today read mainstream newspapers or watch network news than in the past. Hard-core news junkies often get their news online from blog sites or from cable news. Meanwhile, less informed people use social networking tools like Twitter and Facebook for instant, unofficial news, often about popular culture or their favorite celebrities. Another possible source of news is *The Daily Show* and *The Colbert Report*. By presenting information and entertainment together, these shows attract a young audience, especially college-age students who shy away from newspapers or news networks like Fox or CNN. But are these actually good news sources? I will argue that they are, especially for a young audience, because they cover each day's important news and because their satire teaches viewers how to read the news rhetorically. The content on these shows provides up-to-date news stories and compels consumers to recognize that all news has an angle of vision demanding thoughtful processing, not simply blind consumption.

The first thing a good news source does is keep consumers up-to-date on the most important worldwide news. Since *The Daily Show* and *The Colbert Report* both air every weekday except Friday, they constantly present viewers with up-to-date news. Furthermore, all broadcasts are available online, as well as archived—if you missed Tuesday's episode, it's easy to backtrack so that you can stay current. Content published in these shows is trimmed to about 22 minutes (to allow for commercial time), so only the most pertinent information is presented. Consider, for example, the content published in January and February of 2011, which focused almost exclusively on the revolutions in Egypt and the volatile political climate in Tunisia. In these episodes, the shows pulled information from different news sources, both liberal and conservative, showing clips, news anchor commentary, or primary sources just the way other news sources do. In one episode during the turmoil in the Middle East, Stewart interviewed CNN reporter Anderson Cooper, who had just returned from reporting on the revolution from inside Egypt. Viewers watching Stewart might have had more insight into the controversial issues surrounding these revolutions than watchers of network news.

Skeptics, however, may argue that *The Daily Show* and *The Colbert Report* aren't providing real news but just satire. After all, the shows air on Comedy Central. Yet even a satirist needs material to satirize, and these satires always focus on current events, politics, or social trends. Moreover, watching *The Daily Show* offers deeper coverage than many network news programs because it focuses on what is most significant or important in the news. Whereas network news broadcasts tend to move quickly toward sports, weather, humanitarian "feel good" stories, or "breaking news" such as fires, robberies, or traffic accidents, Stewart and Colbert keep their satirical focus on major events with social or political significance.

The satirical methods used by Stewart and Colbert lead to my second and most important reason that *The Daily Show* and *The Colbert Report* are good sources of news: The satire teaches audiences how to "read" the news rhetorically. Unlike conventional news sources, the satire in these two shows unmasks the way that traditional news is packaged and framed, encouraging viewers to be skeptical of news. The satire in these shows functions by pointing out a news source's angle of vision, which promotes specific ideologies and presents news with an agenda. Consider the satirical character played by Stephen Colbert, who presents at one moment a far-right conservative ideology, only to compromise these beliefs at the next moment. His dramatization helps viewers see how rhetorical strategies create an angle of vision. For example, in an interview with Julian Assange, the founder of WikiLeaks, Colbert told his audience that he would show two versions of the interview: one of the unaltered footage and one that deliberately edited the footage to serve an agenda. Network news programs often employ the same tactics as Colbert, but in a much more subtle fashion. Editing may be one strategy, but opinion show hosts like Bill O'Reilly and other conservative news commentators employ a variety of tactics, like selective interviewing, cherry-picking news topics, following "fair and balanced" news with tacit conservative thinking, or any number of other methods. Showing the two versions of Colbert's interview is just one example that reminds viewers that information can be manipulated, presented out of context, edited, or reshaped. Foregrounding these strategies helps viewers criticize and analyze the news they digest.

5   The satire on these shows also points out the absurdities and pretensions of politicians, media commentators, and other public figures. An episode that discussed the Wisconsin labor protests in early 2011 focused on newly elected Republican Governor Scott Walker's decision to slash union benefits and collective bargaining rights to cover deficits in the state budget. When protestors took to the streets, Stewart showed clips from CNN, MSNBC, and CBS that called these protests "inspired by" or "having strong parallels to" revolutionary political action in Egypt or Cairo. However, Stewart rejected this comparison. He pointed out that "no citizens have died, no reporters have been abused, and Republican Governor Scott Walker was elected with 52 percent of the vote—dictators like Mubarak typically hold about 92 percent favor." Stewart's point, in other words, is that comparing two dissimilar things, as traditional news media had done, is unjust to both the Wisconsin protestors and the Tunisian and Egyptian rebels. It belittles those Tunisians or Egyptians who had the courage to raise their voices against dictators just as it distorts the very different political and economic issues and motivations at work in Wisconsin.

Satire also points out inconsistencies in news reporting, or the logical pitfalls into which politicians regularly stumble. In a skit in which Jon Stewart interviewed a conservative political candidate, he exposed inconsistencies in ideological views about when life begins. On the abortion issue, the candidate argued that life begins at conception, but on constitutional issues of citizenship, he argued that life begins at birth. Stewart took these two conflicting Republican ideologies and used a humorous either/or fallacy to show their inconsistency. Stewart argued that Obama was conceived by his mother in Hawaii. Therefore, if pro-life Republicans believe life begins at conception, then logically Obama is a natural citizen of Hawaii. Either Obama is a citizen, or life does not begin at conception, contradicting the fundamental right-to-life belief. Arguments like these help show how poorly constructed arguments or logical fallacies are common tools of news media for political discussions, facilitating a certain agenda or ideological perspective.

Viewers of *The Daily Show* or *The Colbert Report* will not get the same kind of news coverage that they would get from reading hard-copy news or an online newspaper, but they learn a healthy skepticism about the objective truthfulness of news. To many young people, entering a discussion on current affairs can be intimidating. Both Stephen Colbert and Jon Stewart make it easier for younger audiences to analyze the rhetorical dimension of news stories, thus allowing the viewer to see bias and angle of vision. The use of satire is a means of allowing entertainment and information to mingle together on a critical level. These approaches to delivering news are energizing, providing an alternative to lackluster news sources that can make us feel like we're drowning in a sea of information. The conservative Fox News commentator Bill O'Reilly once called my generation "a bunch of stone slackers" who sit at home unengaged in politics and watching *The Daily Show* and *The Colbert Report.* Yeah, right. But I wonder, where did he get his information?

Critiquing "Information Plus Satire"   MyWritingLab™

1. Christopher Moore's first criterion for a good news source is that it should keep viewers up-to-date with significant and important news rather than with ephemeral events like traffic accidents or celebrity divorces. Do you agree with Moore that *The Daily Show* and *The Colbert Report* keep viewers up-to-date with important news?
2. Moore's second criterion is the thought-provoking claim that a good news source teaches viewers to read the news rhetorically. What does he mean by reading the news rhetorically? How does he make his case? Are you persuaded?

Our final readings represent two different ethical arguments emerging from recent research on therapeutic cloning at the Oregon Health and Sciences University. The first article, by Judith Daar and Erez Aloni, appeared as an op-ed piece in the *Los Angeles Times* on March 21, 2014. Judith Daar, a professor of both law and medicine, is a member of the Ethics Committee of the American Society for Reproductive Medicine. Her co-author Erez Aloni is a professor at Whittier Law School. The second article appeared a year earlier (May 17, 2013) in *National Review.* It was written by Catholic writer Samuel Aquila, the archbishop of the Archdiocese of Denver, Colorado.

Three Genetic Parents—For One Healthy Baby

JUDITH DAAR AND EREZ ALONI

Since January, a new California law allows for a child to have more than two legal parents. But children are still limited to two genetic parents. That could change soon, if the Food and Drug Administration approves human clinical trials for a technique known as mitochondrial replacement, which would enable a child to inherit DNA from three parents.

News of the pending application has caused a kind of panic not seen since Dolly the sheep was cloned, raising the possibility of a single genetic parent. But far from being the end of the human race as we know it, the technique might be a way to prevent hundreds of mitochondrial-linked diseases, which affect about one in 5,000 people.

The idea of multi-person reproductive collaborations is not new. Over the last several decades we have acclimated to various forms of assisted reproductive technologies. Indeed, in the U.S. about 75,000 infants are born each year to parents who enlist the aid of egg donors, sperm donors or gestational carriers. These methods, however, still involve the "traditional" merger of DNA from one male and one female

Mitochondrial replacement would alter this two-genetic-parent model by introducing a third set of DNA into the procreative process. The technique would enable women who carry harmful mutations in their mitochondria to have a child without those harmful mutations. As with all human reproduction, the child would carry a combination of genes from one male and one female. However, in this technique, the nucleus of the mother's egg would be injected into a "third parent's" nucleus-free egg containing healthy mitochondrial DNA. As a result, the child would inherit the characteristics of the original male and female but have healthy mitochondria from a third person.

5 Experiments employing the technique conducted on monkeys resulted in healthy offspring that did not carry the harmful mutation. Now, a team at Oregon Health and Sciences University is seeking approval from the FDA to begin human clinical trials.

It seems likely that, if it is proved safe and effective, mitochondrial replacement will eventually join the panoply of techniques facilitating the birth of healthy children through assisted conception. But it should be no surprise that the new technology is causing a furor.

The introduction of assisted reproductive technologies has followed a predictable pattern: initial panic followed by widespread condemnation, followed by gradual acceptance as a technique becomes more widespread. In the 1950s, when reports of pregnancies using donor sperm first appeared in medical journals, lawmakers declared the process "mechanical adultery" and sought its criminalization. Early reports of success with in vitro fertilization in the 1970s provoked editorials that decried the process as totally immoral. In the 1990s, the introduction of preimplantation diagnosis of genetic diseases provoked allegations of a war on disabled individuals.

Today, detractors remain, but the methods have been embraced as the standard of care in reproductive medicine. Once a technique proves safe and effective, its ability to assist in the birth of

healthy children generally paves the way for public approval.

For some, the introduction of a third genetic parent is alarming because the novel genetic configuration could be embedded in the child's DNA in perpetuity, with unknown implications for future generations. But the panic also rests in part on simple discomfort with upending the notion of genetic parenthood involving just two people.

10 A similar anxiety seized the public this year after California authorized judges to recognize more than two people as a child's lawful parents. The law grew out of a horrendous situation in which the court's inability to recognize a third parent diverted a young child into foster care. Though it's hardly on par with the scientific breakthrough represented by mitochondrial replacement, the so-called three-parent law stirred deep fears about the durability of traditional family life in the modern era.

But the fears about three-parent possibilities—both genetic and legal—are likely to subside as people realize that they are aimed at one goal: the well-being of children. The California law orders judges to recognize three parents when not doing so "would otherwise be detrimental to the child." And mitochondrial replacement will be employed to avoid transmission of a heritable disease. If the "power of three" has the ability to improve a child's well-being, isn't that something worth embracing?

The "Therapeutic Cloning" of Human Embryos

SAMUEL AQUILA

Oscar Wilde's *The Picture of Dorian Gray* is the sort of timeless morality tale students read as an antidote, or at least an objection, to the hedonism that seems to follow naturally from youthful ideas about immortality.

The story is familiar to many: Dorian Gray is a narcissist who wishes that a portrait of him—his copy in paint—would age in his place. His wish comes true, and though his life is corrupted by a pursuit of pleasure, only his painted visage bears the effects. Dorian himself is visibly unscathed, though the novel's fatal climax exposes a soul rendered ugly by a life of egoistic debauchery.

The Picture of Dorian Gray took on a particular prescience yesterday. Scientists at Oregon Health and Science University reported a successful incidence of cloning, one that relied on the same method that researchers used 17 years ago to clone Dolly the sheep. This week, the cloned embryos were not sheep; they were human beings. The work is heralded as the success of "therapeutic cloning."

We will hear a lot about therapeutic cloning in the news this week. Researchers distinguish between "therapeutic cloning," which creates embryos in order to harvest their stem cells, and "reproductive cloning," which has the intention of a live birth. The Oregon researchers insist that theirs was not an act of "reproductive cloning."

5 But the distinction is spurious. *Both* types of cloning are reproductive. Both bring a new human being into existence. In fact, so-called therapeutic cloning is the more heinous because the process is intended to create life, exploit it, and then destroy it.

Consider what the cloning breakthrough means. Scientists have discovered how to create perfect human copies, to be used for the sole purpose of growing tissue in the effort to combat disease, and then these copies will be destroyed. From a scientific perspective, this breakthrough could solve, among other problems, that of tissue rejection or a delay that renders organ transplant unfeasible. From the standpoint of materialism, there has been no greater advance in regenerative medicine. Through therapeutic cloning, a person's health can be enhanced immeasurably—and only the copy, the embryo, will suffer the effects.

The problem is that the embryo is not merely a copy. The embryo is not an extension of the patient who donated the DNA, a cell bank to be utilized without consequence. The embryo, though genetically identical, is a new manifestation of human life, endowed by its very being with dignity. The embryo is a human being.

The humanity of the cloned embryo will be aggressively denied in the weeks to come. Though human life demonstrably begins at the embryonic stage of development, the created embryo will be presented as a collection of tissue, a biological tabula rasa from which organs can be grown. Scientists will seek more funding, and the Dickey Amendment, which prohibits federal funding for the creation of cloned embryos, will be attacked.

In 1968, Pope Paul VI warned in *Humanae Vitae* that the sexual revolution, beginning with a cultural acceptance of the contraceptive mentality, would lead to a wholesale denial of human dignity and the family. Now we are cloning embryos to destroy them. It will be only a matter of time before therapeutic cloning will cede to reproductive cloning. If we don't seriously contemplate the ethical consequences of therapeutic cloning now, eventually cloned human beings will be born in America.

The "progress" of therapeutic cloning will not be victimless. But the victims will be hidden from sight, tucked away in the dark like Dorian's decaying portrait.

The first class of victims, and the ones most pressing on our consciences, will be the embryos: brought into existence to be used, and then killed. If nurtured, as in a womb, these embryos would grow into fetuses, and then infants, and then children. They are, no matter their size, human beings. But because they are small and have no voice and offer such tremendous possibility, they will be ignored.

10   The embryos will be a class of human beings created only to be exploited and discarded.

The second class of victims will be the rest of us. We will be the ones remaining healthy and making progress and defeating disease—all by means of killing. We will be the ones who appear beautiful, while our souls embrace the most harrowing kind of social utilitarianism and darkness. If we ignore the problem, as we have done with contraception and abortion, we will only sink into a more violent depravity, like the one that befell vain Dorian Gray. We will be the ones whose portrait grows ever uglier, and who grow ever closer to madness.

Critiquing "Three Genetic Parents—For One Healthy Baby" and "The 'Therapeutic Cloning' of Human Embryos"   MyWritingLab™

1. In "Three Genetic Parents—For One Healthy Baby," Daar and Aloni note that news coming from cloning research at Oregon Health and Science University "has caused a kind of panic not seen since Dolly the sheep was cloned." An example of this panic is the earlier *National Review* article by Archbishop Aquila. Summarize Aquila's objection to both therapeutic and reproductive cloning. What rhetorical strategies do Daar and Aloni use to counter the objections of those like Archbishop Aquila?

2. Identify in both articles examples of arguments from consequence and arguments from principle used either to support the authors' claims or to summarize opposing claims.

3. Aquila acknowledges the health benefits of therapeutic cloning, particularly its potential for curing or preventing certain diseases. He recognizes also that many people will consider therapeutic cloning a moral good because it produces good consequences. To make his case for the moral evil of cloning, he creates an analogy argument based on Oscar Wilde's gothic novel *The Picture of Dorian Gray*. Explain how this analogy functions. What does Aquila compare to what?

MyWritingLab™

Visit Ch. 13 Evaluation and Ethical Arguments in *MyWritingLab* to complete the For Writing and Discussion, Examining Visual Arguments, Critiquing, and Writing Assignments and to test your understanding of the chapter objectives.

Proposal Arguments

14

What you will learn in this chapter:

14.1 To explain the special features and concerns of proposal arguments

14.2 To use a problem-solution-justification structure to develop proposal arguments

14.3 To use heuristic strategies to develop supporting reasons for your proposal argument

14.4 To use words and images to create an advocacy poster or advertisement

14.5 To write your own proposal argument

Proposal arguments are essential for the workings of a free and open society. A proposal argument motivates its audience to recognize a problem and then proposes a solution to the problem. When effective, proposal arguments call an audience to action. Whether you are writing a grant proposal to seek funding for a research project, a practical proposal for remedying a problem at your workplace, or a policy proposal to address a national issue, proposal arguments are among the most important kinds of writing you will ever be called upon to produce.

Case 1   Should the Supreme Court Overturn *Roe v. Wade?*

Among the most heated debates in the United States is whether the due process and privacy protections of the Fourteenth Amendment can be extended to a woman's right to an abortion. The right-to-life movement has intensified its efforts to restrict access to abortions at the state level and to overturn *Roe v. Wade* in the U.S. Supreme Court. Meanwhile, pro-choice advocates such as Planned Parenthood have vigorously defended a woman's right to an abortion. Both sides make effective use of visual arguments. Right-to-life groups frequently use posters showing ultrasound images of unborn babies (often not using the word "fetus"). The poster on the following page, sponsored by Planned Parenthood, features a starkly black question mark that on second look is seen to be made from a coat hanger. It makes an implied proposal claim ("Abortion should remain legal") and supports it with a consequence argument: If abortions are outlawed, women will have abortions anyway—using coat hangers instead of medically safe procedures. The image of the coat hanger (reminiscent of horror stories about abortions prior to *Roe v. Wade*) appeals simultaneously to *logos* and *pathos*.

When
your right
to an abortion
is taken away,
what are you
going to
do

Reproductive rights are under attack. The Pro-Choice Public Education Project. It's pro-choice or no choice.
1(688)253-CHOICE or www.protect.choice.org

Case 2   How Should the United States Reduce the Carbon Footprint of Automobiles?

The concern for climate change—combined with the high price of gasoline—has increased the popularity of small, energy-efficient cars. Much debated among policy makers is the role that federal or state governments should play in further promoting a green transportation system. Some argue that the government should stay out of free markets, letting buyers decide for themselves what kinds of cars they want to buy. Others argue that free markets do not currently make gasoline consumers pay for the "externalities" of gasoline consumption—particularly the cost to the environment of loading more carbon into the atmosphere. Concerned citizens have proposed dozens of ideas for reducing the carbon footprint of cars and trucks. Among the proposals are the following: placing a "green tax" on gasoline; requiring auto manufacturers to increase the fuel efficiency of their fleets; giving tax credits for buying a fuel-efficient car; increasing incentives for carpooling or taking public transportation; increasing the cost of parking; charging different gas prices at the pump (with higher prices for less fuel-efficient cars); retrofitting cars to burn natural gas; and rebuilding cities so that housing is closer to worksites.

The Special Features and Concerns of Proposal Arguments

14.1 Explain the special features and concerns of proposal arguments

Although proposal arguments are the last type of argument we examine, they are among the most common arguments that you will encounter or be called on to write. The essence of proposal arguments is that they call for action. In reading a proposal, the audience is enjoined to make a decision and then to act on it—to *do* something. Proposal arguments are sometimes called *should or ought* arguments because those helping verbs express the obligation to act. They typically have a three-part structure: (1) description of a problem, (2) proposed solution, and (3) justification for the proposed solution. In the justification section of your proposal argument, you develop *because* clauses of the kinds you have practiced throughout this text.

Practical Proposals versus Policy Proposals

For instructional purposes, we distinguish between two kinds of proposal arguments—*practical proposals,* which propose an action to solve some kind of local or immediate problem, and *policy proposals,* which propose a broad plan of action to solve major social, economic, or political problems affecting the common good. A student's proposal to build bike paths on campus would be an example of a practical proposal. In contrast, an argument that the United States should abolish the income tax would be a policy proposal.

The primary difference is the narrowness versus breadth of the concern. *Practical* proposals are narrow, local, and concrete; they focus on the nuts and bolts of getting something done in the here and now. They are often concerned with the exact size of a piece of steel, the precise duties of a new person to be hired, or a close estimate of the cost of paint or computers to be purchased. *Policy* proposals, in contrast, are concerned with the broad outline and shape of a course of action, often on a regional, national, or even international issue. What government should do about overcrowding of prisons would be a problem addressed by policy proposals. How to improve the security alarm system for the county jail would be addressed by a practical proposal.

Learning to write both kinds of proposals is valuable. Researching and writing a *policy* proposal is an excellent way to practice the responsibilities of citizenship, which require the ability to understand complex issues and to weigh positive and negative consequences of policy choices. In your professional life, writing *practical* proposals may well be among your most important duties on the job. Effective proposal writing is the lifeblood of many companies and also constitutes one of the most powerful ways you can identify and help solve problems.

Toulmin Framework for a Proposal Argument

The Toulmin schema is particularly useful for proposal arguments because it helps you support your proposal with reasons linked to your audience's beliefs, assumptions, and values. Suppose that your university is debating whether to banish fraternities and sororities. Suppose further that you are in favor of banishing the Greek system. One of your arguments is that eliminating the Greek system will improve your university's academic reputation. The following chart shows how you might use the Toulmin schema to make this line of reasoning as persuasive as possible.

Toulmin Analysis of the Greek System Argument

ENTHYMEME

CLAIM Our university should eliminate the Greek system

REASON because doing so will improve our university's academic reputation.

GROUNDS

Evidence that eliminating the Greek system will improve our academic reputation:

• Excessive party atmosphere of some Greek houses emphasizes social life rather than studying—we are known as a party school.

• Last year the average GPA of students in fraternities and sororities was lower than the GPA of non-Greek students.

• New pledges have so many house duties and initiation rites that their studies suffer.

• Many new students think about rush more than about the academic life.

CONDITIONS OF REBUTTAL
Attacking the reason and grounds

• Many of the best students are Greeks. Last year's highest-GPA award went to a sorority woman, and several other Greeks won prestigious graduate school scholarships.

• Statistics on grades are misleading. Many houses had a much higher average GPA than the university average. Total GPA was brought down by a few rowdy houses.

• Many other high-prestige universities have Greek systems.

• There are ways to tone down the party atmosphere on campus without abolishing the Greek system.

• Greeks contribute significantly to the community through service projects.

WARRANT

It is good for our university to achieve a better academic reputation.

BACKING

• The school would attract more serious students, leading to increased prestige.

• Campus would be more academically focused and attract better faculty.

• Losing the "party-school" reputation would put us in better light for taxpayers and legislators.

• Students would graduate with more skills and knowledge.

CONDITIONS OF REBUTTAL
Attacking the warrant and backing

• No one will argue that it is not good to have a strong academic reputation.

• However, skeptics may say that eliminating sororities and fraternities won't improve the university's academic reputation but will hurt its social life and its wide range of living options.

Special Concerns for Proposal Arguments

In their call for action, proposal arguments entail certain emphases and audience concerns that you don't generally face with other kinds of arguments. Let's look briefly at some of these special concerns.

- **The need for presence.** To persuade people to *act* on your proposal, particularly if the personal or financial cost of acting is high, you must give your argument presence as well as intellectual force. By *presence* we mean an argument's ability to grip your readers' hearts and imaginations as well as their intellects. You can give presence to an argument through appeals to *pathos,* such as effective use of details, provocative statistics, dialogue, illustrative narratives, and compelling examples that show the reader the seriousness of the problem you are addressing or the consequences of not acting on your proposal.

- **The need to overcome people's natural conservatism.** Another difficulty with proposals is the innate conservatism of all human beings, whatever their political persuasion, as suggested by the popular adage "If it ain't broke, don't fix it." The difficulty of proving that something needs fixing is compounded by the fact that frequently the status quo appears to be working. So sometimes when writing a proposal, you can't argue that what we have is bad, but only that what we could have would be better. Often, then, a proposal argument will be based not on present evils but on the evils of lost potential. And getting an audience to accept lost potential may be difficult indeed, given the inherently abstract nature of potentiality.

- **The difficulty of predicting future consequences.** Further, most proposal makers will be forced to predict consequences of their proposed action. As the "law of unintended consequences" suggests, few major decisions lead neatly to their anticipated results without surprises along the way. So when we claim that our proposal will lead to good consequences, we can expect our audience to be skeptical.

- **The problem of evaluating consequences.** A final problem for proposal writers is the difficulty of evaluating consequences. In government and industry, managers often use a *cost-benefit analysis* to reduce all consequences to a single-scale comparison, usually money. Although this scale may work well in some circumstances, it can lead to grotesquely inappropriate conclusions in other situations. Just how does one balance the environmental benefits of a green tax on gasoline against the suffering of drivers who can't afford to get to work? Also a benefit for one group often entails a cost for others. For example, a higher minimum wage will benefit low-wage workers but at a cost to consumers, who must pay higher prices, or to other low-wage workers who get laid off.

These, then, are some of the general difficulties facing someone who sets out to write a proposal argument. Although these difficulties may seem daunting, the rest of this chapter offers strategies to help you overcome them and produce a successful proposal.

EXAMINING VISUAL ARGUMENTS

MyWritingLab™

A Proposal Claim

This photo of a dead baby albatross on a Pacific island near an albatross nesting ground resembles the photos taken by environmental photographer Chris Jordan in his well-known 2009 exhibit entitled "Midway: Message from the Gyre." The purpose of that exhibit was to draw attention to the effects of the increasing volumes of ocean garbage on albatrosses, who mistake the garbage for food. How could this photo be used to generate concern and activism regarding this environmental problem? The colorful, plastic-filled carcass of the baby albatross creates a complex appeal to *pathos* in the way that it illustrates the problem. What verbal text would you use to interpret the message of the photo and call people to action?

Developing a Proposal Argument

14.2 Use a problem-solution-justification structure to develop proposal arguments

Writers of proposal arguments must focus in turn on three main phases or stages of the argument: showing that a problem exists, explaining the proposed solution, and offering a justification.

Convincing Your Readers that a Problem Exists

There is one argumentative strategy generic to all proposal arguments: calling your reader's attention to a problem. In some situations, your intended audience may already be aware of the problem and may have even asked for solutions. In such cases, you do not need to develop the problem extensively or motivate your audience to solve it. But in most situations, awakening your readers to the existence of a problem—a problem they may well not have recognized before—is your first important challenge. You must give your problem presence through anecdotes, telling statistics, or other means that show readers how the problem affects people or otherwise has important stakes. Your goal is to gain your readers' intellectual assent to the depth, range, and potential seriousness of the problem and thereby motivate them to want to solve it.

Typically, the arguer develops the problem in one of two places—either in the introduction prior to the presentation of the arguer's proposed solution or in the body of the paper as the first main reason justifying the proposed solution. In the second instance the writer's first *because* clause has the following structure: "We should do this action *because* it addresses a serious problem."

Here is how one student writer gave presence to a proposal, addressed to the chair of the mathematics department at her school, calling for redesign of the first-year calculus curriculum in order to slow its pace. She wants the chair to see the problem from her perspective.

Example Passage Giving Presence to a Problem

For me, who wants to become a high school math teacher, the problem with introductory calculus is not its difficulty but its pace. My own experience in the Calculus 134 and 135 sequence last year showed me that it was not the learning of calculus that was difficult for me. I was able to catch on to the new concepts. My problem was that it went too fast. Just as I was assimilating new concepts and feeling the need to reinforce them, the class was on to a new topic before I had full mastery of the old concept.... Part of the reason for the fast pace is that calculus is a feeder course for computer science and engineering. If prospective engineering students can't learn the calculus rapidly, they drop out of the program. The high dropout rate benefits the Engineering School because they use the math course to weed out an overabundance of engineering applicants. Thus the pace of the calculus course is geared to the needs of the engineering curriculum, not to the needs of someone like me, who wants to be a high school mathematics teacher and who believes that my own difficulties with math—combined with my love for it—might make me an excellent math teacher.

By describing the fast pace of the math curriculum from the perspective of a future math teacher rather than an engineering student, this writer brings visibility to a problem. What before didn't look like a problem (it is good to weed out weak engineering majors) suddenly became a problem (it is bad to weed out future math teachers). Establishing herself as a serious student genuinely interested in learning calculus, she gave presence to the problem by calling attention to it in a new way.

Showing the Specifics of Your Proposal

Having decided that there is a problem to be solved, you should lay out your thesis, which is a proposal for solving the problem. Your goal now is to stress the feasibility of your solution, including costs. The art of proposal making is the art of the possible. To be sure, not all proposals require elaborate descriptions of the implementation process. If you are proposing, for example, that a local PTA chapter buy new tumbling mats for the junior high gym classes, the procedures for buying the mats will probably be irrelevant. But in many arguments the specifics of your proposal—the actual step-by-step methods of implementing it—may be instrumental in winning your audience's support.

You will also need to show how your proposal will solve the problem either partially or wholly. Sometimes you may first need to convince your reader that the problem is solvable and not something intractably rooted in "the way things are," such as earthquakes or jealousy. In other words, expect that some members of your audience will be skeptical about the ability of any proposal to solve the problem you are addressing. You may well need, therefore, to "listen" to this point of view in your refutation section and to argue that your problem is at least partially solvable.

In order to persuade your audience that your proposal can work, you can follow any one of several approaches. A typical approach is to use a causal argument to show that your solution is feasible. Another approach is to use a resemblance argument to show how similar proposals have been successful elsewhere. Or, if similar things have failed in the past, you try to show how the present situation is different.

Convincing Your Readers that the Benefits of Your Proposal Outweigh the Costs

The justification phase of a proposal argument will need extensive development in some arguments and minimal development in others, again depending on your particular problem and the rhetorical context of your proposal. If your audience already acknowledges the seriousness of the problem you are addressing and has simply been waiting for the right solution to come along, then your argument will be successful, so long as you can convince your audience that your solution will work and that it won't cost too much. Such arguments depend on the clarity of your proposal and the feasibility of its being implemented.

But what if the costs are high? What if your readers don't think the problem is serious? What if they don't appreciate the benefits of solving the problem or the bad consequences of not solving it? In such cases you have to develop persuasive reasons for enacting your proposal. You may also have to determine who has the power to act on your proposal and apply arguments directly to that person's or agency's immediate interests. You need to know to whom or to what your power source is beholden or responsive and what values your power source holds that can be appealed to. You're looking, in short, for the best pressure points.

Using Heuristic Strategies to Develop Supporting Reasons for Your Proposal

14.3 Use heuristic strategies to develop supporting reasons for your proposal argument

To help you find supporting reasons for your proposal—the pressure points that will move your audience—we offer two heuristic strategies. (A *heuristic* is an exploratory problem-solving technique or invention aid that helps you generate ideas.) We call these heuristics the "claim types" strategy and the "stock issue" strategy.

The "Claim Types" Strategy

In Chapter 10 we explained how evaluation and proposal claims often use claims about category, cause, or resemblance for their supporting reasons. This fact leads to a powerful idea-generating strategy based on arguments from category (particularly from a category of actions that adhere to a certain principle), on arguments from consequences, or on arguments from resemblance. This "claim types" strategy is illustrated in the following chart:

Explanation of Claim Types Strategy for Supporting a Proposal Claim

Claim Type	Generic Template	Example from Biotechnology Issue
Argument from principle or category	We should do this action ■ because doing so adheres to this good principle [or] ■ because this action belongs to this good category	We should support genetically modified foods ■ because doing so values scientific reason over emotion [or] ■ because genetically modified foods are safe [belong to the category of safe things]
Argument from consequences	■ because this action will lead to these good consequences	■ because biotech crops can reduce world hunger ■ because biotech crops can improve the environment by reducing use of pesticides
Argument from resemblance	■ because this action has been done successfully elsewhere [or] ■ because this action is like this other good action	■ because genetic modification is like natural crossbreeding that has been accelerated [or] ■ because genetic modification of food is like scientific advancements in medicine

Before we give you some simple strategies for using this approach, let's illustrate it with another example.

The United States should levy a "carbon tax" on carbon-based fuels.

- Because such a tax accords with the free-market principle that the price of a good should reflect the full cost of production (category/principle)
- Because such a tax will accelerate the transition to cleaner fuels and thus help reduce global warming (cause/consequence)
- Because this approach is similar to the market-based tax on sulfur emissions that helped solve the problem of acid rain (resemblance)

Note how each of these supporting reasons appeals to the value system of different kinds of voters. The writer argues that a carbon tax belongs to the category of things that use free market principles (particularly valued by conservative, pro-business voters); that it will lead to the good consequence of reducing global warming (valued particularly by environmentalists and others worried about climate change); and that it is similar to something that has already proved successful (the market-based approach to fighting acid rain, which has been hailed by both liberals and conservatives). The claim types strategy for generating ideas is easy to apply in practice. The following chart shows you how.

Suggestions for Applying the Claim Types Strategy to Your Proposal

Claim Type	Your Goal	Thinking Strategy
Argument from principle or category	Show how your proposed action follows a principle valued by your audience or belongs to a category valued by your audience.	Think of how your proposed action adheres to an audience-valued rule or principle or belongs to an audience-valued category (for example, "doing this action is kind, just, constitutional, appropriately restrained, safe, efficient," and so forth).
Argument from consequences	Show how your proposed action will lead to consequences valued by your audience.	Brainstorm consequences of your proposal and identify those that the audience will agree are good.
Argument from resemblance	Show how your proposed action has been done successfully elsewhere or is like another action valued by your audience.	Find analogies that compare your proposed action to something the audience already values or find previous places or times that your proposed action (or something similar to it) has been done successfully.

■ ■ ■   **FOR WRITING AND DISCUSSION   Generating Ideas Using the Claim   MyWritingLab™**
Types Strategy

Individual task: Use the strategies of principle/category, consequence, and resemblance to create *because* clauses that support each of the following claims. Try to have at least one *because* clause from each of the claim types, but generate as many reasons as possible. Don't worry about whether any individual reason exactly fits the category. The purpose is to stimulate thinking, not fill in the slots.

Example

Congress should not pass gun control laws (proposal claim)

- because the Second Amendment guarantees the right to own guns (principle or category)
- because owning a gun allows citizens to protect themselves, their homes, and their loved ones from intruders (consequence)

- because laws to ban guns will be as ineffective as laws to ban alcohol during Prohibition (resemblance)

    1. Colleges should require a service learning course for graduation.
    2. Restaurants should be required to post calorie counts and other ingredient information for all menu items.
    3. Division-I college athletes should receive salaries.
    4. Alcohol should not be allowed on campus.
    5. Parents should be heavily taxed for having more than two children.

Group task: Share your efforts with classmates. Then, working in small groups or a whole class, repeat the exercise, taking the opposite position on each issue.

The "Stock Issues" Strategy

Another effective heuristic for a proposal argument is to ask yourself a series of questions based on the "stock issues" strategy. Suppose, for example, you wanted to develop the following argument: "In order to solve the problem of students who won't take risks with their writing, the faculty should adopt a pass/fail method of grading in all writing courses." The stock issues strategy invites the writer to consider "stock" ways (that is, common, usual, frequently repeated ways) that such arguments can be conducted.

Stock issue 1: *Is there really a problem here that needs to be solved?* Is it really true that a large number of student writers won't take risks in their writing? Is this problem more serious than other writing problems such as undeveloped ideas, lack of organization, and poor sentence structure? This stock issue invites the writer to convince her audience that a true problem exists. Conversely, an opponent to the proposal may argue that a true problem does not exist.

Stock issue 2: *Will the proposed solution really solve this problem?* Is it true that a pass/fail grading system will cause students to take more risks with their writing? Will more interesting, surprising, and creative essays result from pass/fail grading? Or will students simply put less effort into their writing? This stock issue prompts a supporter to demonstrate that the proposal will solve the problem; in contrast, it prompts the opponent to show that the proposal won't work.

Stock issue 3: *Can the problem be solved more simply, without disturbing the status quo?* An opponent of the proposal may agree that a problem exists and that the proposed solution might solve it. However, the opponent may say, "Are there not less radical ways to solve this problem? If we want more creative and risk-taking student essays, can't we just change our grading criteria so that we reward risky papers and penalize conventional ones?" This stock issue prompts supporters to show that *only* the proposed solution will solve the problem and that no minor tinkering with the status quo will be adequate. Conversely, opponents will argue that the problem can be solved without acting on the proposal.

Stock issue 4: *Is the proposed solution really practical? Does it stand a chance of actually being enacted?* Here an opponent to the proposal may agree that the proposal would work but contends that it involves pie-in-the-sky idealism. Nobody will vote to change the existing system so radically; therefore, it is a waste of our time to debate it. Following this prompt, supporters would have to argue that pass/fail grading is workable and that enough faculty members are disposed to it that the proposal is worth debating. Opponents may argue that the faculty is so traditional that pass/fail has utterly no chance of being accepted, despite its merits.

Stock issue 5: *What will be the unforeseen positive and negative consequences of the proposal?* Suppose we do adopt a pass/fail system. What positive or negative consequences may occur that are different from what we at first predicted? Using this prompt, an opponent may argue that pass/fail grading will reduce the effort put forth by students and that the long-range effect will be writing of even lower quality than we have now. Supporters would try to find positive consequences—perhaps a new love of writing for its own sake rather than for the sake of a grade.

■ ■ ■   FOR CLASS DISCUSSION   Brainstorming Ideas for a Proposal

The following collaborative task takes approximately two class days to complete. The exercise takes you through the process of creating a proposal argument.

1. In small groups, identify and list several major problems facing students in your college or university.
2. Decide among yourselves which are the most important of these problems and rank them in order of importance.
3. Take your group's number one problem and explore answers to the following questions. Group recorders should be prepared to present their group's answers to the class as a whole:

   a. Why is the problem a problem?
   b. For whom is the problem a problem?
   c. How will these people suffer if the problem is not solved? (Give specific examples.)
   d. Who has the power to solve the problem?
   e. Why hasn't the problem been solved up to this point?
   f. How can the problem be solved? (That is, create a proposal.)
   g. What are the probable benefits of acting on your proposal?
   h. What costs are associated with your proposal?
   i. Who will bear those costs?
   j. Why should this proposal be enacted?
   k. Why is it better than alternative proposals?
4. As a group, draft an outline for a proposal argument in which you

   a. describe the problem and its significance.
   b. propose your solution to the problem.
   c. justify your proposal by showing how the benefits of adopting that proposal outweigh the costs.
5. Recorders for each group should write their group's outline on the board and be prepared to explain it to the class.

Proposal Arguments as Advocacy Posters or Advertisements

14.4 Use words and images to create an advocacy poster or advertisement

A frequently encountered kind of proposal argument is the one-page newspaper or magazine advertisement often purchased by advocacy groups to promote a cause. Such arguments also appear as Web pages or as posters or fliers. These condensed advocacy arguments are marked by their bold, abbreviated, tightly planned format. The creators of these arguments know they must work fast to capture our attention, give presence to a problem, advocate a solution, and enlist our support. Advocacy advertisements frequently use photographs, images, or icons that appeal to a reader's emotions and imagination. In addition to images, they often use different type sizes and styles. Large-type text in these documents frequently takes the form of slogans or condensed thesis statements written in an arresting style. To outline and justify their solutions, creators of advocacy ads often put main supporting reasons in bulleted lists and sometimes enclose carefully selected facts and quotations in boxed sidebars. To add an authoritative *ethos,* the arguments often include fine-print footnotes and bibliographies. (For more detailed discussion of how advocacy posters and advertisements use images and arrange text for rhetorical effect, see Chapter 9 on visual argument.)

Another prominent feature of these condensed, highly visual arguments is their appeal to the audience through a direct call for a course of action: go to an advocacy Web site to find more information on how to support the cause; send an e-mail to a decision maker or political representative; vote for or against the proposition or the candidate; or donate money to a cause.

An example of a student-produced advocacy poster is shown in Figure 14.1. Here, environmental studies student Janie Bube urges residents of her city to build rain gardens to help solve the problem of excess stormwater. At the top of this poster, Janie uses a photo of a flood she took during her internship fieldwork to give the problem presence. She then offers her proposed solution, made visually appealing by another of her own photos—a neighborhood rain garden. She offers three reasons to justify the choice of rain gardens, asserting why and how rain gardens work. The final lines of the poster give readers a Web site for more information. The rhetorical effect of the text, image, and layout is to attract readers' attention, remind them of the problem, and push them toward adopting her proposed solution.

WRITING ASSIGNMENT   A Proposal Argument

MyWritingLab™

14.5 To write your own proposal argument

Option 1: A Practical Proposal Addressing a Local Problem   Write a practical proposal offering a solution to a local problem. Your proposal should have three main sections: (1) description of the problem, (2) proposed solution, and (3) justification. Proposals are usually accompanied by a *letter of transmittal*— a one-page business letter that introduces the proposal to its intended audience and provides some needed background about the writer. Document design is important in practical proposals, which are aimed at busy people who have to make many decisions under time constraints. An effective design helps establish the writer's *ethos* as a quality-oriented professional and helps make the reading of the proposal as easy as possible. For a student example of a practical proposal, see Megan Johnson's argument on pages 322–325.

Is Stormwater Turning Your Street Into a Lake?

Installing green stormwater infrastructure technologies like rain gardens will address this problem.

Install a rain garden to:

- Slow, retain, and absorb runoff
- Replicate the functioning of a forest in cleaning pollutants from the water
- Add natural beauty

For further information contact RainWise through Seattle Public Utilities at rainwise@seattle.gov

FIGURE 14.1   Student advocacy poster

Option 2: A Policy Proposal as a Guest Editorial   Write a two- to three-page policy proposal suitable for publication as a feature editorial in a college or city newspaper, on an appropriate Web site, or in a publication associated with a particular group, such as a church newsletter or employee bulletin. The voice and style of your argument should be aimed at readers of your chosen publication or Web site. Your editorial should have the following features:

1. The identification of a problem (Persuade your audience that this is a genuine problem that needs solving; give it presence.)
2. A proposal for action that will help alleviate the problem
3. A justification of your solution (the reasons why your audience should accept your proposal and act on it)

Option 3: A Researched Argument Proposing Public Policy   Write an eight- to twelve-page proposal argument as a formal research paper, using researched data for development and support. In business and professional life, this kind of research proposal is often called a *white paper*, which recommends a course of action internally within an organization or externally to a client or stakeholder. An example of a researched policy proposal is student writer Ivan Snook's "Flirting with Disaster: An Argument against Integrating Women into the Combat Arms," on pages 326–330.

Option 4: Multimedia Project: A One-Page Advocacy Poster or Advertisement   Using the strategies of visual argument discussed in Chapter 9 and on pages 316–317 of this chapter, create a one-page advocacy advertisement urging action on a public issue. Your advertisement should be designed for publication in a newspaper or Web site or for distribution as a poster or flier. For an example of a student-produced advocacy poster, see Janie Bube's poster shown in Figure 14.1 on page 317.

Option 5: Multimedia Project: A Proposal Speech with Visual Aids   Deliver a proposal argument as a prepared but extemporaneous speech of approximately five to eight minutes, supported with visual aids created on presentation software such as PowerPoint or Prezi. Your speech should present a problem, propose a solution, and justify the solution with reasons and evidence. Use visual aids to give "presence" to the problem and to enhance appeals to *logos*, *ethos*, and *pathos*. Good aids use visual strategies to create encapsulated visual arguments; they are not simply bullet point outlines of your speech. Sandy Wainscott's speech outline and selected PowerPoint slides (pages 333–335) illustrate this genre.

Exploring Ideas

Because *should or ought* issues are among the most common sources of arguments, you may already have ideas for proposal issues. To think of ideas for practical proposals, try making an idea map of local problems you would like to see solved. For initial spokes, try trigger words such as the following:

- Problems at my university (dorms, parking, registration system, financial aid, campus appearance, clubs, curriculum, intramural program, athletic teams)
- Problems in my city or town (dangerous intersections, ugly areas, inadequate lighting, parks, police policy, public transportation, schools)
- Problems at my place of work (office design, flow of customer traffic, merchandise display, company policies)
- Problems related to my future career, hobbies, recreational time, life as a consumer, life as a homeowner

If you can offer a solution to the problem you identify, you may make a valuable contribution to some phase of public life.

To find a topic for policy proposals, stay in touch with the news, which will keep you aware of current debates on regional and national issues. Also, visit the Web sites of your congressional representatives to see what issues they are currently investigating and debating. You might think of your policy proposal as a white paper for one of your legislators.

Once you have decided on a proposal issue, we recommend you explore it by trying one or more of the following activities:

- Explore ideas by using the claim types strategy (see pages 312–314).
- Explore ideas by using the "stock issues" strategy (see pages 314–315).
- Explore ideas using the eleven questions (3a–3k) on page 316.

Identifying Your Audience and Determining What's at Stake

Before drafting your argument, identify your targeted audience and determine what's at stake. Consider your responses to the following questions:

- What audience are you targeting? What background do they need to understand your problem? How much do they already care about it? How could you motivate them to care?
- After they read your argument, what stance do you imagine them holding? What change do you want to bring about in their view or their behavior?
- What will they find uncomfortable or threatening about your proposal? Particularly, what costs will they incur by acting on your proposal?
- What objections might they raise? What counterarguments or alternative solutions will you need to address?
- Why does your proposal matter? What is at stake?

Organizing a Proposal Argument

When you write your draft, you may find it helpful to have at hand an organization plan for a proposal argument. The plan on page 320 shows a typical structure for a proposal argument. In some cases, you may want to summarize and rebut opposing views before you present the justification for your own proposal.

Designing a One-Page Advocacy Poster or Advertisement

As an alternative to a traditional written argument, your instructor may ask you to create a one-page advocacy advertisement. The first stage of your invention process should be the same as that for a longer proposal argument. Choose a controversial public issue that needs immediate attention or a neglected issue about which you want to arouse public passion. As with a longer proposal argument, consider your audience in order to identify the values and beliefs on which you will base your appeal.

When you construct your argument, the limited space available demands efficiency in your choice of words and in your use of document design. Your goal is to have a memorable impact on your reader in order to promote the action you advocate. The following questions may help you design and revise your advocacy ad:

1. How could photos or other graphic elements establish and give presence to the problem?
2. How can type size, type style, and layout be used to present the core of your proposal, including the justifying reasons, in the most powerful way for the intended audience?
3. Can any part of this argument be presented as a memorable slogan or catchphrase? What key phrases could highlight the parts or the main points of this argument?
4. How can document design clarify the course of action and the direct demand on the audience this argument is proposing?
5. How can use of color enhance the overall impact of your advocacy argument? (Note: One-page advertisements are expensive to reproduce in color, but you might make effective use of color if your advocacy ad were to appear as a poster or Web page.)

Designing PowerPoint Slides or Other Visual Aids for a Speech

In designing visual aids, your goal is to increase the persuasive effect of your speech rather than to demonstrate your technical wizardry. A common mistake with PowerPoint presentations is to get enamored with the program's bells and whistles. If you find yourself thinking about special effects (animations, fade-outs, flashing letters) rather than about "at a glance" visual appeals to *logos or pathos*, you may be on the wrong track. Another common mistake is to use slides simply to project a bullet point outline of your speech. Our best advice in designing slides is thus to "think visual argument."

Organization Plan for a Proposal Argument

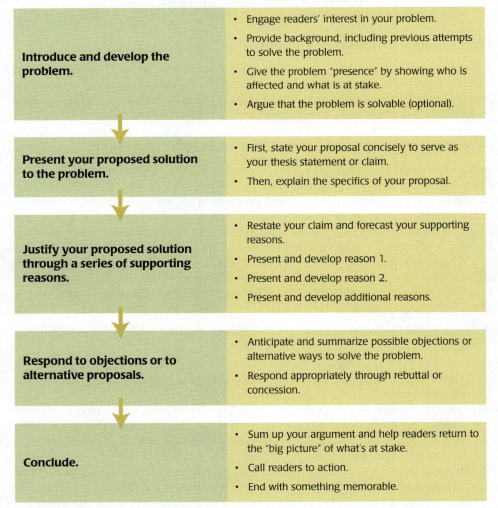

Introduce and develop the problem.

- Engage readers' interest in your problem.
- Provide background, including previous attempts to solve the problem.
- Give the problem "presence" by showing who is affected and what is at stake.
- Argue that the problem is solvable (optional).

Present your proposed solution to the problem.

- First, state your proposal concisely to serve as your thesis statement or claim.
- Then, explain the specifics of your proposal.

Justify your proposed solution through a series of supporting reasons.

- Restate your claim and forecast your supporting reasons.
- Present and develop reason 1.
- Present and develop reason 2.
- Present and develop additional reasons.

Respond to objections or to alternative proposals.

- Anticipate and summarize possible objections or alternative ways to solve the problem.
- Respond appropriately through rebuttal or concession.

Conclude.

- Sum up your argument and help readers return to the "big picture" of what's at stake.
- Call readers to action.
- End with something memorable.

In terms of visual argument, effective presentation slides can usually be placed in three design categories:

- Slides using images (photographs, drawings) to enhance *pathos* or to create a snapshot for visual clarity of a concept (*logos*)
- Slides using graphs or other visual displays of numbers to make numeric arguments
- Slides using bulleted (all-text) subpoints for evidence

All the strategies for visual arguments discussed in Chapter 9 and in this chapter under "Proposal Arguments as Advocacy Posters or Advertisements" (pages 316–317) apply equally to presentation slides.

In most cases, the "title" of the slide should put into words the "take-away point" of the slide—a verbal summary of the slide's visual argument. Most rhetoricians suggest that the title of a slide be a short sentence that makes a point rather than just a topic phrase.

Topic as Title (Weak)	Point as Title (Strong)
Coal and the Environment	Burning Coal Produces Dangerous Greenhouse Gases
The Effect of Money on Happiness	More Money Doesn't Mean More Happiness

Student writer Sandy Wainscott follows these principles in her speech and accompanying PowerPoint slides, shown on pages 333–335. ■

Questioning and Critiquing a Proposal Argument

As we've suggested, proposal arguments need to overcome the innate conservatism of people, the difficulty of anticipating all the consequences of a proposal, and so forth. What questions, then, can we ask about proposal arguments to help us anticipate these problems?

Will a skeptic deny that my problem is really a problem? Be prepared for skeptics who aren't bothered by your problem, who see your problem as limited to a small group of people, or who think you are exaggerating.

Will a skeptic doubt the effectiveness of my solution? A skeptic might agree that your problem is indeed important and worth solving, but might not be convinced that your solution will work. For these skeptics, you'll need to provide evidence that your solution is feasible and workable. Also be prepared for skeptics who focus on the potential negative or unintended consequences of your proposed solution.

Will a skeptic think my proposal costs too much? The most commonly asked question of any proposal is simply, "Do the benefits of enacting the proposal outweigh the costs?" Be wary of the (understandable) tendency to underestimate the costs and exaggerate the benefits of a proposal. Honesty will enhance your *ethos.*

Will a skeptic suggest counterproposals? Once you've convinced readers that a problem exists, they are likely to suggest solutions different from yours. It only makes sense to anticipate alternative solutions and to work out ways to argue why your solution is better. And who knows, you may end up liking the counterproposal better and changing your mind about what to propose!

READINGS

Our first reading, by student writer Megan Johnson, is a practical proposal addressing the problem of an inequitable meal plan on her campus—one that she claims discriminates against women. As a practical proposal, it uses headings and other elements of document design aimed at giving it a finished and professional appearance. When sent to the intended audience, it is accompanied by a single-spaced letter of transmittal following the conventional format of a business letter.

A Practical Proposal

MEGAN JOHNSON (STUDENT)

Ms. Jane Doe

Vice-President for Budgeting and Finance

Certain University

Certain City

Certain State, Zip

Dear Ms. Doe:

Enclosed is a proposal that addresses our university's minimum meal plan requirements for students living on campus. My proposal shows the problems associated with this requirement and suggests a workable solution for the university.

The enclosed proposal suggests a modest plan for allowing students to use their campus cards to purchase items off campus. Currently, students are required to purchase a minimum meal plan of $1,170, even though women eat less than men and often have to donate unspent meal funds back to the university. This proposal would give students the option to spend some of their meal plan money off campus. The benefits of my plan include more fairness to women students, fewer incentives toward binge eating, more opportunities for student bonding, and better relations with the nearby business community.

Through web research, I have discovered that other universities have systems in place similar to what I am proposing. I hope that my proposal is received well and considered as a workable option. A change in the minimum meal plan requirement might make our university a more desirable option for more prospective students as well as ultimately benefit the general welfare of the current student body.

Thank you for your time.

Sincerely,
Megan Johnson (Student)

A Proposal to Allow Off-Campus Purchases with a University Meal Card, Submitted by Megan Johnson (Student)

Problem

The problem with this university's required meal plan is that it is too large for many students, particularly women. For example, at the end of Winter Quarter, my final balance on my meal card was $268.50, all of which, except for $100, I had to donate back to the university. As the current system stands, students have to purchase a minimum meal plan for living on campus. The minimum meal plan totals $1,170 per quarter. During the academic year an amount of $100 may be rolled into the next quarter. At the end of the quarter any remaining funds, excluding the $100, will be removed from the meal plan. Therefore, if students do not spend the money on their meal plans, it will be wasted. As a woman, I am frustrated about having to decide whether to give my money back to the university or to use up my meal card by binge eating at the end of each quarter.

Proposed Solution

I propose that our university create a system in which students are able to use their campus meal plans at local businesses off campus such as local drug stores, grocery stores, and restaurants. As I will note later in this proposal, other universities have such a system, so the technical difficulties should be easy to solve. Basically, the card works as a debit card loaded with the amount of money the student places on the card. Local businesses would swipe a student's card the same way as the on-campus food service currently does, deducting the current charge against the amount still available on the card. It would probably be possible to limit the total number of dollars available for spending off campus.

Justification

My proposal would allow on-campus residential students to use some of their meal plan money on groceries, on non-food related items such as toiletries, or on an occasional off-campus meal at a local restaurant. This proposal would resolve the problem of gender bias in the current system, promote opportunities for more bonding among students, and ultimately help create a healthier student body. Moreover, it would show the university's commitment to its students' welfare.

First of all, the current meal plan policy tends to discriminate against women. All students on campus are required to have a minimum meal plan, even though men and women have clearly different eating habits. Men tend to eat much more than women and frequently have to add money to their meal plans to get through the quarter. In contrast, many women, like myself, don't use up their prepaid amounts. For example, my friend James ran out of his meal plan by the eighth week of the quarter whereas my roommate Blaire still had over $400 left on her card at the end of the quarter. She and I, like many other women, will have to donate our money back to the school. Therefore, women often feel cheated out of their money while men do not. It is discriminatory to require all students, regardless of gender, to have the same minimum meal plan. However, if the university is going to require all students to have the same minimum meal plan, then the university needs to give women more options to spend their money on things other than food purchased in the school dining halls.

5   In addition, my proposal would create more opportunities for bonding. For example, it would allow persons who love to cook, such as me, to use the residence hall kitchens to create "home-cooked meals" for floor mates, thus creating more friendships among students. Personally, I have had the pleasure of helping create such bonds among the women on my floor by cooking a "family dinner" in our floor's kitchen. The aroma of the roasted chicken and homemade mashed potatoes drew the students on the fifth floor into the lounge. After our shared dinner, it seemed as if our floor felt more comfortable being around each other in a more family-like way. I think that cooking on campus gives students a sense of comfort that they do not get when they go to the dining halls and have food pre-made for them. While I would love to cook dinner for my floor more often, the bottom line is that ingredients are too expensive to pay for on my regular credit card when I have already purchased from the university more food than I can eat. If the school were to implement a system where we could use a portion of our meal plans off campus, students would be able to buy groceries from local stores and to put to better use the kitchens already built into the residence halls.

    In addition to creating closer bonds between students, an off-campus option for our meal cards would help women eat more healthfully. The current system promotes bad eating habits causing women to overeat or even to binge in order to use up their extra meal plan money. For example, with the left over money on my card at the end of Fall Quarter, I bought cases of energy drinks which are filled with high fructose corn syrup and other empty calories. As another example, my friend Amber purchases multiple meals such as pizza and a burger for dinner because she doesn't want to waste her money. Overeating is obviously unhealthy and could eventually lead to an increase in obesity or eating disorders. However, if students were able to use their meal card off campus, they could buy items such as shampoo or other toiletries, which would be more beneficial for women than overeating to avoid losing money.

    Despite all these benefits of a new meal plan system, some administrators might be skeptical of the benefits and focus on the drawbacks instead. The biggest drawback is the potential loss of revenue to food services. As it is now, women help subsidize food costs for men. Without that subsidy, the food service might not be able to break even, forcing them to raise food costs for everyone. I don't have the financial expertise to know how to compute these costs. Clearly, however, other universities have thought about these issues and decided that allowing students to spend some of their food money off campus was a benefit worth providing for students. For example, the University of Texas, the University of Minnesota, and the University of Florida allow their meal cards to be used as debit cards at local businesses. As stated on their website, the University of Texas has a system called Bevo Bucks in which students can "purchase food, goods and services at participating locations, both on and off campus" by loading money onto their ID cards. Also according to the University of Minnesota's website, students have a system called FlexDine connected to their ID cards. FlexDine gives students the "convenience … [to eat] at PAPA JOHN's for residence hall residents." If other schools can implement off campus use of dining cards, then the plan is feasible. It might also be possible to limit the number of dollars that could be spent each quarter off campus in order to assure a minimum level of revenue for the food service.

Even if my proposal would be costly in terms of lost revenue to the food service, the benefits of my plan might still outweigh the costs. A revised meal card system might become a recruiting point for prospective students because they would feel as if the university is more personalized to fit the students' needs rather than just the university's needs. My proposal might help prospective students see how close the students at our university are and might draw more students to apply here. (Our website and view books could even include pictures of students cooking in the resident hall kitchens or eating at a local restaurant.) Moreover local off-campus businesses would welcome the opportunity for more student customers and might offer special promotions for students. A new meal card system might even improve the relationship between the university and the surrounding community.

Based on all these reasons, I believe that the university community as a whole would benefit if my proposal were enacted. The new plan would be especially appreciated by women students, many of whom now subsidize the food costs of men. In addition, the new system would bring students closer together by encouraging more creative use of the residence hall kitchens for community meals and by reducing the incentive toward binge eating at the end of each quarter. Finally, if other universities can use this system then our university should be able to use it as well. Although the food service may lose money to local businesses, the university would ultimately benefit by creating a more flexible and attractive meal option— especially for women—and by showing administrative concern for student welfare.

Critiquing "A Proposal to Allow Off-Campus Purchases with a MyWritingLab™ University Meal Card"

1. In your own words, summarize briefly the problem that Megan Johnson addresses, her proposed solution, and her justifying reasons.
2. Megan addresses her proposal to Ms. Jane Doe, an administrator who has the power to change policy. To what extent does Megan develop audience-based reasons that resonate for this audience of university administrators? How effectively does she anticipate and respond to objections her audience might raise?
3. How does Megan establish a positive *ethos* in this argument? To what extent does she appeal to *pathos* as well as *logos*?
4. How effective is Megan's proposal?

Our second reading, by student writer Ivan Snook, is a researched public policy proposal written in response to the option 3 assignment on pages 317–318. Snook's argument is based both on library and Internet research and on personal experience (he is a returning veteran who served as a Marine infantry soldier in Iraq). It is formatted as a formal research paper using the documentation style of the Modern Language Association (MLA). A full explanation of this format is given in Chapter 17.

Ivan Snook

Dr. Johnson

Argumentative Writing

March 31, 2014

Flirting with Disaster: An Argument Against Integrating

Women into the Combat Arms

In 2005 I was a rifleman for the elite 1st Reconnaissance Battalion in Iraq. My deployment was not all bad. When we returned to Camp Fallujah to repair our humvee we ate great chow, enjoyed good entertainment, and drank contraband vodka. I never had a girlfriend, though. I was too busy working in my all-male infantry unit. At the time I wished we had a few girls in the unit. What can I say? I wanted female companionship like the guys in non-combat jobs had. But I realized that women could never serve in the infantry because of the negative impact of boyfriend/girlfriend dramatics on unit morale, cohesiveness, and ultimately combat effectiveness.

However, America's civilian leadership recently moved towards integrating women into frontline combat arms units such as infantry, tanks, and artillery. In January, 2014, Secretary of Defense Leon Panetta lifted the Pentagon's policy on all-male combat arms occupations. "The department's goal...is to ensure that the mission is met with the best qualified and most capable people, regardless of gender," he said. "I'm not talking about reducing the qualifications for the job—if they can meet the qualifications for the job, then they should have a right to serve" (qtd. in Michaels and Vanden Brook). President Obama expanded upon Panetta's sentiment by saying, "Every American can be proud *that our military will grow even stronger*, with our mothers, wives, sisters, and daughters playing a greater role in protecting this country we love" (qtd. in Michaels and Vanden Brook, emphasis mine.)

If this policy change will indeed strengthen our military, every American should support it. However, no one has specified how integrating women into the combat arms will strengthen our military. I wholeheartedly agree with integrationists who claim that women can meet the rigorous physical and mental requirements for frontline combat. Any CrossFit has at least half a dozen women more physically and mentally fit than some of my Marine brothers in arms. If those were the sole criteria by which we evaluate infantrymen, I would endorse integration. But, how an individual soldier affects the combat unit as a whole must be considered. The great military theorist Carl von Clausewitz coined the term "friction" to represent the "[c]ountless minor incidents … [that] combine to lower the general level of performance [of the military machine]." He continues, "We should bear in mind that none of its components is of one piece: each part is composed of individuals, every one of whom retains his potential of friction" (119). Therefore, we must not judge individual soldiers only by their individual physical capabilities, but also by their impact on the unit as a whole.

Introducing women to previously all-male combat units means introducing the friction of romantic relationships. Petty jealousies and other dramatic relational issues combine to lower the general level of performance. In 1997, the non-profit global policy think tank RAND Corporation studied how romantic relationships affect coed military units. The study reported that such relationships "sexualize" the work environment, making it "difficult for colleagues to regard one another as just coworkers. Thus, the cohesion of the unit is negatively affected" (Harrell and Miller 81). One respondent complained, "The [cafeteria] … at night looks more like a singles club or promenade deck than a cafeteria [for a military unit]." Another said, "I get tired of seeing a junior enlisted female and her boyfriend [at the cafeteria].… This place is like high school all over again. Everyone is dating others. To me this is not the military. We are here to do a job not meet our spouse. Guys seem more worried about getting a girl than doing their job" (Harrell and Miller 81-82).

Integrationists claim the military's high level of discipline coupled with strict rules against fraternization will prevent romantic relationships. However, those strict rules have always been in place and have never worked. During the Gulf War, 5 percent of deployed women were sent home early due to pregnancy. The Navy sends home on average 10 percent of deployed female sailors for the same reason. The USS *Theodore Roosevelt,* one of America's largest aircraft carriers, lost 45 of its 300 female sailors to pregnancy leave and became one of the many U.S. Navy ships to earn the nickname "The Love Boat" (Browne 246). My point is not about morality. These statistics demonstrate that despite strict rules against fraternization, 18-25 year olds succumb to their natural urges. What else should one expect when young adults are locked away on ship or deployed to Afghanistan for months at a time? It is analogous to locking the doors on a coed college dormitory for a year and making rules against sex. It is preposterous to expect 18-25 year olds to work, live, and relax together in such close proximity and expect no romantic relationships to sprout.

MLA

These problems are more than just trifling lovers' quarrels. They affect a serious decline in performance and can lead to a total breakdown of command structure. In 2005, Brian Kates of the *New York Daily News* visited Camp Bucca, a military prison in Southern Iraq, which he described as a drunken "out-of-control frat party." "In front of a cheering male audience, two young women wearing only bras and panties threw themselves into a mud-filled plastic kiddie pool and rolled around in a wild wrestling match." Sergeant Emil Ganim, who refereed the match, said other non-commissioned officers "had been lending out their rooms for soldiers to have sex." These were not just young privates, either. A witness told investigators that a drunken first sergeant and master sergeant, two high-ranking non-commissioned officers, were in attendance (Kates). Although Camp Bucca was far away from any actual fighting, it is safe to assume similar sexual antics and command structure breakdowns will occur in coed frontline combat units whose members confront their own mortality on a daily basis.

Still, Camp Bucca is not the worst case scenario. The military is currently battling an epidemic of rape and sexual assault. A study conducted by the Department of Veterans' Affairs reported that one-third of female veterans say they were victims of rape or attempted rape. A third of those claim they were raped multiple times, and 14 percent claim they were gang raped (Browne). Introducing females to frontline combat units will only exacerbate the problem. Dr. David Grossman, one of the world's foremost experts on human aggression and the psychology of combat, has explained how combat stress affects human sex drive. He analogizes the human body's ability to cope with stress to a bathtub: it can hold only so much water before overflowing. When our body overflows with stress the midbrain releases hormones causing a fight or flight response, often followed by a dramatic change in hunger and sex drive. Grossman writes, "Some people lose their appetite for food in response to stress, but many have an enhanced craving to eat. In the same way, some individuals can lose their sex drive in response to great stress, but other people experience a tremendous sex drive, especially after a combat situation in which they were triumphant" (275). Frontline combat is fueled by stress hormones, and the potential for a woman to be sexually assaulted is very high. An inter-unit sexual assault costs the unit two soldiers: the victim is typically transferred to a new unit, the assaulter is sent to prison. Replacing two comrades integrated in a tight-knit unit with two new recruits is a difficult blow to a unit's esprit de corps and trust members have in one another. Thus, to put at risk a female soldier's sexual well-being is to also put at risk her unit's combat ability.

Rather than respond to the physiological realities of preparing for and engaging in combat, integrationists such as CNN's Maren Leed deflect to a false analogy connecting integration of women to past arguments against integrating minorities and homosexuals. Regarding minorities, race is a social construct not a biological difference. Whereas the military somewhat successfully trained its men to not act on racial prejudices, it is improbable that 18-25 year old men can be trained to be not sexually attracted to women. Regarding homosexuals, one homosexual has little effect on a group of heterosexuals, but one female can have a significant impact on a large group of stress hormone driven heterosexual men.

Another integrationist argument is that changes in modern warfare already put women in combat. They say modern warfare is "asymmetric" and attacks can come from anywhere. It is true that women have served in combat in Afghanistan and Iraq, but integrationists erroneously believe the nature of warfare has evolved beyond traditional frontlines. Every American military engagement since World War II has been a limited war, but that does not mean all future wars will be. The wars our military must prepare to fight are global conflicts where combat troops face well-armed and well-trained enemies on traditional frontlines.

Perhaps the most important argument made by integrationists, and one to which I am sympathetic, concerns fairness and equity. It is extremely difficult to be promoted to General without infantry training. Some may say the Army should change its promotion policy, but this would harm overall morale. Frontline troops more enthusiastically follow leaders who are sharing, or have at one time shared, the toils and dangers of war. Thus, high-ranking female officers hit a glass ceiling because no such experience is available to them. However, there is an alternative to break through this glass ceiling without making all combat units coed. The U.S. Army National Guard consists of every imaginable combat arms occupation. If they were opened to aspirant female soldiers, they would have access to the necessary experience for advancement to the military's upper echelon and have the option of transferring from the National Guard to active duty. General John Vessey began his illustrious career in the National Guard infantry and was later selected as Chairman of the Joint Chiefs of Staff. This compromise would give women the opportunity to get infantry training while still protecting our active duty frontline infantry units from the unnecessary friction caused by romantic relationships.

MLA

Snook 5

Although some outsiders call terms like friction, morale, and unit cohesion mere buzzwords, to the Marines they mean life or death. Coed infantry is a parlous experiment with too much at stake. The restriction against women joining the infantry must be reinstated before the policy becomes entrenched and the negative side effects of romantic relationships deteriorate our fighting ability. I fully support gender equality, and I am proud of the brave women in the Marines, Army, Navy, and Air Force who have sacrificed so much defending this country I love. But when one considers the ultimate mission of the military, which is to win wars, we must not risk losing the cohesion of combat units when there is no exigent reason to do so except for the sake of expanding military career opportunities for women.

Snook 6

Works Cited

Browne, Kingsley. *Co-Ed Combat: The New Evidence That Women Shouldn't Fight the Nation's Wars.* New York: Sentinel, 2007. Print.

Clausewitz, Carl von. *On War.* 1832. Trans. Michael Howard and Peter Paret. Princeton: Princeton, 1984. Print.

Grossman, David. *On Combat: The Psychology and Physiology of Deadly Conflict in War and in Peace.* 3rd ed. Millstadt: Warrior Science, 2008. Print.

Harrell, Margaret C., and Laura L. Miller. "New Opportunities for Women: Effects of Gender Integration on Morale." RAND Corporation, 1 Jan. 1997. Web. 15 Mar. 2014

Kates, Brian. "Out of Control at Camp Crazy! Female Soldiers Dress Down & Get Dirty for Mud Romps." *New York Daily News*, 6 Feb. 2005. Web. 15 Mar. 2014.

Leed, Maren. "Will Infantry Men Accept Women as Peers?" CNN, 25 Jan. 2013. Web. 15 Mar. 2014.

Michaels, Jim, and Tom Vanden Brook. "Women, Men Must Meet Same Combat Standards in Military." *USA Today*, 13 Jan. 2014. Web. 15 Mar. 2014.

Critiquing "Flirting with Disaster: An Argument Against Integrating Women into the Combat Arms"

MyWritingLab™

1. What is Ivan Snook's major reason for not integrating women into the combat arms? What evidence does he provide in support of his argument? Do you find that evidence persuasive?
2. What opposing or alternative views does Snook summarize? How effectively does Snook respond to these views?
3. Snook offers as a counterproposal a way that women could get infantry training (for purposes of career advancement) without having to make all infantry units coed. How effective do you find his counterproposal?
4. How effective is Snook's use of audience-based reasons? How would you evaluate his overall appeal to *logos, ethos,* and *pathos*?

Our third reading, from the Save-Bees.org Web site, is the one-page paid advocacy advertisement on page 332. Working in conjunction with other environmental organizations such as Beyond Pesticides, the Center for Food Safety, and Pesticide Action Network, the Save the Bees organization advocates a moratorium on pesticides that are killing off bees. The Web site itself demonstrates how the Internet can be enlisted for education and advocacy. It solicits support for a petition directed to the United States Environmental Protection Agency calling for an immediate discontinuation in the use of certain toxic chemicals deadly to bees. On the Web, this advocacy ad shows a list of organizations in support of this moratorium.

Critiquing the Save the Bees Advocacy Ad

MyWritingLab™

1. How does this advocacy advertisement give "presence" to the problem with bees?
2. What solution does the ad propose for helping the bees? Why hasn't this solution already been adopted? What action does the ad ask readers to take?
3. What reasons and evidence does this advocacy ad provide to persuade readers to take action? How effective is this evidence?
4. How does this proposal argument appeal to personal interest as well as environmental values? How would you say appeals to *logos, ethos,* and *pathos* work together in this advocacy piece?

Our fourth reading, by student Sandy Wainscott, illustrates option 5, a proposal speech supported by visual aids. We have reproduced Sandy's outline for her speech, along with her scripts for the introduction and conclusion. (Although she delivered the body of the speech extemporaneously from her outline, she scripted the introduction and conclusion to reduce nervousness.) We have also reproduced four of her ten PowerPoint slides. She used these four slides to introduce each of the four main points shown on the outline. Note how she has constructed her slides as visual arguments supporting a main point (stated in the slide title).

Bees can't wait 5 *more* years.

And neither can we.

Honey bees, native bees and other pollinators are responsible for 1 out of every 3 bites of food we eat. Bees pollinate 71 of the 100 crops that make up 90% of the world's food supply. Many fruits and vegetables, including apples, blueberries, strawberries, carrots and broccoli, as well as almonds and coffee, rely on bees. These beneficial insects are critical to maintaining our diverse food supply.

Honey bee populations have been in alarming decline since 2006. Widespread use of a new class of toxic pesticides, neonicotinoids, is a significant contributing factor. In addition to killing bees outright, research has shown that even low levels of these dangerous pesticides impair bees' ability to learn, to find their way back to the hive, to collect food, to produce new queens, and to mount an effective immune response.

This week, 15 countries are imposing a two-year restriction on the use of several of these chemicals. Meanwhile, the United States is **stalling**.

The U.S. Environmental Protection Agency estimates it will be **2018, 5 years from now,** before it makes a decision on this deadly class of pesticides.

Bees can't wait 5 more years – they are dying now. The U.S. Environmental Protection Agency has the power and responsibility to protect our pollinators. Our nation's food system depends on it.

HELP PROTECT FOOD CHOICES

✿ **Save-Bees.org**

Why McDonald's Should Sell Meat and Veggie Pies: A Proposal to End Subsidies for Cheap Meat

SANDY WAINSCOTT (STUDENT)

Script for Introduction: McDonald's hamburgers are popular because they're satisfying and pretty darn cheap. But I will argue that the hamburger is cheap because the American taxpayer subsidizes the cost of meat. Uncle Sam pays agribusiness to grow feed corn while not requiring agribusiness to pay the full cost for water or for cleaning up the environmental damage caused by cattle production. If meat producers had to recover the true cost of their product, the cost of meat would be substantially higher, but there would be offsetting benefits: a healthier environment, happier lives for cows and chickens, and healthier diets for all of us.

1. Meat is relatively cheap partly because taxpayers help feed the cows.
   a. U.S. taxpayers give farmers money to grow feed corn, which is fed to cows.
   b. U.S. taxpayers provide farmers with cheap water.
2. Cheap meat threatens health.
   a. Factory-style farms significantly reduce effectiveness of antibiotics.
   b. Antibiotic-resistant pathogens are potentially huge killers.
   c. Factory farms are likely sources of new swine and bird flus.
   d. Meat-related food poisoning harms millions of people per year with thousands of deaths.
3. Cheap meat hurts the environment.
   a. Factory farms create 130 times more sewage than humans.
   b. Animal farming contributes more to global warming than all forms of human transportation combined.
   c. Farming uses much of the world's land and water.
4. Cheap meat requires cruelty to animals.
   a. Ninety-eight percent of egg-laying hens in the U.S. spend their entire lives in stacked cubicle cages with 9-inch sides.
   b. Cruel conditions also exist for pigs and cows.

Script for Conclusion: If we quit giving farmers taxpayer subsidies and required them to pay for the pollution they cause, the cost of meat would be much higher—but with great benefits to our health and to our environment. A restaurant like McDonald's would likely adjust its menus. McDonald's would move the burger off its 99 cent menu and replace it with something like a meat pie, a similarly warm, quick, and satisfying choice, but with a lower proportion of meat than a burger. In a fair market, we should have to pay more for a hamburger than for a meat pie or a stir fry. But we would have the benefit of a healthier Earth.

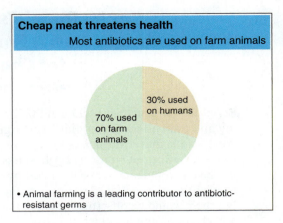

FIGURE 14.2 Sandy's PowerPoint Slides Used to Introduce Main Points

Critiquing "Why McDonald's Should Sell Meat and Veggie Pies: A Proposal to End Subsidies for Cheap Meat"

MyWritingLab™

1. Although it is common to design PowerPoint slides that use topics and bullets to reproduce the speaker's outline, most public speaking experts prefer the approach that Sandy takes in this speech. She uses photographs, drawings, and graphics to create a visual argument that reinforces rather than simply reproduces the verbal message of her speech. How do her slides operate visually to create arguments from both *logos* and *pathos*?

2. Note that the top heading of each slide is a complete sentence making a point rather than a topic phrase without a subject and verb. For example, the

top-left slide in Figure 14.2 might have had the heading "Cheap Meat" or "Role of Subsidies." Do you agree with most experts, who would say that the complete-sentence version ("Meat is relatively cheap because taxpayers help feed the cows") is more effective? Why or why not?

3. How effective do you find Sandy's speech?

Our final reading appeared in the *Wall Street Journal* on February 19, 2011. The authors are both professors of entomology at Wageningen University in the Netherlands. In 2007, Marcel Dicke was awarded the NWO-Spinoza award, often called the Dutch Nobel Prize. He gives speeches (summaries of which are available on the Web) arguing that humans should eat insects rather than meat as one solution to the environmental degradation caused by the meat industry. Coauthor Arnold Van Huis coordinates a research consortium of scientists investigating the nutritional value of insects. He also gives cooking classes featuring bug recipes.

The Six-Legged Meat of the Future

MARCEL DICKE AND ARNOLD VAN HUIS

At the London restaurant Archipelago, diners can order the $11 Baby Bee Brulee: a creamy custard topped with a crunchy little bee. In New York, the Mexican restaurant Toloache offers $11 chapulines tacos: two tacos stuffed with Oaxacan-style dried grasshoppers.

Could beetles, dragonfly larvae and water bug caviar be the meat of the future? As the global population booms and demand strains the world's supply of meat, there's a growing need for alternate animal proteins. Insects are high in protein, B vitamins and minerals like iron and zinc, and they're low in fat. Insects are easier to raise than livestock, and they produce less waste. Insects are abundant. Of all the

known animal species, 80% walk on six legs; over 1,000 edible species have been identified. And the taste? It's often described as "nutty."

Worms, crickets, dung beetles—to most people they're just creepy crawlers. To Brooklyn painter and art professor Marc Dennis, they're yummy ingredients for his Bug Dinners.

The vast majority of the developing world already eats insects. In Laos and Thailand, weaver-ant pupae are a highly prized and nutritious delicacy. They are prepared with shallots, lettuce, chilies, lime and spices and served with sticky rice. Further back in history, the ancient Romans considered beetle larvae to be gourmet fare, and the Old Testament mentions eating

crickets and grasshoppers. In the 20th century, the Japanese emperor Hirohito's favorite meal was a mixture of cooked rice, canned wasps (including larvae, pupae and adults), soy sauce and sugar.

Will Westerners ever take to insects as food? It's possible. We are entomologists at Wageningen University, and we started promoting insects as food in the Netherlands in the 1990s. Many people laughed—and cringed—at first, but interest gradually became more serious. In 2006 we created a "Wageningen—City of Insects" science festival to promote the idea of eating bugs; it attracted more than 20,000 visitors.

Over the past two years, three Dutch insect-raising companies,

which normally produce feed for animals in zoos, have set up special production lines to raise locusts and mealworms for human consumption. Now those insects are sold, freeze-dried, in two dozen retail food outlets that cater to restaurants. A few restaurants in the Netherlands have already placed insects on the menu, with locusts and mealworms (beetle larvae) usually among the dishes.

Insects have a reputation for being dirty and carrying diseases—yet less than 0.5% of all known insect species are harmful to people, farm animals or crop plants. When raised under hygienic conditions—eating bugs straight out of the backyard generally isn't recommended—many insects are perfectly safe to eat.

Meanwhile, our food needs are on the rise. The human population is expected to grow from six billion in 2000 to nine billion in 2050. Meat production is expected to double in the same period, as demand grows from rising wealth.

Pastures and fodder already use up 70% of all agricultural land, so increasing livestock production would require expanding agricultural acreage at the expense of rain forests and other natural lands. Officials at the United Nations Food and Agriculture Organization recently predicted that beef could become an extreme luxury item by 2050, like caviar, due to rising production costs.

Raising insects for food would avoid many of the problems associated with livestock. For instance, swine and humans are similar enough that they can share many diseases. Such co-infection can yield new disease strains that are lethal to humans, as happened during a swine fever outbreak in the Netherlands in the late 1990s. Because insects are so different from us, such risks are accordingly lower.

10   Insects are also cold-blooded, so they don't need as much feed as animals like pigs and cows, which consume more energy to maintain their body temperatures. Ten pounds of feed yields one pound of beef, three pounds of pork, five pounds of chicken and up to six pounds of insect meat.

Insects produce less waste, too. The proportion of livestock that is not edible after processing is 30% for pork, 35% for chicken, 45% for beef and 65% for lamb. By contrast, only 20% of a cricket is inedible.

Raising insects requires relatively little water, especially as compared to the production of conventional meat (it takes more than 10 gallons of water, for instance, to produce about two pounds of beef). Insects also produce far less ammonia and other greenhouse gases per pound of body weight. Livestock is responsible for at least 10% of all greenhouse gas emissions.

Raising insects is more humane as well. Housing cattle, swine or chickens in high densities causes stress to the animals, but insects like mealworms and locusts naturally like to live in dense quarters. The insects can be crowded into vertical stacked trays or cages. Nor do bug farms have to be restricted to rural areas; they could sprout up anywhere, from a suburban strip mall to an apartment building. Enterprising gourmets could even keep a few trays of mealworms in the garage to ensure a fresh supply.

The first insect fare is likely to be incorporated subtly into dishes, as a replacement for meat in meatballs and sauces. It also can be mixed into prepared foods to boost their nutritional value—like putting mealworm paste into a quiche. And dry-roasted insects can be used as a replacement for nuts in baked goods like cookies and breads.

15   We continue to make progress in the Netherlands, where the ministry of agriculture is funding a new $1.3 million research program to develop ways to raise edible insects on food waste, such as brewers' grain (a byproduct of beer brewing), soyhulls (the skin of the soybean) and apple pomace (the pulpy remains after the juice has been pressed out). Other research is focusing on how protein could be extracted from insects and used in processed foods.

Though it is true that intentionally eating insects is common only in developing countries, everyone already eats some amount of insects. The average person consumes about a pound of insects per year, mostly mixed into other foods. In the U.S., most processed foods contain small amounts of insects, within limits set by the Food and Drug Administration. For chocolate, the FDA limit is 60 insect fragments per 100 grams. Peanut butter can have up to 30 insect parts per 100 grams, and fruit juice can have five fruit-fly eggs and one or two larvae per 250 milliliters (just over a cup). We also use many insect products to dye our foods, such as the red dye cochineal in imitation crab sticks, Campari and candies. So we're already some of the way there in making six-legged creatures a regular part of our diet.

Not long ago, foods like kiwis and sushi weren't widely known or available. It is quite likely that in 2020 we will look back in surprise at the era when our menus didn't include locusts, beetle larvae, dragonfly larvae, crickets and other insect delights.

Critiquing "The Six-Legged Meat of the Future"   MyWritingLab™

1. On page 308 we note that a problem faced by all proposal writers is "the need to overcome people's natural conservatism." Their readers' natural conservatism is a major constraint for coauthors Dicke and Van Huis ("Hey, I've never eaten bugs before! If four-legged meat was good enough for my parents, it's good enough for me!") How do the authors use the appeals of *logos*, *ethos*, and *pathos* to try to overcome this natural conservatism?

2. Although this journalistic piece does not have a tightly closed-form structure with transitions and because clauses marking each reason, it still provides a logical progression of separate reasons in support of eating insects. Convert this argument into a bulleted list of because clauses in support of the claim "Westerners should eat insects as a major source of protein."

3. Are you persuaded by this argument? Would you try some mealworm spaghetti or a handful of fried crickets? Why or why not?

MyWritingLab™

Visit Ch. 14 Proposal Arguments in *MyWritingLab* to complete the For Writing and Discussion, Examining Visual Arguments, Critiquing, and Writing Assignments and to test your understanding of the chapter objectives.

The Researched Argument

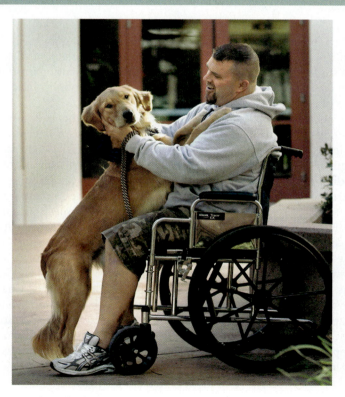

This photo shows a service dog with a disabled veteran. Concern for disabled veterans lies at the center of many public debates about how the country should welcome veterans back into civilian life and reintegrate them after their military service and sacrifice. What medical and social services do disabled veterans require and deserve? What would be the most effective way to help them vocationally and psychologically? What implicit arguments does this photo convey and what claims might it support about service animals for disabled veterans?

Finding and Evaluating Sources

15

Although the "research paper" is a common writing assignment in college, students are often baffled by their professor's expectations. The problem is that students often think of research writing as presenting information rather than creating an argument. One of our business school colleagues calls these sorts of research papers "data dump."

But a research paper shouldn't be a data dump. Like any other argument, it should use information to support a contestable claim. In academic settings (as opposed to arguments in many business or civic settings), a distinguishing feature of a researched argument is its formal documentation. By **documentation**, we mean the in-text citations and accompanying list of references that allow readers to identify and locate the researcher's sources for themselves while also establishing the writer's professionalism and *ethos*.

Fortunately, writing an argument as a formal research paper draws on the same argumentation skills you have already been using—the ability to pose a question at issue within a community, to formulate a contestable claim, and to support your claim with audience-based reasons and evidence. This chapter shows you how to find and evaluate sources. Chapter 16 then shows you how to incorporate your sources skillfully into your own prose using the academic conventions for ethical research. (Knowing and using these conventions will free you from any fears of plagiarism.) Finally, in Chapter 17 we explain the nitty-gritty details of in-text citations and end-of-paper lists of sources.

Formulating a Research Question Instead of a "Topic"

15.1 To formulate a research question instead of a topic

The best way to use your research time efficiently is to pose a question rather than a topic. To appreciate this difference, suppose a friend asks you what your research paper is about. Consider the differences in the following responses:

Topic focus: I'm doing a paper on gender-specific children's toys.

Question focus: I'm researching the effects of gender-specific toys on children's intellectual development. Do boys' toys develop intellectual skills more than girls' toys do?

Topic focus: I'm doing a paper on eating disorders.

Question focus: I'm trying to sort out what the experts say is the best way to treat severe anorexia nervosa. Is inpatient or outpatient treatment more effective?

As these scenarios suggest, a topic focus invites you to collect information without a clear point or purpose—an open road toward data dumping. In contrast, a question focus requires you to make an argument in which you support a claim with reasons and evidence. Your goal as a researcher is to pose an issue question about which reasonable persons may disagree. In many cases, you might not know where you stand yourself. Your research thus becomes a process of inquiry and clarification.

Thinking Rhetorically about Kinds of Sources

15.2 To think rhetorically about kinds of sources

To be an effective researcher, you need to think rhetorically about the different kinds of sources that you might encounter while doing your research.

Identifying Kinds of Sources Relevant to Your Question

At the beginning of your research process think rhetorically about the conversation you will be joining and about the kinds of evidence you might use to support an argument. The following brainstorming questions can help you think of both possible sources for evidence for your argument and for discovering different points of view on your question:

Questions for Identifying Relevant Kinds of Sources

- What personal experiences have you had with this issue? What details from your life or the lives of your friends, acquaintances, or relatives might serve as voices in the conversation or as evidence (personal examples, anecdotes, and so forth)?
- What field research might you undertake that would be relevant to this issue? What might you personally observe, record, count, and so forth?

- What people could you interview to provide insights or expert knowledge on this issue?
- What questions about your issue could be addressed in a survey or questionnaire?
- What useful information on this issue might encyclopedias, specialized reference books, or the regular book collection in your university library provide?
- What evidence might you seek on this issue from magazines, newspapers, scholarly journals, and other sources found through your library's licensed databases? (See pages 349–350.)
- How might an Internet search engine help you research this issue?
- What evidence might you find on this issue from reliable statistical resources such as U.S. Census Bureau data, the Centers for Disease Control, or *Statistical Abstract of the United States?*

Approaching Sources Rhetorically

Whether you interview someone, listen to a speaker, or read a text, you have to approach this source rhetorically, asking questions about the writer's or speaker's purpose, audience, and genre. Particularly when you read, you often need to ascertain a text's genre before you even start to read or decide to select that text as a potential source for your paper. In Chapter 2, we identified the various genres of argument and also explained who writes arguments and why (see pages 26–30). In this section we'll extend our Chapter 2 discussion by explaining ways to distinguish among different genres of sources. An overview of the different genres you might encounter while doing research is shown in Table 15.1 ("A Rhetorical Overview of Sources"). Your payoff for having a basic understanding of source types will be an increased ability to read sources rhetorically and to use them purposefully in your research writing.

To help you appreciate some of the distinctions made among the genres in Table 15.1, consider the following explanations concerning each genre's degree of editorial review, stability, advocacy, and authority.

Degree of Editorial Review

- Note that Table 15.1 begins with "peer-reviewed scholarly sources," which are published by nonprofit academic presses and written for specialized audiences. "Peer review" is a highly prized concept in academia. It refers to the rigorous and competitive selection process by which scholarly manuscripts get chosen for publication. When manuscripts are submitted to an academic publisher, the editor removes the names of the authors and sends the manuscripts to experienced scholars who judge the rigor and accuracy of the research and the significance and value of the argument. In contrast, the other types of sources listed in Table 15.1—in many cases published for profit—are not peer reviewed and may have little if any editorial review from the publisher. However, reputable publishing houses of books, magazines, and newspapers usually employ rigorous editors who oversee the production of trade books and freelance or commissioned magazine articles. Fortunately, it

TABLE 15.1   A Rhetorical Overview of Sources

Genre of Source	Author and Angle of Vision	How to Recognize Them
Peer-Reviewed Scholarly Sources		
ARTICLES IN SCHOLARLY JOURNALS Examples: articles in *Journal of Abnormal Psychology; American Journal of Botany*	**Author:** Professors, industry researchers, independent scholars **Angle of vision:** Scholarly advancement of knowledge; presentation of research findings; development of new theories and applications	• Not sold on magazine racks • No commercial advertising • Academic style with documentation and bibliography • Cover often lists table of contents • Found through licensed online databases
SCHOLARLY BOOKS Example: *Shakespearean Negotiations: The Circulation of Social Identity in Renaissance England* by Stephen Greenblatt	**Author:** Professors, industry researchers, independent scholars **Angle of vision:** Scholarly advancement of knowledge; presentation of research findings; development of new theories and applications	• University press or other academic publisher on title page • Academic style with documentation and bibliography • Found in academic libraries; may be available as e-book
SCHOLARLY WEB SITES Example: http://seasia.museum.upenn.edu (Southeast Asian Archeology Scholarly Web site)	**Author:** Professors or institute scholars **Angle of vision:** Dissemination of research findings; informative access to primary sources	• Usually have a .edu Web address or address of professional scholarly organization • Clearly identified with an academic institution • Material is usually peer reviewed, but may include reports on work-in-progress or links to primary sources
REFERENCE WORKS Example: *The Farmer's Almanac; Statistical Abstract of the United States*	**Author:** Commissioned scholars **Angle of vision:** Balanced, factual overview	• Titles containing words such as *encyclopedia, dictionary, atlas,* and so forth • Found in library reference section or online
Public Affairs Sources		
NEWSPAPERS AND NEWS MAGAZINES Examples: *Time, Newsweek, Washington Post, Los Angeles Times*	**Author:** Staff writers and occasional freelance journalists **Angle of vision:** News reports aimed at balance and objectivity; editorial pages reflect perspective of editors; op-ed pieces reflect different perspectives	• Readily familiar by name, distinctive cover style • Widely available on newsstands, by subscription, and on the Web • Ads aimed at broad, general audience
ARTICLES IN PUBLIC AFFAIRS PERIODICALS Examples: *Harper's, Commonweal, National Review*	**Author:** Staff writers, freelancers, scholars **Angle of vision:** Aims to deepen general public's understanding of issues; magazines often have political bias	• Long, well-researched articles reviewed by editors • Ads aimed at upscale professionals • Often have reviews of books, theater, film, and the arts • Often can be found in online databases or on the Web
ORGANIZATIONAL WHITE PAPERS Examples: "Congressional White Paper on a National Policy for the Environment" (on Web) or "Reform Suggestions for Core Curriculum" (in-house document at a university)	**Author:** Organizational stakeholders; problem solvers for a client **Angle of vision:** Informative document for client or argumentative paper for influencing policy or improving operations	• Desktop-published, internal documents aimed at problem solving; may also be written for clients • Internal documents generally not made available to public • Sometimes posted to Web or published in print medium

(continued)

Genre of Source	Author and Angle of Vision	How to Recognize Them
BLOGS Examples: dailykos.com (liberal blog site); michellemalkin.com (conservative blog site); theladysportswriter.blogspot.com (sports commentary)	**Author:** Anyone; some bloggers are practicing journalists **Angle of vision:** Varies from personal diaries to in-depth commentary on a subject or issues; wide range of views from conservative to liberal	• Usually published on time-stamped blog sites; most sites post responses from readers • Bloggers sometimes use pseudonyms • Often combines text with images or linked videos
NONFICTION TRADE BOOKS Example: *Cheap: The High Cost of Discount Culture* by Ellen Ruppell Shell (a journalism professor)	**Author:** Journalists, freelancers, scholars aiming at popular audience **Angle of vision:** Varies from informative to persuasive; often well researched and respected, but sometimes shoddy and aimed for quick sale	• Published by commercial presses for profit • Popular style; covers designed for marketing appeal • Usually documented in an informal rather than an academic style • May be available as an e-book
DOCUMENTARY FILMS Examples: Michael Moore, *Sicko*; Louie Psihoyos, *The Cove*	**Writer/Director:** Filmmakers, screenwriters trained in nonfiction documentaries **Angle of vision:** Varies from informative "science" documentaries to strong advocacy	• Specifically identified as "documentary" or "nonfiction" • Combines interviews and voice-overs with subject-matter footage
<td colspan="3" align="center">**Advocacy Sources**</td>
NEWSPAPER EDITORIALS, COMMENTARY, AND LETTERS TO THE EDITOR Examples: editorial page, letters to the editor, and op-ed pages of *Washington Post, Los Angeles Times, Wall Street Journal*, and some magazines	**Author:** Editorial writers; citizens writing letters to editor; syndicated or guest columnists **Angle of vision:** Advocacy for certain positions or public policies	• Located in the editorial/op-ed sections of a newspaper • Editorials are often unsigned—they advocate positions held by owners or publishers of the newspaper • Letters and op-ed pieces are signed
EDITORIAL CARTOONS Examples: see www.cagle.com/politicalcartoons/	**Cartoonist:** Usually syndicated artists who specialize in cartoons **Angle of vision:** Varies from conservative to liberal	• Usually located in the op-ed section of newspapers • Occasionally political cartoonists are treated as comics (*Doonesbury*)
ADVOCACY ORGANIZATION WEB SITES, BLOGS, AND ADVERTISEMENTS Examples: NRA.org (National Rifle Association); csgv.org (Coalition to Stop Gun Violence)	**Author/Site Sponsor:** Advocacy organizations; staff writers/researchers; Web developers; guest writers; often hard to identify individual writers **Angle of vision:** Strong advocacy for the site's viewpoint; often encourage donations through site	• .org in URL—denotes advocacy or nonprofit status • Sometimes doesn't announce advocacy clearly on home page • Facts/data selected and filtered by site's angle of vision • Often uses visuals for emotional appeals • Site often includes blogs (or links to blogs) that promote same angle of vision

Genre of Source	Author and Angle of Vision	How to Recognize Them
	Government Sources	
GOVERNMENT AGENCY WEB SITES Example: www.energy.gov (site of the U.S. Dept. of Energy)	**Author:** Development teams employed by agency; sponsoring agency is usually the author (corporate authorship); may include material by individual authors **Angle of vision:** Varies—informational sites publish data and objective documents; agency sites also advocate for agency's agenda	• .gov or .mil in URL—denotes government or military sites • Are often layered and complex with hundreds of links to other sites
LEGAL AND COURT DOCUMENTS	**Author:** Lawyers, judges, persons deposed for trials, trial testimony **Angle of vision:** Trial lawyers take strong advocacy positions; testifiers vow to tell the whole truth; judges defend decisions	• Legal briefs have distinctive formats • Court records can be accessed through www.pacer.gov (public access to court electronic records—requires user to establish an account)
POLITICAL AND LEGISLATIVE SPEECHES	**Author:** Politicians, political candidates, researchers, and aides **Angle of vision:** Reflects politics of speaker	• Widely available through newspapers, Web sites, YouTube videos, congressional records
	Commercial Sources	
TRADE MAGAZINES Examples: *Advertising Age, Automotive Rebuilder, Farm Journal*	**Author:** Staff writers, industry specialists **Angle of vision:** Informative articles for practitioners; advocacy for the profession or trade	• Title indicating trade or profession • Articles on practical industry concerns • Ads geared toward a particular trade or profession
POPULAR NICHE MAGAZINES Examples: *Seventeen, People, TV Guide, Car and Driver, Golf Digest*	**Author:** Staff or freelance writers **Angle of vision:** Varies—focuses on interests of targeted audience; in some cases content and point of view are dictated by advertisers or the politics of the publisher	• Glossy paper, extensive ads, lots of visuals • Popular; often distinctive style • Short, undocumented articles • Credentials of writer often not mentioned
COMMERCIAL WEB SITES AND ADVERTISEMENTS	**Author:** Development teams, in-house writers, contracted developers; advertising agencies **Angle of vision:** Varies from information to advocacy; promotes the viewpoint of the business	• .com or .biz in URL—denotes "commercial" • Advertisements or Web sites often promote corporate image as well as products • Frequent use of visuals as well as text
PERSONAL WEB SITES, BLOGS, OR CORRESPONDENCE	**Author:** Anyone can create a personal Web site or blog or write personal letters/e-mails **Angle of vision:** Varies from person to person	• Researcher using these sources is responsible for citing credentials of source or revealing bias of source

can be profitable for popular presses to publish superbly researched and argued intellectual material written for the general reader rather than for highly specialized scholars. These can be excellent sources for undergraduate research, but you need to separate the trash from the treasure.

Degree of Stability

■ Print sources (books, scholarly journals, magazines, newspapers), which can be stored in archives and retrieved many years later, are more stable than Web-only material, which may change hourly. What complicates the distinction between "print" and "Web only" is that many documents retrievable on the Web are also stable—either because they were originally print sources and made available online in pdf or html formats or because they are produced by a reputable company as e-books, e-journals, or online newspapers that will be archived digitally. As a quick example of a stable versus nonstable source, suppose you write a "letter to the editor" that was published in a major newspaper. Your letter will be archived permanently and retrievable, just as you wrote it, long into the future. But if instead you post a comment on a blog site, that comment (and the whole blog site) might disappear at any time.

Degree of Advocacy

■ In Chapter 1 we explained how arguments combine truth seeking and persuasion. To illustrate these concepts, we charted a continuum from exploratory essays at one end of the continuum to outright propaganda at the other end (see Figure 1.7, page 11). To read a source rhetorically, you should try to determine where on this continuum your source resides. In Table 15.1, we identify as "advocacy sources" those sources that clearly announce their persuasive intentions. But other kinds of sources, such as an article in a public affairs magazine, a trade book, a legal brief, a documentary film, or a political speech, can have a strong advocacy stance. (See pages 352–356 on "Evaluating Sources" for further discussion of how to evaluate the degree of advocacy in a source.)

Degree of Authority

■ Sometimes you turn to a specific genre because you just want the facts. Reputable newspapers are good sources for day-to-day reporting on "what happened." Other kinds of excellent fact-checking sources include encyclopedias, statistical abstracts, or other reference works that provide distilled background or overview information on many topics. For most sources, however, you need to be wary about the author's authority in a field and read rhetorically for angle of vision, accuracy of data, and cherry picking of sources. Be aware too that *Wikipedia* is not a reliable academic source. Although it is a fascinating cultural product that provides rapid overview information, it is often accused of inaccurate information, editorial bias, and shifting content because of constant revisions by its collaborative writers. Most instructors will not accept *Wikipedia* as a factual or informative source.

■ ■ ■ **FOR CLASS DISCUSSION Identifying Types of Sources**

Your instructor will bring to class a variety of print sources—different kinds of books, scholarly journals, magazines, and so forth—and may also show you various kinds of sources retrieved online. Working individually or in small groups, decide to which category in Table 15.1 each piece belongs. Be prepared to justify your decisions on the basis of the clues you used to make your decision.   ■ ■ ■

Finding Sources

15.3 To find sources through field, library, or Web research

In the previous section, we explained differences among the kinds of sources you may uncover in a research project. In this section, we explain how to find these sources through field research (such as interviews and question-naires), through using your campus's library resources (books, reference ma-terials, and online databases for finding articles), and through Web searches.

Conducting Interviews

Conducting interviews is a useful way not only to gather expert testimony and impor-tant data for use in your argument but also to learn about alternative views. To make interviews as productive as possible, we offer these suggestions.

- **Determine your purpose.** Consider why you are interviewing the person and what information he or she is uniquely able to provide.
- **Do background reading.** Find out as much as possible about the interviewee before the interview. Your knowledge of his or her background will help estab-lish your credibility and build a bridge between you and your source. Also, equip yourself with a good foundational understanding of the issue so that you will sound informed and truly interested in the issue.
- **Formulate well-thought-out questions but also be flexible.** Write out before-hand the questions you intend to ask, making sure that every question is related to the purpose of your interview. However, be prepared to move in unexpected directions if the interview opens up new territory. Sometimes unplanned topics can end up being the most illuminating and useful.
- **Come well prepared for the interview.** As part of your professional demeanor, be sure to have all the necessary supplies (notepaper, pens, pencils, perhaps a tape recorder, if your interviewee is willing) with you.
- **Be prompt and courteous.** It is important to be punctual and respectful of your interviewee's time. In most cases, it is best to present yourself as a listener seeking clarity on an issue rather than an advocate of a particular position or an opponent. During the interview, play the believing role. Save the doubting role for later, when you are looking over your notes.
- **Take brief but clear notes.** Try to record the main ideas and be accurate with quotations. Ask for clarification of any points you don't understand.
- **Transcribe your notes soon after the interview.** Immediately after the interview, while your memory is still fresh, rewrite your notes more fully and completely.

When you use interview data in your writing, put quotation marks around any direct quotations. In most cases, you should also identify your source by name and indicate his or her title or credentials—whatever will convince the reader that this person's remarks are to be taken seriously.

Gathering Source Data from Surveys or Questionnaires

A well-constructed survey or questionnaire can provide lively, current data that give your audience a sense of the currency and importance of your views. To be effective and responsible, however, a survey or questionnaire needs to be carefully prepared and administered, as we suggest in the following guidelines.

- **Include both closed-response questions and open-response questions.** To gain useful information and avoid charges of bias, you will want to include a range of questions. Closed-response questions ask participants to check a box or number on a scale and yield quantitative data that you can report statistically, perhaps in tables or graphs. Open-response questions elicit varied responses and often short narratives in which participants offer their own input. These may contribute new insights to your perspective on the issue.
- **Make your survey or questionnaire clear and easy to complete.** Consider the number, order, wording, and layout of the questions in your questionnaire. Your questions should be clear and easy to answer. The neatness and overall formal appearance of the questionnaire will also invite serious responses from your participants.
- **Explain the purpose of the questionnaire.** Respondents are usually more willing to participate if they know how the information gained from the questionnaire will benefit others. Therefore, it is a good idea to state at the beginning of the questionnaire how it will be used.
- **Seek a random sample of respondents in your distribution of the questionnaire.** Think out where and how you will distribute and collect your questionnaire to ensure a random sampling of respondents. For example, if a questionnaire about the university library went only to dorm residents, then you wouldn't learn how commuting students felt.
- **Convert questionnaires into usable data by tallying and summarizing responses.** Tallying the results and formulating summary statements of the information you gathered will yield material that might be used as evidence.

Finding Books and Reference Sources

To find the specialized resources provided by your campus library, your best initial research tool is your campus library's home page. This portal will lead you to two important resources: (1) the library's online catalog for its own holdings of books, periodicals, films, multimedia materials, reference works, and other resources and (2) direct links to the many digital databases leased by the library. (We discuss these databases in the next section.) When searching for books related to your research question, particularly look for recent books that might have helpful indexes and bibliographies. Also be aware of your library's reference materials such as statistical abstracts, biographies, dictionaries, and encyclopedias.

In addition to checking your library's home page, make a personal visit to your library to learn its features and to meet your library's reference librarians, who are a researcher's best friends.

Using Licensed Databases to Find Articles in Scholarly Journals, Magazines, and News Sources

For many research projects, the most useful sources are articles that may be immediately available in your library's periodical collection or online through databases. In either case, you discover the existence of these articles by searching licensed databases leased by your library.

What Is a Licensed Database?

Electronic databases of periodical sources are produced by for-profit companies that index the articles appearing in thousands of periodicals. You can search the database by author, title, subject, keyword, date, genre, and other characteristics. In most cases the database contains an abstract of each article, and in many cases it contains the full text of the article, which you can download and print. These databases are referred to by several different generic names: "licensed databases" (our preferred term), "periodical databases," or "subscription services." Because access to these databases is restricted to fee-paying customers, they can't be searched through Web engines like Google. Most university libraries allow students to access these databases from a remote computer by using a password. You can therefore use the Internet to connect your computer to licensed databases as well as to the World Wide Web.

Although the methods of accessing licensed databases vary from institution to institution, we can offer some widely applicable guidelines. Most likely your library has online one or more of the following databases:

- **Academic Search Complete (Ebsco):** Indexes nearly 8,000 periodicals, including full text of nearly 7,000 peer-reviewed journals. It features a mix of interdisciplinary scholarly journals, magazines, newspapers, and books.
- **Research Library Complete (ProQuest):** Similar to Academic Search Complete except that it includes trade publications and more business and industry materials.
- **LexisNexis Academic Universe:** Primarily a full-text database covering current events, business, and financial news; includes company profiles and legal, medical, and reference information.
- **JSTOR:** Offers full text of scholarly journal articles across many disciplines; you can limit searches to specific disciplines.

Generally, one of these databases is the "default database" chosen by your library for most article searches. Your reference librarian will be able to direct you to the most useful licensed database for your purpose.

Finding Cyberspace Sources: Searching the World Wide Web

Another valuable resource is the World Wide Web, but when using the Web you need to be extra careful to evaluate your sources rhetorically. Web search engines search only the "free-access," ever-changing portions of the Internet known as the World Wide Web. When you type keywords into a Web search engine, it searches for matches in material made available on the Web by all the users of the world's network of computers—government agencies, corporations, advocacy groups, information services, individuals with their own Web sites, and many others. Because different Web search engines search the Web in different ways, your reference librarian can give you good advice on what works well for particular kinds of searches. On the Web, an additional resource is NoodleTools.com, which offers lots of good advice for choosing the best search engine.

■ The following example will quickly show you the difference between a licensed database search and a Web search. When student Ivan Snook (see his proposal argument on pages 326–330) typed "women in combat roles" into Google, he received 5,800,000 hits. When he entered the same keywords into the licensed database *Academic Search Complete*, he received forty-four hits. When he limited the database search to full-text articles appearing in peer-reviewed journals, he received twenty hits. Clearly the search tools are searching different fields. Google picks up, in addition to all the articles that someone may have posted on the Web, all references to material appearing on advocacy Web sites, government publications, newspapers, blogs, chat rooms, student papers posted on the Web, and so forth. In contrast, *Academic Search Complete* searches for articles primarily in scholarly journals and magazines.

Selecting and Evaluating Your Sources

15.4 To use rhetorical awareness to select and evaluate your sources and take purposeful notes.

So far we have explained the importance of posing a good research question, understanding the different kinds of sources, and using purposeful strategies for conducting interviews, for designing questionnaires, and for searching libraries, licensed databases, and the Web. In this final section we explain how to read with rhetorical awareness, how to select and evaluate sources, and how to take purposeful notes. We also provide some additional advice for evaluating Web sources.

Reading with Rhetorical Awareness

How you read a source depends to a certain extent on where you are in the research process. Early in the process, when you are in the thesis-seeking, exploratory stage, your goal is to achieve a basic understanding about your research problem. You need to become aware of different points of view, learn what is unknown or controversial about your research question, see what values or assumptions are in conflict, and build up your store of background knowledge.

Given these goals, at the early stages of research you should select overview kinds of sources to get you into the conversation. In some cases, even an encyclopedia or specialized reference work can be a good start for getting general background information.

As you get deeper into your research, your questions become more focused, and the sources you read become more specialized. Once you formulate a thesis and plan a structure for your paper, you can determine more clearly the sources you need and read them with purpose and direction.

To read your sources rhetorically, you should keep two basic questions in mind:

1. What was the source author's purpose in writing this piece?
2. What might be my purpose in using this piece?

Table 15.2, which sums up the kinds of questions rhetorical readers typically consider, reinforces a point we've made throughout this text: all writing is produced from an angle of vision that privileges some ways of seeing and filters out other ways. You should guard against reading your sources as if they present hard, undisputed facts or universal truths. For example, if one of your sources says that "Saint-John's-wort [an herb] has been shown to be an effective treatment for depression," some of your readers might accept that statement as fact—but many wouldn't. Skeptical readers might ask

TABLE 15.2   Questions Asked by Rhetorical Readers

What was the source author's purpose in writing this piece?	What might be my purpose in using this piece in my own argument?
• Who is this author? What are his or her credentials and affiliations? • What audience is this person addressing? • What is the genre of this piece? (If you downloaded the piece from the World Wide Web, did it originally appear in print?) • If this piece appeared in print, what is the reputation and bias of the journal, magazine, or press? Was the piece peer reviewed? • If this piece appeared only on the Web, who or what organization sponsors the Web site (check the home page)? What is the reputation and bias of the sponsor? • What is the author's thesis or purpose? • How does this author try to change his or her audience's view? • What is this writer's angle of vision or bias? • What is omitted or censored from this text? • How reliable and credible is this author? • What facts, data, and other evidence does this author use and what are the sources of these data? • What are this author's underlying values, assumptions, and beliefs?	• How has this piece influenced or complicated my own thinking? • How does this piece relate to my research question? • How will my own intended audience react to this author? • How might I use this piece in my own argument? • Is it an opposing view that I might summarize? • Is it an alternative point of view that I might compare to other points of view? • Does it have facts and data that I might use? • Would a summary of all or part of this argument support or oppose one or more of my own points? • Could I use this author for testimony? (If so, how should I indicate this author's credentials?) • If I use this source, will I need to acknowledge the author's bias and angle of vision?

whether the author is relying on published research, and if so, whether the studies have been peer reviewed in reputable, scholarly journals. They would also want to know whether a trade association for herbal supplements sponsored the research and whether the author or the researchers had financial connections to companies that produce herbal remedies. Rather than settling the question about Saint-John's-wort as a treatment for depression, this author's assertion may open up a heated controversy about medical research.

Reading rhetorically is thus a way of thinking critically about your sources. It influences the way you evaluate sources, take notes, and shape your argument.

Evaluating Sources

When you read sources for your research project, you need to evaluate them as you go along. As you read each potential source, ask yourself questions about the author's reliability, credibility, angle of vision, and degree of advocacy.

Reliability   "Reliability" refers to the accuracy of factual data in a source. If you check a writer's "facts" against other sources, do you find that the facts are correct? Does the writer distort facts, take them out of context, or otherwise use them unreasonably? In some controversies, key data are highly disputed—for example, the frequency of date rape or the risk factors for many diseases. A reliable writer acknowledges these controversies and doesn't treat disputed data as fact. Furthermore, if you check out the sources used by a reliable writer, they'll reveal accurate and careful research—respected primary sources rather than hearsay or secondhand reports. Journalists of reputable newspapers (not tabloids) pride themselves on meticulously checking out their facts, as do editors of serious popular magazines. Editing is often minimal for Web sources, however, and they can be notoriously unreliable. As you gain knowledge of your research question, you'll develop a good ear for writers who play fast and loose with data.

Credibility   "Credibility" is similar to "reliability" but is based on internal rather than external factors. It refers to the reader's trust in the writer's honesty, goodwill, and trustworthiness and is apparent in the writer's tone, reasonableness, fairness in summarizing opposing views, and respect for different perspectives. Audiences differ in how much credibility they will grant to certain authors. Nevertheless, a writer can achieve a reputation for credibility, even among bitter political opponents, by applying to issues a sense of moral courage, integrity, and consistency of principle.

Angle of Vision and Political Stance   By "angle of vision," we mean the way that a piece of writing is shaped by the underlying values, assumptions, and beliefs of its author, resulting in a text that reflects a certain perspective, worldview, or belief system. Of paramount importance are the underlying values or beliefs that the writer assumes his or her readers will share. You can get useful clues about a writer's angle of vision and intended audience by doing some quick research into the politics and reputation of the author on the Internet or by analyzing the genre, market niche, and political reputation of the publication in which the material appears.

TABLE 15.3   Angles of Vision in U.S. Media and Think Tanks: A Sampling Across the Political Spectrum

Commentators

Left	Left Center	Center	Right Center	Right
Barbara Ehrenreich	E. J. Dionne	David Ignatius	David Brooks	Charles Krauthammer
Michael Moore	Leonard Pitts	Thomas Friedman	Jonah Goldberg	Cal Thomas
(filmmaker)	Eugene Robinson	Kathleen Hall Jamieson	Andrew Sullivan	Glenn Beck (radio/TV)
Bill Moyers (TV)	Nicholas Kristof	Kevin Phillips	George Will	Rush Limbaugh (radio/
Paul Krugman	Maureen Dowd	David Broder	Ruben Navarrette Jr.	TV)
Bill Maher (TV)	Mark Shields	William Saletan	Ross Douthat	Bill O'Reilly (TV)
Rachel Maddow (TV)		Mary Sanchez		Matt Drudge
				Thomas Sowell

Newspapers and Magazines

Left/Liberal	Center	Right/Conservative
Harper's	*Atlantic Monthly*	*American Spectator*
Los Angeles Times	*Business Week*	*Fortune*
Mother Jones	*Commentary*	*National Review*
The Nation	*Commonweal*	*Reader's Digest*
New York Times	*Foreign Affairs*	*Reason*
The New Yorker	*New Republic*	*Wall Street Journal*
Salon	*Slate*	*Weekly Standard*
Sojourners	*Washington Post*	

Blogs

Liberal/Left	Center	Right/Conservative
crooksandliars.com	donklephant.com	conservativeblogger.com
dailykos.com	newmoderate.blogspot.com	drudgereport.com
digbysblog.blogspot.com	politics-central.blogspot.com	instapundit.com
firedoglake.com	rantingbaldhippie.com	littlegreenfootballs.com
huffingtonpost.com	stevesilver.net	michellemalkin.com
talkingpointsmemo.com	themoderatevoice.com	redstate.com
wonkette.com	washingtonindependent.com	townhall.com

Think Tanks

Left/Liberal	Center	Right/Conservative
Center for American Progress	The Brookings Institution	American Enterprise Institute
Institute for Policy Studies	Carnegie Endowment for International	Cato Institute (Libertarian)
Open Society Institute (Soros Foundation)	Peace	Center for Strategic and International
Progressive Policy Institute	Council on Foreign Relations	Studies
Urban Institute	Jamestown Foundation	Heritage Foundation (sponsors
	National Bureau of Economic Research	Townhall.com)
		Project for the New American Century

[1] For further information about the political leanings of publications or think tanks, ask your librarian about Gale Directory of Publications and Broadcast Media or NIRA World Directory of Think Tanks.

[2] Newspapers are categorized according to positions they take on their editorial page; any reputable newspaper strives for objectivity in news reporting and includes a variety of views on its op-ed pages. Magazines do not claim and are not expected to present similar breadth and objectivity.

Determining Political Stance   Your awareness of angle of vision and political stance is especially important if you are doing research on contemporary cultural or political issues. In Table 15.3, we have categorized some well-known political commentators, publications, policy research institutes (commonly known as *think tanks*), and blogs across the political spectrum from left/liberal to right/conservative.

Although the terms *liberal* and *conservative* or *left* and *right* often have fuzzy meanings, they provide convenient shorthand for signaling a person's overall views about the proper role of government in relation to the economy and social values. Liberals, tending to sympathize with those potentially harmed by unfettered free markets (workers, consumers, plaintiffs, endangered species), are typically comfortable with government regulation of economic matters while conservatives, who tend to sympathize with business interests, typically assert faith in free markets and favor a limited regulatory role for government. On social issues, conservatives tend to espouse traditional family values and advocate laws that would maintain these values (for example, promoting a constitutional amendment that would forbid abortions). Liberals, on the other hand, tend to espouse individual choice on many social matters. Some persons identify themselves as economic conservatives but social liberals; others side with workers' interests on economic issues but are conservative on social issues.

Finally, many persons regard themselves as "centrists." In Table 15.3, the column labeled "Center" includes commentators who seek out common ground between the left and the right and who often believe that the best civic decisions are compromises between opposing views. Likewise, centrist publications and institutes often approach issues from multiple points of view, looking for the most workable solutions.

Degree of Advocacy   By "degree of advocacy" we mean the extent to which an author unabashedly takes a persuasive stance on a contested position as opposed to adopting a more neutral, objective, or exploratory stance. For example, publications affiliated with advocacy organizations (the Sierra Club, the National Rifle Association) will have a clear editorial bias. When a writer takes a strong stance on an issue, you need to weigh carefully the writer's selection of evidence, interpretation of data, and fairness to opposing views. Although no one can be completely neutral, it is always useful to seek out authors who offer a balanced assessment of the evidence. Evidence from a more detached and neutral writer may be more trusted by your readers than the arguments of a committed advocate.

Criteria for Evaluating a Web Source   When you evaluate a Web source, we suggest that you ask five different kinds of questions about the site in which the source appeared, as shown in Table 15.4. These questions, developed by scholars and librarians as points to consider when you are evaluating Web sites, will help you determine the usefulness of a site or source for your own purposes.

As a researcher, the first question you should ask about a potentially useful Web source should be, "Who placed this piece on the Web and why?" You can begin answering this question by analyzing the site's home page, where you will often find navigational buttons linking to "Mission," "About Us," or other identifying information about

TABLE 15.4   Criteria for Evaluating Web Sites

Criteria	Questions to Ask
1. Authority	• Is the document author or site sponsor clearly identified? • Does the site identify the occupation, position, education, experience, or other credentials of the author? • Does the home page or a clear link from the home page reveal the author's or sponsor's motivation for establishing the site? • Does the site provide contact information for the author or sponsor such as an e-mail or organization address?
2. Objectivity or Clear Disclosure of Advocacy	• Is the site's purpose clear (for example, to inform, entertain, or persuade)? • Is the site explicit about declaring its point of view? • Does the site indicate whether the author is affiliated with a specific organization, institution, or association? • Does the site indicate whether it is directed toward a specific audience?
3. Coverage	• Are the topics covered by the site clear? • Does the site exhibit a suitable depth and comprehensiveness for its purpose? • Is sufficient evidence provided to support the ideas and opinions presented?
4. Accuracy	• Are the sources of information stated? • Do the facts appear to be accurate? • Can you verify this information by comparing this source with other sources in the field?
5. Currency	• Are dates included in the Web site? • Do the dates apply to the material itself, to its placement on the Web, or to the time the site was last revised and updated? • Is the information current, or at least still relevant, for the site's purpose? For your purpose?

the site's sponsors. You can also get hints about the site's purpose by asking, "What kind of Web site is it?" Different kinds of Web sites have different purposes, often revealed by the domain identifier following the site name:

■ **.com sites:** These are commercial sites designed to promote a business's image, attract customers, market products and services, and provide customer service. Their angle of vision is to promote the view of the corporation or business. Often material has no identified author. (The sponsoring company is often cited as the author.)

■ **.org sites:** These are sites for nonprofit organizations or advocacy groups. Some sites provide accurate, balanced information related to the organization's mission work (Red Cross, World Vision), while others promote political views (Heritage Foundation) or advocate a cause (People for the Ethical Treatment of Animals).

■ **.edu sites:** These sites are associated with a college or university. Home pages aim to attract prospective students and donors and provide a portal into the site. Numerous subsites are devoted to research, pedagogy, libraries, and so forth. The angle of vision can vary from strong advocacy on issues (a student paper, an on-campus advocacy group) to the objective and scholarly (a university research site).

- .gov **or** .mil **sites:** These sites are sponsored by a government agency or military units. They can provide a range of basic data about government policy, bills in Congress, economic forecasts, census data, and so forth. Their angle of vision varies from objective informational sites to sites that promote the agency's agenda.

Because of a new rule by the agency that controls domain identifiers, people and organizations will be able to buy their own unique domain identifiers. Sites with unique identifiers are likely to be commercial sites since the identifiers cost thousands of dollars each.

■ ■ ■ **FOR WRITING AND DISCUSSION** **Analyzing the Rhetorical Elements** MyWritingLab™
of Two Websites

Individual task: Using a Web search engine, find a site opposing gun control (such as the National Rifle Association or Women Against Gun Control) and a site supporting gun control (such as GunVictims Action Council or the Brady Campaign). Peruse each of your chosen sites. Then write out your answers to the following questions:

1. What is the angle of vision and degree of advocacy of each of the sites? How does the selection of images, links to articles, and use of "facts" and "fact sheets" indicate an angle of vision?
2. Look for images of women on each of your sites. How do they construct women differently and imply differences in women's concerns about guns?
3. What range of underlying values does each of the sites appeal to? How do words and images create viewer awareness of these underlying values?
4. How does each of the sites use *logos, ethos,* and *pathos* to sway readers toward its point of view?

Group task: Compare your answers to these questions with those of others in your class. How do your rhetorical observations intersect? Where do they differ?   ■ ■ ■

Taking Purposeful Notes

By reading rhetorically and evaluating your sources as you proceed, you will make purposeful choices about the sources you will use in your researched argument. In this concluding section we offer advice on how to take notes about each of your sources. Many beginning researchers opt not to take notes—a serious mistake, in our view. Instead, they simply photocopy or print articles, perhaps using a highlighter to mark passages. This practice, which experienced researchers almost never use, reduces your ability to engage the ideas in a source and to find your own voice in a conversation. When you begin drafting your paper, you'll have no notes to refer to, no record of your thinking-in-progress. Your only recourse is to revisit all your sources, thumbing through them one at a time—a practice that leads to passive cutting and pasting (and possible plagiarism).

Good note taking includes recording bibliographic information for each source, recording information and ideas from each source, and responding to each source with your own ideas and exploratory writing.

Recording Bibliographic Information   To take good research notes, begin by making a bibliographic entry for each source, following the documentation format assigned by your instructor. Although you will be tempted to put off doing this mechanical task, there are two reasons to do it immediately:

- Doing it now, while the source is in front of you, will save you time in the long run. Otherwise, you'll have to try to retrieve the source, in a late-night panic, just before the paper is due.
- Doing it now will make you look at the source rhetorically. Is this a peer-reviewed journal article? A magazine article? An op-ed piece? A blog? Having to make the bibliographic entry forces you to identify the source's genre. Chapter 17 explains in detail how to make bibliographic entries for both MLA (called "Works Cited") and APA (called "References").

Recording Ideas and Information and Responding to Each Source   To take good research notes, follow the reading habits of summary and exploration discussed in Chapter 2, weaving back and forth between walking in the shoes of the source author and then standing back to believe and doubt what the source says. Think of two categories of notes: informational and exploratory.

- **Your informational notes on each source:** Using the skills of summary writing explained in Chapter 2, summarize each source's argument and record useful information. To avoid the risk of plagiarism later, make sure that you put quotation marks around any passages that you copy word for word (be sure to copy exactly). When you summarize or paraphrase passages, be sure to put the ideas entirely into your own words. (For more on quoting, summarizing, and paraphrasing sources, see Chapter 16, pages 362–364.)
- **Your own exploratory notes as you think of ideas:** Write down your own ideas as they occur to you. Speak back to the source. Record your thinking-in-progress as you mull over ways the source sparked your own thinking.

An approach that encourages both modes of writing is to keep a dialectic or double-entry journal. Divide a page in half; enter your informational notes on one side and your exploratory writing on the other. If you use a computer, you can put your informational notes in one font and your own exploratory writing in another.

Taking effective notes is different from the mechanical process of copying out passages or simply listing facts and information. Rather, make your notes purposeful by imagining how you might use a given source in your research paper. Table 15.5 shows the different functions that research sources might play in your argument and highlights appropriate note-taking strategies for each function.

TABLE 15.5 **Strategies for Taking Notes According to Purpose**

Function That Source Might Play in Your Argument	Strategies for Informational Notes	Strategies for Exploratory Notes
Provides background about your problem or issue	• Summarize the information. • Record specific facts and figures useful for background.	• Speculate on how much background your readers will need.
Gives an alternative view that you will mention briefly	• Summarize the source's argument in a couple of sentences; note its bias and perspective. • Identify brief quotations that sum up the source's perspective.	• Jot down ideas on how and why different sources disagree. • Begin making an idea map of alternative views.
Provides an alternative or opposing view that you might summarize fully and respond to	• Summarize the article fully and fairly (see Chapter 2 on summary writing). • Note the kinds of evidence used.	• Speculate about why you disagree with the source and whether you can refute the argument, concede to it, or compromise with it. • Explore what research you'll need to support your own argument.
Provides information or testimony that you might use as evidence	• Record the data or information. • If using authorities for testimony, quote short passages. • Note the credentials of the writer or person quoted.	• Record new ideas as they occur to you. • Continue to think purposefully about additional research you'll need.
Mentions information or testimony that counters your position or raises doubts about your argument	• Note counterevidence. • Note authorities who disagree with you.	• Speculate how you might respond to counterevidence.
Provides a theory or method that influences your approach to the issue	• Note credentials of the author. • Note passages that sparked ideas.	• Freewrite about how the source influences your method or approach.

Conclusion

This chapter has explained the need to establish a good research question; to understand the key differences among different kinds of sources; to use purposeful strategies for searching libraries, databases, and Web sites; and to use your rhetorical knowledge when you read and evaluate sources and take purposeful notes. It has also discussed briefly the special problems of evaluating a Web site. In the next chapter we focus on how to integrate research sources into your own prose.

MyWritingLab™

Visit Ch. 15 Finding and Evaluating Sources in *MyWritingLab* to complete the For Writing and Discussion and to test your understanding of the chapter objectives.

Incorporating Sources into Your Own Argument

16

What you will learn in this chapter:

16.1 To use your sources for your own purposes
16.2 To summarize, paraphrase, and quote a source
16.3 To punctuate quotations correctly
16.4 To signal your use of sources through rhetorically effective attributive tags
16.5 To avoid plagiarism

The previous chapter helped you pose a good research question, use online databases, search the Web wisely, and evaluate your sources by reading them rhetorically. This chapter teaches you how to incorporate sources smoothly into your own argument.

Using Sources for Your Own Purposes

16.1 To use your sources for your own purposes

To illustrate the purposeful use of sources, we will use the following short argument from the Web site of the American Council on Science and Health (ACSH)—an organization of doctors and scientists devoted to providing scientific information on health issues and to exposing health fads and myths. Please read the argument carefully in preparation for the discussions that follow.

Is Vegetarianism Healthier than Nonvegetarianism?

Many people become vegetarians because they believe, in error, that vegetarianism is uniquely conducive to good health. The findings of several large epidemiologic studies indeed suggest that the death and chronic-disease rates of vegetarians—primarily vegetarians who consume dairy products or both dairy products and eggs—are lower than those of meat eaters....

The health of vegetarians may be better than that of nonvegetarians partly because of nondietary factors: Many vegetarians are health-conscious. They exercise regularly, maintain a desirable body weight, and abstain from smoking. Although most epidemiologists have attempted to take such factors into account in their analyses, it is possible that they did not adequately control their studies for nondietary effects.

People who are vegetarians by choice may differ from the general population in other ways relevant to health. For example, in Western countries most vegetarians are more affluent than nonvegetarians and thus have better living conditions and more access to medical care.

An authoritative review of vegetarianism and chronic diseases classified the evidence for various alleged health benefits of vegetarianism:

- The evidence is "strong" that vegetarians have (a) a lower risk of becoming alcoholic, constipated, or obese and (b) a lower risk of developing lung cancer.
- The evidence is "good" that vegetarians have a lower risk of developing adult-onset diabetes mellitus, coronary artery disease, hypertension, and gallstones.
- The evidence is "fair to poor" that vegetarianism decreases risk of breast cancer, colon cancer, diverticular disease, kidney-stone formation, osteoporosis, and tooth decay.

For some of the diseases mentioned above, the practice of vegetarianism itself probably is the main protective factor. For example, the low incidence of constipation among vegetarians is almost certainly due to their high intakes of fiber-rich foods. For other conditions, nondietary factors may be more important than diet. For example, the low incidence of lung cancer among vegetarians is attributable primarily to their extremely low rate of cigarette smoking. Diet is but one of many risk factors for most chronic diseases.

How you might use this article in your own writing would depend on your research question and purpose. To illustrate, we'll show you three different hypothetical examples of writers who have reason to cite this article.

Writer 1: A Causal Argument Showing Alternative Approaches to Reducing Risk of Alcoholism

Writer 1 argues that vegetarianism may be an effective way to resist alcoholism. She uses just one statement from the ACSH article for her own purpose and then moves on to other sources.

Another approach to fighting alcoholism is through naturopathy, holistic medicine, and vegetarianism. Vegetarians generally have better health than the rest of the population and particularly have, according to the American Council on Science and Health, "a lower risk of becoming alcoholic." This lower risk has been borne out by other studies showing that the benefits of the holistic health movement are particularly strong for persons with addictive tendencies.... [goes on to other arguments and sources]

> Writer's claim
>
> Identification of source
>
> Quotation from ACSH

Writer 2: A Proposal Argument Advocating Vegetarianism

Writer 2 proposes that people become vegetarians. Parts of his argument focus on the environmental costs and ethics of eating meat, but he also devotes one paragraph to the health benefits of vegetarianism. As support for this point he summarizes the ACSH article's material on health benefits.

Not only will a vegetarian diet help stop cruelty to animals, but it is also good for your health. According to the American Council on Science and Health, vegetarians have longer life expectancy than nonvegetarians and suffer from fewer chronic diseases. The Council cites "strong" evidence from the scientific literature showing that vegetarians have reduced risk of lung cancer, obesity, constipation, and alcoholism. The Council also cites "good" evidence that they have a reduced risk of adult-onset diabetes, high blood pressure, gallstones, and hardening of the arteries. Although the evidence isn't nearly as strong, vegetarianism may also lower the risk of certain cancers, kidney stones, loss of bone density, and tooth decay.

> Writer's claim
>
> Identification of source
>
> Summary of ACSH material

Writer 3: An Evaluation Argument Looking Skeptically at Vegetarianism

Here, Writer 3 uses portions of the same article to make an opposite case from that of Writer 2. She focuses on those parts of the article that Writer 2 consciously excluded.

The link between vegetarianism and death rates is a classic instance of correlation rather than causation. While it is true that vegetarians have a longer life expectancy than nonvegetarians and suffer from fewer chronic diseases, the American Council on Science and Health has shown that the causes can mostly be explained by factors other than diet. As the Council suggests, vegetarians are apt to be more health conscious than nonvegetarians and thus get more exercise, stay slender, and avoid smoking. The Council points out that vegetarians also tend to be wealthier than nonvegetarians and see their doctors more regularly. In short, they live longer because they take better care of themselves, not because they avoid meat.

> Writer's claim
>
> Identification of source
>
> Paraphrased points from ACSH

■ ■ ■   **FOR CLASS DISCUSSION**   **Using a Source for Different Purposes**

Each of the hypothetical writers uses the short ACSH argument in different ways for different purposes. Working individually or in small groups, respond to the following questions; be prepared to elaborate on and defend your answers.

1. How does each writer use the original article differently and why?
2. If you were the author of the article from the American Council on Science and Health, would you think that your article is used fairly and responsibly in each instance?
3. Suppose your goal were simply to summarize the argument from the American Council on Science and Health. Write a brief summary of the argument and then explain how your summary is different from the partial summaries by Writers 2 and 3.

Using Summary, Paraphrase, and Quotation

16.2 To summarize, paraphrase, and quote a source

As a research writer, you need to incorporate sources gracefully into your own prose. Depending on your purpose, you might (1) summarize all or part of a source author's argument, (2) paraphrase a relevant portion of a source, or (3) quote small passages from the source directly. To avoid plagiarism, you'll need to reference the source with an in-text citation, put quotation marks around quoted passages, and convert paraphrases and summaries entirely into your own words. Table 16.1 gives you an overview of summary, paraphrase, and quotation as ways of incorporating sources into your own prose. With practice, you'll be able to use all these strategies smoothly and effectively. (For an explanation of in-text citations, see Chapter 17; for more on plagiarism in academic writing and how to avoid it, see pages 370–374.)

Summarizing

Detailed instructions on how to write a summary of an article and incorporate it into your own prose are provided in Chapter 2 (pages 34–36). Summaries can be as short as a single sentence or as long as a paragraph. Make the summary as concise as

TABLE 16.1 Incorporating Sources into Your Own Prose

Strategy	What to Do	When to Use This Strategy
Summarize the source.	Condense a source writer's argument by keeping main ideas and omitting details (see Chapter 2, pages 34–36).	• When the source writer's whole argument is relevant to your purpose • When the source writer presents an alternative or opposing view that you want to push against • When the source writer's argument can be used in support of your own
Paraphrase the source.	Reproduce an idea from a source writer but translate the idea entirely into your own words; a paraphrase should be approximately the same length as the original.	• When you want to incorporate factual information from a source or to use one specific idea from a source • When the source passage is overly complex or technical for your targeted audience • When you want to incorporate a source's point in your own voice without interrupting the flow of your argument
Quote short passages from the source using quotation marks.	Work brief quotations from the source smoothly into the grammar of your own sentences (see pages 364–368).	• When you need testimony from an authority (state the authority's credentials in an attributive tag—see pages 368–370) • In summaries, when you want to reproduce a source's voice, particularly if the language is striking or memorable • In lieu of paraphrase when the source language is memorable
Quote long passages from the source using the block method.	Results in a page with noticeably lengthy block quotations	• When you intend to analyze or critique the quotation—the quotation is followed by your detailed analysis of its ideas or rhetorical features • When the flavor and language of testimonial evidence is important

possible so that you don't distract the reader from your own argument. In many cases, writers summarize only parts of a source, depending on what is relevant to their own argument. Writer 3's summary of the article by the American Council on Science and Health is a good example of a partial summary.

Paraphrasing

Unlike a summary, which is a condensation of a source's whole argument, a **paraphrase** translates a short passage from a source's words into the writer's own words. Writers often choose to paraphrase when the details of a source passage are particularly important or when the source is overly technical and needs to be simplified for the intended audience. When you paraphrase, be careful to avoid reproducing the original writer's grammatical structure and syntax. If you mirror the original sentence structure while replacing occasional words with synonyms or small structural changes, you will be doing what composition specialists call "**patchwriting**"—that is, patching some of your language onto someone else's writing.* Patchwriting is a form of academic dishonesty because you aren't fully composing your own sentences and are thus misrepresenting both your own work and that of the source writer. An acceptable paraphrase needs to be entirely in your own words. To understand patchwriting more fully, track the differences between unacceptable patchwriting and acceptable paraphrase in the following examples.

Original

- The evidence is "strong" that vegetarians have (a) a lower risk of becoming alcoholic, constipated, or obese and (b) a lower risk of developing lung cancer.
- The evidence is "good" that vegetarians have a lower risk of developing adult-onset diabetes mellitus, coronary artery disease, hypertension, and gallstones.

Unacceptable Patchwriting

According to the American Council on Science and Health, there is strong evidence that vegetarians have a lower risk of becoming alcoholic, constipated, or obese. The evidence is also strong that they have a lower risk of lung cancer. The evidence is good that vegetarians are less apt to develop adult-onset diabetes, coronary artery disease, hypertension, or gallstones.

Identification of source

Note phrases taken word for word from original.

---

*We are indebted to the work of Rebecca Moore Howard and others who have led composition researchers to reexamine the use of sources and plagiarism from a cultural and rhetorical perspective. See especially Rebecca Moore Howard, *Standing in the Shadow of Giants: Plagiarists, Authors, Collaborators* (Stamford, CT: Ablex Pub., 1999).

Acceptable Paraphrase

The Council summarizes "strong" evidence from the scientific literature showing that vegetarians have reduced risk of lung cancer, obesity, constipation, and alcoholism. The Council also cites "good" evidence that they have a reduced risk of adult-onset diabetes, high blood pressure, gallstones, or hardening of the arteries.

Identification of source

Doesn't follow original sentence structure

Quotes "strong" and "good" to indicate distinction made in original

Both the patchwriting example and the acceptable paraphrase reproduce the same ideas as the original in approximately the same number of words. But the writer of the acceptable paraphrase has been more careful to change the sentence structure substantially and not copy exact phrases. In contrast, the patchwritten version contains longer strings of borrowed language without quotation marks.

Among novice writers, the ease of copying Web sources can particularly lead to patchwriting. You may be tempted to copy and paste a Web-based passage into your own draft and then revise it slightly by changing some of the words. Such patchwriting won't occur if you write in your own voice—that is, if you convert information from a source into your own words in order to make your own argument.

When you first practice paraphrasing, try paraphrasing a passage twice to avoid patchwriting:

- The first time, read the passage carefully and put it into your own words, looking at the source as little as possible.
- The second time, paraphrase your own paraphrase. Then recheck your final version against the original to make sure you have eliminated similar sentence structures or word-for-word strings.

We'll return to the problem of patchwriting in our discussion of plagiarism (pages 370–374).

Quoting

Besides summary and paraphrase, writers often choose to quote directly in order to give the reader the flavor and style of the source author's prose or to make a memorable point in the source author's own voice. Be careful not to quote a passage that you don't fully understand. (Sometimes novice writers quote a passage because it sounds impressive.) When you quote, you must reproduce the source author's original words exactly without change, unless you indicate changes with ellipses or brackets. Also be careful to represent the author's intention and meaning fairly; don't change the author's meaning by taking quotations out of context.

Punctuating Quotations Correctly

16.3 To punctu-ate quotations correctly

Because the mechanics of quoting offers its own difficulties, we devote the following sections to it. These sections answer the nuts-and-bolts questions about how to punctuate quotations correctly. Additional explanations covering variations and specific cases can be found in any good handbook.

Quoting a Complete Sentence

In some cases, you will want to quote a complete sentence from your source. Typically, you will include an attributive tag that tells the reader who is being quoted. At the end of the quotation, you usually indicate its page number in parentheses (see our later discussion of in-text citations, in Chapter 17).

Original Passage

Many people become vegetarians because they believe, in error, that vegetarianism is uniquely conducive to good health. [found on page 359 of source]*

Writer's Quotation of This Passage

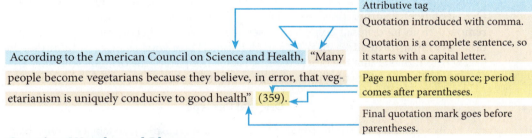

According to the American Council on Science and Health, "Many people become vegetarians because they believe, in error, that vegetarianism is uniquely conducive to good health" (359).

Attributive tag

Quotation introduced with comma.

Quotation is a complete sentence, so it starts with a capital letter.

Page number from source; period comes after parentheses.

Final quotation mark goes before parentheses.

Quoting Words and Phrases

Instead of quoting a complete sentence, you often want to quote only a few words or phrases from your source and insert them into your own sentence. In these cases, make sure that the grammatical structure of the quotation fits smoothly into the grammar of your own sentence.

---

*The cited page is from this text. When quoting from print sources or other sources with stable page numbers, you indicate the page number as part of your citation. To illustrate how to punctuate page citations, we'll assume throughout this section that you found the American Council on Science and Health article in this textbook rather than on the Web, in which case it would not be possible to cite page numbers.

Original Passage

The health of vegetarians may be better than that of nonvegetarians partly because of non-dietary factors: Many vegetarians are health-conscious. They exercise regularly, maintain a desirable body weight, and abstain from smoking. [found on page 359]

Quoted Phrase Inserted into Writer's Own Sentence

The American Council on Science and Health argues that the cause of vegetarians' longer life may be "nondietary factors." The Council claims that vegetarians are more "health-conscious" than meat eaters and that they "exercise regularly, maintain a desirable body weight, and abstain from smoking" (359).

Attributive tag

Quotation marks show where quotation starts and ends.

No comma or capital letter: Punctuation and capitalization determined by grammar of your own sentence.

Period comes after parentheses containing page number.

Modifying a Quotation

Occasionally you may need to alter a quotation to make it fit your own context. Sometimes the grammar of a desired quotation doesn't match the grammar of your own sentence. At other times, the meaning of a quoted word is unclear when it is removed from its original context. In these cases, use brackets to modify the quotation's grammar or to add a clarifying explanation. Place your changes or additions in brackets to indicate that the bracketed material is not part of the original wording. You should also use brackets to show a change in capitalization.

Original Passage

Many vegetarians are health-conscious. They exercise regularly, maintain a desirable body weight, and abstain from smoking. [found on page 359]

Quotations Modified with Brackets

The American Council on Science and Health hypothesizes that vegetarians maintain better health by "exercis[ing] regularly, maintain[ing] a desirable body weight, and abstain[ing] from smoking" (359).

Attributive tag

Brackets show change in quotation to fit grammar of writer's sentence.

Page number from source

According to the American Council on Science and Health, "They [vegetarians] exercise regularly, maintain a desirable body weight, and abstain from smoking" (359).

Attributive tag

Brackets show that writer has added a word to explain what "they" stands for.

Omitting Something from a Quoted Passage

Another way that writers modify quotations is to leave words out of the quoted passage. To indicate an omission, use three spaced periods called an **ellipsis** (. . .). Placement of the ellipsis depends on where the omitted material occurs. In the middle of a sentence, each of the periods should be preceded and followed by a space. When your ellipsis comes at the boundary between sentences, use an additional period to mark the end of the first sentence. When a parenthetical page number must follow the ellipsis, insert it before the final (fourth) period in the sequence.

Original Passage

People who are vegetarians by choice may differ from the general population in other ways relevant to health. For example, in Western countries most vegetarians are more affluent than nonvegetarians and thus have better living conditions and more access to medical care. [found on 359–360]

Quotations with Omitted Material Marked by Ellipses

According to the American Council on Science and Health, "people
| Three spaced periods mark omitted words in middle of sentence. Note spaces between each period.

who are vegetarians by choice may differ . . . in other ways relevant

to health. For example, in Western countries most vegetarians are
| Three periods form the ellipsis. (Omitted material comes before the end of the sentence.)

more affluent than nonvegetarians . . . " (359-360).
| This period ends the sentence.

Quoting Something That Contains a Quotation

Occasionally a passage that you wish to quote will already contain quotation marks. If you insert the passage within your own quotation marks, change the original double marks (") into single marks (') to indicate the quotation within the quotation. The same procedure works whether the quotation marks are used for quoted words or for a title. Make sure that your attributive tag signals who is being quoted.

Original Passage

The evidence is "strong" that vegetarians have (a) a lower risk of becoming alcoholic, constipated, or obese and (b) a lower risk of developing lung cancer. [found on page 360]

Use of Single Quotation Marks to Identify a Quotation within a Quotation

According to the American Council on Science and Health, "The
| Single quotation marks replace the double quotation marks in the original source.

evidence is 'strong' that vegetarians have (a) a lower risk of be-

coming alcoholic, constipated, or obese and (b) a lower risk of
| Double quotation marks enclose the material quoted from the source.

developing lung cancer" (360).

Using a Block Quotation for a Long Passage

If you quote a long source passage that will take four or more lines in your own paper, use the block indentation method rather than quotation marks. Block quotations are generally introduced with an attributive tag followed by a colon. The indented block of text, rather than quotation marks, signals that the material is a direct quotation. As we explained earlier, block quotations occur rarely in scholarly writing and are used primarily in cases where the writer intends to analyze the text being quoted. If you overuse block quotations, you simply produce a collage of other people's voices.

Original Passage

The health of vegetarians may be better than that of nonvegetarians partly because of non-dietary factors: Many vegetarians are health-conscious. They exercise regularly, maintain a desirable body weight, and abstain from smoking. Although most epidemiologists have attempted to take such factors into account in their analyses, it is possible that they did not adequately control their studies for nondietary effects. [found on page 359]

Block Quotation

The American Council on Science and Health suggests that vegetarians may be healthier than nonvegetarians not because of their diet but because of their more healthy lifestyle: ← Block quotation introduced with a colon

Many vegetarians are health-conscious. They exercise regularly, maintain a desirable body weight, and abstain from smoking. Although most epidemiologists have attempted to take such factors into account in their analyses, it is possible that they did not adequately control their studies for nondietary effects. (359) ←

No quotation marks

Block indented 1 inch on left

Page number in parentheses. (Note that parentheses come after the closing period preceded by a space.)

Creating Rhetorically Effective Attributive Tags

16.4 To signal your use of sources through rhetorically effective attributive tags

Throughout the previous examples we've been using attributive tags to indicate words or ideas taken from a source. *Attributive tags* are phrases such as "according to the American Council on Science and Health...," "Smith claims that...," or "the author continues...." Such phrases signal to the reader that the material immediately following the tag is from the cited source. In this section we'll show you why attributive tags are often clearer and more powerful than other ways of signaling a source, such as a parenthetical citation. Particularly, they can also be used rhetorically to shape your reader's response to a source.

Attributive Tags versus Parenthetical Citations

Instead of attributive tags, writers sometimes indicate a source only by citing it in parentheses at the end of the borrowed material—a common practice in the social sciences and some other kinds of academic writing. However, the preferred practice when writing to nonspecialized audiences is to use attributive tags.

Less Preferred: Indicating Source through Parenthetical Citation

Vegetarians are apt to be more health-conscious than nonvegetarians (American Council on Science and Health). *

More Preferred: Indicating Source through Attributive Tag

According to the American Council on Science and Health, vegetarians are apt to be more health-conscious than nonvegetarians.

A disadvantage of the parenthetical method is that it requires readers to wait until the end of the source material before the source is identified. Attributive tags, in contrast, identify the source the moment it is first used, thus marking more clearly the beginning of borrowed material. Another disadvantage of the parenthetical method is that it tends to treat the borrowed material as "fact" rather than as the view of the source author. In contrast, attributive tags call attention to the source's angle of vision. An attributive tag reminds the reader to put on the glasses of the source author—to see the borrowed material as shaped by the source author's biases and perspectives.

Creating Attributive Tags to Shape Reader Response

Attributive tags can be used not only to identify a source but also to shape your readers' attitudes toward the source. For example, if you wanted your readers to respect the expertise of a source, you might say, "According to noted chemist Marjorie Casper...." If you wanted your readers to discount Casper's views, you might say, "According to Marjorie Casper, an industrial chemist on the payroll of a major corporate polluter...."

When you compose an initial tag, you can add to it any combination of the kinds of information in Table 16.2, depending on your purpose, your audience's values, and your sense of what the audience already knows about the source. Our point here is that you can use attributive tags rhetorically to help your readers understand the significance and context of a source when you first introduce it and to guide your readers' attitudes toward the source.

---

*This parenthetical citation is in MLA form. If this had been a print source rather than a Web source, a page number would also have been given as follows: (American Council on Science and Health 43). APA form also indicates the date of the source: (American Council on Science and Health, 2002, p. 43). We explain MLA and APA styles for citing and documenting sources in Chapter 17.

TABLE 16.2 Modifying Attributive Tags to Shape Reader Response

Add to Attributive Tags	Examples
Author's credentials or relevant specialty (enhances credibility)	Civil engineer David Rockwood, a noted authority on stream flow in rivers
Author's lack of credentials (decreases credibility)	City Council member Dilbert Weasel, a local politician with no expertise in international affairs
Author's political or social views	Left-wing columnist Alexander Cockburn [has negative feeling]; Alexander Cockburn, a longtime champion of labor [has positive feeling]
Title of source if it provides context	In her book *Fasting Girls: The History of Anorexia Nervosa,* Joan Jacobs Brumberg shows that [establishes credentials for comments on eating disorders]
Publisher of source if it adds prestige or otherwise shapes audience response	Dr. Carl Patrona, in an article published in the prestigious *New England Journal of Medicine*
Historical or cultural information about a source that provides context or background	In his 1960s book popularizing the hippie movement, Charles Reich claims that
Indication of source's purpose or angle of vision	Feminist author Naomi Wolfe, writing a blistering attack on the beauty industry, argues that

Avoiding Plagiarism

16.5 To avoid plagiarism

In the next chapter, we proceed to the nuts and bolts of citing and documenting sources—a skill that will enhance your *ethos* as a skilled researcher and as a person of integrity. Unethical use of sources—called **plagiarism**—is a major concern not only for writing teachers but for teachers in all disciplines. To combat plagiarism, many instructors across the curriculum use plagiarism-detection software like turnitin.com. Their purpose, of course, is to discourage students from cheating. But sometimes students who have no intention of cheating can fall into producing papers that look like cheating. That is, they produce papers that might be accused of plagiarism even though the students had no intention of deceiving their readers.* Our goal in this section is to explain the concept of plagiarism more fully and to sum up the strategies needed to avoid it.

---

*See Rebecca Moore Howard, *Standing in the Shadow of Giants: Plagiarists, Authors, Collaborators* (Stamford, CT: Ablex Pub., 1999).

Why Some Kinds of Plagiarism May Occur Unwittingly

To understand how unwitting plagiarism might occur, consider Table 16.3, where the middle column—"Misuse of Sources"—shows common mistakes of novice writers. Everyone agrees that the behaviors in the "Fraud" column constitute deliberate cheating and deserve appropriate punishment. Everyone also agrees that good scholarly work meets the criteria in the "Ethical Use of Sources" column. Novice researchers, however, may find themselves unwittingly in the middle column until they learn the academic community's conventions for using research sources.

You might appreciate these conventions more fully if you recognize how they have evolved from Western notions of intellectual property and patent law associated with the rise of modern science in the seventeenth and eighteenth centuries. A person not only could own a house or a horse, but also could own an idea and the words used to express that idea. You can see these cultural conventions at work—in the form of laws or professional codes of ethics—whenever a book author is disgraced for lifting words or ideas from another author or whenever an artist or entrepreneur is sued for stealing song lyrics, publishing another person's photographs without permission, or infringing on some inventor's patent.

This understanding of plagiarism may seem odd in some non-Western cultures where collectivism is valued more than individualism. In these cultures, words written

TABLE 16.3   Plagiarism and the Ethical Use of Sources

	Plagiarism	Ethical Use of Sources
Fraud	Misuse of Sources (*Common Mistakes Made by New Researchers*)	
The writer • buys paper from a paper mill • submits someone else's work as his own • copies chunks of text from sources with obvious intention of not being detected • fabricates data or makes up evidence • intends to deceive	The writer • copies passages directly from a source, references the source with an in-text citation, but fails to use quotation marks or block indentation • in attempting to paraphrase a source, makes some changes, but follows too closely the wording of the original ("patchwriting") • fails to indicate the sources of some ideas or data (often is unsure what needs to be cited or has lost track of sources through poor note taking) • in general, misunderstands the conventions for using sources in academic writing	The writer • writes paper entirely in her own words or uses exact quotations from sources • indicates all quotations with quotation marks or block indentation • indicates her use of all sources through attribution, in-text citation, and an end-of-paper list of works cited

or spoken by ancestors, elders, or other authority figures may be regarded with reverence and shared with others without attribution. Also in these cultures, it might be disrespectful to paraphrase certain passages or to document them in a way that would suggest the audience didn't recognize the ancient wisdom.

However, such collectivist conventions won't work in research communities committed to building new knowledge. In the academic world, the conventions separating ethical from unethical use of sources are essential if research findings are to win the community's confidence. Effective research can occur only within ethical and responsible research communities, where people do not fabricate data and where current researchers respect and acknowledge the work of those who have gone before them.

Strategies for Avoiding Plagiarism

Table 16.4 will help you review the strategies presented throughout Chapters 15 to 17 for using source material ethically and avoiding plagiarism.

TABLE 16.4   **Avoiding Plagiarism or the Appearance of Plagiarism**

What to Do	Why to Do It
At the beginning	
Read your college's policy on plagiarism as well as statements from your teachers in class or on course syllabi.	Understanding policies on plagiarism and academic integrity will help you research and write ethically.
Pose a research question rather than a topic area.	Arguing your own thesis gives you a voice, establishes your *ethos,* and urges you to write ethically.
At the note-taking stage	
Create a bibliographic entry for each source.	This action makes it easy to create an end-of-paper bibliography and encourages rhetorical reading.
When you copy a passage into your notes, copy word for word and enclose it within quotation marks.	It is important to distinguish a source's words from your own words.
When you enter summaries or paraphrases into your notes, avoid patchwriting.	If your notes contain any strings of a source's original wording, you might later assume that these words are your own.
Distinguish your informational notes from your personal exploratory notes.	Keeping these kinds of notes separate will help you identify borrowed ideas when it's time to incorporate the source material into your paper.

TABLE 16.4   Continued

What to Do	Why to Do It
When writing your draft	
Except for exact quotations, write the paper entirely in your own words.	This strategy keeps you from patchwriting when you summarize or paraphrase.
Indicate all quotations with quotation marks or block indentation. Use ellipses or brackets to make changes to fit your own grammar.	Be careful to represent the author fairly; don't change meaning by taking quotations out of context.
Never cut and paste a Web passage directly into your draft. Paste it into a separate note file and put quotation marks around it.	Pasted passages are direct invitations to patchwrite.
Inside your text, use attributive tags or parenthetical citations to identify all sources. List all sources alphabetically in a concluding Works Cited or References list.	This strategy makes it easy for readers to know when you are using a source and where to find it.
Cite with attributive tags or parenthetical citations all quotations, paraphrases, summaries, and any other references to specific sources.	These are the most common in-text citations in a research paper.
Use in-text citations to indicate sources for all visuals and media such as graphs, maps, photographs, films, videos, broadcasts, and recordings.	The rules for citing words and ideas apply equally to visuals and media cited in your paper.
Use in-text citations for all ideas and facts that are not common knowledge.	Although you don't need to cite widely accepted and noncontroversial facts and information, it is better to cite them if you are unsure.

■ ■ ■   **FOR WRITING AND DISCUSSION   Avoiding Plagiarism**   MyWritingLab™

Individual task: Reread the original article from the American Council on Science and Health (pages 359–360) and Writer 3's use of this source in her paragraph about how nondietary habits may explain why vegetarians are healthier than nonvegetarians (page 361). Then read the paragraph below by Writer 4, who makes the same argument as Writer 3 but crosses the line from ethical to nonethical use of sources. Imagine that Writer 4 says in dismay, "How can this be plagiarism? I cited my source." Write a message to Writer 4 explaining how this passage falls into the category of plagiarism.

Writer 4's Argument (Example of Plagiarism)

According to the American Council on Science and Health, the health of vegetarians may be better than that of nonvegetarians partly because of nondietary factors. People who eat only vegetables tend to be very conscious of their health. They exercise regularly, avoid getting fat, and don't smoke. Scientists who examined the data may not have adequately controlled for these nondietary effects. Also in Western countries most vegetarians are more affluent than nonvegetarians and thus have better living conditions and more access to medical care.

Group task: Working in small groups or as a whole class, respond to the following questions.

1. Share with each other your messages to Writer 4.
2. Explore the possible causes of Writer 4's difficulty. Psychologically or cognitively, what may have caused Writer 4 to misuse the source? How might this writer's note-taking process or composing process have differed from that of Writer 3? In other words, what happened to get this writer into trouble?

Conclusion

This chapter has shown you how to use sources for your own purposes; how to summarize, paraphrase, and quote a source; how to signal your use of sources through rhetorically effective attributive tags; and how to punctuate quotations correctly. It has also explained how to use sources ethically to avoid plagiarism and create a professional ethos. In the next chapter we will provide guidelines and formats for citing and documenting your sources.

MyWritingLab™

Visit Ch. 16 Incorporating Sources into Your Own Argument in *MyWritingLab* to complete the For Writing and Discussion and to test your understanding of the chapter objectives.

Citing and Documenting Sources

17

What you will learn in this chapter:

17.1 To understand the correspondence between in-text citations and the end-of-paper list of cited works

17.2 To cite and document your sources using the style and format of the Modern Language Association (MLA)

17.3 To cite and document your sources using the style and format of the American Psychological Association (APA)

The previous chapter showed you how to use sources ethically, incorporating them into your own prose so as to further your argument as well as to avoid plagiarism.

The Correspondence between In-Text Citations and the End-of-Paper List of Cited Works

17.1 To understand the correspondence between in-text citations and the end-of-paper list of cited works

The most common forms of documentation use what are called in-text citations that match an end-of-paper list of cited works (as opposed to footnotes or endnotes). An **in-text citation** identifies a source in the body of the paper at the point where it is summarized, paraphrased, quoted, inserted, or otherwise referred to. At the end of your paper you include a list—alphabetized by author (or by title if there is no named author)—of all the works you cited. Both the Modern Language Association (MLA) system, used primarily in the humanities, and the American Psychological Association (APA) system, used primarily in the social sciences, follow this procedure. In MLA, your end-of-paper list is called **Works Cited.** In APA it is called **References.**

Whenever you place an in-text citation in the body of your paper, your reader knows to turn to the Works Cited or References list at the end of the paper to get the full bibliographic information. The key to the system's logic is this:

■ Every source in Works Cited or References must be mentioned in the body of the paper.

■ Conversely, every source mentioned in the body of the paper must be included in the end-of-paper list.

- The first word in each entry of the Works Cited or References list (usually an author's last name) must also appear in the in-text citation. In other words, there must be a one-to-one correspondence between the first word in each entry in the end-of-paper list and the name used to identify the source in the body of the paper.

Suppose a reader sees this phrase in your paper: "According to Debra Goldstein...." The reader should be able to turn to your Works Cited list and find an alphabetized entry beginning with "Goldstein, Debra." Similarly, suppose that in looking over your Works Cited list, your reader sees an article by "Guillen, Manuel." This means that the name "Guillen" has to appear in your paper in one of two ways:

- As an attributive tag: Economics professor Manuel Guillen argues that....
- As a parenthetical citation, often following a quotation: "...changes in fiscal policy" (Guillen 49).

Because this one-to-one correspondence is so important, let's illustrate it with some complete examples using the MLA formatting style:

If the body of your paper has this:	Then the Works Cited list must have this:
According to linguist Deborah Tannen, political debate in America leaves out the complex middle ground where most solutions must be developed.	Tannen, Deborah. *The Argument Culture: Moving from Debate to Dialogue.* New York: Random, 1998. Print.
In the 1980s, cigarette advertising revealed a noticeable pattern of racial stereotyping (Pollay, Lee, and Carter-Whitney).	Pollay, Richard W., Jung S. Lee, and David Carter-Whitney. "Separate, but Not Equal: Racial Segmentation in Cigarette Advertising." *Journal of Advertising* 21.1 (1992): 45-57. Print.
On its Web site, the National Men's Resource Center offers advice to parents on how to talk with children about alcohol and drugs ("Talking").	"Talking with Kids about Alcohol and Drugs." *Menstuff.* National Men's Resource Center, 1 Mar. 2007. Web. 26 June 2013.

How to format an MLA in-text citation and a Works Cited list entry is the subject of the next section. The APA system is similar except that it emphasizes the date of publication in both the in-text citation and the References entry. APA formatting is discussed on pages 389–396.

MLA Style

17.2 To cite and document your sources using the style and format of the Modern Language Association

An in-text citation and its corresponding Works Cited entry are linked in a chicken-and-egg system: You can't cite a source in the text without first knowing how the source's entry will be alphabetized in the Works Cited list. However, since most Works Cited entries are alphabetized by the first author's last name, for convenience we start with in-text citations.

In-Text Citations in MLA Style

A typical in-text citation contains two elements: (1) the last name of the author and (2) the page number of the quoted or paraphrased passage. However, in some cases a work is identified by something other than an author's last name, and sometimes no page number is required. Let's begin with the most common cases.

Typically, an in-text citation uses one of these two methods:

- **Parenthetical method.** Place the author's last name and the page number in parentheses immediately after the material being cited.

  The Spanish tried to reduce the status of Filipina women, who had been able to do business, get divorced, and sometimes become village chiefs (Karnow 41).

- **Attributive tag method.** Place the author's name in an attributive tag at the beginning of the source material and the page number in parentheses at the end.

  According to Karnow, the Spanish tried to reduce the status of Filipina women, who had been able to do business, get divorced, and sometimes become village chiefs (41).

Once you have cited an author and it is clear that the same author's material is being used, you need cite only the page numbers in parentheses in subsequent citations. A reader who wishes to look up the source will find the bibliographic information in the Works Cited section by looking for the entry under "Karnow."

Let's now turn to the variations. Table 17.1 identifies the typical variations and shows again the one-to-one connection between the in-text citation and the Works Cited list.

When to Use Page Numbers in In-Text Citations   When the materials you are citing are available in print or in pdf format, you can provide accurate page numbers for parenthetical citations. If you are working with Web sources or HTML files, however, do not use the page numbers obtained from a printout because they will not be consistent from printer to printer. If the item has numbered paragraphs, cite them

TABLE 17.1 In-Text Citations in MLA Style

Type of Source	Works Cited Entry at End of Paper (*Construct the entry while taking notes on each source.*)	In-Text Citation in Body of Paper (*Use the first word of the Works Cited entry in parentheses or an attributive tag; add page number at end of quoted or paraphrased passage.*)
One author	Pollan, Michael. *The Omnivore's Dilemma: A Natural History of Four Meals.* New York: Penguin, 2006. Print.	…(Pollan 256). OR According to Pollan,…(256).
More than one author	Pollay, Richard W., Jung S. Lee, and David Carter-Whitney. "Separate, but Not Equal: Racial Segmentation in Cigarette Advertising." *Journal of Advertising* 21.1 (1992): 45-57. Print.	…race" (Pollay, Lee, and Carter-Whitney 52). OR Pollay, Lee, and Carter-Whitney have argued that "advertisers…race" (52). *For the in-text citation, cite the specific page number rather than the whole range of pages given in the Works Cited entry.*
Author has more than one work in Works Cited list	Dombrowski, Daniel A. *Babies and Beasts: The Argument from Marginal Cases.* Urbana: U of Illinois P, 1997. Print. ---. *The Philosophy of Vegetarianism.* Amherst: U of Massachusetts P, 1984. Print.	…(Dombrowski, *Babies* 207)…. …(Dombrowski, *Philosophy* 328). OR According to Dombrowski, …(*Babies* 207). Dombrowski claims that…(*Philosophy* 328). *Because author has more than one work in Works Cited, include a short version of title to distinguish between entries.*
Corporate author	American Red Cross. *Standard First Aid.* St. Louis: Mosby Lifeline, 1993. Print.	…(American Red Cross 102). OR Snake bite instructions from the American Red Cross show that…(102).
No named author (Work is therefore alphabetized by title.)	"Ouch! Body Piercing." *Menstuff.* National Men's Resource Center, 1 Feb. 2001. Web. 17 July 2013.	…("Ouch! Body Piercing"). According to the National Men's Resource Center,…("Ouch!"). <ul><li>*Add "Ouch!" in parentheses to show that work is alphabetized under "Ouch!" not "National."*</li><li>*No page numbers are shown because Web site pages aren't stable.*</li></ul>
Indirect citation of a source that you found in another source *Suppose you want to use a quotation from Peter Singer that you found in a book by Daniel Dombrowski. Include Dombrowski but not Singer in Works Cited.*	Dombrowski, Daniel A. *Babies and Beasts: The Argument from Marginal Cases.* Urbana: U of Illinois P, 1997. Print.	Animal rights activist Peter Singer argues that…(qtd. in Dombrowski 429). <ul><li>*Singer is used for the attributive tag, but the in-text citation is to Dombrowski.*</li><li>*"qtd. in" stands for "quoted in."*</li></ul>

with the abbreviation *par.* or *pars.*—for example, "(Jones, pars. 22–24)." In the absence of reliable page numbers for the original material, MLA says to omit page references from the parenthetical citation. The chart below summarizes the use of page numbers in in-text citations.

Include a page number in the in-text citation:	Do not include a page number:
If the source has stable page numbers (print source or pdf version of print source): • If you quote something • If you paraphrase a specific passage • If you refer to data or details from a specific page or range of pages in the source	• If you are referring to the argument of the whole source instead of a specific page or passage • If the source does not have stable page numbers (articles on Web sites, HTML text, and so forth)

Works Cited List in MLA Style

In the MLA system, you place a complete Works Cited list at the end of the paper. The list includes all the sources that you mention in your paper. However, it does *not* include works you read but did not use. Entries in the Works Cited list follow these general guidelines:

- Entries are arranged alphabetically by author, or by title if there is no author.
- Each entry includes the medium of publication of the source you consulted— for example, *Print, Web, DVD, Performance, Oil on canvas,* and so on.
- If there is more than one entry per author, the works are arranged alphabetically by title. For the second and all additional entries, type three hyphens and a period in place of the author's name.

Dombrowski, Daniel A. *Babies and Beasts: The Argument from Marginal Cases.* Urbana:
U of Illinois P, 1997. Print.

---. *The Philosophy of Vegetarianism.* Amherst: U of Massachusetts P, 1984. Print.

You can see a complete, properly formatted Works Cited list on the last pages of Ivan Snook's paper (pages 326–330).

The remaining pages in this section show examples of MLA citation formats for different kinds of sources and provide explanations and illustrations as needed.

Works Cited Citation Models

Print Articles in Scholarly Journals

General Format for Print Article in Scholarly Journal

Author. "Article Title." *Journal Title* volume number.issue number (year): page numbers.
Print.

Note that all scholarly journal entries include both volume number and issue number, regardless of how the journal is paginated. For articles published in a scholarly Web journal, see page 386. For scholarly journal articles retrieved from an online database, see page 383.

One author

Herrera-Sobek, Maria. "Border Aesthetics: The Politics of Mexican Immigration in Film and
Art." *Western Humanities Review* 60.2 (2006): 60-71. Print.

Two or three authors

Pollay, Richard W., Jung S. Lee, and David Carter-Whitney. "Separate, but Not Equal: Racial
Segmentation in Cigarette Advertising." *Journal of Advertising* 21.1 (1992): 45-57. Print.

Four or more authors

Either list all the authors in the order in which they appear, or use "et al." (meaning "and others") to replace all but the first author.

Buck, Gayle A., et al. "Examining the Cognitive Processes Used by Adolescent Girls and
Women Scientists in Identifying Science Role Models: A Feminist Approach." *Science
Education* 92.4 (2008): 688-707. Print.

Print Articles in Magazines and Newspapers
If no author is identified, begin the entry with the title or headline. Distinguish between news stories and editorials by putting the word "Editorial" after the title. If a magazine comes out weekly or biweekly, include the complete date ("27 Sept. 2011"). If it comes out monthly, then state the month only ("Sept. 2011").

General Format for Magazines and Newspapers

Author. "Article Title." *Magazine Title* day Month year: page numbers. Print.

(Note: If the article continues in another part of the magazine or newspaper, add "+" to the number of the first page to indicate the nonsequential pages.)

Magazine article with named author

Snyder, Rachel L. "A Daughter of Cambodia Remembers: Loung Ung's Journey." *Ms.* Aug.-Sept.
2001: 62-67. Print.

Magazine article without named author

"Sacred Geese." *Economist* 1 June 2013: 24-25. Print.

MLA

Review of book, film, or performance

Schwarz, Benjamin. "A Bit of Bunting: A New History of the British Empire Elevates
  Expediency to Principle." Rev. of *Ornamentalism: How the British Saw Their Empire*, by
  David Cannadine. *Atlantic Monthly* Nov. 2001: 126-35. Print.

Kaufman, Stanley. "Polishing a Gem." Rev. of *The Blue Angel*, dir. Josef von Sternberg. *New
  Republic* 30 July 2001: 28-29. Print.

Lahr, John. "Nobody's Darling: Fascism and the Drama of Human Connection in *Ashes
  to Ashes*." Rev. of *Ashes to Ashes*, by Harold Pinter. The Roundabout Theater Co.
  Gramercy Theater, New York. *New Yorker* 22 Feb. 1999: 182-83. Print.

Newspaper article

Dougherty, Conor. "The Latest Urban Trend: Less Elbow Room." *Wall Street Journal* 4 June
  2013: A1+. Print.

Page numbers in newspapers are typically indicated by a section letter or number as
well as a page number. The "+" indicates that the article continues on one or more
pages later in the newspaper.

Newspaper editorial

"Nearing a Climate Legacy." Editorial. *New York Times* 3 June 2014, New Eng. natl. ed.: A22. Print.

Letter to the editor of a magazine or newspaper

Harvey, Jocelyn. Letter. *New Yorker* 21 Apr. 2014: 11. Print.

Print Books

General Format for Print Books

Author. *Title.* City of publication: Publisher, year of publication. Print.

One author

Pollan, Michael. *The Omnivore's Dilemma: A Natural History of Four Meals*. New York:
  Penguin, 2006. Print.

Two or more authors

Dombrowski, Daniel A., and Robert J. Deltete. *A Brief, Liberal, Catholic Defense of Abortion*.
  Urbana: U of Illinois P, 2000. Print.

Belenky, Mary, et al. *Women's Ways of Knowing: The Development of Self, Voice, and Mind*.
  New York: Basic, 1986. Print.

MLA

If there are four or more authors, you have the choice of listing all the authors in the order in which they appear on the title page or using "et al." (meaning "and others") to replace all but the first author. Your Works Cited entry and the parenthetical citation should match.

Second, later, or revised edition

Montagu, Ashley. *Touching: The Human Significance of the Skin.* 3rd ed. New York: Perennial,
    1986. Print.

In place of "3rd ed.," you can include abbreviations for other kinds of editions: "Rev. ed." (for "Revised edition") or "Abr. ed." (for "Abridged edition").

Republished book (for example, a paperback published after the original hardback edition or a modern edition of an older work)

Hill, Christopher. *The World Turned Upside Down: Radical Ideas during the English*
    Revolution. 1972. London: Penguin, 1991. Print.

Wollstonecraft, Mary. *The Vindication of the Rights of Woman, with Strictures on Political and*
    Moral Subjects. 1792. Rutland: Tuttle, 1995. Print.

The date immediately following the title is the original publication date of the work.

Multivolume work

Churchill, Winston S. *A History of the English-Speaking Peoples.* 4 vols. New York: Dodd,
    1956-58. Print.

Churchill, Winston S. *The Great Democracies.* New York: Dodd, 1957. Print. Vol. 4 of *A History*
    of the English-Speaking Peoples. 4 vols. 1956-58.

Use the first method when you cite the whole work; use the second method when you cite one individually titled volume of the work.

Article in familiar reference work

"Mau Mau." *The New Encyclopaedia Britannica.* 15th ed. 2002. Print.

Article in less familiar reference work

Hirsch, E. D., et al. "Kyoto Protocol." *The New Dictionary of Cultural Literacy.* Boston:
    Houghton, 2002. Print.

Translation

De Beauvoir, Simone. *The Second Sex.* 1949. Trans. H. M. Parshley. New York: Bantam, 1961.
    Print.

Illustrated book

Jacques, Brian. *The Great Redwall Feast.* Illus. Christopher Denise. New York: Philomel, 1996.
Print.

Graphic novel

Miyazaki, Hayao. *Nausicaa of the Valley of Wind.* 4 vols. San Francisco: Viz, 1995-97. Print.

Corporate author (a commission, committee, or other group)

American Red Cross. *Standard First Aid.* St. Louis: Mosby Lifeline, 1993. Print.

No author listed

The Complete Cartoons of The New Yorker. New York: Black Dog & Leventhal, 2004. Print.

Whole anthology

O'Connell, David F., and Charles N. Alexander, eds. *Self Recovery: Treating Addictions Using
Transcendental Meditation and Maharishi Ayur-Veda.* New York: Haworth, 1994. Print.

Anthology article

Royer, Ann. "The Role of the Transcendental Meditation Technique in Promoting
Smoking Cessation: A Longitudinal Study." *Self Recovery: Treating Addictions Using
Transcendental Meditation and Maharishi Ayur-Veda.* Ed. David F. O'Connell and
Charles N. Alexander. New York: Haworth, 1994. 221-39. Print.

When you cite an individual article, give the inclusive page numbers for the article at
the end of the citation, before the medium of publication.

Articles or Books from an Online Database

General Format for Material from Online Databases

Author. "Title." *Periodical Name* Print publication data including date and volume/issue
numbers: pagination. *Database.* Web. Date Month year you obtained the article
from the database.

Journal article from online database

Matsuba, M. Kyle. "Searching for Self and Relationships Online." *CyberPsychology and
Behavior* 9.3 (2006): 275-84. *Academic Search Complete.* Web. 14 Apr. 2007.

To see where each element in this citation was found, see Figure 17.1, which shows the
online database screen from which the Matsuba article was accessed. For articles in
databases, follow the formats for print newspapers, magazines, or scholarly journals,

Matsuba, M. Kyle. "Searching for Self and Relationships Online." *CyberPsychology and Behavior* 9.3 (2006): 275-84. *Academic Search Complete*. Web. 14 Apr. 2007.

FIGURE 17.1   Article downloaded from an online database, with elements identified for an MLA-style citation

as relevant. When the database text provides only the starting page number of a multi-page article, insert a plus sign after the number, before the period.

Broadcast transcript from online database

Conan, Neal. "Arab Media." *Talk of the Nation*. With Shibley Telhami. 4 May 2004. Transcript. *LexisNexis*. Web. 31 July 2014.

The label "Transcript" after the broadcast date indicates a text (not audio) version.

E-book from online database

Hanley, Wayne. *The Genesis of Napoleonic Propaganda, 1796-1799*. New York: Columbia UP, 2002. *Gutenberg-e*. Web. 31 July 2014.

Machiavelli, Niccolo. *Prince*. 1513. *Bibliomania*. Web. 31 July 2014.

Information about the original print version, including a translator if relevant and available, should be provided.

E-book on Kindle, iPad, or other e-reader

Boyle, T. C. *When the Killing's Done*. New York: Viking Penguin, 2011. Kindle file.

Other Internet Sources

General Format for Web Sources

Since Web sources are often unstable, MLA recommends that you download or print out your Web sources. The goal in citing these sources is to enable readers to locate the material. To that end, use the basic citation model and adapt it as necessary.

Author, editor, director, narrator, performer, compiler, or producer of the work, if available.
> *Title of a long work, italicized*. OR "Title of page or document that is part of a larger work, in quotation marks". *Title of the overall site, usually taken from the home page, if this is different from the title of the work*. Publisher or sponsor of the site (if none, use n.p.), day Month year of publication online or last update of the site (if not available, use n.d.). Web. day Month year you obtained the article from the database.

Dyer, Bob, and Ella Barnes. "The 'Greening' of the Arctic." *Greenversations*. U.S. Environmental Protection Agency, 7 Oct. 2008. Web. 11 Oct. 2010.

To see where each element of the Dyer citation comes from, see the Web page in Figure 17.2.

MLA assumes that readers will use a search engine to locate a Web source, so do not include a URL *unless* the item would be hard to locate without it. If you do include a URL, it goes at the end of the citation, after the access date. Enclose it in angle brackets < > followed by a period. If you need to break the URL from one line to the next, divide it only after a slash. Do not hyphenate a URL. See the home page entries on page 387 for an example of a citation with a URL.

Entire Web site

BlogPulse. Intelliseek, n.d. Web. 24 July 2011.

Padgett, John B., ed. *William Faulkner on the Web*. U of Mississippi, 26 Mar. 2007. Web. 25 June 2010.

Documents within a Web site

Marks, John. "Overview: Letter from the President." *Search for Common Ground*. Search for Common Ground, n.d. Web. 25 June 2014.

Gourlay, Alexander S. "Glossary." *The William Blake Archive*. Lib. of Cong., 2005. Web. 21 Jan. 2013.

"Ouch! Body Piercing." *Menstuff*. National Men's Resource Center, 1 Feb. 2001. Web. 17 July 2013.

MLA

URL

Site sponsor

Name of blog

Title of posting

Date of posting

Blog author

Dyer, Bob, and Ella Barnes. "The 'Greening' of the Arctic." *Greenversations*. U.S. Environmental Protection Agency,
7 Oct. 2008. Web. 11 Oct. 2010.

FIGURE 17.2   An item published on the Web, with elements identified for an MLA-style citation

Article from a newspaper or newswire site

Bounds, Amy. "Thinking Like Scientists." *Daily Camera* [Boulder]. Scripps Interactive
Newspaper Group, 26 June 2007. Web. 26 June 2010.

"Great Lakes: Rwanda Backed Dissident Troops in DRC-UN Panel." *IRIN*. UN Office for the
Coordination of Humanitarian Affairs, 21 July 2004. Web. 31 July 2004.

Article from a scholarly e-journal

Welch, John R., and Ramon Riley. "Reclaiming Land and Spirit in the Western Apache
Homeland." *American Indian Quarterly* 25.4 (2001): 5-14. Web. 19 Dec. 2011.

Broadcast transcript from a Web site

Woodruff, Judy, Richard Garnett, and Walter Dellinger. "Experts Analyze Supreme Court Free Speech Rulings." Transcript: Background and discussion. *Online NewsHour*. PBS, 25 June 2007. Web. 26 June 2010.

Blog posting

Goddard, Anne Lynam. "Maya Angelou's Words Were a Comfort to Abducted Aid Worker." *DisruptingPoverty*. Tumblr, 31 May 2014. Web. 4 June 2014.

Social media posting

"Rattlesnake Figure (Aluminum) by Thomas Houseago." *Storm King Art Center*. Facebook, 30 May 2013. Web. 3 June 2013.

Podcast

"The Long and Winding Road: DNA Evidence for Human Migration." *Science Talk*. Scientific American, 7 July 2008. Web. 21 July 2014.

Web video

Beck, Roy. "Immigration Gumballs." *YouTube*. YouTube, 2 Nov. 2006. Web. 23 July 2011.

For films and DVDs, see below.

Home pages

Agatucci, Cora. *Culture and Literature of Africa*. Course home page. Humanities Dept., Central Oregon Community College, Jan. 2007–May 2007. Web. 31 July 2007. <http://web.cocc.edu/cagatucci/classes/hum211/>.

African Studies Program. Home page. School of Advanced International Study, Johns Hopkins U, n.d. Web. 31 July 2013.

E-mail

Daffinrud, Sue. "Scoring Guide for Class Participation." Message to the author. 12 Dec. 2014. E-mail.

Use the subject line as the title of the e-mail. Use "E-mail" as the medium of publication and omit your access date.

Miscellaneous Sources

Television or radio program

Begin with the episode name, if any, in quotation marks, followed by the program name, italicized. Use "Television" or "Radio" as the medium of publication.

"Lie Like a Rug." *NYPD Blue*. Dir. Steven Bochco and David Milch. ABC. KOMO, Seattle. 6

    Nov. 2001. Television.

If you accessed a program on the Web, give the basic citation information without the original medium of publication; then include the Web publication information with an access date.

Ashbrook, Tom. "Turf Wars and the American Lawn." *On Point*. Natl. Public Radio, 22 July

    2008. Web. 23 July 2014.

For podcasts, see page 396.

Film or video recording

Shakespeare in Love. Dir. John Madden. Perf. Joseph Fiennes and Gwyneth Paltrow. Screenplay

    by Marc Norman and Tom Stoppard. Universal Miramax, 1998. Film.

Use "DVD" or "Videocassette" rather than "Film" as the medium of publication if that is the medium you consulted. If you accessed a film or video on the Web, omit the original medium of publication, include the Web site or database name (italicized), the sponsor and posting date, "Web" as medium of publication, and the date of access.

Shakespeare in Love. Dir. John Madden. Perf. Joseph Fiennes and Gwyneth Paltrow. Screenplay

    by Marc Norman and Tom Stoppard. Universal Miramax, 1998. *Netflix*. Netflix, n.d.

    Web. 9 Mar. 2014.

For videos published originally on the Web, see page 387.

Sound recording

Begin the entry with what your paper emphasizes—for example, the artist's, composer's, or conductor's name—and adjust the elements accordingly. List the medium—CD, LP, Audiocassette—last.

Dylan, Bob. "Rainy Day Women #12." *Blonde on Blonde*. Columbia, 1966. LP.

If you accessed the recording on the Web, drop the original medium of publication and include the Web site or database name (italicized), "Web" as the medium of publication, and the access date.

Dylan, Bob. "Rainy Day Women #12." *Blonde on Blonde*. Columbia, 1966. *Lala*. La La Media,

    n.d. Web. 10 Mar. 2014.

Cartoon or advertisement

Trudeau, Garry. "Doonesbury." Comic strip. *Seattle Times* 19 Nov. 2011: B4. Print.

Banana Republic. Advertisement. *Details* Oct. 2001: 37. Print.

Interview

Castellucci, Marion. Personal interview. 7 Oct. 2014.

Lecture, speech, or conference presentation

Sharples, Mike. "Authors of the Future." Conference of European Teachers of Academic
    Writing. U of Groningen. Groningen, Neth. 20 June 2001. Lecture.

Government publications

In general, follow these guidelines:

- Usually cite as author the government agency that produced the document. Begin with the highest level and then branch down to the specific agency:

    United States. Dept. of Justice. FBI.

    Idaho. Dept. of Motor Vehicles.

- Follow this with the title of the document, italicized.
- If a specific person is clearly identified as the author, you may begin the citation with that person's name, or you may list the author (preceded by the word "By") after the title of the document.
- Follow standard procedures for citing publication information for print sources or Web sources.

United States. Dept. of Justice. FBI. *The School Shooter: A Threat Assessment Perspective*. By
    Mary Ellen O'Toole. 2000. Web. 16 Aug. 2011.

MLA-Style Research Paper

As an illustration of a student research paper written in MLA style, see Ivan Snook's argument about women in combat roles on pages 326–330.

APA Style

17.3 To cite and document your sources using the style and format of the American Psychological Association

In many respects, the APA style and the MLA style are similar and their basic logic is the same. In the APA system, the list where readers can find full bibliographic information is titled "References"; as in MLA format, it includes only the sources cited in the body of the paper. The distinguishing features of APA citation style are highlighted in the following sections.

APA

In-Text Citations in APA Style

A typical APA-style in-text citation contains three elements: (1) the last name of the author, (2) the date of the publication, and (3) the page number of the quoted or paraphrased passage. Table 17.2 identifies some typical variations and shows again the one-to-one connection between the in-text citation and the References list.

TABLE 17.2   In-Text Citations in APA Style

Type of Source	References Entry at End of Paper	In-Text Citation in Body of Paper
One author	Pollan, M. (2006). *The omnivore's dilemma: A natural history of four meals*. New York, NY: Penguin.	… (Pollan, 2006, p. 256). OR According to Pollan (2006), … (p. 256).
Two authors	Kwon, O., & Wen, Y. (2010). An empirical study of the factors affecting social network service use. *Computers in Human Behavior, 26*, 254–263. doi:10.1016 /j.chb.2009.04.011	… (Kwon & Wen, 2010, p. 262). OR Kwon and Wen (2010) claim that … (p. 262).
Three to five authors	Pollay, R. W., Lee, J. S., & Carter-Whitney, D. (1992). Separate, but not equal: Racial segmentation in cigarette advertising. *Journal of Advertising, 21*(1), 45–57.	… race" (Pollay, Lee, & Carter-Whitney, 1992, p. 52). OR Pollay, Lee, and Carter-Whitney have argued that "advertisers … race" (1992, p. 52). *For subsequent citations, use* Pollay et al. *For a quotation, use the specific page number, not the whole range of pages.*
Author has more than one work in References list	Dombrowski, D. A. (1984). *The philosophy of vegetarianism*. Amherst, MA: University of Massachusetts Press. Dombrowski, D. A. (1997). *Babies and beasts: The argument from marginal cases*. Urbana: University of Illinois Press.	… (Dombrowski, 1984, p. 207). … (Dombrowski, 1997, p. 328). OR Dombrowski (1984) claims that … (p. 207). According to Dombrowski (1997),… (p. 328).
Indirect citation of a source that you found in another source *You use a quotation from Peter Singer from a book by Dombrowski. Include Dombrowski, not Singer, in References.*	Dombrowski, D. A. (1997). *Babies and beasts: The argument from marginal cases*. Urbana: University of Illinois Press.	Animal rights activist Peter Singer argues that … (as cited in Dombrowski, 1997, p. 429). *Singer is used for the attributive tag, but the in-text citation is to Dombrowski.*

References List in APA Style

The APA References list at the end of a paper presents entries alphabetically. If you cite more than one item for an author, repeat the author's name each time and arrange the items in chronological order, beginning with the earliest. In cases where two works by an author appeared in the same year, arrange them in the list alphabetically by title, and then add a lowercase "a" or "b" (etc.) after the date so that you can distinguish between them in the in-text citations:

Smith, R. (1999a). *Body image in non-Western cultures, 1750–present*. London, England:
Bonanza Press.

Smith, R. (1999b). Eating disorders reconsidered. *Journal of Appetite Studies, 45*, 295-300.

A formatted References list appears on page 271.

References Citation Models

Print Articles in Scholarly Journals

General Format for Print Article in Scholarly Journal

Author. (Year of Publication). Article title. *Journal Title, volume number*(issue number), page
numbers. doi:xx.xxxx/x.xxxx.xx

If there is one, include the **DOI** (digital object identifier), a code that is uniquely assigned to many journal articles in numeric or URL form. Note the style for capitalizing article titles and for italicizing the volume number.

One author

Herrera-Sobek, M. (2006). Border aesthetics: The politics of Mexican immigration in film and
art. *Western Humanities Review, 60,* 60-71. doi:10.1016/j.chb.2009.04.011

Two to seven authors

McElroy, B. W., & Lubich, B. H. (2013). Predictors of course outcomes: Early indicators of delay in online classrooms. *Distance Education, 34*(1). http://dx.doi.org/10.1080/01587919
.2013.770433

When a source has more than seven authors, list the first six and the last one by name, separated by an ellipsis (…) to indicate the authors whose names have been omitted.

Scholarly journal that restarts page numbering with each issue

Pollay, R. W., Lee, J. S., & Carter-Whitney, D. (1992). Separate, but not equal: Racial
segmentation in cigarette advertising. *Journal of Advertising, 21*(1), 45-57.

Note that the issue number and the parentheses are *not* italicized.

Print Articles in Magazines and Newspapers

General Format for Print Article in Magazine or Newspaper

Author. (Year, Month Day). Article title. *Periodical Title, volume number*, page numbers.

If page numbers are discontinuous, identify every page, separating numbers with a comma.

Magazine article with named author

Hall, S. S. (2001, March 11). Prescription for profit. *The New York Times Magazine*, 40-45, 59, 91-92, 100.

Magazine article without named author

Sacred geese. (2013, June 1). *The Economist*, 24-25.

Review of book or film

Schwarz, B. (2001, November). A bit of bunting: A new history of the British empire elevates expediency to principle [Review of the book *Ornamentalism: How the British saw their empire*]. *Atlantic Monthly, 288*, 126-135.

Kaufman, S. (2001, July 30). Polishing a gem [Review of the motion picture *The blue angel*]. *New Republic, 225*, 28-29.

Newspaper article

Dougherty, C. (2013, June 4). The latest urban trend: Less elbow room. *Wall Street Journal*, pp. A1, A12.

Newspaper editorial

Nearing a climate legacy [Editorial]. (2014, June 3). *The New York Times*, p. A22.

Letter to the editor of a magazine or newspaper

Harvey, J. (2014, April 21). The lives of Paul de Man [Letter to the editor]. *The New Yorker*, 7.

Print Books

General Format for Print Books

Author. (Year of publication). *Book title: Subtitle*. City, State [abbreviated]: Name of Publisher.

Brumberg, J. J. (1997). *The body project: An intimate history of American girls*. New York, NY: Vintage.

If the publisher's name indicates the state in which it is located, list the city but omit the state.

Reid, H., & Taylor, B. (2010). *Recovering the commons: Democracy, place, and global justice.* Champaign: University of Illinois Press.

Second, later, or revised edition

Montagu, A. (1986). *Touching: The human significance of the skin* (3rd ed.). New York, NY: Perennial Press.

Republished book (for example, a paperback published after the original hardback edition or a modern edition of an older work)

Wollstonecraft, M. (1995). *The vindication of the rights of woman, with strictures on political and moral subjects.* Rutland, VT: Tuttle. (Original work published 1792)

The in-text citation should read: (Wollstonecraft, 1792/1995).

Multivolume work

Churchill, W. S. (1956–1958). *A history of the English-speaking peoples* (Vols. 1–4). New York, NY: Dodd, Mead.

This is the citation for all the volumes together. The in-text citation should read: (Churchill, 1956–1958).

Churchill, W. S. (1957). *A history of the English-speaking peoples: Vol. 4. The great democracies.* New York, NY: Dodd, Mead.

This is the citation for a specific volume. The in-text citation should read: (Churchill, 1957).

Article in reference work

Hirsch, E. D., Kett, J. F., & Trefil, J. (2002). Kyoto Protocol. In *The new dictionary of cultural literacy.* Boston, MA: Houghton Mifflin.

Translation

De Beauvoir, S. (1961). *The second sex* (H. M. Parshley, Trans.). New York, NY: Bantam Books. (Original work published 1949)

The in-text citation should read: (De Beauvoir, 1949/1961).

Corporate author (a commission, committee, or other group)

American Red Cross. (1993). *Standard first aid.* St. Louis, MO: Mosby Lifeline.

Anonymous author

Complete cartoons of The New Yorker. (2004). New York, NY: Penguin Books.

The in-text citation is (*Complete Cartoons*, 2004).

APA

Whole anthology

O'Connell, D. F., & Alexander, C. N. (Eds.). (1994). *Self recovery: Treating addictions using transcendental meditation and Maharishi Ayur-Veda.* New York, NY: Haworth Press.

Anthology article

Royer, A. (1994). The role of the transcendental meditation technique in promoting smoking cessation: A longitudinal study. In D. F. O'Connell & C. N. Alexander (Eds.), *Self recovery: Treating addictions using transcendental meditation and Maharishi Ayur-Veda* (pp. 221-239). New York, NY: Haworth Press.

Articles or Books from an Online Database

Article from database with digital object identifier (DOI)

Scharrer, E., Daniel, K. D., Lin, K.-M., & Liu, Z. (2006). Working hard or hardly working? Gender, humor, and the performance of domestic chores in television commercials. *Mass Communication and Society, 9*(2), 215-238. doi:10.1207/s15327825mcs0902_5

Omit the database name. If an article or other document has been assigned a digital object identifier (DOI), include the DOI at the end.

Article from database without DOI

Highland, R. A., & Dabney, D. A. (2009). Using Adlerian theory to shed light on drug dealer motivations. *Applied Psychology in Criminal Justice, 5*(2), 109-138. Retrieved from http://www.apcj.org

Omit the database name. Instead, use a search engine to locate the publication's home page, and cite that URL. If you need to break a URL at the end of a line, do not use a hyphen. Instead, break it *before* a punctuation mark or *after* http://.

Other Internet Sources

General Format for Web Documents

Author, editor, director, narrator, performer, compiler, or producer of the work, if available. (Year, Month Day of posting). *Title of web document, italicized.* Retrieved from Name of website if different from author or title: URL of home page

Barrett, J. (2007, January 17). *MySpace is a natural monopoly.* Retrieved from ECommerce Times website: http://www.ecommercetimes.com

Marks, J. (n.d.). "Overview: Letter from the president." Retrieved June 3, 2014, from the Search for Common Ground website: http://www.sfcg.org

Entire Web site

BlogPulse. (n.d.). Retrieved September 3, 2014, from the Intelliseek website:
http://www.intelliseek.com

Article from a newspaper site

Bounds, A. (2007, June 26). Thinking like scientists. *Daily Camera* [Boulder]. Retrieved from
http://www.dailycamera.com

Article from a scholarly e-journal

Welch, J. R., & Riley, R. (2001). Reclaiming land and spirit in the western Apache homeland.
American Indian Quarterly, 25, 5-14. Retrieved from http://muse.jhu.edu/journals
/american_indian_quarterly

Reference material

Cicada. (2004). In *Encyclopaedia Britannica*. Retrieved from http://www.britannica.com

E-book

Hoffman, F. W. (1981). *The literature of rock: 1954–1978*. Retrieved from
http://www.netlibrary.com

E-mail, interviews, and personal correspondence

Cite personal correspondence in the body of your text, but not in the References list:
"Daffinrud (personal communication, December 12, 2014) claims that. . . ."

Blog Posting

Goddard, A. L. (2014, May 31). Maya Angelou's words were a comfort to abducted aid worker
[Web log post]. Retrieved from annegoddard.tumblr.com

Social media posting

Storm King Art Center. (2013, May 30). Rattlesnake figure (aluminum) by Thomas
Houseago [Facebook update]. Retrieved from http://www.facebook.com
/StormKingArtCenter

Web video

Beck, R. (2006, November 2). Immigration gumballs [Video file]. Retrieved from http://www
.youtube.com/watch?v=n7WJeqxuOfQ

APA

Podcast

Funke, E. (Host). (2007, June 26). *ArtScene* [Audio podcast]. National Public Radio. Retrieved from http://www.npr.org

Miscellaneous Sources

Television program

Bochco, S., & Milch, D. (Directors). (2001, November 6). Lie like a rug [Television series episode]. In *NYPD blue*. New York, NY: American Broadcasting Company.

Film

Madden, J. (Director). (1998). *Shakespeare in love* [Motion picture]. United States: Universal Miramax.

Sound recording

Dylan, B. (1966). Rainy day women #12. On *Blonde on blonde* [Record]. New York, NY: Columbia.

Government publications

U.S. Department of Health and Human Services. (2012). *Preventing tobacco use among youth and young adults: A report of the Surgeon General.* Retrieved from http://www.surgeongeneral.gov/library/reports/preventing-youth-tobacco-use/index .html#Full Report

APA-Style Research Paper

An example of a paper in APA style is shown on pages 266–271.

Conclusion

This chapter has shown you the nuts and bolts of citing and documenting sources in both the MLA and APA styles. It has explained the logic of parenthetical citation systems, showing you how to match sources cited in your text with those in your concluding bibliography. It has also shown you the documentation formats for a wide range of sources in both MLA and APA styles.

MyWritingLab™

Visit Ch. 17 Citing and Documenting Sources in *MyWritingLab* to test your understanding of the chapter objectives.

Informal Fallacies

In this appendix, we look at ways of assessing the legitimacy of an argument within a real-world context of probabilities rather than within a mathematical world of certainty. Whereas formal logic is a kind of mathematics, the informal fallacies addressed in this appendix are embedded in everyday arguments, sometimes making fallacious reasoning seem deceptively persuasive, especially to unwary audiences. We begin by looking at the problem of conclusiveness in arguments, after which we give you an overview of the most commonly encountered informal fallacies.

The Problem of Conclusiveness in an Argument

In real-world disagreements, we seldom encounter arguments that are absolutely conclusive. Rather, arguments are, to various degrees, "persuasive" or "nonpersuasive." In the pure world of formal logic, however, it is possible to have absolutely conclusive arguments. For example, an Aristotelian syllogism, if it is validly constructed, yields a certain conclusion. Moreover, if the first two premises (called the "major" and "minor" premises) are true, then we are guaranteed that the conclusion is also true. Here is an example:

Valid Syllogism

Major premise: All ducks are feathered animals.
Minor premise: Quacko is a duck.
Conclusion: Therefore Quacko is a feathered animal.

This syllogism is said to be valid because it follows a correct form. Moreover, because its premises are true, the conclusion is guaranteed to be true. However, if the syllogism follows an incorrect form (and is therefore invalid), we can't determine whether the conclusion is true.

Invalid Syllogism

Major premise: All ducks are feathered animals.
Minor premise: Clucko is a feathered animal.
Conclusion: Therefore Clucko is a duck.

In the valid syllogism, we are guaranteed that Quacko is a feathered animal because the minor premise states that Quacko is a duck and the major premise places ducks within the larger class of feathered animals. But in the invalid syllogism, there is no guaranteed conclusion. We know that Clucko is a feathered animal but we can't know whether he is a duck. He may be a duck, but he may also be a buzzard or a chicken. The invalid syllogism thus commits a "formal fallacy" in that its form doesn't guarantee the truth of its conclusion even if the initial premises are true.

From the perspective of real-world argumentation, the problem with formal logic is that it isn't concerned with the truth of premises. For example, the following argument is logically valid even though the premises and conclusion are obviously untrue:

Valid Syllogism with Untrue Major and Minor Premises

Major premise: The blood of insects can be used to lubricate lawn mower engines.
Minor premise: Vampires are insects.
Conclusion: Therefore the blood of vampires can be used to lubricate lawn mower engines.

Even though this syllogism meets the formal requirements for validity, its argument is ludicrous.

In this appendix, therefore, we are concerned with "informal" rather than "formal" fallacies because informal fallacies are embedded within real-world arguments addressing contestable issues of truth and value. Disputants must argue about issues because they can't be resolved with mathematical certainty; any contestable claim always leaves room for doubt and alternative points of view. Disputants can create only more or less persuasive arguments, never conclusive ones.

An Overview of Informal Fallacies

The study of informal fallacies remains the murkiest of all logical endeavors. It's murky because informal fallacies are as unsystematic as formal fallacies are rigid and systematized. Whereas formal fallacies of logic have the force of laws, informal fallacies have little more than explanatory power. Informal fallacies are quirky; they identify classes of less conclusive arguments that recur with some frequency, but they do not contain formal flaws that make their conclusions illegitimate no matter what the terms may say. Informal fallacies require us to look at the meaning of the terms to determine how much we should trust or distrust the conclusion. In evaluating arguments with informal fallacies, we usually find that arguments are "more or less" fallacious, and determining the degree of fallaciousness is a matter of judgment.

Knowledge of informal fallacies is most useful when we run across arguments that we "know" are wrong, but we can't quite say why. They just don't "sound right." They look reasonable enough, but they remain unacceptable to us. Informal fallacies are a sort of compendium of symptoms for arguments flawed in this way. We must be careful, however, to make sure that the particular case before us "fits" the descriptors for the fallacy that seems to explain its problem. It's much easier, for example, to find informal fallacies in a hostile argument than in a friendly one simply because we are more likely to expand the limits of the fallacy to make the disputed case fit.

In arranging the fallacies, we have, for convenience, put them into three categories derived from classical rhetoric: *pathos, ethos,* and *logos.* Fallacies of *pathos* rest on flaws in the way an argument appeals to the audience's emotions and values. Fallacies of *ethos* rest on flaws in the way the argument appeals to the character of opponents or of sources and witnesses within an argument. Fallacies of *logos* rest on flaws in the relationship among statements in an argument.

Fallacies of *Pathos*

Argument to the People (Appealing to Stirring Symbols)
This is perhaps the most generic example of a *pathos* fallacy. Arguments to the people appeal to the fundamental beliefs, biases, and prejudices of the audience in order to sway opinion through a feeling of solidarity among those of the group. Thus a "Support Our Troops" bumper sticker, often including the American flag, creates an initial feeling of solidarity among almost all citizens of goodwill. But the car owner may have the deeper intention of actually meaning "support our president" or "support the war in _____." The stirring symbol of the flag and the desire shared by most people to support our troops is used fallaciously to urge support of a particular political act. Arguments to the people often use visual rhetoric, as in the soaring eagle used in Wal-Mart corporate ads or images of happy families in marketing advertisements.

Appeal to Ignorance
This fallacy persuades an audience to accept as true a claim that hasn't been proved false or vice versa. "Jones must have used steroids to get those bulging biceps because he can't prove that he hasn't used steroids." Appeals to ignorance are particularly common in the murky field of pseudoscience. "UFOs (ghosts, abominable snowmen) do exist because science hasn't proved that they don't exist." Sometimes, however, it is hard to draw a line between a fallacious appeal to ignorance and a legitimate appeal to precaution: "Genetically modified organisms may be dangerous to our health because science hasn't proved that they are safe."

Appeal to Popularity—Bandwagon
To board the bandwagon means (to use a more contemporary metaphor) to board the bus or train of what's popular. Appeals to popularity are fallacious because the popularity of something is irrelevant to its actual merits. "Living together before marriage is the right thing to do because most couples are now doing it." Bandwagon appeals are common in advertising where the claim that a product is popular substitutes for evidence of the product's excellence. There are times, however, when popularity may indeed be relevant: "Global warming is probably caused by human activity because a preponderance of scientists now hold this position." (Here we assume that scientists haven't simply climbed on a bandwagon themselves, but have formed their opinions based on research data and well-vetted, peer-reviewed papers.)

Appeal to Pity
Here the arguer appeals to the audience's sympathetic feelings in order to support a claim that should be decided on more relevant or objective grounds. "Honorable judge, I should not be fined $200 for speeding because I was distraught from hearing news of my brother's illness and was rushing to see him in the hospital."

Here the argument is fallacious because the arguer's reason, while evoking sympathy, is not a relevant justification for speeding (as it might have been, for instance, if the arguer had been rushing an injured person to the emergency room). In many cases, however, an arguer can legitimately appeal to pity, as in the case of fund-raising for victims of a tsunami or other disaster.

Red Herring   This fallacy's funny name derives from the practice of using a red herring (a highly odiferous fish) to throw dogs off a scent that they are supposed to be tracking. It refers to the practice of throwing an audience offtrack by raising an unrelated or irrelevant point. "Debating a gas tax increase is valuable, but I really think there should be an extra tax on SUVs." Here the arguer, apparently uncomfortable with the gas tax issue, diverts the conversation to the emotionally charged issue of owning SUVs. A conversant who noted how the argument has gotten offtrack might say, "Stop talking, everyone. The SUV question is a red herring; let's get back to the topic of a gas tax increase."

Fallacies of *Ethos*

Appeal to False Authority   Arguers appeal to false authority when they use famous people (often movie stars or other celebrities) to testify on issues about which these persons have no special competence. "Joe Quarterback says Gooey Oil keeps his old tractor running sharp; therefore, Gooey Oil is a good oil." Real evidence about the quality of Gooey Oil would include technical data about the product rather than testimony from an actor or hired celebrity. However, the distinction between a "false authority" and a legitimate authority can become blurred. For example, in the early years of advertising for drugs that treat erectile dysfunction, Viagra hired former senator and presidential hopeful Bob Dole to help market the drug. (You can see his commercials on YouTube.) As a famous person rather than a doctor, Dole would seem to be a false authority. But Dole was also widely known to have survived prostate cancer, and he may well have used Viagra. To the extent a person is an expert in a field, he or she is no longer a "false authority."

Ad Hominem   Literally, *ad hominem* means "to the person." An *ad hominem* argument is directed at the character of an opponent rather than at the quality of the opponent's reasoning. Ideally, arguments are supposed to be *ad rem* ("to the thing"), that is, addressed to the specifics of the case itself. Thus an *ad rem* critique of a politician would focus on her voting record, the consistency and cogency of her public statements, her responsiveness to constituents, and so forth. An *ad hominem* argument would shift attention from her record to features of her personality, life circumstances, or the company she keeps. "Senator Sweetwater's views on the gas tax should be discounted because her husband works for a huge oil company" or "Senator Sweetwater supports tax cuts for the wealthy because she is very wealthy herself and stands to gain." But not all *ad hominem* arguments are *ad hominem* fallacies. Lawyers, for example, when questioning expert witnesses who give damaging testimony, often make an issue of their honesty, credibility, or personal investment in an outcome.

Poisoning the Well   This fallacy is closely related to *ad hominem*. Arguers poison the well when they discredit an opponent or an opposing view in advance. "Before I yield the floor to the next speaker, I must remind you that those who oppose my plan do not have the best interests of working people in their hearts."

Straw Man   The straw man fallacy occurs when you oversimplify an opponent's argument to make it easier to refute or ridicule. Rather than summarizing an opposing view fairly and completely, you basically make up the argument you wish your opponent had made because it is so much easier to knock over, like knocking over a straw man or scarecrow in a corn field. See pages 125–126 for an example of a straw man argument.

Fallacies of *Logos*

Hasty Generalization   This fallacy occurs when someone makes a broad generalization on the basis of too little evidence. Generally, the evidence needed to support a generalization persuasively must meet the STAR criteria (sufficiency, typicality, accuracy, and relevance) discussed in Chapter 5 (pages 92–93). But what constitutes a sufficient amount of evidence? The generally accepted standards of sufficiency in any given field are difficult to determine. The Food and Drug Administration (FDA), for example, generally proceeds cautiously before certifying a drug as "safe." However, if people are harmed by the side effects of an FDA-approved drug, critics often accuse the FDA of having made a hasty generalization. At the same time, patients eager to have access to a new drug and manufacturers eager to sell a new product may lobby the FDA to quit "dragging its feet" and get the drug to market. Hence, the point at which a hasty generalization passes over into the realm of a prudent generalization is nearly always uncertain and contested.

Part for the Whole   Sometimes called by its Latin name *pars pro toto*, this fallacy is closely related to hasty generalization. In this fallacy, arguers pick out a part of the whole or a sample of the whole (often not a typical or representative part or sample) and then claim that what is true of the part is true for the whole. If, say, individuals wanted to get rid of the National Endowment for the Arts (NEA), they might focus on several controversial programs funded by the NEA and use them as justification for wiping out all NEA programs. The flip side of this fallacy occurs when an arguer picks only the best examples to make a case and conveniently forgets about examples that may weaken the case.

Post Hoc, Ergo Propter Hoc   The Latin name of this fallacy means "after this, therefore because of this." The fallacy occurs when a sequential relationship is mistaken for a causal relationship. (See Chapter 12, page 259, where we discuss this fallacy in more depth.) For example, you may be guilty of this fallacy if you say, "Cramming for a test really helps because last week I crammed for my psychology test and I got an A on it." When two events occur frequently in conjunction with each other, we've got a good case for a causal relationship. But until we can show how one causes the other and until we have ruled out other causes, we cannot be certain that a causal relationship is occurring. For example, the A on your psych test may have been caused by something other than your cramming. Maybe the exam was easier, or perhaps you were luckier or more mentally alert. It is often difficult to tell when a *post hoc* fallacy occurs. When the New York police department changed its policing tactics in the early 1990s, the crime rate plummeted. But did the new policing tactics cause the drop in the crime rate? Many experts suggested other clauses, including economist Steven Levitt, who attributes the declining crime rate to the legalization of abortion in the 1970s (and hence to a decline in unwanted children who might grow up to be criminals).

Begging the Question—Circular Reasoning   Arguers beg the question when they provide a reason that simply restates the claim in different words. Here is an example: "Abortion is murder because it is the intentional taking of the life of a human being." Because "murder" is defined as "the intentional taking of the life of a human being," the argument is circular. It is tantamount to saying, "Abortion is murder because it is murder." In the abortion debate, the crucial issue is whether a fetus is a "human being" in the legal sense. So in this case the arguer has fallaciously "begged the question" by assuming from the start that the fetus is a legal human being. The argument is similar to saying, "That person is obese because he is too fat."

False Dilemma—Either/Or   This fallacy occurs when an arguer oversimplifies a complex issue so that only two choices appear possible. Often one of the choices is made to seem unacceptable, so the only remaining option is the other choice. "It's my way or the highway" is a typical example of a false dilemma. Here is a more subtle one: "Either we allow embryonic stem cell research, or we condemn people with diabetes, Parkinson's disease, or spinal injuries to a life without a cure." Clearly, there may be other options, including other approaches to curing these diseases. A good extended example of the false dilemma fallacy is found in sociologist Kai Erikson's analysis of President Truman's decision to drop the A-bomb on Hiroshima. His analysis suggests that the Truman administration prematurely reduced numerous options to just two: either drop the bomb on a major city, or sustain unacceptable losses in a land invasion of Japan. Erikson, however, shows there were other alternatives.

Slippery Slope   The slippery slope fallacy is based on the fear that once we put a foot on a slippery slope heading in the wrong direction, we're doomed to slide right out of sight. The controlling metaphor is of a slick mountainside without places to hold on rather than of a staircase with numerous stopping places. Here is an example of a slippery slope: "Once we allow app-based ride services to compete with regular taxi companies, we will destroy the taxi business and the livelihood of immigrant taxi drivers. Soon anyone who wants to pose as a ride service will be able to do so, using uninspected vehicles and untrained drivers, leading to more accidents and crimes against passengers." Slippery slope arguments are frequently encountered when individuals request exceptions to bureaucratic rules: "Look, Blotnik, no one feels worse about your need for open-heart surgery than I do. But I still can't let you turn this paper in late. If I were to let you do it, then I'd have to let everyone turn in papers late." Slippery slope arguments can be very persuasive—and often rightfully so because every slippery slope argument isn't necessarily a slippery slope fallacy. Some slopes really are slippery. The slippery slope becomes a fallacy when we forget that we can often dig a foothold into the slope and stop. For example, we can define procedures for exceptions to rules so that Blotnik can turn in his paper late without allowing everyone to turn in a paper late. Likewise, a state could legalize app-based ride services, but regulate them to prevent a complete slide down the slope.

False Analogy   In Chapter 11 on definition and resemblance arguments, we explained that no analogy is perfect (see our discussion of analogies on pages 225–226). Any two things being compared are similar in some ways and different in other ways. Whether an analogy is persuasive or false often depends on the audience's initial degree of skepticism. For example, people opposed to gun control may find the following argument persuasive: "Banning guns on the basis that guns accidentally kill people is like banning cars on the basis that cars accidentally kill people." In contrast, supporters of gun control are likely to call this argument a false analogy on the basis of dissimilarities between cars and guns. (For example, they might say that banning cars would be far more disruptive on our society than would be banning guns.) Just when a persuasive analogy turns into a false analogy is difficult to say.

Non Sequitur   The name of this fallacy means "it does not follow." *Non sequitur* is a catchall term for any claim that doesn't follow from its premises or is supported by irrelevant premises. Sometimes the arguer seems to make an inexplicably illogical leap: "Genetically modified foods should be outlawed because they are not natural." (Should anything that is not natural be outlawed? In what way are they not natural?) At other times there may be a gap in the chain of reasons: "Violent video games have some social value because the army uses them for recruiting." (There may be an important idea emerging here, but too many logical steps are missing.) At still other times an arguer may support a claim with irrelevant reasons: "I should not receive a C in this course because I currently have a 3.8 GPA." In effect, almost any fallacy could be called a *non sequitur* because fallacious reasoning always indicates some kind of disconnect between the reasons and the claim.

Loaded Label or Definition   Sometimes arguers try to influence their audience's view of something by creating a loaded label or definition. For example, people who oppose the "estate tax" (which calls to mind rich people with estates) have relabeled it the "death tax" in order to give it a negative connotation without any markers of class or wealth. Or to take another example, proponents of organic foods could create definitions like the following: "Organic foods are safe and healthy foods grown without any pesticides, herbicides, or other unhealthy additives." "Safe" and "healthy" are evaluative terms used fallaciously in what purports to be a definition. The intended implication is that nonorganic foods are not safe and healthy.

■ ■ ■   **FOR WRITING AND DISCUSSION**   **Persuasive or Fallacious?**   MyWritingLab™

Individual task: For each argument on page 404, explain in writing the extent to which you find the argument persuasive or fallacious. If any argument seems doomed because of one or more of the fallacies discussed in this appendix, identify the fallacies and explain how they render the argument nonpersuasive. Remember that it is often hard to determine the exact point where fallacious reasoning begins to kick in, especially when you consider different kinds of audiences. So in each case, consider also variations in audience. For which audiences would any particular argument appear potentially fallacious? Which audiences would be more likely to consider the argument persuasive?

1. Either we invest more money in improving our mental health care system or our society will experience more frequent outbursts of violence in mass shootings.
2. Smoking must cause lung cancer because a much higher percentage of smokers get lung cancer than do nonsmokers.
3. Smoking does not cause cancer because my grandfather smoked two packs per day for fifty years and died in his sleep at age ninety.
4. Society has an obligation to provide housing for the homeless because people without adequate shelter have a right to the resources of the community.
5. Based on my observations of the two renters in our neighborhood, I have concluded that people who own their own homes take better care of them than those who rent. [This arguer provided detailed evidence about the house-caring practices of the two renters and of the homeowners in the neighborhood.]
6. Intelligent design must qualify as a scientific theory because hundreds of scientists endorse it.
7. If we pass legislation requiring mandatory registration of handguns, we'll open the door to eventual confiscation of hunting rifles.
8. Those who support gun control are wrong because they believe that no one should have the right to defend himself or herself in any situation.
9. Most people who have died recently of overdoses of heroin first became addicted to painkillers. Therefore, doctors should drastically reduce their prescription of painkillers.
10. We should question Mr. Robin Albertson's endorsement of charter schools because he is one of the major shareholders in a corporation that develops curriculum used in these schools.

Group task: Share your analyses with classmates.

MyWritingLab™

> Visit Appendix Informal Fallacies in *MyWritingLab* to complete the For Writing and Discussion and to test your understanding.

An Anthology of Arguments

This photo of a SlutWalk in Kolkata, India, taken in June of 2013, depicts a protest against a culture of rape that blames victims for their choice of clothing and behavior instead of blaming the perpetrators. SlutWalks, which began in Toronto, Canada, in 2011, have become a global grassroots protest against societies that deny the prevalence of rape, normalize it, and fault women for provoking it. For furthering the protestors' purpose, what is the function in this photo of the women's red horns, the use of makeup, and the checklist poster? Particularly, how does the word "slut" function rhetorically in this issue? How do SlutWalks attack a complicitous culture of rape as well as support rape victims?

Overview of the Anthology

Part Six, an anthology of engaging arguments addressing a variety of contemporary and classic issues, will let you put into practice your new skills of reading and analyzing arguments, conducting inquiry, and joining an argumentative conversation. You can particularly apply the following skills:

- From Chapter 2: summarizing an argument and applying dialectic thinking to two or more arguments with alternative points of view
- From Chapter 8: writing a rhetorical analysis of an argument
- From Chapter 9: analyzing visual arguments and creating your own visual argument
- From Chapters 10–14: analyzing arguments using insights from the types of claims

The Future of Food and Farming

Food is one of the most intimate and complex relationships we share with the natural world. From farms to factories and from the supermarket to our plates, questions of what we eat and how we produce it dominate our daily lives. One of the most controversial food topics of the last twenty years has been genetically modified (GM) foods. While arguments have raged over whether GM foods should even be created and produced in countries around the world, the widespread genetic modification of commodity crops such as corn, canola, sugar beets, and soy in North America have some researchers estimating that over 70% of the packaged foods in our grocery stores now contain GM ingredients, and the majority of the livestock in the United States now consumes GM feedstuffs. Thus, the conversation has turned recently from "Should we allow genetic modification of our food?" to "How can we make choices about whether we consume GM foods?" Currently, sixty-four other countries require labeling. Yet in the United States, as of 2014, Vermont is the only state to require that food containing GM ingredients be labeled. Connecticut and Maine have passed similar laws that only take effect if other states join in. Voters in both California and Washington have attempted to pass similar legislation and failed. Unwilling to wait for the slow process of state-by-state regulation, Whole Foods Market, whose consumers are willing to pay premium prices for "natural" and organic foods, has vowed that all of their products will be labeled by 2018.

While these movements are taking place at legislative and corporate levels, activists and educators are working at the community level to ensure that children develop and maintain an intimate relationship with our food. School gardens, championed by food activists like chef Alice Waters, have sprung up all over the country in an attempt to reintroduce youth to the pleasures of gardening and eating healthy foods, while simultaneously helping them to learn and apply educational subjects as wide-ranging as literacy, mathematics, biology, chemistry, history, physical education, and art. Yet critics of school gardens view them as merely another educational fad which takes time away from the mastery of skills measured by state testing.

The readings in this unit demonstrate the nuances and complexities of questions related to the seemingly simple task of feeding ourselves. What are the motives behind the surge of genetically modified foods, and what are the concerns? What are our rights and responsibilities when it comes to choosing what we will consume? And how can we ensure that the next generation of Americans will have a strong relationship with food and be empowered to continue to ask such questions?

Genetically Modified Food: Good, Bad, Ugly

ARTHUR L. CAPLAN

Arthur L. Caplan is a professor and head of the Division of Bioethics at New York University's Langone Medical Center. He is the author or editor of 32 books and over 600 papers in peer-reviewed journals of medicine, science, philosophy, bioethics, and health policy. He won the Patricia Price Browne Prize in Biomedical Ethics for 2011 and was chosen as one of the ten most influential people in biotechnology by both the National Journal *and* Nature Biotechnology. *This commentary was published in the* Chronicle of Higher Education *on September 13, 2013.*

Genetically modified food has had a rough year in what has been a fairly miserable decade. In August, 400 farmers in the Philippines stormed a government-owned GM (as it is known) research field. The protesters destroyed 1,000 square meters of Golden Rice, a variety genetically engineered to cut down on vitamin A deficiency.

A 2013 poll in the *New York Times* found that three-quarters of Americans have concerns about genetically modified organisms (GMOs) in their food; most are worried about health effects. Thirty-seven percent of those with worries fear that GM foods cause cancer or allergies.

On the Web site *Counter-Punch* this summer, Katherine Paul wondered what happens when animals are confined in cramped, filthy environments and force-fed monoculture diets of genetically modified corn and soy. A lot, concluded Paul, who is with the Organic Consumers Association: "Calves are born too weak to walk, with enlarged joints and limb deformities. Piglets experience rapidly deteriorating health, a 'failure to thrive' so severe that they start breaking down their own tissues and organs—self-cannibalizing—to survive."

The article described animals with weak bones, dairy cows with mastitis, beef cattle with liver abscesses. "It all adds up to a lot of misery for animals unfortunate enough to be on the receiving end of industrial agriculture's Big GMO Experiment," Paul wrote.

5   A documentary, *Genetic Roulette: The Gamble of Our Lives*, proclaims GMO "the most dangerous thing facing human beings in our generation." And a headline in *Pravda* sneered at the decision to expand GMO agriculture in Russia, under the headline "Russians to proudly poison themselves with their own GM food."

But at the same time, the *Times* also noted that commercial farming of oranges and grapefruit is in dire peril from an insect-borne bacteria that causes a disease known as "citrus greening." An uncontrollable fungal blight is destroying the banana crop around the world. Coffee rust is knocking out plants in Central and South America. Diseases like rice blast, soybean rust, stem rust in wheat, corn smut in maize, and late blight in potatoes destroy at least 125 million tons each year of the world's top five foods. The damage done to rice, wheat, and maize alone costs global agriculture $60 billion per year. The effects are especially catastrophic in the developing world, where 1.4 billion people rely on these foods.

There is a way to get rid of such otherwise unstoppable plant diseases, which waste scarce resources, bring about malnutrition and starvation for hundreds of millions, and cost the world economy billions of dollars. Genetically modified organisms.

Specifically, engineering plants to resist the diseases. So why don't the folks bearing the bad news about GMOs make a connection to the huge problems that could be fixed by genetic engineering? The answer is the bungling mismanagement of a potentially useful breakthrough technology by the GMO industry, alongside market forces that produce GMOs friendly to pesticides rather than hostile to fungi.

On September 10, 1999, I found myself in Switzerland, on a mountaintop overlooking Lake Geneva. A pleasure trip? Nope, I was giving a talk to CEOs about the ethics of GMOs. I spent my time at the summit yelling, literally, at the CEO of Monsanto. He was yelling right back at me—neither of us calmed by the beauty of the setting. Or the horrified looks on the faces of other guests.

10   The subject of the craggy debate was whether foods that contain GMOs should be labeled as such. The head of Monsanto said absolutely not. Since there was nothing unsafe about genetically modified food, there was no reason to label. I thought he was nuts.

I argued that people had a right to know what was in their food, regardless of the safety issue. In a land where you can have a Slurpee and a couple of Slim Jims for lunch, and where E. coli, listeriosis, yersiniosis, and salmonella outbreaks are frequent occurrences, I was not too worried about the safety of GMO food. But safety has little to do with labeling. Plenty of foods are labeled "kosher," "natural," "halal," "made in Vermont," or all manner of other terms not connected to safety.

By not labeling their foods, agricultural companies were creating an environment of suspicion and distrust. The CEO, however, was not convinced. Monsanto did not push labeling or lobby for labeling. No other companies in the GMO business did, either. Only restaurants and supermarkets that threw a "GMO-free" label around, to appeal to consumers made nervous by lack of transparency, bothered to label.

Bad management thus turned a technology that should have been greeted as a way out of chemically based farming into a public-relations nightmare.

I actually had crossed paths with Monsanto years before. When I was at the University of Minnesota, in 1994, the company introduced a genetically engineered form of growth hormone, rBGH, for use in dairy herds. The naturally occurring gene for making rBGH had been inserted into bacteria, E. coli, which went about merrily making as much hormone as anyone could want. Monsanto sold the artificial hormone to dairy farmers with the promise that they could get more milk from their herds.

15   That product had driven me crazy. Why create more milk? My subsidized school lunches at Saxonville Elementary, in Framingham, Mass., in the late 1950s had been built on dairy products—a butter or cheese sandwich every day—since the federal government did not know what else to do with all the surplus. So had my younger sisters' lunches, right through the 1970s. Consumers did not need more milk. rBGH milk is still sold throughout the United States. The Codex Alimentarius Commission,

a UN food-safety agency representing 101 nations, has banned it. So has Canada. Milk, butter, and ice cream remain abundant.

Genetic engineering started out trying to create more of foods that were already abundant. It then tried to sell its products not to consumers, but to farmers. No labeling was involved, no explanation of the genetically engineered cow's milk offered, no value added to what the consumer got on the plate or in the glass. The pattern of ignoring the consumer and selling to the farmer continued with genetically engineered soy, corn, canola, sugar beets, and cotton. No labeling. No value added for the eater.

Even worse, Monsanto, and later DuPont, Bayer, and other big companies focused their GMO efforts on finding synergies between genetic engineering and their existing pesticide, herbicide, and fertilizer businesses. Monsanto's Roundup Ready soybeans, introduced throughout the world in the mid-to-late 1990s, made crops more resistant to herbicides sold by—Monsanto.

The companies making lots of money from the pesticide and fertilizer revolution that swept through agriculture in the 1950s and 1960s were not ready to gamble on losing that business if GMO technology was used to make plants and agriculture greener, cheaper, safer, and more capable of providing nutritious food without their chemicals. GMO, which should have been the next major technological revolution in farming, making the Green Revolution even greener, instead was turned into a handmaiden for an outmoded, highly polluting, and increasingly expensive chemically based agriculture.

Which brings us back to all those diseases and bugs that have figured out ways to defeat our herbicides, pesticides, fungicides, insecticides, and microbicides while thoroughly enjoying global warming, war, and human deforestation. Chemical agriculture has no answer. Nor does organic farming.

20   The only path toward a continuous supply of a variety of foods, more nutritious food, cheaper food, and an environmentally friendlier agriculture is the genetic engineering of plants and seeds. Critics of genetic engineering need to start to separate the technology from its miserable history. Altering genes, which is going on in medicine as a powerful tool against disease, has to be deployed in the same way in the plant world.

The route to getting rid of chemical agriculture can run through organic farming. But it must also incorporate genetic modification, lest entire industries, such as those providing orange juice or coffee products—and their jobs—disappear, and those who eke out a living trying to farm on a warming planet, short on water, with many blight-threatened crops, starve.

There is plenty to argue about regarding GMO foods. Controlling the dissemination of genetically modified plants and animals needs a lot more thought. Getting farmers off monoculture farming and adding back more diversity to vulnerable foods are efforts that need more than a few seed banks. And we must figure out labeling. If it is not always feasible to label foods, trustworthy information should be made available on the Web. Even industry knows that—14 years after my shouting match on the mountaintop, Monsanto has launched a Web site, gmoanswers.com.

That said, the push to make GM food a complement to farming rather than hand-maiden to a rapidly failing form of polluting agriculture must become a priority for all. If industry cannot use the technology in an ethically responsible manner, then either government or a philanthropy like the Bill & Melinda Gates Foundation ought to be urged to step in. (Full disclosure: I receive no support from food companies or agribusiness. But while at the University of Pennsylvania, I did participate in a project with DuPont to establish a code of ethics for its biotechnology business. That project goes on.)

Genetic engineering is not yet solving the food challenges that face humanity. Despite industry bungling, market failure, and a lot of fearmongering, however, it is our last, best, practical, serious hope.

The Threats from Genetically Modified Foods

ROBIN MATHER

Robin Mather is a long-time food columnist and a senior associate editor at Mother Earth News; *this article was published in the April–May 2012 issue. Mather has written about GM crops since the early 1990s, and is the author of* A Garden of Unearthly Delights: Bioengineering and the Future of Food *(1995), one of the first books on genetic modification written for the general public, and* The Feast Nearby *(2011).*

Eighteen years after the first genetically modified food, the Flavr Savr tomato, came to market, the controversy about genetically modified foods rages. The call to label GM foods continues to build, yet the federal government has not responded. GM foods, illegal in many countries, have been part of the American diet for nearly two decades. As GMOs have come to dominate major agribusiness sectors, a handful of chemical/biotech companies now control not only genetically modified seeds but virtually our entire seed supply.

"Genetic modification" refers to the manipulation of DNA by humans to change the essential makeup of plants and animals. The technology inserts genetic material from one species into another to give a crop or animal a new quality, such as the ability to produce a pesticide. These DNA transfers could never occur in nature and are not as precise as proponents make them sound.

Some genetically modified crops have been engineered to include genetic material from BT (*Bacillus thuringiensis*), a natural bacterium found in soil. Inserting the Bt genes makes the plant itself produce bacterial toxins, thereby killing the insects that could destroy it. The first GM crop carrying Bt genes, potatoes, were approved in the United States in 1995. Today there are Bt versions of corn, potatoes and cotton.

Roundup-Ready crops—soybeans, corn, canola, sugar beets, cotton, alfalfa and Kentucky bluegrass—have been manipulated to be resistant to glyphosate, the active ingredient in Monsanto's broadleaf weed-killer Roundup.

5   These two GM traits—herbicide resistance and pesticide production—are now pervasive in American agriculture. The Department of Agriculture's National Agricultural Statistics Service says that, in 2010, as much as 86 percent of corn, up to 90 percent of all soybeans and nearly 93 percent of cotton were GM varieties.

You're eating genetically modified foods almost daily unless you grow all of your food or always buy organic. Federal organic standards passed in 2000 specifically prohibit GM ingredients. Other genetically modified crops—none labeled—now include sweet corn, peppers, squash and zucchini, rice, sugar cane, rapeseed (used to make canola oil), flax, chicory, peas and papaya. About a quarter of the milk in the United States comes from cows injected with a GM hormone, honey comes from bees working GM crops, and some vitamins include GM ingredients. Some sources conservatively estimate that 60 percent or more of processed foods available in the United States contain GM ingredients, because most processed foods contain corn and/or soy products.

Genetically modified foods are not labeled in the United States because the biotech industry has convinced the Food and Drug Administration (FDA) that GM crops are "not substantially different" from conventional varieties. The FDA, however, does no independent testing for human or animal safety and relies strictly on the research conducted by the manufacturers of the products. The main GM producer, Monsanto, makes it nearly impossible for independent scientists to obtain GM seeds to study. Meanwhile, many countries require labeling (the European Union, Australia), and some have even banned all GM foods (Japan, Ireland, Egypt).

Genetic modification technology does have extraordinary potential. In the practice known as "pharming," animals are genetically modified to give milk, meat or blood from which medicines are manufactured, as when GM goats produce milk containing a blood-thinning drug called ATryn. Research laboratories use GM mice to seek cures for diseases. Yet with minimal oversight on the crops and livestock produced, many people have serious worries about GMO technology. Many of us simply want the *right to know* what is in our food.

Bt Crops: Is Built-In Pesticide a Boon or Bane?

Monsanto has led the invasion of Bt crops, starting with corn, cotton and potatoes. Syngenta has developed Bt corn as well, as have Bayer, Dupont

and other companies. Such crops are marketed to growers as pest-resistant.

10 Some researchers have concerns about the effect of Bt crops on human health. Professor Emeritus Joe Cummins of the University of Western Ontario told the U.S. Environmental Protection Agency (EPA) that "there is evidence that [Bt] will impact directly on human health through damage to the ileum [the final portion of the small intestine, which joins it to the large intestine]...[which] can produce chronic illnesses such as fecal incontinence and/or flu-like upsets of the digestive system."

Bt may also harm beneficial insects such as honeybees and lady beetles.

Risky Business?

Roundup is one of Monsanto's powerful broadleaf weedkillers. Because Roundup's patent expired in 2000, a number of companies now manufacture products using Roundup's active ingredient, glyphosate.

Glyphosate is not made using genetic modification. Instead, crops labeled Roundup-Ready are modified to withstand drenching with this weedkiller.

15 In a 2011 report called *Roundup and Birth Defects: Is the Public Being Kept in the Dark?*, eight international scientists cited study after study linking glyphosate to birth defects in birds and amphibians, as well as to cancer, endocrine disruption, damage to DNA, and reproductive and developmental damage in mammals, even at very low doses. Moreover, the report said, Monsanto and the rest of the herbicide industry has known since the 1980s that glyphosate causes malformations in animals, and that governments ignored these studies. Here in the United States, the EPA continues to assert that Roundup is safe.

Another concern is environmental damage. Roundup ends up in wetlands because of runoff and inadvertent spraying. In one study, the recommended application of Roundup sold to homeowners and gardeners killed up to

86 percent of frogs in one day, according to University of Pittsburgh assistant professor Rick Relyea. Roundup also damages soil. Two Purdue scientists, Professor Emeritus Don Huber and G.S. Johal, said in a paper published in 2009 that "the widespread use of glyphosate...can significantly increase the severity of various plant diseases, impair plant defense to pathogens and disease and immobilize soil and plant nutrients rendering them unavailable for plant use." The pair warned that "ignoring potential non-target side effects...may have dire consequences for agriculture such as rendering soils infertile, crops non-productive and plants less nutritious."

Huber is point-blank about glyphosate's dangers. "Glyphosate is the single most important agronomic factor predisposing some plants to both disease and toxins," he said in an interview with *The Organic and Non-GMO Report*. "These toxins can produce a serious impact on the health of animals and humans. The toxin levels in straw can be high enough to make cattle and pigs infertile."

No Independent Review

As the system now stands, biotech companies bring their own research to the government body overseeing their products.

"We don't have the whole picture. That's no accident. Multibillion-dollar agricultural corporations, including Monsanto and Syngenta, have restricted independent research on their genetically-engineered crops. They have often refused to provide independent scientists with seeds, or they've set restrictive conditions that severely limit research options," wrote Doug Gurion-Sherman of the Union of Concerned Scientists in a February 2011 *Los Angeles Times* op-ed.

20 Concern about lack of independent review extends to university-level research, which is often partly funded and/or controlled by the agrochemical companies, which often gives agrochemical companies exclusive rights to academic discoveries—even though universities are taxpayer-funded.

It seems unlikely that scientists whose research is designed and paid for by agrochemical companies would choose to conduct studies that may reduce or remove that funding, even if they could obtain the seeds they needed to do truly independent research. Moreover, the agrochemical companies refuse to release their own research, citing concern that "proprietary information" could be disclosed.

Scientific American called on biotech companies to end restrictions on outside research in a 2009 editorial. "Food safety and environmental protection depend on making plant products available to regular scientific scrutiny," the magazine's editors wrote. "Agricultural technology companies should therefore immediately remove the restriction on research from their end-user agreements. Going forward, the EPA should also require...that independent researchers have unfettered access to all products currently on the market."

When scientists have obtained agrochemical companies' research data, usually through freedom-of-information requests, they have found entirely different conclusions than the company did. Three French scientists analyzed the raw data from three 2009 Monsanto studies on rats and found that three genetically modified corn varieties caused liver and kidney toxicity and other kinds of organ damage. The European Food Safety Authority, at the request of the European Commission, reviewed the French report and said that it "does not raise any new safety concerns," although other scientists continue to insist the French report is correct. All three corn varieties are now in the human food chain in the United States.

GM Milk: rBST

BGH ("bovine growth hormone") is produced in cows' pituitary glands. "Recombinant bovine somatotropin," or rBST, is a genetically modified version of this hormone. Injecting the GM hormone causes cows to produce about 10 percent more milk. The FDA approved the GM hormone in late 1993, saying there was "no significant difference" in milk from injected and uninjected cows. Its ruling meant that dairies could not label their milk as coming from uninjected cows, because doing so, the FDA said, suggested that there is a difference.

25   There is a difference. Injections of rBST in cows raise levels of the naturally occurring IGF-1, (insulin-like growth factor 1), a protein that stimulates cell growth. The IGF-1 in milk from injected cows is easily absorbed in the small intestine. Dr. Samuel Epstein, Professor Emeritus at the School of Public Health, University of Illinois Medical Center in Chicago, has warned for more than 20 years that high levels of IGF-1 raise the risk of cancer, especially breast, colon and prostate cancer. He has said that rBST milk is "super-charged with high levels of abnormally potent IGF-1, up to 10 times the levels in natural milk and over 10 times more potent."

Monsanto began selling rBST in 1994. Later, in 2003, the FDA charged several dairies with "misbranding," and Monsanto sued Oakhurst Dairy in Maine for labeling its milk from cows *not* injected with GMO hormones!

As many people reacted to rBST by reaching for organic milk instead, American retailers began to pledge not to sell rBST milk in response to consumer demands. The synthetic hormone is illegal in Japan, Australia, New Zealand and Canada, and the European Union banned it permanently in 1999.

In 2008, a group of rBST-using farmers formed a group called American Farmers for the Advancement and Conservation of Technology, or AFACT, with help from Monsanto. AFACT tried to ban no-rBST labeling claims in many states, but dropped those efforts in most—except Ohio, where the ban effort ended in a lawsuit. An Ohio circuit court found in 2010 that there *is* a compositional difference between rBST milk and milk from untreated cows, and that the FDA's position was "inherently misleading." The court found higher levels of a cancer-causing compound, lower-quality milk because of higher fat and lower protein, and higher white cell counts, which makes milk spoil faster.

Injecting cows in the same places over and over increases the chance of infection, plus rBST-injected cows frequently suffer from chronic mastitis, an infection of the udder. Mastitis causes the cow's udder to swell and makes it painful. Both of these infections must be treated with antibiotics.

GMOs Feed the World?

30   Fans of GMOs assert that their use in crops and livestock can help end hunger. They also claim that GMOs can help stop climate change, reduce pesticide use and increase crop yields.

Are these claims true? We conclude no.

The international report *The GMO Emperor Has No Clothes* outlined evidence gleaned from many sources. The report is available free at *goo. gl/52wuq*.

GM crops do not produce more food or use fewer pesticides, the report said. As resistant weeds and bugs develop, farmers apply ever more herbicides and insecticides. "The biotech industry is taking us into a more pesticide-dependent agriculture, and we need to be going in the opposite direction," says Bill Freese of the Center for Food Safety.

If GM crops don't increase yield, don't reduce pesticide use and show no significant promise for feeding the world, why do government and industry promote them?

35   If GMOs fail, shareholders in Monsanto, Bayer, Syngenta and other companies will see their investments plummet. According to Yahoo! Finance, more than 80 percent of Monsanto's stock is held by institutional holders such as Vanguard and funds such as Davis, Fidelity and T. Rowe Price.

If GMOs don't benefit the farmers who pay more to buy GM seed, and if they don't benefit the customers who eat them unknowingly, who gains from GMOs?

Stockbrokers. And you, if you have investments that own stock in Monsanto or other biotech companies.

Seed Monopolies

Monsanto now controls so much of the world's seed stock that the U.S. Justice Department launched an "unprecedented series of public meetings" into the company's business practices as part of a formal antitrust investigation in March 2010. "The price of a bag of soybean seed, for example, has roughly quadrupled since Monsanto began licensing genes," the *Wall Street Journal* reported.

The Seed Industry Structure chart (available at https://www.msu.edu/~howardp/seedindustry.html) demonstrates how tightly consolidated the seed industry has become. That's one reason why Monsanto's name comes up again and again in any conversation about GMOs: The company is far and away the largest involved in GM patented seed.

40   *The GMO Emperor Has No Clothes* also includes an appendix detailing Monsanto's long corporate history of misleading research, cover-ups, bribes, and convictions in lawsuits covering a range of issues, from Agent Orange to toxic waste discharge to GM soybeans.

The Right to Know

The FDA and GMO supporters say that labeling GM foods would be cumbersome and costly, ultimately raising food prices.

Labeling proponents point to the European Union, Russia, Brazil, Japan, China, Thailand, Taiwan, South Korea, Australia and New Zealand, all of which require labels for GM foods, and report costs are far lower than the industry and the FDA claim.

Survey after survey and poll after poll have shown that consumers overwhelmingly favor labeling.

In October 2011, the Center for Food Safety filed a petition demanding the FDA require labeling on all food produced using genetic engineering. The center filed the petition on behalf of the Just Label It! campaign, a coalition of more than 350 organizations and individuals concerned about food safety and consumer rights. The FDA's governing rules require it to open a public docket where citizens can comment on the petition. See more about the Just Label It! Campaign in the box below.

45   FDA officials have openly criticized efforts to label GM crops and food. In 2002, when Oregon voters considered Measure 27, a mandatory GMO labeling law, FDA Deputy Commissioner Lester Crawford said in a letter to the governor of Oregon that mandatory labeling could "impermissibly interfere" with the food industry's ability to sell its products, and could violate interstate commerce laws.

The Oregon initiative was soundly defeated, and money was the reason why. "Monsanto took the financial lead against Measure 27, with contributions totaling $1,480,000. Next was Dupont, with $634,000," said Cameron Woodworth in *Biotech Family Secrets*, a report for the Council for Responsible Genetics. Biotech companies Syngenta, Dow Agro Sciences, BASF and Bayer Crop Science, plus the Grocery Manufacturers of America (a trade organization), PepsiCo, General Mills and Nestle USA contributed $900,000 by the reporting date, Woodworth wrote.

Other high-ranking federal officials have lobbied against labeling. "If you label something, there's an implication there's something wrong with it," said Jose Fernandez, the U.S. State Department's assistant secretary for economic, energy and business affairs.

The assertion that labeling somehow implies inferior quality is transparently specious.

Fruits and vegetables labeled "organic" made up the highest growth in sales of all organics in 2010, according to the Organic Trade Association, up 11.8 percent from 2009 sales.

50   If the facts in this article anger you, see the steps in the box below to help you opt out of GM foods.

Have thoughts on genetically modified foods? Post your comments on the online, expanded version of this article.

What You Can Do About GMOs

- If you think GM foods should be labeled, sign on to the Just Label It! campaign. Send letters to the FDA and your congressional representatives to urge them to require labeling of GM foods and products. You'll find sample language and a petition at www.justlabelit.org.
- If you grow your own food, buy your seed from companies that have signed the GMO-free pledge. See the Safe Seed list, maintained by the Council for Responsible Genetics, at *goo.gl/TOePN*.
- Buy organic whenever possible, and look for foods labeled "Non-GMO verified." The Non-GMO Project is an independent nonprofit that requires independent, third-party verification before awarding its label. Find more at www.nongmoproject.org.
- Help combat seed industry monopolies and build local food security by supporting local growers who refuse to use GM products, and work to pass food sovereignty laws in your community. Learn more from food sovereignty expert Dr. Vandana Shiva's blog at *goo.gl/4aXUr*.
- Finally, if you have investments, consider moving out of funds that invest in biotech stock. If you are unable to do so, write letters to your fund's managers to object to this investment strategy.

Wrong-Headed Victory

MICHAEL LE PAGE

Michael Le Page is the environment features editor at New Scientist *magazine, where he covers issues ranging from climate change to genetics. This opinion piece appeared in* New Scientist *on November 17, 2012.*

Imagine there are two plates of food in front of you. One is labelled "natural", the other "genetically modified". Which would you choose? I know what I'd do. Regardless of what the logical side of me knows, I'd feel more comfortable eating "natural" food.

In an ideal world, this wouldn't be a problem. If people don't want to eat GM food, they shouldn't have to, regardless of whether their reasons are rational or not. Food is about so much more than just stuffing down nutrients, after all, and how we feel about what we eat really does matter.

Trouble is, the world is far from ideal. Nearly a billion people go hungry because they cannot grow or buy enough food. And there are problems with the food we do eat. An estimated 2 billion people suffer from a lack of iron, causing everything from tiredness to premature death. Around 250 million preschool children are short of vitamin A, leading to blindness in the worst cases.

The outlook is grimmer still. There will be ever more mouths to feed, and ever more challenges facing farmers. Fuel and fertilisers are becoming more costly, soils are eroding or becoming saline, pests and diseases are evolving to outwit our defences. To add to our woes, the climate is changing and the weather becoming more extreme. In fact, farming is a massive part of this problem—it contributes more to global warming than all the world's cars, trains, ships and planes put together. Rising food prices not only cause suffering, but also threaten political stability.

5   So the world desperately needs better crops. The good news is that they can be improved dramatically. We know it's possible to boost yields by improving the efficiency of photosynthesis, for instance, because some plants have already evolved this improvement. Similarly, there's no doubt we could create crops that need less water, grow in salt water or make their own nitrogen fertiliser, for instance. As for making grains and fruits richer in iron or vitamin A, it's already been done.

So why aren't people in poor countries already eating healthier food, richer in iron and vitamin A? Partly they can't afford to pay for it, so commercial companies have little incentive to develop such crops. Instead, such work has to be funded by public money or philanthropists such as Bill Gates.

A big part of the problem, of course, is the vociferous objection to GM foods. While the line between conventional breeding and genetic engineering is increasingly blurred, it is generally only practical to produce crops with complex new properties by deliberately modifying their DNA, rather than inducing random mutations and hoping a few will have the desired trait (as in conventional breeding).

The opposition to GM crops is making it much harder to get funding to carry out the necessary research and to get over all the regulatory hurdles. Earlier this year, for instance, campaigners attacked the Bill and Melinda Gates Foundation for funding the development of nitrogen-fixing crops that could boost yields without boosting emissions of the highly potent greenhouse gas nitrous oxide. Simply not needed, apparently. Greenpeace, meanwhile, tried to halt field trials of vitamin-A-rich "Golden Rice" in the Philippines, on the ludicrous basis it would deter the consumption of vegetables.

The Monsantos of this world have the economic muscle needed to get crops approved despite protests, but for cash-strapped universities, it's a different story. Their development of the crops we so desperately need is being impeded by anti-GM protesters.

10   How can this opposition be overcome? Not by rational argument, that's for sure. Even for those who understand that nature is the ultimate mad scientist, and that plants are riddled with all kinds of genetic modifications, from mistakes made during DNA replication to insertions of viral DNA, it doesn't make existing GM crops any more appealing.

Rather, we need to win people's hearts as well as their minds. And the way to do that is to make GM foods appealing. Instead of crops designed mainly to boost the profits of large corporations, we need a new generation of GM crops that offers clear benefits to consumers, from looking better to tasting better to being better for us. Scare stories about cellphones causing cancer didn't stop them taking off because they are so useful. Similarly, scare stories about GM foods will lose their power if GM products that help prevent cancer or heart disease can be bought in supermarkets.

The very last way to win hearts is to trick people to eat GM crops by not telling them what's in their food. Californians may have voted down the proposal for mandatory labelling of GM foods—Proposition 37—after food firms spent $45 million on TV ads telling them it would raise food prices, hurt farmers and spark legal wrangles. Few consumers will be any keener on eating GM food, though—quite the contrary.

Prop 37 was flawed, and many of the arguments for it were nonsense. Its opponents argued that the science says there are no ill effects of eating GM, so labelling, which might deter GM consumption, is unnecessary. A triumph for science over anti-science then? No. The argument against Prop 37 really boiled down to something more disturbing: "If we tell people what's in their food, they will make the wrong choice, so we shouldn't give them one."

Why is the US of all places protecting GM foods rather than letting them sink or swim in a free market? Companies should instead persuade people that their new products are better than the alternative.

15   If all countries insisted on GM labelling, corporations would be forced to convince consumers of the benefits. As it stands, in California the companies who have helped engender such rabid distrust of GM foods have been let off the hook. Prop 37 could have been a catalyst for change. Instead the status quo remains—and we'll all be the losers in the end.

Harley, I'm Worried About Gene Transfer

JOHN HAMBROCK

John Hambrock draws the syndicated comic strip The Brilliant Mind of Edison Lee, *a character who is a ten-year-old inventor obsessed with politics and the ironies of life. This strip was published on July 2, 2013.*

Monsanto's Reasons for Fighting GMO Labeling? It Loves You

JOE MOHR

Joe Mohr draws environmentally themed cartoons for publications including Yes! Magazine, *Greenpeace, the Center for Media and Democracy, PBS's* Urban Conversion, *and other publications. He is also the creator of the comic strip* Hank D and the Bee. *This cartoon was published on October 24, 2013.*

We are paying millions to stop GMO labeling in Washington State, just as we did in California, because we want to protect consumers *and* the earth. We feel that seeing GMO labels on food will cause consumers to get on their computer and research what a GMO is—extra computer use means extra electricity use, which is a *major* cause of global warming. If they read the many studies that weren't funded by Monsanto and friends they may get angry, scared, and stressed out—stress is a proven killer. This may lead them to call their friends on their cell phone to share their knowledge of GMOs—meaning extra radiation from said cell phone. To me, *that* is the real hidden killer. In conclusion, not labeling GMOs will keep our planet and its inhabitants safe from stress, global warming, and cellular radiation. You're welcome.

JOEMOHRTOONS.COM

HUGH GRANT
MONSANTO CEO

Cultivating Failure

CAITLIN FLANAGAN

Caitlin Flanagan is a journalist and author of the book To Hell with All That: Loving and Loathing Our Inner Housewife (2006), *an exploration of the lives of modern women based on pieces written for* The Atlantic. *She has established herself as a social critic "unafraid to take on self-indulgence and political correctness," and has been named a finalist for the National Magazine Award five times. This essay appeared in* The Atlantic's *January/February 2010 issue.*

Imagine that as a young and desperately poor Mexican man, you had made the dangerous and illegal journey to California to work in the fields with other migrants. There, you performed stoop labor, picking lettuce and bell peppers and table grapes; what made such an existence bearable was the dream of a better life. You met a woman and had a child with her, and because that child was born in the U.S., he was made a citizen of this great country. He will lead a life entirely different from yours; he will be educated. Now that child is about to begin middle school in the American city whose name is synonymous with higher learning, as it is the home of one of the greatest universities in the world: Berkeley. On the first day of sixth grade, the boy walks through the imposing double doors of his new school, stows his backpack, and then heads out to the field, where he stoops under a hot sun and begins to pick lettuce.

It's rare for an immigrant experience to go the whole 360 in a single generation—one imagines the novel of assimilation, *The White Man Calls It Romaine*. The cruel trick has been pulled on this benighted child by an agglomeration of foodies and educational reformers who are propelled by a vacuous if well-meaning ideology that is responsible for robbing an increasing number of American schoolchildren of hours they might otherwise have spent reading important books or learning higher math (attaining the cultural achievements, in other words, that have lifted uncounted generations of human beings out of the desperate daily scrabble to wrest sustenance from dirt). The galvanizing force behind this ideology is Alice Waters, the dowager queen of the grown-locally movement. Her goal is that children might become "ecogastronomes" and discover "how food grows"—a lesson, if ever there was one, that our farm worker's son might have learned at his father's knee—leaving the Emerson and Euclid to the professionals over at the schoolhouse. Waters's enormous celebrity, combined with her decision in the 1990s to expand her horizons into the field of public-school education, has helped thrust thousands of schoolchildren into the grip of a giant experiment, one that is predicated on a set of assumptions that are largely unproved, even unexamined. That no one is calling foul on this is only one manifestation of the way the new Food Hysteria has come to dominate and diminish our shared cultural life, and to make an educational reformer out of someone whose brilliant cookery and laudable goals may not be the best qualifications for designing academic curricula for the public schools.

Waters, described by her biographer, Thomas McNamee, as "arguably the most famous restaurateur in the United States," is, of course, the founder of Chez Panisse, in Berkeley, an eatery where the right-on, "yes we can," ACORN-loving, public-option-supporting man or woman of the people can tuck into a nice table d'hôte menu of scallops, guinea hen, and tarte tatin for a modest 95 clams—wine, tax, and oppressively sanctimonious and relentlessly conversation-busting service not included. (I've had major surgeries in which I was less scrupulously informed about what was about to happen to me, what was happening to me, and what had just happened to me than I've been during a dinner there.) It was at Chez Panisse that Waters worked out her new American gastronomic credo, which is built on the concept of using ingredients that are "fresh, local, seasonal, and where possible organic." Fair enough, and perfectly delicious, but the scope of her operation—which is fueled not only by the skill of its founder, but also by the weird, almost erotic power she wields over a certain kind of educated, professional-class, middle-aged woman (the same kind of woman who tends to light, midway through life's journey, on school voluntarism as a locus of her fathomless energies)—has widened so far beyond the simple cooking and serving of food that it can hardly be quantified. As McNamee rightly observes, Chez Panisse

> is a much larger enterprise than a restaurant. It is a standard-bearer for a system of moral values. It is the leader of a style of cooking, of a social movement, and of a comprehensive philosophy of doing good and living well.

This notion—that it is agreeably possible to do good (school gardens!) and live well (guinea hens!)—bears the hallmark of contemporary progressivism, a kind of win-win, "let them eat tarte tatin" approach to the world and one's place in it that is prompting an improbable alliance of school reformers, volunteers, movie stars, politicians' wives, and agricultural concerns (the California Fertilizer

Foundation is a big friend of school gardens) to insert its values into the schools.

5   The Edible Schoolyard program was born when Waters noticed a barren lot next to the Martin Luther King Jr. Middle School in Berkeley. Inspired by the notion that a garden would afford students "experience-based learning that illustrates the pleasure of meaningful work, personal responsibility, the need for nutritious, sustainably raised, and sensually stimulating food, and the important socializing effect of the ritual of the table," and spurred on by the school principal, Waters offered to build a garden and help create a curriculum to go along with it.

An Aztec dance troupe performed on the day the first cover crop was planted (imagine it as a set piece for *The White Man Calls It Romaine*), and soon the exciting garden had made its influence felt across the disciplines. In English class students composed recipes, in math they measured the garden beds, and in history they ground corn as a way of studying pre-Columbian civilizations. Students' grades quickly improved at King, which makes sense given that a recipe is much easier to write than a coherent paragraph on *The Crucible*.

Fads in education tend to take off quickly, but nothing else has come into our public schools at the rocket-blast rate of school gardens, particularly here in my home state of California. To be sure, this was hardly a new phenomenon in California, where school gardens waxed and waned over the years, propelled by the state's agricultural interests, the back-to-the-land movement of the 70s, and so on. But by the time Waters came onto the scene, organic food, nutrition, and sustainability were becoming the pet issues of the volunteering set. In the 1990s, Waters found a powerful ally in Delaine Eastin, the newly elected state superintendent of instruction (herself a "devoted gardener, home cook and recycler"), who called for "A Garden In Every School" the same year the Edible Schoolyard began.

Together, the bureaucrat and the celebrity paved the way for an enormous movement: by 2002, 2,000 of the state's 9,000 schools had a garden, and by 2008 that number had risen to 3,849, and it continues to grow. Waters, with her charisma and high political profile (which includes her friendship with the Clintons), has been hailed as one of the most important educational innovators not just in the state, but in the nation. In 1998, she received an Excellence in Education Award from Senator Barbara Boxer, as well as an Education Heroes Award from the U.S. Department of Education; the Smithsonian has sponsored an Edible Schoolyard exhibit on the National Mall in Washington, D.C. Only four school gardens across the country bear the coveted Chez Panisse Foundation imprimatur (just two of them in California), but their influence has been profound. Not only has the foundation published a mind-numbingly earnest series of books on lesson planning, policy planning, and public policy, but it also has a teacher-training program and offers regular tours of the garden at King. In July, a *Los Angeles Times* article was titled "A New Crop of School Gardens: Even as State Funds Are Wilting, Support for School Gardens Is Still Growing." Maria Shriver, the first lady of California, is a strong supporter and, like all the proponents of this kind of education, she urges schools to use the gardens across all disciplines.

Of course, Waters herself is guilty of nothing more terrible than being a visionary and a woman of tremendous persuasive abilities. It's the state's Department of Education that is to blame for allowing these gardens to hijack the curricula of so many schools. But although garden-based curricula are advanced as a means of redressing a wide spectrum of poverty's ills, the animating spirit behind them is impossible to separate from the haute-bourgeois predilections of the Alice Waters fan club, as best expressed in one of her most oft-repeated philosophies: "Gardens help students to learn the pleasure of physical work." Does the immigrant farm worker dream that his child will learn to enjoy manual labor, or that his child will be freed from it? What is the goal of an education, of what we once called "book learning"? These are questions best left unasked when it comes to the gardens.

10   Hispanics constitute 49 percent of the students in California's public schools. Ever since the state adopted standards-based education (each child must learn a comprehensive set of skills and material) in 1997—coincidentally, at the same moment that garden learning was taking off—a notorious achievement gap has opened between Hispanic and African American students on the one hand, and whites and Asians on the other. Indeed, Hispanic students do particularly poorly at King Middle School. According to the 2009 Federal Accountability Requirements, statewide, more than 39 percent of Latinos are proficient in English and 44 percent in math, but at the King school, those numbers are a dismal 30 percent and 29 percent, respectively. Where do Berkeley's African American and Hispanic middle-schoolers do well? At a garden-less charter school called Cal Prep, where 92 percent of the students are black or Latino, where the focus is on academic achievement, and where test scores have been rising steadily.

The garden-based curriculum has good news for the state's catastrophically underachieving students: a giant team of volunteers is ready to help them. Here is how our garden-loving, home-cooking, recycling superintendent of instruction describes one of the program's principal advantages in the introduction to A *Child's Garden of Standards,* a gargantuan compendium of charts and lesson plans intended to link the beloved method of gardening with the hard-ass objectives of the state standards:

> Some families, particularly those from other countries, may feel uncomfortable when asked to help out at school because their English skills or educational background do not give them a solid classroom footing. For these families, the living classroom of a garden can be a much more inviting environment in which to engage in their children's education.

If this patronizing agenda were promulgated in the Jim Crow South by a white man who was espousing a sharecropping curriculum for African American students, we would see it for what it is: a way of bestowing field work and low expectations on a giant population of students who might become troublesome if they actually got an education.

Here is the essential question we must ask about the school gardens: What evidence do we have that participation in one of these programs—so enthusiastically supported, so uncritically championed—improves a child's chances of doing well on the state tests that will determine his or her future (especially the all-important high-school exit exam) and passing Algebra 1, which is becoming the make-or-break class for California high-school students? I have spent many hours poring over the endless research on the positive effects of garden curricula, and in all that time, I have yet to find a single study that suggests classroom gardens help students meet the state standards for English and math. Our kids are working in these gardens with the promise of a better chance at getting an education and a high-school diploma but without one bit of proof that their hard work will result in either. We should remember, by the way, that the California high-school exit exam, which so many are failing, is hardly onerous: it requires a mastery of eighth-grade math (students need to score a mere 55 percent on that portion of the test) and 10th-grade English language and composition (on which they need to score 60 percent or higher). And so I would say this to our state's new child farm laborers: ¡*Huelga!* Strike!

The ever-evolving rationale behind the school-garden movement mushes together two emotionally stirring ideas: first, that kids will learn by doing, and second, that millions of poor kids have so little access to fruits and vegetables that if they don't spend their school day growing some on campus, they will never get any at all. As a pro-Waters friend observed to me in a recent e-mail, "There's only 7-Eleven in the hood."

15   As it happens, I live fewer than 20 miles from the most famous American hood, Compton, and on a recent Wednesday morning I drove over there to do a little grocery shopping. The Ralphs was vast, well-lit, bountifully stocked, and possessed of a huge and well-tended produce section. Using my Ralphs card, I bought four ears of corn for a dollar, green grapes and nectarines (both grown in the state, both 49 cents a pound), a pound of fresh tortillas for $1.69, and a half gallon of low-fat milk for $2.19. The staff, California friendly, outnumbered the customers, and the place had the dreamy, lost-in-time feeling that empty American supermarkets often have.

But across Compton Boulevard, it was a different story. Anyone who says that Americans have lost the desire and ability to cook fresh produce has never been to the Superior Super Warehouse in Compton. The produce section—packed with large families, most of them Hispanic—was like a dreamscape of strange and wonderful offerings: tomatillos, giant mangoes, cactus leaves, bunches of beets with their leaves on, chayóte squash, red yams, yucca root. An entire string section of chiles: serrano, Anaheim, green, red, yellow. All of it was dirt cheap, as were the bulk beans and rice. Small children stood beside shopping carts with the complacent, slightly dazed look of kids whose mothers are taking care of business.

What we see at Superior Super Warehouse is an example of capitalism doing what it does best: locating a market need (in this case, poor people living in an American inner city who desire a wide variety of fruits and vegetables and who are willing to devote their time and money to acquiring them) and filling it.

But the existence of the monastically quiet Ralphs in Compton reflects something quite different: advocacy. Over the past decade, many well-intentioned factions have made a focused effort to bring supermarkets—and with them, abundant fresh produce—to poor urban areas. Although the battle is far from over, there has been some progress. This seems to me a more sensible approach to getting produce to children than asking the unfortunate tykes to spend precious school hours growing it themselves. Why not make them build the buses that will take them to and from school, or rotate in shifts through the boiler room?

This notion of the school day as an interlude during which children can desperately attempt to cheat ignorance and death by growing the snap peas and zucchini flowers that are the essential building blocks of life comes with a lofty set of ideals. It is a grand vision, which Waters is happy to expand upon to any reporter who takes an interest, and it was described in the following way in last July's *Los Angeles Times*:

> Waters says there is a shift in priorities that needs to happen within federal policy to give garden programs longevity. In the 1960s, John F. Kennedy implemented the President's Council on Physical Fitness to instill values of physical fitness. She considers the current prevalence of childhood obesity and early-onset Type 2 diabetes to be signals for immediate action similar to the fitness council.

20   Well, there's a leap of logic. Waters calls for a new federal program based on an old one, but the new one is necessary only because the old one has obviously failed: American kids are fatter and sicker than ever.

Why are obesity and Type 2 diabetes so closely related to low incomes in this country? Surely a good part of the answer lies in a heartrending truth about the experience of poverty that many conservatives (and not a few liberals) either don't know or choose not to know, and it is something I see at my volunteer job in a Los Angeles food bank, where the clients scoop as many candies out of the basket on my desk as I'll let them have (if I didn't set a limit, only the first person would get any) before glumly turning to the matter of filling out their food order form, which offers such basic and unexciting items as tuna, rice, and (yes) fresh fruits and vegetables, often including delicious oranges, pears, and peaches that people with fruit trees donate the day they're picked. The simple truth is expressed clearly by George Orwell in *The Road to Wigan Pier,* his book about the grinding poverty experienced in the North of England in the 1930s:

> The peculiar evil is this: that the less money you have, the less inclined you feel to spend it on wholesome food…When you are unemployed, which is to say when you are underfed, harassed, bored, and miserable, you don't *want* to eat dull wholesome food. You want something a little bit "tasty." There is always some cheaply pleasant thing to tempt you. Let's have a three pennorth of chips! Run out and buy us a two-penny ice cream! Put the kettle on and we'll all have a nice cup of tea…Unemployment is an endless misery that has got to be palliated.

The suicidal dietary choices of so many poor people are the result of a problem, not the problem itself. The solution lies in an education that will propel students into a higher economic class, where they will live better and therefore eat better.

I started to ask Michael Piscal, founder and CEO of the Inner City Education Foundation Public Schools, which runs 15 successful charter schools in South Los Angeles, what he thought about the Edible Schoolyard and school gardens in general, but he cut me off. "I ignore all those e-mails," he told me bluntly. "Look," he said, when pressed, "there's nothing wrong with kids getting together after school and working on a garden; that's very nice. But when it becomes the center of everything—as it usually does—it's absurd. The only question in education reform that's worth anything is this: What are you doing to prepare these kids for college? If I can get a kid to read Shakespeare and laugh at the right places, I can get him to college. That's all that matters to me."

With the Edible Schoolyard, and the thousands of similar programs, the idea of a school as a venue in which to advance a social agenda has reached rock bottom. This kind of misuse of instructional time began in the Progressive Era, and it has been employed to cheat kids out of thousands of crucial learning hours over the years, so that they might be indoctrinated in whatever the fashionable idea of the moment or the school district might be. One year it's hygiene and another it's anti-Communism; in one city it's safe-sex "outercourse," and in another it's abstinence-only education. (Sixth-graders at King spend an hour and a half each week in the garden or the kitchen—and that doesn't include the time they spend in the classroom, in efforts effective or not, to apply the experiences of planting and cooking to learning the skills and subjects that the state of California mandates must be mastered.) But with these gardens—and their implication that one of the few important things we as a culture have to teach the next generation is what and how to eat—we're mocking one of our most ennobling American ideals. Our children don't get an education because they're lucky, or because we've generously decided to give them one as a special gift. Our children get an education—or should get an education—because they have a right to one. At the very least, shouldn't we ensure that the person who makes her mark on the curricula we teach be someone other than an extremely talented cook with a highly political agenda?

25   I have spent my life, it seems, in and around schools. For complicated reasons, I attended a score of them, both in the United States and abroad; I taught in Louisiana and Los Angeles for more than a decade; I have volunteered in all sorts of schools, and am now a mother of elementary-school students. I have never seen an entire school system as fundamentally broken and rudderless as the California public schools, a system in which one out of five high-school students drops out before graduation, and in which scarcely 60 percent of the African American and Hispanic students leave school with a diploma. These young people are cast adrift in a $50 billion system in which failure is almost a foregone conclusion.

So why not give these troubled kids a bit of engagement and excitement out in the nourishing gardens, which if nothing else might slim them down and thus extend their lives? Really: How can that hurt?

Last October, we lost the greatest educational reformer of the late 20th century, Theodore Sizer, the founder of the Essential Schools movement, who was brave enough to say that when a school is in crisis, its leaders should strip away every program and resource that is not essential to the mission of schooling. He wrote in his classic 1984 book, *Horace's Compromise*:

> If students have yet to meet the fundamental standards of literacy, numeracy and civic understanding, programs should focus exclusively on these. Some critics will argue that the school must go beyond these subjects to hold the interest of the pupils...but a fourteen year old who is semiliterate is an adolescent in need of intensive, focused attention.

My state is full of semiliterate 14-year-olds. Let their after-school hours be filled with whatever enriching programs the good volunteers and philanthropic organizations of California care to offer them: club sports, choruses, creative-writing workshops, gardens. But until our kids have a decent chance at mastering the essential skills and knowledge that they will need to graduate from high school, we should devote every resource and every moment of their academic day to helping them realize that life-changing goal. Otherwise, we become complicit—through our best intentions—in an act of theft that will not only contribute to the creation of a permanent, uneducated underclass but will rob that group of the very force necessary to change its fate. The state, which failed these students as children and adolescents, will have to shoulder them in adulthood, for it will have created not a generation of gentleman farmers but one of intellectual sharecroppers, whose fortunes depend on the largesse or political whim of their educated peers.

A Defense of School Gardens and Response to Caitlin Flanagan's "Cultivating Failure" in *The Atlantic*

BONNIE HULKOWER

Bonnie Hulkower is a marine scientist and environmental planner whose work focuses on ensuring that public housing and water resource projects comply with environmental regulations. This blog entry on Treehugger.com *was posted on February 1, 2010.*

The Edible Schoolyard program, which began in 1995 at Martin Luther King public middle school in Berkeley, has inspired growth of garden programs in other communities throughout the county during the past 15 years. The program teaches children valuable lessons as they learn to grow food. However, Caitlin Flanagan's diatribe against school gardens, "Cultivating Failure," in the latest edition of *The Atlantic* attacks the program through two main arguments. The first is that in a troubled school system every resource should be funneled into the core disciplines of "literacy, numeracy, and civic understanding." Whether school gardening "works" to educate children does not seem to merit consideration to Flanagan. Presumably, like art, music, and anything else that is not in the state performance exams, working and learning in the school garden is a sham activity that betrays the true needs of students, mostly minority, to prove their testing competence in our brave new world. In doing so, Flanagan ignores the entirety of mainstream educational reform in the 20th century and beyond. It is knowledge common to most educators that children learn through a variety of modalities and thrive in supportive and interactive environments. Patsy Benveniste, vice president of Community Education Programs at the Chicago Botanic Gardens offers a response from within the ongoing movement to strengthen schools through gardening:

> One of the main ideas behind school gardening is to allow the child—constrained in an utterly artificial "learning" environment that denies most requirements of genuine physical and psychic development—a little freedom and play; a little sensory exploration and experimentation; a little socialization around a joint effort to create something that is tangible and valued by others and maybe even edible. Flanagan seems to think that our only recourse in the face of massive educational failure by this country is to close the blinds, lock the doors and drill more work on the captives. She does not seem to understand that the kids who are being failed by the system will never profit by her remedy.

This argument is ignorant of developmental theory and understanding of how children learn and grow. E.F. Schumacher said in *Small Is Beautiful* that the task of education was not the process of creating "know how." The task of education is "first and foremost, the transmission of ideas of value, of what to do with our lives." Frederick Froebel knew in the early 19th century that children must be nurtured outside of rigid patterns. Heck, Cicero knew it ... "If you have a garden and a library, you have everything you need."

The second basic premise of Ms. Flanagan's article involves torching a straw woman by the name of Alice Waters. Yes, it seems that Alice Waters, the Edible Schoolyard program at MLK Middle School, and school gardens throughout the country are responsible for all that ails the American Public School System. However, the expansion of school gardens in America does not stem from some mesmeric, cult-of-personality influence of Alice Waters on school districts, but rather because it works. School boards and principals have seen success stories and have chosen to incorporate gardening activities into our public schools one school at a time. A garden can reinforce many lessons learned in a classroom. Furthermore, through a garden a student can also learn responsibility, self-sufficiency, teamwork, volunteerism, and environmental stewardship.

5   Adding insult to injury, Flanagan's article condescends terribly to the people she purports to defend. She chafes at the colonial, exploitative horror of asking Hispanic students to harvest lettuce in the school garden. By using this analogy, Flanagan denigrates labor and laborers with her view that hard work is an activity that should be avoided, instead of an action that deserves our respect. She quotes Orwell on the tendency of the poor to choose empty, consoling calories over real nutrition. According to Flanagan, the sheer misery of the poor overwhelms their appetite for "boring, wholesome food." Flanagan also attempts to attack the food desert theory by insisting that poor people do have access to produce, her empirical proof being a one-time visit to two grocery stores in Compton.

In fact, in an age of diabetes, obesity, and under-funded school lunch programs, Edible Schoolyard can transform kids' dietary habits and provide them with adequate nutrition which will keep their minds alert and aid them in excelling in their studies. All this can be achieved by spending an hour or so a week tending the arugula.

Finally, Flanagan has fallen onto the pendulum swing syndrome that captures many educational critics. Our pluralistic society educates a broad spectrum of students who require differentiated strategies to meet their specific learning needs and strengths. Proponents of a particular perspective frequently propose the exclusive use of their preferred method.

However, educators do not need to follow a simplistic approach that limits programs to "either/or." Rather, an inclusive curriculum embracing several educational philosophies can foster a lifetime love of learning. School gardening might also be offered as an elective in the grade levels that present curriculum options. Students learn best when they are encouraged to follow their interests after exposure to a variety of subject matter. Educators using best practices can and do use experiential learning in the garden to support a multitude of learning opportunities involving, but not limited to, literacy, numeracy, biology, chemistry, history, economics, botany, art, culture, and community.

Yes, at times the locavore movement can feel tiresome, but having had a bad dinner experience at Chez Panisse is not a reason to attack school gardens. For all her entertaining rhetoric, Flanagan has brought no new insight to the table. Her cure—increased standardization of education—merely swings outdated pendulum theories.

Thoughts on *The Atlantic's* Attack on School Gardens

TOM PHILPOTT

Tom Philpott is the cofounder of Maverick Farms, a center for sustainable food education in North Carolina. He has been a columnist and editor for Grist, *an online environmental news site, and has been published in* Newsweek, Gastronomica, *and the* Guardian. *He is the food and agriculture correspondent for* Mother Jones. *This response appeared on* Grist *on January 13, 2010.*

For several years starting in the early '90s, I worked as a remedial math and writing teacher at Austin Community College. At that time—and, for all I know, now—the Texas public education system was mercilessly stratified: high-income districts lavished resources on schools, while their counterparts in low-income districts scraped by on bare-bones budgets. Predictably, college acceptance rates were much higher in the high-income districts.

That brazenly unequal system churned out plenty of customers for our remedial services. What struck me about many of my students was that they seemed to have never really been engaged before in a classroom: they expected rote, mechanistic, abstract assignments. And they expected to do poorly on them.

So I tried to engage them—cast around for topics they were interested in, concrete things, and use them to explain math concepts, or inspire an essay. And, more often than not, it worked—the students and I would hit upon something, amid much back and forth, that sparked genuine interest, and then they would be off and running, giddy in the pursuit of ideas. Which, of course, is exactly the kind of teaching that goes on in lots of private schools—the ones that routinely send students to esteemed universities, and not remedial programs at community colleges.

It's not exactly a radical idea. Teaching is a form of communication; and focusing on concrete things has long been a favored communication strategy. In their celebrated guidebook to writing *The Elements of Style*, Strunk and White advise, "use definite, specific, concrete language." The advice seems impeccable.

5   The Edible Schoolyard program, launched in Berkeley public schools by Alice Waters, is an attempt at putting that principle in action. It makes food, a material reality that everyone interacts with daily, an object of hands-on study. See that lettuce on your plate? Where did it come from? How do seeds germinate? What variety of lettuce is it? Why this variety and not another one? Why are only one or two available at the grocery store? Who owns grocery stores—and who decides what they offer. What makes plants grow? And so on.

The idea of having kids grow and cook food as part of the curriculum seems brilliant: a way to make concrete such potentially abstract topics as biology, chemistry, history, economics, and botany. It also promises leverage in another direction: in an age of defunded, low-quality school lunches and surging diabetes rates among children, Edible Schoolyard has the potential to transform kids' dietary habits.

Has it worked in practice? That's a fair question. The program has been around for nearly 15 years now—it started in 1995 at Martin Luther King public middle school in Berkeley, and has expanded to affiliates in New Orleans, among other places across the country. Similar programs have sprouted up elsewhere, inspired by its example. Has it succeeded in catching students' interest and making them better learners? Has it helped them develop healthier eating habits?

In a scathing piece in *The Atlantic*, the writer Caitlin Flanagan raises those questions but doesn't answer them. Or, more properly, she declares the program a disaster—the piece is titled "Cultivating Failure"—without even coming close to driving home her case.

In her 3500-word polemic, the only hard evidence she brings to bear for her verdict of failure is this:

> Indeed, Hispanic students do particularly poorly at King Middle School. According to the 2009 Federal Accountability Requirements, statewide, more than 39 percent of Latinos are proficient in English and 44 percent in math, but at the King school, those numbers are a dismal 30 percent and 29 percent, respectively. Where do Berkeley's African American and Hispanic middle-schoolers do well? At a gardenless charter school called Cal Prep, where 92 percent of the students are black or Latino, where the focus is on academic achievement, and where test scores have been rising steadily.

10 So at King, Latinos are underperforming on standardized tests, while over at Cal Prep, "test scores have been rising steadily." You don't need to be a social-sciences graduate student to marvel at the logical gymnastics on display here. Correlation does not show causation; students could be underperforming at King because of the garden program—or because of some other reason. And so on. The numbers she cites may call into question the efficacy of Edible Schoolyard, but they by no means settle the case.

And that's her last nod to bringing empirical evidence to bear. (In another jaw-dropping section, she seeks to debunk the concept of food deserts—the idea that residents of low-income areas tend to have less access to fresh food—not by scrutinizing the considerable academic research on the topic, but rather by making a 20-mile trip to "the most famous American hood [sic], Compton," to check out the grocery scene.)

Her point seems to be this: working the land and cooking are lowly tasks, work that should be fled and not aspired to. It's unconscionable to urge Latino students, some of whose parents may work as migrant laborers, to garden as a form of learning. Students, particularly those struggling with basic reading and math, should be forced to hit the books, not weed the carrots.

That line of reasoning seems brutally reductionist—and certainly doesn't reflect my own experience as a remedial teacher. More importantly, Flanagan makes no effort to actually engage the program she is trashing (or, indeed, the book she's ostensibly reviewing—her piece is ludicrously packaged as a review of Thomas McNamee's 2008 biography of Alice Waters).

And the idea that farming and cooking—and even getting one's hands dirty in the garden—are beneath respectable middle-class aspiration is deeply problematic. Such thinking reinforces an unjust food system that exploits cheap labor as a matter of course, propped up by a largely invisible army of migrant workers who do the dirty work of tending fields, slaughterhouses, and kitchens.

15 The sustainable-food movement has matured enough and gained enough force that it's coming under withering criticism from a variety of quarters. That's good for the movement—hard questions need to be asked, assumptions questioned, received ideas reconsidered. And authors who perform those tasks will find a market from editors desperate to generate attention with contrarian poses.

But I wish we could expect more thoughtfulness, and less hack work, from such critics.

Atlantic Gets It Wrong!: School Gardens Cultivate Minds Not Failure

JESSE KURTZ-NICHOLL

Jesse Kurtz-Nicholl joined the Center for a Livable Future while getting his Master's in Public Health at the Johns Hopkins Bloomberg School of Public Health. While at the Center, he worked on writing a food system curriculum for high school students. This response was posted on the Center's blog on January 13, 2010.

As a disclaimer, I used to be a high school teacher in Richmond, California in the exact urban schools of which Caitlin Flanagan writes about.

This post is in response to the recently published article in *The Atlantic* magazine by Caitlin Flanagan titled, "Cultivating Failure."

Ms. Flanagan makes the argument that the school garden movement building in California and nationwide is somehow stripping students of valuable time to become "educated," dooming urban students to a life of poverty and "cultivating failure" as her title expresses. She begins with the idea that immigrant students from Mexico, who come to the United States in search of an education are being pushed back into the fields of manual labor through their middle school garden. I wish I could just claim how ridiculous this viewpoint is and be done with it, but I take her feelings seriously and feel the need to correct the record.

In her article, she makes the claim that she traveled to deeply urban areas near Compton, Calif., and found a bountiful harvest of cheap, healthy produce in the local Ralphs and other supermarkets backing up her claim that there is no need for school gardens that provide "access" to healthy food because it is everywhere. There are some serious flaws with this argument. First off, a recent study released by the U.S. Department of Agriculture tells us that 14.6 percent of American households, approximately 17 million households are "food insecure" meaning that they can't afford a healthful diet or lack dependable access. Many communities like West Oakland, Calif., Baltimore and Richmond, Calif., lack supermarket chains within a reasonable distance. Her contention thus smacks of a very dangerous fallacy of composition. A second problem I have with Ms. Flanagan's assessment is that even if there was incredible access of all of our urban and rural residents to great healthy produce, which there is not, it would not diminish the importance and need for school gardens and even more intensive food production-focused endeavors like The Food Project in Boston, Urban Roots in Austin, Urban Tilth in Richmond, Calif., and Alice Waters' edible schoolyard. With staggering obesity rates in the United States, our children have not just lost access, they have lost their connection to food. Gardening is less about manual labor than it is about re-connecting to your body, to food and to health.

5   We know from programs like Head Start and research that young people will perform better in school if they are well-fed. After watching throngs of students come into my classes every morning with a breakfast of chips and a soda, I know the true value of garden programs that change the way children and adolescents think about their body, what they put in it and how it affects them. If Ms. Flanagan claims that the garden "takes away" an hour and a half each week of class time, (all of which is spent outside, doing physical activity, I remind you) I claim that hour and a half, if anything, only acts to engage the student further, cement their connection with the school (which is lacking in many urban areas), beautify their learning environment, and even, yes, provide them with healthy food and snacks that will help them maintain better health, choose better nutrition and be more focused when it comes time to engage in their in-class learning.

All of this tacitly acknowledges Flanagan's argument that urban agriculture and school gardens are somehow a break from learning, and that you must sacrifice scholarly learning when you are in the garden. I completely disagree with this most fundamental of Ms. Flanagan's arguments.

In fact, after running an Urban Agriculture and Food Systems class last year with high school students, I'm convinced that you could teach not only a Biology class, a Chemistry class, but a U.S. History class, Art classes and elements of English classes and even Math classes in various ways through the garden and sacrifice nothing of which Ms. Flanagan contends. I agree with her that the California school system is deeply broken. Why she decides to pin it on school gardens and Alice Waters is beyond me. How about blasting the state for drastically underfunding our schools, or Prop 13 for emptying the coffers of valuable school revenue and forcing class sizes into the dangerous territory of 40 students or more, or low teacher pay that won't attract the young bright minds we should have educating our children, or myriad other concerns. I wish every school had a substantial thriving school garden class and program, but the fact is that there are very few schools that actually have a substantial food production program like MLK middle school in Berkeley; most are small gardens that never get used, or gardens used during after-school time. While I wish every school could have an Alice Waters supporting their wonderful food-focused garden, sadly that's not the case.

Lastly, we are starting to learn that it is our food environment and not lack of exercise that is the main cause of our overweight society. Recent studies from Johns Hopkins have begun to illuminate that point. Well, I ask you, where is the food environment for our children? Some would say the home, which is true, but students also spend 1/3 of their day at school. Considering another 1/3 of their time is spent sleeping, I would contend that the food environment of the school is incredibly important in developing a healthy lifestyle for our urban students. Take a deep look at this article, and try to answer the question of how learning about food and our connection to it somehow cultivates a life of failure. I can't come to that conclusion.

■ ■ ■   **FOR CLASS DISCUSSION** **The Future of Food and Farming**

1. Many of the readings about genetically modified foods in this unit focus on the rights and responsibilities of consumers to know what they are eating. How important do you believe it is to know what is in your food or how it was produced? What do you believe to be the responsibilities of government or corporations when it comes to telling us what is in the food we eat? What are our responsibilities as consumers?

2. Look at the foods in your cupboard or refrigerator. Choose one package and rhetorically analyze the information available to you. What information appears to be regulated or required? What information is designed to appeal to you as a consumer? What information would you like to know that is not available on the packaging? Bring the package or photos of the package to class to work in groups. What might your classmates notice that you did not when purchasing this item?

3. Map out the positions of the different authors and artists on the issue of GM foods. Where do they agree and disagree? To what extent are they focusing on the larger question of GMOs, and to what extent are certain authors focusing on a specific aspect of the issue? Which authors seem to share underlying values and assumptions about GM foods, even if they are not focusing on the same question? Which arguments seem to make the strongest appeals to *logos*?

4. Some readers might say that Caitlin Flanagan's argument resembles a polemic, even a rant, an impassioned statement of a viewpoint with more emphasis on expressing and evoking emotion than on making a rational case for a position. Consider the reasons offered by Caitlin Flanagan. What points do you think have merit and are supported with evidence? What are the values and assumptions of an audience who would find her argument persuasive? What concerns seem included merely to "stir the pot"? Three readings in this unit were written directly in response to Flanagan. Where do these other writers offer effective rhetorical critiques of Flanagan's argument? (See Chapter 8 for a discussion of rhetorical analysis points.) Where and how well do these writers rebut Flanagan's reasoning and evidence?

WRITING ASSIGNMENT   **Peer Review: A Rhetorical Analysis Letter to Caitlin Flanagan**

Almost immediately upon its publication, Caitlin Flanagan's article, "Cultivating Failure," was met with controversy. Responses such as those provided in this unit appeared online; another writer for *The Atlantic* took her to task; and even a Berkeley school administrator responded to Flanagan's charges in an open letter. Imagine you are in a writers' workshop with Caitlin Flanagan, and she has shared her essay with you. Write her a letter in which you provide peer feedback on her work. From your position as a citizen interested in the issue and an attentive reader, what changes might she make to her essay that would strengthen the quality of her argument? How could she anticipate and respond to the objections raised by other writers in a rebuttal paragraph or paragraphs? What research could she include that might reinforce her claims and enhance her positive *ethos*? ■

Higher Education: How and Why We Learn Matters

As many students know from firsthand experience, the costs of a college education continue to rise while the job market for recent college graduates reels from a global recession. This growing economic insecurity has led to increased scrutiny of the decision to seek a higher education. More than ever, students must carefully weigh the costs and benefits of attending college. In the process, students face pressures to define their educational goals and values, choose institutions likely to lead to their vocational paths, and consider alternatives to attending college altogether.

The ways that a college education is delivered are also changing. While most colleges still offer traditional face-to-face courses, more and more colleges and universities are expanding their online course options, and a few are entirely online. The most recent development in online education is the MOOC, or massive open online course, offered by both traditional universities such as Stanford, Harvard, and MIT, and by for-profit corporations. Such courses have been touted by their supporters as innovative and as a way to equalize education, but their critics view them as cynical attempts to profit from learners who cannot afford the time or expense of a traditional degree or to help legislators save money at the expense of actual learning.

This unit offers a range of voices in the conversations about attending college and the decisions students face if they choose to enroll. Across different genres ranging from a speech to college freshmen to a contribution to a roundtable discussion, the readings explore related questions: What makes education valuable beyond economic incentive? How should students approach their higher education to get the most out of the experience? What values should determine how decisions are made about delivering education to the next generation of learners?

Learning by Degrees

REBECCA MEAD

As a staff writer for The New Yorker *since 1997 and author of* My Life in Middlemarch, *Rebecca Mead has explored a wide variety of journalistic subjects. From the infertility egg industry to God-based diets, Mead carefully analyzes cultural phenomena. In this comment, published in the* Talk of the Town *section of* The New Yorker *on June 10, 2010, Mead addresses the cultural trend of viewing college for its financial benefits rather than for its impact on self-worth.*

A member of the Class of 2010—who this season dons synthetic cap and gown, listens to the inspirational words of David Souter (Harvard), Anderson Cooper (Tulane), or Lisa Kudrow (Vassar), and collects a diploma—need not be a statistics major to know that the odds of stepping into a satisfying job, or, indeed, any job, are lower now than might have been imagined four long years ago, when the first posters were hung on a dorm-room wall, and having a .edu e-mail address was still a novelty. Statistically speaking, however, having an expertise in statistics may help in getting a job: according to a survey conducted by the National Association of Colleges and Employers, graduates with math skills are more likely than their peers in other majors to find themselves promptly and gainfully employed.

The safest of all degrees to be acquiring this year is in accounting: forty-six percent of graduates in that discipline have already been offered jobs. Business majors are similarly placed: forty-four percent will have barely a moment to breathe before undergoing the transformation from student to suit. Engineers of all stripes—chemical, computer, electrical, mechanical, industrial, environmental— have also fared relatively well since the onset of the recession: they dominate a ranking, issued by Payscale.com, of the disciplines that produce the best-earning graduates. Particular congratulations are due to aerospace engineers, who top the list, with a starting salary of just under sixty thousand dollars—a figure that, if it is not exactly stratospheric, is twenty-five thousand dollars higher than the average starting salary of a graduate in that other science of the heavens, theology.

Economics majors aren't doing badly, either: their starting salary averages about fifty thousand a year, rising to a mid-career median of a hundred and one thousand. Special note should be taken of the fact that if you have an economics degree you can, eventually, make a living proposing that other people shouldn't bother going to college. This, at least, is the approach of Professor Richard K. Vedder, of Ohio University, who is the founder of the Center for College Affordability and Productivity. According to the *Times*, eight out of the ten job categories that will add the most employees during the next decade—including home-health aide, customer-service representative, and store clerk—can be performed by someone without a college degree. "Professor Vedder likes to ask why fifteen percent of mail carriers have bachelor's degrees," the paper reported.

The argument put forth by Professor Vedder (Ph.D., University of Illinois) is, naturally, economic: of those overly schooled mail carriers, he said, "Some of them could have bought a house for what they spent on their education." Another economist, Professor Robert I. Lerman, of American University (Ph.D., M.I.T.), told the *Times* that high schools, rather than readying all students for college, should focus on the acquisition of skills appropriate to the workplace. According to the *Times*, these include the ability to "solve problems and make decisions," "resolve conflict and negotiate," "cooperate with others," and "listen actively."

5   It may be news that the academy is making a case for the superfluity of the academy, but skepticism about the value of college, and of collegians, is hardly novel. Within the sphere of business, a certain romance attaches to the figure of the successful college dropout, like Steve Jobs, who was enrolled at Reed for only a semester, or Bill Gates, who started at Harvard in 1973 but didn't get his degree until it was granted, honorarily, thirty-four years later. On the political stage, too, having spent excessive hours in seminar rooms and libraries is widely regarded as a liability. *Vide* Peggy Noonan's celebration, during the 2004 Presidential campaign, of George W. Bush's lack of cerebration. "He's not an intellectual," Noonan wrote in the *Wall Street Journal*. "Intellectuals start all the trouble in the world."

The candidates' education, or the insufficiency thereof, came up again during the most recent Presidential election. Sarah Palin told Katie Couric that she was "not one of those who maybe came from a background of, you know, kids who perhaps graduate college and their parents get them a passport and give them a backpack and say go off and travel the world"—even though Palin evidently considered college important enough to have tried out five different ones within three years. Meanwhile, Barack Obama's degrees from prestigious universities were, to his critics, evidence of his unfitness for office. "The last thing we need are more pointy-headed intellectuals running the government," the political scientist Charles Murray (B.A., Harvard; Ph.D., M.I.T.) said during the closing months of the campaign. As President, Obama has rightly noted that too many Americans are already skipping college or dropping out, even without economists having advised them to do so; within weeks of the Inauguration, he pledged to increase the national graduation rate, which is significantly lower than that of many other developed nations, including Canada, Japan, and Korea.

The skip-college advocates' contention—that, with the economic downturn, a college degree may not be the best investment—has its appeal. Given the high cost of attending college in the United States, the question of whether a student is getting his or her money's worth tends to loom large with whoever is paying the tuition fees and the meal plan bills. Even so, one needn't necessarily be a liberal-arts graduate to regard as distinctly and speciously utilitarian the idea that higher education is, above all, a route to economic advancement. Unaddressed in that calculus is any question of what else an education might be for: to nurture critical thought; to expose individuals to the signal accomplishments of humankind; to develop in them an ability not just to listen actively but to respond intelligently.

All these are habits of mind that are useful for an engaged citizenry, and from which a letter carrier, no less than a college professor, might derive a sense of self-worth. For who's to say in what direction a letter carrier's thoughts might, or should, turn, regardless of the job's demands? Consider Stephen Law, a professor of philosophy at the University of London, who started his working life delivering mail for the British postal service, began reading works of philosophy in his spare time, decided that he'd like to know more, and went on to study the discipline at City University, in London, and at Oxford University. (A philosophy graduate in the Class of 2010, by the way, stands to earn an average starting salary of forty thousand dollars a year, rising to a lifetime median of seventy-six thousand. Not exactly statistician money, but something to think about.) Indeed, if even a professionally oriented college degree is no longer a guarantee of easily found employment, an argument might be made in favor of a student's pursuing an education that is less, rather than more, pragmatic. (More theology, less accounting.) That way, regardless of each graduate's ultimate path, all might be qualified to be carriers of arts and letters, of which the nation can never have too many.

What Do You Do with a B.A. in History?

KEN SAXON

Ken Saxon, a graduate of Princeton and Stanford's Graduate School of Business, has been both an entrepreneur and a leader in the nonprofit sector for more than 20 years. He currently heads Courage to Lead, a leadership and support program for executives of nonprofit organizations based in California. Saxon delivered this speech in 2010 to the freshman class of the University of California, Santa Barbara. A transcript of the speech can be found on Andy Chan's blog The Heart of the Matter.

"What do you do with a B.A. in English,
What is my life going to be?
Four years of college and plenty of knowledge,
Have earned me this useless degree.
I can't pay the bills yet,
'Cause I have no skills yet,
The world is a big scary place."

That's a cute song in a funny Broadway show, *Avenue Q.* But it sends a message that's quite different from what I've experienced in my own life. I went off to college, and unencumbered by personal or parental concerns that I come out with a professional skill, I majored in History.

What did I do with a B.A. in European History?

I got myself a job in corporate finance at the largest real estate company in America.

I attended Stanford Business School.

5   I started and built a company that stores business files and records and expanded it up and down the West Coast.

I sold the business, and got deeply involved with community nonprofit organizations.

I founded and run a leadership and renewal program for nonprofit executive directors, and I became Chairman of the Board of a local foundation working on global development issues, and recently went to Kenya visiting health clinics serving the poorest of the poor.

None of this journey (none of it!) was even a glimmer in my mind's eye when I was sitting in a lecture hall in my freshman year at college. Life journeys are rarely predictable, and they inevitably have lots of twists and turns. It doesn't hurt at all to head out in a certain direction—as a matter of fact, clear goals and ambition are a good thing—but to act with high confidence that you will end up where you plan to at the start of college is folly.

So if you buy into my premise about life's uncertainty, what consequence does this have for how you approach your four or so years at a university like UCSB? Well my talk this evening will explore the benefits of taking a liberal arts approach to college.

And if you already feel confident what your professional path will be, I'm going to encourage you to broadly explore a lot of other academic fields during your time here.

10   In this talk, I'm going to focus on three things:

1. The purpose of a college education, and what the liberal arts is all about,
2. The downside of focusing on college as a pre-professional or technical education experience, and
3. I want to talk about some questions I think are fundamental to your education, and how a liberal arts approach to college can help you get some answers.

First, let's talk about what college is for. I think our society does many young people a disservice. Kids constantly get the message that if they want to get at what life has to offer, they need to go to college. Supposedly, according to the data, your income will be higher, you'll be more likely to have a successful marriage, and more likely to live a happy life.

But then tons of young people head off to college—record numbers in the last decade—without really thinking about why, and what they want out of it. That was certainly the case for me. In my family, it was just expected that I go to college. And I went to the best one I got into—Princeton.

So what would I say that the purpose of a college education is? I'd start by saying that it's about discovering who you are, what you're passionate about, what's important to you, and what doesn't interest you in the slightest. Answering such questions is a life-long journey. But the fact is that this is a unique moment in your life. *[READ SLOWLY]* Compared to your time here at UCSB, there will likely be no other time in your life when it will be easier to try so many interesting things, to find out what you like and don't like, and be influenced by so many incredible potential mentors.

To me, college is a time for experimentation and paying attention. I can't think of any way better to do all of this than by taking a liberal arts approach to college.

15   According to Wikipedia—and as a liberal arts guy, I love Wikipedia, that giant storehouse of general knowledge—"the term liberal arts denotes a curriculum that imparts general knowledge and develops the student's rational thought and intellectual capabilities, unlike a professional, vocational, technical curricula emphasizing specialization."

So let's pick that apart. First of all, it makes clear what liberal arts is not:

- professional, vocational, technical curricula emphasizing specialization. I think they're talking about a couple things here. One is a type of curriculum—like pre-med or engineering—that focuses on specific learning to prepare for a certain kind of career. The other part of this is specialization—a narrow approach to education, as opposed to a broad approach. If you think about it, grad school is 100 percent specialized or focused in a certain discipline. In college, in contrast, you have a choice as to whether you go narrow or broad.

In terms of what the liberal arts IS, the definition also says a few things. First, it says that the approach imparts general knowledge—once again, broad over narrow.

But it says something else that's really important, that it develops the student's rational thought and intellectual capabilities.

So, what's that all about? I think they're talking about things like critical thinking, analytical reasoning, and creativity. They're talking about complexity, and the ability to learn and adapt.

There's no question a liberal arts education is a great place to develop your critical faculties, taking in a lot of information and making informed judgments about complex questions. This is a skill-set that is integral to succeeding in the broader world, and certainly in my world of business and of leadership.

20   Now I know many of you are hearing other messages that really conflict with the liberal arts approach. The University of California, as you know better than anyone, has gotten ridiculously expensive, and some of you may feel pressure—either personally, or from your parents—to get a good return on that investment by pretty quickly getting a good-paying job. And, of course, there are student loans to repay. I also know what the economy is like right now, and that you may be more focused on developing marketable skills than you may have been just a few years ago.

But even if you want to go out and quickly make a good amount of money, I have some cautions about a pre-professional approach to college.

First of all, how can you be sure you know where the better paying fields are going to be in five years? From my experience at Stanford Business School, I can't tell you how many times I've seen that the industry that everyone wants to get into one year is headed for a fall the next. All the students in the late '80s that wanted to get into real estate development. CRASH! The flood of students in the late '90s that wanted to go into Internet startups. OUCH! How about the house flippers of a few years ago? It all looked like easy money. But that's how markets work—tons of people and money follow such bullish signals, leading to a glut of that kind of business, leading to a hyper-competitive market, and then a crash. It's the nature of markets, and it has happened since the beginning of time. So the question here is—even if you wanted to, how could you know the best fields for making money in the future? Even pre-med students today can't be sure of what the career path of a doctor will look like in the more than a decade it will take until they finish their residency.

Now, let's say you want to go into business one day, as I ultimately did. What would be the best preparation for that? I can tell you that as a hiring employer, here are things I looked for:
Evidence of:

Initiative and leadership,
Work ethic,
Communication skills, and
Emotional intelligence and interpersonal skills.

None of those is linked to a specific line of study.

25   It is true that there are some prospective employers who will be searching for narrow lines of study in their hiring. But many, many do not. When I applied as a senior

in college for a newly created finance job at the world's largest real estate development company based in Dallas, Texas, I don't know what they thought when they saw I was a European History major from Princeton. But I do know that something in my letter and resume led them to want to interview me, and somehow I was able to stand out from the six finalists they flew down to Dallas. You can try to predict such things, but everyone's different, and you just never know. I found out later that the hiring manager—a high-level executive in a Texas-based global real estate company—graduated college with a B.A. in English. Go figure.

I also want to ask how can you know what you like at this point in your life? My experience is that people who like what they do, who love what they do, are much more likely to be successful at it, in addition to being happier. And if you're going to spend a third of your life working, why not like what you do? Seems like a no-brainer to me.

So to pick the bulk of your curriculum now based upon your guess as to what you might want to do in the working world, when you really haven't tried that many things and don't likely know what will make you happy later in life, seems foolhardy to me. If it turns out you're wrong, you may have wasted a big opportunity. Tons of my friends changed their majors, and tons have changed careers. One of my best friends in business school went through med school first, only to discover that he hated it. He didn't want to quit, so he graduated—and then went to business school. This stuff happens, and it may happen to you.

And so often the best things that happen to you, the things that make all the difference, happen by chance, or result from failure—not the result of careful planning.

I want to play something for you. Who here has seen on the Internet the commencement speech that Steve Jobs gave at Stanford in 2005? It's really quite an extraordinary talk, and I encourage you to watch the whole 15-minute Steve Jobs video sometime. He tells three stories of his life, and I want to play the first one for you.

30   I dropped out of Reed College after the first 6 months, but then stayed around as a drop-in for another 18 months or so before I really quit. So why did I drop out?

It started before I was born. My biological mother was a young, unwed college graduate student, and she decided to put me up for adoption. She felt very strongly that I should be adopted by college graduates, so everything was all set for me to be adopted at birth by a lawyer and his wife. Except that when I popped out they decided at the last minute that they really wanted a girl. So my parents, who were on a waiting list, got a call in the middle of the night asking: "We have an unexpected baby boy; do you want him?" They said: "Of course." My biological mother later found out that my mother had never graduated from college and that my father had never graduated from high school. She refused to sign the final adoption papers. She only relented a few months later when my parents promised that I would someday go to college.

And 17 years later I did go to college. But I naively chose a college that was almost as expensive as Stanford, and all of my working-class parents' savings were being spent on my college tuition. After six months, I couldn't see the value in it. I had no idea what I wanted to do with my life and no idea how college was going to help me figure it out. And here I was spending all of the money my parents had saved their entire life. So I decided to drop out and trust that it would all work out OK. It was pretty scary at the time, but looking back it was one of the best decisions I ever made. The minute I dropped out I could stop taking the required classes that didn't interest me, and begin dropping in on the ones that looked interesting.

It wasn't all romantic. I didn't have a dorm room, so I slept on the floor in friends' rooms, I returned coke bottles for the 5¢ deposits to buy food with, and I would walk the 7 miles across town every Sunday night to get one good meal a week at the Hare Krishna temple. I loved it. And much of what I stumbled into by following my curiosity and intuition turned out to be priceless later on. Let me give you one example:

35   Reed College at that time offered perhaps the best calligraphy instruction in the country. Throughout the campus every poster, every label on every drawer, was beautifully hand calligraphed. Because I had dropped out and didn't have to take the normal classes, I decided to take a calligraphy class to learn how to do this. I learned about serif and san serif typefaces, about varying the amount of space between different letter combinations, about what makes great typography great. It was beautiful, historical, artistically subtle in a way that science can't capture, and I found it fascinating.

None of this had even a hope of any practical application in my life. But ten years later, when we were designing the first Macintosh computer, it all came back to me. And we designed it all into the Mac. It was the first computer with beautiful typography. If I had never dropped in on that single course in college, the Mac would have never had multiple typefaces or proportionally spaced fonts. And since Windows just copied the Mac, it's likely that no personal computer would have them. If I had never dropped out, I would have never dropped in on this calligraphy class, and personal computers might not have the wonderful typography that they do. Of course it was impossible to connect the dots looking forward when I was in college. But it was very, very clear looking backwards ten years later.

Again, you can't connect the dots looking forward; you can only connect them looking backwards. So you have to trust that the dots will somehow connect in your future. You have to trust in something—your gut, destiny, life, karma, whatever. This approach has never let me down, and it has made all the difference in my life.

I shared this story with you NOT to encourage you to drop out of college—although it shows that that's not necessarily the end of the world. I mean, I've been to one of Steve Jobs['s] houses, and I can assure you he's no longer eating at the Hare Krishna temple. No, I shared this story with you because it embodies an important point—that we can't always understand or explain the practical purpose of our choices to others as we go along. All we can do is listen to our hearts, follow our instincts and make the best judgments we can. It's all part of the experience of getting to know ourselves.

And that leads us back to some of what I suggested were the important life questions to make some progress answering while you're in college.

Who am I?
What am I passionate about?
What's important to me?
What doesn't interest me at all?

40   For me, embracing a liberal arts education was a great way to find some answers.

As part of putting this talk together, I did something I haven't done in decades—I pulled out my college transcript. It turns out I took courses in 16 different academic departments at Princeton. Clearly, I took the liberal arts seriously!

So let me share a few examples of how these experiences in the liberal arts helped me learn about myself.

From studying philosophy, I learned that abstract theories were intellectually interesting to me, but not so satisfying. Turns out, I'm a doer, an entrepreneur. I had the same experience with mathematics. Though I was good at it, once the classes got too deep into the abstract realm and I couldn't figure out the real world application, I lost interest.

From working week after week with a pigeon in a Psychology lab, I learned about Behaviorism, where our habits and behaviors came from and how they can be molded. It turns out that I love figuring out people, how they think and make decisions, and how to motivate them and bring out their best. My studies of Psychology and the brain have helped me be a better employer, a better negotiator, and a better parent—and they've helped me better understand myself.

45   From studying history, I learned that every struggle my society and I are going through is not new, that I am part of a story much larger than myself, and I learned humility about my role in that story. Interestingly to me, when I lost my bearings when the Twin Towers fell on 9/11, it was from history that I regained my sense of perspective—reading about how other societies survived much greater horrors over the centuries. It helped get me out of my own grief, and reminded me of the power of human resilience.

By writing a senior thesis and doing historical research leafing through primary source material in national archives in London and in Washington, I learned about how hard it is to understand the "truth" when relying on secondhand sources, like books and newspapers (and now on the Internet), where everything is filtered through other people's perspectives and biases. I also learned I was capable of original research, and of finding my own voice. And just like the marathons I've run, writing a 130-page thesis built endurance and expanded my sense of my own capabilities.

And what of studying music and art and architecture and literature? They helped me learn about what I find beautiful, and how that enhances my life. A couple years ago, I finally got to Barcelona, Spain [to] see the Gaudi-designed buildings whose pictures amazed me in Architecture class almost 30 years ago. It was a personal thrill.

Each academic subject is a window, a lens, through which to see the world. As you broaden yourself, you will notice things you wouldn't have noticed—you will appreciate things you would have completely missed—and you will meet and connect with more interesting people, possibly because you may be a more interesting person yourself!

And I don't know if you all will value this or not, but as you broaden yourself, you will be able to be a much more productive citizen. One of our biggest national problems is that we have become more self-focused as a people, and less able and willing to understand and care about others. Taking a liberal arts education—for example, my classes in Politics, East Asian Studies, Religion and Sociology—made me a less provincial and more worldly person. And the more connected you become to the world, the more you know and the more you care.

50   And by the way, one of the ways your generation is way ahead of mine is how global you are. Many times more of you will study abroad than my peers did in college. Were I in your seat right now, I would definitely study abroad, and I think it's one of the most encouraging indicators in our country that so many more American students do so today.

One more suggestion—take classes from the best teachers you can find, no matter what they teach. My experience is that they are the classes you will remember. Every college has iconic professors who know who they are, why they are teaching, and who love to open young minds. At Princeton, if you ask me the classes that most impacted how I see the world, they were not in my major. One of them was a Civil Engineering class. Why did I, a History major with no professional interest in science and engineering, take a Civil Engineering class? Because fellow students I respected told me to. They said David Billington was an incredible teacher. Billington loved how structures like buildings and bridges, when designed well, could come to symbolize a place and its people. His course "Structures and the Urban Environment" filled a 400-person lecture hall each spring. One of our homework assignments was to walk across his favorite built American structure—the Brooklyn Bridge—and write about our experience of it. Billington had a big impact on how I see my surroundings. Now I don't know who they are, but I know there are teachers like this at UCSB. Find them and spend time with them. They are the professors you will remember, and who will impact how you view yourself and the world.

Personally, I happen to be someone who loves to learn, so for me getting exposed by excellent teachers to varied subjects was a lot of fun. One last encouragement for each of you, no matter what your field of study, is to go through the course offerings and take something off the wall that just sounds fun to you—not because it's easy, not because you think it might get you a job, but just because it piques your interest. This is the time to do it. You are very privileged to be here at UCSB, and you have a unique opportunity.

Think forward. In 15 or 20 years, many of you will be buried in responsibilities—work, family. You may have a desire to expand yourself, to be a more stimulated and interesting person, to expose yourself to the new. At that point in your life, it's not impossible, but it's really hard.

Here, it's easy. It's right at your fingertips. Don't take it for granted. This opportunity will be gone before you know it.

55   Good wishes to each of you on your journey.

The MOOC Moment and the End of Reform

AARON BADY

Aaron Bady is a postdoctoral fellow at the University of Texas, Austin. He works on African literature and is a blogger and editor for the New Inquiry. *This article was adapted from the author's remarks at "MOOCs and For Profit Universities: A Closer Look," a roundtable discussion and event sponsored by the University of California-Irvine Humanities Collective in May 2013. The article appeared in* Liberal Education *in Fall 2013.*

The MOOC phenomenon has happened very quickly, to put it mildly. Last November, the *New York Times* declared 2012 to be "the Year of the MOOC" (Pappano, 2012), and while it feels (at least to me) like we've been talking about MOOCs for years now, the speed by which the MOOC has become the future of higher education is worth thinking carefully about, both because it's an important way to frame what is happening and because that speed warps the narrative we are able to tell about what is happening. Coursera, Udacity, and edX are all just over a year old, and while the first two—which are Silicon Valley startups out of Stanford, essentially—have already enrolled millions of students, the nonprofit consortium edX has grown just as prodigiously. Beginning as a partnership between Harvard and MIT, edX now includes a dozen different universities, and that number will surely grow. The MOOC phenomenon is also a shift in discourse, a shift that's happened so quickly and so recently that it fills up our mental rear-view mirror. When the word "MOOC" was first coined in 2008, by a set of Canadian academics who needed a term to describe the experiment in pedagogy they were putting together, the word itself was a niche term that most people in higher education would not hear about, or need to. In the last year, the MOOC has gone from a rather singular experiment in connectivist and distributed learning to a behemoth force that we are told is reshaping the face of higher education. And whether MOOCs are disrupting education through innovation—as

Clay Christensen's model of disruptive innovation in business would have it—or simply representing the disruption of education as it is embedded in the market, the phenomenon under discussion has changed quite dramatically as it has migrated from Canada to Silicon Valley.

This is why it's interesting to note that *Inside Higher Ed*'s new booklet of essays, "The MOOC Moment," introduces its subject by observing that "the acronym MOOC (for massive open online course) first appeared in *Inside Higher Ed* in December 2011, in reference to a course offered by a Stanford University professor. These days, the acronym is omnipresent and—to many—needs no definition" (*Inside Higher Ed,* 2013, 3). I would say in response that this apparent lack of a need for a definition is exactly why we need to slow things down and figure out what the heck we're talking about. For one thing, when we start the story in 2011, we forget about the 2008 MOOCs, and if the MOOCs are the future and the future is now, then it tends to have little to do with what was happening at the University of Manitoba in 2008, or why.

The MOOC that debuted in *Inside Higher Ed* in December 2011 was Sebastian Thrun's "Artificial Intelligence" MOOC, a course that was offered at Stanford but opened up to anyone with a broadband Internet connection. The way this story is usually told is that his incredible success—160,000 students from 190 countries—encouraged Thrun to leave Stanford in order to try the new model of pedagogy he had stumbled upon. After seeing a TED talk given by Salman Khan, the founder of Khan Academy, Thrun decided to give it a whirl, and it was a huge success. In January 2012, he founded the startup Udacity, and the rest is history.

However, another way to tell the story is that Thrun was a Google executive—already well known for his work on Google's driverless car project—and that he had already resigned his tenure at Stanford in April 2011, before he even offered that artificial intelligence class. Ending his affiliation with Stanford could be described as completing his transition to Silicon Valley proper. In fact, despite *Inside Higher Ed*'s singular "a Stanford University professor," Thrun co-taught the famous course with Google's director of research, Peter Norvig. It's important to tell the story this way, too, because the first story makes us imagine a groundswell of market forces and unmet need, a world of students begging to be taught by a Stanford professor and Google, and the technological marvels that suddenly make it possible. But it's not education that's driving this shifting conversation. As the MOOC became something very different in migrating to Silicon Valley, it's in stories told by the *New York Times*, the *Wall Street Journal*, and *Time* magazine that the MOOC comes to seem like an imminent revolution whose pace is set by necessity and inevitability.

5   It would be an exaggeration to say that a David Brooks column and a few articles in the *Wall Street Journal* were the cause of the abrupt firing of the president of the University of Virginia (UVa) in June 2012, for example, but it would not be that much of an exaggeration. As we can now roughly reconstruct—from e-mails obtained through a Freedom of Information Act request by the UVa student newspaper—UVa's rector and vice rector essentially engineered Teresa Sullivan's resignation because they decided she was moving too slowly on online education. And what you get from reading these e-mails is an overwhelming sense of speed, which they are repeating, verbatim,

from the articles they are e-mailing and forwarding to each other. The rector e-mailed a *Wall Street Journal* column titled "Higher Education's Online Revolution" with the subject line "good piece in *WSJ* today—why we can't afford to wait," for example, an article she had gotten from a major donor who suggested that it was "a signal that the on-line learning world has now reached the top of the line universities and they need to have strategies or will be left behind." She immediately replied: "Your timing is impeccable—the BOV is squarely focused on UVa's developing such a strategy and keenly aware of the rapidly accelerating pace of change." At a meeting of UVa deans and vice presidents, UVa's rector said, "The board believes this environment calls for a much faster pace of change in administrative structure, in governance, in financial resource development and in resource prioritization and allocation....We do not believe we can even maintain our current standard under a model of incremental, marginal change. The world is simply moving too fast."

Where does such a person get this kind of conviction? You find the best examples of this kind of rhetoric in the *New York Times*. For example, Thomas Friedman (2013) recently argued that the "MOOCs revolution...is here and is real" and remarked on "how much today's traditional university has in common with General Motors of the 1960s, just before Toyota used a technology breakthrough to come from nowhere and topple G.M." This kind of comparison has become common sense. MOOCs are a "campus tsunami," to use columnist David Brooks's (2012) term, one that we all need to pay attention to before it's too late.

A Strange Temporality

Where this urgency comes from, however, might be less important than what it does to our sense of temporality, how we experience and talk about the way we are, right now, in "the MOOC moment." In the MOOC moment, it's already too late—always already too late. The world not only will change, but it has changed. In this sense, it isn't simply that "MOOCs are the future" or that "online education is changing how we teach." Those kinds of platitudes are chokingly omnipresent, but the interesting thing is the fact that the future is already now, that it has already changed how we teach. If you don't get on the MOOC bandwagon, yesterday, you'll have already been left behind. The world has already changed. To stop and question that fact is to be already belated, behind the times.

The first thing I want to do, then, is to slow us down and go through the last year or so with a bit more care than we're usually able to do—to do a "close reading" of the year of the MOOC, as it were—because, to be blunt, the MOOC only makes sense if you don't think about it too much, if you're in too much of a hurry to go deeply into the subject.

The logic of the MOOC is a function of shallow thinking, of arguments that go no deeper than a David Brooks or Thomas Friedman column. But they also valorize and reward that level of depth, even make it compulsory. MOOCs are literally built to cater to the attention span of a distracted, multitasking teenager who pays attention in cycles of ten to fifteen minutes. This is not a shot at teenagers, just an observation about what the form anticipates—and, therefore, rewards and reproduces. In place of the fifty-minute lectures that are the norm at my university, for example, a MOOC will break a unit of pedagogy down into YouTube-length clips that can be more easily digested, whenever and wherever. Much longer than that, and it falls apart; the TED talk is essentially the gold standard. But I want to suggest that the argument in favor of MOOCs can't handle all that much complexity either. It makes sense at the speed of a TED talk or the length of a *New York Times* column, but starts to come apart very quickly if you go any deeper or longer than that.

10   The "MOOC moment" relies on a belated temporality where we're always already behind the times, which is necessary to make the MOOC

seem like the kind of self-fulfilling prophecy it has become. If Harvard, Stanford, and MIT are making MOOCs, then anyone who doesn't jump on the bandwagon will be left behind. We don't have to understand why it's happening, where it's going, or where it came from; the fact that it's happening there is all the reason we need. Framed by this temporality, the MOOC becomes a kind of fetish object: because we treat its existence as self-evident fact—or to the extent that we treat its existence as a kind of self-evident fact—its objective reality obscures the contingencies of its production and the ideological formations that make it seem to exist. Why are Harvard, Stanford, and MIT making MOOCs? It doesn't matter. Only the fact that they are making them is important.

This is a logic that particularly appeals to universities that aren't in the Ivy league but see themselves at the forefront of higher education. But it's also an argument that only works at the depth (or non-depth) of a David Brooks column, because its claims only work if you don't interrogate their foundational premises too much.

For example, David Brooks (2012) began his "Campus Tsunami" column in this way: "Online education is not new. The University of Phoenix started its online degree program in 1989. Four million college students took at least one online class during the fall of 2007. But, over the past few months, something has changed. The elite, pace-setting universities have embraced the Internet. Not long ago, online courses were interesting experiments. Now online activity is at the core of how these schools envision their futures." This is a sophisticated piece of discourse, in its way. By acknowledging that "online education is not new," Brooks is working to distinguish the thing that is not new (online education) from the form of online education that is new, the MOOC. To rebrand online education—which has generally had a well-deserved bad reputation—he has to conjure forth this distinction, creating space between the old kind of online education (the University of Phoenix) and the new kind, which, because it is new, can shed that baggage. He therefore opens by acknowledging online education's lack of novelty so he can then resituate our perspective in a different place, just ahead of the cutting edge: if the University of Phoenix's online program is decades old—and, therefore, not cutting edge—the kind of online education that he's interested in discussing, which is different from the University of Phoenix, is cutting edge. And the difference is a shift from the bottom to the top, from low prestige to high prestige: "over the past few months, something has changed....The elite, pace-setting universities have embraced the Internet."

What he's not saying, of course—what he's working very hard to un-say—is that Harvard is actually struggling to get where the University of Phoenix already was in 1989. You have to read him against the grain to draw that out, but it's there. He's essentially observing the way that Harvard is emulating the University of Phoenix. But, of course, that can't be, can it? After all, by definition, Harvard, Stanford, and MIT are cutting-edge, while the University of Phoenix—a for-profit, low-prestige university that markets to nontraditional students and employs a no-name teaching staff—well, they can't be the cutting edge, by definition.

These definitional "facts" allow Brooks to finesse a truly jaw-dropping rhetorical move: though he began with the statement that "online education is not new," he manages, in only four sentences, to write the words: "Not long ago, online courses were interesting experiments." How does he get from "online education is not new" (old hat, established, conventional) to the line "Not long ago, online courses were interesting experiments"? How does online education go from something older than most of our students to a temporality where it's just on the cusp of being developed, where in very recent memory, it was pure speculative futurity, where it's the future we [are] hurtling backward into?

15   The key to this piece of rhetorical alchemy is that you can't overthink it, in the way I just have.

Brooks is taking something that lacks prestige and cultural capital—a mode of education that is not valuable, only expensive, not innovative or exciting—and placing the name "Harvard" around it, thereby making it into something that suddenly is both valuable and worthwhile, as a function of Harvard's symbolic role in American higher education. And when he writes "Now online activity is at the core of how these schools envision their futures," he means that because these schools are envisioning it—because attached to that brand—online education is now the future we must emulate and pursue. Because it's at Harvard, it's "now" instead of being where the University of Phoenix already was the year the Berlin Wall fell, before our students were born.

If I have one overarching takeaway point in this article, it's that there is almost nothing new about the kind of online education that the word MOOC now describes. It's been given a great deal of hype and publicity, but that aura of "innovation" poorly describes a technology—or set of technological practices, to be more precise—that is not that distinct from the longer story of online education, and which is designed to reinforce and reestablish the status quo, to make tenable a structure that is falling apart.

If you read the people who were creating MOOCs in 2008, by contrast—as I've been doing—you'll actually see a lot of thinking that's kind of out there, as far as how we conceptualize what education is for and what it does. But the innovations in pedagogy that produced the first MOOC in 2008 at the University of Manitoba had to be forgotten and erased from the historical timeline if the MOOCs that we're talking about were to become the standard bearer for "cutting edge." When *Inside Higher Ed* writes about the MOOC moment, after all, that moment has to begin not in 2008, but in December 2011, and in Silicon Valley, where and when the hype machine really gets into gear.

Things are moving so fast because if we stopped to think about what we are doing, we'd notice that

MOOCs both are not the same thing as normal education and are being positioned to replace "normal" education. But the pro-MOOC argument is always that it's cheaper and almost never that it's better. The most utopian MOOC boosters will rarely claim that MOOCs are of equivalent educational value; the most they'll say is that someday they might be. This point is crucial to unpacking the hype: columnists, politicians, university administrators, educational entrepreneurs, and professors who are hoping to make their name by riding out this wave can all talk in such glowing terms about the onrushing future of higher education only because that future hasn't actually happened yet. It's still speculative in the sense that we're all speculating about what it will look like. This means that the MOOC can be all things to all people because it is, literally, a speculation about what it might someday become.

To put my cards on the table, the MOOC seems to me like a speculative bubble, a product that's being pumped up and overvalued by pro-business legislators, overzealous administrators, and a lot of hot air in the media. But like all speculative bubbles—especially the ones that originate in Silicon Valley—it will eventually burst. The only question is what things will look like when it does.

MOOCs and the Future of Public Education

20 A bill currently before the California State Senate—SB520—will, if it passes, require all three sectors of California's public university system to accept MOOCs from a certain approved list for course credit. The details are yet to be determined, and it seems most likely that the final bill will be something different from what was originally introduced. But the assumptions and ambitions of SB520 offer a useful way to frame the direction the MOOC tsunami is taking: the capture of public education.

For the Twenty Million Minds Foundation, one of the drivers behind the bill, SB520 is all about options, opportunity, and choice for students. The bill's sponsor, Senate Pro-Tem President Darrell Steinberg, cites the very real problems of access to over-enrolled courses—and the fact that students are failing to graduate on time, because they cannot get required courses for their majors—and uses this as a rhetorical wedge to argue that MOOCs should actually be acceptable as replacements for normal college classes. As he put it, "We want to be the first state in the nation to make this promise: No college student in California will be denied the right to move through their education because they couldn't get a seat in the course they needed" (quoted in Lewin, 2013). But the irony of Steinberg's formulation is that even he admits that instead of solving a problem that has a very simple definition—which is basically reducible to a number, the fact that there are more students than there are chairs and classrooms—they are simply redefining the problem, imagining into existence a chairless classroom.

The problem is real: years of consistent budget cuts have left public universities without the money to buy "chairs" (and everything that represents), so public universities have shifted the financial burden onto the backs of individual students, whose tuition now pays much more of the cost. Since educating more students would cost money—and it would also cost money to fully staff the necessary courses—there is no solution to the problem that does not require spending more money on chairs, classrooms, and teachers. MOOCs enter the picture, then, as a kind of fantasy solution to this unsolvable problem. Instead of addressing the problem by either admitting fewer students or adding more courses, we will define the problem differently: chairless classrooms! Everyone is happy.

In this case, the cliché that California is where everything happens first has some truth to it. If SB520 passes, it will define the shape of things to come not only by creating a model for other states to follow, but also by creating a kind of market value for MOOCs that didn't exist before and that wouldn't exist otherwise. By making certain selected MOOCs convertible into course credit—at California Community Colleges, California State Universities, and the University of California system—the legislature will quite literally create value where it didn't exist before, by making MOOCs a thing that are worth paying for. This shift is important. But mandating that a MOOC is the same thing as college—that it can be literally credited as a college class—not only changes what a MOOC is, it changes what college is.

After all, if a MOOC is simply a free educational resource that you can find on the web—which is what MOOCs presently are—then there's nothing to object to in them, and everything to like. Such a MOOC is an almost wholly good addition to the universe. Other than opportunity costs and the costs of a computer—which are not nothing, but they are also not that much—it's simply a free and useful thing, available to those who want it. But the moment that such a use value becomes a market value, when it becomes something that can be exchanged for the kinds of course credits that students pay very high tuition for, MOOCs become a radically different beast with a radically different kind of economic value. It'll be much easier to charge for them, on the one hand, and almost unthinkable that associated costs won't rise, as they did with the once free California public universities (especially since Udacity and Coursera are literally for-profit enterprises). And on the other hand, they will radically devalue the resource that they can now be used to replace. If you can replace "chairs" (by which I mean the brick-and-mortar campus) with a chairless university—if those things are literally exchangeable—then the market value of "chairs" goes down, at the same time as the actual costs stay the same. If we can't fully staff our classrooms now, how will we staff them in the future, when they have to compete with free?

25 To put it slightly differently, pumping up the value of MOOCs in this way—declaring, by legislative fiat, that MOOCs are now interchangeable with "real courses"—actually does have an important cost. If the platonic ideal of the classroom experience is the gold standard, then declaring that a bunch of other unrelated metals are also gold will lower its value, especially if those metals are freely available in infinite supplies. Why would someone pay a teacher to give one-on-one attention to students when those students could get the same formal credential from an online course? You can point out that there is an actual and effective difference between a student-to-professor ratio of seventeen to one and a ratio of ten thousand to one online. But once market equivalency has entered the equation, once the market recognizes an equivalence between a MOOC and an in-person class, pointing out the difference that is experienced by the student will be trumped by the equivalence of market logic, which will dictate paying for the cheaper of the two. An in-person education will become an unnecessary luxury, an ornamental marker of elite status.

To legislators, MOOCs can seem like a win-win solution to an otherwise intractable fiscal crisis. Students who are locked out of over-enrolled required courses can complete their degrees by taking those classes with an online provider, possibly even at a lower cost and at no extra cost to the state. Meanwhile, allowing Silicon Valley start-ups like Coursera and Udacity to offer courses that will transfer into the California State University and the University of California systems will give those companies a legitimacy in the education marketplace that they have never had before. When you see that Sebastian Thrun is one of the people who helped write SB520 and that Darrell Steinberg held his press conference announcing the bill on "Google Hangout," a lot of things become clearer.

If this bill passes, the winners will be Silicon Valley and the austerity hawks in the California legislature. While the former will have privileged access to the largest student market in the state, the latter will be relieved of the burden of having to educate the state's young people. The losers will be teachers and students.

The Value of MOOCs

MOOC boosters live in the future. Actually existing MOOCs are a far cry from what their champions promise they will someday become, which allows us to gloss over any troubling trends in their present day iteration. After all, MOOC boosters like to brag about the thousands of students—even hundreds of thousands—who sign on to learn from super-professors like Harvard's Michael Sandel or Sebastian Thrun. But completion rates for these courses consistently hover in the single digits. A software engineering MOOC taught by University of California–Berkeley professor David Patterson in May 2012, for example, may have enrolled over fifty thousand students, but fewer than four thousand actually completed the course—and this is typical. What's more, as Patterson himself was quick to observe, his MOOC was a "cheating-rich environment" (quoted in Meyer 2012). It's safe to assume that the number of students who actually completed the course is somewhat lower than even the 7 percent who received a completion certificate.

This doesn't mean that MOOCs are without value, of course. Just because most of Patterson's students didn't complete his course doesn't mean they didn't benefit from taking it, and it seems reasonable to assume that many online learners are not interested in completion certificates. Patterson observed, for example, that many of his students already had degrees, and that some were instructors themselves. For learners wishing to brush up skills or keep abreast of new pedagogy, a MOOC might be just the thing. In applied fields like software engineering, where the ability to code is a valuable enough skill that course credit becomes almost irrelevant—and where the material lends itself naturally to online instruction—the free availability of high-quality course materials is an almost pure social good.

30   It does, however, demonstrate what the technology is not good at: accreditation and mass education. The MOOC rewards self-directed learners who have the resources and privilege that allow them to pursue learning for its own sake. But if you want it to function as a gate-keeping mechanism, which is one of the things that universities do, it's not very good at that. A MOOC is almost designed to make cheating even easier than ever before. MOOCs are also a really poor way to make educational resources available to underserved and underprivileged communities, which has been the historical mission of public education. Historically, public systems like California's have provided high-quality education to citizens of the state who could not have gotten the equivalent anywhere else. MOOCs promise to see to it that what the public universities are able to provide is not, in every sense, the equivalent of what rich people's kids get.

The irony is that when the term was first coined in 2008, this was all quite well understood. The MOOC came into existence as something that, by its very nature, could never be used to replace a normal college class. The whole point was that it was something fundamentally different from a college class.

Dave Cormier originally suggested the name for an experiment in open courseware that George Siemens and Stephen Downes were putting together at the University of Manitoba, a class of twenty-five students that was opened up to over 1,500 online participants. For them, this MOOC was part of a long-running engagement with connectivist principles of education, rooted in the idea that we learn best when we learn collaboratively, in networks, because the process of learning is less about acquiring new knowledge—the commodified "content" that a Udacity or edX MOOC tries to reify and market—and much more about building the social and neural connections that will allow knowledge to circulate, be used, evolve, and grow. A class that's animated by a contractual agreement that spells out the costs, requirements, and credential to be acquired is one thing, and it may even be a good thing; but the goal of these original MOOCs was to foster an educational process that was something totally different. It would be as exploratory and creative as its participants chose to make it. It was about building a sense of community investment in a particular project, a fundamentally socially driven enterprise, and its outcomes were to be fluid and open-ended. I would argue that getting a "grade" for such a thing—or charging money for it—would be fundamentally to change what it is.

Today's MOOC looks very different, starting with the central narrative of "disruption" and "unbundling." Instead of building social information networks, the neoliberal MOOC is driven by a desire to liberate and empower the individual, breaking apart actually existing academic communities and refocusing on the individual's acquisition of knowledge. The MOOC being praised by utopian technologists in the *New York Times* might be the diametric opposite of what Siemens, Downes, and Cormier said they were trying to create, in this sense, even though it deploys some of the same idealistic rhetoric. Rather than transferring course content from expert to student, the original MOOCs stemmed from a connectivist desire to decentralize and de-institutionalize education, creating fundamentally open and open-ended networks of circulation and collaboration. But the MOOCs being developed by Silicon Valley startups Udacity and Coursera, as well as by nonprofit initiatives like edX, aim to do exactly the same thing that traditional courses have done—transfer course content from expert to student—only to do so massively more cheaply and on a much larger scale.

This is why, instead of de-institutionalizing education or making learning less hierarchical, we see some of the most prestigious institutions of higher learning in the world treating the MOOC as a lifeline in troubled economic waters, leveraging the figure of the "super-professor" to maintain their position of excellence atop the educational field and even to create new hierarchical arrangements among universities. These MOOCs are just a new way of maintaining the status quo, of

re-institutionalizing higher education in an era of budget cuts, sky-rocketing tuition, and un-employed college graduates burdened by student debt. If the MOOC began in the classroom as an experimental pedagogy, it has swiftly morphed into a process driven from the top down, imposed on faculty by university administrators or even imposed on administrators by university boards of trustees and regents.

35 From within academia, the MOOC phenomenon is all about dollars and cents, about doing more of the same with less funding. And while MOOC boosters like to deride the "sage on the stage" model of education delivery—as if crowded lecture halls are literally the only kind of classroom there is—most of the actually existing MOOCs being marketed are not much more than a massive and online version of that very same "sage on a stage" model. And what could be more hierarchical than a high-prestige university like Harvard lecturing to less prestigious institutions?

Conclusion

I've titled this article "The MOOC Moment and the End of Reform" because I had to call it something; I couldn't just say that the MOOCification of Higher Education is a Terrible No Good Very Bad Thing, although I think you have a sense of what I think about it. But MOOCs really are more like an end of something than a beginning. Instead of a transition between old and new, they represent the end of a process of constant change that has defined higher education for as long as it has existed. At the micro level, MOOCs are cheap because you record them once and then reuse them. They don't grow and evolve, and they don't require the hiring of academic faculty, whose intellectual lives keep intellectual inquiry moving forward. This is what makes them cheap, but it's also what will make them solidify hierarchy by placing a pantheon of academic superstars at the center of pedagogical practice, reifying knowledge into a commodity that, because it has value, cannot be allowed to change. If academic life is anything, it's a devotion to endless process: the scientific method tells you how to take the next step, not where to stop. MOOCs are structurally devoted to pinning knowledge down like a butterfly, putting it on file, putting a price on it, and floating it on the market.

MOOCs also represent the end of reform at the macro level. The University of California, for example, is a profoundly recent creation. It was basically a two-campus university until the 1950s; today, there are eleven campuses. The same is true of the California State University (CSU) system and the California Community College system. Between 1957 and 1965, California established eight new CSU campuses—out of an eventual twenty-three—while more than half its present complement of 112 community colleges was built in the period between 1957 and 1978. California's public university system is, in many ways, the biggest and best expression of a moment in time when futurity was incredibly important and possible. It

represented a massive investment of public funds in the state's collective future. The 1960 Donahoe Act, better known as the Master Plan for Higher Education, was a complex piece of legislation, but at its heart was, quite simply, a blanket commitment from the state to educate all the California students who wanted an education. And as society grew, the university was to grow with it, adapting to changing needs by staying in a permanent state of reformulation.

Even though California State Senate Bill 520 begins by citing the Master Plan, this piece of legislation represents a refusal of futurity: because the future is now, there is nothing to plan for. The only reality is the economic reality that a funding shortfall must be dealt with. And instead of solving this problem, SB520 seeks to institutionalize it, to render it permanent. We solve the problem of frustrating ambitions by foreswearing ambition, by refusing to have desires that can be frustrated.

References

Brooks, D. 2012. "The Campus Tsunami." *New York Times*, May 3. http://www.nytimes.com/2012/05/04/opinion/brooks-the-campus-tsunami.html.

Department of Philosophy, San Jose State University. 2013. "An Open Letter to Professor Michael Sandel from the Philosophy Department at San Jose State U." *Chronicle of Higher Education*, May 2. http://chronicle.com/article/The-Document-an-Open-Letter/138937.

Friedman, T. L. 2013. "The Professors' Big Stage." *New York Times*, March 5. http://www.nytimes.com/2013/03/06/opinion/friedman-the-professors-big-stage.html?_r=0.

Inside Higher Ed. 2013. *The MOOC Moment: A Selection of Inside Higher Ed Articles and Essays on Massive Open Online Courses.* Washington, DC: Inside Higher Ed.

Lewin, T. 2013. "California Bill Seeks Campus Credit for Online Study" *New York Times*, March 12. http://www.nytimes.com/2013/03/13/education/california-bill-would-force-colleges-to-honor-online-classes.html?pagewanted=all.

Meyer, R. 2012. "What It's Like to Teach a MOOC (and What the Heck's a MOOC?)." *The Atlantic*, July 18. http://www.theatlantic.com/technology/archive/2012/07/what-its-like-to-teach-a-MOOC-and-what-the-hecks-a-MOOC/260000/.

Pappano, L. 2012. "The Year of the MOOC." *New York Times*, November 2. http://www.nytimes.com/2012/11/04/education/edlife/massive-open-online-courses-are-multiplying-at-a-rapid-pace.html?pagewanted=all&_r=0.

A Plea for "Close Learning"

SCOTT L. NEWSTOK

Scott L. Newstok is an associate professor of English at Rhodes College, teaching courses in Shakespeare and his Renaissance contemporaries. This article, which was published in Liberal Education *in Fall 2013, was adapted from an essay that originally appeared in* Inside Higher Ed *on July 11, 2013.*

What an exciting year for distance learning! Cutting-edge communication systems allowed universities to escape the tired confines of face-to-face education. Bold new technologies made it possible for thousands of geographically dispersed students to enroll in world-class courses. Innovative assessment mechanisms let professors supervise their pupils remotely. All this progress was good for business, too. Private entrepreneurs leapt at the chance to compete in the new distance-learning marketplace, while Ivy League universities bustled to keep pace.

True, a few naysayers fretted about declining student attention spans and low course-completion rates. But who could object to the expansively democratic goal of bringing first-rate education to more people than ever before? The new pedagogical tools promised to be not only more affordable than traditional classes, but also more effective at measuring student progress. In the words of one prominent expert, the average distance learner "knows more of the subject, and knows it better, than the student who has covered the same ground in the classroom." Indeed, "the day is coming when the work done [via distance learning] will be greater in amount than that done in the class-rooms of our colleges." The future of education was finally here.

2013, right? Think again: 1885. The commentator quoted above was Yale classicist (and future University of Chicago President) William Rainey Harper, evaluating correspondence courses. That's right: you've got (snail) mail. Journalist Nicholas Carr has chronicled the recurrent boosterism about mass mediated education over the last century: the phonograph, instructional radio, televised lectures.

All were heralded as transformative educational tools in their day. This should give us pause as we recognize that massive open online courses, or MOOCs, are but the latest iteration of distance learning.

In response to the current enthusiasm for MOOCs, skeptical faculty (Aaron Bady, Ian Bogost, and Jonathan Rees, among many others) have begun questioning venture capitalists eager for new markets and legislators eager to dismantle public funding for American higher education. Some people pushing for MOOCs, to their credit, speak from laudably egalitarian impulses to provide access for disadvantaged students. *But to what are they being given access?* Are broadcast lectures and online discussions the sum of a liberal education? Or is it something more than "content" delivery?

"Close Learning"

5   To state the obvious: there's a personal, human element to liberal education, what John Henry Newman once called "the living voice, the breathing form, the expressive countenance." (2001, 14). We who cherish personalized instruction would benefit from a pithy phrase to defend and promote this millennia-tested practice. I propose that we begin calling it close learning, a term that evokes the laborious, time-consuming, and costly but irreplaceable proximity between teacher and student. Close learning exposes the stark deficiencies of mass distance learning, such as MOOCs, and its haste to reduce dynamism, responsiveness, presence.

Techno-utopians seem surprised that "blended" or "flipped" classrooms—combining out-of-class media with in-person discussions—are more effective than their online-only counterparts, or that one-on-one tutoring strengthens the utility of MOOCs. In spite of all the hype about interactivity, "lecturing" à la MOOCs merely extends the cliché of the static, one-sided lecture hall, where distance learning begins after the first row. As the philosopher Scott Samuelson (2013) suggests, "The forces driving online education, particularly MOOCs, aren't moving us toward close learning. We should begin by recognizing that close learning is the goal and then measure all versions of our courses by that standard. Many giant lecture-hall courses are going to be found wanting, as will many online courses, and all (or almost all) MOOCs. In the end, we're still going to need a lot of face-to-face learning if want to promote close learning."

The old-fashioned Socratic seminar is where we actually find interactive learning and open-ended inquiry. In the close learning of the live seminar, spontaneity rules. Both students and teachers are always at a crossroads, collaboratively deciding where to go and where to stop; how to navigate and how to detour; and how to close the distance between a topic and the people discussing it. For the seminar to work, certain limits are required (most centrally, a limit in size). But these finite limits enable the infinity of questioning that is close learning. MOOCs claim to abolish those limits, while they paradoxically reinstate them. Their naïve model assumes that there is always total transparency, that passively seeing (watching a lecture or a virtual simulation) is learning.

A Columbia University neuroscientist, Stuart Firestein, recently published a polemical book titled *Ignorance: How It Drives Science*. Discouraged by students regurgitating his lectures without internalizing the complexity of scientific inquiry, Firestein created a seminar to which he invited his colleagues to discuss what they don't know. As Firestein repeatedly emphasizes, it is informed ignorance, not information, that is the genuine "engine" of knowledge. His seminar reminds us that mere data transmission

from teacher to student doesn't produce liberal learning. It's the ability to interact, to think hard thoughts alongside other people.

In a seminar, a student can ask for clarification, and challenge a teacher; a teacher can shift course when spirits are flagging; a stray thought can spark a new insight. Isn't this the kind of nonconformist "thinking outside the box" that business leaders adore? So why is there such a rush to freeze knowledge and distribute it in a frozen form? Even Coursera cofounder Andrew Ng concedes that the real value of a college education "isn't just the content. . . . The real value is the interactions with professors and other, equally bright students" (quoted in Oremus 2012).

10   The business world recognizes the virtues of proximity in its own human resource management. (The phrase "corporate campus" acknowledges as much.) Witness, for example, Yahoo's controversial decision to eliminate telecommuting and require employees to be present in the office. CEO Marissa Mayer's memo reads as a mini-manifesto for close learning: "To become the absolute best place to work, communication and collaboration will be important, so we need to be working side-by-side. That is why it is critical that we are all present in our offices. Some of the best decisions and insights come from hallway and cafeteria discussions, meeting new people, and impromptu team meetings. Speed and quality are often sacrificed when we work from home. We need to be one Yahoo!, and that starts with physically being together" (quoted in Swisher 2013).

Why do boards of directors still go through the effort of convening in person? Why, in spite of all the fantasies about "working from anywhere" are "creative classes" still concentrating in proximity to one another: the entertainment industry in Los Angeles, information technology in the Bay Area, financial capital in New York City? The powerful and the wealthy are well aware that computers can accelerate the exchange of information and facilitate "training," but not the development of knowledge, much less wisdom.

Close learning transcends disciplines. In every field, students must incline toward their subjects: leaning into a sentence, to craft it most persuasively; leaning into an archival document, to determine an uncertain provenance; leaning into a musical score, to poise the body for performance; leaning into a data set, to discern emerging patterns; leaning into a laboratory instrument, to interpret what is viewed. MOOCs, in contrast, encourage students and faculty to lean back, not to cultivate the disciplined attention necessary to engage fully in a complex task. Low completion rates for MOOCs (still hovering around 10 percent) speak for themselves.

Technology as Supplement

Devotion to close learning should not be mistaken for an anti-technology stance. (Contrary to a common misperception, the original Luddites simply wanted machines that made high-quality goods, run by trained workers who were adequately compensated.) I teach Shakespeare, supposedly one of the mustiest of topics. Yet my students navigate the vast resources of the Internet, evaluate recorded performances, wrestle with facsimiles of original publications, listen to pertinent podcasts, survey decades of scholarship in digitized form, circulate their drafts electronically, explore the cultural topography of early modern London, and contemplate the historical richness of the English language. Close learning is entirely compatible with engaging in meaningful conversations outside the classroom: faculty can correspond regularly with students via e-mail and keep in close contact via all kinds of new media. But this is all in service of close learning, and the payoff comes in the classroom.

Teachers have always employed "technology"—including the book, one of the most flexible and dynamic learning technologies ever created. But let's not fixate upon technology for technology's sake, or delude ourselves into thinking that better technology overcomes bad teaching. At no stage of education does technology, no matter how novel, ever replace human attention. Close learning can't be automated or scaled up. As retrograde as it might sound, gathering humans in a room with real time for dialogue still matters. As educators, we must remind ourselves—not to mention our legislators, our boards, our administrators, our alumni, our students, and our students' parents—of the inescapable fact that our "product" is close learning. This is why savvy parents have always invested in intensive human interaction for their children. (Tellingly, parents from Silicon Valley deliberately restrict their children's access to electronic distractions, so that they might experience the free play of mind essential to human development.)

15   What remains to be seen is whether we value this kind of close learning at all levels of education enough to defend it, and fund it, for a wider circle of Americans—or whether we will continue to permit the circle to contract, excluding a genuinely transformative intellectual experience from those without means. Proponents of distance education have always boasted that they provide access, but are they providing access to *close learning*?

References

Firestein, S. 2012. *Ignorance: How It Drives Science*. New York: Oxford University Press.

Newman, J. H. 2001. "What Is a University?" In *Rise and Progress of Universities and Benedictine Essays*, edited by M. K. Tilman, 6–17. Notre Dame, IN: University of Notre Dame Press.

Oremus, W. 2012. "The New Public Ivies: Will Online Education Startups Like Coursera End the Era of Expensive Higher Education?" *Slate*, July 17. http://www.slate.com/articles/technology/future_tense/2012/07/coursera_udacity_edx_will_free_online_ivy_league_courses_end_the_era_of_expensive_higher_ed_.html.

Samuelson, S. 2013. Comment on S. L. Newstok, "A Plea for 'Close Learning.'" *Inside Higher Ed*, July 11. http://www.insidehighered.com/views/2013/07/11/essay-calls-alternative-massive-online-learning.

Swisher, K. 2013. "'Physically Together': Here's the Internal Yahoo No-Work-From-Home Memo for Remote Workers and Maybe More." *AllThingsD*, February 22. http://allthingsd.com/20130222/physically-together-heres-the-internal-yahoo-no-work-from-home-memo-which-extends-beyond-remote-workers.

Melissa Misunderstands Massive Open Online Courses

DAVE BLAZEK

Dave Blazek is a syndicated cartoonist who is best known for his comic strip Loose Parts. *He also wrote for* Dr. Katz Professional Therapist *for Comedy Central. This cartoon was posted on the Post University blog on February 7, 2013.*

The Changing Face of Higher Education: The Future of the Traditional University Experience

CHRISSIE LONG

Chrissie Long is a freelance journalist who covers higher education for University World News. *Her work has appeared in the* Christian Science Monitor *and the* Miami Herald. *She is also a Master in Public Policy candidate at the Kennedy School of Government at Harvard. This essay was published in the 2013 issue of the* Kennedy School Review.

Sarah Cummings sat at the kitchen table, her Web browser open and a handful of graduate school brochures strewn about. A senior manager at an education firm based in Cambridge, Massachusetts, Cummings was wrestling with [the] idea of returning to school. "People have always told me that you need a master's degree," said the twenty-eight-year-old California native. "But given the business climate, I am just not sure it is worth it."

Cummings is not alone in her hesitation: enrollment in graduate school programs has dropped for the second year in a row, according to the Council of Graduate Schools. Experts say the decline is a result of rising tuition (since 2000, there has been a 49 percent increase at private universities and 73 percent rise at public universities) coupled with a struggling economy.

But there's a third factor that may be affecting enrollment figures.

Today, more so than ever, digital course offerings are becoming a valid alternative. Prospective students no longer need to leave their jobs or forgo a salary to pursue higher education. This is supported by the recent entry of the so-called elite colleges into the space, which is giving online learning greater credibility.

5   In fact, the rush to stake a flag in the online higher education movement led the *New York Times* to label 2012 "the year of the MOOCs" (massive online open courses): "MOOCs have been around for a few years," the *Times* wrote in a November 2012 article, "but this is the year everyone wants in."

In April 2012, former Snapfish photo company CEO Ben Nelson introduced Project Minerva, an initiative to create the next Ivy League university entirely online. With $25 million in start-up money from Benchmark Capital and a board of advisors that includes former Harvard University President Larry Summers and the former New School President Bob Kerrey, Nelson is preparing to enlist "the smartest, hardest-working students worldwide" in a highly selective, transcontinental learning experience.

In the fall, Harvard University and the Massachusetts Institute of Technology teamed up to release their first seven courses as part of a not-for-profit venture called edX. The online platform extends the elite academic experience to the general public—tuition free. Those who complete the courses receive a "certificate of mastery," though no degrees are awarded.

Then there's the more well-known Khan Academy, a five-year-old nonprofit with bite-sized videos and mini-tutorials directed at secondary school students; Coursera, a private, fee-based, certificate-issuing platform launched in 2011 and used by thirty-five universities around the world, and Udacity, a computer science–focused, free online system that introduced its first two courses in February 2012.

With so many video-streaming online platforms, learning analytics, and interactive exercises delivered at a fraction of the cost (or sometimes free), a crucial question arises: are higher education programs putting themselves out of business?

10   Stephen Carson, external relations director at MIT OpenCourseWare (one of the first MOOC projects), says no. "It's going to be a long time before a graduate school experience can be replicated online," he said. "Some of the best experiences [at least at MIT] are in labs, using the equipment, designing and creating things, and that is not going to go online very easily or very quickly."

The Impact on Campus-Based Education

The academic fields that may suffer most from this movement online are education, management, and arts and sciences. Unlike medicine or science, where you need a lab, you don't need a physical infrastructure to learn in humanities-based courses. Despite edX's "Introduction to Biology" or Coursera's "Fundamentals of Electrical Engineering," training the nation's doctors, scientists, and engineers entirely through virtual spaces—when so much of their work is hands-on—seems a far way off.

But beyond displacing fields of study, there is some concern that the rise of online learning will purge institutions. While it certainly will not threaten an MIT or a Harvard, it may put pressure on lesser-known institutions. When you can learn from the so-called elite universities for free and without going through the rigorous application process, will there still be interest in a $40,000 degree from a lesser-known college?

"There is a lot of anxiety in the higher education community about people and jobs and academics being supplanted by these tools," Carson says. "I think they are going to challenge schools at the middle of the pack to better articulate the value that they bring to the table."

These middle-of-the-road institutions have one thing going for them: most of the interest in online courses is not coming from the United States but from areas that may not necessarily have access to campus-based learning. For example,

according to self-reported statistics from both MIT OpenCourseWare and edX, 60 percent of each venture's traffic is international, stemming from countries such as India and Colombia.

15   Within the United States, there has yet to be a massive movement toward supplanting campus-based education. But if online learning continues on its current trajectory and students exchange their pricy campus-based education for an online degree, the universities that have thrived on low-cost tuition, night classes, and low entry barriers may see their enrollments taper off.

As far as learning at the undergraduate level, the ivy-covered brick towers, dorm-room keg parties, and large lecture halls still have their place. Experts agree that campuses serve as an important venue for the transition from adolescence to adulthood. It is a rite-of-passage for the nation's youth and a safe environment in which young minds can experiment.

That is good news for disciples of campus-based education, who say there is nothing like sitting around a small table with a handful of students and discussing the merits of Immanuel Kant's "Transcendental Aesthetic" or John Rawls' "Veil of Ignorance." The four-year undergraduate experience—though it may be transformed—is not going anywhere.

The Changing Face of Higher Education

But while campuses still serve a role in educating the nation's young people, the structure of their classes is much different from those who graduated just ten years earlier.

Not only is online learning allowing students to more easily study abroad or take time off due to personal issues, it is also tailoring the learning experience to an individual style or pace. Concepts not grasped immediately can be relearned through programs online or processed through a variety of formats (online questions and answers, brief summaries, and additional readings or videos). By offering greater flexibility in teaching mechanisms, students are better equipped to take their learning in stride.

20   Surfacing alongside the online education movement are new ideas about how to use classroom time. Today, fewer courses are being taught in the traditional lecture style; many are moving toward a discussion-based seminar or are adopting the notion of the "flipped classroom." According to Allison Pingree, director of professional pedagogy at the John F. Kennedy School of Government at Harvard University, a flipped classroom is a new teaching method in which lectures are moved outside of class (in the form of online videos or readings) and class time is spent on problem sets with the professor serving as a guide.

"So much of our educational model in the past has been to sit and be passive recipients," Pingree said. "Today, we are recognizing that how we spend that face-to-face time is a really precious resource, and technology can help us enhance student learning by having students get caught up to speed outside of class."

Online learning is also changing the relationship between student and teacher. Rather than the instructor serving as the sole source of knowledge in a classroom, professors are increasingly encouraging information sharing between students.

In fact, online platforms have cited situations of "massive meetups" where students enrolled in a particular class will meet for a coffee in Argentina, a tutoring session in Germany, or class discussion over beers in India: instead of all learning being done between a professor and a student, peer-to-peer guidance is becoming increasingly important.

"The idea that learning revolves around one central figure disseminating expertise was already on its way out," Pingree said. "Technology has sped that up exponentially."

Higher Education Is Changing the World

25   As state and federal policy makers wrestle with higher costs of public institutions and shrinking budgets, many are exploring digital platforms as a tool to keep tuition costs low.

In the spring of 2013, forty public universities offered credits for online courses through the MOOC2Degree/Academic Partnerships. A central idea of the platform is to ensure that those high costs and low budgets don't threaten academic quality or enrollment rates.

The Florida state legislature recently discussed online education as a means to grow a more educated workforce and keep pace with high demand for a university education. Already the state has a virtual K-12 school with a 122,000-student enrollment.

California legislators are considering a bill that gives students at state universities credit for courses taken online. The credits would only be offered to students who were denied access to oversubscribed courses, and the online classes would have to be pre-approved by faculty. According to bill sponsors, the change is one way to answer challenges of funding and over-enrollment in the state's higher education institutions.

In November 2012, edX announced it would partner with the Massachusetts Community Colleges for open access courses. Beginning in spring 2013, both Bunker Hill and MassBay Community Colleges will offer a computer science and programming course from the edX platform that will be complimented by in-class exercises and discussion.

30   "The growth in student borrowing and student debt levels has been of great concern both to the general public and to the federal government," said James Honan, a senior lecturer at the Harvard Graduate School of Education. "There is a gigantic push toward online resources...Can [digital tools] be deployed to reduce the cost of traditional higher education or tuition even in a marginal way? That is of great interest to policy makers and to leaders."

But the real opportunity for online education is in developing countries. Today, even the daughter of a farm laborer in rural Thailand can access the classrooms of an Ivy League school, provided the local Internet café connection is fast enough and she has the patience to learn English. No longer does an eight-hour bus ride to the closest urban center stand as an obstacle to greater learning. And no longer do the hurdles of poverty keep all determined learners on the sidelines of higher education.

Perhaps it's a bit idealistic to think that online offerings could lead to scholarship opportunities, employment opportunities, or the development of new industries in emerging markets. But the tools are there and enough institutions are working to facilitate access that it does not seem so far-fetched anymore. For anyone who has traveled to developing countries and interacted with Internet-savvy youth, the aspiration of global equality does not seem so far off.

Governments and universities around the world are experimenting with online education as a means of reaching their more rural populations and overcoming infrastructure challenges, where the number of classroom seats is not enough to meet demand.

Though questions of quality of education arise from a heavy dependence on online platforms, university administrators are simultaneously re-examining accreditation standards and ways to internalize new technology.

So while a Coursera and Udacity will never replace the bricks and mortar of centuries-old universities, they are offering access to elite education in many corners of the world. They are reshaping how classes are taught and how students learn. And they are leading graduate students to rethink the hefty price tag of campus-based learning.

35   For now, there is still a need for ivy-covered towers, large campus quads, and wood-paneled lecture halls. But how those spaces are used and how students learn is changing. Largely because universities and academics are now embracing the Internet, higher learning will never be the same.

■ ■ ■   **FOR CLASS DISCUSSION HIGHER EDUCATION** How and Why We Learn Matters

1. Many of these readings attempt to challenge commonly held beliefs, assumptions, and values about education. As you read, ask yourself: What are the stated and unstated assumptions about education that each author is challenging? Keep a list of the commonly held beliefs, assumptions, and values that these readings engage and note similarities and differences among the readings.

2. After reading Ken Saxon and Rebecca Mead, summarize Saxon's and Mead's definitions of a liberal arts education. Where do Saxon's and Mead's ideas differ? How would you define the features and supposed benefits of a liberal arts education? Now reread Saxon and Mead and consider how your understanding of a liberal arts education has changed, deepened, or become reinforced by your readings?

3. MOOCs (massive open online courses) have generated much public controversy, especially in higher education circles. What features of MOOCs have the potential to be innovative? Where do they seem simply to return to old, lecture-style pedagogies? Consider how you learn best, and whether you believe you would benefit from a MOOC-style course. How does your major or intended field of study shape your response?

4. Financial concerns are at the heart of many of this unit's readings. What is the value of a liberal arts education? What is the value of a college degree, and will it pay off in future earnings? Do MOOCs level the educational playing field, or are they merely a profit center for business and an easy solution for underfunded public systems? Using the readings in this unit, sketch out the reasons and evidence that build cases for different answers to these questions.

■ ■ ■

WRITING ASSIGNMENT Speech on MOOCs to a Committee of Student Body Officers

Imagine that your university is considering offering credit for MOOCs. As a representative student, you have been asked to research this issue and present a case for or against this idea to a committee of student body officers at your university who are investigating various educational issues and sharing perspectives with the university's administration. Drawing on the readings in this unit, articles from the *Chronicle of Higher Education*, *Inside Higher Ed*, and other publications that are exploring this issue, compose a five-minute speech that takes a reasoned stand on MOOCs for credit. ■

Immigration in the Twenty-First Century

Immigration and immigration reform remain some of the most contentious issues in the United States. Political leaders debate immigration policy and strategies for stopping the flow of illegal immigrants across our borders while immigrants themselves, human rights groups, and social justice organizations work for the just treatment of immigrants, legal and illegal, highlighting such issues as immigrants' right to drive, to receive an education, or to obtain health care. One ongoing reform issue is the DREAM (Development, Relief, and Education for Alien Minors) Act, a federal bill introduced in Congress several times since 2001 that would provide a path to citizenship for illegal immigrants who arrived in the U.S. by the age of 15. The path would involve either the completion of a college degree or military service. Advocates in Congress and beyond have pledged to continue their support until a version of the DREAM legislation can be enacted.

Numerous factors contribute to the complexity of the United States' immigration policy and treatment of immigrants. Cultural and religious differences often complicate perceptions and acceptance of immigrants. The economic and political debates over which immigrants to welcome (high-tech workers versus agricultural laborers, for instance) are compounded by concerns over our identity as a nation of immigrants. Should humanitarian values govern the United States' policies toward immigrants and refugees? Should illegal immigrants be deported, separating families? By virtue of the Fourteenth Amendment, whether their parents arrived in the United States by legal or illegal means, children born on U.S. soil are citizens. Currently, one of the most pressing issues facing the United States is what to do with the tens of thousands of child immigrants from Central America? Should they be regarded as refugees seeking asylum from the violence of drug gangs in their countries? Should they be reunited with parents who are in the United States illegally or sent back to their countries?

The readings in this unit ask you to consider the issues and challenges of immigration in a country that prides itself on its immigrant origins but struggles to welcome people with unfamiliar appearances, languages, and practices and to balance humane concerns with social, economic, and political pressures. How well is the United States accommodating its immigrant population? And when determining policy, what or whose concerns should take precedence?

460

Scarfing It Down

FATEMEH FAKHRAIE

Fatemeh Fakhraie founded a Web site called Muslimah Media Watch: Looking at Muslim Women in the Media and in Pop Culture, *a forum for critiquing images of Muslim women. "We're tired," says the site, "of seeing ourselves portrayed in the media in ways that are one-dimensional and misleading." She has also been a regular contributor to the blog* Racialicious.com *and she blogs at* fatemahfakhraie.com. *Her research interests revolve around identity, appearance, and style, especially regarding Islamic attire.*

Even before Pakistani-Canadian teen Aqsa Parvez was killed by her father last December because of her alleged refusal to wear hijab, provinces in Canada were hopping on the headscarf-banning bandwagon set in motion by countries like France and Turkey where women in hijab are not allowed in public institutions like schools and government buildings. Exclusionary rulings have also affected non-governmental entities: Many female sports teams (in both Canada and the United States) with members who wear hijab have been subject to short- or long-term rulings by sports federations banning them from playing on the basis that hijab is unsafe, despite the development of sport-safe hijabs. This past January, Washington, D.C. high-school track competitor Juashaunna Kelly was disqualified from a meet after officials deemed her custom-made uniform unfit for competition—even though she'd worn it the previous three seasons.

The idea of banning the hijab is an exclusionary and ignorant one. But a good share of the ignorance comes as much from the media's coverage of these bans as from those implementing them. News stories on hijab bans are always ready to skew the issue by focusing on the hijab ban as a "freedom of religion" issue. More important, the stories nearly always take away the voices of those who should have a say in these bans— namely, Muslim women themselves. How can we know what a particular person or group thinks about something that concerns them if we don't talk to them about it?

Another problem with the coverage is that the stories often call the hijab "a traditional Muslim garment" or "an Islamic obligation." While many Muslims do see hijab as a mandatory obligation, others do not. There are many devout women who don't observe hijab for whatever reason, and decrying hijab bans on the pretext of religious freedom leaves these women out—are they not Muslims, despite the fact that they don't wear a headscarf?

When you get right down to it, banning a headscarf is banning an item of clothing, which is an issue of personal, not religious, freedom. But banning the hijab specifically targets women. It's kind of like not allowing women to wear long-sleeved shirts; or, if you want to add a religious dimension to it, it's like banning Christmas sweaters. (A tempting idea sometimes, but not one most people would take seriously.)

5   So the next time you hear about a hijab ban (and sadly, there will be a next time), think about your best pair of jeans or your faded t-shirt with the logo of your favorite band. Then think about being forbidden by law to wear them.

Veiled Voices

STEPHANIE PAULSELL

Stephanie Paulsell is a professor of the Practice of Ministry Studies at Harvard Divinity School. She is the author of Honoring the Body: Meditations on a Christian Practice *(2003). This commentary was published in* Christian Century *on July 12, 2011.*

On a summer evening late in the 1990s, Harvard Divinity School professor Leila Ahmed was walking with a friend—a feminist scholar visiting from a Muslim-majority country—when they came across a large gathering on the Cambridge Common. As they stood to watch, they began to notice that all the women were in hijab, the head covering worn by some Muslim women. Ahmed's friend turned to her in dismay, saying, "To them, we are the enemy. That's how they see us. All of us, people like us, feminists, progressives."

Ahmed shared her friend's discomfort. The only veiled women Ahmed remembers seeing during her childhood and youth in Cairo in the 1940s and '50s were women associated with the Muslim Brotherhood. The sight of Muslim women with their heads covered stirred childhood memories of the bombing of cinemas and the assassination of Egypt's prime minister, Mahmoud al-Nuqrashi Pasha, a friend of her father's. The hijab seemed to her a symbol of the gender hierarchy and gender separation advocated by Islamists in her home country.

How to explain, then, the sight of more and more women wearing the hijab in the United States? Ahmed began researching the return of the veil in the Middle East and its growing presence in the West. The result is *A Quiet Revolution: The Veil's Resurgence, from the Middle East to America* (Yale University Press), a book fascinating both for the story it tells and for its story of a scholar who has her own assumptions upended through her research. Her deliberate seeking out of a variety of "angles of observation" on the veil results in what she describes as "a complete reversal of my initial expectations."

The discomfort Ahmed and her friend felt on that summer night in the late 1990s mirrors the discomfort many Egyptians felt when the hijab began to appear on university campuses in the '70s. These young women disturbed their elders just as American students of the '60s disturbed theirs, and for many of the same reasons: through their unusual manner of dress they seemed to be doing more than just challenging and critiquing the status quo. Inspired by the activism of resurgent Islamism, many of the students who put on the hijab reported feeling powerful in it. Some of these young women were studying for professions like medicine and engineering: they felt empowered to enter public spaces and join the public discourse about creating a society based on Islamic values.

5   Ahmed is not romantic about this. She acknowledges that some women felt pressure to dress differently, and she notes that some women report that members of the Muslim Brotherhood paid women to wear the veil. She sees that by the '80s a movement that began among women was being co-opted by men who had their own political and religious agenda. These findings did not surprise her. What did surprise her were the ways in which women extended the meaning of Islamic dress far beyond what many Islamists intended, using the veil as a way of cultivating identities as socially active Muslims and transcending traditional limits to their freedom.

Ahmed follows the veil as it accompanied Muslim immigrants to North America after immigration quotas were abolished in 1965 and its presence in American society increased, especially after the attacks of 9/11. Some Muslim women unveiled after 9/11 as violence against Muslims flared, but others began wearing the hijab. Some women chose to wear it in solidarity with Muslims throughout the world, or to publicly claim their Muslim identity, or to be recognizable to other Muslims. Some wore it as a way of challenging stereotypes and inviting conversation about Islam. Some turned their attention more closely to Islam and experienced a spiritual awakening that the hijab helped them to express. Other women articulated reasons for veiling that had little to do with 9/11. Amina Wadud, an African-American scholar of Islam who leads Friday prayers in New York City, explained that she covered her body as a way of claiming her "historical identity, personal dignity, and sexual integrity" as a descendant of slave women whose bodies had been bought and sold.

For many women the veil that Ahmed and her friend regarded as a symbol of patriarchy and oppression has become a symbol of their striving for gender and racial justice. It is "they and not us, the secular or privately religious Muslims," writes Ahmed, who have integrated Islam with American traditions of social and political activism. They opened new "possibilities of belief, practice and interpretation for the rising generation."

The image of the veiled Muslim woman has been invoked to justify colonialism and war from the colonial period to our own day—reason enough to read this book. By allowing veiled women to speak for themselves, Ahmed reminds us that human beings and their religious practices are always more complex than we imagine. *A Quiet Revolution* illustrates the creativity that can be evoked by the life of faith, the ways religious ideas are transformed as they move across place and time, and the power of scholarship to overturn our assumptions and open us to each other in new ways.

Unauthorized Immigrant Arrivals Are on the Rise, and That's Good News

MADELINE ZAVODNY

Madeline Zavodny is a professor of economics at Agnes Scott College in Atlanta, Georgia, and a prolific author on immigration and economics. She coauthored Beside the Golden Door: U.S. Immigration Reform in a new Era of Globalization *(2010) with Pia Orrenius as well as numerous articles included in books analyzing immigration policy, economics, and border issues. This opinion editorial appeared on the Web site for* Forbes *on October 1, 2013.* Forbes *is an Internet media company providing insightful commentary and analysis for global business leaders.*

New estimates from the Pew Research Center suggest that the number of unauthorized immigrants is once again rising in the U.S. Although this turnaround from the sharp decline in the unauthorized population during the Great Recession is likely to be condemned by many, it's actually good news.

Unauthorized immigration is a bellwether of the strength of the economy. Unlike legal immigrants who may have waited years or even decades for a visa, illegal immigrants respond quickly to changes in economic conditions. Inflows rise faster when the economy, especially the construction sector, is growing, and slow down when the economy is shrinking. This turnaround is consistent with other signs that the economy is recovering and that residential construction activity in particular is gaining steam—good news for homeowners.

The possible increase in the unauthorized population is also good news in that it may finally spur the House to pass immigration reform. But it's critical that the House not use these numbers as a justification for even tougher border security. Economic forces, not border enforcement, drive illegal inflows. The Great Recession played a far bigger role in reducing unauthorized immigration than the tenfold increase in the Border Patrol's budget over the last decade. The House Homeland Security Committee had the right idea to support a bill that removes last-minute additions to the Senate bill that double the number of Border Patrol agents along the U.S.-Mexico border and expand the fence.

Instead, the House should focus on addressing the fundamental factor that motivates most illegal immigration: jobs. Employers turn to undocumented immigrants because current immigration policy makes it impossible to bring in foreign workers quickly and legally when employers can't find Americans to fill jobs. The current H-2A and H-2B temporary foreign worker programs require planning months in advance and following complicated rules. It's far easier to hire an unauthorized immigrant.

5   To reduce unauthorized immigration, immigration policy needs to reproduce the flexibility that employers value in unauthorized workers. Allowing temporary foreign workers to easily move across employers is critical. Current policy ties H-2A and H-2B visa holders to their employers, increasing the potential for abuse and weakening market forces. If temporary foreign workers could freely move to an employer who offered them a higher wage or better working conditions, they would. Such mobility would force employers to raise wages when labor markets tighten, which would benefit competing American workers, too. The Senate bill creates far more mobility than current programs but still allows only pre-approved employers hire temporary foreign workers, not the spot labor market that employers need when trying to get motel rooms cleaned, meals cooked, or crops picked.

Keeping employers from turning to cheaper unauthorized workers requires more enforcement, but in the interior instead of along the U.S.-Mexico border. At the state level, policies requiring the use of E-Verify, such as the 2007 Legal Arizona Workers Act, appear to have been effective at reducing the number of unauthorized immigrant workers. The rise of such state laws has coincided with increased use of the H-2A system by farmers who can no longer rely on a ready supply of unauthorized immigrants. Requiring all employers to use E-Verify, as the Senate bill does, would help choke off the demand for unauthorized workers.

The third part of successfully reducing unauthorized immigration is increasing the scale of temporary foreign worker programs. Before the Great Recession, the unauthorized labor force was growing by about 350,000 workers per year. This dwarfed the roughly 110,000 H-2A and H-2B visas issued annually. The difference is even bigger when considering stocks instead of flows: from 2003 to 2007, the U.S. gained about 1.4 million unauthorized workers whereas there was virtually no change in the number of H-2A and H-2B visa holders, who have to return home every year.

When the economic recovery picks up steam, immigration policy should ensure enough foreign workers can enter legally. The new programs the Senate bill creates for less-skilled agricultural and non-agricultural workers are capped at levels roughly commensurate with previous inflows of low-skilled immigrant workers. However, the construction industry gets special adverse treatment in the Senate bill, with a maximum of only 15,000 visas annually regardless of the level of construction activity.

Finally, Congress needs to keep the issue of unauthorized immigration in perspective. Yes, it's problematic to have some 12 million people living here illegally and it would be good to reduce future illegal inflows. But it's at least as important to adopt an immigration policy that encourages more highly skilled immigrants to enter and remain in the U.S. The greatest economic gains will come from allowing more engineers, scientists and other professionals to come to the U.S., not from focusing on less-skilled immigrants.

10 Unauthorized immigrants have become a safety valve for the U.S. economy: they enter in greater numbers when needed, and they go where the jobs are. Their arrival in greater numbers is good news indeed. But sensible immigration reform that reduces the supply of and demand for unauthorized immigrants and admits more highly skilled immigrants would be even better news.

Processing Undocumented Children

CHIP BOK

Chip Bok is an editorial cartoonist and 1997 Pulitzer Prize finalist. His work appears worldwide in newspapers and magazines, including The New York Times, The Washington Post, The Times of London, Time, *and* Newsweek. *This cartoon appeared on July 7, 2014. Elian Gonzalez, mentioned in the first frame of the cartoon, is a Cuban boy who reached the United States illegally when his Cuban mother drowned in the crossing. His case became embroiled in both international laws and the U.S. court system, and he was forcefully returned to Cuba. Citing Elian's name raises questions about the treatment of immigrant children. On his Web site, Bok explains the context for the cartoon as follows: "Fifty-two thousand undocumented children have crossed the border so far this year. A union spokesman for the Border Patrol claims agents are now spending most of their time babysitting."*

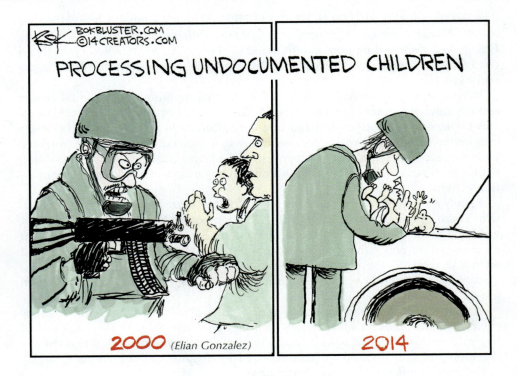

DREAM On

MARK KRIKORIAN

Mark Krikorian is executive director of the Center for Immigration Studies and the author of The New Case Against Immigration, Both Legal and Illegal *(2008). He is also a contributor to the* National Review Online, *a source for "Republican/conservative news, commentary, and opinion," where this commentary appeared in December 2010.*

Harry Reid and Nancy Pelosi have pledged a vote as early as this week on the DREAM Act (Development, Relief and Education for Alien Minors), a bill that would legalize illegal aliens who arrived here before the age of 16 and who comply with certain educational or military-service requirements.

The core principle behind this amnesty proposal is that it is aimed at those who have grown up here and are, psychologically and emotionally, Americans. In the words of America's Voice, a hard-left open-borders group, the beneficiaries of the measure are "patriotic young Americans in all but paperwork."

There's no doubt that this is the most sympathetic group of illegal immigrants. That is precisely why DREAM has been dangled as bait for the more general amnesty proposals described as "comprehensive immigration reform," with amnesty advocates brandishing the situation of these young people as justification for a broader amnesty. (Though no one seems to have stopped to ask: If such a comprehensive bill would provide amnesty for all illegals, then why would we need DREAM?)

Nonetheless, now that the amnesty crowd has belatedly decided to move ahead on DREAM as a standalone measure, many in the public and Congress are open to the idea of addressing the situation of such young people. But the DREAM Act, in every one of its iterations over the years, has four fatal flaws.

5   1. The act is billed as legalizing those brought as infants or toddlers, and yet it covers people brought here up to age 16. The examples used by advocates are nearly always people who were brought here very young. The student-body president at Fresno State University, Pedro Ramirez—who was "coincidentally" revealed to be an illegal alien just as the DREAM Act lame-duck effort got under way—came here at age three. Harvard student Eric Balderas was brought here at age four. Yves Gomes was brought here at 14 months, Juan Gomez at two years, Marie Gonzalez at five, Dan-el Padilla at four, and so on.

So why set the age cutoff at 16? If the point is to provide amnesty to those whose identity was formed here, then you'd need a much lower age cutoff. I have a 15-year-old, and if I took him to live illegally in Mexico (and living illegally is a lot harder to do there than here), he would always remain, psychologically, an American, because his identity is already formed. The Roman Catholic Church and English common law set the age of reason at seven. That, combined with a requirement of at least ten years' continuous residence here, seems like a much more defensible place to draw the line. Unless, of course, you're just using those who came as young children to bootstrap a larger amnesty.

2. Next, all amnesties have at least three harmful consequences, and the DREAM Act ignores all three. The first of these is massive fraud. Perhaps one-fourth of those legalized under the 1986 Immigration Reform and Control Act received amnesty fraudulently, including Mahmud Abouhalima, a leader of the first World Trade Center attack. The fraud in that first big amnesty program was so pervasive as to be almost comical, with people claiming work histories here that included picking watermelons from trees and digging cherries out of the ground.

And yet what does the DREAM Act say about fraud? As Sen. Jeff Sessions (R., Ala.) points out in "Ten Things You Need To Know about S-3827, the DREAM Act," the measure "prohibits using any of the information contained in the amnesty application (name, address, length of illegal presence that the alien admits to, etc.) to initiate a removal proceeding or investigate or prosecute fraud in the application process." This is like playing a slot machine without having to put any money in—any illegal alien can apply, and if he wins, great, but if he loses, he can't be prosecuted *even if he lied through his teeth about everything*. No amnesty proposal can be taken seriously unless applicants are made to understand, right up front, that any lies, no matter how trivial, will result in arrest and imprisonment.

3. Another problem with DREAM, which all amnesties share, is that it will attract new illegal immigration. Prospective illegal immigrants, considering their options, are more likely to opt to come if they see that their predecessors eventually hit the jackpot. In 1986, we had an estimated 5 million illegals, 3 million of whom were legalized. We now have more than twice as many as before the last amnesty, and they've been promised repeatedly that if they hold out a little longer they'll be able to stay legally. Any new amnesty, even if only for those brought here as children, will attract further illegal immigration.

10   There's really no way to prevent this, but to minimize it, you need stringent enforcement measures. This was the logic of the 1986 law and the recent "comprehensive immigration reform" proposals. The critique of such "grand bargains" has been that the illegals get their amnesty but the promised enforcement never materializes—and that critique remains valid. But if the sponsors of DREAM were serious about addressing the plight of people brought here as infants and toddlers, they would include muscular enforcement measures as proof of their bona fides. These would include mandatory use of E-Verify for all new hires, explicit authorization of state and local governments to enforce civil immigration law, and full implementation of an exit-tracking system for all foreign visitors, for starters. And the legal status of all the amnesty beneficiaries would remain provisional until the enforcement measures were up and running and passed judicial muster. Even these might not be sufficient to turn back a new wave of illegal immigration sparked by the amnesty, but the lack of such measures speaks volumes about the real intentions of the DREAM Act's sponsors.

4. Finally, all amnesties reward illegal immigrants—in this case, both those brought here as children *and* the adults who subjected them to this limbo. Any serious proposal to legalize young people brought here as infants or toddlers would need to prevent the possibility that their parents and other adults responsible for bringing them here illegally would ever receive any benefit from the amnesty, namely, future sponsorship as legal immigrants. This could be done in two ways: Either the amnesty recipients would not be put on a "path to citizenship" at all, but instead be given a time-limited work visa, indefinitely renewable so long as they stay out of trouble. This would mean they could not petition for any relatives to immigrate in the future. Alternatively, the amnesty beneficiaries could receive green cards and eventual citizenship, but we would abolish all the legal-immigration categories for family members other than spouses and minor children of U.S. citizens. Either way, the adults who knew what they were doing would never be rewarded.

A DREAM Act 2.0 that addressed these problems—that prosecuted fraud, implemented enforcement, prevented downstream legal immigration, and focused much more narrowly on those who came very young—would possibly be something that even I, were I a congressman, might be able to vote for. But the lack of these elements is clear proof that the amnesty crowd isn't interested in fixing the specific problem of a sympathetic but small group of people; rather, these young people are simply poster children who have been used for years to try to justify a general amnesty for all illegal aliens. And when the DREAM Act fails, as it will, Pedro Ramirez and his fellows will need to ask the pro-amnesty politicians and lobbying groups why they were sacrificed on the altar of "comprehensive immigration reform."

Immigration, America's Advantage

LEE HABEEB AND MIKE LEVEN

Lee Habeeb is the vice president of content development at Salem Radio Network, which specializes in news and talk radio and Christian programming. He is also a columnist for Townhall.com *and* National Review. *Mike Leven is the president and chief operating officer of the Las Vegas Sands and a member of the Job Creators Alliance. This commentary was posted at* National Review Online, *a conservative commentary Web site, on April 25, 2014.*

It was the *Inconvenient Truth* of its day. The book was *The Population Bomb,* by Paul Ehrlich, published in 1968. Ehrlich made some apocalyptic predictions about resource depletion and mass starvation resulting from population growth. A frightened public devoured the book.

But Ehrlich got some things wrong. He didn't factor into his thinking technological change and the growth of free enterprise around the world, both of which have done much to ameliorate global poverty and hunger. The biggest thing he got wrong, though, was that he failed to foresee this: The population is now shrinking in many parts of the world. Entire nations, even continents, are committing slow-motion suicide by not making babies.

A more prescient title of Ehrlich's book would have been "The Population Bust."

Take Russia. According to the United Nations, its adult population will fall from 90 million today to 20 million by the end of the century. Eighty percent of the population of the Russian Federation are ethnic Russians, but fertility is higher among Central Asian Muslim minorities. Some experts predict a Muslim majority in Russia by 2040. This past year, more babies were aborted in Russia than were born.

5 These facts might help explain President Vladimir Putin's recent aggression in the Ukraine. Maybe he's looking to lift a depressed nation's spirits, but maybe he's also looking for more Russians, to ward off a population decline of nearly 700,000 a year.

Japan's numbers are almost as bleak. In 2013, its population shrank for the third year running, with the elderly, people over 65, making up a quarter of the total for the first time in its history. That number will reach 40 percent by 2060. Meanwhile, the proportion of people aged 14 or younger dropped to a record low of 12.9 percent. The number of deaths this past year exceeded the number of births.

The baby bust is ravaging Europe and spreading to the developing world. Governments have tried to offer incentives to drive up fertility rates but to little avail. Many countries are now in the grip of an impending crisis: how to pay for the needs of an aging population as the ratio of workers plummets? The ratio of workers to retirees is falling fast in America, too. While there were 16 workers for every retiree in 1950, the ratio is now 3 to 1. As more baby boomers approach retirement age, that ratio will fall to 2.5.

America's secret weapon on the all-important population front is our immigrant advantage. It's our immigrant population that has kept America from falling over the demographic cliff of late. Today, there are roughly 38 million people in the U.S. who were born somewhere else; two-thirds of them are here legally.

"Consider that just four million babies are born annually in the U.S.," Jonathan Last wrote in *The Weekly Standard* last year. "If you strip these immigrants—and their relatively high fertility rates—from our population profile, America suddenly looks an awful lot like continental Europe."

10   Immigrants help ease our impending demographic and entitlement problems in two critical ways. First, most immigrants come here at the beginning of their working years, and few come with elderly parents, which immensely helps our worker-to-retiree ratio. Second, and equally important, immigrants have more children than do native-born Americans, and their children, too, will pay into our Social Security system.

All of this was confirmed last year in a report of the trustees of the Social Security Administration. In addition, SSA's chief actuary, Stephen Goss, predicted that new legal and illegal immigrants, who currently come to the U.S. at the net rate of 1.08 million each year, will increase the Social Security trust fund by $500 billion over 25 years and by $4 trillion over 75 years. Even in Washington, D.C., that's real money.

There are three categories of immigrants we must examine separately to understand the opportunity before us.

First and foremost are the nearly 12 million undocumented residents who live here, the vast majority of whom work, pay taxes, and contribute to the American economy. Those who argue that undocumented immigrants crossed a desert only to live off the state are wrong. Proof of that assertion is the near-sudden end to illegal immigration after the Great Recession of 2007–09. The jobs dried up, and so too did the workers chasing them.

We know that we're not going to deport all of these people. Why we're waiting so long to make these de facto citizens legal makes no political sense. And leaving entire families in limbo as we're doing makes no moral sense. Creating a path to citizenship for those who came here is common sense and would be in keeping with the soul of a nation enriched by its immigrant heritage.

15   Then there are the two categories of immigrants who wish to come here but are blocked by current policies — the skilled and the so-called unskilled.

Let's address the skilled immigrants first, mostly in the technology, science, and engineering fields. In 2013, our government received 124,000 applications for the H-1B program in four days. But we took 85,000 as a result of a self-imposed cap.

That means some other country was the beneficiary of all of that human capital that wished to come to America—but was rejected.

What do those skilled immigrant workers who come here contribute? One-quarter of our technology firms established since 1995 have had at least one foreign-born founder, according to Matthew Slaughter, professor at the Tuck School of Business at Dartmouth, writing recently in the *Wall Street Journal*. "These new companies today employ 450,000 people and generate more than $50 billion in sales. Immigrants or their children founded 40% of today's Fortune 500 companies, including firms behind seven of the 10 most valuable global brands."

What's the cost of our Scrooge-like approach to H1-B visas? Back in 2008, Bill Gates told members of Congress that for every immigrant hired at technology companies, an average of five additional employees were added. Slaughter calculated that approximately 500,000 jobs a year are lost thanks to our restrictive immigration policy regarding skilled workers.

But America should do more than simply cherry-pick from the world's "best and brightest" workers. We should increase our numbers of "unskilled" immigrants, too. No one takes a berth in steerage because he heard that in America the government gives you stuff. It takes courage to leave your country and cross an ocean. Most immigrants do it not for themselves but for their families. That kind of selflessness and risk-taking is a perfect American skill set, perfectly reflecting our national character.

Amnesty?

Let Us Be Vigilant and Charitable

JOHN F. KAVANAUGH

The following article by Roman Catholic priest and professor of philosophy John F. Kavanaugh, appeared in the March 10, 2008 issue of America, *a Jesuit publication that describes itself as "the only national Catholic weekly magazine in the United States."*

Let's call her María. She was illegally brought into the United States at the age of 2. Now 27, she is a vital member of her parish and has three young children. María was recently deported to Ciudad Juárez, where, in the last 15 years, 600 young women have been kidnapped, raped, murdered and buried in the desert. Luckily, she was able to find a way into the United States, again illegally, to be with her children. If she is discovered again, she will spend five years in a U.S. federal prison.

My Jesuit friend and neighbor, Dick Vogt, has told me of people like María and many others of the 12 to 14 million "undocumented aliens." She is not necessarily typical of the masses who have illegally entered this country. Some, no doubt, are drunks and dealers; many are incarcerated for other crimes than their immigrant status. But most have come at great risk to their lives, because their lives were already at risk from poverty and displacement. They want to make a living, form a family, and help their families back home.

The Catholic bishops of Mexico pointed out in January that the recent surge of immigration is a direct effect of the North American Free Trade

Agreement. Open trade, while benefiting the most powerful and technologically advanced, has threatened poor farmers and their small rural communities. They cannot compete with heavily subsidized U.S. and Canadian producers. It is this phenomenon that drives so many to leave their homeland for a livelihood in the United States, despite, as the bishops put it, "its anti-humane immigration program."

The U.S. bishops, witnessing everything from evictions in California to employment raids in Massachusetts, have stirred the consciences of their dioceses and taken stands in conscience of their own. The bishop of Oklahoma City and 10 of his pastors have publicly professed defiance of a punitive state law that makes felons of all who "aid, assist, or transport any undocumented person." The bishops of Missouri have expressed their alarm over politicians "who vie to see who can be tougher on illegal immigrants." Cognizant of the economic pressures on many families in rural Mexico, they call for a more compassionate, fair, and realistic reform of our immigration system, including education and humanitarian assistance to all children, "without regard to legal status."

5   There has been some resistance to the bishops' proposals and some resentment. It is reminiscent of the outrage directed by anti-immigrant groups toward last year's immigration reform bill, a very harsh measure that they nonetheless condemned for proposing what they called amnesty.

Some of the resentment is understandable. There are householders, especially on the border, who have had their land and yards trashed. Residents of some towns feel flooded with immigrants they cannot engage or manage. A few businesspersons who have refused to hire undocumented or cheaper labor have lost sales and customers.

But this does not explain the seething hostility that can be read in some nativist opinion columns and popular books or heard on radio talk shows: "They are criminals, felons; and that's that."

"They have broken the law." This is an interesting standard of ethics, justice or charity for a nation that sees itself as Judeo-Christian and humane. It is puzzling that we do not think of the Good Samaritan or of the "least of our brothers and sisters" in Matthew 25, or of the passage from Leviticus that the Missouri bishops quote: "The stranger who sojourns with you shall be to you as the native among you, and you shall love him as yourself."

10   As for making the law our bottom line, do Christians know how many times Jesus was in trouble with the law? Do they know that the natural law tradition, articulated in the work of Thomas Aquinas, holds an unjust law to be no law at all? Do they forget that our nation was founded upon an appeal to a higher law than positive law, an appeal shared by the labor movement, by Martin Luther King Jr., and by Elizabeth Cady Stanton and Susan B. Anthony?

A nation has every right to secure its borders. Unrestrained immigration will hurt our country, the immigrants, and their homeland. So let us indeed protect our borders (even though that will not solve the problem of those who enter legally and overstay their visa). Let us also honestly face the multiple causes of illegal immigration. As an excellent position paper from the Center for Concern notes, illegal immigration involves many factors: trade negotiation, the governments involved, the immigrants who break the law by entering our country, employers who take advantage of them, corporate leaders who profit from them, and consumers who benefit from lower food and service costs.

We must devise ways to offer legal status to anyone who contributes to our common good, whether as a future citizen or a temporary guest worker. If that means using the dirty word "amnesty," so be it.

As to those who sojourn in our midst, let us be vigilant if they are threats and charitable if they are friends. It would be a good, if unusual, move if our legislators had the imagination to call for citizen panels before which an illegal immigrant could request amnesty, leniency, and a path to citizenship based on his or her contribution to the community, solid employment record, faithful payment of taxes, family need, and crime-free record.

Instead of fearing some abstract horde of millions, we might see the faces of people like María and hear their stories. If we turn them away, we will have to face the fact that we are not so much a nation of Judeo-Christian values as a punitive and self-interested people hiding under the protection of lesser, human-made laws.

Young, Alone, and in Court

This editorial appeared in the Los Angeles Times *on March 14, 2014.*

Until about three years ago, federal agents annually intercepted some 8,000 unaccompanied minors entering the United States illegally. By last year, the number had jumped to nearly 26,000. This year's projection: As many as 60,000 youngsters may attempt to cross into this country without parents or papers.

This surge of under-age humanity presents two problems. First is understanding the forces propelling it, which experts say include narco-trafficking, Central American gang violence and abusive homes. Parents desperate to raise their children outside the reach of powerful gangs are packing them off to the north, making the calculated gamble that the trip will be safer than staying put. Other youths are caught up in sex-trafficking or similarly exploitative or abusive situations, and they come to this country to escape.

The United Nations high commissioner for refugees released a report Wednesday spotlighting

5 the problem and calling on the governments of the United States, El Salvador, Guatemala, Honduras and Mexico to work together to stem the flow; acknowledge that more than half the minors likely have internationally recognized cause to be granted refugee status based on the risks they face at home; and adopt procedures to identify those with legitimate claims for asylum or refugee status. Regrettably, the report did not offer suggestions on what the nations should do to address the root causes.

It's sensible to seek a regional approach to a humanitarian issue that is beyond the power of a single government to control. A joint effort holds greater potential to address the causes of this migration trend, and the affected governments should work together to find a solution before it becomes a migration crisis.

The second problem the U.S. faces is what to do with the youngsters once they get here. Unlike people charged with criminal offenses, those detained on immigration violations do not have the right to a court-appointed attorney during deportation proceedings, so if the detained person can't afford a lawyer, he or she often faces the judge alone. There are real consequences: A 2007 Georgetown University Law Center study found that people represented by lawyers were three times more likely to win protection.

The issue is compounded when the defendant is a child. Children barely of school age have been compelled to argue alone in immigration court why they should be allowed to stay. Often, the children can't even understand the language, let alone the process, which means there is a very real chance that minors who qualify for asylum or other protections are being booted out of the country without a fair hearing.

This is wrong. There are reasons for and against providing indigent adults with legal help as they seek permission to remain in the country, a debate we won't join here. How unaccompanied children are processed within the U.S. immigration system is a different issue that needs addressing out of fairness, if not a sense of humanity.

The federal government should develop a system under which unaccompanied minors have access to a lawyer or experienced advocate (as happens in child-welfare court proceedings) to defend their interests. A number of nonprofit organizations, such as Kids in Need of Defense, have been training and coordinating pro bono lawyers to help children. While the number of available lawyers falls far below the need, that pro bono system could offer a framework for the government to build on—much like a targeted public defender system—to ensure that all detained unaccompanied minors have someone in their corner during deportation proceedings.

Border Crisis in Texas

This editorial appeared in the National Review Online *on June 10, 2014.*

The Obama administration and its allies on immigration—both Democrats and Republicans—have justified their call for a "path to citizenship" for illegal aliens by boasting of new, tight control of the border. The message has been that new illegal immigration has effectively come to an end, so it's time to tie up the loose ends of past mistakes and move forward.

Would that were so.

Instead, the United States is experiencing a surge in illegal immigration, especially in South Texas. A large share of new arrivals are families with children, teenagers traveling alone, and younger children brought here by professional smugglers. In the first five months of this year, 47,000 unaccompanied minors were apprehended, double the number for the same period the year before. A Border Patrol memo estimates that up to 90,000 could be apprehended this fiscal year and 140,000 next year.

The administration claims that this surge is driven entirely by outside factors—i.e., poverty and violence in the sending countries, particularly Guatemala, Honduras, and El Salvador. Because they imagine it to be a refugee flow beyond their control, officials are responding as they would to a humanitarian crisis. The president has directed FEMA to lead the response, with the Office of Refugee Resettlement (part of the Department of Health and Human Services) housing the unaccompanied minors until family members in the U.S.—legal or illegal—can be found to take the youngsters in.

5   But this crisis is not simply a response to conditions in Central America, deplorable as they might be. Senator Jeff Sessions correctly asserted that "the rising crisis at the border is the direct and predictable result of actions taken by President Obama." The administration has essentially halted immigration enforcement in the interior of the country for anyone not a murderer or drug dealer. In the words of John Sandweg, until recently the acting director of Immigration and Customs Enforcement, "If you are a run-of-the-mill immigrant here illegally, your odds of getting deported are close to

zero." Add to this the unilateral amnesty for illegal immigrants claiming to have come before their 16th birthday, and you have a powerful magnet for illegal immigration.

The administration response is actually feeding the frenzy. The Justice Department is hiring lawyers to represent the youngsters in immigration court, to maximize the number who will receive formal permission to stay. A federal judge late last year berated the administration for abetting human trafficking by delivering illegal-immigrant children to their illegal-immigrant parents.

Word of Obama's permissive approach to illegal immigration has filtered south. The *New York Times* quoted one teenager in Honduras whose mother had sent for him: "If you make it, they take you to a shelter and take care of you and let you have permission to stay."

The only way to stanch the flow is to change such expectations. All illegal aliens caught at the border must be detained, and the adults prosecuted. Illegal-immigrant parents should be reunited with their illegal-immigrant children and returned as a family unit to their own countries. Border officials must be permitted to exercise the statutory power of "expedited removal" to keep new arrivals out of the immigration-court system and ensure their quick return.

And any talk of amnesty must end until order is restored.

■ ■ ■ **FOR CLASS DISCUSSION** Immigration in the Twenty-First Century

1. Fatemeh Fakhraie and Stephanie Paulsell's commentary on Leila Ahmed's book refer to aspects of Muslim culture and beliefs that mark them as different from the mainstream, particularly the choice to wear hijab. How does the media give us insight into other cultures, yet also create perceptions that may distance us from truly understanding the lived experience of someone from that culture?

2. Lee Habeeb and Mike Leven view immigrants as an economic and social advantage for the country; Madeline Zavodny also takes an economic perspective on illegal immigration, arguing for changes in policy and laws to benefit employers and immigrant workers, while Mark Krikorian explains why he believes reform of one aspect, the so-called DREAM Act, will affect all other aspects of immigration policy. While these articles point to the complexities of immigration reform, they also raise questions. What would a humane immigration policy look like, in your view? Should there be different rules for different categories of immigrants?

3. John F. Kavanaugh, Chip Bok, and the editors of the *Los Angeles Times* and the *National Review* provide different scenarios for the circumstances under which immigrants and their families may arrive or live in the United States and use different terms to describe the situation and status of illegal immigrants. What is the rhetorical effect of these competing definitions and the language employed? How might these rhetorical strategies cause the intended audience for each piece to feel more or less sympathetic toward these immigrant families?

4. Read Mark Krikorian's essay, "DREAM On," as both a believer and a doubter. Working in small groups or as a class, discuss the following questions: What are the warrants for believing his argument—that is, what other beliefs or values must one hold in order to buy his contentions about the consequences of granting amnesty to illegal immigrants? What beliefs and values would enable one to doubt Krikorian's argument?

5. What activities or privileges do citizens of the United States take for granted that might be difficult or impossible for illegal immigrants or their children? How might these barriers perpetuate or even create some of the problems stemming from illegal immigration in the United States?

WRITING ASSIGNMENT White Paper Summarizing and Analyzing the Arguments about an Immigration Policy Proposal

A number of the readings in this unit deal with U.S. immigration laws and policies. Research one recent proposal to change federal or state immigration laws (such as the federal DREAM Act, proposals for handling the crisis of thousands of immigrant children on the border, or a specific element of comprehensive reform such as the E-Verify system or the H-2A Seasonal Agricultural Worker program) and read about it in both popular news commentary and scholarly sources. Identify and characterize the stakeholders in the debate: Who are they? What do they stand to gain or lose? Then analyze the arguments used by these stakeholders. What are their strengths and weaknesses? Finally, write a white paper in which you summarize the proposal and the arguments for and against it for a citizen wanting to be better informed. You might find the following resources helpful as a starting place: the White House Web site on immigration reform at http://www.whitehouse.gov/infocus/immigration, the Federation for American Immigration Reform site at www.fairus.org, the National Immigration Law Center at www.nilc.org, or the League of Women Voters Immigration Study at www.lwv.org. ■

Millennials Entering Adulthood

The Millennial Generation is also known as Generation Y (or the group following Generation X), the Net Generation, the Echo Boomers (children of Baby Boomers), or even the Boomerang Generation (based on the number of young adults who return home to live with their parents). These terms generally refer to people born between 1980 and 1999, although some writers include people born as early as 1976 and as late as 2004. This generation has been called optimistic and idealistic, but also "entitled" and "unable to take criticism." They are skilled multitaskers, but they must constantly be connected to their technology and social networks. They aim high in their careers, but sometimes find that the opportunities available to recent graduates don't match their expectations for success.

As the first waves of Millennials enter the workforce, a number of books and articles have come out aimed at helping employers manage these new, technologically savvy employees who have grown up accustomed to intensive parental involvement ("helicopter parents") and frequent praise and feedback. In 2008, *Wall Street Journal* columnist Ron Alsop popularized the term "Trophy Kids" to identify young workers accustomed to getting trophies for participation rather than achievement.

The readings that follow will ask you to consider the following questions: What are the challenges and opportunities facing the Millennial Generation as they enter a job-scarce workplace? What are the expectations for Millennials—what are they called to be or to do? Are the stereotypes associated with Millennials fair? Are these stereotypes grounded in actual generational difference or merely an expression of developmental stages that have always been present if not always acknowledged?

The Tethered Generation

KATHRYN TYLER

Kathryn Tyler is a freelance writer with a background in human resources and training. She identifies herself as a member of Generation X. She is a frequent contributor to HR Magazine, *a magazine for human resources professionals, in which this article appeared in May 2007.*

At 11 years old, Kate Achille had a pager for her parents to reach her when necessary. At 13, she had a cell phone. Now 22 and working for a school, she e-mails her mother as many as five times a day and calls her on the cell phone several times a week.

Her mother, Jeanne Achille, CEO of Shrewsbury, N.J., public relations firm The Devon Group, says technology allows her to communicate regularly with Kate and her other daughter, who is 18. "I know where my daughters are constantly because we use these communications technologies to update each other: 'I'm still at work,' 'I'm going to the gym,' 'I'm picking up dinner,' etc."

"I would have never given my parents visibility into this level of detail in my day!" she admits.

But this is a different day. Kate Achille and her sister are part of the so-called millennial generation, now ages 8 to 29. This group, also called Generation Y and the Net Generation, is made up of 80 million people in the United States born between 1978 and 1999. They are the first generation to use e-mail, instant messaging (IM) and cell phones since childhood and adolescence.

5   Especially as millennials born since 1985 begin to show up in the workforce, HR professionals and psychologists are just beginning to see what effect the constant "tethering" to technology has had on the way millennials work, communicate, make decisions and interact. That effect, along with a tethered relationship to their peers and parents—sometimes to the extent that they have been deemed "helicopter parents"—presents challenges for HR professionals integrating millennials into the workplace.

For those who remember life without cell phones and the Internet, it may be difficult to understand how ingrained technology is in millennials' lives. To prepare for millennials, it's important to understand how cell phones and computers have changed their brain development, the enormous role their parents play in their lives well into adulthood, and what policies and training programs HR professionals will need to implement to transition these young people into the workplace.

Millennial Connectivity

Older generations that couldn't wait to proclaim their independence can't comprehend this generation's need for parental guidance and influence. Years ago, "most college dorm rooms had one land line, and, if parents were lucky, kids called home once a week. Now, students may be going across the country, but they call their parents on the cell phone three to five times per day" says Claire Raines, author of *Generations at Work* (AMACOM, 2000).

Another big influence on this generation is their peers. While previous generations also looked to their friends for advice and direction, today's technology allows a perpetual connection to peers, leaving little time for autonomy. "Except for their mothers, these kids don't have relationships with people outside of their generation. They spend 72 hours per week of connected time—by phone and IM—seeking advice and input on the smallest decisions," says Jim Taylor, a futurist, author and vice chairman of Waterbury, Conn.-based The Harrison Group, a marketing consulting and research services firm, which has consulted for large companies on tapping the teen market.

What could be wrong with young people using cell phones and IM to keep mom and dad abreast of their every move? New research reveals a lot.

10   Scientists once believed the brain was almost completely formed by age 13. But, in the past two years, neuroscientists have discovered that parts of the brain—specifically the prefrontal lobes, which are involved in planning and decision-making—continue to develop well into the late teens and early 20s.

"The prefrontal cortex is important for decision-making, planning, reasoning and the storage of knowledge," explains Jordan Grafman, chief of the Cognitive Neuroscience section at the National Institute of Neurological Disorders and Stroke in Bethesda, Md.

That means millennials' brains are still developing reasoning, planning and decision-making capabilities while they are depending heavily on technology—cell phones, IM and e-mail—as well as parents and friends at the other end of the technology. As a result, some experts believe millennials struggle to make decisions independently.

When parents give teens cell phones, it's a double-edged sword. "On the one hand, this arrangement gives the adolescent new freedoms. On the other, the adolescent doesn't have the experience of having only herself to count on; there's always a parent on speed dial," says Sherry Turkle, licensed clinical psychologist and professor of the social studies of science and technology at the Massachusetts Institute of Technology in Cambridge.

Stephen P. Seaward, director of career development for Saint Joseph College in West Hartford, Conn., agrees. "The majority of millennials never experienced life without a microwave, computer, ATM card or television remote control. Many had their first cell phones in their early teens with parents footing the bill," he says. "This instantaneous gratification…may have fostered unrealistic expectations with respect to goal-setting and planning. That, in conjunction with extreme parental influence, can prohibit creative problem-solving and decision-making."

15   A 2006 research report bears this out. Roughly three-quarters of executives and HR managers at 400 companies surveyed said that recent four-year college graduates displayed only "adequate" professionalism and work ethic, creativity and innovation, and critical thinking and problem-solving. Only one-quarter reported an "excellent" display of those traits in recent college graduates, according to *Are They Really Ready to Work?*, a report by the Society for Human Resource Management, The Conference Board, Corporate Voices for Working Families and the Partnership for 21st Century Skills.

Helicopter Parents

While technology has enabled children's dependency, it has also abetted parental oversight, making it easier for overbearing parents to "hover" well into adulthood. "Some hovering is good since some mistakes can be catastrophic. But small errors induce critical thinking," and if children are not allowed to make small errors, they don't learn through experience, argues Grafman.

"Parents' most important task is to help young people to become independent and autonomous. When we infantilize our young, we stifle their development," says Robert Epstein, visiting scholar at the University of California in San Diego, and West Coast editor of *Psychology Today*.

Epstein tells the story of a helicopter parent meddling in his college-aged daughter's courses. "In class, I announced I expect hard work and sacrifice from my students and any professor who said less than that was cheating his students. This young woman's father—a California Superior Court judge—sent a letter to the chair of my department saying his daughter was intimidated by my warning. His letter arrived on judicial stationery."

Epstein brought the matter to the attention of the judicial regulatory board, which later reprimanded the judge. Imagine when this young woman enters the workforce and her father dislikes her workload, he wonders.

20 "Parental involvement in the lives of their off-spring seems to be increasing every year. I've seen parents come to campus protesting a low grade. When I caught one student cheating on a paper, his mom called and demanded I let him write a new paper," says Epstein.

Most colleges now hold orientation sessions for freshman students and their parents, separately. The parent orientation talks about how to "cut the apron strings."

However, it often doesn't achieve the desired effect, says Robert W. Wendover, director of The Center for Generational Studies, a research and training company in Aurora, Colo.

"The kids leave everything to mom and dad," says Wendover. "The kids encourage it; they're used to it. It's easier to use the parent as a surrogate than to think for yourself. There is a point at which the child fails to learn resourcefulness. It's a learned helplessness."

Not everyone agrees this is detrimental or even prevalent. Barbara Dwyer, CEO of The Job Journey, a soft-skills training firm for high-school and community college students in El Macero, Calif., says, "This generation is closer to their parents than any other generation. They see their parents as friends. It's a good thing." Dwyer believes helicopter parents are a small percentage of the total parenting population.

25 However, many college professors and career counselors say otherwise. "Parents have called to set up interview appointments for their children. The students lose a sense of self-reliance," says Toni McLawhorn, director of career services at Roanoke College in Salem, Va.

Helicoptering in the Workforce

As millennials move into the workforce, their hovering parents do, too. "Parents are writing resumes, applying to jobs and even attending interviews," reports Steven Rothberg, president and founder of the CollegeRecruiter.com career site, headquartered in Edina, Minn.

Ann Reynolds, director of university career services at Texas Christian University in Fort Worth, says she has received feedback from employers about "parents calling to find out why their child was not hired or offered more money. A few want to be involved in negotiating salary."

Susan Revillar Bramlett, PHR, an HR generalist for a defense research contractor in Fort Wayne, Ind., and a millennial herself, "overheard a parent yell at the HR person because her daughter was turned down for a promotion."

Wendover has another disquieting but increasingly common tale from a pharmaceutical company. "They had a 23-year-old new employee with a pharmacy doctoral degree show up for the first day of work with her dad. He wanted to see where she worked. The dad stayed for about four hours. The manager was aghast," he says.

30 Another HR professional, who asked not to be identified, tells of withdrawing a job offer from a young candidate after he failed a required drug test. "Within 24 hours, his mother called me to say their family takes a lot of herbal supplements and we shouldn't hold this against him. Then she kept talking about what a good person her son was and how he could do great things for our company. After I refused to discuss the situation with her, I didn't hear from them again."

When it comes to dealing with helicopter parents, there are two schools of thought: beat 'em or join 'em. HR professionals will need to decide to which school they subscribe and develop policies and procedures accordingly.

Some companies are courting the parents and applicants simultaneously. At many Enterprise Rent-A-Car offices, for instance, the company offers to provide information to the parents of prospective candidates, and about half of the candidates accept. Remember, though, any parental involvement should always be at the request or discretion of the candidate.

In contrast, if a company chooses not to communicate with helicopter parents, it will need to enforce strong privacy policies and train managers on how to deflect parental interference. The unnamed HR professional above refuses to discuss anyone's employment with his or her parents. "I remain polite and explain we don't discuss employment-related issues with [outsiders]. If they continue to push, I suggest they discuss the matter with their [child]. If the employee follows up with me, I say why it's inappropriate, and I hope it won't happen again."

How to Prepare for the Millennials

Policies to manage helicopter parents aren't the only preparation companies will need to consider for the millennial generation. Experts suggest HR professionals plan to:

35 ■ Increase basic skills training. Many millennials may lack basic spelling and writing skills because they have come to rely on spell check. Moreover, some millennials have become so accustomed to using IM abbreviations, such as "b/c" for "because," that some don't know how to spell it correctly. Wendover recommends asking candidates to write a letter from scratch without the benefits of grammar or spell check. "Then, you'll know what their writing skills are," he says.

In addition, millennials need to learn how to conduct old-fashioned research in books and other primary sources. "It doesn't occur to them to go to the library, but there's a whole bunch of stuff not on the web," says Wendover.

Millennial Bramlett agrees. "New college grads strongly believe all Internet information is valid, and if it's not available on the Internet, then it doesn't exist. This can create problems in work quality if someone is relying 100 percent on Internet resources."

■ Explain the reasons behind processes. To gain compliance from millennials, you need to give the rationale behind your instructions, says Wendover. If you tell a person to stock a grocery shelf but to be cautious opening the boxes, he won't be. "This person takes a box knife to open

a case of Wheaties and slices across all the boxes. Then you have to discount that box. But, if you explain, 'In the grocery industry you only have a 1 percent profit margin, the box sells for $5, you're only making 5 cents, and by being forced to discount the box you have lost any profit that could have been made,' [this is how] you engage them. You need to teach them why they're doing what they're doing," says Wendover.

■ Place clear parameters on communication frequency and methods, particularly DVI. Millennials need to be told when it is acceptable to call and how to reach their superiors. Don't assume they have traditional standards for appropriate behavior, such as knowing it isn't acceptable to make a business call in the restroom.

40 "Some of our interns expect staff members to be available to them instantly, even when the issue is not urgent. They don't appreciate that our workdays are full and we need to prioritize our tasks. Sometimes, their requests must wait," says Rothberg.

■ Provide more frequent job performance appraisals and other feedback. "This generation has grown up sitting in front of a monitor playing video games. Players always know how they're doing by the score on the screen," says college career director Seaward. "Therefore, this generation won't want to wait for a semiannual or annual performance review. They will require ongoing feedback."

Bramlett agrees: "If I do something wrong, I expect my manager to let me know immediately, not at my next performance evaluation. If I've given a major presentation to company executives, I immediately follow up with someone who sat in on the call to gain feedback on how I did and how I can improve."

■ Focus on outcomes. "They can do their job, surf the web, IM friends, have a chat with colleagues on the side and pay attention to everything," says Wendover. "It's unrealistic to expect them to have no personal calls during the workday."

HR must measure outcome-based performance. "If they are getting the job done faster than you anticipated, give them more to do," says Wendover. Don't settle for poor quality, but don't fuss if they are also conducting personal conversations while they're working."

45 ▪ Keep them engaged. "I will stay with a company as long as my skills are developing. If something major doesn't change, I move on. This happened with my last HR position," says Bramlett. "The only reason I didn't leave [right away] was because I felt responsible for a major project where employees were depending on me. Millennials can be loyal, but it's based more on relationships than on the company."

Therefore, HR professionals will need to be vigilant about helping millennials with career planning and job rotation assignments. "If a company doesn't have a good internal placement program, they may find many of these folks leaving to gain new experiences," says Bramlett.

▪ Expand work/life balance programs. According to a study by Spherion, a recruiting and staffing firm headquartered in Fort Lauderdale, Fla., millennials highlight "time and flexibility" as the most important thing in keeping them loyal to their employers (followed by financial compensation and benefits). No other age group named "time and flexibility" in their top three retention drivers.

Bramlett confirms this. "Just because a person is single or doesn't have kids doesn't mean they will accept responsibility of having to work a majority of the overtime or travel more than others in the same position," she says. "Work/life balance is important to this generation, and it shouldn't matter why they want the time off."

Great Expectations

"My generation is going to be high-maintenance," acknowledges Bramlett. "We were brought up to reach for the stars. Many millennials don't recognize the idea of starting at the bottom and working their way up. Millennials come to work on their first day with great ideas on how they're going to change the world. Management will need to be sensitive to their aspirations when responding to their ideas so as to not shoot them down."

50 Dwyer agrees: "This generation is going to come to work with higher expectations than any other. They will be quickly disappointed if it's not as good as they had hoped. With one click of the mouse, they can tell thousands of other people, 'Don't go to work for XYZ company.' It's going to be challenging."

Concludes Taylor, "The main thing HR people have to deal with is how to take people who are well-educated, intelligent and quick to draw remarkably accurate conclusions and immerse them in the organization."

Millennials and Mentoring: Why I'm Calling Out "Bullpucky!" on Generational Differences and Professional Development

ERIN BURNS

Erin Burns is a reference librarian at Penn State University, Shenango. The following commentary appeared in Pennsylvania Libraries: Research and Practice, *a peer-reviewed, open-access journal, in Fall 2013.*

In my experience, most assumptions about the millennial label are faulty, especially with respect to professional development and support. There is no shortage of webpages talking about millennials, also known as "Generation Y," in which experts in the field of generational cohorts cannot even agree on which dates the label should be applied. While most may agree that the age cohort can be defined as those born between 1980 and 2000, even this is disputed (EchoBoom, 2010; Generation Y, 1993; Hoover, 2009; Howe & Strauss, 2000; Strauss & Howe, 1991). As I was born in 1983, I tend to fall into the millennial cohort, however it may be defined.

Lately, millennials are portrayed "as entitled whiners who have been spoiled by parents who overstoked their self-esteem, teachers who granted undeserved A's and sports coaches who bestowed trophies on any player who showed up" (Warner, 2010). *Time* magazine even went so far as to run a cover story by Joel Stein (2013) about "The Me Me Me Generation." These articles suggest that there is something far more narcissistic and lazy about contemporary youth than older generations. Closer examination reveals that these articles are relying on the pseudoscience of generational cohorts—which, in some opinions, has as much scientific rigor as horoscopes or reading tea leaves (Granger, 2011). This reliance on faulty assumptions about generational cohorts can cause many overgeneralizations about young professionals. Countless articles appear to be obsessive attempts at exempting older generations from the same issues that they themselves faced in their own youth. Millennials have been trashed in the media and even within my own profession of librarianship, and as a millennial, I am putting my foot down and saying "generational differences are BULLPUCKY and I'm not going to take it anymore!"

Millennials are being categorized by Stein (2013) as different than other generations because they are "narcissistic," "materialistic," "selfish," and "lazy" in addition to having a "technology addiction" (p. 27). These types of generalizations about millennials made Elspeth Reeve (2013) at the *Atlantic Wire* declare, "It's like doing a study of toddlers and declaring those born since 2010 are *Generation Sociopath: Kids these days will pull your hair, pee on walls, throw full bowls of cereal without even thinking of the consequences*." Additionally, Matt Bors (2013) stated in a cartoon on CNN that "the only thing more lazy than a 20-something is the generational slander that takes place anew every two decades or so to fill column inches and create a new demographic to market to," suggesting that the only reason these generational cohorts exist at all is for selling magazines and generating webpage traffic. However, if we as a society stop despairing over the younger generations, we realize that *all* generations have been disparaged by their elders. Older generations tell familiar stories, scoffing at the younger ones with phrases like "back in my day..." and "kids these days...." Sound familiar?

Considerable research exists about millennials, including how these people fit into the workplace, how we should be educating them, what they like and dislike, and so forth. The book *Generation Me* by Jean Twenge (2006) speaks of a narcissistic quality among millennials and has been heavily cited. However, it has been shown in research by Roberts, Edmonds, and Grijalva (2010) that the narcissism that Twenge spoke of is actually related to developmental changes and not generational ones. "Every generation of young people is substantially more narcissistic than their elders, not because of cultural changes, but because of age-related developmental trends" (p. 100). Their research delves into these trends and shows that across one's lifespan, a person's narcissism decreases an entire standard deviation. Developmentally and psychologically speaking, all young people are narcissistic, and the reason that older people do not realize this is because one gets less narcissistic with age. Roberts et al. go on to discuss that "the fact that one can find complaints about the younger generation being more narcissistic going back to Hesiod helps make the point that every generation is Generation Me. That is, until they grow up" (p. 101) which, coincidentally, millennials are doing in the workplace right now.

5   The faulty and misunderstood assumptions about millennials lead many companies and institutions to assume that they must somehow creatively change current and widely accepted practices in order to reach out across generational differences. Bell (2013) posited that millennials are not looking for help from senior members of their institutions. Specifically, he mentions how millennials might not want to be a part of a mentoring program, so administrators might want to consider other options for them. Further, he suggests that peer-mentoring and speed-mentoring could be possible replacements for a formal mentoring program.

These kinds of generalizations tend to be suspect, especially when they are being used as convenient excuses to change what is currently in practice. Do not misunderstand me: I am entirely for change. I am a millennial, after all. Additionally, librarianship is a field that has become reliant upon the technology that millennials have grown-up with and has indeed transformed with that technology over time. It would seem that one needs to be familiar with change if one wants to be successful, but why change mentoring programs when they have been proven to work? Changing an established mentoring program that provides one-on-one support from a senior colleague to peer-mentoring, speed-mentoring, or reverse-mentoring is not going to fix the perceived problems of generational differences. Perhaps these kinds of mentoring programs can be used to complement current long-term programs. Nevertheless, I do not think that these programs can replace the indispensable one-on-one support senior colleagues can provide to the newly hired.

Of course millennials, like previous generations, look to senior colleagues for mentors. It would be foolish not to! It is also completely typical for a newly hired millennial colleague to befriend others in their age cohort. But this occurs with any new hire, regardless of age. How exactly is peer-mentoring to work when, by definition, we have all been hired at the same time with the same experience? While millennials can share experiences because they are of a generational cohort, these relationships do not provide the same perspective as someone who has been in the organization for years. This elder perspective is crucial for a new librarian, especially at large institutions like Pennsylvania State University or within state and national organizations. New to the field, these librarians will need the guidance of older professionals who know the vocation, the organizations, and the library. Why would we spurn their advice?

Further, the assumption that millennials' social relationships resemble Twitter and Facebook statuses, and then claiming that mentoring should operate more like their social network relationships, is bullpucky. Online presence is only one of a multitude of ways people keep in contact with each other. My experiences as a millennial tell me that we are complex because we are human, and this complexity provides us with rich social networks, ranging from the brief and informal to the long-lasting relationships that will span a career, or even a lifetime. Bell's statement (2013) that we might "avoid deep, close, personal one-on-one mentoring" seems to be ignoring human nature. We are actively seeking deep and personal relationships, formally and informally. Everyone needs strong personal relationships in their lives, and if a formal mentoring relationship can turn into a personal one, both parties win. Why would anyone avoid deep, close, personal relationships with a mentor? Personality, rather than age group, would seem to be a deciding factor. In addition, most professionals will have a higher number of informal mentors to formal ones because they will meet many people over the course of their careers. We have all had more than one person we go to for career advice. It is almost a given that some of them are bound to become mentors. If these informal mentors were more suited to you, it is because you were the one who chose them.

Most formal mentoring relationships will only succeed when clear goals exist for the relationship, such as promotion, tenure, or other professional involvement. The expanded mentoring program within the University Libraries at Penn State attempts to do just that. The goals of this program have been two-fold: to welcome and provide guidance to new librarian faculty hires not on the tenure-track, and to prepare them to successfully attain a tenure-track position, either within the institution or outside of it. This program is an extension of the tenure-track mentoring program that has been in place for many years, which includes an assigned mentor and guidance along the six-year tenure track. Moreover, there has been some discussion about expanding current mentoring initiatives to include staff members.

10   Much has been written about what works in a successful mentoring program, as well as how to have successful mentor-mentee relationships. A quick search of the literature for the phrase "successful mentor mentee relationships" returned numerous results. What is clear across many of these pages, books, and articles, is that regardless of profession, communication is important on both sides of this relationship. This includes factors such as being open to communication, providing professional and personal support, getting to know each other, being honest and tactful, defining expectations about the relationship, maintaining contact and actively participating in the relationship, and being reliable and consistent (American Massage Therapy Association, 2013; Metros & Yang, 2006; Smallwood & Tolley-Stokes, 2012; Zerzan, Hess, Schur, Phillips, & Rigotti, 2009). Moreover, it is clear that this communication must go both ways. A mentor has to be open to the relationship, but so does the mentee. Age labels do not seem to matter when it comes to this relationship, but rather communication through these perceived differences.

For newly hired faculty librarians at Penn State, it can be difficult and daunting to see how one fits into a complex organization with more than 130 librarians across the state. Worries arise about how one can be successful or secure a tenure-track position if he/she has not been given guidance on how to get there. While we can develop informal relationships with our colleagues, the expanded mentoring program within the University Libraries provides a platform for a more formal relationship. This formal relationship allows for both parties to become comfortable communicating with each other. It also allows for the development of talent and the sharing of knowledge and skills. Strategically, having a formal mentoring program is a way to continue the excellent leadership, collaboration, and professional practice for which Penn State University Libraries is renowned.

Not only has the Penn State University Libraries been extremely supportive of me and my career goals, my newly assigned mentor has been with me along my journey, checking in on me, keeping tabs on both my personal life and professional progress. It is this formal relationship that has given me the courage to expand professionally, with the goal of reaching for a tenure-track position and taking a more active leadership role within both the university and the Pennsylvania Library Association. I would argue that this is why mentor-mentee relationships can be successful. One has to put the time and communication into making the relationship last. Checking in on your mentee only twice a year can be a prescription for mentorship breakdown. If you are a mentor but are too busy to check in on your mentee, failure is a probable result. However, this relationship goes both ways. A mentee needs to make time, reach out, and feel welcomed by the mentor. If the mentee gets the feeling that the mentor is too busy to bother answering questions or otherwise assist him/her, the mentee is not going to go to the assigned mentor for help when it is needed. Both parties need to be able to put the time and effort into making the relationship work. Blaming a failed mentoring relationship on the fact that the mentee is a millennial strikes me as just another example of bullpucky.

It is important to keep in mind that mentor-mentee relationships may fizzle out over time. In fact, if there are clear goals for the relationship, this is bound to happen. For non-tenured librarians, the mentoring relationship may end after a few years, either after the newly hired faculty member is more comfortable with participating in such a large organization or has achieved his/her professional goals. As another example, if one is assigned a mentor within a national organization, the mentor-mentee relationship will probably end when the mentee is comfortable seeking out and succeeding in committee assignments, research and publication opportunities, and the like. This would normally occur within the first few years of the new member's initiation into the organization. When the formal relationship ends, it should not be considered a failure, but rather a designed part of the relationship.

Once familiar within an organization, the mentee is introduced to people within the organization. Knowing the right people can be key, after which the mentee can make his/her own decisions about place and activity within the organization. But this usually happens only when an experienced member provides support and guidance.

What matters most is that a senior colleague supplied the support early in the librarian's career, whether this relationship is formal or informal. This is not just a millennial thing. It is a professional thing.

15   In the case of Bell (2013) and many others, the millennial label appears to be a convenient excuse for laziness and complacency from older generations to the current one regarding leadership opportunities. Just because mentoring relationships may fizzle after two years does not mean that those relationships were not useful. Organizations offering mentoring programs are providing their members with professional benefits and leadership opportunities. While these programs may be changing, it does us a disservice to think that because of an arbitrary demographic we are generalizing how a mentoring program works and succeeds.

The millennial label should not be applied lightly. Yes, millennials have grown up with technology and have differing social connections, but this does not mean that a formal mentor is unwelcome. Organized mentoring programs allow new professionals to gain formal guidance in the profession, acceptance from predecessors, and a safe place to discuss career goals. All these can enable success, no matter age or career. Whether these relationships are formal or informal should not matter, and neither should a generational label.

References

American Massage Therapy Association. (2013). Ten tips for a successful mentor/mentee relationship. Retrieved from http://www.amtamassage.org/mentor/Ten-Tips-for-a-Successful-Mentor-Mentee-Relationship.html

Bell, S. (2013, April 24). The next generation may not want your mentoring. *Library Journal*. Retrieved from http://lj.libraryjournal.com/2013/04/opinion/leading-from-the-library/the-next-generation-may-not-want-your-mentoring-leading-from-the-library

Bors, M. (2013, July 9). The generation we love to dump on. *CNN Opinion*. Retrieved from http://www.cnn.com/2013/07/09/opinion/bors-millenial-comic-strip

EchoBoom. (2010, September 21). Date/age range of Baby Boomers, Generation X, and Generation Y. Retrieved from http://theechoboom.com/2010/09/dateage-range-of-baby-boomers-generation-x-and-generation-y

Generation Y. (1993, August 30). *Advertising Age*, 16.

Granger, S. (2011, April 3). The rubbish science of generational dynamics. HR.com. Retrieved from http://www.hr.com/en/app/blog/2011/04/the-rubbish-science-of-generational-dynamics_gm2m2zwb.html

Hoover, E. (2009, October 11). The millennial muddle: How stereotyping students became a thriving industry and a bundle of contradictions. *The Chronicle of Higher Education*. Retrieved from http://chronicle.com/article/The-Millennial-Muddle-How/48772

Howe, N., & Strauss, W. (2000). *Millennials rising: The next great generation*. New York: Vintage Books.

Metros, S., & Yang, C. (2006). The importance of mentors. In C. Golden (Ed.), *Cultivating careers: Professional development for campus IT*. Boulder, CO: EDUCAUSE. Retrieved from http://www.educause.edu/research-publications/books/cultivating-careers-professional-development-campus-it/chapter-5-importance-mentors

Reeve, E. (2013). Every every every generation has been the me me me generation. *Atlantic Wire*. Retrieved from http://www.theatlanticwire.com/national/2013/05/me-generation-time/65054

Roberts, B. W., Edmonds, G., & Grijalva, E. (2010). It is developmental me, not generation me: Developmental changes are more important than generational changes in narcissism— Commentary on Trzesniewski & Donnellan. *Perspectives on Psychological Science*, 5(1), 97-102. doi:10.1177/1745691609357019

Smallwood, C., & Tolley-Stokes, R. (Eds.). (2012). *Mentoring in librarianship: Essays on working with adults and students to further the profession*. Jefferson, NC: McFarland & Company.

Stein, J. (2013, May 20). Millennials: The me me me generation: Why Millennials will save us all. *Time* 181(19), 26-34.

Strauss, W., & Howe N. (1991). *Generations: The history of America's future, 1584 to 2069*. New York: William Morrow and Company.

Twenge, J. (2006). *Generation me: Why today's young Americans are more confident, assertive, entitled— and more miserable than ever before*. New York: Free Press.

Warner, J. (2010, May 28). The why-worry generation. *New York Times Magazine*. Retrieved from http://www.nytimes.com/ 2010/05/30/magazine/30fob-wwln-t.html

Zerzan, J. T., Hess, R., Schur, E., Phillips, R. S., & Rigotti, N. (2009). Making the most of mentors: A guide for mentees. *Academic Medicine*, 84(1), 140-144. doi:10.1097/ACM.0b013e3181906e8f

Generation S

This editorial appeared in the March 2, 2009, edition of America, *a national Catholic weekly magazine published for over one hundred years. It is a forum for discussion of religion, society, politics, and culture, and considers itself "a resource for spiritual renewal and social analysis guided by the spirit of charity."*

In his inaugural address, President Obama spoke of ours as "a moment that will define a generation." He pointed specifically to the men and women in the armed forces as those who "embody the spirit of service; a willingness to find meaning in something greater than themselves." "Precisely this spirit of generosity," the president explained, "must inhabit us all." His is a clear call to service, quite the opposite of so much we have witnessed during the past year, which might be called the year of Generation G, for greed.

Consumerism, greed and self-centeredness have surely contributed to the economic morass in which we find ourselves. Is it time now to move to a new spirit? Can we foster a culture or civilization of service, a civic generation? Generation X produced the pop culture of the 80s and 90s. Then came the millennials of Generation Y, born between 1980 and 2000. What might we call the new generation? Instead of C for cellphone, I for Internet, V for virtual or D for digital, how about Generation S—for service?

This spirit is already in the air. The Peace Corps (founded in 1961), which enlists college graduates and retirees, continues to labor in 76 countries, working in education, development and care for the environment. Habitat for Humanity, begun in 1976, has built more than a million homes for the poor. Campus Compact, begun in 1985 with four universities (Georgetown among them), now includes 1,200 colleges committed to involving college students in tutoring, home building and caring for the sick and elderly. Princeton University now encourages its incoming freshmen to spend a precollegiate year in social service in a foreign country.

A number of educational institutions at the high school and college level encourage or even require students to dedicate a designated number of hours to community service as a prerequisite for receiving a diploma. Faculty members are encouraged to accompany and guide students on overseas visits and volunteer projects. Fraternities and sororities may take up a specific charity or need in their community. In classrooms, the concept of service-learning is growing. Staff members and students integrate community service with reflection on the experience and instruction. Students, to give just one example, assist in collecting trash and cleaning rivers and lots, and then examine what makes up the trash and study better ways to reduce waste and
5 pollution.

Such organizations as the Jesuit and Ignatian Volunteer Corps and the Lutheran, Franciscan and Mercy Volunteer Corps are only a few of the religious-based programs that are leading the way, inspiring and enabling persons of every age to give time and energy to projects at home and abroad.

The new administration, in addition to the creation of five new service corps in the fields of teaching, health care, clean energy, veterans' assistance and emergency preparedness, also plans a major increase in AmeriCorps to 250,000 from its current level of 75,000. This will enable adults of all ages to meet critical needs in communities by engaging with nonprofit groups in teaching, mentoring, improving health service and building housing. Those who complete a year of service are eligible to receive an education award of $4,725 toward college tuition. Teach for America places approximately 4,000 graduating college seniors in teaching positions in needy schools. Large corporations and small businesses are also joining in. A growing sense of corporate social responsibility leads an increasing number of companies to encourage and even reward employees for community service beyond the workplace.

In the face of the economic downturn and hardships, with cutbacks in programs for the needy and for teachers, the need for Generation S becomes all the greater. Part of the economic stimulus, in addition to adequate salaries for teachers, might be to legislate tax benefits for them and for other employees who can demonstrate hours given to community service.

Some years ago, the Nobel Prize-winner Albert Schweitzer, already famous as a Scripture scholar and musician, became a medical doctor and served in Gabon, West Africa. He once addressed a group of students in the United States: "I do not know what your destiny will be, but one thing I know; the only ones among you who will really be happy are those who have sought and found how to serve."

A revolution is taking place with a new set of values. This is our hope: that schools, corporations, businesses, churches and faith-based groups will take up the torch and encourage, empower and shape Generation S. In 1994 Congress declared Martin Luther King Jr. Day a National Day of Service. Such a day could lead to years of service. The label Generation S should not be reserved to persons grouped by age, but should designate multitudes of young and old Americans who are civic-minded and dedicated to serving the common good.

Lip Service Useless for Millennials

RAFFI WINEBURG

Raffi Wineburg is a recent graduate of the University of British Columbia, an intern with The Jerusalem Post, *and a freelance journalist who blogs his social and political commentaries for* The Times of Israel. *Wineburg published this op-piece in* The Seattle Times *on June 19, 2014.*

My face broke out today. Not since the hormonal rollercoaster ride of high school have so many angry red marks marred my skin. I'm not surprised, though. Lately I've been stressed, anxious and moody. It's high school all over again.

This time, I'm not applying for college, I'm searching for jobs. Well, not jobs, internships. Don't scoff; they don't just hand these things out.

I'm actually a recent college graduate, which puts me at a disadvantage. Most internships are available only to current students. I've had three of those type of internships already. Somehow, I still grasp at straws when writing cover letters for the internships I want: The paid ones.

I'm not alone. Millennials are all struggling on the job front. It's so bad that *The New York Times* Sunday issue ran not one, but two pieces on this topic. The first, a column by Frank Bruni titled "Dear Millennials, We're Sorry," was a punchline-filled apology for a disastrous economy and impending environmental collapse. The editorial board then offered "Starting Out Behind," which detailed an outrageously dire situation for young job-seekers.

Here is how I would paraphrase the editorial: A lot of things are bad for young people. To make matters worse, other things are also bad for young people. In the end, things are bad, and we should do something to change them.

I apologize for the sarcasm, but the constant scrutiny isn't helping. Every day there's something new published about millennials, dissecting our brains and examining them for clues. One day, we're all just selfish, selfie-snapping pipsqueaks of the "Me Generation." The next, we're selfless and deserve an official apology from *The New York Times*.

At this point, debating who or what millennials are is just dilly-dallying. Unemployment for 16- to 24-year-olds is roughly 15 percent. Nothing inherent to our generation will explain that harrowing statistic. Diagnosing us only muddies debate around policy solutions. And solutions are what we need.

The nonprofit organization Young Invincibles recently published a policy brief with a number of concrete, tangible recommendations: investing more in AmeriCorps, reinstating Youth Opportunity Grants and expanding the Department of Labor's Registered Apprenticeship program.

The Labor Department's own fact sheet on the program estimates that the federal government receives $50 in revenue for every federal dollar invested in the program. That's a 4,900 percent return on investment.

But if young people want to apply, they should "visit, write, or call the local Job Service Office, the nearest OA or SAA office (listed in the blue pages of the telephone directory), or employer or union engaged in the trade you want to enter."

Seriously, the blue pages?

There's a lot of room for improvement, not just in the Department of Labor's application process. Apologies and inspirational commencement addresses are nice, but if writers aren't offering sound advice, or concrete solutions, then, really, they're just profiting from our misfortune—the same misfortune they are so sorry about.

Things are tough, we all get that. But telling us that we're poor doesn't change the fact that we're poor.

Millions of millennials, myself included, are working hard every day so that there will be no reason to apologize. If the previous generation made a big doo-doo pile out of the environment and the economy, we'll make it our jobs to clean things up.

Eventually, I'll find something, even if it's underpaid or underappreciated. That's OK. Like most millennials, I'm more interested in finding purposeful work than in making millions.

Until that time, let's let up on the millennial microscope, and start looking at the bigger picture—for the sake of my skin, and for all of ours.

Where Have the Good Men Gone?

KAY S. HYMOWITZ

Kay S. Hymowitz is a fellow at The Manhattan Institute (a conservative think tank) and a contributing editor of City Journal. *She writes on childhood, family issues, poverty, and cultural change in America. The following essay, which appeared in the* Wall Street Journal *on February 19, 2011, is adapted from her book* Manning Up: How the Rise of Women Has Turned Men into Boys.

Not so long ago, the average American man in his 20s had achieved most of the milestones of adulthood: a high-school diploma, financial independence, marriage and children. Today, most men in their 20s hang out in a novel sort of limbo, a hybrid state of semi-hormonal adolescence and responsible self-reliance. This "pre-adulthood" has much to recommend it, especially for the college-educated. But it's time to state what has become obvious to legions of frustrated young women: It doesn't bring out the best in men.

"We are sick of hooking up with guys," writes the comedian Julie Klausner, author of a touchingly funny 2010 book, *I Don't Care About Your Band: What I Learned from Indie Rockers, Trust Funders, Pornographers, Felons,* *Faux-Sensitive Hipsters and Other Guys I've Dated.* What Ms. Klausner means by "guys" is males who are not boys or men but something in between. "Guys talk about 'Star Wars' like it's not a movie made for people half their age; a guy's idea of a perfect night is to hang around the PlayStation with his bandmates, or a trip to Vegas with his college friends.... They are more like the kids we babysat than the dads who drove us home." One female reviewer of Ms. Klausner's book wrote, "I had to stop several times while reading and think: Wait, did I date this same guy?"

For most of us, the cultural habitat of pre-adulthood no longer seems noteworthy. After all, popular culture has been crowded with pre-adults for almost two decades. Hollywood started the affair in the early 1990s with movies like "Singles," "Reality Bites," "Single White Female" and "Swingers." Television soon deepened the relationship, giving us the agreeable company of Monica, Joey, Rachel and Ross; Jerry, Elaine, George and Kramer; Carrie, Miranda, et al.

But for all its familiarity, pre-adulthood represents a momentous sociological development. It's no exaggeration to say that having large numbers of single young men and women living independently, while also having enough disposable income to avoid ever messing up their kitchens, is something entirely new in human experience. Yes, at other points in Western history young people have waited well into their 20s to marry, and yes, office girls and bachelor lawyers have been working and finding amusement in cities for more than a century. But their numbers and their money supply were always relatively small. Today's pre-adults are a different matter. They are a major demographic event.

5   What also makes pre-adulthood something new is its radical reversal of the sexual hierarchy. Among pre-adults, women are the first sex. They graduate from college in greater numbers (among Americans ages 25 to 34, 34 percent of women now have a bachelor degree but just 27 percent of men), and they have higher GPAs. As most professors tell it, they also have more confidence and drive. These strengths carry women through their 20s, when they are more likely than men to be in grad school and making strides in the workplace. In a number of cities, they are even out-earning their brothers and boyfriends.

Still, for these women, one key question won't go away: Where have the good men gone? Their male peers often come across as aging frat boys, maladroit geeks or grubby slackers—a gender gap neatly crystallized by the director Judd Apatow in his hit 2007 movie *Knocked Up.* The story's hero is 23-year-old Ben Stone (Seth Rogen), who has a drunken fling with Allison Scott (Katherine Heigl) and gets her pregnant. Ben lives in a Los Angeles crash pad with a group of grubby friends who spend their days playing videogames, smoking pot and unsuccessfully planning to launch a porn Web site. Allison, by contrast, is on her way up as a television reporter and lives in a neatly kept apartment with what appear to be clean sheets and towels. Once she decides to have the baby, she figures out what needs to be done and does it. Ben can only stumble his way toward being a responsible grownup.

So where did these pre-adults come from? You might assume that their appearance is a result of spoiled 24-year-olds trying to prolong the campus drinking and hook-up scene while exploiting the largesse of mom and dad. But the causes run deeper than that. Beginning in

Women now outpace their male peers in getting through college ...

☐ Men   ☐ Women

Americans with a bachelor's degree or higher, by age

... and thus have better employment prospects.

Unemployment rates, age 20 or older

Men

Women

The percentage of those of both sexes who marry in their 20s has declined dramatically ...

Americans age 25–29 who were never married

Source: U.S. Census Bureau (bachelor's, degrees never stated): Bureau of Labor Statistics (Unemployment rates): UN, Economic Commissions for Europe (mean marriage age)

the 1980s, the economic advantage of higher education—the "college premium"—began to increase dramatically. Between 1960 and 2000, the percentage of younger adults enrolled in college or graduate school more than doubled. In the "knowledge economy," good jobs go to those with degrees. And degrees take years.

Another factor in the lengthening of the road to adulthood is our increasingly labyrinthine labor market. The past decades' economic expansion and the digital revolution have transformed the high-end labor market into a fierce competition for the most stimulating, creative and glamorous jobs. Fields that attract ambitious young men and women often require years of moving between school and internships, between internships and jobs, laterally and horizontally between jobs, and between cities in the U.S. and abroad. The knowledge economy gives the educated young an unprecedented opportunity to think about work in personal terms. They are looking not just for jobs but for "careers," work in which they can exercise their talents and express their deepest passions. They expect their careers to give shape to their identity. For today's pre-adults, "what you do" is almost synonymous with "who you are," and starting a family is seldom part of the picture.

Pre-adulthood can be compared to adolescence, an idea invented in the mid-20th century as American

teenagers were herded away from the fields and the workplace and into that new institution, the high school. For a long time, the poor and recent immigrants were not part of adolescent life; they went straight to work, since their families couldn't afford the lost labor and income. But the country had grown rich enough to carve out space and time to create a more highly educated citizenry and work force. Teenagers quickly became a marketing and cultural phenomenon. They also earned their own psychological profile. One of the most influential of the psychologists of adolescence was Erik Erikson, who described the stage as a "moratorium," a limbo between childhood and adulthood characterized by role confusion, emotional turmoil and identity conflict.

Like adolescents in the 20th century, today's pre-adults have been wait-listed for adulthood. Marketers and culture creators help to promote pre-adulthood as a lifestyle. And like adolescence, pre-adulthood is a class-based social phenomenon, reserved for the relatively well-to-do. Those who don't get a four-year college degree are not in a position to compete for the more satisfying jobs of the knowledge economy.

But pre-adults differ in one major respect from adolescents. They write their own biographies, and they do it from scratch. Sociologists use the term "life script" to describe a particular society's ordering of life's large events

and stages. Though such scripts vary across cultures, the archetypal plot is deeply rooted in our biological nature. The invention of adolescence did not change the large Roman numerals of the American script. Adults continued to be those who took over the primary tasks of the economy and culture. For women, the central task usually involved the day-to-day rearing of the next generation; for men, it involved protecting and providing for their wives and children. If you followed the script, you became an adult, a temporary custodian of the social order until your own old age and demise.

Unlike adolescents, however, pre-adults don't know what is supposed to come next. For them, marriage and parenthood come in many forms, or can be skipped altogether. In 1970, just 16 percent of Americans ages 25 to 29 had never been married; today that's true of an astonishing 55 percent of the age group. In the U.S., the mean age at first marriage has been climbing toward 30 (a point past which it has already gone in much of Europe). It is no wonder that so many young Americans suffer through a "quarterlife crisis," a period of depression and worry over their future.

Given the rigors of contemporary career-building, pre-adults who do marry and start families do so later than ever before in human history. Husbands, wives and children are a drag on the footloose life required for the early career track and identity search. Pre-adulthood has also confounded the primordial search for a mate. It has delayed a stable sense of identity, dramatically expanded the pool of possible spouses, mystified courtship routines and helped to throw into doubt the very meaning of marriage. In 1970, to cite just one of many numbers proving the point, nearly seven in ten 25-year-olds were married; by 2000, only one-third had reached that milestone.

American men have been struggling with finding an acceptable adult identity since at least the mid-19th century. We often hear about the miseries of women confined to the domestic sphere once men began to work in offices and factories away from home. But it seems that men didn't much like the arrangement either. They balked at the stuffy propriety of the bourgeois parlor, as they did later at the banal activities of the suburban living room. They turned to hobbies and adventures, like hunting and fishing. At midcentury, fathers who at first had refused to put down the money to buy those newfangled televisions changed their minds when the networks began broadcasting boxing matches and baseball games. The arrival of *Playboy* in the 1950s seemed like the ultimate protest against male domestication; think of the refusal implied by the magazine's title alone.

In his disregard for domestic life, the playboy was prologue for today's pre-adult male. Unlike the playboy with his jazz and art-filled pad, however, our boy rebel is a creature of the animal house. In

the 1990s, *Maxim*, the rude, lewd and hugely popular "lad" magazine arrived from England. Its philosophy and tone were so juvenile, so entirely undomesticated, that it made *Playboy* look like Camus.

15   At the same time, young men were tuning in to cable channels like Comedy Central, the Cartoon Network and Spike, whose shows reflected the adolescent male preferences of its targeted male audiences. They watched movies with overgrown boy actors like Steve Carell, Luke and Owen Wilson, Jim Carrey, Adam Sandler, Will Farrell and Seth Rogen, cheering their awesome car crashes, fart jokes, breast and crotch shots, beer pong competitions and other frat-boy pranks. Americans had always struck foreigners as youthful, even childlike, in their energy and optimism. But this was too much.

What explains this puerile shallowness? I see it as an expression of our cultural uncertainty about the social role of men. It's been an almost universal rule of civilization that girls became women simply by reaching physical maturity, but boys had to pass a test. They needed to demonstrate courage, physical prowess or mastery of the necessary skills. The goal was to prove their competence as protectors and providers. Today, however, with women moving ahead in our advanced economy, husbands and fathers are now optional, and the qualities of character men once needed to play their roles—fortitude, stoicism, courage,

fidelity—are obsolete, even a little embarrassing.

Today's pre-adult male is like an actor in a drama in which he only knows what he shouldn't say. He has to compete in a fierce job market, but he can't act too bossy or self-confident. He should be sensitive but not paternalistic, smart but not cocky. To deepen his predicament, because he is single, his advisers and confidants are generally undomesticated guys just like him.

Single men have never been civilization's most responsible actors; they continue to be more troubled and less successful than men who deliberately choose to become husbands and fathers. So we can be disgusted if some of them continue to live in rooms decorated with "Star Wars" posters and crushed beer cans and to treat women like disposable estrogen toys, but we shouldn't be surprised.

Relatively affluent, free of family responsibilities, and entertained by an array of media devoted to his every pleasure, the single young man can live in pig heaven—and often does. Women put up with him for a while, but then in fear and disgust either give up on any idea of a husband and kids or just go to a sperm bank and get the DNA without the troublesome man. But these rational choices on the part of women only serve to legitimize men's attachment to the sand box. Why should they grow up? No one needs them anyway. There's nothing they have to do.

They might as well just have another beer.

You *Can* Go Home Again

EVE TUSHNET

Eve Tushnet is a freelance writer most frequently cited for her views as a gay, celibate, Catholic convert. She blogs at Patheos.com *and is a frequent contributor to* The Weekly Standard, *a conservative news and opinion magazine. This commentary appeared in the magazine's September 2, 2013 edition.*

A few years ago I was getting a ride home from a party with a guy in his early twenties. I lived in a gentrified neighborhood I could no longer pretend to afford, and he lived, it emerged, with his parents. "Good for you," I said. "I think that's great."

We hit a stoplight and he turned to look at me. "Do you?" he asked, with a sudden edge of cynicism in his voice. "Do you *really*?" I could hear what he was thinking: *I guess you're trying to be nice or whatever, but nobody thinks it's "great" when a guy—who should be a man—lives with Mommy and*

Daddy. One of us was making a foolish choice that was destroying her savings, but the more frugal one bore the weight of societal stigma.

The proportion of young adults (aged 18 to 31) who live with one or both parents stayed basically the same between 1968, the earliest year for which we have data, and 2007. What proportion was normal for those four decades? About a third, 32 percent. A recent Pew Research report found that in 2012 that number had risen to 36 percent, a noticeable increase but not necessarily a sign of social crisis—especially not when you consider that college students living in dorms are still counted as "living with their parents," and college enrollment has been rising since 2007 as well. More men than women live with Mom and/ or Dad, which might seem like an effect of the ongoing "mancession"—in which men's labor-force participation has plummeted—but men have been more likely to live with their parents as adults since at least 1968, partly because men typically marry later than women. In fact, the gender gap was greater in 1968 than today.

Americans believe that adults who live with their parents have "failed to launch"; man-boys spend their days playing *World of Warcraft* while Mom does their laundry. This narrative is persuasive in part because many of the trends driving the increase in "returning to the nest" are bad, so returning is correlated with bad things, like unemployment and underemployment. If you see an unemployed young adult living with his parents, maybe he's living with them because he's unemployed—or maybe his unemployment and his living situation have a common cause, which is that he's an immature loser.

5   And living with your parents can make it harder to grow up. There's less pressure to take responsibility for yourself, and pressure often forces us past what we believe to be our limitations. A 2008 study interviewing young adults who lived at home found that few contributed financially to the household or did chores. One young woman explained, "I was excited to have my mother to cook for me, and always having a full refrigerator."

These attitudes are by no means universal (and the study itself wasn't intended to be representative), as some young adults paid rent and utilities even against their parents' wishes. And part of the problem in stigmatizing "returning to the nest" is that the category lumps together a huge range of circumstances. A 2011 study found that older "parental co-residers" (those who live with their parents after age 27) were likelier to be disabled, and so were their parents; the parents were also more likely to be single-never married, divorced, or widowed. This paints a different picture, of families with limited resources banding together to get through tough times.

Given the powerful trends of rising part-time work and job instability, rising university attendance, and delayed or disappearing marriage, I don't think there's much reason to believe that the modest rise in living at home is the result of some sudden onslaught of millennial laziness or unwillingness to start at the bottom of the career ladder.

In fact, starting your adult life in your parents' home was not historically stigmatized, precisely because it offered young adults an oasis of stability in a chaotic economy. The economic journalist Megan Mc Ardle writes,

> My grandfather worked as a grocery boy until he was 26, in the depths of the Great Depression. For six years, he supported a wife on that salary—and no, it's not because You Used To Be Able To Support A Family On A Grocery Boy's Wages Until These Republicans Ruined Everything. He and my grandmother moved into a room in his parents' home, cut a hole through the wall for their stovepipe and set up housekeeping. They got married on Thanksgiving, because that was the only day he could get off.

Two huge differences between the Depression era and today leap out from McArdle's account. One is the sense that what her grandparents did was normal, not shameful. But the other is that they did it as young marrieds. This is perhaps the biggest negative effect of living at home these days: It postpones marriage and, in many cases, childbearing. Today, young adults believe that they can't get married—that it's *wrong* to get married—before they've achieved economic independence. For reasons that can be crudely summarized as "terror of divorce," young adults believe that it's only morally acceptable to get married once you've undergone an extensive period of finding yourself and attaining financial stability.

10   The belief that young adults must be able to live independently before they can marry is new, and it's damaging. At the pregnancy center where

I volunteer, about half of the women intend to marry their children's father eventually. What are they waiting for? A steady job, an escape from welfare and charity, a sense of financial solid ground. But if a woman names one specific goal she must attain before she can marry, 9 times out of 10 that goal is an apartment of her own: moving out from under Mom's roof. So she puts her name on the years-long waiting list for Section 8 subsidized housing, and she applies for yet another part-time job, and she goes back to community college, and she hopes that her relationship with her baby's father will survive. Without marriage, it usually doesn't.

Almost every form of dependence is stigmatized in America's individualist culture. This particular form of dependence has also been redefined to be as individualist as possible (you can't marry *and* you're not expected to care for your parents) and then shamed both for its dependence and for its narcissism. But the stigma hasn't worked. Everybody doing it feels it to be shameful, yet the shame has not made us do it less. Expecting and then *honoring* mutual dependence might be a better option.

Shortly after that awkward car ride, I finally left my fancified neighborhood. I was older than most "boomerang kids," but like many of them I was single and dealing with personal problems—I'd gotten sober a few months earlier and desperately wanted a break from the surroundings in which I'd done my worst drinking—and I fled back home seeking both financial and emotional relief. I paid no rent and did exactly one chore, cleaning the catbox, so I am the problem. But I also exemplified "returning to the nest" as a useful adaptive strategy: Six months later I moved out, much improved in both spirit and bank account. This is one way the boomerang story ends well. But it would be an equally happy ending, although more radically challenging to American norms of independence, if I had remained at home and begun to make real household contributions of money and care.

■ ■ ■ **FOR CLASS DISCUSSION**   **Millennials in the Workplace**

1. The articles by Kathryn Tyler and Erin Burns and the *America* editorial outline characteristics typically associated with a Millennial employee. Choose one of the characteristics and explore its value for a new employee first as a believer and then a doubter. How might the characteristic you've chosen be seen as a liability by a potential employer? How might that same characteristic be viewed as an asset to an employer?

2. Raffi Wineburg and Eve Tushnet discuss the effects of the current job-scarce economy on the job market for younger workers. Do some research on the job outlook for your field or for recent college graduates. What are the challenges facing job seekers right now? What are some of the opportunities? Based on your research, what advice would you give to a friend just entering the job market?

3. To what extent do the stereotypes associated with Millennials seem fair? What do you think is the origin of these stereotypes? To what degree do the pop culture examples cited by Hymowitz contribute to the creation of stereotypes or the building of expectations? To what degree do Millennials contribute to or define themselves by these same pop culture depictions of young adults?

4. When discussing the challenges of the Millennial Generation, some of the authors in this unit are themselves Millennials, while others view Millennials

from the perspective of an older generation. How would you characterize the rhetorical differences between such articles? How do writers from within the Millennial Generation frame the issues differently from those outside the generation?

WRITING ASSIGNMENT **Multimodal Argument: A Storyboard or Cartoon**

Many of the arguments presented in this unit are made by members of older generations (Generation X, Baby Boomers) as they seek to understand the Millennial Generation. But how does the Millennial Generation (of which you may be a member) view itself in relation to the world? Construct a visual argument in the form of a cartoon or storyboard of at least four frames in which you respond to one of the claims made about Millennials or present your own argument about a challenge or opportunity facing this generation. For instance, you might respond to the claim about Millennial employees' lack of loyalty through a storyboard that illustrates the high number of layoffs and the reduced number of career opportunities available to recent graduates. Or you might draw a cartoon illustrating the expectations placed upon young adults in their twenties. You may wish to consult Chapter 9 on "Analyzing Visual Arguments" in this book for tips on constructing a visual argument. ◼

Choices for a Sustainable World

In *Climate Change 2013*, the most recent report of the U.N. Intergovernmental Panel on Climate Change, the world's leading climate researchers re-affirm the scientific conclusion that human-influenced climate change threatens our global environment. Much of the public debate has now shifted from arguing about causes of global warming to arguing about potential consequences and solutions. The dominant question is no longer whether climate change is happening but what actions we should take to mitigate its impact. What choices should we make as a society? What actions should we expect of our government? What life choices should we make as ethical members of society when we consider how our individual actions affect both our close neighbors and those who live around the globe?

At stake for humanity is whether humans can live more sustainably, preserving the environment without ruining the world's economies. A focus on sustainability means recognizing that the earth's resources are limited, that these resources are being over-drawn, that some countries such as the United States and China are responsible for a much larger percentage of environmental damage than others, and that solutions to the environmental crisis ought not to lead to an economic collapse that plunges people into chaos and poverty. Awareness of the suffering caused by either environmental damage or economic collapse leads us to reevaluate the traditional choices we have made in using the world's resources.

The readings in this unit invite you into controversies sparked by three questions: (1) Can the world's energy needs be feasibly met with renewable sources and, if so, how soon? (2) What is the environmental and economic role of natural gas (obtained through fracking of shale structures) as a bridge toward a sustainable future? And (3) to what extent can individual citizens create their own sustainable local communities that constrain the excesses of corporate capitalism? This last question, which focuses on permaculture and farming, connects the issue of sustainability to the earlier unit on food production (pages 406–431).

A Path to Sustainable Energy by 2030

MARK Z. JACOBSON AND MARK A. DELUCCHI

Mark Z. Jacobson is a professor of civil and environmental engineering and director of the Atmosphere/Energy Program at Stanford University. He is also a senior fellow at the Woods Institute for the Environment and the Precourt Institute for Energy, both at Stanford. The main goal of his research is to better understand severe atmospheric problems such as air pollution and global warming, and to develop and analyze large-scale renewable energy solutions to them. Mark A. Delucchi is a research scientist at the Institute of Transportation Studies, University of California, Davis. He specializes in economics, environmental, engineering, and planning analyses of transportation systems and technologies. The essay that follows appeared in Scientific American *in November, 2009.*

Wind, water and solar technologies can provide 100 percent of the world's energy, eliminating all fossil fuels. Here's how.

In December leaders from around the world will meet in Copenhagen to try to agree on cutting back greenhouse gas emissions for decades to come. The most effective step to implement that goal would be a massive shift away from fossil fuels to clean, renewable energy sources. If leaders can have confidence that such a transformation is possible, they might commit to an historic agreement. We think they can.

A year ago former vice president Al Gore threw down a gauntlet: to repower America with 100 percent carbon-free electricity within 10 years. As the two of us started to evaluate the feasibility of such a change, we took on an even larger challenge: to determine how 100 percent of the world's energy, for all purposes, could be supplied by wind, water and solar resources, by as early as 2030. Our plan is presented here.

Scientists have been building to this moment for at least a decade, analyzing various pieces of the challenge. Most recently, a 2009 Stanford University study ranked energy systems according to their impacts on global warming, pollution, water supply, land use, wildlife and other concerns. The very best options were wind, solar, geothermal, tidal and hydroelectric power—all of which are driven by wind, water or sunlight (referred to as WWS). Nuclear power, coal with carbon capture, and ethanol were all poorer options, as were oil and natural gas. The study also found that battery-electric vehicles and hydrogen fuel-cell vehicles recharged by WWS options would largely eliminate pollution from the transportation sector.

5   Our plan calls for millions of wind turbines, water machines and solar installations. The numbers are large, but the scale is not an insurmountable hurdle; society has achieved massive transformations before. During World War II, the U.S. retooled automobile factories to produce 300,000 aircraft, and other countries produced 486,000 more. In 1956 the U.S. began building the Interstate Highway System, which after 35 years extended for 47,000 miles, changing commerce and society.

Is it feasible to transform the world's energy systems? Could it be accomplished in two decades? The answers depend on the technologies chosen, the availability of critical materials, and economic and political factors.

Clean Technologies Only

Renewable energy comes from enticing sources: wind, which also produces waves; water, which includes hydroelectric, tidal and geothermal energy (water heated by hot underground rock); and sun, which includes photovoltaics and solar power plants that focus sunlight to heat a fluid that drives a turbine to generate electricity. Our plan includes only technologies that work or are close to working today on a large scale, rather than those that may exist 20 or 30 years from now.

To ensure that our system remains clean, we consider only technologies that have near-zero emissions of greenhouse gases and air pollutants over their entire life cycle, including construction, operation and decommissioning. For example, when burned in vehicles, even the most ecologically acceptable sources of ethanol create air pollution that will cause the same mortality level as when gasoline is burned. Nuclear power results in up to 25 times more carbon emissions than wind energy, when reactor construction and uranium refining and transport are considered. Carbon capture and sequestration technology can reduce carbon dioxide emissions from coal-fired power plants but will increase air pollutants and will extend all the other deleterious effects of coal mining, transport and processing, because more coal must be burned to power the capture and storage steps. Similarly, we consider only technologies that do not present significant waste disposal or terrorism risks.

In our plan, WWS will supply electric power for heating and transportation—industries that will have to revamp if the world has any hope of slowing climate change. We have assumed that most fossil-fuel heating (as well as ovens and stoves) can be replaced by electric systems and that most fossil-fuel transportation can be replaced by battery and fuel-cell vehicles. Hydrogen, produced by using WWS electricity to split water (electrolysis), would power fuel cells and be burned in airplanes and by industry.

Plenty of Supply

10   Today the maximum power consumed worldwide at any given moment is about 12.5 trillion watts (terawatts, or TW), according to the U.S. Energy Information Administration. The agency projects that in 2030 the world will require 16.9 TW of power as global population and living standards rise, with about 2.8 TW in the U.S. The mix of sources is similar to today's, heavily dependent on fossil fuels. If, however, the planet were powered entirely by WWS, with no fossil-fuel or biomass combustion, an intriguing savings would occur. Global power demand would be only 11.5 TW, and U.S. demand would be 1.8 TW. That decline occurs because, in most cases, electrification is a more efficient way to use energy. For example, only 17 to 20 percent of the energy in gasoline is used to move a vehicle (the rest is wasted as heat), whereas 75 to 86 percent of the electricity delivered to an electric vehicle goes into motion.

Even if demand did rise to 16.9 TW, WWS sources could provide far more power. Detailed studies by us and others indicate that energy from the wind, worldwide, is about 1,700 TW. Solar, alone, offers 6,500 TW. Of course, wind and sun out in the open seas, over high mountains and across protected regions would not be available. If we subtract these and low-wind areas not likely to be developed, we are still left with 40 to 85 TW for wind and 580 TW for solar, each far beyond future human demand. Yet currently we generate only 0.02 TW of wind power and 0.008 TW of solar. These sources hold an incredible amount of untapped potential.

The other WWS technologies will help create a flexible range of options. Although all the sources can expand greatly, for practical reasons, wave power can be extracted only near coastal areas. Many geothermal sources are too deep to be tapped economically. And even though hydroelectric power now exceeds all other WWS sources, most of the suitable large reservoirs are already in use.

The Plan: Power Plants Required

Clearly, enough renewable energy exists. How, then, would we transition to a new infrastructure to provide the world with 11.5 TW? We have chosen a mix of technologies emphasizing wind and solar, with about 9 percent of demand met by mature water-related methods. (Other combinations of wind and solar could be as successful.)

Wind supplies 51 percent of the demand, provided by 3.8 million large wind turbines (each rated at five megawatts) worldwide. Although that quantity may sound enormous, it is interesting to note that the world manufactures 73 million cars and light trucks every year. Another 40 percent of the power comes from photovoltaics and concentrated solar plants, with about 30 percent of the photovoltaic output from rooftop panels on homes and commercial buildings. About 89,000 photovoltaic and concentrated solar power plants, averaging 300 megawatts apiece, would be needed. Our mix also includes 900 hydroelectric stations worldwide, 70 percent of which are already in place.

15   Only about 0.8 percent of the wind base is installed today. The worldwide footprint of the 3.8 million turbines would be less than 50 square kilometers (smaller than Manhattan). When the needed spacing between them is figured, they would occupy about 1 percent of the earth's land, but the empty space among turbines could be used for agriculture or ranching or as open land or ocean. The nonrooftop photovoltaics and concentrated solar plants would occupy about 0.33 percent of the planet's land. Building such an extensive infrastructure will take time. But so did the current power plant network. And remember that if we stick with fossil fuels, demand by 2030 will rise to 16.9 TW, requiring about 13,000 large new coal plants, which themselves would occupy a lot more land, as would the mining to supply them.

The Materials Hurdle

The scale of the WWS infrastructure is not a barrier. But a few materials needed to build it could be scarce or subject to price manipulation.

Enough concrete and steel exist for the millions of wind turbines, and both those commodities are fully recyclable. The most problematic materials may be rare-earth metals such as neodymium used in turbine gearboxes. Although the metals are not in short supply, the low-cost sources are concentrated in China, so countries such as the U.S. could be trading dependence on Middle Eastern oil for dependence on Far Eastern metals. Manufacturers are moving toward gearless turbines, however, so that limitation may become moot.

Photovoltaic cells rely on amorphous or crystalline silicon, cadmium telluride, or copper iridium selenide and sulfide. Limited supplies of tellurium and indium could reduce the prospects for some types of thin-film solar cells, though not for all; the other types might be able to take up the slack. Large-scale production could be restricted by the silver that cells require, but finding ways to reduce the silver content could tackle that hurdle. Recycling parts from old cells could ameliorate material difficulties as well.

Three components could pose challenges for building millions of electric vehicles: rare-earth metals for electric motors, lithium for lithium-ion batteries and platinum for fuel cells. More than half the world's lithium reserves lie in Bolivia and Chile. That concentration, combined with rapidly growing demand, could raise prices significantly. More problematic is the claim by Meridian International Research that not enough economically recoverable lithium exists to build anywhere near the number of batteries needed in a global electric-vehicle economy. Recycling could change the equation, but the economics of recycling depend in part on whether batteries are made with easy recyclability in mind, an issue the industry is aware of. The long-term use of platinum also depends on recycling; current available reserves would sustain annual production of 20 million fuel-cell vehicles, along with existing industrial uses, for fewer than 100 years.

Smart Mix for Reliability

20   A new infrastructure must provide energy on demand at least as reliably as the existing infrastructure. WWS technologies generally suffer less downtime than traditional sources. The average U.S. coal plant is offline 12.5 percent of the year for scheduled and unscheduled maintenance. Modern wind turbines have a down time of less than 2 percent on land and less than 5 percent at sea. Photovoltaic systems are also at less than 2 percent. Moreover, when an individual wind, solar or wave device is down, only a small fraction of production is affected; when a coal, nuclear or natural gas plant goes offline, a large chunk of generation is lost.

The main WWS challenge is that the wind does not always blow and the sun does not always shine in a given location. Intermittency problems can be mitigated by a smart balance of sources, such as generating a base supply from steady geothermal or tidal power, relying on wind at night when it is often plentiful, using solar by day and turning to a reliable source such as hydroelectric that can be turned on and off quickly to smooth out supply or meet peak demand. For example, interconnecting wind farms that are only 100 to 200 miles apart can compensate for hours of zero power at any one farm should the wind not be blowing there. Also helpful is interconnecting geographically dispersed sources so they can back up one another, installing smart electric meters in homes that automatically recharge electric vehicles when demand is low and building facilities that store power for later use.

Because the wind often blows during stormy conditions when the sun does not shine and the sun often shines on calm days with little wind, combining wind and solar can go a long way toward meeting demand, especially when geothermal provides a steady base and hydroelectric can be called on to fill in the gaps.

As Cheap as Coal

The mix of WWS sources in our plan can reliably supply the residential, commercial, industrial and transportation sectors. The logical next question is whether the power would be affordable. For each technology, we calculated how much it would cost a producer to generate power and transmit it across the grid. We included the annualized cost of capital, land, operations, maintenance, energy storage to help offset intermittent supply, and transmission. Today the cost of wind, geothermal and hydroelectric are all less than seven cents a kilowatt-hour (¢/kWh); wave and solar are higher. But by 2020 and beyond wind, wave and hydro are expected to be 4¢/kWh or less.

For comparison, the average cost in the U.S. in 2007 of conventional power generation and transmission was about 7¢/kWh, and it is projected to be 8¢/kWh in 2020. Power from wind turbines, for example, already costs about the same or less than it does from a new coal or natural gas plant, and in the future wind power is expected to be the least costly of all options. The competitive cost of wind has made it the second-largest source of new electric power generation in the U.S. for the past three years, behind natural gas and ahead of coal.

25   Solar power is relatively expensive now but should be competitive as early as 2020. A careful analysis by Vasilis Fthenakis of Brookhaven National Laboratory indicates that within 10 years, photovoltaic system costs could drop to about 10¢/kWh, including long-distance transmission and the cost of compressed-air storage of power for use at night. The same analysis estimates that concentrated solar power systems with enough thermal storage to generate electricity 24 hours a day in spring, summer and fall could deliver electricity at 10¢/kWh or less.

Transportation in a WWS world will be driven by batteries or fuel cells, so we should compare the economics of these electric vehicles with that of internal-combustion-engine vehicles. Detailed analyses by one of us (Delucchi) and Tim Lipman of the University of California, Berkeley, have indicated that mass-produced electric vehicles with advanced lithium-ion or nickel metal-hydride batteries could have a full lifetime cost per mile (including battery replacements) that is comparable with that of a gasoline vehicle, when gasoline sells for more than $2 a gallon.

When the so-called externality costs (the monetary value of damages to human health, the environment and climate) of fossil-fuel generation are taken into account, WWS technologies become even more cost-competitive.

Overall construction cost for a WWS system might be on the order of $100 trillion worldwide, over 20 years, not including transmission. But this is not money handed out by governments or consumers. It is investment that is paid back through the sale of electricity and energy. And again, relying on traditional sources would raise output from 12.5 to 16.9 TW, requiring thousands more of those plants, costing roughly $10 trillion, not to mention tens of trillions of dollars more in health, environmental and security costs. The WWS plan gives the world a new, clean, efficient energy system rather than an old, dirty, inefficient one.

Political Will

Our analyses strongly suggest that the costs of WWS will become competitive with traditional sources. In the interim, however, certain forms of WWS power will be significantly more costly than fossil power. Some combination of WWS subsidies and carbon taxes would thus be needed for a time. A feed-in tariff (FIT) program to cover the difference between generation cost and wholesale electricity prices is especially effective at scaling-up new technologies. Combining FITs with a so-called declining clock auction, in which the right to sell power to the grid goes to the lowest bidders, provides continuing incentive for WWS developers to lower costs. As that happens, FITs can be phased out. FITs have been implemented in a number of European countries and a few U.S. states and have been quite successful in stimulating solar power in Germany.

30   Taxing fossil fuels or their use to reflect their environmental damages also makes sense. But at a minimum, existing subsidies for fossil energy, such as tax benefits for exploration and extraction, should be eliminated to level the playing field. Misguided promotion of alternatives that are less desirable than WWS power, such as farm and production subsidies for biofuels, should also be ended, because it delays deployment of cleaner systems. For their part, legislators crafting policy must find ways to resist lobbying by the entrenched energy industries.

Finally, each nation needs to be willing to invest in a robust, long-distance transmission system that can carry large quantities of WWS power from remote regions where it is often greatest—such as the Great Plains for wind and the desert Southwest for solar in the U.S.—to centers of consumption, typically cities. Reducing consumer demand during peak usage periods also requires a smart grid that gives generators and consumers much more control over electricity usage hour by hour.

A large-scale wind, water and solar energy system can reliably supply the world's needs, significantly benefiting climate, air quality, water quality, ecology and energy security. As we have shown, the obstacles are primarily political, not technical. A combination of feed-in tariffs plus incentives for providers to reduce costs, elimination of fossil subsidies and an intelligently expanded grid could be enough to ensure rapid deployment. Of course, changes in the real-world power and transportation industries will have to overcome sunk investments in existing infrastructure. But with sensible policies, nations could set a goal of generating 25 percent of their new energy supply with WWS sources in 10 to 15 years and almost 100 percent of new supply in 20 to 30 years. With extremely aggressive policies, all existing fossil-fuel capacity could theoretically be retired and replaced in the same period, but with more modest and likely policies full replacement may take 40 to 50 years. Either way, clear leadership is needed, or else nations will keep trying technologies promoted by industries rather than vetted by scientists.

A decade ago it was not clear that a global WWS system would be technically or economically feasible. Having shown that it is, we hope global leaders can figure out how to make WWS power politically feasible as well. They can start by committing to meaningful climate and renewable energy goals now.

Vaclav Smil: "The Great Hope for a Quick and Sweeping Transition to Renewable Energy Is Wishful Thinking"

ASHUTOSH JOGALEKAR

Ashutosh (Ash) Jogalekar is a chemist interested in the history and philosophy of science. He maintains the popular science blog The Curious Wavefunction *as part of the Scientific* American Blog Network. *The following blog post, which appeared on January 13, 2014, is Jogalekar's response to a* Scientific American *article by Vaclav Smil, a Distinguished Professor Emeritus at the University of Manitoba in Canada. Smil is widely admired for his data-rich (but often bleak) analyses of contemporary issues related to energy and food production.*

That's Vaclav Smil, the prolific University of Manitoba thinker writing in this month's issue of *Scientific American*. When Smil says something I usually listen. In the last two decades he has written more than 30 books on almost every imaginable aspect of energy, the environment and the biosphere. The typical Smil approach—and one that has recently led Bill Gates to call him one of the authors whose books he most looks forward to—is to wrap an energy related topic in a tight blanket of facts and figures, transporting discussion from speculation and wishful thinking into hard data. Vaclav Smil is where the clouds of starry eyed energy dreams meet the cold mountain of numbers and reality.

Smil's core argument is simple and one which I have often advanced on this blog: While reasonably promising, renewable energy is simply not quick and widespread enough. It has delivered very little in terms of overall contributions to the nation's energy portfolio, and barring unexpected breakthroughs or radical policy changes, it seems set to continue on this excruciatingly slow track. This is contrary to the starry eyed dreams of renewable enthusiasts who seem to think that a renewables-dominated energy future is right around the corner.

Smil starts by noting an underappreciated fact, that only *3.35%* of the 10% or so energy that renewables are providing right now comes from "new" renewables, namely solar, wind and liquid biofuels. The majority of renewables are still of the "old" variety, hydroelectric power and wood chips. We are unlikely to see any significant expansion in the latter category, so all the promise projected for renewables would have to come from the new ones, especially from solar and wind. Sadly these two currently provide a tiny fraction of national energy needs (wind: 1.19%, solar: 0.16%).

These numbers also seem consistent with the history of energy usage. When it comes to dreams of rapid renewable expansion, as Smil tells us, history is not on our side. Even traditional sources like coal, oil and natural gas took about 50 to 75 years to contribute significantly to the energy portfolio, and unlike renewables these were sources for which base load was not a problem and the technology was largely available and cheap. The latter two factors are already stacked against renewables, which makes any possibility of their expansion in just a few decades a very tenuous proposition to say the least.

5   Smil describes the three major challenges for renewables that make their projected rapid growth murky and pessimistic. The first factor is simply the sheer growth required to meet energy needs; it's a point that cannot be stressed [too] often, but the stark fact is that increasing the share of say wind from 1.19% to 50% is not simply a matter of additional investment. Given the history of energy, the whole energy infrastructure and political establishment would have to be shaken up to even try to effect this kind of change. Concomitantly world demand, especially in the developing countries, is increasing so rapidly that even fossil fuels have a hard time keeping up, so renewables are already trying to inch uphill.

Nor are these efforts likely to bear fruit in the face of what was always a constant headache for renewables: their inability to provide base load power, something which was handily accomplished by fossil fuels as soon as they appeared on the grid:

> Wind and solar can contribute to the base load, but they alone cannot supply all of it, because the wind does not always blow, the sun is down at night and that supply cannot be predicted reliably. In countries such as Germany, where renewables have already grown substantially, wind and solar may supply anywhere from a negligible amount to roughly half of all demand during certain sunny and windy hours. These large fluctuations require backup from other power plants, typically coal- or gas-fired, or increased electricity imports. In Germany, all this variability can cause serious disruptions in electricity flow for some neighboring countries.

The third reason why renewables will face stiff opposition is largely a political and economic one, but it's still one that's daunting since it involves rejecting a way of life that has been ingrained in the economic and corporate life of this country for more than a century.

> The final factor leading to a prolonged shift is the size and cost of existing infrastructure. Even if we were given free renewable energy, it would be economically unthinkable for nations, corporations or municipalities to abandon the enormous investments they have made in the fossil-fuel system, from coal mines, oil wells, gas pipelines and refineries to millions of local filling stations—infrastructure that is worth at least $20 trillion across the world.

10   The scenario for renewables, especially as it pertains to measurable and quick expansion, thus looks rather dismal. What can we do to make this transition at least somewhat easier? Energy efficiency for one is a very pressing need; as Smil says, "Recent studies have shown that there are no insurmountable technical problems to reducing energy use by a third, both in the affluent world and in rapidly modernizing countries, notably through efficiency gains."

The second solution is to stop heavily subsidizing renewables. As Todd Myers wrote in the *Wall Street Journal,*

> *Why is solar popular? Huge taxpayer subsidies hide the actual cost. Other renewables receive a subsidy of about one cent per kwh, solar energy receives about 96 cents per kwh. We pay solar's cost in the form of taxes instead of as electric rates.*

Last year a study led by eminent environmental economist William Nordhaus pointed out that subsidies on green energy can actually increase carbon emissions, a good example if there was any of the law of unintended consequences.

The problem with subsidies actually highlights a bigger issue noted by Smil. We live in [an] era where fashions often trump facts, where governments, corporations and a public which is often fed biased information love to pick favorites. Solyndra is only one example of wasteful spending and dashed hopes engendered by wishful thinking. Technology is an unpredictable and fickle beast and its development cannot be engineered by bureaucratic fiat.

15   One way to do this (to avoid investing in failed energy policies) is to avoid picking energy winners. Governments cannot foresee which promising research and development activities will make it first to the free market, and hence they should not keep picking apparent winners only to abandon them soon for the next fashionable option (remember fast breeder reactors or fuel-cell cars running on hydrogen?). Spending on a variety of research activities is the best strategy: Who would have guessed in 1980 that during the next three decades the best return on federal investment in energy innovation would come not from work on nuclear reactors or photovoltaic cells but from work on horizontal drilling and hydraulic fracturing ("fracking") of shale deposits?

That last line actually tells us why it is indeed dangerous to hold our dreams hostage to the promise of uncertain dreams of renewable energy. In 2000, who would have foreseen the enormous and wholly unexpected economic windfall resulting from fracking, a technology that has not only led to unprecedented energy gains and independence but has also made a measurable dent in reducing greenhouse gas emissions and power plant pollution. The tale of renewables and fracking confirms something that Niels Bohr told us decades ago: prediction is very tough, especially about the future.

The U.S. Energy Story in Numbers: Energy Supply and Disposition by Type of Fuel, 1975 to 2010

U.S. ENERGY INFORMATION ADMINISTRATION

The following table tells a wealth of stories about energy production and consumption in the United States. Note how the table lets you track the growth of energy consumption from 1975–2010 or compute the rising or declining gap between domestic production of energy and domestic consumption.

TABLE 1 Energy Supply and Disposition by Type of Fuel: 1975 to 2010

[In quadrillion British thermal units (Btu) (61.32 represents 61,320,000,000,000,000). For definition of Btu, see source and text, this section]

Year	Production											Consumption					
						Renewable energy[4]											
	Total[1]	Crude oil[2]	Dry natural gas	Coal[3]	Nuclear electric power	Total[1]	Hydro-electric power[5]	Biomass[6]	Solar/ photo-voltaic	Wind	Net imports, total[7]	Total[1,8]	Petro-leum[9]	Dry natural gas[10]	Coal	Nuclear electric power	Renew-able energy,[4] total
1975	61.32	17.73	19.64	14.96	1.90	4.69	3.16	1.50	(NA)	(NA)	11.71	71.97	32.73	19.95	12.66	1.90	4.69
1980	67.18	18.25	19.91	18.60	2.74	5.43	2.90	2.48	(NA)	(NA)	12.10	78.07	34.21	20.24	15.42	2.74	5.43
1985	67.70	18.99	16.98	19.33	4.08	6.08	2.97	3.02	(Z)	(Z)	7.58	76.39	30.93	17.70	17.48	4.08	5.43
1990	70.71	15.57	18.33	22.49	6.10	6.04	3.05	2.74	0.06	0.03	14.07	84.49	33.55	19.60	19.17	6.10	6.04
1995	71.17	13.89	19.08	22.13	7.08	6.56	3.21	3.10	0.07	0.03	17.75	91.03	34.44	22.67	20.09	7.08	6.56
1996	72.49	13.72	19.34	22.79	7.09	7.01	3.59	3.16	0.07	0.03	19.07	94.02	35.68	23.09	21.00	7.09	7.01
1997	72.47	13.66	19.39	23.31	6.60	7.02	3.64	3.11	0.07	0.03	20.70	94.60	36.16	23.22	21.45	6.60	7.02
1998	72.88	13.24	19.61	24.05	7.07	6.49	3.30	2.93	0.07	0.03	22.28	95.02	36.82	22.83	21.66	7.07	6.49
1999	71.74	12.45	19.34	23.30	7.61	6.52	3.27	2.97	0.07	0.05	23.54	96.65	37.84	22.91	21.62	7.61	6.52
2000	71.33	12.36	19.66	22.74	7.86	6.10	2.81	3.01	0.07	0.06	24.97	98.81	38.26	23.82	22.58	7.86	6.11
2001	71.74	12.28	20.17	23.55	8.03	5.16	2.24	2.62	0.06	0.07	26.39	96.17	38.19	22.77	21.91	8.03	5.16
2002	70.77	12.16	19.44	22.73	8.15	5.73	2.69	2.71	0.06	0.11	25.74	97.69	38.22	23.56	21.90	8.15	5.73
2003	70.04	12.03	19.63	22.09	7.96	5.98	2.83	2.81	0.06	0.12	27.01	97.98	38.81	22.83	22.32	7.96	5.98
2004	70.19	11.50	19.07	22.85	8.22	6.07	2.69	3.00	0.06	0.14	29.11	100.15	40.29	22.91	22.47	8.22	6.08
2005	69.43	10.96	18.56	23.19	8.16	6.23	2.70	3.10	0.06	0.18	30.15	100.28	40.39	22.56	22.80	8.16	6.24
2006	70.79	10.80	19.02	23.79	8.22	6.61	2.87	3.23	0.07	0.26	29.81	99.62	39.96	22.22	22.45	8.22	6.66
2007	71.44	10.72	19.83	23.49	8.46	6.54	2.45	3.49	0.08	0.34	29.22	101.36	39.77	23.70	22.75	8.46	6.55
2008	73.11	10.51	20.70	23.85	8.43	7.21	2.51	3.87	0.09	0.55	25.93	99.27	37.28	23.83	22.39	8.43	7.19
2009	72.60	11.35	21.10	21.63	8.36	7.60	2.67	3.92	0.10	0.72	22.74	94.48	35.40	23.34	19.69	8.36	7.59
2010[11]	75.03	11.67	22.10	22.08	8.44	8.06	2.51	4.31	0.11	0.92	21.62	98.00	35.97	24.64	20.82	8.44	8.05

NA Not available. Z Less than 5 trillion. [1] Includes other types of fuel, not shown separately. [2] Includes lease condensate. [3] Beginning 1989, includes waste coal supplied. Beginning 2001, also includes a small amount of refuse recovery. [4] Electricity net generation from conventional hydroelectric power, geothermal, solar, and wind; consumption of electricity from wood, waste, and alcohol fuels; geothermal heat pump and direct use energy; and solar thermal direct use energy. [5] Conventional hydroelectricity net generation. [6] Organic nonfossil material of biological origin constituting a renewable energy source. [7] Imports minus exports. [8] Includes coal coke net imports and electricity net imports, not shown separately. [9] Petroleum products supplied, including natural gas plant liquids and crude oil burned as fuel. Does not include biofuels that have been blended with petroleum—biofuels are included in "Renewable Energy." [10] Excludes supplemental gaseous fuels. [11] Preliminary.

Source: U.S. Energy Information Administration, "Monthly Energy Review," May 2011, http://www.eia.gov/totalenergy/data/monthly/.

The Real Energy Revolution Shrinking Carbon Dioxide Emissions? It's Fracking

ROBERT BRYCE

Robert Bryce is a senior fellow with the Center for Energy Policy and the Environment at the Manhattan Institute, a conservative think tank. A prolific writer and sought-after public speaker, he has been writing about energy for two decades. He is a critic of "green energy," believing that renewable sources cannot be scaled up to meet energy demands. He argues that natural gas and nuclear power are the only viable alternatives to coal and oil. The article appeared as an op-ed piece in The Seattle Times *in July 2014.*

WHEN it comes to the issue of climate change, it's easy to bash the United States. Yes, the U.S. emits a lot of carbon dioxide—about 5.9 billion tons in 2013 alone, second only to China's 9.5 billion tons.

But it's also easy to overlook this fact: The U.S. is leading the world in reducing its carbon dioxide emissions. And those reductions are largely due to the innovation that is happening not in green energy, but in the oil and gas sector's ability to produce hydrocarbons from shale deposits.

Indeed, thanks to soaring domestic production of natural gas—up by 27 percent, or about 2.7 million barrels of oil equivalent per day since 2003—the U.S. has been able to reduce the amount of coal it consumes for electricity generation. Since 2003, according to the latest data from the *BP Statistical Review of World Energy*, U.S. coal consumption has declined by about 2.1 million barrels of oil equivalent per day. Put another way, the U.S. is now burning about the same amount of coal as it did back in 1987.

That reduced coal consumption has resulted in major reductions in carbon-dioxide emissions, even when compared to Germany, a country that many environmentalists consider an example to be copied. Over the past decade or so, German consumers have subsidized renewable energy programs to the tune of about $100 billion, according to a *Financial Times* report.

5   And, while it's true that Germany is now producing more solar energy than any other country, it's also true that the U.S. has achieved far greater emissions reductions, in absolute terms, than Germany has.

Since 2003—again, according to the latest *BP Statistical Review of World Energy*—the U.S. has reduced its carbon-dioxide emissions by six times what Germany has achieved, and it has done so at far lower cost.

When it comes to energy, the U.S. is now the envy of the rest of the world. Over the past two years or so, U.S. natural gas prices, measured at the Henry Hub in Louisiana, have averaged about $4 per million BTU (British thermal unit). In the European Union, that same 1 million BTUs of gas will cost roughly three times as much. In Japan, it will cost about four times as much.

To be clear, the dramatic increase in domestic oil and gas production is creating some friction. Many people are concerned about the possibility of water contamination. But remember that in 2011 the head of the Environmental Protection Agency, Lisa Jackson, in testimony before the U.S. Senate, said, "I'm not aware of any proven case where the fracking process itself has affected water."

Continuing improvements in horizontal drilling and hydraulic fracturing are allowing the U.S. to produce record quantities of natural gas. And that flood of gas is stimulating the economy, creating large numbers of jobs and attracting tens of billions of dollars in foreign investment.

10   Last fall, Wallace Tyner, an energy economist at Purdue University, estimated in a study that the shale revolution was adding some $473 billion per year to the U.S. economy, or about 3 percent of the gross domestic product. Energy consulting firm IHS recently estimated that more than 2.1 million jobs in the U.S. are now supported by shale-related oil and gas activity. To cite just one example of foreign investment: Sasol, a South African company, is spending $21 billion on a new gas-to-liquids facility in Lake Charles, La.

Over the past few years, a myriad of pundits and politicians have claimed that the U.S. would see big economic gains due to breakthroughs in renewable-energy production. While it's true that the cost of solar photovoltaic modules has fallen from more than $20 per watt in the 1980s, to less than $1 per watt today, the energy story of today is the resurgence of America's oil and gas production.

That resurgence has occurred due to continuing innovation in everything from better drilling rigs and drill bits to improved seismic techniques and more powerful pumps. Those innovations may not be glamorous, but they are giving the U.S. a major competitive advantage in the world economy while also helping the country reduce its carbon-dioxide emissions.

Fracking: A Key to Energy Independence?

ABRAHM LUSTGARTEN

Abrahm Lustgarten in an investigative journalist for ProPublica, *an online, independent, nonprofit newsroom that, in the words of its Web site, "produces investigative journalism in the public interest." Lustgarten's investigation into fracking for natural gas was recognized with the George Polk award for environmental reporting, a National Press Foundation award for best energy writing, and a Sigma Delta Chi award. This article appeared in February 2012 in the* World Energy Monitor *produced by the World Energy Forum.*

First, a wave of new natural gas drilling swept across the US. Mountain and pastoral landscapes were transformed into landscape-scale factories that optimistically promised a century's worth of clean-burning fuel and a risk-free solution to dependence on imported oil. In 2008, it seemed the ultimate win-win in an era of hard choices. Later, more sobering facts began to complicate things. The drilling relies on an invasive process called hydraulic fracturing or "fracking" that uses brute force and dangerous chemicals to crack open the Earth and extract the gas from previously unreachable deep deposits.

Where the drilling and fracturing happened, water wells sometimes became contaminated. Waste pits leaked into aquifers. Large quantities of fresh water were used. Mountain glaciers and Wyoming valleys became shrouded in smog. Reports began to emerge that natural gas might cause almost as much greenhouse gas pollution as coal. Now, the industry is at a crucial point. Even as the hard lessons have come into focus, the myriad opportunities presented by this vast fuel source have made its development inevitable. In the US, President Barack Obama stands firmly behind expanded natural gas use and the local economic development it brings. In the next

10 years, the US will use the fracturing technology to drill hundreds of thousands of wells in cities, rivers and watersheds. Drilling—along with fracking—is fast expanding across Europe, South Africa and Russia. And it will not stop while oil prices are at record highs, the Middle East is in turmoil and nuclear energy is bogged down by global distrust after the Fukushima crisis.

The industry and governments need to figure out how to scale up gas drilling safely and how to learn from the mistakes in the US where the fracturing technology was first put to commercial use. The problem is that despite their head start, US scientists and regulators have not answered crucial questions about the risks. Where will the vast amounts of water for fracturing come from and how will the waste water be safely disposed of? Are regulations in place to make sure the industry extracts the gas as safely as possible and that underground sources of drinking water are protected? And what, exactly, happens when bedrock is shattered and filled with chemicals deep underground?

It remains unclear, for example, how far the tiny fissures that radiate through the bedrock from hydraulic fracturing might reach. Or whether they can connect underground passageways or open cracks into groundwater aquifers that could allow the chemical solution to escape into drinking water, as methane from these wells has been proven to have done. And it is not certain that the chemicals—some, such as benzene, are known to cause cancer—are adequately contained by either the well structure beneath the Earth or by the people, pipelines and trucks that handle it on the surface. Almost no research exists into these issues.

5   Rather than learning from the environmental problems, the drilling industry has insisted they are not its fault. It maintains the fracturing happens thousands of feet from water supplies and below layers of impenetrable rock that seal the world above from what happens down below. There is no reason for concern, they say. Yet there is. And the frequent cases of contamination and well control problems across the US that have come to light through several *ProPublica* investigations prove it. Even if layers of rock can seal water supplies from the layer where fluid is injected, the gas well itself creates an opening in that layer.

The well bore is supposed to be surrounded by cement, but often there are large empty pockets or the cement cracks under pressure. In many instances, the high pressure of the fluids being injected into the ground has created leaks of gas—and sometimes fluids—into surrounding water supplies. This is partly why the US Environmental Protection Agency has undertaken a nationwide study into the life-cycle impacts of fracking, for the first time. The next step will be to use the findings to inform a rigorous system of oversight so drilling happens in the best, most technologically advanced and safest way possible.

In the US that is going to be tough, because the federal government does not regulate hydraulic fracturing. Oversight is left to states where regulations vary widely. Europe, where disparate governments oversee a shared continuous natural landscape, may face similar challenges. The energy industry already knows how to prevent water pollution and how to sharply reduce toxic air emissions, for example. Drilling companies have figured out how to drill wells with fewer toxic chemicals, enclose waste water so it can [be managed]. In the US, legislators are considering a baseline set of rules with higher standards which would make fracturing slightly more expensive than the industry has wanted, but also offer an opportunity for consistency, predictability, and the streamlining of operations.

For places already coping with the environmental consequences of drilling, that will boost confidence that natural gas can be harvested safely. It will also lead to political and regulatory stability that will end up saving the industry money. And only then can drilling for gas be the win-win it was promised to be.

The Problem Is the Solution: Cultivating New Traditions Through Permaculture

JASON POWERS

Jason Powers wrote this article for Clamor, *a small independent magazine in the alternative press. Published largely through volunteer efforts for the seven years of its existence,* Clamor *was nominated by* Utne Reader *for its Independent Press awards each year of its existence, first in the category of Best New Title and subsequently in the category of Culture/Social Coverage. Permaculture, the topic of this article, engages the values of* Clamor, *in that it promotes change based on the action of those without political or governmental power. The article was published in the May/June 2006 issue.*

Irresponsible traditions of waste, conquest, and over-consumption have dominated much of human history, leading to the collapse of many past societies. History has shown us that a civilization that undermines its land and resource base through wasteful and exploitative habits eventually will collapse. Today, the destruction hinges upon our wasteful and exploitative economy, based on perpetual growth, and the fossil fuel–dependent industrial agriculture that strips our soils and poisons our waters. Agribusiness corporations are consolidating ownership of the world's seed stock, while the genetically altered organisms they produce silently embed themselves into the wild gene pool, with yet unknown consequences for global food security and biodiversity. Oil and natural gas production, the cheap energy that our agriculture, industry, and transportation systems depend on, has most likely peaked and begun to regress. Extinction of species is drastically increasing due to pollution, ecological

devastation, and weather change. Extinction of cultures due to conquest—euphemistically termed, "development"—and resource extraction is likewise increasing.

In many ways shielded from the effects of the global economy by our relative wealth, most in the "developed" world live unaware of the effects of our lifestyle, not knowing or caring where our food, water, energy, and consumer products come from, nor what is done to bring us these things. Even as we imagine progress and technological salvation, our systems and the culture they've created perpetuate denial.

Clearly, whether we choose to change or not, we will have to eventually. It's just a matter of when we're able to leave denial behind and look honestly at how we live. From this we will hopefully (re)develop skills and traditions that teach us to value and care for what sustains us: the land, our communities, and our relationships.

Permaculture arose from the realization that prevailing agricultural systems were fundamentally unsustainable and creating worldwide catastrophe. Based on observations of the sustainable systems of nature, as well as many of the traditions of indigenous cultures, permaculture was developed and applied in the 1970s by Australians Bill Mollison, a forestry worker and scientist, and David Holmgren, then a 20-year-old student. As initially conceived, "Permaculture is the conscious design and maintenance of agriculturally productive ecosystems which have the diversity, stability, and resilience of natural ecosystems. It is the harmonious integration of landscape and people providing their food, energy, shelter, and other material and non-material needs in a sustainable way," according to Mollison's *Designers' Manual,* the "bible" of permaculture.

5   Originally an attempt to return to systems of small-scale intensive gardens, permaculture now incorporates numerous techniques for ecologically sustainable living: grey water, recycling, solar energy, rainwater catchment, natural building, and local food networks. "You could say it's a rational man's approach to not shitting in his bed…a framework that never ceases to move, but that will accept information from anywhere," explained co-founder Mollison in an interview with In Context. Coined in 1976 as a conjunction of "permanent agriculture," the word permaculture has evolved to signify a "permanent culture," one that has since spread into a de-centralized global movement, adapted and implemented by peoples in nearly every ecosystem, and socioeconomic level, by rural and urban, rich and poor.

Toby Hemenway, a permaculture teacher, designer and author of *Gaia's Garden: A Guide to Home-Scale Permaculture* likens permaculture to "a toolbox that helps organize [techniques] and helps you decide when to use them." Aiding this are four simple ethical tenets: caring for the earth, caring for people, limiting growth and consumption, and sharing surplus (goods, energy, time,

etc.). Design principles derived from these tenets incorporate no-till and perennial gardening, use of natural patterns, energy efficiency, and intelligent use of space and resources. As in nature, stability is created through diversity and the relationships between the elements in the system. "The philosophy behind permaculture is one of working with, rather than against, nature; of protracted and thoughtful observation rather than protracted and thoughtless action; of looking at systems in all their functions, rather than asking only one yield of them; and of allowing systems to demonstrate their own evolutions," Mollison writes. Practitioners try to integrate the different elements into harmonious relationships where cooperation and mutual support are encouraged, multiple functions are filled by one element, and multiple elements fill one function. This is seen in the "guild," a permaculture-specific technique which uses vertical space to stack and layer mutually beneficial plants.

To be sustainable, a system must create as much or more energy than it consumes, so closing energy and resource loops becomes very important. Problems are reframed as solutions and waste is redirected as inputs for other processes. "I have become increasingly aware of how the output/waste of my activities can be reused as inputs useful in other activities," admits Leopoldo Rodriguez, an economics professor at Portland State University with three years of permaculture experience. "I think a lot more about the placement of different elements in the process of putting a garden together, planting a tree in the yard or building a chicken coop." Beyond understanding one's own systemic impact, permaculture bolsters people's self-sufficiency. "Grow food or learn how to forage wild food yourself. The empowerment of this one act will have a great effect on you," says courthouse clerk Carla Bankston, an eight-year permaculture devotee.

In addition to this focus on sustainability and DIY [do it yourself] practicality, successful application of permaculture depends on continuous feedback, adjustment and involvement with the design. "One key aspect is to reassess at every step and make sure that you're still in line with what your original goals were," Hemenway says. "You stay with the project for long after it's up and running because it's always going to change. It creates a long-term relationship which will in the long run wind up being cheaper." He contrasts that with how things are typically done. "Our culture does a cost benefit analysis where we say 'Okay, this is the cheapest way to do it so let's do it like that.' It makes it very difficult to [do] anything resembling what sustainable cultures do."

Always site and system specific, permaculture is incredibly versatile. Its principles are broad enough to be applied to various systems—economics, home building, human relationships, and food distribution systems. Mayans in Guatemala, post-Soviet Cubans, and villagers in rural Zimbabwe have all successfully bolstered their communities' food security by ceasing to use expensive chemical-based processes. Instead they combine production-intensive and energy-saving permaculture techniques like mulching, composting and water harvesting with their traditional farming methods, concentrating once again on subsistence rather than producing commodities for export. City Repair in Portland, Oregon, applies it to urban planning with community-guided creation of public spaces and the integration of natural building into the cityscape. The Permaculture Credit Union in New Mexico invests in their community rather than destructive companies, offering loan discounts for fuel-efficient automobiles and second mortgages for energy efficient upgrades on houses. "I've seen businesses and organizations where people have applied permaculture principles that have helped them get a lot more functional," says Hemenway, "It works with so-called invisible structures as well as with visible things like landscapes or buildings."

10 "[Permaculture] involves rediscovering a lot of things we have lost," Linda Hendrickson, a Portland weaver and recent permaculturist, says. While it is true the philosophy challenges many of our modern habits, it is by no means anachronistic. "You look at the inputs and the outputs and embedded energy," explains Hemenway. "What did it take to build that solar panel? Is there more energy being consumed in the creation of it than you're going to get back from its use? I don't rule out any technology simply because it's technology, but we look at it as how much really does it cost to be using this, and who gets hurt by it." Rather than reject modern know-how, permaculture examines both negative and positive impact, a more conscientious approach than our current mass delusion of "progress" as endless and thoughtless expansion.

This broad integration of technique and application, as well as the inclusion of ethics in design originally captivated Hemenway. While leaving his job at a biotech company, he stumbled across Bill Mollison's *Designers' Manual* at the public library. "I leafed through the pages and said, 'This is it. This is everything I've ever wanted to do. This is ecology and appropriate technology and design and gardening. It puts it all together.'"

It's easy to be overwhelmed by the many facets of permaculture design at first. Karen Tilou, who applies permaculture techniques to the orchard she manages, explains, "There's so much you can do, so people end up feeling like 'Wow, I'm not doing anything if I'm not doing all of it.'" To avoid this, "Find what aspect of permaculture's ethics and principles you can apply to what you really love. It doesn't have to be about gardens or solar energy."

Ultimately, permaculture is responsible to earth and home, wherever that may be. Joseph and Jacqueline Freeman, who live and garden on a ten-acre farm, advise, "Start paying attention to the small things, like where your water comes from and where it goes. Keep your septic outflow nontoxic by using low-impact detergent when you wash clothes. Be aware of packaging when you make purchases. Develop relationships with elders and others of like mind so you can keep adding to your knowledge. Build community in whatever ways you can." Though nice to have the space rural areas offer, permaculture is especially important in urban areas. "The cities and suburbia are the places where the resources are being consumed," Hemenway observes. "It's where everybody lives in this country. If those places can't change then we're not going to get there."

By no means the solution, permaculture offers a valuable approach to restructuring our lives and counters the deleterious habits of our society by simultaneously looking forward to new technology and backward to older agricultural traditions and indigenous wisdom. In contrast to our current pathologies of short-term profit, waste, perpetual growth, oversimplification and reductionism, permaculture teaches us to slow down, observe, evaluate our actions and consumption patterns, to value the land, the local and relationships.

The Soil vs. the Sensex

VANDANA SHIVA

Vandana Shiva is an internationally known voice for environmentalism and social justice, espousing the rights of the third-world poor who suffer at the hands of international corporations. With a doctorate in physics, she has expertise in both scientific and social issues and writes regularly on political, economic, and environmental topics. Her most recent books are Staying Alive: Women, Ecology, and Development *(2010),* Soil Not Oil: Environmental Justice in a Time of Climate Crisis *(2008),* Earth Democracy: Justice, Sustainability, and Peace *(2005), and* Water Wars: Privatization, Pollution and Profit *(2002). Shiva's article, "The Soil vs. the Sensex" reflects her concern for the farmer who works the land as opposed to powerful business interests represented by the Sensex, which is India's stock exchange. It was published in the October 2010 issue of* India Currents.

The earth, the source of all nourishment and sustenance, is seen as a mother in most cultures. She is Terra Madre and Gaia, Dharti, and Vasundhara. Even today, in parts of India not destroyed by the Green Revolution, tribals and peasants apologize to the earth at the beginning of every agriculture season for hurting her with their plough, and promise [to] take no more than their need.

But the culture of the sacred earth is under severe threat, and this threat looms over the communities who depend on the land. As India grows at 9 percent, and the Sensex (the stock exchange index in Mumbai) becomes the measure of the state of the people and the state of the land, the rich and the privileged often forget that the majority in India depends neither on the Sensex nor the state. They depend on the Maati Ma (Mother Earth). Yet the dominant culture of the land and the earth is being marginalized; our biodiversity and cultural diversity are at risk; our very future is threatened.

The war against the land is cultural and material. The culture of the sacred earth is one of nonviolence and restraint, of compassion and care for all life that the earth creates and supports. The bird and the tree, the earthworm and the elephant, all have their space and their share in the gifts of Mother Earth. We referred to this culture as Vasundhaiva Kutumbkam. I call it Earth Democracy.

Materially a sacred earth invites us to create technologies and economies that sustain the fertility and productivity of the soil and the land. An agrarian economy is a highly evolved economy in the yardstick of the sacred earth because it is the only economy in which humans can give back to the earth. Every other economy—urban, industrial—is an economy of taking. All that urban and industrial society gives back to the land is waste and pollution.

5   The earth is no longer seen as the source of soil fertility. Instead synthetic fertilizers made in chemical factories are viewed as the source of soil fertility, even though they kill soil fauna and flora, the real creators of fertility. The farmers and the earth are no longer seen as the source of food. Nestle and Cargill, Lever and ITC become the "food providers." The farmer is no longer the annadata (grain provider, giver of food). Food is no longer the sacred gift that creates and maintains life. It is just another commodity.

Maximization of profits, not maximization of well being, determines what we eat. No wonder there is increasing hunger and malnutrition of the poor, who do not get enough food, and the malnutrition of the rich, who live on junk food and processed food. India is emerging as the epicenter of the diabetes epidemic. Changes in food cultures and diets have a lot to do with these new diseases.

The farmer is no longer seen as the source of seed—the 200,000 rice varieties we have grown, or the 15,000 mangoes, or the 15,000 banana varieties disappear from science and from the earth. Monsanto becomes the "inventor" of seed, the "owner" of life through intellectual property and patents. It does not matter if 200,000 Indian farmers commit suicide because they have been pushed into debt by costly, unreliable, nonrenewable seed and the related destruction of their seed sovereignty and seed freedom. All that matters is that the profits of seed corporations keep increasing.

Farmers who have tilled the land for generations, and want to continue taking care of the earth, refuse to be uprooted. The new rich, the big corporations, think that they have the right to dispossess every tribal and every farmer of their land and resources, bury the soil under the concrete jungle of new luxury townships, and literally kill the earth. From the perspective of Maati Ma, this is matricide. And no society can flourish if it destroys the very source of its sustenance.

The Sensex will rise and fall. The earth has sustained life for billions of years and can continue to do so. While wealthy Indians are high on the recent climb of the stock market they need to remember the collapse of the financial markets in South East Asia in 1997.

10   We as a society and as a civilization based on the sacred earth are on the threshold of destroying our very ecological foundation by worshipping money and markets. These are becoming the new sacred. And false sacred emerge when society loses its anchor.

We need to re-anchor ourselves in the earth. We need to stop uprooting those who are anchored in the land, our peasants and tribals.

We need to return to the Earth, our mother.

■ ■ ■ **FOR CLASS DISCUSSION** Choices for a Sustainable World

1. Mark Z. Jacobson and Mark A. Delucchi argue that it is technologically feasible to use renewable sources to meet the world's energy needs. In their own words, "A large-scale wind, water and solar energy system can reliably supply the world's needs, significantly benefiting climate, air quality, water quality, ecology and energy security. As we have shown, the obstacles are primarily political, not technical." Based on your reading of other essays in this unit (particularly Jogalekar and Bryce) and your own knowledge and research, make a list of the "social and political" constraints that work against rapid conversion to renewable resources.

2. Imagine a forum on United States energy policy with a panel that includes Jacobson (or Delucchi), Jogalekar, Bryce, and Lustgarten. An audience member asks the panel what role fracking should play in the nation's energy policies for the next fifty years. For these panelists prepare one-paragraph answers that you think best represents each person's position. Finally, what would your own one-paragraph answer be?

3. The table on page 514 tells many energy stories. Find one that you found surprising, unexpected, or particularly troubling. Tell the story vividly in a graph (line graph, pie chart, bar graph) and share your graphic with classmates. (See Chapter 9 for guidance in constructing meaningful numerical graphics.)

4. The first two sequences of readings in this unit focus on sustainability from the perspective of energy policy, government regulations, free markets, and federal or state policies. On a different path, Powers and Shiva see sustainability achieved through the ethical/spiritual transformation of individuals. They propose making local communities, not corporations, responsible for the care of the earth and the harvest of its abundance. In essence, Powers and Shiva present ethical arguments. What reasons do they use in appealing to the reader? What rhetorical strategies do they use to influence the reader? What values do they appeal to in their audience?

■ ■ ■

WRITING ASSIGNMENT Proposal Argument or Rogerian Letter in Response to an Argument

1. **Option 1: Proposal Argument Taking Your Own Stand on a Sustainability Issue.** Write an op-ed piece or a longer researched white paper in which you present and defend your own proposal on one of the energy or sustainability issues or sub-issues raised in this unit.

2. **Option 2: Rogerian Letter in Response to an Argument.** Write a Rogerian letter addressed to the writer of one of the readings in this unit with which you particularly disagree. Begin your letter by setting up the problem the writer is addressing. Then write an accurate summary of the writer's argument and identify the values you share with the writer to establish common ground. Write to share your perspective and open a channel for collaborative problem solving and future communication. ■

Digital Literacies

Young adults today constitute the first generation raised in a digital environment. In 2001, writer Marc Prensky coined the term "Digital Natives" to describe the first generation of "native speakers" of digital language. Prensky and others have posited that such immersion in digital environments has created differences in brain function between digital natives and the "digital immigrants" for whom learning these technologies was like learning a foreign language. Other researchers deny the existence of a "digital divide" between generations, but share concerns that the Web environment has negatively affected our ability to learn from traditional teaching methods, to process print text, and to assess information critically.

The advent of Web 2.0, a collective term for Web sites that allow user-generated content, has complicated matters even further. From their Instagram and Twitter feeds to their Tumblr accounts, from their Facebook postings about athletics competitions, parties, and student projects to their Yelp reviews and YouTube uploads, teenagers and young adults are creating trackable online identities available to anyone with a search engine. With so much of their personal lives exposed on the Web, how safe are teenage and youth users, and how might their digital footprint impact them in the future? And how has participating in social interactions online impacted the ability of digital addicts to interact offline and face to face?

Critics also continue to question the value of the information we are sharing online, particularly through social media. Do our postings reveal narcissistic over-sharing, as some claim, or are we creating new opportunities for individual self-expression and beneficial social change? Also, to what extent can new digital literacies be harnessed for productive political action?

The readings in this unit ask you to consider the issues and questions raised by this still-recent and constantly evolving platform.

Digital Demands: The Challenges of Constant Connectivity
An Interview with Sherry Turkle

Sherry Turkle, Director of MIT's Initiative on Technology and Self, is a scholar, researcher, and longtime observer of technology's impact on people. Her 2011 book, Alone Together: Why We Expect More from Technology and Less from Each Other, *posits a potential downside to human reliance on digital technologies and poses the question: Is our perpetual connectedness actually making us feel more alone? The following interview is excerpted from a PBS* Frontline *TV/Web report, "Digital Nation."*

SHERRY TURKLE: What I'm seeing is a generation that says consistently, "I would rather text than make a telephone call." Why? It's less risky. I can just get the information out there. I don't have to get all involved; it's more efficient. I would rather text than see somebody face to face.

There's this sense that you can have the illusion of companionship without the demands of friendship. The real demands of friendship, of intimacy, are complicated. They're hard. They involve a lot of negotiation. They're all the things that are difficult about adolescence. And adolescence is the time when people are using technology to skip and to cut corners and to not have to do some of these very hard things. One of the things I've found with continual connectivity is there's an anxiety of disconnection; that these teens have a kind of panic. They say things like, "I lost my iPhone; it felt like somebody died, as though I'd lost my mind." The technology is already part of them.

And with the constant possibility of connectivity, one of the things that I see is a very subtle movement from "I have a feeling. I want to make a call" to "I want to have a feeling. I need to make a call"—in other words, people almost feeling as if they can't feel their feeling unless they're connected. I'm hearing this all over now so it stops being pathological if it becomes a generational style.

FRONTLINE: Some would say most of the [university] lectures, most of the classes, most of the books are unnecessarily long and boring, and the stuff that's great you could fit in a couple of hands, and that's the stuff they should really commit to and memorize and study. The rest of it is better short and quick and to the point. Look at haiku. It's much harder to do something quickly than it is to do something for hours. And who's to say that it's better to take your time and not be distracted?

5 **TURKLE:** The ability to trace complicated themes through a literary work, through a poem, through a play—these pleasures will be lost to us because they become pleasures through acquired skills. You need to learn how to listen to a poem, read a [Fyodor] Dostoevsky novel, read a Jane Austen novel. These are pleasures of reading that demand attention to things that are long and woven and complicated. And this is something that human beings have cherished and that have brought tremendous riches. And to just say, "Well, we're of a generation that now likes it short and sweet and haiku. Why? Just because the technology makes it easy for us to have things that are short and sweet and haiku." In other words, it's an argument about sensibility and aesthetics that's driven by what technology wants.

I don't really care what technology wants. It's up to people to develop technologies, see what affordances the technology has. Very often these affordances tap into our vulnerabilities. I would feel bereft if, because technology wants us to read short, simple stories, we bequeath to our children a world of short, simple stories. What technology makes easy is not always what nurtures the human spirit.

I've been an MIT professor for 30 years; I've seen the losses. There's no one who's been teaching for 25 years and doesn't think that our students aren't different now than they were then. They need to be stimulated in ways that they didn't need to be stimulated before. No, that's not good. You want them to think about hard things. You want them to think about complicated things. When you have the ability to easily do showy, fabulous things, you want to believe they're valuable because that would be great. I think that we always have to ask ourselves, when technology makes something easy, when its affordances allow us to do certain things, is this valuable? What are the human purposes being served? And in the classroom, what are the educational purposes being served?

One of the most distressing things to me in looking at K–12 is the use of PowerPoint in the schools. I believe that PowerPoint is one of the most frequently used pieces of software in classrooms. Students are taught how to make an argument—to make it in bullets, to add great photos, to draw from the popular culture, and show snippets of movies and snippets of things that [he or she] can grab from the Web, and funny cartoons and to kind of make a mélange, a pastiche of cropped cultural images and animations and to make a beautiful PowerPoint. And that's their presentation.

PowerPoints are about simple, communicable ideas illustrated by powerful images, and there's a place for that. But that isn't the same as

critical thinking. Great books are not fancied-up PowerPoint presentations. Great books take you through an argument, show how the argument is weak, meet objections, and show a different point of view. By the time you're through with all that, you're way beyond the simplicities of PowerPoint.

10   Computers are seductive; computers are appealing. There's no harm in using the seductive and appealing to draw people in, to get them in their seats, and to begin a conversation. The question is, what happens after that?

FRONTLINE: What about multitasking?

TURKLE: Because technology makes it easy, we've all wanted to think it is good for us, a new kind of thinking, an expansion of our ability to reason and cycle through complicated things—do more and be more efficient. Unfortunately, the new research is coming in that says when you multitask, everything gets done a little worse; there's a degradation of all functions. Did we need to really go through 10 years of drinking the Kool-Aid on the educational wonders of multitasking and forgetting about everything we knew about what it takes to really accomplish something hard?

At MIT, I teach the most brilliant students in the world. But they have done themselves a disservice by drinking the Kool-Aid and believing that a multitasking learning environment will serve their best purposes because they need to be taught how to make a sustained, complicated argument on a hard, cultural, historical, psychological point. Many of them were trained that a good presentation is a PowerPoint presentation—you know, bam-bam-bam—it's very hard for them to have a kind of quietness, a stillness in their thinking where one thing can actually lead to another and build and build and build and build. There are just some things that are not amenable to being thought about in conjunction with 15 other things. And there are some kinds of arguments you cannot make unless you're willing to take something from beginning to end.

We're becoming quite intolerant of letting each other think complicated things. I don't think this serves our human needs because the problems we're facing are quite complicated. To hear someone else out, you need to be able to be still for a while and pay attention to something other than your immediate needs. So if we're living in a moment when you can be in seven different places at once, and you can have seven different conversations at once on a back channel here, on a phone here, on a laptop, how do we save stillness? How threatened is it? How do we regain it?

15   Erikson is a psychologist who wrote a great deal about adolescence and identity, and he talks about the need for stillness in order to fully develop and to discover your identity and become who you need to become and think what you need to think. And I think stillness is one of the great things in jeopardy.

[Henry David] Thoreau, in writing about Walden Pond, lists the three things that he feels the experience is teaching him to develop fully as the man he wants to become. He wants to live deliberately; he wants to live in his life; and he wants to live with no sense of resignation. But on all of those dimensions, I feel that we're taking away from ourselves the things that Thoreau thought were so essential to discovering an identity.

We're not deliberate; we're bombarded. We have no stillness; we have resignation.

Kids say: "Well, it has to be this way; we have no other way to live. We're not living fully in our lives. We're living a little in our lives and a little bit in our Facebook lives." You know, you put up a different life, you put up a different person. So it's not to be romantic about Thoreau, but I think he did write, as Erikson wrote, about the need for stillness; to be deliberate; to live in your life and to never feel that you're just resigned to how things need to be.

When we're texting, on the phone, doing e-mail, getting information, the experience is of being filled up. That feels good. And we assume that it is nourishing in the sense of taking us to a place we want to go. And I think that we are going to start to learn that in our enthusiasms and in our fascinations, we can also be flattened and depleted by what perhaps was once nourishing us but which can't be a steady diet. If all I do is my e-mail, my calendar, and my searches, I feel great; I feel like a master of the universe. And then it's the end of the day, I've been busy all day, and I haven't thought about anything hard, and I have been consumed by the technologies that were there and that had the power to nourish me.

20   The point is we're really at the very beginning of learning how to use this technology in the ways that are the most nourishing and sustaining. We're going to slowly find our balance, but I think it's going to take time. So I think the first discipline is to think of us as being in the early days so that we're not so quick to yes, no, on, off, good, good, and to just kind of take it slowly and not feel that we need to throw out the virtues of deliberateness, living in life, stillness, solitude.

There is a wonderful Freudian formulation, which is that loneliness is failed solitude. In many ways we are forgetting the intellectual and emotional value of solitude. You're not lonely in solitude. You're only lonely if you forget how to use solitude to replenish yourself and to learn. And you don't want a generation that experiences solitude as loneliness. And that is something to be concerned about, because if kids feel that they need to be connected in order to be themselves, that's quite unhealthy. They'll always feel lonely, because the connections that they're forming are not going to give them what they seek.

Diagnosing the Digital Revolution: Why It's So Hard to Tell if It's Really Changing Us

ALISON GOPNIK

Alison Gopnik, a professor of psychology and affiliate professor of philosophy at the University of California at Berkeley, is a widely recognized researcher and scholar in the field of children's learning and development. She has published many books and articles in these areas, including The Philosophical Baby: What Children's Minds Tell Us about Love, Truth, and the Meaning of Life. *In this article, published in* Slate *in February 2011, she examines and questions some of Sherry Turkle's pessimistic claims for the impact of technology on young people.*

They gave her The Device when she was only 2 years old. It sent signals along the optic nerve that swiftly transported her brain to an alternate universe—a captivating other world. By the time she was 7 she would smuggle it into school and engage it secretly under her desk. By 15 the visions of The Device—a girl entering a ballroom, a man dying on the battlefield—seemed more real than her actual adolescent life. She would sit with it, motionless, oblivious to everything around her, for hours on end. Its addictive grip was so great that she often stayed up half the night, unable to put it down.

When she grew up, The Device dominated her house: no room was free from it, no activity, not even eating or defecating, was carried on without its aid. Even when she made love it was the images of The Device that filled her mind. Psychologists showed that she literally could not disengage from it—if The Device could reach the optic nerve, she would automatically and inescapably be in its grip. Neuroscientists demonstrated that large portions of her brain, parts that had once been devoted to understanding the real world, had been co-opted by The Device.

A tale of the dystopian technological future? No, just autobiography. The Device is, of course, the printed book and I've been its willing victim all my life. But this might be how Sherry Turkle would describe it in her new book, *Alone Together*, and, in some ways, she'd be right.

The story illustrates why it's so hard to know how new technologies will affect us. Some technologies really have reshaped our lives, minds, and societies. Print did change everything. So did the telegraph. Information had always traveled at the speed of a fast horse; suddenly, it traveled at the speed of electricity, from 10 miles an hour to millions. (The old movie newspaper clichés "Get me rewrite!" "Tear up the afternoon edition!" seem like part of a timeless past, but they actually reflect the elaborate and ingenious technologies that took advantage of telegraphic immediacy—"Extra, extra!" was a ping and a pop-up.)

5   But other changes that seemed equally profound at the time have turned out, in retrospect, to be minor. The radio was an improvement on the telegraph but it didn't have the same exponential, transformative effect. How do we know when and how changing your technology will change your life?

Sherry Turkle has been chronicling the impact of the digital revolution for some 20 years. In her *Alone Together* she focuses on two developments, social robots and Internet communications (texting, Second Life, e-mail, Facebook). Her method is ethnographic—she interviews people, especially children and adolescents, at length about how they feel about those technologies. Turkle is a sensitive interviewer and an elegant writer, and her book captures the anxiety and ambivalence that children and adolescents (and adults, too) feel about the new developments. Her general conclusion is that those anxieties are justified. Both robots and the Web will have a profound, and bad, effect on human psychology. Technology will lead to devalued and alienated lives rather than enriched ones.

When the ethnographic "clinical interview" method is done well, as Turkle does it, it can give us an excellent picture of what people think about the effects of technology. The trouble is that it doesn't tell us what those effects actually are. The children she talks to are remarkably thoughtful, but they are also contradictory: Robots are sort of people, but then again they're just machines; cell phones make parents more intrusive, or maybe more distant. Turkle quotes Niels Bohr's statement that the opposite of a profound truth is sometimes another profound truth, but fails to mention his preamble that the opposite of a fact is a falsehood. Facts about the effects of technology are thin on the ground. For example, there are remarkably few firm scientific conclusions from 50 years of psychological research on children and television.

There is also the problem of what psychologists call the "cultural ratchet effect." We learn differently as children than as adults. For grown-ups, learning a new skill is painful, attention-demanding, and slow. Children learn unconsciously and effortlessly. Because of this, each new generation rapidly acquires all the accumulated innovations of the past without even knowing it. The story of The Device is startling because we were born with print. The new generation, in turn, will consciously alter those earlier practices and invent new ones. They can take the entire past for granted as they move toward the future.

These generational shifts are the engine of cultural innovation, and they are particularly relevant for technological change—our children will talk digital as a native language, while we speak it haltingly with an immigrant accent. But generational shifts go beyond technology. They also produce entirely arbitrary changes, like the historical changes from Elizabethan words or dances or dresses to ours. Even in the Neolithic period, pottery decorations changed over generations. These changes can feel significant even though they actually don't alter much of anything. The telegraph really did mean The End of Civilization As We Knew It, but the waltz and the crinoline caused just as much angst.

10   This immediate generational transformation, the click of the ratchet, is so vivid that the long historical changes and constancies are hard to see. The year before you were born looks like Eden, the year after your children were born looks like Mad Max.

Which of the effects that Turkle and other digital pessimists attribute to technology really are radical transformations, and which are relatively small changes magnified by the ratchet effect? Is the Internet the telegraph or just the crinoline? Some of the stories Turkle tells seem awfully like false nostalgia. A young woman feels guilty because she surreptitiously writes e-mail while she is Skyping (for hours!) with her distant grandmother. A teenager complains that her mother is distracted by her cell phone when she picks her up from school. Did we really once listen to our grandmothers with undivided attention? Were adolescent girls delighted by the rich and meaningful conversations they had with their mothers? Is the teenager who comes home from school and IMs her friends while she updates her Facebook page really much worse off than the one who came home and watched *Gilligan's Island* reruns? (More autobiography there.)

Turkle and her interviewees sometimes seem to treat minor variations on human nature like threatening psychological revolutions. For example, Turkle and many of her subjects worry that people might interact with nonhuman simulacra, like robots, as if they were people, and might lose themselves in imaginary worlds like Second Life.

But, after all, a majority of young children communicate extensively with imaginary companions, creatures who are even more elusive than robots since they don't exist at all. All normal children become immersed in unreal pretend worlds. And their elders do the same. Is the Turklean child who cries over a Furby really all that different from the Dickensian one who weeps for a doll? Is the lonely widow who talks to a robot really all that different than the one who talks to her dead husband's picture? Or religiously follows the lives of soap opera characters? Is a Second Life romance all that different from a Harlequin one?

And what about the fact that we communicate through highly abstract signals, rather than face to face? Take texting, surely the most baffling technological success of our age. We've harnessed vast computational power to let us write telegrams with our thumbs. Turkle and the teenagers contrast texting nostalgically, not only with live conversation, but with that day-before-yesterday Eden of the telephone—a technology that once seemed equally threatening.

15   But, at least since writing began, perhaps even since language itself began, human beings have conducted their most intimate lives through abstract, digital symbols. Bertrand Russell and Lady Ottoline Morrell carried on their love affair through the London post, writing several times a day, and Proust used the equally rapid and frequent pneumatic petits bleus of Paris. London letters were delivered 12 times a day and a petit bleu arrived two hours after it was sent (not much more slowly than an AT&T connection and probably more reliably). The Henry James story "The Great Good Place" is a utopian fantasy about unhooking from the grid and begins with a bitter lament at the inundation of telegrams and overflow of obligations that will be familiar to anyone with a bulging inbox.

Another worry is about attention. It is certainly true that by the time we're adults attention is a limited resource and attentional patterns are hard to change. But the exaggerated highly focused attention we consider appropriate in a contemporary classroom is itself a recent cultural invention, and one with costs as well as benefits. Guatemalan Mayan mothers successfully teach their children to divide their attention, as Western mothers teach children to focus theirs.

Despite all this, Turkle and the digital pessimists may be on to something. There is something about the Internet that seems genuinely different—a telegraphlike transformation. But it isn't the result of changes in the speed or character of communications. Texts and e-mails travel no faster than phone calls and telegrams, and their content isn't necessarily richer or poorer.

Turkle may be right, though, that there is a transformative difference in how many people we interact with, though it would be nice to have some objective evidence. There is an anthropological observation that most of us can keep track of only a couple of hundred people—a village-worth. The rise of cities just led us to define that village sociologically instead of geographically. City dwellers learn not to acknowledge, or even see, most of the people they pass on the street, a skill that seems baffling and obnoxious to rural visitors. The post and the petit bleu connected a relatively small urban literary circle.

The Web expands that circle exponentially. When we do a Google search we aren't consulting a brilliant computer, but the aggregated opinions of millions of other people. Facebook, which began as a way of digitally defining your social network, rapidly increases it beyond recognition. On the Web we communicate with the planet relying on a psychology that was designed for the village. You used to listen to your friends and Walter Cronkite, and, unless you were Walter, you could assume that your friends were the ones listening to you. Now it's much harder to tell whom we should listen to and who is listening to us, or at least we haven't yet figured out how to do it. We can edit out the obnoxious guy on the street more easily than the anonymous flame on the blog. On the Web we all become small-town visitors lost in the big city.

20   Even these reactions aren't completely new, though. City dwellers never entirely succeeded in turning Manhattan into Peoria, and they didn't really want to. The contradictory emotions Turkle describes are the characteristic urban emotions—excitement, novelty, and possibility balanced against loneliness, distraction, and alienation, and they seem to have arisen almost as soon as cities themselves. We were alone together in ancient Rome and 11th-century Kyoto. Long before even the printed book, Horace and Lady Murasaki reacted to the life of their physical cities by yearning for simplicity, mindfulness, and meaning. Turkle's children also seem to yearn for a digital version of the classical pastoral retreat, or the Buddhist monastery. Maybe that would do us all some good. But the villa and the monastery would be much less appealing if we didn't have the big city and the Web of the wide world to return to.

Deconstructing Digital Natives

MARY ANN HARLAN

Mary Ann Harlan is the coordinator of the Teacher Librarian Program at San José State University. Her doctoral research focused on the ways teens use information to learn and create in an online environment. This article was published in the Spring 2013 issue of the California School Library Association Journal.

When the term digital native first emerged it seemed a useful metaphor (Prensky, 2001). After all, the youth we saw everyday seemed to be eternally connected. They sent thousands of text messages, navigated browsers with ease, they were googling and spending hours on MySpace (remember, it was 2001).

Librarians, however, knew there were problems with the metaphor. In our schools students often defaulted to a Google search for academic papers. They typed into the address bar or search box entire questions rather than using strategic search terms, often wondering why their search did not work. They settled for the first entries they found, despite the fact that the source might have limited relevance, be of poor quality and/or even inaccurate.

Digital natives proved to be uncritical consum- 5 ers of online information and content. And so we struggled to teach information and digital literacy skills to a generation of students being told by the media and adults around them that they were digital natives, comfortable and capable in online environments, despite evidence to the contrary. We have come a long way in a short time. Prensky has acknowledged the limitation of the digital native metaphor, although he still argues its usefulness (Prensky, 2011). The youth we see in our libraries have a wider variety of skills and knowledge than the word "native" suggests. Despite having never experienced a time before the World Wide Web, or even the ease of participation and content creation,

they do not enter school as critical consumers or capable producers of information. They may be able to locate the web site of their favorite entertainer, or play online games but they may not be able to access and evaluate information to support academic subjects, much less evaluate the point of view and bias of that information.

Matt Williams, Educational Technologist at KQED, recently provided me with a different framing, an interesting way of understanding the role school librarians might have in a digital age. He suggested that youth today are tech savvy, not digitally literate. A look at the research into the skills and interests of youth in a digital way will shed some light on this difference.

Tech Savvy Youth

It is undeniable that youth have access and are accessing digital technologies. In 2010, 84 percent of 8–18 year olds reported having home access to the Internet (Rideout, Foehr, & Roberts, 2010), and this does not take into account school and after school environments. Furthermore, 66 percent of youth had mobile phones (Rideout, et al., 2010). As youth age, the numbers increase. Ninety-three percent of teens have home access to the Internet and 78 percent report having a cell phone with an increasing number of these phones being smart phones (Madden, Lenhart, Duggan, Cortesi, & Gasser, 2013). What these numbers suggest is that the majority of American youth are engaged in using both at-home online technologies and mobile technologies. However, the numbers do not reflect the quality of their access; for instance, the number of teens with access to broadband is much lower.

Furthermore, the numbers are not reflective of the quality of their engagement with digital information. In a follow up to the Digital Native article, Prensky indicates we should be encouraging "digital wisdom" and maintains that the digital native metaphor was indicative of "young people's comfort with digital technology." This is a tech savvy youth construction. However, even as a metaphor there are some concerns with this generalization and it is time to retire the concept of a digital native, and recognize that tech savvy doesn't mean digitally literate (and perhaps not ALL youth are tech savvy).

Digitally Literate Youth

As stated above, being a technically savvy student does not mean one is a digitally literate student. Literacy suggests a capacity to be competent in a particular context (Erstad, 2011; Gee, 1996). Digital literacy suggests that one has both the basic skills to navigate an online environment but can also communicate, collaborate, and produce in online communities (Erstad, 2011; Harlan, 2012).

However, research indicates a lack of competence in being critical consumers, and a lack of involvement in collaborative production (Head & Eisenberg, 2009; Kennedy & Judd, 2011). We must recognize that competence goes beyond access, that in order to be digitally literate we have roles as critical consumers, and producers of information. Schools, and libraries, have an opportunity to contribute to developing this literacy.

It isn't just consuming and producing information that youth must consider in regard to digital literacy. There are issues of safety and privacy that relate to the role of circulator or the sharing of information in online environments. For example, reports on cyberbullying indicate that while a majority of youth have seen cyberbullying, 66 percent report that teens are mostly nice to each other in online environments (Lenhart, Madden, Smith, Purcell, & Rainie, 2011).

As youth participate in spreading information they need to understand the responsibility implicit in sharing, particularly since it is so easy. This has implications not just in safety and responsibility to others but issues of copyright and fair use as well. Teacher librarians are positioned to help youth understand legal and ethical consequences in circulating information.

Today's youth need to understand the opportunities of the online environment (Livingstone, 2008); however, they also need to understand the risks (Palfrey & Gasser, 2008). They need instruction in identity management. They need support in managing a network that supports learning and personal interests. They need to understand how the content they share represents them. They need to understand how personal information is gathered and used for corporate interests so they can make informed choices. They need to be digitally literate, not just technologically savvy.

Dispelling the Myth, Breaking Down the Metaphor

I respect Prensky's defense of the digital native as a metaphor, his emphasis that he was trying to indicate the comfort youth have with technology. However the metaphor has its limitations, and has become shorthand for moral panic and rose-colored optimism. We need to embrace the nuance the metaphor lacks, and we need to promote a critical vision of youth's skills in online and mobile environments. Teacher librarians are particularly well located to challenge the myth and help youth become digitally literate. But first we must retire the digital native.

References

Erstad, O. (2011). Citizens navigating in literate worlds: The case of digital literacy. In M. Thomas (Ed.), *Deconstructing digital natives: Young people, technology, and the new literacies*. New York: Routledge.

Gee, J. P. (1996). Social linguistics and literacies: Ideology in discourses. Retrieved from Amazon.com

Harlan, M. A. (2012). *Information practices of teen content creators: The intersection of action and experiences*. PhD, Queensland University of Technology, Queensland, Aus.

Head, A. J., & Eisenberg, M. (2009). Finding context: What today's college students say about conducting research in the digital age. Retrieved from http://projectinfolit.org/publications/

Kennedy, G. E., & Judd, T. S. (2011). Beyond Google and the "satisficing" searching of digital natives. In M. Thomas (Ed.), *Deconstructing digital natives: Young people, technology, and the new literacies*. New York: Routledge.

Lenhart, A., Madden, M., Smith, A., Purcell, K., & Rainie, L. (2011). Teens, kindness and cruelty on social network sites. Retrieved from http://pewinternet.org/Reports/2011/Teens-and-social-media.aspx

Livingstone, S. (2008). Taking risky opportunities in youthful content creation: Teenagers use of social networking sites for intimacy, privacy, and self-expression. *New Media and Society*, 10(3), 393. Retrieved from Sage Journals Online.

Madden, M., Lenhart, A., Duggan, M., Cortesi, S., & Gasser, U. (2013). Teens and Technology. *Pew Internet and American Life Project*. Retrieved from http://www.pewinternet.org/Reports/2013/Teens-and-Tech.aspx

Palfrey, J., & Gasser, U. (2008). *Born digital: Understanding the first generation of digital natives*. New York, NY: Basic Books.

Prensky, M. (2001). Digital natives, digital immigrants. *On the Horizon*, 9. Retrieved from http://www.marcprensky.com/writing/default.asp

Prensky, M. (2011). Digital wisdom and Homo Sapiens digital. In M. Thomas (Ed.), *Deconstructing digital natives: Young people, technology, and the new literacies*. New York: Routledge.

Rideout, V. J., Foehr, U. G., & Roberts, D. F. (2010). Generation M2: Media in the Lives of 8-18 year olds. Retrieved from http://www.kff.org/entmedia/upload/8010.pdf

Help Teens Erase Their Web Indiscretions

The Christian Science Monitor *produces a weekly news magazine and a Web site dedicated to independent, international journalism. This editorial was published on November 19, 2013.*

Most states allow someone to expunge his or her record of being arrested or convicted for a crime committed as a minor. The idea is simple: You can reclaim your innocence as an adult after a youthful indiscretion. Coming of age earns you a clean slate, a presumption of probity.

In September, California approved a law that applies the idea to what teenagers often post on social media. It requires websites to let teens delete images or words they have come to regret and that might be used against them if they apply for college, a job, a mortgage, or a credit card.

Other states, such as New Jersey and Utah, now have similar legislation pending. And last week, a group of bipartisan lawmakers introduced a bill in Congress, known as the Do Not Track Kids Act, that would extend the concept nationwide.

The federal bill would not only prohibit Web companies from collecting personal information from teens under 16 without their consent, but it would also create an "erase button" to let them delete embarrassing content from a site where it was posted. (For technical reasons, the law does not extend to copies of content that end up on other sites or other people's computers.)

5   Such measures are well timed. Most teenagers now have smart phones, which allow easier access to Twitter, Facebook, Instagram, Google+, and similar sites. The number of teens who worry about Internet privacy has jumped to 43 percent from 35 percent last year. And many more teens may now regret their digital footprints, which helps account for the popularity of Snapchat. Users of that site can send a photo to a friend and have it disappear for good within seconds.

Young people may welcome laws that help them better navigate their evolving use of the Internet as they mature and wish to expunge previous postings, e-mails, or text messages. Many sites already allow such deletions, but the law would ensure they happen.

But in a sign of why the laws are needed, Facebook was forced last week to amend the public description of its new privacy policy after critics said the social network was trying to collect more information on teens without their consent in order to boost advertising revenue.

Another approach to the problem, now gaining ground in some states, is to bar employers from using old personal data in hiring decisions. And a few public schools are debating whether to start teaching proper ethics and etiquette in the use of social media.

A minor's mistakes on the Web should not follow them into adulthood, just as the criminal record of a teen can be sealed for good. Being able to erase a past error has long been society's way to support an individual's redemption.

10   Many teens may come to regret a photo on social media or other Internet postings. But a new California law, which requires websites to let teens "erase" their digital past, may be catching on in other states.

An Internet "Eraser" Law Would Hurt, Not Help, Oregon Teens

SUSAN NIELSEN

Susan Nielsen is an associate editor and columnist for the Portland Oregonian *newspaper, and the publication's lead editorial writer on law and education. This commentary appeared in the September 28, 2013 edition.*

California just passed a law giving teenagers the right to erase their online mistakes. This makes the Golden State a national leader not just in digital privacy, but in helicopter parenting.

Oregon shouldn't follow California's example on this unenforceable, misleading law. It's corrosive to imply to teenagers that being a good person is just a matter of proper image management. It also

doesn't do teens any favors to enable their most immature online behavior, as if the hurt they inflict could be deleted with video-game ease.

Last week, California Gov. Jerry Brown signed into law a bill with a right-to-delete, or "eraser," provision for minors. It would require Web sites to give users under 18 a way to delete photos, comments and other material they wish they hadn't posted.

"Kids and teenagers often self-reveal before they self-reflect," says James Steyer, director of Common Sense Media, a San Francisco–based group that lobbied for the bill. "Too often, young people post information they later regret but can't delete from the online and mobile world. All of us—especially kids—should be able to delete what we post."

5   Steyer's argument swayed a California lawmaker who's the father of a teenage girl. He sponsored the bill and found plenty of support among colleagues with their own concerns about the online impulsiveness of their college-bound darlings.

Now this groundbreaking law is making headlines nationwide, as California's digital regulations always do. Oregon may be tempted to follow suit, enticed by the notion of protecting teenagers from themselves. However, a special right-to-delete law for teens suffers from two fatal flaws.

First, few things can be permanently deleted from the Internet. They can be removed from a particular site, yes. (In fact, most social-media sites do offer ways to take down damaging content, which is a very good thing, especially in instances of online bullying.) But it's almost impossible to "erase" something that has been shared with friends and stored in big server farms. To imply otherwise to teenagers is grossly irresponsible.

Second, the idea of giving your children their own handy-dandy Internet eraser shares the same quality of most other helicopter-parent schemes: It is doomed to backfire by enabling more childish behavior which, in turn, triggers the need for more rescuing.

I don't mean to minimize the problem of teenagers paying an outsized price for the dumb things they say or do online. A single photo can wreck a kid's reputation; a string of cruel comments, left to simmer online, can drive a kid to despair. More companies are recognizing their moral responsibility here, which is why Facebook and other social-media sites have made it easier to report and scrub regrettable content.

10   But giving teenagers special Internet privileges isn't the right remedy, particularly when those privileges are illusory. If anything, we should take the opposite approach: We should make it more clear to teenagers that they are real and other people are real, and the things they say and do have a lasting impact—both online and in person.

Staring at a screen can mess with your head a little. You start to think of people as "people," and you can persuade yourself that deleting an email or ignoring a text is a reasonable way to deal with a conflict. You can forget about your actual self, sitting there, the permanent understudy to your online persona. You can make this mistake with your kids, too, and accidentally spend more energy polishing their image than developing their character.

I don't think that was the motive behind California's right-to-delete law. But that's probably how a group of otherwise sane adults might buy into the idea of a magical eraser.

Meet Jack

GARY VARVEL

Gary Varvel is the editorial cartoonist for The Indianapolis Star, *and his cartoons have appeared in many other publications, including* Newsweek, The New York Times, *and* National Review. *In the past twelve years, he has won the Indiana Society of Professional Journalists' Award for Best Editorial Cartoon ten times.*

Meet Jack

He studied hard at College

Jack earned a Degree

It cost him 4 years and Tens of Thousands of Dollars

Jack partied hard at College

He put it all on FaceBook

Potential Employers found it

It cost him 4 years and Tens of Thousands of Dollars

The Age of the Selfie: Taking, Sharing Our Photos Shows Empowerment, Pride

ADRIENNE SARASY

Adrienne Sarasy was a junior at Healdsburg High School and joint editor-in-chief of the school's newspaper, The Hound's Bark, *when this editorial appeared in February 2014. It was reprinted in the Santa Rosa* Press Democrat, *along with its companion piece by Robert Wilcox, on March 9, 2014.*

With the proliferation of social media outlets like Facebook, Twitter and Instagram, there has been a whirlwind of photos cataloging people's lives, meals and, most importantly, appearances.

Selfies, most often those of women and girls, can be found within any popular social media site. The idea behind the selfie is to capture a photo in which you feel extraordinary, beautiful and confident, and share it with the world. In fact, it is an act of pride and even empowerment for those who post these selfies.

However, this empowerment is viewed by some selfie-critics as a narcissistic act of self-indulgence. Indeed, by taking a photo of yourself and posting it into the world of social media, you may give off the impression that you are attention-seeking and self-absorbed, but who doesn't enjoy the compliments and feeling of receiving a significant amount of likes on a photo?

As individuals, we are inherently attention-seeking, whether we like to think so or not. We seek attention in all aspects of the ways in which we present ourselves to society. More often than not, this venture toward attention is interpreted as a form of self-expression and uniqueness, but it still is rooted within the same soils of self-indulgence. The selfie allows those who take selfies to proclaim their confidence and love for themselves via the Internet, while redefining the ways in which society defines beauty as a whole.

A recent Dove campaign harnessed the power of the selfie to address the growing issues involving low self-esteem in teens and young women.

In this campaign, they interviewed teenaged girls and their mothers, and asked them to define their own, personal beauty. The majority of the girls and their mothers addressed their unique attributes as their flaws, feeling that these flaws failed to make them beautiful.

Big eyebrows, red cheeks, frizzy hair, and freckles were just some of the attributes which these girls wanted to alter about themselves. The girls picked these features because they did not fit the criteria of "normal beauty," which society and the fashion industry have established as the anorexic, photoshopped faces of models. They felt they themselves were not beautiful. Yet through the employment of the selfie, Dove showed the girls and their mothers where true beauty lies—not in the photoshopped figures of models, but in the faces of real women.

The power behind the selfie is far greater than simply that of narcissism. In truth, the selfie has proliferated the images of real people who have found beauty within their own skin, rather than carefully edited images of supermodels. They are these images, these selfies, which are working to redefine the ways in which society views beauty. Selfies from people young and old, male and female are the catalysts to changing the established notions of beauty as a whole, and are the entities which will improve self esteem and confidence within this generation of Google babies.

So maybe selfies seem self-indulgent, and a tad annoying on your Instagram feed, but when the true power of the selfie is harnessed, the ways in which society perceives and defines beauty will forever be altered for the better.

The Age of the Selfie: Endless Need to Share Tears Society's Last Shred of Decency

ROBERT WILCOX

Robert Wilcox was a senior at Healdsburg High School and entertainment editor of the school's newspaper, The Hound's Bark, *when this editorial appeared in February 2014. It was reprinted in the Santa Rosa* Press Democrat, *along with its companion piece by Adrienne Sarasy, on March 9, 2014.*

The epidemic known as "the selfie" is destroying the last shreds of decency in our society. "Selfie" was Oxford Dictionaries' word of the year in 2013, and is defined as a photograph that one has taken of oneself, typically one taken with a smartphone or webcam and uploaded to a social media website.

The very fact that the word "selfie" is now in the dictionary—not to mention that it is word of the year—is a disgrace. Even worse is the speed and ferocity with which this terrible trend has consumed the lives of millions of people.

Since the creation of mega-social sites like Facebook and Twitter, the Internet has gradually transformed us to an exhibition-ist and self-obsessed people, who feel the need to share every single aspect of their daily lives with the world. Girls post promiscuous pictures of themselves dressed in risqué outfits, guys flex in the mirror half-naked, and many more reveal intimate aspects of their lives that could potentially endanger both their reputation and their physical well-being. The first thing selfie fanatics need to realize is that almost no one else in the world cares to see photos of them at all, let alone self-taken pixelated portraits taken with a smartphone camera. I know it's hard to believe, but really, we don't care if you just got out of the shower, or if you've been working out!

By broadcasting racy images of yourself on all of your social networking accounts, not only are you annoying all of your friends, you are opening up your life to the rest of the world, which can be dangerous. Though you may think that that "special someone" is admiring the close-up of your lips that you just took, it may actually be some creep in his basement doing God knows what with all of your pictures. It is scary to think about how many people can see all of your photos on the Internet; do you really want the entire world to be able to see the innermost workings of your daily lives?

5   The danger of releasing these photos of yourself becomes more apparent on a daily basis. Social media sites now post the location and time your photos were taken, giving anyone—including predators—access to very personal information, like where you live and your daily routines. The consequences of posting selfies could be much greater than you ever imagined; someone could rob your home when they know you are out, or even find and kidnap you based on the location of that "harmless" photo you just took.

This issue of exhibitionism not only extends to selfies, but to the rest of our social networking lives as well. The societal trend of documenting our entire lives on the Internet is becoming more prevalent, and it's more of an issue than most people think. Every second, millions of people tweet about their mundane lives, parents post photos of their children on Facebook, and countless others upload selfies to Instagram. Why is it so important that everyone else in the world know every nuance of your daily life?

While it is generally virtuous to be "an open book," in this case we need to be more protective of our personal information. Releasing pictures and detailed information about yourself can be dangerous, and even if you are never subject to these dangers, it is an extremely annoying habit.

If you are a chronic selfie taker, do yourself and the rest of your friends a favor; stop taking close-ups of your face.

The Rise of "Great Potential": Youth Activism Against Gender-Based Violence

AASHIKA DAMODAR

Aashika Damodar is an anthropologist, artist, and social activist interested in creative uses of technology for positive social impact. Among other accomplishments, she is the founder of Freedom Connect, a nonprofit organization working to develop and extend innovative technology platforms for the anti-trafficking movement. She also received the United Nations Association Community Human Rights Award in 2008 for her anti-trafficking work. This article appeared in the Fall 2012 issue of the Harvard International Review.

On February 12, 2012, thousands of young people watched the Grammys in anticipation of who would win the year's most coveted awards, such as Best Artist and Best Album of the year. The Grammy telecast encouraged Tweeters to participate in a parallel awarding process based on snap judgments of all the performances and awards, grounded in personal taste. One commentator wrote, "Twitter, after all, is like a T-shirt whose slogan you can keep changing: every new tap of the keyboard trumpets your tastes." When Chris Brown accepted the award for Best R&B Album for his latest record "F.A.M.E" there was a surge of tweets across the "twitterverse" both in celebration and disgust. Brown's assault on his ex-girlfriend, Rihanna, after a pre-Grammy party back in 2009 had made him the most contentious character of this year's awards.

Youth across the world hurled various responses all over Twitter and Facebook, some in disgust at every mention and sight of Brown. Others shouted overwhelming support for the award. Perhaps the most upsetting to witness were the women who made his history of abuse light and trivial by stating their willingness to allow him to beat them.

Their rawness and insensitivity prompted several bloggers and activists to write about the incident. This surge in dialogue in the twitterverse was indicative of several issues, the most important being how complex and nuanced gender-based violence actually is, and how far we still have to go as a movement to end it.

Shortly after this episode, BET.com temporarily dropped Dream Hampton's "The Trouble with Chris Brown," which discussed the origins of Brown's manchildish behavior and his rash attempt to replace critically needed therapy with a small team of tweeters using the hashtag *#teambreezy* to show he still had support. "Team Breezy" is simply a group of Chris Brown supporters.It is often referred to as a digital team of fans, whose primary goal is to tell everyone about their position, and share their passion both on- and offline as much as possible.

5   BET's permissiveness, the slew of young women and girls who made up *#teambreezy*, female bloggers

(and commenters on blogs), and twitter followers who unwaveringly stood by Chris Brown amidst domestic violence charges and uncontrolled violent outbursts are very telling of some of the issues youth will face, and how they will address it in the future. Nearly 10 million @chrisbrown followers drove his album "F.A.M.E" to the number one spot, but failed to hold him accountable, relentlessly displacing responsibility for his actions onto others.

In this paper, I will attempt to unpack the parameters of what social media and connective technologies do for youth and youth activists. As a practitioner who has seen a diverse range of uses of connective technologies against human rights violations and gender-based violence, it is clear that social media has been important in recent social movements. Numerous cases show that opportunities for participation by youth and members of the public are greatly expanding through social media. However, the "youth" cannot be described as a homogenous category, and the use of connective technology among them is diverse and heavily contingent on context and level of access. I will explain how social media is creating new possibilities and practices among youth and its role in promoting and prompting progressive social change. With regular access to social media, the youth are influential "enablers" and have the greatest potential of spurring change. I will also outline the limited functionality of social media, the need for associated offline action and clear targets, and cases of success and failure in which technology is involved. Gender-based violence both in the developed and developing world are a complex blend of structural and cultural challenges, many of which are enhanced and enabled by communicative technology.

What Is Social Media?

It is first important to define what we mean by social media. Kaplan and Haenlein define social media as "a group of Internet-based applications that build on the ideological and technological foundations of Web 2.0, and that allow the creation and exchange of User Generated Content." There are different types of social media, including collaborative web-based projects such as Wikipedia, Pinterest, and Reddit, which are content communities that constantly evolve based on the information that people contribute. Online collaboration platforms, blogs, video, and traditional social networking platforms such as Twitter and Facebook are included in the category of social media. According to this definition of social media, email and short messaging services or texting would not be included because it is content not readily exchangeable by the public. However, this is increasingly changing, as people are using short messaging services as a means of mass public broadcasting and collaboration.

While there are varying definitions of social media, it seems no matter what the tool, the tool itself has no original intent towards a specific end. Facebook, Twitter, Youtube, and other platforms were not necessarily established for activism. This may seem obvious, but to those immersed in youth activism, it is easy to lose sight of this. Low barriers to access and use now means that there is a lot of positive and negative noise on the web. Youth, who I call "the great potential," utilize technology to create positive and negative social environments. The proceeding findings apply to all the following forms of technology, including: mobile phones, picture messaging, social sharing spaces, and crowd-sourced platforms.

So how do youth and young adults pick and chose which social media platforms they will use? Usually, it starts with a personal recommendation. People are inclined to join social platforms under the influence of their friends and family. Usage of various platforms is also largely dependent on accessibility, cost, and ease of use. There are several economic and social rationales for using different platforms. These rationales combined inform the context in which they are operationalized. Any analysis of youth movements can and should begin there.

Activating Social Media

10 Digital communication technology offers a wide range of capabilities: increased accessibility and opportunities to disseminate information, coordinate action, make decisions, and to build trust and a sense of collective identity. Before an individual considers going through these steps, an original motive is needed. At minimum, people need to feel excited, aggrieved, or worried about something. In today's digital age, how does anyone become aggrieved about issues beyond what is happening to them directly? It usually starts with a personal connection. It starts with information, and an explanation of how this issue is a violation of his or her rights, the rights of others, and is causing an injustice that has an impact on issues important to them. Social media can both generate and share information, where mainstream news may not reach. This is particularly important when working with young people, who may not be avid newsreaders, but rely heavily on social media as a source of news.

There are countless examples of people using social media to share their grievances. Whether it is activists in Iran or users of Weibo in China, as information on issues such as government corruption or human rights violations swarms over social media networks, these people can mobilize to realize an alternative. Two of my favorite examples of such action include HarassMap in Egypt, and Mensajes de Paz in Guatemala.

In countries like Egypt and Guatemala, regular text messaging, data maps, and social networking platforms are being used to address sexual harassment and report sexual assault. Most women who live here are constantly exposed to a range of offensive and endangering behavior.

The Egyptian Center for Women's Rights in Cairo called harassment in Egypt a "dangerous social cancer" in a survey from 2008. This survey found that 83 percent of Egyptian women and 98 percent of foreign women experience sexual harassment in Egypt. As a response to the rampant levels of harassment, several women came together to found a project called HarassMap, which is a crowdsourcing project that utilizes open-source technologies such as Ushahidi, a web crowd-map and mobile technology to encourage women to report and document incidents of harassment via the web, Twitter, and text. The technology empowers and enables women to share experiences and raise awareness through pro-active reporting. Women can report anonymously in real time, and will receive an automated message that reads: "Thank you for reporting harassment. If you would like to receive legal or psychological assistance or other services, please contact the NGO Task Force on Sexual Harassment at 33464901." All reports are published (without names or phone numbers) on an online map, which shows the areas where complaints are coming from.

Mensajes de Paz, which translates to "Messages of Peace," works in as similar manner. Mensajes de Paz is a project of Justice for My Sister (JFMS), a women's collective and film documentary addressing gender-based violence. At its core, *Justice for my Sister* is a David versus Goliath story. A courageous woman named Rebeca takes on a giant system to demand answers for her sister's brutal murder, and she has all the odds stacked against her, but her resilience and power is unstoppable. Violence against women, and specifically femicide (gender-based killing) is an epidemic in Guatemala; nearly 6000 women have been murdered in the last decade and only two percent of the killers were sentenced. The film documents one of the few successful cases from beginning to end. Survivors Connect collaborated with producers of the film to create a text message-based reporting and awareness campaign. The film is regularly screened in villages and communities where violence is rampant and access to resources is bleak.

15 At each of the film screenings, volunteers at JFMS collected phone numbers of viewers who wished to stay in touch with the campaign, receive regular alerts of resources near them, and report instances of violence, which are then mapped.

In both cases of action, connective technology has offered a flexible and decentralized communication infrastructure, which gives way for the public to report, shape opinion, and more easily facilitate action. The Internet has facilitated rapid and cheap communication across vast geographical boundaries and has transformed the dissatisfaction of women in Egypt and Guatemala into collective action quickly and effectively. These online movements helped people find and disseminate information, recruit participants, organize, coordinate, and make decisions.

Though both cases have combined various connective technologies and social media in innovative ways, there is an integral element to their success, which often goes unacknowledged. Both movements include durable activist networks, and the use of technologies alone does not necessarily guarantee this stability. Regular "grass roots" level meetings, online spaces for collaboration, and coordination around well-defined projects and goals can help make networks long-lasting, and achieve impact on violence are also addressed, such as what constitutes rape or harassment, and how women are not "asked" to be harassed based on what they wear. Volunteers distribute pamphlets and flyers about the project, and many people have been receptive to this type of messaging. In both countries, communities have organized themselves with neighborhood safety groups and protecting the streets. Youth-led activism has also been critical, where the skills and access to technologies are higher than in other populations. In these contexts, there is an economic and demo this issue, which is constantly evolving with new targets, opponents, and struggles. In both examples, there is a strong element of the "face-to-face" connection, which works to sustain their momentum.

In the case of efforts like HarassMap and Mensajes de Paz, participants have explained that while direct advocacy on the issue is key, the solution lies much more in the shifting of cultural perspectives on gender relations. Women argue that the social stigma is no longer widespread and contemporary society tends to trivialize gender-based violence. In order to "re-create the stigma" as some activists have put it, they rely on one-to-one interactions so that interpersonal relationships are built between activists and new recruits. Images, stories, emails, comments on Facebook and Twitter, films and statements convey the mission, and their interactions around the issues, contribute the process of identifying and defining the movement.

The online piece on its own however, is heavily prone to a problem called "flaming" where exchanges online consist of highly inflamed attacks on opinion, rather than discussion. While a degree of conflict is necessary in any social movement, whether it is a coalition or advocacy campaign, flaming does not happen nearly to the same degree when people are forced to talk with each other in person. Discussions happen, forcing people to overcome differences, build relationships and understanding, ultimately resulting in incremental change.

How do HarassMap and Mensajes de Paz encourage people to report? Has the reporting itself made a difference? Not so surprisingly, much of their success can be attributed to its proactive approach on the streets where the violence actually occurs. In the case of HarassMap, over 500 volunteers speak to people as neighbors and remind men of traditional Egyptian values of safety, pride and dignity. Mensajes de Pas works with a collective of women who hold community screenings and discussions about the film in schools, universities, unions, prisons and other youth groups. Misconceptions about gender-based graphic imperative for the power of mobile technology. The tools match the goals, the targets, and the context.

Combining Online Activism and Offline Action

In the previous sections, I discussed how powerful combinations of online and offline tactics have helped create sustained youth-led movements against gender-based violence. Of the various tools available today in an activist's tool box—such as e-petitions, emails, crowdsourcing and crowdfunding, SMS, targeted tweets or Facebook statuses, special avatars and more—these movements chose tactics that fit their target population, context, and need. Though, often times, these forms of activism are considered to be passive, compared to the more aggressive offline tactics of past movements. Malcolm Gladwell, a thought leader in this camp, is skeptical that digital tactics can really make a difference. Several call this pool of tactics as "slacktivism," "clicktivism" or my personal favorite, "armchair activism."

I am not quite as pessimistic as Gladwell. Social media and connective technologies for youth activism against gender-based violence can work, especially when the target is easily defined and the goals are clear. Digital tactics are not always passive. Social media and digital tactics work best in the instances where activists are mindful of who their target(s)/opponent(s) are, and what they are likely to see, where they are located, and what their sensitivities are. The phrase, "keep your friends close but keep your enemies closer" could not be more relevant here. Cases such as protests against Village Voice and sex trafficking (in progress), or GoDaddy and its support for Stop Online Piracy Act (SOPA) worked because public outrage made it easy for clients to take their business elsewhere, which was a direct threat they would listen and respond to. In the case of Susan G. Komen, who relies on donors, the foundation was severely put at risk with the wave of bad publicity after revoking critical funds to Planned Parenthood. E-petitions, Facebook shares and tweets were well heard by the opponents, and there was no choice but to respond.

Activists were smart in placing the tactic to fit the context. This sadly is not always the case. Digital activist scholar Mary Joyce has observed that other forms of digi-activism such as changing Facebook or Twitter icons green did not help much with pro-democracy activists in Iran in

2009. These tactics are the least threatening to the target. Though this act did not have a direct impact on the movement, it should be understood that this action is one of solidarity, and does not make the action wrong. A Facebook status change, changing of a profile picture or a tweet is a symbol of a specific outcome and change one wishes to see. The underlying lesson here is that of all the tactics available, activists should make decisions based on their relative strengths and weaknesses in relation to their fellow activists, their opponents or targets, and the context in which the tactic is operationalized.

Often times, activism on gender-based violence (or any issue) is incredibly difficult because the movement lacks clearly defined targets. In the cases of HarassMap and Mensajes de Paz, their targets are not specific individuals or institutions, but rather a culture. This is harder to change, further making a compelling case for smarter offline work. Digital communication tools and social media however, are integral now because it creates a short stepladder of engagement for people new to the cause, which is giving rise to "the great potential." A tweet to an elected official may not necessarily do much, but it also requires very little of activists in terms of the personal time, resources, and commitment, which in the case of offline action, such as a rally or meeting, are incredibly high. Today, the first step of engagement with many social movements is risk-free and as easy as clicking a button. One may be inclined to continue their involvement, however it is up to good organizers to keep people engaged and demonstrate impact.

Perhaps this is where we should be looking towards our predecessors who organized without social media, and remind ourselves of how they spurred change. In the span of just under 50 years, the British Government outlawed the slave trade and went on to abolish the practice throughout its colonies. It is still by far one of the most successful reform movements of the 19th century. This win was tremendous for its time; people believed that

25

the nation's economy and the economies of its colonies would collapse if slavery ended, vital labor would be lost, and that it was a right to have a slave. Against all odds, the Society for Abolition of the Slave Trade tasked itself to create a constituency of anti-slavery activists through what we would now call traditional means of organizing through distribution of books, pamphlets, prints, and artifacts. It took courage for people to participate in the movement. They had a network of country committees scattered throughout the country working on getting vital petition signatures, and had travelling agents who served as links to the organizing hubs, offering advice to newly-joined activists. If youth plan on creating movements for the long haul, they will need to remember these challenges, strategies, and tactics. Given the widespread accessibility of social media and connective technologies, I fear that youth may become increasingly predisposed towards "slacktivism." Technology is usually the first medium of entry to causes and news, because this is also where their social relations are. Technologies can be effective in getting people to be more active participants, however, sustained and meaning ful progress will always rely on good organizers.

Conclusion

The Internet offers an unprecedented flexible and decentralized communication infrastructure, facilitating rapid and cheap communication across vast geographical boundaries. The Internet can transform dissatisfaction to a mass collective action quickly, as well as organize, coordinate, and spread information. While the digital revolution provides us with a plentiful box of tactics and tools, it doesn't necessarily mean that these attempts at activism are any more successful than before. It may possibly lead to faster responses from well-defined targets, in the case of GoDaddy or Susan

G. Komen. For larger, more broadly defined social ills of society, such as sexual violence, we need durable activist networks. Social change is never achieved just through one action alone.

We must abandon the idea that digital communication tools will bring about radical change to our generation. Successful youth-led movements will be predicated on how new tools and old practices are combined in modular and innovative ways. The most important consequence of digital technologies for youth movements will be neither a creation of a futuristic digital politics nor full-scale transformation of politics as usual, but rather in the integration of novel practices and technology, creating a new normal for youth going forward; this is where "the great potential" lives.

Powerful technology-driven initiatives such as HarassMap, Mensajes de Paz, and others will be important steps in recording and combating gender-based violence. If these small steps succeed in the countries of origin, I am positive that youth will seek to follow suit in further exploration of how technology can increase awareness, shift public opinion and attitudes about violence, and create safer communities. I am reminded by the Chris Brown example that his fans and youth are the most influential "enablers" of all, however, in some cases, at their own dismay. It is a testament to young men and boys across the country that this is what women indeed want, and that the behavior can be acceptable and tolerated because Chris Brown can. We often refuse to call abuse when we see it, and refuse to acknowledge the problem because of the regular depictions in our entertainment. We have a long way to go, but when youth stop accepting, and defend the behavior less, the change will be obvious on the web and in our culture. The ways in which youth and social movements balance their presence on and offline will be integral to their success.

■ ■ ■ **FOR CLASS DISCUSSION Digital Literacies**

1. Think about the articles in this unit as well as your own experiences with digital technologies. In what specific ways do you think these technologies affect interpersonal relationships, for better or worse? What claims of danger or harm are made in these readings? What arguments can you identify that counter these claims? Which arguments are most convincing and why?

2. Log your own use of communication technologies over twenty-four hours—social networking, e-mailing, texting, tweeting, talking over a device, Web surfing, TV watching. Come to class prepared to discuss the ways in which you use these various technologies (e.g., social interaction, information or news gathering, education, movies or television, music, gaming, consumer activity, business communication, work, other). How do you feel these activities enhance your development and learning socially, academically, or professionally? How might they impede or interfere with development and learning? Did you multitask? If so, do you feel you were more productive or more distracted?

3. Much has been made in the mainstream media about the dangers of revealing too much personal information on social networking sites such as Facebook or Twitter. Discuss your own experience of identity sharing on social networking spaces: What do you reveal? What do you conceal? If you are sharing your information willingly, what responsibility, if any, do governments or Web service providers have to protect your privacy or help you manage your online identity? Should the rules be different if the person in question is a teen or young adult?

4. Think of an instance where social media have been employed to raise awareness of an issue or to address an injustice. (Consider, for example, Adrienne Sarasy's positive analysis of selfies or Aashika Damodar's explanation of social media to combat gender violence in Cairo.) How effective are the campaigns that you have encountered via social media? Has on online campaign ever spurred you to take offline action?

■ ■ ■

WRITING ASSIGNMENT Researched Argument

Research a recent instance of political activism that employed a significant social media campaign. You might consider one of the movements cited by Aashika Damodar. Other possibilities include campaigns for marriage equality, for GMO labeling in various states, for protesting Russia's anti-gay laws leading up to the Sochi 2014 Olympics, for stopping the African cult leader Joseph Kony (Kony 2012), for protesting income inequality (Occupy Wall Street), or a host of other examples. What social media tactics were employed? Was there a corresponding offline campaign? What have critics cited as significant and/or controversial about your chosen campaign or about social media campaigns in general? Then, write a researched argument evaluating the effectiveness of your campaign. Alternatively, you might reimagine the campaign and propose a set of tactics that you believe would be more effective. ■

Argument Classics

In this unit we present four arguments that have been particularly effective at influencing public opinion, presenting uncomfortable truths to their audiences, and demonstrating powerful strategies of persuasion. Each of these arguments has made a difference in the world, either because it has persuaded people of the justice of its claims or has evoked powerful resistance and counterargument. Richly suitable for classroom analysis, each of these classic arguments can move students and teachers alike to introspection and to agreement or dissent.

Lifeboat Ethics: The Case Against Aid That Does Harm

GARRETT HARDIN

Garrett Hardin's "Lifeboat Ethics: The Case Against Aid That Does Harm" has been influential in changing the debate about foreign aid, in stimulating new thinking about the causes of poverty and about ways to combat it, and in promoting wider understanding of the "tragedy of the commons." It has also sparked dozens of impassioned counterarguments. Based on an unflinching analysis of consequences, Hardin presents his anti-liberal thesis against foreign aid and open borders. Rhetorically, Hardin's argument is famous for its extended use of analogy—in this case a lifeboat filled with people representing rich countries and an ocean of swimmers (poor countries) clamoring to get in the boat. The article was originally published in Psychology Today *in 1974.*

Environmentalists use the metaphor of the earth as a "spaceship" in trying to persuade countries, industries and people to stop wasting and polluting our natural resources. Since we all share life on this planet, they argue, no single person or institution has the right to destroy, waste, or use more than a fair share of its resources.

But does everyone on earth have an equal right to an equal share of its resources? The spaceship metaphor can be dangerous when used by misguided idealists to justify suicidal policies for sharing our resources through uncontrolled immigration and foreign aid. In their enthusiastic but unrealistic generosity, they confuse the ethics of a spaceship with those of a lifeboat.

A true spaceship would have to be under the control of a captain, since no ship could possibly survive if its course were determined by committee. Spaceship Earth certainly has no captain; the United Nations is merely a toothless tiger, with little power to enforce any policy upon its bickering members.

If we divide the world crudely into rich nations and poor nations, two thirds of them are desperately poor, and only one third comparatively rich, with the United States the wealthiest of all. Metaphorically each rich nation can be seen as a lifeboat full of comparatively rich people. In the ocean outside each lifeboat swim the poor of the world, who would like to get in, or at least to share some of the wealth. What should the lifeboat passengers do?

First, we must recognize the limited capacity of any lifeboat. For example, a nation's land has a limited capacity to support a population and as the current energy crisis has shown us, in some ways we have already exceeded the carrying capacity of our land.

Adrift in a Moral Sea

So here we sit, say 50 people in our lifeboat. To be generous, let us assume it has room for 10 more, making a total capacity of 60. Suppose the 50 of us in the lifeboat see 100 others swimming in the water outside, begging for admission to our boat or for handouts. We have several options: we may be tempted to try to live by the Christian ideal of being "our brother's keeper," or by the Marxist ideal of "to each according to his needs." Since the needs of all in the water are the same, and since they can all be seen as "our brothers," we could take them all into our boat, making a total of 150 in a boat designed for 60. The boat swamps, everyone drowns. Complete justice, complete catastrophe.

Since the boat has an unused excess capacity of 10 more passengers, we could admit just 10 more to it. But which 10 do we let in? How do we choose? Do we pick the best 10, "first come, first served"? And what do we say to the 90 we exclude? If we do let an extra 10 into our lifeboat, we will have lost our "safety factor," an engineering principle of critical importance. For example, if we don't leave room for excess capacity as a safety factor in our country's agriculture, a new plant disease or a bad change in the weather could have disastrous consequences.

Suppose we decide to preserve our small safety factor and admit no more to the lifeboat. Our survival is then possible although we shall have to be constantly on guard against boarding parties.

While this last solution clearly offers the only means of our survival, it is morally abhorrent to many people. Some say they feel guilty about their good luck. My reply is simple: "Get out and yield your place to others." This may solve the problem of the guilt-ridden person's conscience, but it does not change the ethics of the lifeboat. The needy person to whom the guilt-ridden person yields his place will not himself feel guilty about his good luck. If he did, he would not climb aboard. The net result of conscience-stricken people giving up their unjustly held seats is the elimination of that sort of conscience from the lifeboat.

This is the basic metaphor within which we must work out our solutions. Let us now enrich the image, step by step, with substantive additions from the real world, a world that must solve real and pressing problems of overpopulation and hunger.

The harsh ethics of the lifeboat become even harsher when we consider the reproductive differences between the rich nations and the poor nations. The people inside the lifeboats are doubling in numbers every 87 years; those swimming around outside are doubling, on the average, every 35 years, more than twice as fast as the rich. And since the world's resources are dwindling, the difference in prosperity between the rich and the poor can only increase.

As of 1973, the U.S. had a population of 210 million people, who were increasing by 0.8 percent per year. Outside our lifeboat, let us imagine another 210 million people (say the combined populations of Colombia, Ecuador, Venezuela, Morocco, Pakistan, Thailand and the Philippines) who are increasing at a rate of 3.3 percent per year. Put differently, the doubling time for this aggregate population is 21 years, compared to 87 years for the U.S.

The harsh ethics of the lifeboat become harsher when we consider the reproductive differences between rich and poor.

Multiplying the Rich and the Poor

Now suppose the U.S. agreed to pool its resources with those seven countries, with everyone receiving an equal share. Initially the ratio of Americans to non-Americans in this model would be one-to-one. But consider what the ratio would be after 87 years, by which time the Americans would have doubled to a population of 420 million. By then, doubling every 21 years, the other group would have swollen to 3.54 billion. Each American would have to share the available resources with more than eight people.

But, one could argue, this discussion assumes that current population trends will continue, and they may not. Quite so. Most likely the rate of population increase will decline much faster in the U.S. than it will in the other countries, and there does not seem to be much we can do about it. In sharing with "each according to his needs," we must recognize that needs are determined by population size, which is determined by the rate of reproduction, which at present is regarded as a sovereign right of every nation, poor or not. This being so, the philanthropic load created by the sharing ethic of the spaceship can only increase.

The Tragedy of the Commons

The fundamental error of spaceship ethics, and the sharing it requires, is that it leads to what I call "the tragedy of the commons." Under a system of private property, the men who own property recognize their responsibility to care for it, for if they don't they will eventually suffer. A farmer, for instance, will allow no more cattle in a pasture than its carrying capacity justifies. If he overloads it, erosion sets in, weeds take over, and he loses the use of the pasture.

If a pasture becomes a commons open to all, the right of each to use it may not be matched by a corresponding responsibility to protect it. Asking everyone to use it with discretion will hardly do, for the considerate herdsman who refrains from overloading the commons suffers more than a selfish one who says his needs are greater. If everyone would restrain himself, all would be well; but it takes only one less than everyone to ruin a system of voluntary restraint. In a crowded world of less than perfect human beings, mutual ruin is inevitable if there are no controls. This is the tragedy of the commons.

One of the major tasks of education today should be the creation of such an acute awareness of the dangers of the commons that people will recognize its many varieties. For example, the air and water have become polluted because they are treated as commons. Further growth in the population or per-capita conversion of natural resources into pollutants will only make the problem worse. The same holds true for the fish of the oceans. Fishing fleets have nearly disappeared in many parts of the world, technological improvements in the art of fishing are hastening the day of complete ruin. Only the replacement of the system of the commons with a responsible system of control will save the land, air, water and oceanic fisheries.

The World Food Bank

In recent years there has been a push to create a new commons called a World Food Bank, an international depository of food reserves to which nations would contribute according to their abilities and from which they would draw according to their needs. This humanitarian proposal has received support from many liberal international groups, and from such prominent citizens as Margaret Mead, U.N. Secretary General Kurt Waldheim, and Senators Edward Kennedy and George McGovern.

A world food bank appeals powerfully to our humanitarian impulses. But before we rush ahead with such a plan, let us recognize where the greatest political push comes from, lest we be disillusioned later. Our experience with the "Food for Peace program," or Public Law 480, gives us the answer. This program moved billions of dollars worth of U.S. surplus grain to food-short, population-long countries during the past two decades. But when P.L. 480 first became law, a headline in the business magazine *Forbes* revealed the real power behind it: "Feeding the World's Hungry Millions: How It Will Mean Billions for U.S. Business."

And indeed it did. In the years 1960 to 1970, U.S. taxpayers spent a total of $7.9 billion on the Food for Peace program. Between 1948 and 1970, they also paid an additional $50 billion for other economic-aid programs, some of which went for food and food-producing machinery and technology. Though all U.S. taxpayers were forced to contribute to the cost of P.L. 480 certain special interest groups gained handsomely under the program. Farmers did not have to contribute the grain; the Government or rather the taxpayers, bought it from them at full market prices. The increased demand raised prices of farm products generally. The manufacturers of farm machinery, fertilizers and pesticides benefited by the farmers' extra efforts to grow more food. Grain elevators profited from storing the surplus until it could be shipped. Railroads made money hauling it to ports, and shipping lines profited from carrying it overseas. The implementation of P.L. 480 required the creation of a vast Government bureaucracy, which then acquired its own vested interest in continuing the program regardless of its merits.

Extracting Dollars

Those who proposed and defended the Food for Peace program in public rarely mentioned its importance to any of these special interests. The public emphasis was always on its humanitarian effects. The combination of silent selfish interests and highly vocal humanitarian apologists made a powerful and successful lobby for extracting money from taxpayers. We can expect the same lobby to push now for the creation of a World Food Bank.

However great the potential benefit to selfish interests, it should not be a decisive argument against a truly humanitarian program. We must ask if such a program would actually do more good than harm, not only momentarily but also in the long run. Those who propose the food bank usually refer to a current "emergency" or "crisis" in terms of world food supply. But what is an emergency? Although they may be infrequent and sudden, everyone knows that emergencies will occur from time to time. A well-run family, company, organization or country prepares for the likelihood of accidents and emergencies. It expects them, it budgets for them, it saves for them.

Learning the Hard Way

What happens if some organizations or countries budget for accidents and others do not? If each country is solely responsible for its own well-being, poorly managed ones will suffer. But they can learn from experience. They may mend their ways, and learn to budget for infrequent but certain emergencies. For example, the weather varies from year to year, and periodic crop failures are certain. A wise and competent government saves out of the production of the good years in anticipation of bad years to come. Joseph taught this policy to Pharaoh in Egypt more than 2,000 years ago. Yet the great majority of the governments in the world today do not follow such a policy. They lack either the wisdom or the competence, or both. Should those nations that do manage to put something aside be forced to come to the rescue each time an emergency occurs among the poor nations?

"But it isn't their fault!" Some kind-hearted liberals argue. "How can we blame the poor people who are caught in an emergency? Why must they suffer for the sins of their governments?" The concept of blame is simply not relevant here. The real question is, what are the operational consequences of establishing a world food bank? If it is open to every country every time a need develops, slovenly rulers will not be motivated to take Joseph's advice. Someone will always come to their aid. Some countries will deposit food in the world food bank, and others will withdraw it. There will be almost no overlap. As a result of such solutions to food shortage emergencies, the poor countries will not learn to mend their ways, and will suffer progressively greater emergencies as their populations grow.

Population Control the Crude Way

On the average poor countries undergo a 2.5 percent increase in population each year; rich countries, about 0.8 percent. Only rich countries have anything in the way of food reserves set aside, and even they do not have as much as they should. Poor countries have none. If poor countries received no food from the outside, the rate of their population growth would be periodically checked by crop failures and famines. But if they can always draw on a world food bank in time of need, their population can continue to grow unchecked, and so will their "need" for aid. In the short run, a world food bank may diminish that need, but in the long run it actually increases the need without limit.

Without some system of worldwide food sharing, the proportion of people in the rich and poor nations might eventually stabilize. The overpopulated poor countries would decrease in numbers, while the rich countries that had room for more people would increase. But with a well-meaning system of sharing, such as a world food bank, the growth differential between the rich and the poor countries will not only persist, it will increase. Because of the higher rate of population growth in the poor countries of the world, 88 percent of today's children are born poor, and only 12 percent rich. Year by year the ratio becomes worse, as the fast-reproducing poor outnumber the slow-reproducing rich.

A world food bank is thus a commons in disguise. People will have more motivation to draw from it than to add to any common store. The less provident and less able will multiply at the expense of the abler and more provident, bringing eventual ruin upon all who share in the commons. Besides, any system of "sharing" that amounts to foreign aid from the rich nations to the poor nations will carry the taint of charity, which will contribute little to the world peace so devoutly desired by those who support the idea of a world food bank.

As past U.S. foreign-aid programs have amply and depressingly demonstrated, international charity frequently inspires mistrust and antagonism rather than gratitude on the part of the recipient nation (see "What Other Nations Hear When the Eagle Screams," Kenneth J. and Mary M. Gergen, PT, June).

Chinese Fish and Miracle Rice

The modern approach to foreign aid stresses the export of technology and advice, rather than money and food. As an ancient Chinese proverb goes: "Give a man a fish and he will eat for a day; teach him how to fish and he will eat for the rest of his days." Acting on this advice, the Rockefeller and Ford Foundations have financed a number of programs for improving agriculture in the hungry nations. Known as the "Green Revolution," these programs have led to the development of "miracle rice" and "miracle wheat," new strains that offer bigger harvests and greater resistance to crop damage. Norman Borlaug, the Nobel Prize winning agronomist who, supported by the Rockefeller Foundation, developed "miracle wheat," is one of the most prominent advocates of a world food bank.

Whether or not the Green Revolution can increase food production as much as its champions claim is a debatable but possibly irrelevant point. Those who support this well-intended humanitarian effort should first consider some of the fundamentals of human ecology. Ironically, one man who did was the late Alan Gregg, a vice president of the Rockefeller Foundation. Two decades ago he expressed strong doubts about the wisdom of such attempts to increase food production. He likened the growth and spread of humanity over the surface of the earth to the spread of cancer in the human body, remarking that "cancerous growths demand food; but, as far as I know, they have never been cured by getting it."

Overloading the Environment

Every human born constitutes a draft on all aspects of the environment: food, air, water, forests, beaches, wildlife, scenery and solitude. Food can, perhaps, be significantly increased to meet a growing demand. But what about clean beaches, unspoiled forests, and solitude? If we satisfy a growing population's need for food, we necessarily decrease its per capita supply of the other resources needed by men.

India, for example, now has a population of 600 million, which increases by 15 million each year. This population already puts a huge load on a relatively impoverished environment. The country's forests are now only a small fraction of what they were three centuries ago and floods and erosion continually destroy the insufficient farmland that remains. Every one of the 15 million new lives added to India's population puts an additional burden on the environment, and increases the economic and social costs of crowding. However humanitarian our intent, every Indian life saved through medical or nutritional assistance from abroad diminishes the quality of life for those who remain, and for subsequent generations. If rich countries make it possible, through foreign aid, for 600 million Indians to swell to 1.2 billion in a mere 28 years, as their current growth rate threatens, will future generations of Indians thank us for hastening the destruction of their environment? Will our good intentions be sufficient excuse for the consequences of our actions?

My final example of a commons in action is one for which the public has the least desire for rational discussion—immigration. Anyone who publicly questions the wisdom of current U.S. immigration policy is promptly charged with bigotry, prejudice, ethnocentrism, chauvinism, isolationism or selfishness. Rather than encounter such accusations, one would rather talk about other matters leaving immigration policy to wallow in the crosscurrents of special interests that take no account of the good of the whole, or the interests of posterity.

Perhaps we still feel guilty about things we said in the past. Two generations ago the popular press frequently referred to Dagos, Wops, Polacks, Chinks and Krauts in articles about how America was being "overrun" by foreigners of supposedly inferior genetic stock (see "The Politics of Genetic Engineering: Who Decides Who's Defective?" PT, June). But because the implied inferiority of foreigners was used then as justification for keeping them out, people now assume that restrictive policies could only be based on such misguided notions. There are other grounds.

A Nation of Immigrants

Just consider the numbers involved. Our Government acknowledges a net inflow of 400,000 immigrants a year. While we have no hard data on the extent of illegal entries, educated guesses put the figure at about 600,000 a year. Since the natural increase (excess of births over deaths) of the resident population now runs about 1.7 million per year, the yearly gain from immigration amounts to at least 19 percent of the total annual increase, and may be as much as 37 percent if we include the estimate for illegal immigrants. Considering the growing use of birth-control devices, the potential effect of education campaigns by such organizations as Planned Parenthood Federation of America and Zero Population Growth, and the influence of inflation and the housing shortage, the fertility rate of American women may decline so much that immigration could account for all the yearly increase in population. Should we not at least ask if that is what we want?

For the sake of those who worry about whether the "quality" of the average immigrant compares favorably with the quality of the average resident, let us assume that immigrants and native-born citizens are of exactly equal quality, however one defines that term. We will focus here only on quantity; and since our conclusions will depend on nothing else, all charges of bigotry and chauvinism become irrelevant.

Immigration vs. Food Supply

World food banks move food to the people, hastening the exhaustion of the environment of the poor countries. Unrestricted immigration, on the other hand, moves people to the food, thus speeding up the destruction of the environment of the rich countries. We can easily understand why poor people should want to make this latter transfer, but why should rich hosts encourage it?

As in the case of foreign-aid programs, immigration receives support from selfish interests and humanitarian impulses. The primary selfish interest in unimpeded immigration is the desire of employers for cheap labor, particularly in industries and trades that offer degrading work. In the past, one wave of foreigners after another was brought into the U.S. to work at wretched jobs for wretched wages. In recent years the Cubans, Puerto Ricans and Mexicans have had this dubious honor. The interests of the employers of cheap labor mesh well with the guilty silence of the country's liberal intelligentsia. White Anglo-Saxon Protestants are particularly reluctant to call for a closing of the doors to immigration for fear of being called bigots.

But not all countries have such reluctant leadership. Most educated Hawaiians, for example, are keenly aware of the limits of their environment, particularly in terms of population growth. There is only so much room on the islands, and the islanders know it. To Hawaiians, immigrants from the other 49 states present as great a threat as those from other nations. At a recent meeting of Hawaiian government officials in Honolulu, I had the ironic delight of hearing a speaker who like most of his audience was of Japanese ancestry, ask how the country might practically and constitutionally close its doors to further immigration. One member of the audience countered: "How can we shut the doors now? We have many friends and relatives in Japan that we'd like to bring here some day so that they can enjoy Hawaii too." The Japanese-American speaker smiled sympathetically and answered: "Yes, but we have children now, and someday we'll have grandchildren too. We can bring more people here from Japan only by giving away some of the land that we hope to pass on to our grandchildren some day. What right do we have to do that?"

At this point, I can hear U.S. liberals asking: "How can you justify slamming the door once you're inside? You say that immigrants should be kept out. But aren't we all immigrants, or the descendants of immigrants? If we insist on staying, must we not admit all others?" Our craving for intellectual order leads us to seek and prefer symmetrical rules and morals: a single rule for me and everybody else; the same rule yesterday, today and tomorrow. Justice, we feel, should not change with time and place.

We Americans of non-Indian ancestry can look upon ourselves as the descendants of thieves who are guilty morally, if not legally, of stealing this land from its Indian owners. Should we then give back the land to the now living American descendants of those Indians? However morally or logically sound this proposal may be, I, for one, am unwilling to live by it and I know no one else who is. Besides, the logical consequence would be absurd. Suppose that, intoxicated with a sense of pure justice, we should decide to turn our land over to the Indians. Since all our other wealth has also been derived from the land, wouldn't we be morally obliged to give that back to the Indians too?

Pure Justice vs. Reality

Clearly, the concept of pure justice produces an infinite regression to absurdity. Centuries ago, wise men invented statutes of limitations to justify the rejection of such pure justice, in the interest of preventing continual disorder. The law zealously defends property rights, but only relatively recent property rights. Drawing a line after an arbitrary time has elapsed may be unjust, but the alternatives are worse.

We are all the descendants of thieves, and the world's resources are inequitably distributed. But we must begin the journey to tomorrow from the point where we are today. We cannot remake the past. We cannot safely divide the wealth equitably among all peoples so long as people reproduce at different rates. To do so would guarantee that our grandchildren, and everyone else's grandchildren, would have only a ruined world to inhabit.

To be generous with one's own possessions is quite different from being generous with those of posterity. We should call this point to the attention of those who, from a commendable love of justice and equality, would institute a system of the commons, either in the form of a world food bank, or of unrestricted immigration. We must convince them if we wish to save at least some parts of the world from environmental ruin.

Without a true world government to control reproduction and the use of available resources, the sharing ethic of the spaceship is impossible. For the foreseeable future, our survival demands that we govern our actions by the ethics of a lifeboat, harsh though they may be. Posterity will be satisfied with nothing less.

The Obligation to Endure

RACHEL CARSON

"The Obligation to Endure" is the second chapter of Rachel Carson's influential book Silent Spring. *A marine biologist, meticulous researcher, and powerful writer, Carson is regarded as one of the world's most influential environmentalists.* Silent Spring *(1962) exposed the subtle, insidious dangers of DDT, a pesticide that since its discovery in the 1940s had been hailed as a miracle substance that could wipe out mosquitoes and other disease-bearing or crop-destroying insects. According to the Natural Resources Defense Council, whose Web site contains an inspiring story about Carson's work,* Silent Spring *"eloquently questioned humanity's faith in technological progress and helped set the stage for the environmental movement." In "The Obligation to Endure," which precedes the more technical portions of the book, Carson presents her causal argument showing how apparently beneficial chemicals can have disastrous unanticipated consequences. Her work was strenuously attacked by the chemical industry, which argued that if we followed Carson's recommendations we would return to the dark ages of insect-borne diseases and famine from failed agriculture. But Carson's carefully documented research defended her against the charges of the chemical industry. According to the Natural Resources Defense Council, the "threats Carson had outlined—the contamination of the food chain, cancer, genetic damage, the deaths of entire species—were too frightening to ignore. For the first time, the need to regulate industry in order to protect the environment became widely accepted, and environmentalism was born."*

The history of life on earth has been a history of interaction between living things and their surroundings. To a large extent, the physical form and the habits of the earth's vegetation and its animal life have been molded by the environment. Considering the whole span of earthly time, the opposite effect, in which life actually modifies its surroundings, has been relatively slight. Only within the moment of time represented by the present century has one species—man—acquired significant power to alter the nature of his world.

During the past quarter century this power has not only increased to one of disturbing magnitude but it has changed in character. The most alarming of all man's assaults upon the environment is the contamination of air, earth, rivers, and sea with dangerous and even lethal materials. This pollution is for the most part irrecoverable; the chain of evil it initiates not only in the world that must support life but in living tissues is for the most part irreversible. In this now universal contamination of the environment, chemicals are the sinister and little-recognized partners of radiation in changing the very nature of the world—the very nature of its life. Strontium 90, released through nuclear explosions into the air, comes to earth in rain or drifts down as fallout, lodges in soil, enters into the grass or corn or wheat grown there, and in time takes up its abode in the bones of a human being, there to remain until his death. Similarly, chemicals sprayed on croplands or forests or gardens lie long in soil, entering into living organisms, passing from one to another in a chain of poisoning and death. Or they pass mysteriously by underground streams until they emerge and, through the alchemy of air and sunlight, combine into new forms that kill vegetation, sicken cattle, and work unknown harm on those who drink from once pure wells. As Albert Schweitzer has said, "Man can hardly even recognize the devils of his own creation."

It took hundreds of millions of years to produce the life that now inhabits the earth—eons of time in which that developing and evolving and diversifying life reached a state of adjustment and balance with its surroundings. The environment, rigorously shaping and directing the life it supported, contained elements that were hostile as well as supporting. Certain rocks gave out dangerous radiation; even within the light of the sun, from which all life draws its energy, there were short-wave radiations with power to injure. Given time—time not in years but in millennia—life adjusts, and a balance has been reached. For time is the essential ingredient; but in the modern world there is no time.

The rapidity of change and the speed with which new situations are created follow the impetuous and heedless pace of man rather than the deliberate pace of nature. Radiation is no longer merely the background radiation of rocks, the bombardment of cosmic rays, the ultraviolet of the sun that have existed before there was any life on earth; radiation is now the unnatural creation of man's tampering with the atom. The chemicals to which life is asked to make its adjustment are no longer merely the calcium and silica and copper and all the rest of the minerals washed out of the rocks and carried in rivers to the sea; they are the synthetic creations of man's inventive mind, brewed in his laboratories, and having no counterparts in nature.

5   To adjust to these chemicals would require time on the scale that is nature's; it would require not merely the years of a man's life but the life of generations. And even this, were it by some miracle possible, would be futile, for the new chemicals come from our laboratories in an endless stream; almost five hundred annually find their way into actual use in the United States alone. The figure is staggering and its implications are not easily grasped—500 new chemicals to which the bodies of men and animals are required somehow to adapt each year, chemicals totally outside the limits of biologic experience.

Among them are many that are used in man's war against nature. Since the mid-1940's over 200 basic chemicals have been created for use in killing insects, weeds, rodents, and other organisms described in the modern vernacular as "pests"; and they are sold under several thousand different brand names.

These sprays, dusts, and aerosols are now applied almost universally to farms, gardens, forests, and homes—nonselective chemicals that have the power to kill every insect, the "good" and the "bad," to still the song of birds and the leaping of fish in the streams, to coat the leaves with a deadly film, and to linger on in soil—all this though the intended target may be only a few weeds or insects. Can anyone believe it is possible to lay down such a barrage of poisons on the surface of the earth without making it unfit for all life? They should not be called "insecticides," but "biocides."

The whole process of spraying seems caught up in an endless spiral. Since DDT was released for civilian use, a process of escalation has been going on in which ever more toxic materials must be found. This has happened because insects, in a triumphant vindication of Darwin's principle of the survival of the fittest, have evolved super races immune to the particular insecticide used, hence a deadlier one has always to be developed—and then a deadlier one than that. It has happened also because, for reasons to be described later, destructive insects often undergo a "flareback," or resurgence, after spraying, in numbers greater than before. Thus the chemical war is never won, and all life is caught in its violent crossfire.

Along with the possibility of the extinction of mankind by nuclear war, the central problem of our age has therefore become the contamination of man's total environment with such substances of incredible potential for harm—substances that accumulate in the tissues of plants and animals and even penetrate the germ cells to shatter or alter the very material of heredity upon which the shape of the future depends.

10   Some would-be architects of our future look toward a time when it will be possible to alter the human germ plasm by design. But we may easily be doing so now by inadvertence, for many chemicals, like radiation, bring about gene mutations. It is ironic to think that man might determine his own future by something so seemingly trivial as the choice of an insect spray.

All this has been risked—for what? Future historians may well be amazed by our distorted sense of proportion. How could intelligent beings seek to control a few unwanted species by a method that contaminated the entire environment and brought the threat of disease and death even to their own kind? Yet this is precisely what we have done. We have done it, moreover, for reasons that collapse the moment we examine them. We are told that the enormous and expanding use of pesticides is necessary to maintain farm production. Yet is our real problem not one of *overproduction*? Our farms, despite measures to remove acreages from production and to pay farmers *not* to produce, have yielded such a staggering excess of crops that the American taxpayer in 1962 is paying out more than one billion dollars a year as the total carrying cost of the surplus-food storage program. And is the situation helped when one branch of the Agriculture Department tries to reduce production while another states, as it did in 1958, "It is believed generally that reduction of crop acreages under provisions of the Soil Bank will stimulate interest in use of chemicals to obtain maximum production on the land retained in crops."

All this is not to say there is no insect problem and no need of control. I am saying, rather, that control must be geared to realities, not to mythical situations, and that the methods employed must be such that they do not destroy us along with the insects.

The problem whose attempted solution has brought such a train of disaster in its wake is an accompaniment of our modern way of life. Long before the age of man, insects inhabited the earth—a group of extraordinarily varied and adaptable beings. Over the course of time since man's advent, a small percentage of the more than half a million species of insects have come into conflict with human welfare in two principal ways: as competitors for the food supply and as carriers of human disease.

Disease-carrying insects become important where human beings are crowded together, especially under conditions where sanitation is poor, as in time of natural disaster or war or in situations of extreme poverty and deprivation. Then control of some sort becomes necessary. It is a sobering fact, however, as we shall presently see, that the method of massive chemical control has had only limited success, and also threatens to worsen the very conditions it is intended to curb.

15   Under primitive agricultural conditions the farmer had few insect problems. These arose with the intensification of agriculture—the devotion of immense acreages to a single crop. Such a system set the stage for explosive increases in specific insect populations. Single-crop farming does not take advantage of the principles by which nature works; it is agriculture as an engineer might conceive it to be. Nature has introduced great variety into the landscape, but man has displayed a passion for simplifying it. Thus he undoes the built-in checks and balances by which nature holds the species within bounds. One important natural check is a limit on the amount of suitable habitat for each species. Obviously then, an insect that lives on wheat can build up its population to much higher levels on a farm devoted to wheat than on one in which wheat is intermingled with other crops to which the insect is not adapted.

The same thing happens in other situations. A generation or more ago, the towns of large areas of the United States lined their streets with the noble elm tree. Now the beauty they hopefully created is threatened with complete destruction as disease sweeps through the elms, carried by a beetle that would have only limited chance to build up large populations and to spread from tree to tree if the elms were only occasional trees in a richly diversified planting.

Another factor in the modern insect problem is one that must be viewed against a background of geologic and human history: the spreading of thousands of different kinds of organisms from their native homes to invade new territories. This worldwide migration has been studied and graphically described by the British ecologist Charles Elton in his recent book *The Ecology of Invasions*. During the Cretaceous Period, some hundred million years ago, flooding seas cut many land bridges between continents and living things found themselves confined in what Elton calls "colossal separate nature reserves." There, isolated from others of their kind, they developed many new species. When some of the land masses were joined again, about 15 million years ago, these species began to move out into new territories—a movement that is not only still in progress but is now receiving considerable assistance from man.

The importation of plants is the primary agent in the modern spread of species, for animals have almost invariably gone along with the plants, quarantine being a comparatively recent and not completely effective innovation. The United States Office of Plant Introduction alone has introduced almost 200,000 species and varieties of plants from all over the world. Nearly half of the 180 or so major insect enemies of plants in the United States are accidental imports from abroad, and most of them have come as hitchhikers on plants.

In new territory, out of reach of the restraining hand of the natural enemies that kept down its numbers in its native land, an invading plant or animal is able to become enormously abundant. Thus it is no accident that our most troublesome insects are introduced species.

20   These invasions, both the naturally occurring and those dependent on human assistance, are likely to continue indefinitely. Quarantine and massive chemical campaigns are only extremely expensive ways of buying time. We are faced, according to Dr. Elton, "with a life-and-death need not just to find new technological means of suppressing this plant or that animal"; instead we need the basic knowledge of animal populations and their relations to their surroundings that will "promote an even balance and damp down the explosive power of outbreaks and new invasions."

Much of the necessary knowledge is now available but we do not use it. We train ecologists in our universities and even employ them in our governmental agencies but we seldom take their advice. We allow the chemical death rain to fall as though there were no alternative, whereas in fact there are many, and our ingenuity could soon discover many more if given opportunity.

Have we fallen into a mesmerized state that makes us accept as inevitable that which is inferior or detrimental, as though having lost the will or the vision to demand that which is good? Such thinking, in the words of the ecologist Paul Shepard, "idealizes life with only its head out of water, inches above the limits of toleration of the corruption of its own environment...Why should we tolerate a diet of weak poisons, a home in insipid surroundings, a circle of acquaintances who are not quite our enemies, the noise of motors with just enough relief to prevent insanity? Who would want to live in a world which is just not quite fatal?"

Yet such a world is pressed upon us. The crusade to create a chemically sterile, insect-free world seems to have engendered a fanatic zeal on the part of many specialists and most of the so-called control agencies. On every hand there is evidence that those engaged in spraying operations exercise a ruthless power. "The regulatory entomologists...function as prosecutor, judge and jury, tax assessor and collector and sheriff to enforce their own orders," said Connecticut entomologist Neely Turner. The most flagrant abuses go unchecked in both state and federal agencies.

It is not my contention that chemical insecticides must never be used. I do contend that we have put poisonous and biologically potent chemicals indiscriminately into the hands of persons largely or wholly ignorant of their potentials for harm. We have subjected enormous numbers of people to contact with these poisons, without their consent and often without their knowledge. If the Bill of Rights contains no guarantee that a citizen shall be secure against lethal poisons distributed either by private individuals or by public officials, it is surely only because our forefathers, despite their considerable wisdom and foresight, could conceive of no such problem.

25   I contend, furthermore, that we have allowed these chemicals to be used with little or no advance investigation of their effect on soil, water, wildlife, and man himself. Future generations are unlikely to condone our lack of prudent concern for the integrity of the natural world that supports all life.

There is still very limited awareness of the nature of the threat. This is an era of specialists, each of whom sees his own problem and is unaware of or intolerant of the larger frame into which it fits. It is also an era dominated by industry, in which the right to make a dollar at whatever cost is seldom challenged. When the public protests, confronted with some obvious evidence of damaging results of pesticide applications, it is fed little tranquilizing pills of half truth. We urgently need an end to these false assurances, to the sugar coating of unpalatable facts. It is the public that is being asked to assume the risks that the insect controllers calculate. The public must decide whether it wishes to continue on the present road, and it can do so only when in full possession of the facts. In the words of Jean Rostand, "The obligation to endure gives us the right to know."

Apocalypse Now / Letter to a Southern Baptist Minister

E. O. WILSON

Edward Osborne (E. O.) Wilson is an American biologist often called "the father of sociobiology." Among his many awards, he has twice won the Pulitzer Prize. He is considered the world's leading authority on ants, and has controversially and influentially argued that all animal behavior, including that of humans, is the product of heredity, environmental stimuli, and past experiences. In The Diversity of Life *(1992), he describes how an intricately interconnected natural system has been threatened by human encroachment, and calls our current environmental crisis the "sixth extinction," after the well-known fifth extinction that wiped out the dinosaurs. He is known for his environmental advocacy as well as his secular-humanist and deist views in relation to religion and ethics. This excerpt, which has appeared in various publications under the names "Apocalypse Now" and "Letter to a Southern Baptist Minister," originally came from Wilson's book,* The Creation: An Appeal to Save Life on Earth *(2006). In it, Wilson calls for an end to the differences between science- and faith-based explanations, because "Science and religion are two of the most potent forces on Earth and they should come together to save the creation." Note his use of ethical argument and Rogerian communication to negotiate with an audience, an imagined member of the clergy, who has views very different from his.*

Dear Pastor:

We have not met, yet I feel I know you well enough to call you friend. First of all, we grew up in the same faith. As a boy I too answered the altar call; I went under the water. Although I no longer belong to that faith, I am confident that if we met and spoke privately of our deepest beliefs, it would be in a spirit of mutual respect and good will. I know we share many precepts of moral behavior. Perhaps it also matters that we are both Americans and, insofar as it might still affect civility and good manners, we are both Southerners.

I write to you now for your counsel and help. Of course, in doing so, I see no way to avoid the fundamental differences in our respective worldviews. You are a literalist interpreter of Christian Holy Scripture. You reject the conclusion of science that mankind evolved from lower forms. You believe that each person's soul is immortal, making this planet a way station to a second, eternal life. Salvation is assured those who are redeemed in Christ.

I am a secular humanist. I think existence is what we make of it as individuals. There is no guarantee of life after death, and heaven and hell are what we create for ourselves, on this planet. There is no other home. Humanity originated here by evolution from lower forms over millions of years. And yes, I will speak plain, our ancestors were apelike animals. The human species has adapted physically and mentally to life on Earth and no place else. Ethics is the code of behavior we share on the basis of reason, law, honor, and an inborn sense of decency, even as some ascribe it to God's will.

For you, the glory of an unseen divinity; for me, the glory of the universe revealed at last. For you, the belief in God made flesh to save mankind; for me, the belief in Promethean fire seized to set men free. You have found your final truth; I am still searching. I may be wrong, you may be wrong. We may both be partly right.

Does this difference in worldview separate us in all things? It does not. You and I and every other human being strive for the same imperatives of security, freedom of choice, personal dignity, and a cause to believe in that is larger than ourselves.

Let us see, then, if we can, and you are willing, to meet on the near side of metaphysics in order to deal with the real world we share. I put it this way because you have the power to help solve a great problem about which I care deeply. I hope you have the same concern. I suggest that we set aside our differences in order to save the Creation. The defense of living Nature is a universal value. It doesn't rise from, nor does it promote, any religious or ideological dogma. Rather, it serves without discrimination the interests of all humanity.

Pastor, we need your help. The Creation—living Nature—is in deep trouble. Scientists estimate that if habitat conversion and other destructive human activities continue at their present rates, half the species of plants and animals on Earth could be either gone or at least fated for early extinction by the end of the century. A full quarter will drop to this level during the next half century as a result of climate change alone. The ongoing extinction rate is calculated in the most conservative estimates to be about a hundred times above that prevailing before humans appeared on Earth, and it is expected to rise to at least a thousand times greater or more in the next few decades. If this rise continues unabated, the cost to humanity, in wealth, environmental security, and quality of life, will be catastrophic.

Surely we can agree that each species, however inconspicuous and humble it may seem to us at this moment, is a masterpiece of biology, and well worth saving. Each species possesses a unique combination of genetic traits that fits it more or less precisely to a particular part of the environment. Prudence alone dictates that we act quickly to prevent the extinction of species and, with it, the pauperization of Earth's ecosystems—hence of the Creation.

You may well ask at this point, Why me? Because religion and science are the two most powerful forces in the world today, including especially the United States. If religion and science could be united on the common ground of biological conservation, the problem would soon be solved. If there is any moral precept shared by people of all beliefs, it is that we owe ourselves and future generations a beautiful, rich, and healthful environment.

I am puzzled that so many religious leaders, who spiritually represent a large majority of people around the world, have hesitated to make protection of the Creation an important part of their magisterium. Do they believe that human-centered ethics and preparation for the afterlife are the only things that matter? Even more perplexing is the widespread conviction among Christians that the Second Coming is imminent, and that therefore the condition of the planet is of little consequence. Sixty percent of Americans, according to a 2004 poll, believe that the prophecies of the book of Revelation are accurate. Many of these, numbering in the millions, think the End of Time will occur within the life span of those now living. Jesus will return to Earth, and those redeemed by Christian faith will be transported bodily to heaven, while those left behind will struggle through severe hard times and, when they die, suffer eternal damnation. The condemned will remain in hell, like those already consigned in the generations before them, for a trillion trillion years, enough for the universe to expand to its own, entropic death, time enough for countless universes like it afterward to be born, expand, and likewise die away. And that is just the beginning of how long condemned souls will suffer in hell—all for a mistake they made in choice of religion during the infinitesimally small time they inhabited Earth.

For those who believe this form of Christianity, the fate of ten million other life forms indeed does not matter. This and other similar doctrines are not gospels of hope and compassion. They are gospels of cruelty and despair. They were not born of the heart of Christianity. Pastor, tell me I am wrong!

However you will respond, let me here venture an alternative ethic. The great challenge of the twenty-first century is to raise people everywhere to a decent standard of living while preserving as much of the rest of life as possible. Science has provided this part of the argument for the ethic: the more we learn about the biosphere, the more complex and beautiful it turns out to be. Knowledge of it is a magic well: the more you draw from it, the more there is to draw. Earth, and especially the razor-thin film of life enveloping it, is our home, our wellspring, our physical and much of our spiritual sustenance.

I know that science and environmentalism are linked in the minds of many with evolution, Darwin, and secularism. Let me postpone disentangling all this (I will come back to it later) and stress again: to protect the beauty of Earth and of its prodigious variety of life forms should be a common goal, regardless of differences in our metaphysical beliefs.

To make the point in good gospel manner, let me tell the story of a young man, newly trained for the ministry, and so fixed in his Christian faith that he referred all questions of morality to readings from the Bible. When he visited the cathedral-like Atlantic rainforest of Brazil, he saw the manifest hand of God and in his notebook wrote, "It is not possible to give an adequate idea of the higher feelings of wonder, admiration, and devotion which fill and elevate the mind."

That was Charles Darwin in 1832, early into the voyage of HMS *Beagle*, before he had given any thought to evolution.

And here is Darwin, concluding *On the Origin of Species* in 1859, having first abandoned Christian dogma and then, with his newfound intellectual freedom, formulated the theory of evolution by natural selection: "There is grandeur in this view of life, with its several powers, having been originally breathed into a few forms or into one; and that, whilst this planet has gone cycling on according to the fixed law of gravity, from so simple a beginning endless forms most beautiful and most wonderful have been, and are being, evolved."

Darwin's reverence for life remained the same as he crossed the seismic divide that divided his spiritual life. And so it can be for the divide that today separates scientific humanism from mainstream religion. And separates you and me.

You are well prepared to present the theological and moral arguments for saving the Creation. I am heartened by the movement growing within Christian denominations to support global conservation. The stream of thought has arisen from many sources, from evangelical to unitarian. Today it is but a rivulet. Tomorrow it will be a flood.

I already know much of the religious argument on behalf of the Creation, and would like to learn more. I will now lay before you and others who may wish to hear it the scientific argument. You will not agree with all that I say about the origins of life—science and religion do not easily mix in such matters—but I like to think that in this one life-and-death issue we have a common purpose.

The Morality of Birth Control

MARGARET SANGER

Margaret Sanger was a nurse who became a birth control activist, believing that the ability to limit family size would free working-class women from the economic and physical burden of unwanted pregnancy. In 1921, Sanger founded the American Birth Control League, which is now known as the Planned Parenthood Federation of America. As a courageous proponent of sex education and the distribution of contraceptives, Sanger ran afoul of the 1873 Federal Comstock Law, which made it a crime to "import or distribute any device, medicine, or information designed to prevent conception or induce abortion, or to mention in print the names of sexually transmitted infections." "The Morality of Birth Control" was originally scheduled to be delivered at the close of the First American Birth Control Conference on November 12, 1921, but police raided the Town Hall and arrested Sanger. The speech was then delivered a week later at the Park Theatre in New York City on November 18, 1921. In arguing for the morality of birth control, Sanger also, in the last section of the speech, argues for eugenics (a social movement advocating improvement of the human genetic stock through selective breeding)—a position that generated controversy even among supporters of the birth control movement. Sanger's speech reveals the historical complexity of an era in which women's liberation, sexual freedom, eugenics, poverty eradication, and racism were intermixed.

The meeting tonight is a postponement of one which was to have taken place at the Town Hall last Sunday evening. It was to be a culmination of a three day conference, two of which were held at the Hotel Plaza, in discussing the Birth Control subject in its various and manifold aspects.

The one issue upon which there seems to be most uncertainty and disagreement exists in the moral side of the subject of Birth Control. It seemed only natural for us to call together scientists, educators, members of the medical profession and the theologians of all denominations to ask their opinion upon this uncertain and important phase of the controversy. Letters were sent to the most eminent men and women in the world. We asked in this letter, the following questions:

1. Is over-population a menace to the peace of the world?
2. Would the legal dissemination of scientific Birth Control information through the medium of clinics by the medical profession be the most logical method of checking the problem of over-population?
3. Would knowledge of Birth Control change the moral attitude of men and women toward the marriage bond or lower the moral standards of the youth of the country?
4. Do you believe that knowledge which enables parents to limit the families will make for human happiness, and raise the moral, social and intellectual standards of population?

We sent such a letter not only to those who, we thought, might agree with us, but we sent it also to our known opponents. Most of these people answered. Every one who answered did so with sincerity and courtesy, with the exception of one group whose reply to this important question as demonstrated at the Town Hall last Sunday evening was a disgrace to liberty-loving people, and to all traditions we hold dear in the United States. I believed that the discussion of the moral issue was one which did not solely belong to theologians and to scientists, but belonged to the people. And because I believed that the people of this country may and can discuss this subject with dignity and with intelligence I desired to bring them together, and to discuss it in the open.

When one speaks of moral[s], one refers to human conduct. This implies action of many kinds, which in turn depends upon the mind and the brain. So that in speaking of morals one must remember that there is a direct connection between morality and brain development. Conduct is said to be action in pursuit of ends, and if this is so, then we must hold the irresponsibility and recklessness in our action is immoral, while responsibility and forethought put into action for the benefit of the individual and the race becomes in the highest sense the finest kind of morality.

We know that every advance that woman has made in the last half century has been made with opposition, all of which has been based upon the grounds of immorality. When women fought for higher education, it was said that this would cause her to become immoral and she would lose her place in the sanctity of the home. When women asked for the franchise it was said that this would lower her standard of morals, that it was not fit that she should meet with and mix with the members of the opposite sex, but we notice that there was no objection to her meeting with the same members of the opposite sex when she went to church.

The church has ever opposed the progress of woman on the ground that her freedom would lead to immorality. We ask the church to have more confidence in women. We ask the opponents of this movement to reverse the methods of the church, which aims to keep women moral by keeping them in fear and in ignorance, and to inculcate into them a higher and truer morality based upon knowledge. And ours is the morality of knowledge. If we cannot trust woman with the knowledge of her own body, then I claim that two thousand years of Christian teaching has proved to be a failure.

We stand on the principle that Birth Control should be available to every adult man and woman. We believe that every adult man and woman should be taught the responsibility and the right use of knowledge. We claim that woman should have the right over her own body and to say if she shall or if she shall not be a mother, as she sees fit. We further claim that the first right of a child is to be desired. While the second right is that it should be conceived in love, and the third, that it should have a heritage of sound health.

Upon these principles the Birth Control movement in America stands. When it comes to discussing the methods of Birth Control, that is far more difficult. There are laws in this country which forbid the imparting of practical information to the mothers of the land. We claim that every mother in this country, either sick or well, has the right to the best, the safest, the most scientific information. This information should be disseminated directly to the mothers through clinics by members of the medical profession, registered nurses and registered midwives.

Our first step is to have the backing of the medical profession so that our laws may be changed, so that motherhood may be the function of dignity and choice, rather than one of ignorance and chance. Conscious control of offspring is now becoming the ideal and the custom in all civilized countries. Those who oppose it claim that however desirable it may be on economic or social grounds, it may be abused and the morals of the youth of the country may be lowered. Such people should be reminded that there are two points to be considered. First, that such control is the inevitable advance in civilization. Every civilization involves an increasing forethought for others, even for those yet unborn. The reckless abandonment of the impulse of the moment[,] and the careless regard for the consequences, is not morality. The selfish gratification of temporary desire at the expense of suffering to lives that will come may seem very beautiful to some, but it is not our conception of civilization, [n]or is it our concept of morality.

In the second place, it is not only inevitable, but it is right to control the size of the family for by this control and adjustment we can raise the level and the standards of the human race. While Nature's way of reducing her numbers is controlled by disease, famine and war, primitive man has achieved the same results by infanticide, exposure of infants, the abandonment of children, and by abortion. But such ways of controlling population is no longer possible for us. We have attained high standards of life, and along the lines of science must we conduct such control. We must begin farther back and control the beginnings of life. We must control conception. This is a better method, it is a more civilized method, for it involves not only greater forethought for others, but finally a higher sanction for the value of life itself.

Society is divided into three groups. Those intelligent and wealthy members of the upper classes who have obtained knowledge of Birth Control and exercise it in regulating the size of their families. They have already benefited by this knowledge, and are today considered the most respectable and moral members of the community. They have only children when they desire, and all society points to them as types that should perpetuate their kind.

The second group is equally intelligent and responsible. They desire to control the size of their families, but are unable to obtain knowledge or to put such available knowledge into practice.

The third are those irresponsible and reckless ones having little regard for the consequence of their acts, or whose religious scruples prevent their exercising control over their numbers. Many of this group are diseased, feeble-minded, and are of the pauper element dependent entirely upon the normal and fit members of society for their support. There is no doubt in the minds of all thinking people that the procreation of this group should be stopped. For if they are not able to support and care for themselves, they should certainly not be allowed to bring offspring into this world for others to look after. We do not believe that filling the earth with misery, poverty and disease is moral. And it is our desire and intention to carry on our crusade until the perpetuation of such conditions has ceased.

We desire to stop at its source the disease, poverty and feeble-mindedness and insanity which exist today, for these lower the standards of civilization and make for race deterioration. We know that the masses of people are growing wiser and are using their own minds to decide their individual conduct. The more people of this kind we have, the less immorality shall exist. For the more responsible people grow, the higher do they and shall they attain real morality.

■ ■ ■   **FOR CLASS DISCUSSION**   Argument Classics

1. Each of the arguments in this unit is trying to persuade its audience to adopt the writer's values and position on a major problem. Working in small groups or as a whole class, explore your answers to the following questions for one of the arguments selected by your instructor:

    a. What is the question or problem addressed by the writer?
    b. What are the writer's values and assumptions behind his or her argument?
    c. What is the core of the writer's argument (claims and reasons)?
    d. What is at stake?

2. Then, working with the same argument, analyze its author's use of rhetorical strategies to persuade his or her audience and evaluate the effectiveness of these strategies. To generate ideas for this discussion, use the "Questions for Rhetorical Analysis" in Chapter 8, pages 155–157.   ■ ■ ■

WRITING ASSIGNMENT   Exploratory Essay

Classic arguments often raise questions that are complicated by historical contexts different from that of the contemporary reader. Articulate a puzzling question of truth or value that is sparked by your reading of one of the arguments in this unit (or another classic argument chosen by your instructor). Then write an exploratory essay in which you narrate in first-person, chronological order the evolution of your thinking about the issue or problem. Begin with a question and then describe your inquiry process as you work through sources or different views. Some enduring issues broached by these authors include questions about immigration, population control, humanitarian ethics, the environment and its carrying capacity, pesticides, genetic engineering, birth control, sex education, and others. Follow the instructions and guidelines for an exploratory essay as explained in Chapter 2, pages 42–50.   ■

Credits

Text

Page 5. Juan Lucas

Pages 22, 23, 36, 37, 44. Trudie Makens

Page 33. James Surowiecki, "The Pay is Too Damn Low," *The New Yorker*. Reprinted with permission of the Chris Calhoun Agency.

Page 40. Michael Saltsman, "To Help the Poor, Move Beyond 'Minimum Gestures'," Huffington Post. Reprinted by permission of the author.

Page 55. Pearson Education

Pages 66, 81, 82. Carmen Tieu

Page 129. Trudie Makens, "Bringing Dignity to Workers: Make the Minimum Wage a Living Wage"

Page 140. Colleen Fontana, "An Open Letter to Robert Levy in Response to His Article 'They Never Learn'." Used by permission.

Page 145. Lauren Shinozuka, "The Dangers of Digital Distractedness"

Page 149: Monica Allen, "An Open Letter to Christopher Eide in response to His Article 'High-Performing Charter Schools Can Close the Opportunity Gap'"

Page 159. Kathryn Jean Lopez, "Egg Heads," *National Review*. (c) 1998 National Review, Inc. Reprinted by permission.

Page 171. Zachary Stumps, "A Rhetorical Analysis of Ellen Goodman's 'Womb for Rent'." Reprinted with permission of the author.

Page 217. Alex Hutchinson, "Your Daily Multivitamin May Be Hurting You—The Debate Is On: Just Useless, or Truly Dangerous?" *Outside Magazine*, Oct. 8, 2013. Used with permission.

Page 242. John Bean

Page 244. Alex Mullens, "A Pirate but Not a Thief: What Does 'Stealing' Mean in a Digital Environment?" Reprinted by permission of the author.

Page 257. LA Times Editorial Board, "College Football...Yes, It's a Job." Reprinted by permission of *LA Times*.

Page 257. "Buying Sex Causes Sex Trafficking" from Free the Captives. Used by permission.

Page 266. Julee Christianson, "Why Lawrence Summers Was Wrong." Used by permission.

Page 272. Deborah Fallows, "Papa, Don't Text: The Perils of Distracted Parenting." (c) 2013 The Atlantic Media Co., as first published in *The Atlantic* Magazine. All rights reserved. Distributed by Tribune Content Agency, LLC

Page 274. Carlos Macias, "'The Credit Card Company Made Me Do It!'—The Credit Card Industry's Role in Causing Student Debt." Used by permission.

Page 294. Lorena Mendoza-Flores, "Silenced and Invisible: Problems of Hispanic Students at Valley High School"

Page 297. Christopher Moore, "Information Plus Satire: Why The Daily Show and The Colbert Report Are Good Sources of News for Young People." Reprinted with permission.

Page 300. Judith Daar, "Three Genetic Parents for One Healthy Baby," *Los Angeles Times,* March 21, 2014. Reprinted with permission of the author.

Page 302. Samuel Aquila, "The 'Therapeutic Cloning' of Human Embryos," *National Review,* May 17, 2013. Reprinted with permission.

Page 322. Megan Johnson, "A Practical Proposal"

Page 326. Ivan Snook, "Flirting with Disaster: An Argument Against Integrating Women into the Combat Arms." Reprinted by permission of the author.

Page 333. Sandy Wainscott, "Why McDonald's Should Sell Meat and Veggie Pies: A Proposal to End Subsidies for Cheap Meat." Used by permission.

Page 335. Marcel Dicke and Arnold Van Huis, "The Six-Legged Meat of the Future," *The Wall Street Journal,* February 19, 2011. Reprinted with permission.

Page 384. Used with permission of EBSCO.

Page 386. United States Environmental Protection Agency

Part 6 An Anthology of Arguments

Page 407. Arthur L. Caplan, "Genetically Modified Food: Good, Bad, Ugly," *Chronicle of Higher Education,* 2013, Edition 60(2). Reprinted by permission of the author.

Page 410. Robin Mather, "The Threats from Genetically Modified Foods," *Mother Earth News,* April/May 2012. Reprinted with permission.

Page 415. Michael Le Page, "Wrong-Headed Victory," *New Scientist.* (c) 2012 Reed Business Information–UK. All rights reserved. Distributed by Tribune Content Agency, LLC.

Page 418. Caitlin Flanagan, "Cultivating Failure: How School Gardens Are Cheating Our Most Vulnerable Students," *The Atlantic,* Jan/Feb 2010. Reprinted by permission of Tribune Content Agency.

Page 424. Bonnie Hulkower, "A Defense of School Gardens and Response to Caitlin Flanagan's 'Cultivating Failure' in *The Atlantic*," Treehugger.com. Reprinted with permission.

Page 426. Tom Philpot, "Thoughts on *The Atlantic*'s Attack on School Gardens," *Grist,* Jan. 13, 2010. Reprinted with permission.

Page 428. "*Atlantic* Gets It Wrong! School Gardens Cultivate Minds, Not Failure" by Jesse Kurtz-Nicholl. This article first appeared in Johns Hopkins Center for a Livable Future Blog, January 2010. Used with permission.

Page 433. Rebecca Mead, "Learning by Degrees," (c) The New Yorker/Rebecca Mead/Conde Nast. Reprinted with permission.

Page 435. Ken Saxon, "What Do You Do with a B.A. in History?" Reprinted by permission of the author.

Page 442. Reprinted with permission from *Liberal Education,* vol 99, no 4. Copyright 2013 by the Association of American Colleges and Universities.

Page 451. Reprinted with permission from *Liberal Education,* vol 99, no 4. Copyright 2013 by the Association of American Colleges and Universities.

Page 455. Chrissie Long, "The Changing Face of Higher Education," John F. Kennedy School of Government. Reprinted with permission.

Page 461. Lara Fatemeh Fakhraie, "Scarfing It Down," Bitch: Feminist Response to Pop Culture. Reprinted by permission of the author.

Page 462. Copyright (c) 2011 by the *Christian Century.* "Veiled Voices" by Stephanie Paulsell is reprinted by permission from the July 12, 2011, issue of the *Christian Century.*

Page 463. Madeline Zavodny, "Unauthorized Immigrant Arrivals Are on the Rise, and That's Good News," *Forbes,* Oct. 2013. Reprinted with permission of the author.

Page 466. Mark Krikorian, "Dream On." (c) National Review. Reprinted by permission.

Page 469. Lee Habeeb and Michael Leven, "Immigration, America's Advantage." © 2014 by National Review, Inc. Reprinted by permission.

Page 471. John Kavanaugh, "Amnesty? Let Us Be Vigilant and Charitable," *America* Magazine. March 10, 2008. Reprinted with permission of America Press, Inc. 2008. All rights reserved. For subscription information, call 1-800-627-9533 or visit www.americamagazine.org

Page 473. LA Times Editorial Board, "Young, Alone and in Court." Reprinted with permission of *LA Times.*

Page 474. Editors, "Border Crisis in Texas." © 1955 by National Review, Inc. Reprinted by permission.

Page 549. Chapter 2: "The Obligation to Endure" from *Silent Spring* by Rachel Carson. Copyright (c) 1962 by Rachel Carson, renewed 1990 by Roger Christie. Reprinted by permission of Houghton Mifflin Harcourt Publishing Company. Used by permission of Frances Collin, Trustee. Unauthorized electronic copying or distribution of this text is expressly forbidden. Reprinted by permission of Pollinger Ltd. (www.pollingerltd.com) on behalf of the Estate of Rachel Carson. All Rights Reserved.

Page 554. From *The Creation: An Appeal to Save Life on Earth* by Edward O. Wilson. Copyright 2006 by Edward O. Wilson. Used by permission of W.W. Norton & Company, Inc.

Page 557. Margaret Sanger, "The Morality of Birth Control"

Images

Page 1. AP Photo/StephanSavoia

Page 4. United Steelworkers Union

Page 6. Top, GHoneywell Design. Bottom, AP Photo/Hans Pennink.

Page 7. www.cartoonstock.com

Page 20. Employment Policies Institute. Reprinted with permission.

Page 21. www.cartoonstock.com

Page 22. Shmitt, John and Janelle Jones. 2012. "Low-Wage Workers are Older and Better Educated Than Ever." Washington, DC: Center for Economic and Policy Research. Used with permission.

Page 51. Andreas Rentz/Getty Images

Page 63. Top, Deborah Thompson/Alamy. Bottom, Juniors Bildarchiv GmbH/Alamy.

Page 98. Top, AP Photo/Toby Talbot. Bottom, AP Photo/Branimir Kvartuc.

Page 114. AP Photo/Bullit Marquez

Page 115. Men Can Stop Rape. Reprinted with permission.

Page 143. Top left, AP Photo/Evan Vucci. Top right, AP Photo/J. Scott Applewhite. Bottom left, AP Photo/Ross D. Franklin, File. Bottom right, AP Photo/The News Tribune, Thomas Soerenes.

Page 153. Peter Byrne/PA Wire URN:187 98732 (Press Association via AP Images)

Page 175. John Bean

Page 179. Ad Council

Page 181. Save the Children

Page 183. Ad Council/National Highway Traffic Safety Administration

Page 185. National Library of Medicine

Page 187. Figure 9.6, Art Wolfe Travels to the Edge/Getty Images. Figure 9.7, FramePool. Figures 9.8–9.10, ©2010 Nissan North America, Inc. Nissan, Nissan model names and the Nissan logo are registered trademarks of Nissan. Figure 9.11, Sterling Artists Management.

Page 191. Figure 9.12, Blend Images/Alamy. Figure 9.13, Radius Images/Alamy. Figure 9.14, Eric Basir/Alamy. Figure 9.15, DCPhoto/Alamy.

Page 193. Photos 12/Alamy

Page 195. Gretchen Ertl

Page 196. TXTResponsibly.org

Page 197. Milt Prigee/Cagle Cartoons

Page 206. John Ramage

Page 209. © Kathy deWitt/Alamy

Page 220. Bagley/Cagle Cartoons

Index

READINGS AND VISUAL ARGUMENTS

Unless otherwise indicated, the readings or visual arguments appear in the Anthology.

PROFESSIONAL READINGS

Scholarly Articles
Erin Burns, "Millenials and Mentoring"
Mary Ann Harlan, "Deconstructing Digital Natives"

Articles by Journalists or Freelancers
Alex Hutchinson, "Your Daily Multivitamin May Be Hurting You" (Ch. 10)
Fallows, Deborah, "Papa, Don't Text: The Perils of Distracted Parenthood" (Ch. 12)
Caitlin Flanagan, "Cultivating Failure"
Kathryn Tyler, "The Tethered Generation"
Abrahm Lustgarten, "Fracking: A Key to Energy Independence?"
Jason Powers, "The Problem Is the Solution: Cultivating New Traditions through Permaculture"
Aashika Damodar, "The Rise of 'Great Potential'"

Op-Ed Commentary from Journalists
James Surowiecki, "The Pay is Too Damn Low" (Ch. 2)
Ross Douthat, "Islam in Two Americas" (Ch. 7)
Kathryn Jean Lopez, "Egg Heads" (Ch. 8)
Ellen Goodman, "Womb for Rent" (Ch. 8)
Los Angeles Times Editorial Board, "College Football—Yes, It's a Job" (Ch. 12)
Robin Mather, "The Threats from Genetically Modified Foods"
Michael Le Page, "Wrong-Headed Victory"
Tom Philpott, "Thoughts on The Atlantic's Attack on School Gardens"
Rebecca Mead, "Learning by Degrees"
Chrissie Long, "The Changing Face of Higher Education: The Future of the Traditional University Experience"
Fatemeh Fakhraie, "Scarfing It Down"
Mark Krikorian, "DREAM On"

Lee Habeeb and Mike Leven, "Immigration, America's Advantage"
Los Angeles Times, "Young, Alone, and in Court"
National Review, "Border Crisis in Texas"
America, "Generation S"
Kay Hymowitz, "Where Have the Good Men Gone?"
Christian Science Monitor, "Help Teens Erase Their Web Indiscretions"
Susan Nielsen, "An Internet 'Eraser' Law Would Hurt, Not Help, Oregon Teens"

Op-Ed Commentary from Concerned Citizens
Michael Saltsman, "To Help the Poor, Move Beyond 'Minimum' Gestures" (Ch. 2)
Judith Daar and Erez Aloni, "Three Genetic Parents—For One Healthy Baby" (Ch. 13)
Samuel Aquila "The 'Therapeutic Cloning' of Human Embryos" (Ch. 13)

PROFESSIONAL VISUAL ARGUMENTS

Advocacy Advertisements or Posters
Employment Policies Institute, "Why Robots Could Soon Replace Fast Food Workers" (Ch. 2)
Men Can Stop Rape, "Where Do You Stand?" (Ch. 6)
StopBullying.gov, "You're a Dumb Piece of Trash" (Ch. 9)
Save the Children, "Help One, Save Many" (Ch. 9)
National Highway and Traffic Safety Administration, "Buzzed Driving is Drunk Driving" (Ch. 9)
War Department, "Never Give Germ a Break" (Ch. 9)
Txtresponsibly.org, "Be a Part of the Solution" (Ch. 9)
FreeTheCaptivesHouston.com, "Buying Sex Causes Sex Trafficking" (Ch. 12)
Planned Parenthood, "Reproductive Rights Under Attack" (Ch. 14)
Save-Bees.org, "Bees Can't Wait 5 More Years" (Ch. 14)

Product Advertisements
Nicolites Electronic Cigarettes (Part 4)
Nissan Leaf Commercial (Ch. 9)

Posters
Genetically Engineered Food (Ch. 1)
The Hunger Games: Catching Fire (Ch. 9)
District 9 (Ch. 13)

Cartoons
Aaron Bacall, "Do You John Promise" (Ch. 1)
Paul Fell, "Job Killer!" (Ch. 2)
Milt Priggee, "New Theory as to How the Dinosaurs Died" (Ch. 9)
Pat Bagley, "Climate Change Frogs" (Ch. 11)
Randy Bish, "Heroin" (Ch. 11)
John Hambrock, "Harley, I'm Worried About Gene Transfer"
Joe Mohr, "Monsanto's Reasons for Fighting GMO Labeling? It Loves You"
Dave Blazek, "Melissa Misunderstands Massive Open Online Courses"

Chip Bok, "Processing Undocumented Children"
Gary Varvel, "Meet Jack"

Photos
Stand with Fast Food Workers (Part 1)
Protect Our Kids (Ch. 1)
Occupy Wall Street Protestors (Ch. 1)
Orca Performance at Marine Park (Ch. 3)
Jumping Orcas (Ch. 3)
Mosh Pit Photos (Ch. 5)
Boy after Typhoon Haiyan (Ch. 6)
Illegal Immigration Demonstrations (Ch. 7)
Frack Will Seriously Damage Your Health (Part 3)
Polar Bear Parade (Ch. 9)
Self-Defense Photos (Ch. 9)
Young Girls with Toy Bows (Ch. 9)
Stephen Colbert and Jon Stewart (Ch. 13)
Dead Baby Albatross (Ch. 14)
Disabled Veteran with Dog (Part 5)
Things Causing Rape (Part 6)